English and International:
Studies in the Literature,
Art and Patronage of
Medieval England

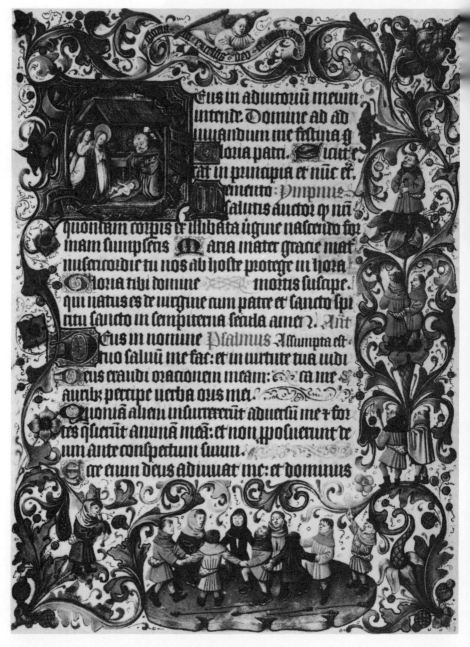

Rustic Festival, Annunciation to Shepherds, Nativity. Oxford, Bodl. MS Douce 93, fo. 28r; Utrecht, mid-fifteenth century.

English and International: Studies in the Literature, Art and Patronage of Medieval England

Elizabeth Salter

edited by
Derek Pearsall
· and
Nicolette Zeeman

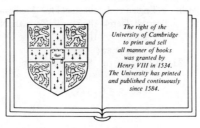

The right of the
University of Cambridge
to print and sell
all manner of books
was granted by
Henry VIII in 1534.
The University has printed
and published continuously
since 1584.

CAMBRIDGE UNIVERSITY PRESS

Cambridge

New York   New Rochelle   Melbourne   Sydney

Published by the Press Syndicate of the University of Cambridge
The Pitt Building, Trumpington Street, Cambridge CB2 1RP
32 East 57th Street, New York, NY 10022, USA
10 Stamford Road, Oakleigh, Melbourne 3166, Australia

© Cambridge University Press 1988

First published 1988

Printed in Great Britain at
the University Press, Cambridge

British Library cataloguing in publication data
Salter, Elizabeth, *1925–1980*
English and international: studies in the
literature, art and patronage of medieval England.
1. English poetry – Middle English, 1100–1500
– History and criticism   2. Art, Medieval
I. Title   II. Pearsall, Derek   III. Zeeman, Nicolette
821'.1'09   PR311

Library of Congress cataloguing in publication data
Salter, Elizabeth.
English and international: studies in the literature, art, and
patronage of Medieval England / Elizabeth Salter; edited by Derek
Pearsall and Nicolette Zeeman.
p.   cm.
'Bibliography of the published writings of Elizabeth Salter'.
Includes index.
ISBN 0–521–34375–5
1. English literature – Middle English, 1100–1500 – History and
criticism.   2. English literature – European influences.   3. Authors
and patrons – England.   4. Art and literature – England.   5. Art
patronage – England.   6. Art, Medieval – England – Themes, motives.
7. Art, English.   8. England – Intellectual life – Medieval period,
1066–1485.   I. Pearsall, Derek Albert.   II. Zeeman, Nicolette,
1956–   .   III. Title.
PR251.S24   1988
820'.9'001 – dc 19   87–24625   CIP

ISBN 0 521 34375 5

FP

Contents

Contents

vi

Plates

Rustic Festival, Annunciation to the Shepherds, Nativity. Oxford, Bodleian Library, MS Douce 93, fo. 28r; Utrecht, mid-fifteenth century.   *frontispiece*

BETWEEN PAGES 266 AND 267

1   Virgin and Child, Pilgrimage in margin. Hours of Marguerite of Orléans, Paris, Bibliothèque Nationale, MS Lat. 1156B, fo. 25r; French, after 1426.

2   Harrowing of Hell. 'Paduan Psalter', Cambridge, Fitzwilliam Museum, MS 36/1950, fo. 103v; German, in Italianate style, c. 1260.

3   Crucifixion. Holkham Bible Picture Book, London, British Library, MS Add. 47682, fo. 32v; English, first half of the fourteenth century.

4   Events surrounding the Resurrection. Eadwine Psalter (or Canterbury Psalter), Cambridge, Trinity College, MS R.17.1, fo. 24r; Canterbury, c. 1150.

5   'The Cart of the Faith'. London, British Library, MS Add. 37049, fo. 83r; English, early fifteenth century.

6   'The Tree of Life'. London, British Library, MS Add. 37049, fo. 19v.

7   'The Tree of Love'. London, British Library, MS Add. 37049, fo. 25r.

8   Virgin and Child. Talbot Hours, Cambridge, Fitzwilliam Museum, MS 40/1950, fo. 73r; French, c. 1450.

9   *Troilus* Frontispiece. Cambridge, Corpus Christi College, MS 61, fo. IV; English, first quarter of the fifteenth century.

10   Copy of the *Itinerary*, a leaf added in about 1410 by the Limbourgs to the *Très Belles Heures de Notre Dame*. Paris, Bibliothèque Nationale, MS nouv. acq. lat. 3039 (French, late fourteenth century); now lost, the leaf is known only in the lithograph published by Auguste, Comte de Bastard d'Estang, *Peintures et ornements des manuscrits . . . depuis le VIe siècle jusqu'à la fin du XVIe* (Paris, 1832–69).

11   Ascension. Breviary of Jean sans Peur, London, British Library, MS Harley 2897, fo. 188v; French, c. 1413–17.

12   Poet and Audience. *Oeuvres* of Adam de la Halle, Paris, Bibliothèque Nationale, MS f. fr. 25566, fo. 10r; French, c. 1300.

13   Poet and Audience. *Poésies* of Guillaume de Machaut, Paris, Bibliothèque Nationale, MS f. fr. 22545, fo. 75v; French, c. 1380.

14   Poet and Audience. *Pèlerinage de vie humaine* of Guillaume de Deguileville, London, British Library, MS Add. 38120, fo. 1r; French, c. 1415.

vii

Plates

31   Annunciation to the Shepherds. Rohan Hours, Paris, Bibliothèque Nationale,
      MS Lat. 9471, fo. 85v; French, c. 1420–30.

32   Annunciation to the Shepherds. *Passion d'Arras* of Eustache Mercadé, Arras,
      Bibliothèque d'Arras, MS 697, fo. 28v; French, mid-fifteenth century.

PLATE ACKNOWLEDGEMENTS

We are indebted to the following museums, galleries, libraries, and other copyright-holding institutions, for the supply of photographs, and for permission to reproduce in this volume illustrations from works in their possession:

Arras, Bibliothèque d'Arras   32; Brussels, Bibliothèque Royale Albert Ier   24, 26; Cambridge, Fitzwilliam Museum   2, 8, 28; Cambridge, The Master and Fellows of Trinity College   4, 19; Cambridge, The Master and Fellows of Corpus Christi College   9, 16a, 17a, 18a; Cambridge, Mass., Houghton Library, Harvard University   30; London, The British Library   3, 5, 6, 7, 11, 14, 20a and b, 23; New York, The Metropolitan Museum of Art, Cloisters Collection   22; Oxford, Bodleian Library   *Frontispiece*, 27; Paris, Bibliothèque Nationale   1, 12, 13, 15, 16b, 16c, 17b, 18b–d, 25a–b, 31; Rome, Vatican Library   21; Vienna, Nationalbibliothek   29.

Acknowledgements

There are many who have helped to bring this volume to publication, and we are particularly glad of the encouragement we have received from Elizabeth Salter's colleagues, friends and pupils in pursuing our design to bring out this collection. We are particularly grateful to Dr J. J. G. Alexander and to Dr H. R. Beadle, who read the draft of the essay on Shepherds, and made many helpful suggestions, and to Dr J. W. Binns, who assisted with the translation of some of the Latin passages in Chapters 1, 2 and 3 of this book. The staff of the Cambridge University Press, especially Mr Kevin Taylor, have been unfailingly helpful and courteous.

Foreword

The essays of Elizabeth Salter contained in this volume are made up of materials published after 1966 but also of materials which remained unpublished at her death in 1980. Gathering these pieces together in one book reveals powerfully not merely the coherence of her writing on many different subjects, but also the strength and consistency of purpose which characterises her thinking.

Elizabeth Salter began her university education at Bedford College, University of London, and it was here that she went on, under the supervision of Phyllis Hodgson, to write a dissertation for the degree of MA on Nicholas Love's prose translation of the pseudo-Bonaventuran *Meditationes vitae Christi*. Material derived from and inspired by her dissertation constituted the basis of her journal publication during the early years of her scholarly career, and the whole dissertation was subsequently published in revised form in 1974. Elizabeth Salter's early teaching years, from 1950 onwards, were spent at Cambridge, where she contributed significantly to the development of medieval studies in the University; here she developed the ideas on Chaucer and Langland which found expression in her book on the *Knight's Tale* and the *Clerk's Tale* and her book on *Piers Plowman*, published in 1962 and 1963 respectively. These two works first established her as a scholar of international reputation.

In 1964 she moved to the University of York, where the high reputation of the growing department of English owed much to the brilliance of her teaching and lecturing. In 1969 she was appointed to a professorial chair; she was also the moving force behind the creation of the postgraduate Centre for Medieval Studies at the University of York, whose first director she became in 1972. Elizabeth Salter was prodigal with her time and talent as a supervisor of postgraduate research, and the impress of the radiant warmth of her personality as well as the zeal and dedication of her scholarship will remain with the many students she taught and trained.

The years at York saw much collaborative and editorial publishing activity, and also a number of essays and articles, especially on Chaucer and Langland, where she developed her earlier insights into the poet's creative engagement with the sometimes intractable matter of his reading and experience. But she also began to explore the territories where literature is essentially, and often enigmatically embedded in its social and historical environment, where matters of patronage, for instance, become vital. Many of her numerous articles on alliterative literature reflect these preoccupations; nevertheless the more ambitious of these explorations into the wider cultural contexts of both art and literature were only just being put into written form towards the end of her life, as can be seen in the posthumously published work *Fourteenth-Century English Poetry: Contexts and Readings*, and in the essays which appear for the first time in the present book. These years at York, too, saw the maturing of Elizabeth Salter's work on the relationships between literature and the visual arts in the Middle Ages. In 1973 she published, in collaboration with her colleague Derek Pearsall, *Landscapes and Seasons of the Medieval World*; the last essay in the present volume is a continuous prose version of some of her many lectures on literature and the visual arts – lectures which were perhaps the pinnacle of her achievement as a teacher.

In 1978, Elizabeth Salter returned to the University of Connecticut at Storrs, where she had been a visitor 1963–4, to take up a year's appointment as distinguished visiting professor. From this time until her death from cancer in 1980 she maintained an extraordinary vigour in research and writing. She had made interdisciplinary methods of study very much her own, bringing literary texts and historical documents into a conjunction both complex and stimulating: her writing was characterised throughout by an unflinching regard for the sometimes surprising interpretative insights and problems revealed by such cross-connections. The evidence of these developments in her scholarly powers is to be found in many pieces presented here, in the reprinted essays on *Winner and Waster* and *A Complaint against Blacksmiths*, but above all in the unpublished material which appears here for the first time.

Some parts of this book will need no introduction or explanation. In the central part of the volume we have reprinted all the major articles and essays published by Elizabeth Salter in books and journals from 1966 onwards. In reprinting this series of published writings we hope to make more readily accessible those of her important and influential later works which have up till now been scattered in many different publications. We have grouped them according to the main issues which preoccupied her in the later part of her career, but a complete bibliography of Elizabeth Salter's writings is appended to the volume so that readers can see the original chronology of the pieces.

We have also taken this opportunity, as we have said, to introduce two major pieces of unpublished writing, which stand at the beginning and end of the collection. These two pieces need some further comment.

When Elizabeth Salter died in 1980, she left unfinished a new book on the cultural contexts of literature in medieval England. It was to be a book which would fully explore the continental elements in those cultural contexts; provisionally entitled *An Obsession with the Continent* (in allusion to a phrase used by G. O. Sayles), it was to give prominence throughout to the fact that the literature of medieval England was written in Anglo-Norman, French and Latin as well as in English. The book began as a sweeping revision of one that Elizabeth Salter had completed some years before, principally on fourteenth-century English poetry. As she became more preoccupied with the international and polyglot dimensions of her subject she grew increasingly dissatisfied with this book, and her revisions, characteristically, involved a comprehensive and radical rethinking of the whole pattern of writing in medieval England. Although she felt that the earlier book did not represent her most fully developed views on the subject, we, as her literary executors, were nevertheless very content to have it published in 1983 by Oxford University Press as *Fourteenth-Century English Poetry: Contexts and Readings*. Our task there was comparatively simple, since nearly all of the text and most of the notes were already in typescript and ready for the printer.

What we had for the revised volume was rather different. In effect, there was a brief introduction; a first chapter, complete, in corrected typescript, with annotation fairly full; a second chapter, unfinished, in manuscript, with annotation partly complete and partly in the form of hints and suggestions; and a third chapter, unfinished, in manuscript, with annotation somewhat less full. The third chapter was left unfinished when Elizabeth Salter returned from the United States in September 1979; the second chapter she was still working on in 1980. We have therefore had a good deal to do in completing the annotation. As far as the text is concerned, however, it has been a matter of correcting a very small number of mistakes or infelicities of expression that we know would have been corrected in the author's own final version.

The last piece in the present book, 'The Annunciation to the Shepherds in later medieval art and drama', has a different history again. Essentially, it is a rendering in continuous prose of the quite extraordinary series of lectures that Elizabeth Salter was giving in the last years of her life: in these lectures she studied the portrayal of the shepherd in the literary and visual arts of the later Middle Ages and the social and cultural assumptions, especially late medieval attitudes towards the peasantry, implicit in such portrayal. Any who were present at these lectures will have been conscious of the privilege of listening to the reflections and questions of a scholar who had spent many years asking what kinds of common ground could be discovered between the disciplines of art and literature. The text which we possessed for these lectures comprised several versions of partly-written-out lecture notes, largely unannotated; we believed, nevertheless, that the evolution of ideas behind the lectures was sufficiently clear to warrant presenting them together. Preparing them for publication, therefore, has involved fairly continuous interpretative amplification and reorganisation of the materials, while the annotation has been filled out either from works referred to in Elizabeth Salter's own manuscript notes or from works which it seems likely that she read. We make no apology for our editorial activity here, though it goes further than anything else that we have attempted; we believe that the justification is to be found in a study that could properly be called epoch-making.

DEREK PEARSALL   NICOLETTE ZEEMAN

Abbreviations

ANTS	Anglo-Norman Text Society
BJRL	*Bulletin of the John Rylands Library*
BL	British Library (London)
BN	Bibliothèque Nationale (Paris)
ChauR	*Chaucer Review*
CUL	Cambridge University Library
DNB	*Dictionary of National Biography*
EETS, ES, OS, SS	Early English Text Society, Extra Series, Original Series Supplementary Series
EHR	*English Historical Review*
HLF	*Histoire littéraire de la France*, ed. Petit de Julleville
JEGP	*Journal of English and Germanic Philology*
JWCI	*Journal of the Warburg and Courtauld Institutes*
LSE	*Leeds Studies in English*
MED	*Middle English Dictionary*
MGH	Monumenta Germaniae Historica
MLN	*Modern Language Notes*
MLR	*Modern Language Review*
MP	*Modern Philology*
MS	*Mediaeval Studies*
NQ	*Notes and Queries*
OED	*Oxford English Dictionary*
PBA	*Proceedings of the British Academy*
PL	*Patrologia Latina*, ed. J.-P. Migne
PMLA	*Publications of the Modern Language Association of America*
PRO	Public Record Office (London)
RES	*Review of English Studies*
SATF	Société des anciens textes français
TRHS	*Transactions of the Royal Historical Society*
VCH	*Victoria County History*

Part I An obsession with the continent*

Introduction

No study of medieval literature which intends more than a brief excursion into familiar territory can afford to spend long debating the advantages of travelling as critic or historian. When the journey proposed is one of exploration, with so much ground to cover and so various a landscape to comprehend, no skills, no disciplines are irrelevant. The co-operative parts played by historical scholarship and evaluative criticism in dealing with works of the past are no less easily demonstrable in the field of literature than in that of the visual arts. And it seems, therefore, quite as appropriate to accept, at the outset, Panofsky's statement about this relationship as to argue, with some sense of urgency, and in the expectation of battles yet to be won, that such a relationship should exist:

Archaeological research is blind and empty without aesthetic recreation, and aesthetic recreation is irrational and often misguided without archaeological research.[1]

There are, however, special reasons why, when the study is focussed upon English literature of the thirteenth and fourteenth centuries, the balance of parts in this relationship might often have to be adjusted in favour of 'archaeological research'. Or, at the very least, why an extremely flexible attitude might have to be adopted towards the handling of the works in question as exercises in historical or literary modes. For the period 1150–1400, a view of English culture which relied exclusively upon writing in the English language for basic evidence would be an impoverished one indeed. The history of these centuries is rich and exciting: during those years England became closely enmeshed in European dynastic affairs, and acted out a most complex and sometimes contradictory series of roles in its encounters with continental politics, trade, learning, art and literature. But only a limited amount of the richness and excitement of the age is conveyed to us by English vernacular literature. Not until the later fourteenth century did England produce, in Geoffrey Chaucer, a poet whose range and sophistication in the English language was comparable with those who had worked in French and Italian before him. And even then, it must be said, Chaucer was as much a recognisable and conscious product of a European cultural situation as he was 'the firste fyndere of our faire langage',[2] the 'father of English poetry'.[3]

Under such conditions, we can be tempted to dramatise the importance of what English literature exists, and to see its 'history' in an evolutionary way, as

---

* This introduction and the three following chapters are published here for the first time: their provenance is described in the Preface above.

I

developing through lean periods of foreign domination to a national triumph after 1350. Theories of 'hidden continuity' can become a useful way of disguising what appear to be empty spaces; artificial emphases can produce a false impression of the literary contexts of apparently isolated English works. The powerful attractions of an evolutionary point of view must be admitted. When we consider how confidently Old English vernacular literature responded to the immensely varied needs of Anglo-Saxon England, and then consider how tentatively, during the thirteenth and fourteenth centuries, Middle English literature served comparable needs, we are almost bound to find ourselves looking with some eagerness towards the emergence of a stable situation, in which a dominant literary language, based firmly upon dominant spoken usages, had achieved national and international status. We are bound, therefore, to anticipate with pleasure the decades in which *Troilus and Criseyde*, the *Pearl*, and the *Cloud of Unknowing* were written, and to feel, however imprecisely, that here, once more, we are in touch with an 'English tradition' which will lead us naturally to Shakespeare and to the religious poets of the seventeenth century. But the limitations of such a view must also be admitted, if, in fact, it directs the eye only towards the recognition of certain kinds of literary excellence in a selected language, and in incompletely documented settings.

The examination and presentation of medieval works of art customarily involves a very wide variety of procedures: the studies of Millard Meiss, for instance, over recent years, have examined French court painting of the fourteenth and early fifteenth centuries by means of historical research: into the society for which it was produced – the patrons, their family ties, their administration of estates: into the economic conditions which controlled the quality and availability of the artists who worked for such patrons: into the iconographic and stylistic traditions – traditions which affected, equally, book and panel painting, sculpture, metal-work, ivories – which these artists both inherited and modified. Thus evaluative judgements of particular fifteenth-century paintings – the dazzling Calendar series, for the *Très Riches Heures* of Jean, Duc de Berry, by the Limbourg brothers, or the strangely expressionist miniatures of the Rohan master, as we find them in the *Grandes Heures de Rohan* – are founded firmly upon knowledge of a whole complex of relationships, personal, geographical, economic and aesthetic, which we are helped to trace over the preceding fourteenth century. And this knowledge can be proved to be relevant to evaluative judgement: it is not simply a pleasing arabesque to critical analysis.

Ideally, we should expect medieval works of literature to be treated in a similarly comprehensive and rigorous way. Literary criticism, at its most generous, should involve many of the inquiries felt to be essential by those scholars and critics (the separation of their roles is encouragingly difficult) who have done most to illuminate and elucidate for us the art of the Middle Ages and of the Renaissance – Panofsky, Gombrich, Meiss. In practice, medieval works of literature are more often subjected to separate kinds of scrutiny – those directed by specialist scholarly interest and those directed by what Matthew Arnold expressed as an interest in 'a real, not a historic estimate' of their nature.[4]

It would not be useful to discuss at any length the cruder ways in which a disregard for the historical life of this literature and the past operates in certain kinds of literary criticism. More important is an affirmation that medieval literature, as medieval art, has a life which is often far more complicated than narrower forms of literary criticism and stylistic analysis can reveal. If we believe that it is the task of scholar and critic to co-operate in the revelation of a living culture as much as in the assessment of particular artistic quality, we must expect to achieve no more than modest triumphs in our crucial campaigns of rediscovery. It would be dangerous to assume, for instance, that the most traditionally accessible of medieval poetry, that of Chaucer, reveals more than a part of its original meaning and its original artistry to us, however well-educated our responses to later literature. The most recent studies of 'Chaucer in his age' suggest, in the very variety of materials put before us, that we have still far to go, and will perhaps never agree as to the distance travelled, in our search for the whole life of his poetry.

There are structures of life, art, and thought which support the most seemingly fragile, even insignificant medieval text, and give it that substance which purely evaluative criticism must deny. Indeed it may well be that the silences which seem to surround and isolate many English writings of the thirteenth and early fourteenth centuries are, to the attentive ear, filled with the sounds of an active world which is only partly English, partly literary. The chapters which follow will often be dedicated to those silences.

1 Cultural patterns in twelfth-century England: Norman and Angevin

T H E heavy conditioning of all medieval English literature by social, political and religious factors is a plain historical truth. Nowhere is this conditioning more clearly demonstrable than in its variable cultural status over the period. Indeed, the complex, often enigmatic relationship of the English language to English as a respected literary medium dominates the 'history of English literature' from the twelfth to the fifteenth centuries; in long perspective, the literary role of English was not securely redefined until the sixteenth century. Before the Norman Conquest, the security of its position was real enough. But unlike art and architecture, which from an early period have proved themselves capable of assimilating new materials and forms without internal damage, English literature was, of necessity, profoundly affected by the changes which followed the introduction of new ruling classes and a new spoken and written vernacular language into the country at 1066. In the special case of native English poetry, with its reliance upon Germanic prosodic systems, linguistic change meant ultimately, if not immediately, some measure of serious disturbance. It would be easy to represent the position of English literature in the twelfth and thirteenth centuries, with some remarkable exceptions, as precarious, even depressed: to illustrate continuing composition from texts of either fragmentary or uncertain quality, compared with the splendid vernacular works of the pre-Conquest period. It would also be easy to misrepresent both the nature and the context of those 'remarkable exceptions', seeing them either as monuments to a stubborn sense of national survival or as bold pretenders to a literary distinction which was only to be fully claimed by English works of the next century. Texts such as Laȝamon's verse chronicle, the *Brut*, the prose *Ancrene Riwle*, and the debate poem, the *Owl and the Nightingale*, all probably composed between the late twelfth and earlier thirteenth centuries, could be singled out for such kinds of attention, which would, nevertheless, fail to do justice to them in their historical time-contexts. We cannot, of course, exaggerate the overall literary importance of the establishment of a new aristocracy in England, after 1066, and the continuous strengthening of that aristocracy from continental sources over the next two centuries. Settlement may have declined somewhat in intensity during the thirteenth century, but the importation of Frenchmen from regions as far distant as Provence and Savoy into all branches of English administration – ecclesiastical, military, political – was constant, well into the age of Chaucer. One of the immediate and long-lasting effects of this was to put incentives for the patronage of English literature into great doubt. In particular, it meant that the whole cultural context for English poetry of any but the most useful instructional genres became problematic. If, however, our search for evidences of 'the survival of English after the Norman Conquest' must meet with as many disappointments as rewards, we should perhaps respond by questioning the usefulness of a strict approach to what, at this time, is 'English'. This chapter attempts to use generous definitions of the term.

Historians stress the positive and creative significance of the fact that the Norman Conquest 'compelled (England) to become an intimate part of the European state system', redefining the context in which England was hencefor-ward to operate:

the power which became of European account was not England . . . not even Normandy, but the Anglo-Norman Empire, and, after it, the Angevin Empire . . . it was as a member of these Empires that England participated in continental politics . . .[1]

England's 'obsession with the continent'[2] from the eleventh to the fifteenth centuries is a fact to be reckoned with, rather than regretted, and this must have consequences in our attitudes to literary no less than political situations in this country during those years. It would, in these changed circumstances, be a poor account of the twelfth century in England which concentrated upon the processes of literary decay in one vernacular language and failed to give some idea of the processes of new creation at work in other vernaculars, already widely acceptable at many levels of insular society, for written and spoken purposes. There is an excitement in recognising that 'l'explosion littéraire du XIIe siècle en Angleterre' was a mainly French affair, dependent basically upon the vigour and 'precocity' of Anglo-Norman literature, produced under new and demanding conditions in an occupied country.[3] And there is an excitement in recognising the extent to which this 'explosion' affected all European literatures of subsequent centuries, whether English or continental. Beside this, the tracing of dubious 'continuities' which would hope to establish the tenacity of a specifically English literary culture seems over-fastidious.[4]

For twelfth-century England was as decisively international in its intellectual and artistic temper as in its political. Under both Norman and Angevin rule, statesmen, theologians, philosophers, mathematicians, poets and artists moved naturally between England and the continent: further, too, for the dynastic ties between the royal houses of England, northern France, Spain and Sicily were strong, and encouraged free interchange in every sphere of activity.[5] The concept of a European Internationalism need not, of course, rule out that of continuity with certain aspects of an Anglo-Saxon past. If we seek continuities, they are there to find, but they are continuities set into larger patterns of change. There were some ways in which the new aristocracy and those who served it were content, even eager, to identify with the history, both political and cultural, of pre-Conquest England. So, George Zarnecki has shown that, in the field of architectural sculpture, the deeply-rooted Anglo-Saxon traditions of low-relief designs, allied to equally strong traditions of line-drawing and draughtsmanship, not only resisted the implantations of the monumental Romanesque styles of the continent, but also affected, by example, twelfth-century Normandy and Northern France. Native sculptors 'found employment and favour with the Normans'.[6] Earlier, Francis Wormald had demonstrated that the Norman patrons of the Bayeux tapestry employed Anglo-Saxon artists and Anglo-Saxon two-dimensional styles for this great record of their military achievement.[7] The first chroniclers of the Anglo-Norman Kingdom – men such as Ordericus Vitalis, Henry of Huntingdon and William of Malmesbury – accepted that their kings were the legitimate successors of the Anglo-Saxon royal line.[8] Patrons and public showed no reluctance for literature, sober or romantic, which presented them with the varied subject matter of England's earlier centuries – whether Anglo-Saxon, Scandinavian or Celtic, and whether drawn from chronicle, legend or saga. The Anglo-Normans, supported by their chroniclers and romance writers, found some good reasons to regard themselves as the inheritors of late Anglo-Saxon tradition. From such a point of view, the great *Historia Regum Britanniae* of Geoffrey of Monmouth, and the vernacular *Chronicles* of Geoffrey Gaimar and of Wace confirmed the desire of the Normans to enter into their new inheritance, rather than to advertise their role as continental conquerors:

Le public de l'Angleterre préféra l'histoire des rois du pays, anglais, danois ou normands, à l'histoire des ducs de Normandie, dont les derniers furent par hasard rois d'Angleterre.[9]

Something similar could be said of the enthusiasms of a slightly later period, when Anglo-Norman families, by then firmly settled in England, employed poets to celebrate the stability of their position in 'ancestral romances' which are 'insular, provincial and independent of the continental tradition from which they derive'.[10]

But it is also true that many of those very historians and verse chroniclers who celebrated, for the Anglo-Normans, a newly-acquired past, were themselves, either by birth or education, products of the mixed situation created by that kingdom. Ordericus Vitalis, a Shropshire man, whose French father, Odelier, came to Mercia as a member of the household of Robert Montgomery, the Count of Shrewsbury, spent most of his life as a monk of St Evroult, in Normandy, with occasional visits to England and France. William of Malmesbury was the son of a French knight and an English mother: 'Ego autem, quia utriusque gentis sanguinem traho . . .'[11] Henry of Huntingdon, of Norman origin, but brought up at the Abbey of Ramsey, passed into the service of Robert Bloet, Norman Chancellor of William Rufus, and Bishop of Lincoln.[12] If these men feel that they are

'English', and also 'partisans très nets de la nouvelle dynastie',[13] their allegiances clearly operate in a very wide field of 'national' consciousness. Just how wide that consciousness was, we can begin to imagine, from the pages of Ordericus Vitalis, as he looks both north and south to Norman kingdoms in England and Sicily, and enables us to grasp 'the unity of the Norman achievement'.[14] Only a generous concept of national identity makes intelligible those early twelfth-century situations in which St William of York, who was related to both King Stephen of England and King Roger of Sicily, could be received as an honoured guest of the Chancellor of the Norman Sicilian Kingdom, the Yorkshire clerk, Robert of Selby.[15]

It is, therefore, still proper to maintain that the fullest sense of English culture during the twelfth century must be conveyed by the phrase 'international exchange' – an exchange which concerns the relationships between England and the continent, and, no less, between England, the continent and Scandinavia.[16] Twelfth-century art and literature in England, no less than twelfth-century politics, are dependent upon a web of connections between the royal and ecclesiastical households of Europe. Paths of art and devotion can sometimes be traced most precisely across England and the continent. The Latin *Prayers and Meditations* of St Anselm, Archbishop of Canterbury and himself an Italian, one of the founders of that 'affective devotion' to Christ which was to take such firm root as an 'English' tradition,[17] were sent to Mathilda, Countess of Tuscany, in 1104, by the hand of an English monk of Canterbury, and with graceful illustrations by an English manuscript painter. At the time of their sending, St Anselm was in temporary exile, at Lyons, and it has been conjectured, therefore, that he had access to English miniaturists, working in Southern France. The pictures were later used as models for other manuscripts of the *Meditations*, in Salzburg and, again, in England, where one particular copy came to rest at a priory of Benedictine Nuns, near Oxford.[18]

Journeys of English churchmen on business, and secular administrators on pilgrimage, to Italy and Spain across the rich kingdoms of France are as swiftly recorded in the art of the English countryside as in the art of the English cloister. A Romanesque church facade from Pavia serves an English illuminator as the model for the City of God, as he works with St Augustine's text at Canterbury just after 1100.[19] The appearance, in small Herefordshire churches of the earlier twelfth century, of decorative programmes and figure-sculpture directly reminiscent of the grander Romanesque of south-western France, reminds us of the travels of west-country gentry, whose background would, in any case, have been as much continental as newly 'English'. Oliver de Merlimond, steward of Hugh de Mortimer, Lord of Wigmore, who had been given the 'vile' of Shobdon, in Herefordshire in return for services to his lord – 'pur ly lealement servir' – went on pilgrimage to St James of Compostella, shortly after deciding to build a new church at Shobdon:

dount Olyver esteit mout pensifs de fer lever une novele eglise en Schobbedon . . . Deentre ceo sa veyt meymes cely Olyver devociun et talent de prendre le vyage al seinct Jake en Pelrimage . . .[20]

Even in their present fragmented state, the remains of de Merlimond's lavishly decorated building seem 'to reflect observations made on foreign travel'.[21] The exuberant sculpted interlace of birds, beasts and zodiac signs, their elongated Apostle figures, comment upon de Merlimond's route through Poitou and Aquitaine, taking in the deeply carved facades of larger French churches and cathedrals. At nearby Kilpeck, south-west of Hereford, the Shobdon craftsmen worked again, producing on the chancel-arch evangelists whose mournful, expressive faces can only be meaningfully compared with those of sculpted figures on the great tympana and portals of churches such as Parthenay-le-Vieux, near Poitiers, Beaulieu, Moissac and Marcilhac, on the pilgrimage ways through the Auvergne and Guyenne districts.[22] To recognise the complex European affiliations of Herefordshire art during the earlier years of the twelfth century (Shobdon was consecrated before 1143) is only to fill in one small detail of a picture which will enlarge but not substantially change over the next two centuries. The sculpted arches and columns of Shobdon and Kilpeck, the tympana of the neighbouring villages of Fownhope and Brinsop, with their majestic seated figures and triumphant St George, register powerful native responses to south-western French traditions and symbols.

And these were not the only responses encouraged by Oliver de Merlimond. On his journey back to England, he visited the Abbey of St Victor, in Paris, and was much impressed by what he saw and heard there. His invitation of two canons of St Victor to Shobdon, to found a religious house there, had important results: after some movement between various sites in the area, an Abbey of Austin Canons was finally settled at Wigmore, in Herefordshire, with the help of de Merlimond's overlord, Hugh de Mortimer. The House at Wigmore came to immediate fame by the appointment of Andrew of St Victor as its first Prior, for the writings of Andrew, who died in 1175, were important in the widest European contexts of learned Biblical study.[23] It may be no contradiction of this that Wigmore appears, during the next century, to take special interest in some of the finest kinds of English vernacular writing of the time (see below, p. 71): its connection with the Mortimer family remained close – many Mortimers, including five Earls of March, were buried there, and benefactions were frequent.[24]

The nature of twelfth-century 'Internationalism' can be, and frequently has been, illustrated in a highly dramatic form from the rich years of the reign of Henry of Anjou and Eleanor of Aquitaine (1154–79) and no-one would question the political and intellectual significance of 'the converging tendencies, English, Celtic, Norman, Angevin, which came together in the Angevin empire'.[25] But, as we may see, rehearsals for that brilliant performance were already under way in the reign of Henry I (1100–35) and preparations had been made even earlier than the Conquest itself. There were royal and ducal precedents in the courts of the early twelfth century for the wealthy international patronage of Henry and Eleanor, and precise structures were already in place which would help, ultimately, to stage their more ambitious international scenes.

An important piece of research, published in 1966, presented hitherto unnoticed evidence for the existence in the British Isles, from a very early date, of a class of professional interpreters or *latimarii*, both English and Celtic, 'acting as intermediaries and translators between one race and another'. The need for such a class of men in Britain 'polyglot . . . from at least the fifth century . . .', and probably extending its range of languages, by the time of Edward the Confessor, even to French, was sharpened after the Conquest:

William I and the majority of his men spoke French, but scores of his followers spoke Breton. The languages to be heard in the lands he had conquered were English, Welsh, Scandinavian, Scottish, Cornish and some Irish. The resident and incoming clergy, in addition to their vernaculars, naturally spoke Latin. If any man had need of interpreters, William surely had.[26]

The extensive use of *latimarii* made by the Normans and the Angevins in the business of government might seem to have only historical interest of a specialised sort. But, as Dr Bullock-Davies argues convincingly, the overlap of political and literary history is here significantly large. The ease with which materials concerning Arthur and other Celtic heroes passed into the 'neo-Celtic' literature of the French and Anglo-French writers of the twelfth century may find its most likely explanation in the 'royal and baronial *latimers*, with whom important poets like Wace, Thomas the author of *Tristan*, Marie de France and Chrétien de Troyes would have come into personal contact' (ibid., p. 10). Her study brings to life for us the interpenetration of cultures, dependent often upon mixed marriages – French and Welsh: the journeys between the courts of Wales and Poitou in the early twelfth century, the daily contacts, in the noble households of Wales and the border country, between *latimers*, French, Welsh and English minstrels, which may account for the rapid assimilation of Celtic story into the verse of continental French, Anglo-Norman and, ultimately, English poetry. The telling of the tale of *Perceval* by a visiting Welsh poet and *latimer* to the Count of Poitou, who may have been the troubadour, William VII: the gathering of materials for her *lais* by Marie de France from interpreters in the Cardiff castle of William Consul, Lord of Glamorgan: these are more than daring conjectures, given what we know of their historical framework (ibid., pp. 5–6, 12, 15). When that framework admits the strong possibility, for instance, that the mother of Robert, Earl of Gloucester, illegitimate son of Henry I, and one of the most famous patrons of his time, was Nesta, sister of Staffyd ap Rhys, king of south-Wales, it may be even easier to understand why Geoffrey of Monmouth first dedicated his legendary history of Celtic Britain, the *Historia Regum Britanniae*, to Robert.[27]

But of course the dedication and the family circumstances which may have prompted it were not simply expressions of parochial interest. Robert of Gloucester was a great prince, half-brother to the Empress Matilda, and deeply involved in the political struggles over the succession to his father's throne, a cultivated and respected man, to whom the Anglo-French historian, William of Malmesbury, also dedicated his work, remarking admiringly upon his daily reading hours, snatched from a busy life of action:

Litteras ita fovetis, ut cum sitis tantarum occupationum mole districti, horas tamen aliquas vobis surripiatis, quibus aut ipsi legere, aut legentes possitis audire.[28]

(You cherish letters to such an extent that, although you are perplexed by the burden of such great business, nonetheless you snatch a few hours for yourself, in which you can either read yourself, or listen to others reading.)

His munificence to the abbey church at Tewkesbury was also remarked upon in his own time –

Munificentiae vestrae pecuniaeque contemptum praetendit Teochesbiriae coenobium (ibid., p. 520)

(And in addition to your munificence, the monastery at Tewkesbury shows your contempt for money . . .)

and Tewkesbury's 'unfamiliar beauty', its 'external felicities', have been more recently associated with his 'wealth and enlightenment'.[29] Geoffrey of Monmouth's *Historia* received subsequent dedications to Waleran, Count of Meulan, later Earl of Worcester, and to King Stephen himself: it was immediately as well-known on the continent as in England, in contexts both monastic and seigneurial. A copy was at the Abbey of Bec, in Normandy, by 1139; of its ninety manuscripts, forty-eight can be dated to the twelfth century, and their circulation among the Anglo-Norman magnates of England charted with some precision.[30]

But if the 'matter' of Celtic Britain was in demand by those who had recently come to regard it as their own heritage, so too was the 'matter' of France. We have been reminded that some of the earliest and the best manuscripts of the French *chansons de geste* are Anglo-Norman:

l'Alexis et nos poèmes épiques antérieurs à 1150 (*Gormont et Isembart, Roland, Guillaume, Pèlerinage*) ne nous sont parvenus que dans des copies anglo-normandes le plus souvent uniques . . .[31]

The poem on the *Life of St Alexis* in the famous Albani manuscript and the Oxford text of the *Chanson de Roland* offer substantial and various proof that literary tastes and needs on either side of the Channel were not remarkably different.

The most direct testimony comes from the famous Oxford manuscript of the *Roland*:[32] copied by an Anglo-Norman scribe, most probably for the d'Oilli family,[33] Constables of Oxford during the late eleventh and early twelfth centuries, it shows us that the continental pride of perspective which typifies the spirit of *Roland* was still very much to the liking of those who had settled in that 'offshore island', Charlemagne's 'private retreat':

> Jo l'en cunquis e Escoce e Vales Islonde,
> E Engletere, que il teneit sa cambre.[34]

The *Alexis*, which is a continental French poem with an Anglo-Norman prose *Prologue*, was probably composed for the dedication of the Chapel of St Alexis, at St Albans, before 1119 and sung after the ceremony of consecration.[35] Later bound in with the splendidly illuminated Albani Psalter, it provides a striking example of how a great English centre such as St Albans in the early twelfth century could bring together the work of a northern French poet, an Anglo-French commentator, and three painters, two of whom are certainly English, from the St Albans scriptorium, and one more probably continental, under strong Byzantine influence.[36] Such a confluence is understandable in terms of the Norman 'patrons' involved: Abbot Paul of St Albans (1077–93), who came from the Abbey of St Etienne, Caen, and is known to have collected artists for St Albans from all over the continent; and Abbot Richard de Albini, who came to St Albans from Bec, home of the cult of St Alexis. The occasion for which the poem was composed, though set in England, had an international character: it was attended by the King and Queen of England, the Archbishop of Rouen. The Albani manuscript is similarly international, though its home and its powerful influence were in twelfth-century England.[37]

It is above all, however, from the royal and aristocratic courts of England and northern France in the earlier twelfth century that the ease and the wealth of cultural interchange can be most decisively illustrated. Here the interlocked fortunes of England, Normandy and France, and the consequent fact that 'the same kind of people, and very often the same people themselves, were patronizing writers on both sides of the Channel'[38] make the distinguishing of separate histories extremely difficult, and often quite unnatural. Something has already been said of the patronage of Robert, Earl of Gloucester: the case of Geoffrey of Monmouth's *Historia*, dedicated both to him and to Waleran, Count of Meulan and Earl of Worcester, focusses the nature of the situation very neatly. Both Robert and Waleran had strong continental ties and affiliations: we hear of Robert, who was also seigneur of Caen and Torigny, visiting the monastery of Bec, in Normandy, as his father and grandfather had done. The early appearance of a copy of Geoffrey's *Historia* at Bec may record his personal presentation, since he was at Rouen in 1135 and 1137.[39] Waleran, after a life of active engagement both in Normandy and England, died as a monk at Préaux, the abbey founded by his grandfather, who was one of the Conqueror's chief vassals. Robert and Waleran are praised in similar terms by the historians William of Malmesbury and Ordericus Vitalis: it seems not entirely inappropriate that Geoffrey of

Monmouth should also address them similarly, admiring their educated interests: Robert, whom 'Philosophia liberalibus artibus erudivit . . .' (Philosophy instructed in the liberal arts . . .), Waleran whom 'mater Philosophia in gremio excepit, scientiarumque subtilitatem suarum edocuit' (Philosophy as a mother took in her lap, and taught the subtlety of her branches of learning).[40]

With regard to the highest in the realm, we can trace the shared literary tastes, the shared poets, of Maud, first queen of Henry I, and her sister-in-law, Adela of Blois, daughter of William I. Writers as diverse as Aelred of Rievaulx and William of Malmesbury wrote respectfully of the learning, piety and generosity of Maud, a Scottish princess who was daughter of St Margaret, and convent-educated. Her court at Westminster was the centre of literary and artistic life: large numbers of poets and musicians were attracted to it, many of whom were continental, for her reputation as a patroness spread far and wide over Europe:

Westmonasterio multis annis morata. Nec tamen quicquam ei regalis magnificentiae deerat . . . Erat ei in audiendo servitio Dei voluptas unica ideoque in clericos bene melodos inconsiderate provida; blande quoscunque alloqui, multa largiri, plura polliceri. Inde, liberalitate ipsius per orbem sata, turmatim huc adventabant scholastici tum cantibus tum versibus famosi; felicemque se putabat qui carminis novitate aures mulceret dominae. Nec in his solum expensas conferebat, sed etiam omni generi hominum, praesertim advenarum: qui, muneribus acceptis, famam ejus longe per terras venditarent.[41]

(She dwelt at Westminster for many years. She lacked nothing of regal magnificence . . . She took a unique pleasure in hearing the service of God, and thus she provided unsparingly for clerics with melodious voices, all of whom she spoke courteously to, bestowed many gifts on, and promised more. With her liberality thus planted throughout the world, scholars celebrated not only for their songs but also for their verses came hither in throngs; and he who could soothe the ears of his lady by the newness of his song thought himself a happy man. She lavished money not only on these, but also on all kinds of men, especially strangers: and they, having received her gifts, proclaimed her fame far and wide throughout the lands.)

Two of the most celebrated continental poets of the age, Marbod, Bishop of Rennes, and Hildebert of Lavardin, Bishop of Mans, eulogised her in Latin verses. Marbod praises her speech, her natural beauty, in the midst of feminine artificiality:

> Egregios mores, ac melle fluentia verba
>   Plus reticere juvat, quam minus inde loqui.
> Affectant aliae quod eis natura negavit,
>   Purpureas niveo pingere lacte genas;
> Fucatosque trahit facies medicata colores . . .
> Comprimit exstantes quarundam fascia mammas . . .
> Tu regina, quod es, metuis formosa videri.[42]

(I had rather remain silent about her outstanding manners and her honeyed words than speak inadequately about them. Other women affect what nature has denied them –

brightly coloured painted cheeks with snow-white milk. A face that is painted uses colours that are false . . . Certain ladies have their prominent breasts bound in by a strip of cloth . . . You, O queen, because you *are* beautiful, fear to *seem* so.)

Hildebert corresponded with her, sending, on request, a sermon, and receiving in return two elaborate gold candlesticks; occasionally his letters are decorous versions of love-longing – 'Hinc est. quod mari ac terra separatus a te, in Christo diligo te'[43] ('Thus it is, since I am separated from you by sea and land, that I love you in Christ') – and his poem to celebrate the birth of her son, William, uses language which brushes both Marian hymn and secular love-lyric:

> Est rosa de radice rosae, de relligione
>   Relligio: pietas de pietate fluit,
> De stella splendor, de magno nomine majus.   (ibid., col. 1444)

(A rose comes from the root of a rose; religion comes from religion; piety flows from piety; splendour comes from a star; from a great name comes a greater.)

That rose was offered again, by Hildebert, in his epitaph for her sister-in-law, Adela, Countess of Blois:

> Mens humilis, blandus sermo, benigna manus.
> Exempli speculum, patriae rosa . . .   (ibid., col. 1394)

(A humble mind, courteous speech, a kindly hand, the mirror of example, the rose of her native land.)

He had corresponded with Adela also, consoling her for the absence of her husband, in a letter thick with quotation from Seneca (ibid., col. 1444). For she was, like Maud of England, 'litteris erudita', worthy to have an Ecclesiastical History dedicated to her.[44] And she was much loved and admired, if we can judge from the warmth of her husband's Latin, as he writes to her on Crusade:

Pauca certe sunt, carissima, quae tibi de multis scribo, et quia tibi exprimere non valeo quae sunt in animo meo, carissima.[45]

(These are a few of the things which I write to you about out of many, most dear lady, and because I cannot express to you the things which are in my mind, most dear lady.)

and from the wide-ranging compliment of the verses of Baudri de Bourgueil, later Bishop of Dol,[46] who not only saw her renowned literary patronage as exalting her above her famous father:

> Una tamen res est qua praesit filia patri,
>   Versibus applaudet, scitque vacare libris.
> Haec etiam novit sua merces esse poetis,
>   A probitate sua nemo redit vacuus.
> Rursus inest illi dictandi copia torrens,
>   Et praeferre sapit carmina carminibus.[47]

(There is, however, one matter in which the daughter excels her father – she will favour verses, and she knows how to have leisure for books. She also knows how to reward poets: no-one returns empty-handed from her uprightness. Again, she possesses copious powers of [prose] composition, and she knows how to distinguish one poem from another.)

but acknowledged her as the source of his materials, the breath of his inspiration:

> Grandia dico quidem, sed grandia dicere novi,
> Ex quo materiam mihi sumpsi de comitissa.
> Ipsa mihi carmen, calamum mihi suggeris ipsa,
> Ipsa dabis flatus, os ipsa replebis hiulcum.[48]

(I speak on a mighty topic indeed, but I have known how to speak on a mighty topic from the time when I took my material from the countess. You yourself suggest to me my poem, you yourself suggest to me my pen, you yourself will give me inspiration, you yourself will fill my gaping mouth.)

His vision of her is deeply romantic: he remembers how she had appeared before him, as insubstantial as the slip of a new moon, as fleeting as a dream:

> Sic me saepe novam lunam vidisse recordor,
> Vel cum vix video meve videre puto.[49]

(Thus I remember that I have often seen the new moon, either when I scarcely see it or when I think that I see it.)

He goes on to imagine her, reading his poetry in her bed-chamber at the Château of Blois, surrounded by beauty and learning – tapestries depicting universal history, ceilings painted with the planets and zodiac signs, marble floors inset with a *mappa mundi*, a bed carved with signs of philosophy and the Seven Liberal Arts, and hung with gold-brocaded silk into which is woven the story of her father's conquest of England. Baudri's description is probably, itself, a lavish compliment to Adela: he presents her with a setting ideally worthy of her qualities:

> Dum tibi desudo, dum sudans, Adela, nugor,
> Depinxi pulchrum carminibus thalamum
> . . .
> Nempe decet talem talis thalamus comitissam
> At plus quod decuit quam quod erat cecini.
> (lines 1342–3, 1352–3)

(Whilst I sweat [out poems] for you, whilst I trifle sweating, Adela, I depicted a beautiful bed-chamber in my poems . . . Surely such a bed-chamber becomes such a countess, but I sang rather of what was becoming than of what was.)

Some of his sources lie, no doubt, in classical and late-classical poetry – Ovid, Lucan, Claudian, Isidore of Seville. But there is no reason to suppose that Adela would not have been familiar with, perhaps lived with, palace-art of this kind. One of the tapestries 'imagined' by Baudri recalls vividly the Bayeux Tapestry –

an Anglo-Norman masterpiece of secular pictorial narrative. The *chansons de geste* of the time, no less than the ecclesiastical complaints against 'pulchra tapetia variis coloribus depicta' ('beautiful tapestries painted with various colours'), remind us that monasteries, churches and castles were frequently decked with figured hangings just as elaborate as those provided for Adela in her poem.[50] The detail of Baudri's account – the *mappa mundi* on the floor is protected from dust by glass, 'tota fuit vitrea tecta superficie' ('Adelae', line 728: 'the whole was covered by a glassy surface') – is suggestive perhaps of something more precise than ordinary dream-vision material.

The courts of Maud of England and Adela of Blois, antedating as they do by half a century those of Marie of Champagne and Eleanor of Aquitaine, are clearly of some importance to the history of a certain kind of sensibility – to 'la naissance de la courtoisie, de l'amour courtois et de la poésie qui l'exprimera . . .'[51] More broadly viewed, for themselves and for their immediate products and their ultimate consequences, they belong to a world of almost unlimited geographical and intellectual horizons, in which the harsh realities, the narrow choices of feudal life and crusading venture cannot be denied, but can be released into moving forms of art, a world in which, through literature, religion, learning and tender sentiment can tolerantly enrich each other. The benefits of the lives they nourished and of the poetry and art they inspired were bestowed generously, irrespective of country or language. It has been suggested that the account by Ordericus Vitalis of the scene between Adela and Stephen of Blois, when the countess persuaded her reluctant husband to return to crusading, and, as it turned out, to his death, may have prompted a similar scene in Chrétien de Troyes' *Erec*, when Enid urges her husband, Erec, towards renewed 'deeds of chivalry'.[52] The splendid decorations of Adela's bedchamber at Blois recorded or imagined for us by Baudri de Bourgueil – its ceiling and carvings done to the late-antique prescriptions of Isidore and Martianus Capella, conjure up for us similar embroideries upon the coronation robe of Chrétien's Erec, and similar sculptures at the Cathedrals of Sens, Laon, and Chartres.[53] But even this distinguished sequence does not exhaust their interest. They may, of course, have most to tell us about the learned and colourful imagination of Adela's poet Baudri de Bourgueil, who was, we discover, as familiar with the English west-country at Worcester as he was with the abbeys of Normandy and the court of Blois.[54] Or they may turn us to think of the reputation of Adela's son, Henry of Blois, connoisseur of fine art, who was appointed Abbot of Glastonbury in 1126, and Bishop of Winchester three years later.[55] It is tempting to suppose that, if we may make anything more of the evidence supplied by Baudri than literary compliment, the civilised surroundings of his mother's court, her interest in classical as well as Biblical subjects in art, might have influenced Henry as much as his years as a monk of Cluny, the Burgundian Abbey whose metalwork and sculpture were the special object of St Bernard's famous complaint against the luxury and impropriety of twelfth-century ecclesiastical art.[56] The chroniclers recognise his magnificence as a builder of palaces, and a designer of elaborate water-gardens in the grounds of those palaces, at Wolvesey and Bishop's Waltham:

Praeterea opera mira, palatia sumptuosissima, stagna grandia, ductus aquarum difficiles, hypogeosque varia per loca meatus . . .[57]

(Furthermore, wonderful works, most sumptuous palaces, large pools, intricate aqueducts, and cellars and passages through various places . . .)

They describe his menageries and aviaries, his fascination with the 'varied monsters of the earth', in a way which recalls his mother's marbled floor at Blois, and its *mappa mundi*,

où figuraient la terre avec . . . ses animaux et ses bêtes fabuleuses, la mer avec ses poissons et ses monstres . . .[58]

But they are most impressed with his art-purchases – treasures from all over Europe: classical sculptures from Rome, probably intended for his palaces outside Winchester, manuscripts, reliquaries, cameos, Saracen carpets for his churches at Glastonbury and Winchester.[59] Giraldus Cambrensis becomes almost breathless with admiration:

Item cathedralem ecclesiam suam palliis purpureis et olosericis, cortinis et aulaeis pretiosissimis textis, philateriis, crucibus aureis massatis et argenteis, miro et exquisito artificio longe materiam exsuperante fabricatis et gemmatis . . . exornavit.[60]

(He enriched his cathedral church with brightly-coloured hangings made entirely of silk, with curtains and most precious woven tapestries, with phylacteries, with heavy gold and silver crosses, made and bejewelled with a wondrous and exquisite artifice far surpassing the material.)

The likelihood that he was the original owner of the Winchester Psalter (British Library MS Cotton Nero C. iv)[61] focusses attention once again upon his international status and tastes. The paintings in the Psalter, which were certainly executed at Winchester during Henry's life-time, are highly characteristic of English Romanesque – a lively blend of dramatic and often grotesque elements with those ornamental and formal. But they are related to northern French wall-painting and to miniature work 'from the Plantagenet Empire',[62] and in two cases, clearly copy a Byzantine icon. The availability of Byzantine models to artists at Winchester presents no problem since 'the Bishop, Henry of Blois, was a well known collector of curiosities and antiques':[63] and we can recall the picture offered by John of Salisbury, of Henry, disappointed in a petition to the Pope but solacing himself in Rome by selecting 'old statues', 'veteres statuas', to be sent home to adorn his now practically vanished palaces.[64] In the case of the Winchester Psalter with its probable patron, Henry of Blois, it is easy to see how the nature of English art of the twelfth century could be determined to a great extent by curial circumstances. What is painted in England can depend intimately upon the character and tastes of a prince brought up in central France.

But what is written in France can equally well depend upon the character and tastes of a queen brought up in a Scottish court, and in English convents. To Queen Maud of England, the patroness of Hildebert and Marbod, the poet 'Benedeiz' dedicated his romantic *Voyage of St Brendan*; in Anglo-Norman verse, probably translated for the Queen's household from his own original Latin version, he describes the wanderings of the Irish saint, as he searches for a sight of Heaven and Hell. Its exotic subject matter – a deserted city, a magic spring, sea-monsters, volcanoes, frozen seas – foreshadows that of later romances of the century: Béroul and Chrétien de Troyes may both be indebted.[65] The interest in the *Voyage* was international: dedicated over again to Henry I's second wife, Adeliza of Louvain, it was still being read on the continent in the thirteenth century, for of its five manuscripts the latest is a Picard version.[66]

Nothing which happened after 1150 would radically alter situations or processes characteristic of the earlier part of the century. In most respects, the reign of Henry of Anjou and Eleanor of Aquitaine intensified and enlarged what was already existent – in politics or in patronage of the arts. It is certainly true that with their accession, and the consequent welding of such powerful interests in one Angevin court, some further rationalisation and even a measure of institutionalisation was inevitable.

In the relationship between the Angevin and the Sicilian kingdoms during Henry's reign, for instance, historians have seen some loss of earlier spontaneity, represented nicely by the substitution of learned and political adventure on the roads to Sicily for adventure of a much more military and opportunist kind. Knights, '... happy and joyful on their horses as they rode up and down to seek their fortunes...'[67] were replaced by careerists and scholars, seeking benefices, administrative posts, manuscripts and teachers: both Norman kingdoms, northern and southern European, had expanded and formalised. This is, however, a change which could only clarify the 'internationalism' we can observe in earlier twelfth-century England. The international careers of some Englishmen spanned both halves of the century: Thomas Brown, 'Kaid Brun' of the Sicilian royal records, and judge and chaplain to Roger II of Sicily between 1137 and 1158, moved on to high position in the Exchequer of Henry II.[68] It is probably more important to stress the fulfilment of earlier twelfth-century promise, after 1150, than to particularise minor differences of organisation and outlook. One of the most spectacular careers of all later twelfth-century Englishmen was that of Gervase of Tilbury: scholar, jurist, administrator, he served William II of Sicily, Otto IV of Brunswick and Henry II of England. His *Otia Imperialia* (c. 1211) look back with some shrewdness of observation at the people he had lived among in Sicily – the great king Roger II, who sponsored learning and scientific experiment, the Sicilians themselves, paradoxical as their bitter and beautiful landscape. And we hear of summer journeys through Italy with English friends – with Philip, son of the Earl of Salisbury, for instance, whom he meets by chance at Salerno: a journey to Naples which even at this distance has genuine touches of authenticity. Its marvels of sightseeing are interspersed with the same details of the unchanging life and the Italian countryside that we find in Lorenzetti's frescoes, over a century later – the donkey laden with firewood which forces these travellers to pass through the propitious side of the miraculous Virgilian entrance to Naples:

Cum ad ipsam veniremus portam, et paratior nobis ad sinistram pateret ingressus, occurrit ex improviso asinus lignorum strue oneratus, et ex occursu compulsi sumus ad dextram declinare.[69]

(When we came to the gate itself, and a readier entry lay on the left for us, we suddenly met an ass burdened with a heap of wood, and, meeting it, we were compelled to turn to the right.)

Nothing could represent better the spirit of the whole twelfth century than the epitaph of the Englishman, Richard Palmer, who, after a life spent in the schools of France and the sees of Sicily, died in Messina. He had kept close contacts with visiting Englishmen in Sicily, assisted those in exile over the Becket controversy, officiated at the wedding of Joan of England and William of Sicily in 1177:

> Anglia me genuit, instruxit Gallia, fovit
> Trinacris; huic tandem corpus et ossa dedi.[70]
>
> (England bore me, Franche schooled me, Sicily
> Cherished me: to the last I leave my body's dust.)

This sense of a completely open western world, in which only the transitory terrors of brigands or mountain weather disturb the paths of travellers across Europe, is very strong. The plain words of John of Salisbury, describing the journeys made necessary by his own restless career, are anything but plain in what they tell us of the supporting political and intellectual structures which made such flexibility and 'openness' possible:

For I crossed the Alps ten times; leaving England I went successfully as far as Apulia; I often did business in the Roman church for my lords and my friends; and, as various causes arose, I traveled many times about England and France.[71]

Papal official, member of the households of Theobald and Thomas of Canterbury, and ultimately Bishop of Chartres, the life and writings of John of Salisbury ask us to understand how the learning and culture centred in the courts of great English Archbishops such as Theobald (1139–62) and Thomas Becket (1162–70) were expressive of a situation which was generously European rather than distinctively English. Paris, Chartres and Canterbury, Palermo and Catania were points on a map which had no need to concern itself with national boundaries.

John of Salisbury's intellectual temper, his passionate love of classical literature, his resistance to the rising enthusiasm of the schools for logical disciplines as the crown of all learning, his comprehensive and sympathetic view of human society – all of this must be associated with his years in France, and particularly with the programmes of study he knew first hand, at Paris and at Chartres. It must also be associated with his journeys further south, to Apulia, where not only was he entertained with all kinds of delicacies from the Eastern world, but learnt Greek.[72] There were few of the distinguished men who surrounded Theobald and Thomas Becket who had not travelled widely for political and scholarly reasons: when the Canterbury court is praised by them as 'crown of the realm, home of justice' ('caput est regni iustitiaeque domus'),[73] 'a camp of God, none other than the house of God and the gate of heaven',[74] this praise of its learned as well as its pious character must be glossed by what we know of the European training and status of those who made it so.[75] Again, it is probably less significant to describe John of Salisbury's 'tolerance . . . gravity and . . . judicial quality' of mind as 'thoroughly English'[76] than to see them as products of the humane philosophies of Chartres, in which 'l'exil de l'homme c'est l'ignorance: sa patrie est la science'.[77] If he stands out from his contemporaries at Chartres for his special eminence as a 'littéraire', and his convictions about the divine gift of eloquence –

les hommes deviendraient des bêtes, s'ils étaient privés de l'eloquence dont ils ont été doués.[78]

there is no way of accounting for this as peculiarly 'English'.

In fact, it might well be proposed, as a general statement, that what is 'peculiarly and significantly English' in the second half of the twelfth century is also peculiarly Angevin, and to that extent, therefore, European. To what exact degree the family relationships and the policies of the Angevin court played a determining role in shaping a literary scene which belonged as much to Champagne, Aquitaine and Poitou as it did to England is, of course, open to discussion.[79] And no doubt some simplification is involved in any very precise correlation of dynastic ties with literary developments. The immensely complex growth of the Arthurian legends, for instance, over the whole of the twelfth century, cannot be more than partially clarified by the curial and political situations of the Angevin royal house. Yet it is suggestive, if only that, to discover how early and strong are the connections of Eleanor of Aquitaine and her family with poetry making familiar reference to Arthurian materials: those allusions, to Arthur, to Tristan and Iseut, to Perceval, in the elegies and the love complaints of poets such as Marcabru, Cercamon, Bernart de Ventadour and Raimbaut d'Orange,

lead us again and again to the court of Poitou or to the domains of Eleanor, Countess of Poitou and Duchess of Aquitaine. It was her father, William, who was the subject of

Marcabru's elegy. He was also the patron of Cercamon. To Eleanor herself Bernart de Ventadour addressed the lyrics in which Tristan is named . . . From her lands in the Auvergne . . . it was easy for the Arthurian legend to pass down the Rhone to Provence . . .[80]

When Wace presented his *Roman de Brut* to the new Queen of England in 1155, he may have calculated upon Eleanor's known interest in that period of Celtic history which dominates his chronicle – the Arthurian period. And it was probably for Eleanor that the Anglo-Norman poet, Thomas, wrote his much-admired and imitated romance of *Tristan*.[81] To this we may add the likelihood that it was her husband's half-sister, Marie, Abbess of Shaftesbury, if she may be identified with Marie de France, who worked Celtic Arthurian tales into her sophisticated *lais*, for a 'nobles reis', perhaps Henry II.[82] When we deal with courts which have such powerful interests in Arthurian legend, we can quite reasonably suppose that the strategic marriages of the royal princesses into distinguished European families would accelerate the processes by which these legendary themes were disseminated across Western Europe, or, at the very least, would help to confirm tastes already formed. Thus the marriages of the princesses – Eleanor to Alfonso VIII of Castile, Matilda to Henry, Duke of Saxony, and Joan to William II of Sicily – do seem to provide a pattern into which some of the literary facts can fit. By 1170, the knights of the Round Table were celebrated in Catalonia. Guiraut III de Cabrera, Catalan nobleman, prescribed a list of them as proper subjects for his jongleurs: Erec, Tristan, Artus.[83] By 1210, the German poet, Gottfried von Strassburg, was building upon Thomas's *Tristan* to produce his richer and more haunting version of the lovers' story: '. . . their life, their death, their joy, their sorrow . . .'[84] And by the end of the twelfth century, the legends of Arthur were as much at home in Sicily as in Wales.[85] There is not, for these Angevin ladies and Arthurian literature, the same kind of exact evidence which links Chrétien de Troyes' composition of *Lancelot* with Eleanor's most famous daughter, by Louis of France – Marie of Champagne. But it has been claimed that there are the strongest reasons, both historical and literary, for associating the earliest German poem on the Tristan theme, the *Tristant* of the Brunswick knight, Eilhart d'Oberg, with the court of the Duchess Mathilda of Saxony – especially since that court lived in exile, between 1182 and 1184, in Normandy, paying frequent visits to the Angevin court in England, and moving with it in its progresses from London to Winchester, Reading, and Windsor.[86]

We do not, however, have to rely upon the attractive but often elusive evidence of Arthurian materials to support the view that the Angevin court of Henry and Eleanor was, in 'an age of great literary activity: of very learned and acute men, *and* of culture enough to appreciate and conserve the fruits of their labours',[87] an important international centre, both intellectually and politically. The work of Bishop Stubbs and, later, that of Charles Haskins[88] upon learning, literature and patronage at Henry's court has established this beyond doubt. The range of Latin texts dedicated to or associated with Henry of Anjou is impressive. Moral, historical, scientific, legal, administrative, they highlight some of the most famous authors of the later twelfth century: Adelard of Bath and William of Conches, who were writing for the young Henry before he had reached the age of seventeen; Aelred of Rievaulx, Henry of Huntingdon, Peter of Blois, Giraldus Cambrensis, Joseph of Exeter, Walter Map and Roger of Hoveden.[89] They remind us that the intellectual background to the literature of the secular courts of the twelfth century was often of a very comprehensive nature and that such literature was often connected with and supported by the learned activities of the contemporary schools, whether monastic or secular. Bezzola has pointed to the fact that the early flourishing of courtly culture in Aquitaine was dependent upon the existence of the monastic schools of the Loire valley and of Chartres.[90] Benton's study of the court of Henry and Marie of Champagne, in the second half of the twelfth century, lays similar stress upon the interaction of monastic and cathedral schools and the court at Troyes, and describes a situation in which the patronage of the Count and Countess was extended to men such as Nicolas de Clairvaux and Pierre de Celle, both important churchmen, educated in monastic schools and deeply versed in the Classics, the Fathers, and Scripture. Both held high office in monasteries on the outskirts of Troyes, and both dedicated works to Count Henry, 'the Liberal', as well as conducting official business on his behalf.[91] Benton's insistence that a medieval courtly society was, of necessity, of an extremely mixed and flexible make-up, with a resident 'core', but with many famous writers loosely and temporarily attached to it, is equally relevant to the court of Henry and Eleanor of England and to the court of Henry and Marie of Champagne, where 'the variety and complexity' of the literature associated with the princely patrons must indicate an easy commerce at this time between all kinds of intellectual and literary centres, whether predominantly religious or secular, and a courtly audience 'partly composed of clerics, who may to some degree have shared the literary interests and attitudes which they had learned in monastic and cathedral schools'.[92]

As might be expected, the quality of vernacular texts dedicated to Henry and to Eleanor does not disgrace the situation already described. Written in Provençal, French and Anglo-Norman, they record not only the extent of the lands over which the Angevin house ruled, or with which it had close ties, but also, probably, the strongly peripatetic nature of the court routines. The detailed itineraries of king and queen, during the years between 1154 and 1189, outlining constant journeys between England, Poitou, Maine, Gascony and Aquitaine,[93] make the variousness of the Angevin literary scene quite understandable. During the two decades 1152–73, Eleanor spent substantially more than half her time holding her court, 'vagabonde, mais fastueuse',[94] in Angevin territories abroad. The same restlessness employed in Henry's case to military and political ends may account for the fact that a Provençal poet of the early thirteenth century refers to a work on falconry, lost, but known to have been written for 'rei Enric/d'Anclaterra lo pros el ric'.[95] The vernacular authors who served Henry and Eleanor came from widely disparate areas. But they produced similar kinds of literature for both king and queen. The reputation of Eleanor as patroness of the French troubadour poets should not obscure for us the fact that Henry, too, was addressed directly by some of the most famous of these men. Five lyrics by Bernart de Ventadour name Henry; only one names Eleanor.[96] Raimon Vidal of Bezaudun praises Henry as a liberal rewarder of poets:

> Et yeu auzi, com En Enricx,
> Us reis d'Englaterra, donava
> Cavals e muls e com sercava . . .[97]

(And I heard, how Sir Henry, a King of England, gave horses and mules as gifts . . .)

The aggressive and bold-speaking poet, Bertrand de Born of Perigord, was involved in a different way with Henry – fostering strife between him and his sons, Henry, Richard and Geoffrey: 'fetz mesclar lo paire e.l filh d'Englaterra'.[98] But it is important to register that these poets of Poitou and the south feel politically and poetically involved with both Henry and Eleanor: Bernart de Ventadour puts it strongly,

> Pel rei sui engles e normans.[99]

(On the king's account I am an Englishman and a Norman.)

Chronicle and chronicle-romance are dedicated to both. Wace, the clerk from Jersey, who was educated at Caen and Paris, and then spent most of his life at Caen as a 'clerc lisant', or teacher and lector, during the reigns of Henry I and Henry II, is said to have presented his long verse-chronicle, the *Roman de Brut*, to 'the noble Eleanor, high King Henry's queen . . .'[100] His later and unfinished work, the *Roman de Rou*, begun in 1160 at the request of Henry II for a semi-historical account of his Norman ancestors, is prefaced by a eulogy of both Henry and Eleanor – even if the eulogy is followed by a hint that their patronage is not quite lavish enough to put him out of need.[101] The French poet, Benoît de Ste Maure, from the country between Tours and Poitiers, wrote of Eleanor in his long and influential *Roman de Troie* as 'riche dame de riche rei', and presented her as a discriminating patroness, beautiful, generous and learned: 'en cui tote science abonde'.[102] Benoît was 'un clerc très savant':[103] his labour to release classical antiquity into a wider though still courtly European world is both reminiscent of and distinct from that earlier situation, in which another learned poet paid deference to a noble lady's interest in the history of Troy, by creating for her a room tapestried with its legends.[104] Adela's Latin verses, Eleanor's French, record a continuity of educated taste, expressed in differing artistic forms.

For Henry, vernacular history sometimes began nearer home: it might, however, be no less adjusted to romance and *chanson de geste* patterns. Jordan Fantosme, a clerk of Henry of Blois, probably born in England, but educated in the Chartres schools under Gilbert de la Porrée, devised for Henry, in 1175, his Anglo-Norman verse *Chronique de la Guerre entre les Anglois et les Ecossois*.[105] This unusual work, which celebrates Henry as 'the best king that ever lived' and compares him with Moses and Charlemagne, aspires to a tragic view – in the medieval sense – of the historical events of Henry's reign, and shapes his Scottish victories as rewards for sincere penitence after Becket's death: his enemies were vanquished justly, by Fortuna acting for God, on account of their pride. The similarities between Fantosme's *Chronique* and a later fourteenth-century English Arthurian poem with a theme of pride, Fortune and military disaster, the alliterative *Morte Arthure*, are striking.

One must stress the lively and various felicities of the vernacular poetry associated with Henry II: it is by no means ruled out that he himself, and not his son, the 'young king', crowned in 1170, was intended in the dedication of the *Lais* of Marie de France to a 'nobles reis'. The tradition of Henry as patron of vernacular works is intriguingly witnessed to in the prologue to the early thirteenth-century French prose romance, *Palamedes*: the author, who presents himself as 'Elie de Borron', 'chevaleur pecheor', knows at least that Walter Map was 'clerc le roi henri', even if his account of the development of Arthurian romance under the patronage of Henry is suspect indeed, and even if his assertion that Henry has already given him two castles as a reward for his literary labours wins no scholarly support.[106]

In proposing that such are the contexts for the significant literary activity, Latin or vernacular, of later twelfth-century England, we must not over-emphasise the royal *curia* to the neglect of other centres of culture. The households of archbishops, bishops and magnates – at Canterbury, Salisbury, Lincoln, Monmouth, Winchester and Gloucester – were already firmly established, and engaged in forms of literary patronage, even during the reigns of Henry I[107] and Stephen. Not only for the kinds of work produced to their approval, but also for the 'literary geography' they mark, these provincial centres are to be of permanent importance – and, perhaps, of particular importance to the development of vernacular composition, over the next two centuries – whether in French, Anglo-Norman, English, or Welsh. The court of Alexander of Blois, Bishop of Lincoln after 1123, is an excellent example: for this great prince of the Church, 'pater patriae, princeps a rege secundus', Henry of Huntingdon wrote his *Historia Anglorum*: to him, Geoffrey of Monmouth dedicated his *Prophetiae Merlini*, which were to go into almost every language of Europe and Scandinavia by the end of the medieval period.[108] The association of Lincoln and its bishops with famous vernacular texts will be well-documented in the thirteenth century, during the episcopate of Robert Grosseteste;[109] meanwhile, in the mid-twelfth century, evidence of literary patronage in Lincoln and Lincolnshire among the households of the 'grands et petits barons féodaux' is abundant, and sometimes refers us to other more distinguished provincial courts. Thus we learn that for Alice de Condet, lady of Thorngate Castle, on the outskirts of Lincoln, the poet – and perhaps chaplain – Sanson de Nantuil translated the *Proverbs of Solomon* into French couplets. His graceful version, as he tells us, was made specifically at the request of Alice, 'noble damme enseigne e bele', whose life seems to have been full of the disturbing and dramatic incident of the baronial struggles of Stephen's reign.[110] Her first marriage, to Richard FitzGilbert of Clare, associated her with a family of known literary interests, and with an even more important act of literary patronage. The first vernacular translation of Geoffrey of Monmouth's *Historia* – into Anglo-Norman verse – was made for a Lincolnshire noblewoman, Constance FitzGilbert, by Geoffrey Gaimar, who was probably one of the clerks of her husband, Ralph FitzGilbert. Ralph FitzGilbert seems to have had connections with the de Clare family, possibly through his Lincolnshire 'over-lord', Gilbert de Gaunt.[111] The circumstances in which Gaimar's lost *Estorie des Bretuns* was undertaken depend upon further ties: between Ralph FitzGilbert and the northern baron, Walter Espec of Helmsley in Yorkshire, and between Walter Espec and Robert, Earl of Gloucester, who from his court at Bristol exercised a powerful influence over what Bezzola describes as the 'vie littéraire' of England at that time. Robert's direct patronage, as we have seen, was extended to Latin writers such as Geoffrey of Monmouth – for his *Historia Regum Britanniae* – and to William of Malmesbury, for his *Gesta Regum Anglorum*. But his loan of a copy of Geoffrey's *Historia* to Walter Espec, who in turn passed it on to Ralph FitzGilbert, had a decisive though indirect effect upon the vernacular literary situation, and reminds us how crucial are the links between these twelfth-century magnates in relation to the availability of texts for translation and adaptation into the vernacular.[112]

The map which can be drawn in from what we know of such links – a map of provincial communications, between Gloucestershire, Yorkshire, Lincolnshire, Kent – is not, however, exclusive of reference to the royal *curia*. It was at the court of his uncle, Robert Earl of Gloucester, that Henry II received his early training – from the age of nine to sixteen he was at the Bristol household under the tutorship of a certain Master Matthew. There, perhaps, he received specialised instruction from the famous scholar, Adelard of Bath, whose *Treatise on the Astrolabe* begins 'Intelligo iam te, Heynrice, cum sis regis nepos, a philosophia id plena percepisse nota . . .' (I now understand that you, Henry, since you are the grandson of a king, have fully perceived this lesson from philosophy [the lesson being that kings ought to be acquainted with the liberal arts and philosophy]).[113] Many who wrote in the contexts of the episcopal courts of Canterbury and Lincoln wrote also in that of the royal court: Henry of Huntingdon's *Historia Anglorum* was first dedicated to Alexander of Blois, Bishop of Lincoln, and, in its final edition, to Henry II. Similarly, Peter of Blois: his career could be seen as yet another summing-up of all that has been said about the 'internationalism' of the worlds of scholarship, religion and politics in the twelfth century – student at the Universities of Bologna and Paris, tutor and later Clerk of the Seal to William of Sicily, archdeacon of Bath, Clerk and later Chancellor to the Archbishop of Canterbury, and royal chaplain to Henry of England, his descriptions of Becket's court, its learning, its magnificence, are rivalled by those of Henry's. For this king, who encouraged, according to Peter, 'constant conversation of the best scholars and discussion of questions', 'quotidiana eius schola est litteratissimorum conversatio jugis et discussio quaestionum',[114] he collected his *Letters*, wrote his *Compendium in Job*, and his *Dialogue*, between Henry and the Abbot of Bonneval.[115]

And with Peter of Blois we return to the subject of the Angevin and Sicilian kingdoms, reaffirming what this chapter has been substantially concerned to describe – the powerful determining forces exerted by Angevin situations, policies, and events upon the widest range of what we must define as 'English' literature and art, during the twelfth century. Peter himself, who, once settled in England, maintained a wry and critical attitude towards certain aspects of Sicily – its volcanic landscapes, its unfriendly people, its harsh climate – and refused to return, kept nevertheless a strong interest in Sicilian affairs, corresponding regularly with Walter, the English Archbishop of Palermo, and with his own brother, William of Blois, who remained on the island as Abbot of a Monastery at the foot of Mount Etna, writing sermons and theological works, and, quite surprisingly, a comedy, and a curiously-named tragedy, *Mark and Flora*, upon which his brother compliments him. William visited England, according to Giraldus Cambrensis;[116] considering his dramatic aspirations, and the lively gifts of his more famous brother, we would indeed like to know more in detail of the learned and literary circles which such a visit from abroad might have involved.[117] It may be, however, that we can be more precise about other matters concerning Peter of Blois: his appointment as Chancellor of the Archbishop of Canterbury in 1173 may shed some light upon the kind of close connection between Canterbury and Sicily which must account for the equally close connections between Canterbury wall-painting and Sicilian mosaic at this date. Thus the dramatically-bent figure of St Paul, in the Cathedral Chapel of St Anselm, at Canterbury, is clearly modelled, and probably directly, upon a similar figure in the Capella Palatina, at Palermo.[118]

But perhaps the most dazzling literary testimonies to the importance of the relationships between Angevin England and Sicily in the twelfth century are provoked by the marriage of Joan, daughter of Henry II and Eleanor, to William II, in 1177. This was the finale of a whole century of splendid international occasions, political, scholarly, ecclesiastical, in which the two kingdoms expressed their mutual concerns and interests. Not only did it catch the imagination of monastic chroniclers, such as Roger of Hoveden, who reported it as a 'fairy-tale of splendour' – the lavish entertainment of the Sicilian ambassadors in London, the dowry of gold and silver plate, the triumphant entry of the bride into Palermo, on horseback, the ceremony itself in the glittering Capella Palatina at Palermo, with the new queen seated on her golden chair.[119] Beyond that, it set a fashion for romance in the 'mode sicilienne' – a fashion as well represented in the provincial courts of the borderlands of England and Wales as in those of northern and central France. The most spectacular working of these real-life materials into a romance format comes slightly later than this period from the Picard poem, *Floriant et Florete*, which moves between Cardigan, London, Monreale and Palermo in an elaborate picturing of the life of the royal courts of England and Sicily.[120] But in the Anglo-Norman *Ipomedon*, written by a Herefordshire clerk, Hue de Rotelande, we have a work more nearly contemporary with the royal betrothal and wedding, set in Apulia, Calabria and Sicily, and concerned with the love-adventures of Ipomedon, heir to the throne of Calabria.[121] *Ipomedon* confirms the 'literary geography' we have been discussing, by suggesting, once more, how the larger themes of Angevin royal history come to shape the literary tastes and habits of the 'petits barons féodaux' of the English kingdom. For Hue, writing near Hereford, 'a Credehulle a ma meisun',[122] dedicated his two romances, *Ipomedon* and its sequel, *Protheselaus*, to Gilbert Fitz-Baderon, lord of Monmouth, 1177–91. Gilbert was related, through his mother, Rohaise, to the important de Clare family, whose patronage of writers such as Sanson de Nantuil and Geoffrey Gaimar has already been proposed.[123] The statement by Hue that *Protheselaus* was translated, at Gilbert's request, from a Latin book in his well-stocked castle library could just conceivably be more than 'conventional compliment':[124]

> Cest lyvre me comaunda feire
> E de latyn [fist] translater
> D'un livre q[u]'il me fist moustrer
> Dount sis chastels est mult manauntz
> E de latyn e de romaunz . . .[125]

Certainly he seems to intimate that *Ipomedon* was based, in part at least, upon a French book: was this also found in Gilbert's library at Hereford Castle? We have seen how sophisticated the results of west-country patronage could be, over the span of the twelfth century, whether expressed in the sculptural schemes of Herefordshire parish churches, or in the historical works associated with Robert, Earl of Gloucester. It is worth recalling also that Gilbert Fitz-Baderon was related, through his wife, Bertha de Briouze, to a family quite as distinguished as that of de Clare for political and devotional commitments which can be documented well into the next century.[126]

With regard to the art of these later years of the twelfth century, it might be thought, at first sight, that it resists any particularly Angevin 'interpretation'. The early appearance of Aquitainian motifs in the Herefordshire school of sculpture was not followed up by similar full-scale sculptural borrowings, except in the Rochester area after 1177 where the style and iconography of Rochester Cathedral tympanum, with its deeply-carved, monumental Christ supported by angels and evangelist symbols, and its voussoir decoration of strangely contorted bird-forms, is reminiscent only of churches in Herefordshire and in Poitou. The south doorway of nearby Barfreston repeats with fresh conviction a Romanesque programme of imagery – labours of the month, bestiary figures, animal musicians – from south-western France.[127]

By contrast, the affiliations of much of the manuscript painting of the time are with work from parts of France outside the Angevin empire, with 'books produced in the Capetian areas of Ponthieu, Vernandois, Flanders and Paris . . .': here, we might agree, stylistic developments at last run 'curiously counter to political divisions'.[128] The overriding of Angevin 'political divisions' for the characteristic book-painting styles of St Albans and Canterbury during the last quarter of the century may, indeed, be a sign of the 'growing supremacy of Paris as a cultural centre', and the direct interchange of artists and manuscripts between, for instance, the Abbey of St Victor, in the very heart of the Paris schools, and English centres. We have seen how the first Prior of the Austin Abbey of Wigmore was Andrew of St Victor: at St Albans, Abbot Simon (1167–83) corresponded with Richard of St Victor: we know that one Canterbury artist, 'Manerius, son of Wigmund', was head of a considerable group of Parisian craftsmen.[129] To that extent, we should perhaps see some change of emphasis which may be important for the future. Even in manuscript illumination some things remain unchanged, however: in Winchester, for instance, the influence of Byzantine art, transmitted through the old channels of communication between England and Sicily, continued undiminished. It has been pointed out that even the later twelfth-century 'expressionistic' phase of Byzantine painting is directly represented in the work of some of the initial artists of the Winchester Bible.[130]

Although the formation of what is commonly known as the 'channel style' of illumination, best exemplified in the Herbert of Bosham and Thomas Becket manuscripts, given by them to Christ Church, Canterbury, proposes channels of cultural interchange not precisely Angevin in nature, we may add an Angevin postscript to this: the manuscripts in question could very easily have been produced in the Sens diocese of northern France, where Thomas Becket and Herbert of Bosham spent their years of enforced exile, during the quarrel with Henry II.[131] Angevin political issues are powerful in their effect here, even if the Becket and Bosham books were made in France, and remind us of the part which Paris will play in the history of cultural interchange over the next two English centuries. Their styles were of course rapidly adopted and copied: manuscripts with delicate, neat initials, pink, white and blue on burnished gold backgrounds, thin, decorative spirals and coils, and a more angular script, become as familiar in England as in France, moving out of Romanesque vigour and solidity into a new 'gothic' refinement.

But this chapter began by suggesting that it was necessary, for the twelfth century, to take a generous definition of the term 'English' as far as the rich and characteristic products of the age and of the northern kingdom are concerned. The emphasis has been upon the pleasures of discovering likenesses between continental and 'English' literary and artistic situations rather than upon those of distinguishing separable identities, signs of emergent national individuality in the arts of the time. It is not, therefore, important that so far no work in the English language has been discussed. For the twelfth and, indeed, for the thirteenth century in England, all that matters is that we should note the fact of composition in a vernacular language, whether French, Anglo-Norman, or English. Increasingly, over those centuries, literature in all three languages maintained an i..ricate pattern of relationships – a pattern which was itself always partly controlled by a larger relationship to Latin literature. We shall have ample opportunity to observe how major vernacular writings, French or English, do not fill rigidly compartmented roles, but often share both functions and qualities, and are often similarly indebted to materials from a common European-Latin stock.

2   Culture and literature in earlier thirteenth-century England: national and international

IT was possible, in the first chapter, to write with confidence of the relationships between historical events, art and literature – especially as they were fostered by the European courts of the twelfth century. A particularly stable situation was observed at the Angevin court of Henry II and Eleanor of Aquitaine, where cultural and political strengths seem to have been almost inseparable. It is the reverse side of that stable situation which accounts for our inability to distinguish signs of much more than a 'holding operation' in the field of mid-twelfth-century English vernacular literature. Only monastic and 'clerical didactic'[1] traditions were receptive – often in smaller provincial centres – to the copying and 'modernising' of Old English homiletic prose, and to the fresh composition of a modest kind of moral and penitential verse.[2] But other vernacular literatures, as we have seen, pursued a vigorous and distinguished life in contexts which were frequently courtly, learned and international, asking us, in company with much twelfth-century art, to consider new definitions of 'English' work during those years.

HISTORICAL SITUATIONS

Historians have demonstrated that the 'greatness and permanence' of Henry II's monarchical system survived his death (in 1189) and the absentee reign of his son, Richard (1189–99), ensuring administrative order through a trained class of government officials.[3] But the same kind of survival cannot be demonstrated for the English royal court in its function as a centralising cultural influence, whose willingness to promote and encourage literary endeavour has often been associated with its larger political aspirations and responsibilities. The death of Henry, and the disgrace of Eleanor, his queen, seem to have signalled the beginning of some change in both the location and the emphasis of high-class patronage, as far as literary matters are concerned. We could not say that the initiative in literary patronage passed entirely from the royal to the baronial courts of England, but baronial patronage certainly begins to assume a new prominence, and to define itself rather differently from royal patronage. It frequently occupies itself with specific 'English' interests, which are now to be served by that vernacular language newly developed as an independent and 'English' version of continental French: Anglo-Norman. The Anglo-Norman 'ancestral romances' which are the major result of this movement belong to the first half of the thirteenth century and the second half of the twelfth, and differ in interesting and decisive ways from

29

both the older *geste* narratives, and the increasingly popular chivalric romances of France. Successors to both literary traditions, their authors work out for themselves a characteristic form which has been usefully described as 'historical romance'.[4] At the same time, royal patronage begins to look increasingly to writers of 'foreign' origin, who may come to England for periods of their lives, but whose allegiances are predominantly continental French. These developments will make for a pattern of literary activity in thirteenth-century England markedly more complex than that of the preceding century, which, though diverse, had a very real unity to it.

There is some irony in the fact that the son who succeeded Henry, Richard 'coeur de lion', was himself both poet and friend of poets, destined to be long celebrated in the romantic legend of England. Richard's literary tastes, however, were of minimal significance to England during his ten-year reign. Of that reign, he spent five months only in the country. He remained, as he had been brought up, a seigneur in the continental style: passionately devoted to warfare, his courts at Poitiers and at Argentan were frequented by some of the most famous of the 'midi' poets, including the notorious and brilliant Bertrand de Born, who had helped him in his earlier rebellious campaigns against his father.[5] The pattern is essentially French, and flamboyant – that of a Prince of Poitou and Aquitaine – and it is certain that just as Richard was able to retain the loyalty of Norman barons because he conformed to the familiar feudal concept of a 'warrior-king', so too he appealed to French poets in the familiar role of 'seigneur-troubadour'.[6] The *sirventes* which is attributed to him shows some talent in a southern-French mode[7] and there is at least one fragment of another *sirventes*, addressed to the 'Dauphin d'Auvergne', son of Guillaume VII, Comte d'Auvergne, in which Richard reproaches the 'Dauphin' for not coming to his support in France. The 'Dauphin' replied in another *sirventes*, defending his course of action.[8]

We should not exaggerate the cultural as distinct from the political consequences for England of the disintegration of the Angevin Empire, begun in the reign of Richard, and quickly completed in that of his successor, John. But it did mean that the place of the English royal court as part of a firm structure of international relationships was weakened, and this was bound to have a wide range of repercussions.

The years during which John was on the throne (1199–1216) saw the rise of Paris as the acknowledged intellectual centre of Christendom: they saw, also, the rise of a strong Capetian monarchy, centred upon Paris, and the secession of all former Angevin possessions in France, except for Gascony and Aquitaine. It is true that the dominant interests of the English royal house of the thirteenth century were still based upon an 'obsession with the Continent',[9] but it was an obsession which had to come to terms with changed continental conditions, and which had to assert itself against a slowly awakening consciousness, among some sections of the church and baronage, of a specifically 'English' identity. The loss of Normandy, in 1204, forced a recognition of some degree of separateness for England; nothing could illustrate this better than the outcome of the civil war in the later years of the reign of John and the early years of the minority of Henry III, when the attempt of Louis VIII of France to claim England in the name of his wife, Blanche of Castile, granddaughter of Henry II, was repudiated as an invasion of the country in spite of its ultimate Angevin sanction.[10] There are moments when things look different, in an old-fashioned way: Powicke reminds us that a few years later than the Treaty of Kingston (1217), by which peace was made with Louis at the price of 10,000 marks, the cry of 'Louis of France' could still be heard among rioting Londoners.[11] Henry III was to make a serious, though abortive, attempt to 'restore the ancient glories of his house across the Channel',[12] and he would be encouraged back by the *sirventes* of an unknown troubadour which welcomed him as king claiming his own right.[13] But even the filling of the royal court of Henry in the middle years of the thirteenth century with Provençals, Savoyards and Poitevins can be seen as a product of a changed world: 'it was as though the king, debarred from going to the Continent, was determined to redress the balance by having the Continent come to England'.[14]

Continental yearnings, both political and cultural, would continue to be part of the ambitions and tastes of English kings, from Henry III to Richard II, but there can be no doubt that the break-up of the Angevin empire in the early thirteenth century was of crucial importance in compelling the barons

to concentrate on English interests. They would continue to think feudal thoughts and work in feudal ways, but their problems were at last basically English, and English ways and traditions would sooner or later influence the manner in which those problems were solved.[15]

The administrative, as well as the political, history of the thirteenth century is full of events which augur strongly the eventual unification of the country; the *Provisions of Westminster*, for instance, in 1259, put the authority of seigneurial courts, in legal matters, under the jurisdiction of national laws, and can be seen as a 'step towards the unity of England'.[16]

It is natural, then, to expect that this 'concentration on English interests', attended as it was, from a political point of view, by a narrowing of international horizons, would have some important compensations in literary matters, and, not least, in the development of vernacular modes apt for the expression of 'national identity'. But if we supposed that these compensations would register most rapidly in the development of English vernacular modes, we should be mistaken – or prematurely optimistic. The retention of French – in either its continental or its insular form – as powerful and perhaps dominant literary languages for most of the thirteenth century in England was probably inevitable, considering the position of French at this time as 'almost the universal vernacular of Christendom'[17] with a hundred years of fine poetry to its credit. In thirteenth-

31

century Italy, for example, it only just failed to become that country's official literary medium: there were more substantial reasons for such recognition in England, where hereditary claim to the language was constantly being reinforced by royal and aristocratic marriages into continental families. Consequently, while the closer circles about the royal house in the thirteenth century looked habitually to the continent for their literature of entertainment and edification – they were, after all, substantially composed of Provençals, Poitevins, Savoyards and Castilians – the magnates and their families looked to England, but to a class of authors writing about them and their history in Anglo-Norman. Even here, of course, there is some overlap. The queens of Henry III and Edward I were also addressed in Anglo-Norman by their resident clerks and by eminent English Churchmen; for the first Eleanor (of Provence), John of Howden, her clerk, wrote the graceful Anglo-Norman religious poem, *Rossignos*,[18] and for the second Eleanor (of Castile), John Pecham, Archbishop of Canterbury, made an Anglo-Norman exposition of the pseudo-Dionysian *Heavenly Hierarchies*.[19] There will be other examples.

But leaving aside for the time being the question of the extent and significance of the patronage of continental French literature by the royal court, we may concentrate upon the acceptance of Anglo-Norman by a wide spectrum of literate public, and propose that it is here we shall find the effect of changing historical patterns most strikingly manifested.

Indeed, as we have briefly noticed, even before the end of the twelfth century, some identification of 'the consciousness of being English' with a particular kind of literary genre, in a particular language, had already begun in the Anglo-Norman 'ancestral romances', whose clerkly authors catered for the need of Norman and French families, now settled in castles and manor-houses throughout England, to feel pride in both a distinguished continental past and an English present.[20] At a more popular level, Anglo-Norman poetry was as quick to respond to the great public events of the time – the death of Simon de Montfort, Earl of Leicester, at the Battle of Evesham, the death of Edward I – as it was to great contemporary issues such as taxation, the baronial opposition to Henry III, and commissions of Trailbaston.[21]

This, then, is one vernacular literary language of England in which we can hope to chart some of the processes of social and political change in the passage between the twelfth and thirteenth centuries. Its very existence speaks to us of confidence in newly emergent national status, and its literary range speaks of confidence in a series of well-assured milieux. By comparison, the definition of status and milieu for the English language as a literary medium during those years, and, indeed during the whole of the thirteenth century, presents difficulties. The evidence upon which a definition can be based is extremely varied, and, at first sight, even contradictory. Thus it would be possible, taking account of certain kinds of English composition, to propose that the major role of English literature throughout the thirteenth century was to provide for those who were incapable of reading continental French or Anglo-Norman texts. Anglo-Norman often takes the lead, and English follows not as an alternative, but as a substitute. Robert of Greatham's collection of verse-sermons, the Anglo-Norman *Miroir* or *Evangiles des Domnees*, written for 'Aline', wife of his patron, exists in seven complete manuscripts – its English translation in only four.[22] The original work suggests an early well-documented relationship between social classes of some standing and their chaplains who served them in an appropriate language:

> A sa trechere dame, Aline,
> Saluz en la vertu divine.
> Ma dame, bien l'ai oï dire
> Ke mult amez oïr e lire
> Chancon de geste e d'estoire,
> E mult i metez la memoire.[23]

Although the Prologue is carried over into the translation, the English version changes its list of 'romances', and makes its references less specific: 'Mani men it ben þat han wille to here rede romaunce and gestes þat is more þan idelschip'.[24]

Robert Grosseteste, Bishop of Lincoln, scientist and theologian, wrote his Anglo-Norman *Treatise on Husbandry* for the Countess of Lincoln, and his spiritual allegory, the *Chasteau D'Amour*, for young noblemen such as the sons of Simon de Montfort who were brought up in his household.[25] Eleven manuscripts of the Anglo-Norman verse *Chasteau* are still extant; its Prologue makes it clear that it is written in French for those who are not scholars:

> En romanz comenz ma reson
> Pur ceus ki ne sevent mie
> Ne lettreüre ne clergie.[26]

But the composure and brevity of its statement contrasts with the anxious emphasis of the Prologue to one of the later English adaptations, done, as the author says, 'for lewede mennes byhoue':[27]

> þauh hit on Englisch be dim and derk
> Ne nabbe no sauur bifore a clerk,
> for lewed men þat luitel connen
> On Englisch hit is þus bigonnen.   (lines 71–4)

The apologetic tone of the English translator is marked; we note also that the version is intended as a substitute for Grosseteste's Anglo-Norman version:

> For him þat con not iknowen
> Nouþer French ne Latyn . . .   (lines 36–7)

Even after the turn of the thirteenth century, adjustments are sometimes made in English renderings of Anglo-Norman materials which indicate a change of class

33

of audience: a *Lament* for the death of Edward I excises learned references in its last stanza, and is altogether more popular in appeal:

> Si Aristotle fust en vie,
> E Virgile qe savoit l'art,
> Les valurs ne dirrent mie
> Del prudhomme la disne part.
>
> þah mi tunge were mad of stel,
> ant min herte yȝote of bras,
> þe godnesse myht y neuer telle
> þat wiþ kyng edward was . . .[28]

But any hasty relegation of thirteenth-century English, both as a spoken and a literary language, to permanently low standing compared with Anglo-Norman, would ignore the complexities of the situation in that century. It may only have been practical disadvantages which weighed with John Pecham of Canterbury when, in 1282, he refused to accept Bartholomeo de Ferentino as papal tax-collector on account of the fact that he 'knew neither Latin nor English'.[29] English, however, was of no small importance as a qualification for the post. And we are faced with the strongest evidence of bilingualism, from the twelfth and the thirteenth centuries, at widely different levels of society. Clearly if, after 1066, the acquisition of English was considered a necessity by many of the new Norman rulers, French had become increasingly accessible to substantial sections of the English population. No doubt one class of people could speak only English; another class may have been limited, perhaps, to French or to Anglo-Norman – the French or Spanish-born wives of kings and magnates and their households make up the class in question. Between such classes, a large proportion of the population may have come to feel at home in both English and Anglo-Norman – even if continental French was beyond them.[30] There is, in fact, no other way of accounting for what might otherwise appear to be isolated but high-class English compositions at the turn of the twelfth century – compositions quite different in quality and intent from any of the English adaptations of Anglo-Norman material considered above, and capable of supporting the view of Hope Emily Allen that, as the twelfth passed into the thirteenth century, 'no sharp demarcation could have existed of social distinction between the two languages'.[31]

There are one or two impressive records which suggest that facility in the three languages – Latin, French and English – was admired in men of culture and education: as early as 1181–2, Walter Map commented of Gilbert Foliot, Bishop of London, that he was 'vir trium peritissimus linguarum, Latine, Gallice, Anglice, et lucidissime disertus in singulis . . .',[32] and the same may have been true of Grosseteste. Roger Bacon in his *Compendium Studii Philosophiae* (1271–2) takes it for granted as desirable that the English should speak three languages: English, French and Latin 'sicut maternam in qua natus est'; it may be significant

34

that he places English first – 'ut nos loquimur Anglicum, Gallicum et Latinum'.[33] The sophisticated literary evidence to be considered below could only have come into existence in some such situation, which would have guaranteed that 'the literature of the two vernaculars would reach much the same public and be characteristic of much the same environment'.[34] The close similarities, for instance, between the Anglo-Norman and the English religious lyric during the thirteenth century must bring us to conclude that 'the Anglo-Norman and Middle English authors were subject to much the same influences, as would be natural, as they were both Englishmen'.[35]

We are clearly dealing here with cultural contexts which allowed alternatives in the choice of literary media, and which were able to reconcile issues such as the growing political nationalism of the time with a flexibility of literary practice. There is much to point to the conclusion that, by the thirteenth century, Anglo-Norman had become widely acceptable as an 'English' vernacular, and that, in its local characteristics, Anglo-Norman literature was often 'thoroughly English in everything but the medium'.[36] We should be mistaken if we thought that the mid-thirteenth-century resentment of the great numbers of 'alienigenae' who followed Henry III's relatives to England might have had any effect upon the common use of a language not identical with that of the foreigners but certainly closely related to it. Galbraith has emphasised that the consolidation of 'national' feeling during the mid-century years of opposition to Henry III's preferment of Poitevins to high office 'took place at a time when England enjoyed three literary languages and three competing cultures . . . The country was loyal, patriotic, anti-Welsh, anti-Scottish, anti-French. It showed in fact all the essentials of national feeling, except that, so far as education allowed, it preferred Latin to French, and French to English.'[37] If we may adjust Galbraith's statement in so far as it relates to the vernacular, modifying the concepts of 'competition' and 'preference' in the interests of larger concepts of 'coexistence' and 'choice', it may stand as an excellent summary of the thirteenth-century position.

LITERARY TEXTS

Texts written to many different kinds of social (and sometimes satirical) demand illustrate this: the thirteenth-century 'mime-poem', *La Paix aux Anglais*, for instance, in which 'un Anglais parle', using recognisably 'Marlborough French', and describing Henry III's ambitions for the reconquest of Normandy. The means by which the author identifies English sentiments with a kind of French which, in grammar and syntax, is already familiar to us from twelfth- and thirteenth-century insular compositions, is neat and confident; he knows that his derisive purposes will be well served by this 'provincial' version not only of a continental language, but also of its literary conventions:

Or vint la tens de may que ce ros panirra,
Que ce tens serra beles, roxinol chanterra,
Ces prez il serra verdes, ces gardons florrirra.
J'ai trova a ma cul .I. chos que je dirra.
De ma ray d'Ingleters, qui fu a bon naviaus
Chivaler vaelant, hardouin et leaus,
Et d'Adouart sa filz qui fi blont sa chaviaus,
M'ai covint que je faites .I. dit troute noviaus,
Et de ce rai de Frans, cestui longue baron,
Qui tenez Normandi a tort par mal choison.[38]

In a quite different vein, an Anglo-Norman life of Edward the Confessor, *La Estoire de Seint Aedward le Rei*,[39] translated from the Latin of Aelred of Rievaulx by the chronicler and artist of St Albans, Matthew Paris, and dedicated before 1250 to Eleanor of Provence, speaks proudly of Henry III as head of a united people:

Now are king, now are barons, and the kingdom, of a common blood of England and of Normandy.[40]

This book, from notes on the flyleaf, was in circulation between the Queen and her aristocratic friends and relatives, the Countesses of Arundel and Cornwall. The illustrations to the text are in a style which blends earlier English and contemporary French elements: fluid, elegant outline drawing and warm, varied colouring.[41] Work such as this can stand just as authentically to represent the 'Englishness' of the thirteenth century, interpreted in a high social context, as can, in their different context, the *Owl and the Nightingale*, or the romance *Floriz and Blanchefleur*.

But we should not neglect to stress that the possibility of English taking its place beside Anglo-Norman as a vernacular of equal literary standing is unlikely to be a witness to the dogged persistence of an underprivileged language struggling to survive in lean political times. Rather it witnesses to the hospitality of newly-constructed cultural settings, able to provide matter and motifs for a vernacular literature which might otherwise have been destined to cater for only a severely limited range of public. We have noticed that the twelfth century provides ample illustration of what might have become of English literature – an area dedicated to monastic antiquarianism and to clerical didacticism – had not a mixture of social, religious and political forces brought it into contact with more richly related cultural traditions. There is no really significant way in which the 'updated' versions of Old English religious prose, made in the twelfth and earlier thirteenth centuries, can serve as a context for the prose of the *Ancrene Wisse* or that of the *Wohunge of Ure Louerde*, written at the turn of the twelfth century for women recluses and/or nuns: nor is there any significant way in which the *Worcester Fragments*, probably composed in the earlier twelfth century on homiletic and elegiac themes, can introduce the great heroic chronicle-poem of about

1225, Laȝamon's *Brut*. No later Old English debate-poem has anything to tell us of the *Owl and the Nightingale*: in company with the *Ancrene Wisse*, and the *Brut*, it belongs to a different European world, in which works of the English vernacular are now able to assume a place. And it is in this way that the processes of historical change affect English composition of these crucial years. They do not operate to single out English as the vernacular medium most worthy to express the newly coherent consciousness of 'English interests'; rather they help to associate English with Anglo-Norman in this role, by virtue of bilingualism on many levels of the educated clergy and laity. They also ensure that whatever the vicissitudes of political dealings between England and France, authors writing in England will have not only a choice of vernacular medium, but, whether they elect to write in English or in Anglo-Norman, a sense of writing in a European, not a defensively insular tradition of thought and learning. Many English texts of the thirteenth century come out of a relaxed cultural situation, in which they inherit, as do their Anglo-Norman counterparts, the legacy of that great period of twelfth-century internationalism with its wealth of European-Latin and continental French materials.

Nothing could better illustrate the significance of such a statement than the English debate poem, the *Owl and the Nightingale*, probably written about 1200, in the south of England, perhaps in Dorset.[42] It would be easy to exaggerate the almost miraculous nature of its appearance, if we viewed it only as a kind of sequel to the instructional and penitential debates between *Body and Soul* from the Old English period and the 'transitional' years of the earlier twelfth century. Its most recent editor has, however, warned us against seeing it 'in isolation' (ibid., p. 25). And it is true, of course, that medieval Latin literature of the twelfth and thirteenth centuries is full of verse-debates which dispute, sometimes through personifications, 'problems to which there are sides but no solutions' (p. 24). The genre of the *conflictus* is of classical antiquity, and although the medieval period frequently developed it as a set rhetorical exercise, individual examples can always prove the imaginative potential of the form. The beautiful *Conflictus Veris et Hiemis*, traditionally ascribed to Alcuin, scholar of York and Aachen (d. 804), debates the seasonal pleasures of spring and winter in terms of the return of the cuckoo, and resists a symbolic interpretation of weather and landscape, touching gracefully and memorably upon the contrasting joys of ease by the warm hearth and lengthening days in the sun: the victory of spring is celebrated by the shepherd-arbiters of the debate, with some of the characteristic medieval sharpness of distaste for the winter – 'prodigus, atrox', 'spendthrift and foul'. But the sense of the poem, finally, is of inevitable seasonal change, in which winter's rigours serve as a preface to the serenity of spring:

> Desine plura, Hiems: rerum tu prodigus, atrox.
> et veniat cuculus, pastorum dulcis amicus.

37

collibus in nostris erumpant germina laeta,
pascua sint pecori, requies et dulcis in arvis:
et virides rami praestent umbracula fessis.[43]

(Have done, have done, Winter, spendthrift and foul,
And let the shepherd's friend, the cuckoo, come.
And may the happy buds break on our hills,
Green be our grazing, peace in the ploughed fields,
Green branches give their shadow to tired men.)

It is worth pausing over earlier Latin poems such as these, since literary historians frequently give the impression that the Latin debate-tradition is characterised only by works of school-exercise, formal and stilted, with predictable outcomes.[44] The majority are of this character.[45] But one poet, in particular, at the court of Henry II, Peter of Blois, wrote several debates, of both an internalised and externalised nature, remarkable for the free and subtle flow of their arguments, in which 'it is no longer a question of two set positions neatly contrasted, but rather of two attitudes of life that in a host of ways reveal themselves to be incompatible'.[46] Peter of Blois' debate of the courtier and the critic of court-life, *Dialogus inter dehortantem a curia et curialem*, presents a generous and, at times, surprisingly uninhibited case for worldly attentiveness. The courtier defends himself against the violent and orthodox attack of the critic –

si vis ut te perhennibus
absorbeant suppliciis
mors et inferna palus,
confidas in principibus
et in eorum filiis,
in quibus non est salus.[47]

(If you want to be swallowed up
in lasting torment
by death and the marsh of hell,
then put your trust in princes
and in their sons –
they won't bring you salvation!)

– by arguments which are not only composed, but intelligent: who knows if these tales of torment in hell are reliable – 'neminem ab inferis / revertentem vidimus . . .' ('we've never seen anyone / coming back from the world below . . .'); why should God have given us abilities, only to trick us into damnation – 'benignus dei spiritus / non dedit ista celitus / ut in dolo nos eludat / et per ista nos detrudat / in puteum interitus!'[48] By comparison, as the most recent editor of the poem has pointed out, the horrified warnings of the critic seem almost 'lifeless': a new context for the *memento mori*, 'Astat mors in ianuis / et diffluis / in omne desiderium' ('Death is standing in the doorway,/ and you melt / to every craving!'), has been given,[49] and we are by no means certain, at the end of the debate, whether the courtier and the world have been vanquished. If we compare with this another poem by Peter of Blois, the *Cantilena de luctu carnis et spiritu*, the originality of the *Dialogus* becomes apparent: running closer to the traditional 'Body and Soul' debate form, the *Cantilena* ends on a sternly conclusive note:

> Cessa, caro, lascivire,
> quia dies instat ire . . .
> Ne templum dei polluat
> aut destruat
> Christi fundamenta.[50]

(Cease, o flesh, to wanton, for the day draws on apace . . . Let it not pollute the temple of God, nor destroy the foundation-stones of Christ.)

In the first chapter we have frequently argued for the intricate relationships of the vernacular literatures, whether French, Anglo-Norman or English, and for their indebtedness to a common European-Latin stock. While we cannot prove that any of the vernacular debate-poems written in England at the turn of the twelfth and thirteenth centuries show a detailed knowledge of the Latin of Peter of Blois, it is interesting that at least two of them, the *Petit Plet* and the *Owl and the Nightingale*, show an unusual flexibility of approach to the themes of their choice. Peter of Blois served not only Henry II, but Queen Eleanor, becoming her secretary in 1189, when Henry died; his close contact with late twelfth-century circles in which vernacular French literature was highly prized is important to note. It would not have been difficult for his Latin debate-poem on an anti-curial theme to have found a way of influencing vernacular writers of that time, and slightly later; its subject matter was of universal interest.[51] What may certainly be said, however, is that the first debate-poem that comes to us in a recognisable version of Middle, as opposed to Old, English, is strikingly reminiscent in mode of handling subject matter and, perhaps, in underlying philosophy, of distinguished *exemplars* of the genre in Latin and Anglo-Norman: its 'Englishness' is of that international brand we have had cause to trace in both the art and the literature of the twelfth and thirteenth centuries.

The manuscripts of the *Owl and the Nightingale* reinforce this general impression of associative processes at work in the literary background of the poem, but in a more precise way – giving us some facts about the collection and preservation of the text in the later thirteenth century, and about its probable original reception by an early thirteenth-century reading public. Jesus College, Oxford, MS 29, and British Library, MS Cotton Caligula A.ix, are closely connected:[52] both contain a mixture of Anglo-Norman and English works, with one Latin item in the Oxford manuscript; both belong to the second half of the thirteenth century. The contents of these miscellanies are interesting for a number of reasons – all relevant to arguments in favour of a thirteenth-century reading public of comprehensive tastes. One poem, however, common to both manuscripts, has particular importance for the *Owl and the Nightingale* – the *Petit Plet*, an Anglo-Norman debate, written as its author tells us by 'Chardri'.[53] Whoever he was, his materials are those we might expect to be accessible to a clerk of some kind; two other poems of his occur in the same manuscripts under discussion – *Josaphaz* and *Les Set Dormanz* – and both are presented as parts of a sermon on the moral life, in which the 'seinnurs' and the 'beaus duz seinnurs' of England are given more substantial food for thought than the fables of Ovid or the stories of Tristan and of Renard:

> Mes voil de Deu e sa vertu
> Ki est pussant e tuz jurs fu
> E de ses seinz, les Set Dormanz.[54]

The difficulty of determining the identity of the author of the Anglo-Norman *Petit Plet*, with his cheerful lack of any more specific reference than the bare mention of a name, must immediately remind us of the situation we meet in the *Owl and the Nightingale*, where there is the same confident assumption of a known relationship between poet and public: in all probability, further comment was unnecessary for either. Our only clue in the English poem is in the complimentary referral of the dispute between the two birds to one who may have been the recipient of the work, or who may or may not have been the poet himself – 'maister Nichole, þat is wis'; he lived 'at Porteshom . . . ine Dorsete', and was apparently a cleric of some reputation with either legal or ecclesiastical responsibilities in the Guildford area.[55] Both clerkly poets administer to their intended publics a skilful mixture of entertainment and edification; Chardri is explicit about his aims:

> .... por vus dedure
> Vus cunterai un esveisure
> De un veillard e de un enfant ...   (lines 1–3)

Basically, the theme of both the *Petit Plet* and the *Owl and the Nightingale* (which describes itself as a 'plait' in its opening lines) is one which would later receive a self-conscious and elegant treatment by Milton, in *L'Allegro* and *Il Penseroso*: the opposition of contrary views of life, two different outlooks upon man and society, man and religion, with characteristically different emotional stresses and different ranges of literary and spiritual associations. Both medieval poems take up serious issues, but the manner of handling them is lightly reflective, even ironical. The *Petit Plet* is a debate between Old Age and Youth: 'un veillard e un enfant'. And it might be expected to produce its arguments in true homiletic fashion, working towards a stern, foreseeable conclusion. In fact, it honours the announcement made at the very beginning of its narrative –

> si fu le estrif mult delitius
> Del veillart e del jofne tus.   (lines 9–10)

The play of opinions is agile and surprisingly unconventional: the poem aims to divert as well as teach. In the *Owl and the Nightingale*, the very nature of the bird-disputants, who are constantly thrown back from dignified discussion of life and religion to assert their own limited 'bird-existence', raises a delicate but firm barrier against strong didacticism. The puncturing of solemnity or brash confidence is deftly managed, time after time, as the poet reminds us of the distance between the vigorously expressed opinions and the frail creatures of the woodland who hold them – often in such strange juxtapositions. So, the Owl's defence of her role in urging penitence upon man as the high-road to heaven –

> And þan sunfulle ich helpe alswo
> Vor ich him teche ware is wo   (lines 891–2)

is perfectly acceptable as an orthodox part of Church doctrine. What makes the difference here is that it exists alongside other claims by the Owl which range from delusions of martial grandeur – her voice is like a 'grete horne' (line 318), and she sees herself as a bird of battle-omen, travelling with armies by night: 'Ich folȝi þan aȝte manne / An flo bi niȝte in hore banne' (lines 389–90) – to convictions about superior sanitary arrangements:

> Men habbet, among oþer iwende,
> A rumhus at hore bures ende,
> Vorþat hi nelleþ to uor go;
> An mine briddes doþ also.   (lines 651–4)

It is not surprising that the lively and permissive Nightingale is able to detect the possibility that pride is the flaw in the virtuous Owl's character, and she makes a spirited attack upon hypocrisy:

> Moni man is of his flesche clene
> þat is mid mode deouel imene.   (lines 1411–12)

But, as with all triumphs in this poem, that of the Nightingale evaporates: although pride and hypocrisy are solemn human subjects, a proud and hypocritical Owl has distinctly comic dimensions. The Nightingale is less vulnerable to these sleights of the poet's hand; even the Owl's derisive remarks about her drab plumage –

> þu art dim an of fule howe,
> An þinchest a lutel soti clowe   (lines 577–8)

– cannot really make her espousal of the high cause of romantic love seem ridiculous. Indeed, there is something enduringly attractive about the combination of humble exterior and splendid song: nothing the Owl says about the 'squeaking and crowing' of the Nightingale –

> So longe so þe niȝt is long,
> & eure croweþ þi wrecche crei . . . (lines 334–5)

– has any power to shut out the centuries of literature celebrating the poignant beauty of her voice. The thirteenth-century reader would have his own memories of songs, both religious and secular, in which 'the little brown nightingale amorous' tirelessly urges man to be spendthrift of his love.[56]

Consequently, criticism of the Nightingale has to bear upon her fluttering nervous energy, her rapidly rising passions, her fastidious preference for warm seasons and southerly lands: when the Owl scores confidently against her, she is distraught:

> þe Niȝtingale at þisse worde
> Was wel neȝ ut of rede iworþe; (lines 659–60)

she bristles with aggression – would have fought 'mid sworde an mid speres orde' had she been a man (line 1068). The Owl's taunt 'Hong up þin ax! Nu þu miȝt fare' (line 658) presses home the point. But it is the Nightingale's frank recognition that she comes only with the flowers of spring, and departs with the onset of autumn –

> þe blostme ginneþ springe & sprede,
> Both ine tro & ek on mede.
> þe lilie mid hire faire wlite
> Wolcumeþ me
> . . .
> Wane mon hoȝeþ of his sheue,
> An falew icumeþ on grene leue,
> Ich fare hom & nime leue.
> Ne recche ich noȝt of winteres reue . . . (lines 437–40, 455–8)

that characterises her special graces and at the same time helps the Owl to demonstrate her own sturdy year-round dependability. In the poet's evocation of the winter world over which the Owl alone presides – the bright evergreens, the night-frosts, the indoor warmth and conviviality – there is just a hint of that sharply-etched pastoral of *Love's Labour's Lost* – 'When icicles hang by the wall . . .' The uncertain nature of the medieval response to the beauty and pleasure of winter inhibits the thirteenth-century poet in his selection of winter detail. We miss the sensuous particularity – frozen milk, hissing apples – and the dramatic range – shepherds, kitchen-maids, church congregations – of Shakespeare's version. But the raw materials are being collected, even if their transformation into clear, strong images – 'Then nightly sings the staring owl . . .' – is yet to be achieved:

> 'Ac wane niȝtes cumeþ longe
> & bringeþ forstes starke an stronge
> . . .

Ich habbe at wude trou wel grete
Mit þicke boȝe no þing blete,
Mid iui grene al bigrowe,
þat eure stont iliche iblowe
An his hou neuer ne uorlost,
Wan hit sniuþ, ne wan hit frost'
. . .

'þu aishest me', þe Hule sede,
'Wi ich a winter singe & grede.
Hit is gode monne iwone –
An was from þe worlde frome –
þat ech god man his frond icnowe
An blisse mid hom sume þrowe
In his huse, at his borde
. . .

& hure & hure to Cristes masse,
þane riche & þoure, more & lasse,
Singeþ cundut, niȝt & dai,
Ich hom helpe what ich mai.'

(lines 523–4, 615–20, 473–9, 481–4)

('But when the nights are long, and bring heavy, bitter frosts . . . I shelter in an enormous tree, with great branches thickly covered in green ivy; it never loses its leaves or its colour, even when snow or frost is on the ground' . . . 'You ask me', said the Owl, 'why I sing and wail in winter-time. It is a well-established custom – and has been since the beginning of the world – for man to welcome and entertain his friends in his house, and at his table . . . and especially at Christmas, when rich and poor, high and low, sing their dance-songs night and day. I take part (in all of this) as much as I can.')

It is a mark of the happy and accidental quality of medieval observation on such winter themes that the most striking image of the poem comes not from the Owl herself, but from the Nightingale, who pictures the Owl singing as miserable as a hen in snow –

þu singest a winter 'wolawo';
þu singest so doþ hen a snowe –
Al þat ho singeþ hit is for wowe. (lines 412–14)

Only the later medieval miniaturists would rival this, with their desolate February farm-yards and anxious birds pecking for stray grains in the snow-drifts.[57]

Part of the poet's intention, as he manipulates the 'estrif', is to engage in reversals of accepted associations. The Nightingale, creature of spring and love, perched on a flowering spray –

. . . up one vaire boȝe,
þar were abute blosme inoȝe . . . (lines 15–16)

is accused by the Owl of nesting behind the privy, in the weed-filled hedges:

43

> I mai þe uinde ate rumhuse;
> Among þe wode, among þe netle
> þu sittest & singst bihinde þe setle. (lines 592–4)

Her song is not of love, but of lechery:

> ... of golnesse is al þi song. (line 498)

And the Nightingale's denials do not completely answer the charge that she tempts and excites by her song. The Owl also, for all the sobriety, even severity of her stance upon moral problems, can be unusually sympathetic to human lapses. We might expect the Nightingale to defend the peccadilloes of a wife locked up by a jealous husband:

> He hire bileck in one bure,
> þat hire was boþe stronge & sure.
> Ich hadde of hire milse an ore,
> An sori was for hire sore ... (lines 1081–4)

It is more impressive to find the Owl pitying the ill-used wife to the extent of understanding, if not condoning, her adultery:

> Me hire mai so ofte misbeode
> þat heo do wule hire ahene neode.
> La, Godd hit wot! heo nah iweld
> þah heo hine makie kukeweld. (lines 1541–4)

Critics have devoted time to analysing what we can deduce about the poet's favour of one or other of the contestants. This seems a wasteful business. We are certainly meant to enjoy the comedy of contrasts in their respective natural histories, the quick-change of their thrust and parry in argument. There may, however, be a deeper and unified meaning to all of this. Together the birds describe, represent and intervene in all areas of human activity, secular and religious. It would have been no simple decision for the poet to make that initial choice of 'Owl' and 'Nightingale': they are both 'double' in significance. The Owl of bestiary lore is the symbol of Jewish unbelief, the bird of both darkness and heresy; she keeps her ancient reputation for wisdom, as the goddess Athene's bird. The Nightingale is celebrant of human passion and the Passion of Christ.[58] We need not read the poem intently to search out hidden messages; on the other hand, the poet relies upon an acknowledgement of the richly composite nature of truth, and the impossibility of holding narrow views about how to live, and how to judge life. On the question of religion, for instance, it is clear that both Owl and Nightingale have relevant things to say about different functional parts of the Christian's life: worship and praise are no less important than repentance. The bliss of heaven is as much of a reality as the pain of hell, as the two kinds of song, the one ecstatic, the other admonitory, indicate (lines 716–42, 854–92). Sometimes the poet seems simply to be showing us how the same phenomena can be interpreted from different points of view: the fact that the dead Owl is often used as a scare-crow on a stick is seen as a contemptible end by the Nightingale (line 1648); it is presented by the Owl herself as a last humble service to man (lines 1625–30). The unresolved conclusion to the poem is nothing unusual in the tradition of debate literature, but it comes here with special appropriateness: Owl and Nightingale are component parts of life, as they are also complementary ways of regarding it.

The *Petit Plet* accomplishes some of the same things as the *Owl and the Nightingale* by refusing to bow to convention, and present its debaters, the Young and the Old Man, as simple stages in the experience of man on earth; instead, it engages in surprising inversions of their traditional roles, in 'reversals of accepted associations' similar to those we have encountered in the English poem. The opening, admittedly, runs on accepted lines: Youth and Age meet in a pretty orchard, where a fountain sends forth clear water to run over gravel; the grass bordering it is starred with flowers; the bird-song is loud along the banks of the stream. And it seems as if the debate is going to take the usual form of Youth defending a life of delight, Age recommending meditation upon the end of life. Thus the Young Man invokes the popular *Disticha Catonis* to justify his amusements:

> Ben savez cum il est escrit,
> Si cum Catun enseinne e dit:
> 'Entremedlez vostre cure
> De joie u de aukun enveisure ...'   (lines 153–6)

And he would rather go laughing to God, dying early, than finish out his life in miserable old age:

> Meuz voil aler a Deu riant
> Ke veuz chanu a chef de tur
> Finir ma vie a grant dolur.   (lines 194–6)

But his sense of the naturalness of death seems to be a turning point in the argument; from then on, it is the Young Man who comforts the complaining voice of Age, and often wisdom and common-sense seem to be on his side. The Old Man is anxious, morbidly so, about the decay of the corpse, and the danger of its disinterment by birds and animals of prey:

> Si mun cors n'est tost mis en terre.
> Les oiseals mei depincerunt
> E les gros luus mei devurrunt,
> E les mastins tut ensement ...   (lines 628–31)

The Young Man knows such fears are irrelevant; all is well 'si vostre alme est a eise ...' (line 652). In the grim fable of the meeting of 'The Three Living and the

Three Dead',[59] it is usual for the aged cadavers to remind the heedless youths of the terrors of the grave; here the Old Man admires the Young Man's wisdom:

> Jo di por veir ke mult plus sage
> Est ta juvente ke mun veil age. (lines 683–4)

While sad tales 'de ceus ke vivent en grant destreit' (line 700) are all that the Old Man can offer, the Young Man delivers a brisk and bracing sermon on divine providence, which takes care of all living creatures and would do the same for man, if only he were not so 'curius' – so ambitious and discontented:[60]

> Deu nule creature ne fist
> Ke vitaille ne li porveist
> . . .
> As bestes pert e as oiseals volanz
> E en la mer as peissuns nuanz,
> Car quant le jur apert tut cler,
> Ne sevent pas de quei disner
> . . .
> Si ert chescune creature
> E beauz e runz en sa nature.
> Mes vus, ki dussez guverner
> Quanke vit en terre e en mer
> . . .
> Vus memes ne savez meintenir
> . . .
> Savez por quei?
> . . .
> Quant vus en estes trop curius,
> Deus em pensera le meins de vus.
> (lines 913–14, 923–6, 929–32, 934, 937, 939–40)

It is, however, in the exchanges between the two characters on the subject of human loss that the special quality of the poem is best appreciated. The Old Man mourns the death of his 'duce amie', who was more beautiful than other women 'si cum saphir fet la gravele' (line 1192); the Young Man's duty is to remind him that 'death has cut short her career so that she should not henceforth change her heart like February of the thirteen moods':

> La mort li ad recopé sun eire
> Ke ele ne changast sun quor avant,
> Cum feverer tredze covenant. (lines 1296–8)

The unusual distribution of the images – 'Sapphire' for the Old Man, 'February of the thirteen moods' for the Young – prepares us for the later development of the debate, when the Old Man's persistent grief is brusquely jolted by a piece of antifeminist satire of the liveliest sort. The Young Man imagines how much worse than death would be the transformation of the 'duce amie' into a middle-aged shrew, reviling her husband for his parsimony; she cannot go out, her clothes are so shabby:

> E si dirra: 'La male hart
> Vus pende, mauveis putre vilein
> . . .
> Car vus me hunissez entre gent
> Ke vus mei vestez si povrement.' (lines 1494–5, 1497–8)

The vigour of the little scene is too much for the Old Man; he capitulates and thanks the Young Man for his salutary lesson.

Critics have often praised the 'Chaucerian' characteristics of the *Owl and the Nightingale*: the 'subtlety and irony' of its approach to its themes, the 'variety and crispness' of its poetic couplet.[61] But there is equal reason to praise Chaucerian qualities in the *Petit Plet* – perhaps stronger historical reason, for it must have been from earlier French, not English, poetry that Chaucer learnt the rudiments of his art. Chardri controls his short octosyllabic line marvellously well, breaking into dramatic dialogue with that same ease we recognise in Chaucer's first major creative adventure – the *Book of the Duchess*:

> 'Savez coment?' 'Beau fiz, nenal!'
> 'Jo le vus dirrai', fet il, 'sanz mal . . .' (lines 1009–10)

And there is more than metrical expertise to remind us of Chaucer; nothing until the moment of final comprehension in the *Book of the Duchess* –

> Is that youre los? Be God, hyt ys routhe! (line 1310)

rivals the moment in the *Petit Plet* when the Old Man reveals the death of his son, and halts, temporarily, the Young Man's fluent moralising:

> Li prudum atant se tut,
> E l'enfant la teste mut
> Vers le prudum e dist en haut:
> 'Sire', fet il, 'Si Deu me saut,
> De tute vostre aventure
> Ceste resemble la plus dure.' (lines 1087–92)

The debate ends almost as conventionally as it began; the Young Man is allowed a pious summing-up, which makes room for some pleasure in the beauty of God's world. In between beginning and end, however, more unusual paths have been travelled; like the poet of the *Owl and the Nightingale*, Chardri alerts his readers not simply to the delight of following the quick changes of a virtuoso performance. He and his English counterpart are also concerned to disturb and challenge norms of thought and belief in the interests, perhaps, of a larger truth which is left unspoken for the best of formal and informal reasons.

But the Cotton Caligula manuscript which contains both Chardri's *Petit Plet* and the *Owl and the Nightingale* gives us in addition one of the two extant copies of another work much featured in older arguments for the continuing life of English literary tradition during these French-dominated years of the twelfth and thirteenth century: the *Brut* of Laȝamon, priest of Areley Kings in Worcestershire.[62] More recently, Eric Stanley has stressed the deliberate element of archaising present in Laȝamon's immense verse-chronicle – his choice, not only of English language, but also of a basically accentual verse-line, his taste for alliterative diction and, most remarkable, for the kind of poetic compound typical of Old English usage. All of this is contrasted with the 'foreign ways of expression' to which other contemporary English poets had turned, and is seen as a special statement in keeping with Laȝamon's view of his subject matter: 'his antiquarian sentiments seem to have led him to the creation of an idiom in tune with his love of the English past'.[63]

As we shall see, there is sufficient room for debate about the precise nature of Laȝamon's allegiances to 'the English past' to make any identification of them with a particular language and poetic idiom no easy matter. We have suggested, when dealing with the *Owl and the Nightingale*, that the creation, in the thirteenth century, of wealthy cultural contexts made possible the free association of literature in one or more vernacular languages: a relationship in which languages and works within them are alternatives rather than substitutes for each other. The same kind of 'equality' may hold good for literary form and, perhaps, even for diction. What precisely motivated Laȝamon, for instance, as he made his choice of a literary medium for the translation of his main source, the French *Roman de Brut* by Wace, clerk to Queen Eleanor, we cannot know. His opening lines give little away – except that they express his admiration of Wace, 'þe wel couþe writen',[64] and refrain from any apology for using the English language and a verse line quite distinct, in origins and general characteristics, from that of Wace. But the *Brut* is an extremely varied composition; if, as Stanley argues, Laȝamon was at times self-consciously 're-animating fossils of an extinct art form' and advertising the English past 'by putting up *ye olde* signs'[65] he was also at other times assimilating that past, with its pre-Conquest literary traditions, into the present. In fact, we might reasonably hold that while parts of the *Brut* bear witness to an 'antiquarian activity' by Laȝamon, other parts witness to his equally strong concern with the adaptation of older literary forms for newer purposes. Laȝamon writes of himself primarily as a translator and compiler, and this is probably not far from a just estimate of his labours with his multiple sources:[66]

> ... þa soþere word.   sette to-gadere ...
> ... he þeos soþfeste word.   segge to-sumne.   (lines 27, 32)

Similarly, it is the compilation and modulation of multiple literary styles that we notice in the *Brut*, rather than the single-minded advocacy of one particular style, resuscitated from a moribund past. What Laȝamon achieves is as much an extension of the range of English verse-writing, under the influence of twelfth-century materials and forms, both French and Latin, as is the *Owl and the Nightingale*. In that sense, at least, he cannot be said to be a 'massive erratic in the history of English poetry'[67] but very much a man of his time.

A closer look at Laȝamon's formal verse affiliations bears this out. The two existing manuscripts of the *Brut* recognise, by their punctuation, certain basic features of his verse; although using a 'continuous' format,[68] they mark out a long line, divided by a strong caesural pause:

> An preost wes on leoden.   Laȝamon wes ihoten.   (line 1)

The line avoids end-rhyme, but is frequently given to internal rhyme, thus often appearing 'broken' as a quasi-couplet:

> Stanes heo letten seoððen.   sturnliche winden.
> seoððen speren chrakeden,   sceldes brastleden.
> helmes to-helden.   heȝe men uellen.
> burnen to-breken.   blod ut ȝeoten.   (lines 13706–9)

It is alliterated in a very variable manner: the range of variation is from nothing –

> His moder wes ihoten Creusa.   Priames kinges dohter   (line 107)

to a full three alliterating staves:

> Wondrede ȝeond þat wald.   iwundede cnihtes ouer-al.   (line 13711)

As we have already noted, certain features of this system allied to Laȝamon's occasional use of traditional poetic diction have persuaded scholars of the important relationship of his verse to that of pre-Conquest England: the 'classical' verse of the Old English poets. Thus both Eric Stanley and Carolyn Friedlander, while giving very different accounts of this relationship, stress a kind of conscious 'nostalgia' for the past in Laȝamon and some of his English contemporaries[69] which acts as a powerful determining force in literary matters.

Certainly it is undeniable that there are passages in the *Brut* which ask to be accounted for in terms of Laȝamon's access to rhetorical conventions most memorably displayed either in the 'classical' verse of the Old English period or in that of the later pre-Conquest years: martial episodes have always provided good hunting-ground. In the following passages, both dealing with the campaigns of Arthur, formulae reminiscent of a poem such as *The Battle of Brunanburh* (entered in the Old English Chronicle for 937) can be picked out:

> fastliche on-sloȝen.   snelle heore kempen.
> feollen þa uaeie.   uolden to grunde.
> þer wes muchel blod-gute.   balu þer wes riue.
> brustlede scaeftes.   beornes þer ueollen.   (lines 10017–20)

þa gon þat folc sturien.   þa eorðen gon to dunien.
bemen þer bleowen.   bonneden ferden.   (lines 13696–7)

Here we must assume some knowledge, at however many removes, of the lines

faege feollon, feld dennede
secga swate . . .   (*Brunanburh*, lines 12–13)

Moreover, Laȝamon's battle-scenes, it has been noted, are often less technical than those of his immediate source, Wace's *Roman* – especially when siege-warfare is the subject. He also shows a reluctance to render Wace's expert accounts of cavalry fighting, and tends, in these cases, to give a fairly repetitive and stylised battle-narrative, which we could only loosely regard 'in terms of the old (English) poetic tradition'.[70] On a few occasions it is true he actually refers to particular features of pre-Conquest warfare – his 'sceld-trume' (line 13729) is probably the 'scyldburh', or phalanx formation with massed shields, described in the *Battle of Maldon* (c. 991) as a 'wihaga' (lines 102, 242). Moreover, heroic sentiments such as those of Byrhtwold and his companions in that poem seem in some powerful, if undefined way, to have been the basis for Laȝamon's expansions of his original, when he writes fresh speeches for the Britons in similar situations:

for leouere us is here.   mid manscipe to fallen.
þanne we heonne i-sunde farren.   ure frenden to scare . . .
                                              (lines 2909–10)

But having said this, we should recognise that his battle-episodes are far less carefully composed than the most famous examples from Old English poetry; here the differences between Wace and Laȝamon are not simply the result of a close adherence to older English models. Laȝamon produces his own brand of set-piece for these occasions, in which variation is really less important than repetition of component units. In the following passage from Arthur's last campaign, practically all of the details are already thoroughly familiar, and have furnished many earlier battles with their basic sequence of events:

Uppe þere Tambre.   heo tuhte to-somne.
heuen here-marken.   halden to-gadere.
luken sweord longe.   leiden o þe helmen.
fur ut sprengen.   speren brastlien.
sceldes gonnen scanen.   scaftes to-breken.
þer faht al to-somne.   folc vnimete.
Tambre wes on flode.   mid vnimete blode . . .   (lines 14244–50)

A. C. Gibbs points out (see n. 70, p. 106), that only 'luken sweord longe' is repeated elsewhere in the poem less than twice; the rest is made up of favourite formulas in a rather deliberate way which contrasts sharply with the effort of Old

English poets in comparable situations to vary and enrich their subject matter by means of elaborate, often synonymic, vocabulary.

The same is true of Laȝamon's descriptive techniques when applied to another well-known area of composition in both Old and Middle English: the sea-voyage. When he sets his hero Arthur on his last journey to the continent, he departs dramatically from his source, omitting most of Wace's nautical terminology, and reducing nearly all of the accurate account of navigation in the French text to two, or at most, two and a half, lines of very vague reference:

> Weder stod on wille.   wind wex an honde.
> ankeres heo up droþen.   drem wes on uolken.
> Wunden in-to widen sæ.   þeines wunder bliðe.
> scipen þer forð þrungen.   gleo-men þer sungen.
> seiles þer tuhten.   rapes þer rehtten.
> Wederen alre selest.   and þa sæ sweuede.   (lines 12745–50)

The passage is quite unlike Wace in its disregard for the special business of managing a troop-carrying vessel:

> Dunc veissiez ancres lever,
> Estrens traire, hobens fermer,
> Mariniers saillir par cez nés,
> Deshenechier veilles e trés;
> Li un s'esforcent al windas,
> Li altre al lof e al betas;
> Detriés sunt li guverneür,
> Li maistre esturman li meillur.
> Chescuns de guverner se peinne
> Al guvernal, ki al nef meine:
> Avant le hel si curt senestre
> E sus le hel pur cure a destre.
> Pur le vent es trés acuillir
> Funt les lispruez avant tenir
> E bien fermer es raelinges
> Tels i ad traient les gurdinges,
> E alquant abaissent le tref
> Pur la nef curre plus oüef...[71]

Its almost 'impressionistic' nature might lead us to suppose that Laȝamon had an alternative convention in mind: the vaguer more generalised treatments of sea-faring in Old English poetry. If we compare, for instance, one of the voyages described in *Beowulf* with Laȝamon's lines, it looks as if he could have found in this earlier verse a way of celebrating joyful harmonies of weather and seamanship which allowed him to avoid Wace's more restless catalogue of sailors-at-work. The earlier poet has a grasp of the effectiveness of the springing rhythms of the half-line units for conveying rapid movement, and he knows how to achieve a

51

sense of swift but steady progress by packing those units with important nouns and verbs:

> þa waes be maeste merehraegla sum,
> segl sale faest; sundwudu þunede;
> no þaer wegflotan wind ofer yðum
> siðes getwaefde; saegenga for,
> fleat famigheals forð ofer yðe
> bundenstefna ofer brimstreamas ... (*Beowulf*, lines 1905–10)

What distinguishes the two extracts is, however, as interesting as what links them. Laȝamon has no store of metaphor for his ships – the 'wegflota', 'saegenga', 'famigheals' which totally absorbs the *Beowulf* poet's attention is for him 'the sturdy vessel' which bears the army rejoicing to the shores of France. Moreover, once more we notice the importance of repetition to Laȝamon; he deals, as the Old English poet does not, in open parallelisms of structure, reinforced by rhymed endings: 'scipen þer forð þrungen / gleomen þer sungen / seiles þer tuhten / rapes þer rehtten...' It may be, of course, that those repetitions tell us something about the difficulties experienced by a writer who sets out, at a later date, to reproduce the compression of Old English verse, without the necessary aid of a fully inflected language. In such circumstance, there could have been a real temptation to resort to simple formulas, resoundingly repeated, when more adventurous, more complex structures would have to introduce a proportion of light connecting words, and dissipate the essential and traditional strength of the passage. But we cannot be sure that this is all there is to be said about Laȝamon's intentions and strategies. The prominence in the *Brut* of repetition as a device on every level of the process of composition – from basic grammar and syntax through to descriptive formulas – makes better sense if we associate it with Laȝamon's knowledge of stylistic theory and practice circulating within his own life-time. Even his French source, Wace's *Roman*, could demonstrate to him the interest and desirability of repetition as a literary device, especially when allied with rhyme; here the character of Arthur is elegantly analysed:

> Cuntre orguillus fu orguillus
> E cuntre humles dulz e pitus;
> Forz e hardiz e conqueranz,
> Large dunere e despendanz;
> E se busuinnus le requist,
> S'aidier li pout, ne l'escundist.
> Mult ama preis, mult ama gloire,
> Mult volt ses faiz mettre en memoire,
> Servir se fist curteisement,
> Si ce cuntint mult noblement. (*Roman*, lines 9019–28)

But there are times when it is Laȝamon's fondness for the accumulative rhetoric of the catalogue, each section introduced by the same word, which persuades him to depart from a close following of the *Roman*: A. C. Gibbs (see n. 70, p. 132) has stressed the 'echoing, patterned' quality of Laȝamon's description and it would be difficult to resist the conclusion, in a passage such as the following, that he is deliberately trying for stylistic effects not unknown, certainly, to earlier vernacular poets, but newly emphasised in the prescriptive treatises of the twelfth and thirteenth centuries:[72]

> Brutus hine bi-þohte.   & þis folc bi-heold.
> bi-heold he þa muntes.   feire & muchele.
> bi-heold he þa medewan.   þat weoren swiðe maere.
> bi-heold he þa wateres.   & þa wilde deor.
> bi-heold he þa fisches.   bi-heold he þa fuȝeles.
> bi-heold he þa leswa.   & þene leofliche wode.
> bi-heold he þene wode hu he bleou.   bi-heold he þat corn hu hit greu.
>
> (lines 1002–8)

Indeed, if Laȝamon can be said unreservedly to be an 'archaist', it is on a fairly limited type of evidence. His substitution of traditional names for Wace's 'seneschal' and 'buteiller' does alert us to places in the *Brut* where older structures of insular society seem to be very much on his mind; when presenting Arthur's court, for instance, he is just as likely to work within specifically Anglo-Saxon terms as to follow Wace's feudal pattern:

> Aelc of his birlen.   & of his bur-þaeinen.
> & his ber-cnihtes.   gold beren an honden.
> to ruggen and to bedde.   iscrud mid gode webbe...   (lines 9951–3)

And in occasional passages of prayer, reference back to Old English religious poetry seems direct and almost ostentatious; the clustering of epithets in the style of the Old English 'kenning' marks out this speech of Arthur's as something to be recognised for its special and – in the *Brut* – unusual qualities:

> Lauerd Drihten Crist.   domes waldende.
> midelarde mund.   monnen froure.
> þurh þine aðmode wil.   walden aenglen.
> let þu mi sweuen.   to selþen iturnen.   (lines 12760–3)

But his forays into older English poetry did not provide him with material for sustained composition of an imitative sort. It is true that we are sometimes reminded of that poetry as we travel with Laȝamon through centuries of battle description and panegyric, but the reminders themselves are of short duration. On reflection, we may wish to lay greater stress upon the significance of the fact that he moves so easily from one stylistic mode to another. Is it, we may ask, a sign of unsettled allegiances, or is it genuine striving for variety – stimulated, perhaps, by his familiarity with a number of literary models, only some of which are drawn out of the pre-Conquest past? On the question of metre, for instance, there were other twelfth-century English poets working with some knowledge of an Old English alliterative system, but overlaying it with rhyme in an apparently arbitrary way so as to give an uneven sequence of unrhymed accentual and couplet lines. *The Proverbs of Alfred* pose problems of formal definition not entirely unlike those we encounter in the *Brut*:

> Alured. he wes in englene lond.
> and king. wel swiþe strong.
> He wes king. and he wes clerek.
> Wel he luuede godes werk.
> He wes wis on his word.
> and war on his werke.
> he wes þe wysuste mon.
> þat wes englelonde on.
> þus queþ Alured/englene frouer.
> wolde ye mi leode/lusten eure louerde
> he ou wolde wyssye wisliche þinges.
> hw ye myhte worldes w[u]rþsipes welde.[73]

There is similar variation of metrical form in the late twelfth-century English *Bestiary* poem, though here the metrical changes that are rung throughout may be in rough imitation of the Latin original, which contains a variety of metrical forms.[74] It may also be important that certain of the *chansons de geste* circulating in the twelfth and thirteenth centuries do not confine themselves to a single unvarying metrical form: *Aiol*,[75] for example, uses both decasyllabic and dodecasyllabic lines. We shall have occasion to notice how one Anglo-Norman chronicle writer, Jordan Fantosme, perhaps an older contemporary of Laȝamon, availed himself of three different metres for his treatment of the years of rebellion against Henry II.[76] We could here be recording a number of twelfth-century attempts to satisfy a taste for stylistic diversity within the single long vernacular work. And this focusses a problematic subject: the nature and the range of literature influential upon Laȝamon.

We have suggested that whatever first-hand knowledge he had of Old English poetry – either in its 'classical' or in its later stages – he did not base his verse norm upon it, but occasionally used it as a guide to special stylistic effects. Poems such as *Beowulf* or the *Battle of Brunanburh*, separated by perhaps two centuries, can indicate something of the kind of sources from which Laȝamon may have drawn vocabulary and formulaic phrases, and, perhaps, a general sense of how to pack the long alliterative line: they cannot help us to understand the 'mixed', almost protean character of his verse-structurings. A recent study has looked outside the more famous named poems of the earlier period to find 'the seeds of Laȝamon' in a minor species of Old English verse – represented by certain pieces embedded in manuscripts of the prose *Chronicle* between entries for 959 and 1086.[77] Here the unevenness already remarked upon for the *Proverbs of Alfred* appears in a more confused form; the long line with linking alliteration is rare:

> of his land-leode.   for littelre neode[78]

and if a 'norm' can be discovered, it is probably the half-line, which sometimes rhymes emphatically:

> Sume hi man wið feo sealde,
> Sume hreowlice acwealde,
> Sume hi man bende,
> Sume hi man blende,
> Sume hamelode
> Sume haettode . . .[79]

and sometimes exists as an isolated unit with or without its own alliteration:

> Her Eadgar gefor
> Anglia reccent
> West Seaxena wine
> & Myrcene mundbora.
> Cuð waes þet wide
> geond feola þeoda.[80]

The possibility cannot be ruled out that we have here a collection of transitional verse-forms, representing, in a fragmentary way, a once much larger corpus of writing from which Laȝamon, in the next century, selected and developed what elements appealed to him. His rhymed passages could be said to resemble, if rather generally, the rhymed entry for 1036:

> Her wes fiðelinge and song.   her wes harpinge imong.
> pipen & bemen.   murie þer sungen.
> Scopes þer sungen.   of Arthure þan kingen.   (lines 11328–30)

And his subordination of alliteration in the long line to rhyming patterns –

> He letten stronge walles.   he lette bulden halles.   (line 8459)

is not unconvincingly anticipated by

> Castelas he let wyrcean
> & earme men swiðe swencean.[81]

The ultimately unsatisfying nature of such a theory lies in the fact that it has to rely upon a century of 'lost literature', in order to argue a continuity of existence into Laȝamon's life-time. It also has to rely upon quite unprovable assumptions about the quality and status of that literature. The five scraps of evidence we have, all brief 'insertions' into manuscripts of the Old English Chronicle, hardly encourage us to see great potential in such verse for an extensive narrative project; Laȝamon must surely have had more substantial testimony than this if, indeed, he did elect to work with it for the *Brut*. Without exaggerating his decision into a 'high choice' of momentous artistic consequence, we are probably right to insist that he had a reputable alternative to Wace's own verse medium. It is still true that between the entry for 1086 and the *Brut* nothing remains to indicate how or whether English historical verse flourished, in that same loose, mixed style, furnishing Laȝamon with some kind of literary precedent.

If we prefer, on the other hand, a hypothesis which lays emphasis upon existing, rather than lost, literature, there is at least one other major possibility: that the basic form of his verse line, with its characteristic systems of stress and alliteration, is inherited from a type of rhythmic composition, related to, but not identical with, Old English poetry. This 'rhythmical prose' was invented, as far as is known, by Aelfric, Abbot of Eynsham, in the early eleventh century, and widely disseminated through the manuscript copies of his *Homilies*, some of which were certainly being read, modernised and glossed, over the twelfth and thirteenth centuries in monastic libraries of the west of England.[82]

J. C. Pope's description of this literary medium is strikingly apposite to any study of the make-up of Laȝamon's verse:

a loosely metrical form resembling in basic structural principles the alliterative verse of the Old English poets, but differing markedly in the character and range of its rhythms as in strictness of alliterative practice, and altogether distinct in diction, rhetoric and tone.[83]

Pope stresses the way in which this style of Aelfric's adjusts itself easily to the demands of different kinds of material; 'too insistently regular to be disregarded', it can drop into unobtrusiveness, and 'lapse for a moment into ordinary prose' (Pope, pp. 135, 122). And it is clearly a style which might recommend itself for a long work – a situation in which resilience and stamina rather than idiosyncrasy might be valued. Pope's analysis of this 'rhythmic' prose might, in fact, be an analysis of a good deal of Laȝamon's verse: variable – indeed unpredictable – stress and syllabic content in the half-line; little enjambement; a contained syntactical structure for both half-lines and full-lines; a free range of alliterative conventions, with alliteration allowable on minor syllables, in the second stave of the second half-line, and as a device which often 'distinguishes half-lines but fails to unite them . . .' (Pope, pp. 117, 122, 124, etc.). Many of those features are present in the following passage, from Aelfric's Homily *De Falsis Deis*, a homily which was certainly given a twelfth-century circulation in the west country:

> Se Iouis waes swa swiðe gal þaet he on hys
>   swustor gewifode;
> Seo waes gehaten Iuno, swiðe healic gyden.
> Heora gedohtra waeron Minerua and Uenus.
> þa forlaeg se faeder fullice buta,
> and manega his magan manlice gewemde.

þas manfullan menn waeron þa maeroston godas
þe þa haeþenan wurðodan, and worhton him to godum . . .
His sunu hatte Mars, se macede aefre saca,
and wrohte and wawan he wolde aefre styrian.

(Homilies, II, 682–3: lines 113–19, 126–7)

If we now juxtapose a passage from the *Brut* in which Laʒamon is not striving, as he was in those extracts quoted above, for special effects of style, basic similarities become apparent:

þe king was ihoten Latin.   þe on þan londe wes.
hey wes and riche.   & he wes redesful.
mid wintre he wes bi-weaued.   swo hit wolde Godd.
þar com Eneas.   & grette þen alde king.
& he hine feire on-feng.   mid allen his folke.
Muche lond he him ʒef.   & mare him biheyte.
an-long þare sea.   siden & widen.
þare quene hit of-þouhte.   noþeles heo hit þolede.
þe king heuede ane douter.   þe him was swiþe deore.
Eneam he heo biheyte.   to habben to wife.
& after his daye.   al his drihliche lond.   (lines 65–75)

Both Homilist and Chronicle-writer could here be said to be 'mildly readjusting the rhythmic sequences of his ordinary prose' (Pope, p. 118). The syntax and grammar is, on the whole, that of 'ordinary prose' discourse: there is no consistent system of line stresses, reinforced by alliteration; the alliterative content of the lines varies from nothing to two or three staves in patterns which include conventional poetic types ('þas manfullan menn waeron þa maeroston godas', aa:ax) and disallowed poetic types ('þe king heuede ane douter. þe him was swiþe deore', xa:xa). In both cases, alliteration upon weakly-stressed syllables is permitted.

It would be perverse, it seems to me, if, in the face of such strong evidence, we resisted the conclusion that we are under obligation to find acceptable historical reasons for Laʒamon's extensive use, nearly two centuries later, of a rhythmical mode substantially similar to that employed by Aelfric in his *Homilies*. Here, as N. F. Blake has proposed,[84] rigid compartmentation into 'verse' or 'prose' is unhelpful; we are dealing with a species of composition which combines elements traditionally associated with one or other of those forms. Yet it would also be perverse if we ignored the fact that there are certain marked elements in Laʒamon's style which cannot have been derived from a developed version of this later Old English homiletic literature – in particular, his predilection for 'breaking' the long line with internal rhyme.[85] For this, he must have gone to very different models. It is, of course, not out of the question that he found those models in English vernacular poetry; although we have had reservations about accepting a theory of his indebtedness which has to call up a substantial body of

English historical verse out of a void, there can be no guarantee that rhymed composition, of the sort and of the scope of the pieces in the Old English Chronicle, did not continue to be written over the next century and a half. We should not, however, confine our searches and our speculations to one twelfth-century vernacular area only.

We have already raised the possibility of French and Anglo-Norman models for Laʒamon when touching upon the subject of repetitious half-lines, reinforced by rhyme (see above, p. 52). We might now come more exactly to the point: Laʒamon's own main source, the *Roman de Brut*, would have kept the attractions of rhyme firmly in his attention even if it could not apparently persuade him to imitate systematically its own regular and rhymed octosyllabic couplets. Laʒamon's use of internal rhyme produces uneasy couplets ranging from five to seven or eight syllables, in an unpredictable medley. It looks as if he intended the long line to remain as a unit, but with diversification from internal rhyme. The quick changes of rhythmical organisation which take place almost from line to line, even sometimes from half-line to half-line, in the following extract would seem to bear this out; there is no way of presenting it as a series of conventionally regular rhymed couplets:

> Ma þer aqueðen.   of Arðures iueren.
> þene sixti þusende.   segges mid horne.
> þa wolcne gon to dunien.   þa eorðe gon to biuien.
> To-somne heo heolden.   swulc heouene wolde uallen.
> aerst heo lette fleon to.   feond-liche swiðe.
> flan al swa þicke.   swa þe snau adun ualleð.
> stanes heo letten seoððen.   sturnliche winden.
> seoððen speren chrakeden.   sceldes brastleden.
> helmes to-helden.   heʒe men uellen.
> burnen to-breken.   blod ut ʒeoten.
> ueldes falewe wurðen.   feollen here-maerken.
> Wondrede ʒeond þat wald.   iwundede cnihtes ouer-al.
> sixti hundred þar weoren.   to-tredene mid horsen.   (lines 13700–12)

This highly characteristic passage defies easy generalisation about the kind of metrical 'norm' to which it subscribes. And, indeed, we can hardly resist the conclusion that at least two separate models are here involved – and perhaps, in some cases, superimposed: a long accentual, alliterative and unrhymed line, derived, at however many removes, from one or more Old English traditions; a long line, broken by internal rhyme derived from Anglo-Norman tradition which itself is probably dependent upon Latin. Among some of the earliest vernacular works of the twelfth century in England are the Anglo-Norman *Cumpoz* and the *Bestiaire* of Philippe de Thaon – the one a treatise on calculation, the other a version of the Latin *Physiologus*: both are written in a metre which has been described as 'a hexasyllabic rhymed couplet', or alternatively, 'a dodecasyllable with internal rhyme', an imitation of Latin verses such as those of Marbod of Rennes.[86] When we read Philippe's verses it is easy to hear the rhythm of some, at least, of Laȝamon's lines:

> Philipes de Thaün at fait une raisun
> Pur pruvaires guarnir de la lei maintenir.
> A sun uncle l'enveiet, que amender la deiet,
> Se rien i at mesdit en fait u en escrit
> A Hunfrei de Thaün le chapelein Yun.[87]

By comparison, the rhyming passages of the *Brut* are far less regular in syllabic content within the half-line, but they often read, on these occasions, more like a version of Philippe's metre than like a rough approximation to Wace's octo-syllabic couplet or to the rhymed doggerel of earlier English pieces:

> We habbað for eower luuen.   ilosed ure leoden.
> cnihtes i þissen londe.   an hundred þusende.
> seoððen Iulius Cesar.   aerst bicom her.
> ah swa we ibiden are.   nulle we no mare.
> ah we wulleð sone.   uaren in-to Rome.   (lines 6233–7)

It may easily be that Laȝamon had a strong sense of the appropriateness of a long-line format for his chronicle but was also aware of the need for metrical variation in a work of such length. The adoption of multiple formats in order to achieve that variousness created its own difficulties: when his verse escapes the charge of monotony, it is often accused of insecurity. But the important fact to stress is that the *Brut* bears witness to processes of metrical experimentation which are, in their own way, adventurous. No doubt, when making his choice of a suitable medium, Laȝamon was faced with many different alternatives and considerations. His serious historical intent in the *Brut*, with its patriotic and heroic emphasis, must have been one important determining factor; we shall later seek to establish his knowledge of twelfth-century Latin heroic verse – this might have bred in him dissatisfaction with the short couplets of his original, although complex Latin hexameters could hardly have provided him with a practical model. More practical in this role would have been heroic verse in the vernacular languages of both continental French and Anglo-Norman: he must have been familiar with the spacious decasyllabics and alexandrines of the *chansons de geste*, and he might even have known that the ultimate source of his own material, Geoffrey of Monmouth's *Historia*, had been turned into *chanson de geste* form by an anonymous Anglo-Norman poet.[88] The range of possible overlap between *chansons de geste* and chronicle had already been demonstrated by the work of Jordan Fantosme, from Lincolnshire in the 1170s, which dealt with the sombre events of the later years of Henry II's reign in a mixture of decasyllabics, alexandrines and 'fourteeners'.[89] But all of these use either assonance or rhyme at the end of the long line, and Laȝamon seems to have wished to avoid that feature. What has been called his 'compromise' was the adoption of a loosely-articulated, unrhymed line, which could be wrought up for more elaborate purposes by recourse to a number of vernacular styles, some of nostalgic, antiquarian and learned interest, perhaps, and some of more recent origin and reputation. Later medieval English poets would achieve their own versions of that same compromise.[90]

We said earlier that 'acceptable historical reasons' would have to be found for Laȝamon's use of a stylistic 'ground-bass' which had been invented and developed to deal with homiletic, not historical subject-matter. But it may be truer to say that acceptable reasons are needed to explain why this should not have been both possible, and even natural, for him to do. In the first place, it is doubtful whether he would have made any very rigid demarcation of the provinces of homily and chronicle, or whether he would have had a very keen sense of the impropriety of exchanges of literary forms between them. He must have been conscious, on the contrary, of many hospitable inter-genre arrangements: the Anglo-Norman *Sermon* or *Romaunz de Tentaciuns de Siecle*, written about 1200 by a monk of Beaulieu Priory for a noble lady of that district, delivers its homiletic messages about the decay of the world in *laisses* of rhymed alexandrines, borrowed from *chansons de geste*.[91] Although Laȝamon does not intend to subject his historical narratives to the judgement of the homilist, there are moments in the *Brut* when we are reminded that his statement of sources refers to Bede (line 16). Whether in fact he used Bede's *Historia Ecclesiastica* or not, he must have been conscious of a strong medieval tradition of historical writing which crossed the boundaries of chronicle and homily; he must also have been conscious of other literary traditions such as that of the Saint's Life, in which history, sermon and heroic drama are inextricably mingled. There seems no serious obstacle to the idea that he met the demands of his historical subject matter with a form already proved for its durability and flexibility in a homiletic field; those demands were often, in any case, the same as the demands made by homily. The many common areas of narrative and simple explication would prove the point, where theoretical objections might remain. In the following passages, what separates homily from chronicle? Certainly, neither content nor style:

> On þam halgan godspelle þe ge gehyrdon nu raedan
> us segð be Lazare, þe seoc laeg
> þa he waes in Bethania-wic wuniende [þa]
> [and] waes Marðan broðor and Marian [soþlice]
> and þaet waes seo Maria þe mid micelre arwurðnysse
> mid deorwurþre sealfe urne Drihten smyrode
> and mid hyre fexe wipode hys fet.
>
> (Aelfric, *Homilies*, I, 311–12, lines 1–7)

Siluius Eneas.   for ae[ð]elen he wes ihoten.
Ascanius his broþer.   þe mid his fader com from Troie.
mid muchele worscipe.   þis kine-bearn bi-wiste.
Asscanius wes þes childes broþer.   ah heo nefden noht ane moder.
His moder wes ihoten Creusa.   Priames kinges dohter.
þe Eneas his fader in Troie for-leas.
inne þane fehte.   his feon heo him binomen.

(Brut, lines 103–9)

The alternatives are to believe either that Laȝamon had to hand an established species of English accentual verse, probably on historical themes, but now completely lost to us, or that he can be credited with the same kind of 'creative step' as Aelfric had taken two centuries before him, divorcing 'the rhythm and alliteration of Old English poetry from its traditional vocabulary and syntax', and associating them with 'the vocabulary and syntax of prose'.[92] It seems more natural to believe that the truth is both less dramatic and les mysterious; that the context in which Laȝamon lived and wrote – the west midlands of the twelfth and early thirteenth centuries – allowed for the coming-together of diverse but essentially traceable literary influences: French, Anglo-Norman, English and Latin may all be involved.

Not only the metrical aspects of Laȝamon's art suggest that this is so. One of the most frequently praised ornaments of his style is the extended simile – a feature which is concentrated, although not isolated, in that part of the poem dealing with Arthur's campaign against the Saxons. The effect of these elaborately designed passages, set as they often are into a continuum of plainer writing, is arresting, and several suggestions have been made as to the possibility that Laȝamon was, in this particular stretch of the *Brut*, drawing upon special, but as yet unidentified, texts.[93] The long simile is not characteristic of his immediate source, Wace's *Roman de Brut*, nor indeed of Geoffrey of Monmouth's *Historia*, which lies behind the *Roman*. Admittedly, short similes, many of which use material from the animal world similar to that favoured by Laȝamon, do occur in the *Historia* and the *Roman*, but they are not clustered in the Saxon campaign section, and they are often considerably reduced in Wace's translation. It is reasonable to think that Laȝamon learnt something of the simile from either his immediate or ultimate source; here for instance, he adapts one which in Wace describes the aggressive Saxon leader, Corineus, as a 'lion attacking sheep', 'come leuns fait de berbiz':[94]

Corineus heom rasde to.   swa þe rimie wulf.
þane he wule on scheapen.   scaðe-werc wrchen.   (lines 774–5)

And here it looks as if a simile from the *Historia* has been worked over and sharpened with additional pictorial detail: Geoffrey of Monmouth sees the marauding Saxons setting about the Britons 'just as wolves attack sheep which the shepherds have forsaken':

> quemadmodum lupi oues, quas pastores
> deseruerunt.[95]

Laȝamon transfers the simile to Arthur:

> & he gon to rusien.　swa þe runie wulf.
> þenne he cumeð of holte.　bi-honged mid snawe.
> and þencheð to biten.　swulc deor swa him likeð.　(lines 10041–3)

But the existence of short similes, and a rare example of an extended version – Wace surprisingly, on one occasion, invents without prompting from Geoffrey[96] – cannot wholly account for what we find in Laȝamon's *Brut*. Familiarity with other kinds of works must have persuaded Laȝamon towards large-scale trans- formations and relocations of subject matter. For it is not only the range of his illustrative topics but also the ingenuity with which he develops them which distinguishes his simile-making from that of his most obvious sources. The effect of these descriptive 'excursions', many of them drawn from the animal world – whether in its active role as natural aggressor or in its passive role as victim of the chase – is both decorative and enlarging in an imaginative sense. The fleeing Saxons wander as blindly as the wild crane does in the moor-fen, separated from his flock and pursued by dogs and hawks:

> þenne nis him neouðer god.　no þat lond no þat flod.
> hauekes hine smiteð.　hundes hine biteð.
> þenne bið þe kinewurðe foȝel.　faeie on his siðe.　(lines 10065–7)

Neither land nor water offers him refuge; hawks and dogs tear at him; the noble bird is on his last journey. Arthur exults over the rout of Childric, the Saxon commander, in an elaborate simile, likening him to the once-proud fox, harried by men and hounds, and finally dug out of his hole. The passage takes us through the life of the fox: his freedom in the wild landscapes, his lordship over other lesser creatures and the misery of his final raucous hunting-down:

> hunten þar talieð.　hundes þer galieð.
> þene vox driueð.　ȝeond dales & ȝeond dunes.
> he ulih to þan holme.　& his hol isecheð.　(lines 10407–9)

Arthur himself, frequently referred to as a lion – a simile which is most likely to have come to Laȝamon from Geoffrey's *Historia*[97] – is once dramatically pre- sented as the wild boar playing havoc among the domestic swine as they feed in the beech-wood:

> Al waes þe king abolȝen.　swa bið þe wilde bar.
> þenne he i þan maeste.　monie swin imeteð . . .　(lines 10609–10)

But the most famous lines from the *Brut*, conjured up as part of Arthur's account of the defeated Saxon leaders, gazing down at their drowned troops in the river Avon, come in the form of metaphor rather than simile. Here the inversion of scaled fish and mailed warriors is quite remarkable; if Laȝamon found the basic idea in something similar to Geoffrey of Monmouth's description of the drowning of the children of Henry I, in 1120 –

the lion's whelps shall be transformed into fishes of the sea . . .[98]

the credit for fully realising its dramatic potential is his alone:

> þa ȝet c[l]eopede Arður.   aðelest kingen.
> ȝurstendaei wes Baldulf.   cnihten alre baldest.
> nu he stant on hulle.   & Auene bi-haldeð.
> hu ligeð i þan straeme.   stelene fisces.
> mid sweorde bi-georede.   heore sund is awemmed.
> heore scalen wleoteð.   swulc gold-faȝe sceldes.
> þer fleoteð heore spiten.   swulc hit spaeren weoren.   (lines 10637–43)

We might almost be tempted to believe that the inspiration for Laȝamon's elegant 'conceit' came from contemporary visual, rather than literary, sources. A striking miniature in a mid-thirteenth-century manuscript of the *Roman de Toute Chevalerie*, by Thomas of Kent, shows Alexander in the water, fully armed, and surrounded by fishes; the floating subaqueous shapes, similarly decorated with scales or chain-mail, suggest a direction for the development of Laȝamon's image.[99]

Certainly, when we look to those vernacular literary sources which have been canvassed by some experts as influential upon the *Brut*, we meet with little success. Old English poetry is not much given to long similes, except as translations from the Bible and patristic works; homiletic prose of the period will occasionally use them as *exempla*, but there are no instances of long similes in secular literary contexts.[100] Old French *chansons de geste* offer only brief and repetitious examples:

> plus se fait fiers que leon ne leupart . . .
> plus est isnels que nen est uns falcuns . . .[101]

There is, however, one species of medieval literature which is famous for its extended similes – Latin heroic poetry. Inspired by the epic of the classical and late classical worlds – by that of Virgil, but most frequently by that of Statius, Claudian, Lucan – it is represented in the twelfth century by the verse of two authors associated with the court of Henry II: Joseph of Exeter and Walter of Châtillon. Walter of Châtillon's *Alexandreis*, or life of Alexander in hexameters, was probably the most popular of all medieval Latin 'epics'.[102] Written between 1178 and 1182, it was dedicated to William, Archbishop of Sens and later of Rheims; interestingly enough, William was grandson of a patroness we have already encountered – Adela of Blois. Walter had worked for Henry II, in his Chancellery; he came to England in 1160, but returned to France after Henry's quarrel with Becket. Although the *Alexandreis* was not a direct result of Angevin patronage, it was extremely well-known on both sides of the Channel; extant manuscript copies are numerous, often annotated copiously. Joseph of Exeter's *Frigii Daretis Yliados*, more commonly referred to as the *De Bello Troiano*, was written at Henry II's court, dedicated in the mid-1180s to Baldwin, Archbishop of Canterbury, who was preparing to depart on the Third Crusade; it tells in six books of the history of the Trojan war from the rejection of the Argonauts to the dispersal of the Trojans.[103] Joseph's poem in hexameters is 'extrèmement riche de contents rhétoriques' (Bezzola, III, 149), and maintained its popularity throughout the medieval centuries.

Joseph uses both the long and the short simile: Hercules, meditating revenge upon the Trojans, is likened to a bull:

the outcast leader of his herd, lamenting his exile from the stamping-grounds that he loves . . . Imagining glorious battles, he rages with his horns, and considers it shame if he does not shatter the trees that he charges.[104]

Antilochus and Achilles are assailed by the Trojans as a double-oak is set-upon by fifty peasants, and 'a great destruction of men and forest follows its fall'.[105] Men in rage are compared to lions, eagles, Hyrcanian tigers, and Scythian bears. Walter of Châtillon, using all the devices of Latin epic to present his hero, Alexander, as a god-like creature who merited nothing but unbounded admiration, invokes Hyrcanian lions, menacing stags, and twin bulls. Armies are as carefully deployed as sheep, let out of pasture, are counted and watched-over by shepherd and faun.[106]

Many of the similes of Joseph and Walter are not entirely original, and there is, of course, no over-riding reason why a thirteenth-century English priest could not have had access to the older Latin materials upon which these twelfth-century poets drew. The 'Silver Age' Statius and Lucan, the fourth-century Claudian, were widely read in educated circles of twelfth- and thirteenth-century England.[107] They all lavishly employ the long 'Virgilian' simile to dignify and diversify their heroic verse: the *Thebaid* of Statius, for instance, is packed with *similitudines* to an almost grotesque degree. Apart from a number of subjects from natural phenomena such as storms at sea and on land, hurricanes, and mountain torrents, Statius works tirelessly over the predatory animal world producing variation after variation on the themes of wolves, tigresses, bulls, lions, serpents, boars and bears, attacking either each other, or milder domestic creatures – heifers and sheep.[108] Some of these similes and others more recently invented were mediated to the twelfth century through the works of Claudian. His *Contra Rufinum* and *De Raptu Proserpinae*[109] were particularly popular, and most writers at the Angevin court, from John of Salisbury and Gerald of Wales to

Joseph of Exeter, were influenced by him. To the corpus of familiar examples – lions, wolves, bulls and tigresses – Claudian added a few fresh subjects: ostriches, whales and arena animals.

None of Laȝamon's extended similes can be precisely tracked down to passages in twelfth-century Latin poetry or in its classical and late-classical sources. And yet we are led irresistibly to the conclusion that he must have based his practice upon some knowledge of Latin stylistic tradition. If the detailed development of his similes cannot be exactly paralleled in the works we have been considering, the basic themes can often be compared. And here we should not rule out entirely the possibility that he could have come across some of these themes in the parent text itself – Virgil's *Aeneid*. The *Aeneid* was in everyday reading use throughout the Middle Ages for the teaching of Grammar in the Schools; it was constantly excerpted for the illustration of modes of high style.[110] Laȝamon's interesting simile about the pursuit of the wild crane, for instance, reminds us that 'Strymonian cranes', fleeing before the south winds, are the subject of a more peaceful simile in Book X of the *Aeneid*.[111] Lucan and Claudian, after all, certainly imitate Virgil. One of the rare similes outside the 'Arthurian' sections of the *Brut*, applied early on to the warrior Brutus, who is 'as enraged as the wild boar when hounds have him at bay in the forest' (lines 850–1), reads like a shortened version of Virgil's splendid description of Mezentius, fighting against great odds 'velut ille canum morsu de montibus altis / actus aper ...' (X.707 – 8). It is even tempting to juxtapose Laȝamon's dramatic metaphor of arrows showering the Romans 'al swa þicke. swa þe snau adun ualleð' (lines 13705–6), with that of Virgil – 'fundunt simul undique tela / crebra nivis ritu' (XI.610–11), 'at once from all sides they shower darts as thick as snowflakes'.

Of course, there must also have been many less well-known productions of the age in heroic hexameters – battle-poems, lives of kings, panegyrics – which could have come within Laȝamon's range of knowledge, and which could have certainly provided him with simile material. Guillaume le Breton's Latin verse *Life of Philip Augustus* (the *Philippidos*), written about 1213, pictures the army of Simon de Montfort moving against the Toulousains in a lengthy and ferocious simile:

like a wolf who having broken into a sheepfold by night, does not care to slake his belly with meat, but is content to tear open the throats of the sheep, adding dead to the dead, lapping-up blood with his tongue, so the army, consecrated to God...[112]

And, even nearer home, a Latin poem on the 'Battle of Lincoln', in which the cause of Louis of France was finally defeated (1216/17), ventures upon a metaphor quite as startling, for all its ultimate Virgilian origin,[113] as that of Laȝamon's fish-warriors in the River Avon; the victorious English are the 'iron-clad bees of war':

fundunt examina Christi
Ferrigeras Mavortis apes, stimulisque timendis
Hostiles penetrant tunicas, squamosaque ferri
Texta secant . . .[114]

(The hives of Christ send forth the iron-girt bees of war, and with fearful stings they
penetrate the hostile shirts, and cut the scaly textures of iron . . .)

If nothing else is absolutely clear, what is beyond doubt is that Laȝamon's use
of extended simile (and metaphor) in certain areas of his poem was a deliberate
attempt to heighten and dignify particular stretches of British history; beyond
doubt, too, is the fact that he did this in imitation of Latin heroic verse practice.

Reluctance to look to such a tradition for Laȝamon's exemplars is part of a
general tendency to regard the *Brut* as the eccentric work of an obscure country
priest, isolated in the west midlands, and celebrating, in a rather old-fashioned
way, the glories of this island's past. And it must be admitted that Laȝamon did
not help matters by making a confused, if not misleading, opening statement
about the authors to whom he was indebted:

> He nom þa Englisca boc. þa makede Seint Beda.
> An-oþer he nom on Latin. þe makede Seinte Albin.
> & þe feire Austin. þe fulluht broute hider in.   (lines 16–18)

What this seems to mean is that he had seen Bede's *Ecclesiastica Historia*, and the
Old English translation; he may have done no more than look at the Preface to the
Latin text, since he mistakenly assumes that it had been written by 'Seinte Albin
& þe feire Austin'.[115] In fact, he makes no use of either the Latin or the
vernacular in his poem as a whole. His next announcement – that he turned to the
work of a 'Frenchis clerc/Wace wes ihoten' – is demonstrably reliable. But we
need not assume, from his irrelevant invocation of Bede and Augustine, that he
was unable to read and had no access to Latin literature. It is not unusual for
medieval authors to try to win for themselves the sober reputation of being
scrupulous consulters of Latin historical sources: nor to be silent about their
reading and borrowing from other kinds of literature, both Latin and vernacular.
Laȝamon wishes, no doubt, to set himself apart from the French clerk, Wace, and
stress the essentially historical and even religious nature of his great project: he
wishes to

tell of the great men of England . . . who they were, and whence they came, after the Flood
which the Lord sent, and which drowned all living men except Noah, Shem, Japhet and
Ham . . .   (lines 7–12)

On the question of Laȝamon's humble country status and his western 'isola-
tion', we should also make cautious judgements. The two manuscripts tell us that
Laȝamon was priest of a 'fine church', 'aeðelen are chirechen' (Cotton Caligula,
A.ix, line 3), and that he dwelt at Areley-Kings 'with the good knight', 'wid þan

gode cniþte' (Cotton Otto, c. xiii, line 3). There he 'read books', 'bokes radde'. In medieval times, and indeed until 1684, Areley-Kings was part of the manor of Martley, and in the diocese of Worcester.[116] Martley seems to have been a royal manor in its earliest days: a fishery at 'Ernel', or Areley, with lands attached to it, was granted by the Empress Maud to the Cistercian Abbey of Bordesley on its foundation in 1136, and the Abbot of Bordesley is recorded as paying an annual sum to the Exchequer in the twelfth and thirteenth centuries for those fishing and property rights. The manor of Martley remained in the King's hands until 1196; various grants of land within the manor were, however, made during this time: to Roger de Mortimer, for instance, in 1175. In 1197, land worth £33 was granted to Philip de Aire, but by 1200 the whole manor seems to have passed to the de Frisa or Frise family, who kept it until 1233. After that time, having apparently lapsed to the Crown, it was granted, by Henry III, to the Despencers.

A member of the de Frisa family, or one of the Despencers, or any of their dependents, could qualify as Laȝamon's 'good knight' of the Cotton Otho manuscript: we have no means of verifying the manuscript reference, nor of identifying the person who may have been meant. It was perhaps as true for the thirteenth century as for the seventeenth that 'the lord of Martley is the lord of Areley'.[117] Certainly the rector of Martley had the right to present an incumbent to Areley-Kings, and as late as 1283 Areley church was called the 'chapel' of Areley.[118] Laȝamon was dead by 1268[119] but his time at Areley-Kings could have spanned the de Frisa and Despencer years as lords of the manor of Martley. His avowed intent to 'tell of the heroes of England, who they were and whence they came – they who first conquered the land...' (*Brut*, lines 7–9), would have been to the taste of noble secular patrons who, as a class, had already shown themselves so interested in commissioning and accepting the Anglo-Norman 'ancestral romances'. Lay enthusiasm for Laȝamon's ultimate source, Geoffrey of Monmouth's *Historia Regum Britanniae*, had also been great.[120] It could be objected, however, that Laȝamon's choice of English for his work, and the lack of any dedicatory formula, would rule out the patronage of a family as important as the Despencers. And although we have been stressing the interchangeability of the various vernacular languages in use in England during the early thirteenth century, Anglo-Norman would have been a more likely choice at the Despencer level. There were many less distinguished landowners in the area, and it is probably to one of those that we should look if we decide to believe that the 'good knight' of the Cotton Otho manuscript was a real person.

In the preceding account of the shaping of Laȝamon's metre and of his poetic style, a fairly wide range of composition in English, French, Anglo-Norman and Latin has been mentioned. It has been suggested that for Laȝamon, no less than for the poet of the *Owl and the Nightingale*, we should look to cultural contexts of some interest in order to explain the newly variable nature of his art. We may well ask, in the first place, how he came across books of any sort – both those which he mentions, and those which are unnamed, but must have been somewhere, in a west-midland collection, available to him. The two manuscripts of his *Brut* tell us that he read books at Areley-Kings or perhaps at nearby Redstone – the punctuation does not make this absolutely clear:

> He wonede at Ernleʒe.   at aeðelen are chirechen.
> vppen Seuarne staþe.   sel þar him þuhte.
> on-fest Radestone.   þer he bock radde.
>
> (Cotton Caligula MS, lines 3–5)

> He wonede at Ernleie wid þan gode cniþte.
> uppen Seuarne. merie þer him þohte.
> faste bi Radistone þer heo bokes radde.
>
> (Cotton Otho MS, lines 3–5)

They also say that he travelled far and wide to collect other books for his work: 'Laʒamon gon liðen. wide ʒond þas leode/& biwon þa aeðela boc...'; 'Loweman gan wende. so wide so was þat londe./and nom þe Englisse boc...' (Cotton Caligula, Cotton Otho MSS, lines 14–15 respectively). In spite of the unreliability of the references to Bede/Albinus/Augustine (see page 66 above), it may be worth attending to other details of the manuscript accounts. The possibilities are that he had books at 'home', whether he was a domestic chaplain to a 'gode cniþte' of Areley-Kings, or whether he was simply a parish priest of Areley: moreover that he supplemented his local store by searching outside his immediate district. None of this is entirely unlikely. His major source, Wace's *Roman de Brut*, could easily have been in secular hands during the twelfth and thirteenth centuries; evidence for lay ownership and patronage of similar works in the twelfth century has been discussed above (see pp. 19–25) and we know that Guy Beauchamp gave a copy of the *Roman de Brut*, among a large number of romances, *chansons de geste*, and religious works, to the Cistercian Abbey of Bordesley, in 1305.[121] The Beauchamps, Earls of Warwick, were powerful land-owners throughout the west-midlands, during Laʒamon's life-time: Bordesley Abbey lay about twenty miles due east of Areley-Kings. However, the very fact that Bordesley received a 'Romaunce de Brut' from Guy Beauchamp alerts us to the fact that Laʒamon could just as easily have found his French book in a local religious library. The Cathedral Library of Canterbury had a copy in the thirteenth century;[122] it was clearly not an unusual acquisition. If Laʒamon did, in fact, move further afield than Areley-Kings for his books, west-midland religious houses could have provided him with rich fare. Worcester, with its Cathedral and conventual libraries, was only ten miles away; here, Old English devotional texts were preserved alongside patristic and classical volumes.[123] Laʒamon's adaptation of a loose kind of later Old English rhythmical prose for his own special purposes may have been made possible in less formal ways than by access to prose texts in west-midland libraries; it is interesting, however, that not only at Worcester but also at Lanthony, near Gloucester, 'Old English prose was understood and valued...'[124] The library of Lanthony Priory, a house of Augustinian Canons consecrated in 1136, and endowed by a succession of wealthy local families from the Chaundos of Brockworth to the Bohuns of Hereford and Essex, contained, according to an early fourteenth-century library list, an exceptionally large section of classical and late classical texts, including Cicero, Ovid, Horace, Lucan, Dares Phrygius and Aristotle.[125] Lanthony seems to have had a very hospitable relationship with the outside world during the whole of its history; a thirteenth-century manuscript, still extant, with Latin and English contents, is thought to have been owned by a schoolmaster from the grammar-school maintained by the Priory from the twelfth to the thirteenth centuries.[126] The libraries of the houses of Augustinian Canons are often very wide-ranging in their taste for historical as well as theological works; St Oswald's, Gloucester, had a number of volumes dealing with the conquests of Alexander and the Trojan Wars, and Lanthony Priory had, as item 156 in its early fourteenth-century list, 'Duo libelli que vocantur Brut'.[127]

What all of this goes to show is that west-midland book collections, built up over the twelfth and thirteenth centuries predominantly by religious houses but, in one exceptional instance, by a magnate, were eclectic in nature. Like their counterparts in other areas of England, they enlivened patristic and theological holdings with classical materials, with medieval history and even romance; they did not entirely neglect the vernacular languages, although works in Old French and Anglo-Norman are more in evidence than those in English. Professor Rodney Hilton, writing of a slightly later period in the west midlands, tells us that 'no centre is more likely (than Worcester) to have stimulated the west-midland school of poetry than this, even if it were not the only one'.[128] His study of the close relationships between lay and ecclesiastical lords, the special function of religious houses as 'meeting places for local notabilities', could have something to tell us of the thirteenth century too, and how a country priest, who may have had a 'good knight' as patron, and who may have had access to some kinds of local libraries, decided to undertake a project as ambitious as the *Brut*.

Laȝamon's insistence that he lived 'near to Redstone', and, indeed, the ambiguity of the punctuation at that point in both manuscripts, so that it is impossible to know whether he 'read books' at Areley-Kings or at Redstone, raises a little speculation as to the exact significance of the references. Earlier historians were led to conclude that he had some close connection with the remarkable series of cliff-dwellings at Redstone, which housed a number of hermits as early as the twelfth and thirteenth centuries.[129] Some recognised community must have dwelt there in Laȝamon's time; in 1182, Simon, clerk of 'Reddestan', is mentioned, and in 1260, protection was granted for 'the brethren of the House of Radestone'.[130] The 'House of Radestone' never apparently developed into any more formal institution, although J. C. Dickinson cites several instances of houses of regular canons evolving out of original hermitages.[131] We do not have to go as far as Nash and suggest that Laȝamon actually wrote the *Brut* in Redstone Hermitage; it is, however, intriguing to know that he specifically mentions a place which had some kind of community during his life-time, and we may wonder whether he had any useful contact with the 'clerk' and the 'brethren' of a literary sort.

Neither Redstone nor Areley-Kings were entirely secluded places; the ford over the Severn at Redstone was at one time the chief road across the river and, as the fourteenth-century *Gough Map* indicates, Areley-Kings must have been on the main road and water routes from Worcester to Bridgnorth.[132] Even the little that remains of the twelfth-century church of Laȝamon's day – a few features absorbed into a nineteenth-century structure – allows us to suppose that his references to a 'fine church', 'aeðelen are chirechen' (line 3), were not perhaps misjudged.

Although their milieux are no longer courtly in any real sense, in these vernacular compositions of the twelfth and thirteenth centuries we hear the echoes of the high literatures of the European courts. Laȝamon could not have designed the best part of his chronicle in a heroic frame, ornamented by the figures of style most clearly appropriate to the celebration of a great hero and his people, if texts such as the *Alexandreis* and the *De Bello Troiano* had not been written. As in the case of the *Petit Plet* and *Owl and the Nightingale*, where the clerkly debates of the twelfth-century Angevin court pass into more widely acceptable vernacular versions, here in the *Brut* Laȝamon is able to give his west-midland patron or readers a taste of the fine and varied writing they could expect to find in the Latin epic, dedicated within his life-time to Archbishops and Kings of England and France. The cultural energies of twelfth-century courts are productive in vernacular situations of the earlier thirteenth century.

But perhaps the crowning example of this process at work comes from a body of prose texts of the period 1190–1220: the so-called 'Katherine Group' of Saints' lives and meditative treatises, and the rule of life for three Anchoresses of Herefordshire – the *Ancrene Wisse*. E. J. Dobson's brilliant reconstruction of the historical context in which these compositions existed presents us with a picture of 'a feudal society of the Welsh Marches'[133] with powerful overlords in patronal situations and religious foundations promoting scholarship and literary culture 'in intimate contact with the main centres of contemporary thought, including especially the University of Paris'.[134] Older accounts of the comprehensive and elegantly written English texts produced by authors from this area for women in conventual life tended to dwell on the way in which they illustrated the strength of the English language and English literary tradition reasserting themselves after a period of foreign domination and native decline.[135] We have seen how, in the case of contemporary English poetry, nothing could be further from the truth. Dobson's study of the origins of the *Ancrene Wisse* tells a story which begins in

1148, with the first moves by Oliver de Merlimond, steward of Hugh de Mortimer, Baron of Wigmore and the most influential Marcher Lord in that territory, to found a house of Victorine Canons in the village of Shobdon in north-western Herefordshire. We have already noticed how de Merlimond's zeal for travel abroad and building at home resulted in the importation of southern-French sculptural styles for his church at Shobdon, completed about 1140.[136] But another more important link with France was established by de Merlimond's invitation to the Abbey of St Victor in Paris to send a small number of Canons to Shobdon, and establish a house there. Two came; the site was found unsatisfactory, and after further attempts to settle the Canons a permanent site for what was to become Wigmore Abbey was decided upon – one mile north of Wigmore village and the Mortimer castle of Wigmore. The provision of the final site for the Abbey was made by de Merlimond's overlord, Hugh de Mortimer, who became a generous benefactor to the house and was often regarded as its founder. The building went on rapidly, and the new Abbey Church was finished by 1179. The first abbot of Wigmore came direct from Paris and was the learned Andrew of St Victor, who died at Wigmore in 1175. Dobson is able to substantiate that, 'though it was neither very large nor very wealthy, Wigmore Abbey was large enough to have been able to develop its own literary form of English and to assemble a group of trained scribes . . .'[137] By a 'process of exclusion' (p. 133) of the most rigorous kind, he locates the composition of the *Ancrene Wisse* and its related writings at the Abbey. For the *Ancrene Wisse* he shows how the 'erudition and width of reading' of the author, who is familiar with Biblical commentaries, the writings of Augustine, Gregory, Anselm, Bernard of Clairvaux, Stephen Langton and Alexander of Bath, are especially appropriate to his Victorine calling. For he is also significantly indebted to the great Victorine masters of the twelfth century – Hugh and Richard of St Victor. And all of this demonstrates 'how closely he was in touch with the intellectual activity of the later twelfth century, of which the most eminent centre was the University of Paris' (p. 144).

The clerical authors of the *Ancrene Wisse* and the 'Katherine group' of texts can be convincingly placed in Wigmore Abbey; the women religious for whom they wrote are probably the nuns of Limebrook or Lingbrook, a small house of Augustinian Canonesses four miles from the Abbey, founded by a local landowner, Ralph of Lingen, in 1190. The *Ancrene Wisse* itself, however, seems to have been specifically intended for the three sisters of an 'offshoot' of the nunnery – an anchorage and chapel dedicated to the Virgin and St Leonard, endowed by Roger de Mortimer, son of Hugh, about 1200. Only rarely, for this early period, has historical research so successfully documented the intimate relationships between patrons, authors and readers: between Latin theological and meditative works and vernacular treatises: between universities of international repute and small religious houses of the English west country. The range and quality of this vernacular literature argue for the existence of a decent library at Wigmore

Abbey, and, as Dobson points out, a library which must have contained not only Latin but some earlier English religious materials. Varieties of native alliterative and rhythmical composition, probably from homilies and saints' lives, must lie behind the three *Lives* of Saints Katherine, Juliana and Margaret. Indeed, alliterative language is a feature common to all of these texts, although only the saints' lives systematise it thoroughly. The preservation of Old English religious texts in the libraries of the west country is well-proven; as with Laȝamon, so with the authors of these saints' lives – access would have been easy.

But the truth is that wherever we look in this large collection of English works what we observe is the modification, even the transformation, of any native inheritance by newer subject-matter, and correspondingly new stylistic modes. The three alliterative saints' lives, for instance, dependent though they may be to some extent upon a knowledge of the tradition of Aelfric's alliterative *Saints' Lives*, use alliteration in a heavier, more extravagant way, and in combination with other verbal devices not favoured by Aelfric. Comparison of specimen passages illustrates this:

> Man ledde to his breostum brade isene clutas
> swiðe glowende þaet it sang ongean.
> & hi þa teartan wita mid witum ge-eacnodon.
> & his aerran wunda mid wundum ofsettan.
> & into his innoðum hine gewundodon.
> swa þaet on his lichaman nan dael ne belaf
> ne naere gewundod on ðaere witnunge.

wite hit tu nu ȝif þu wult – for he hit wat ful wel, he þe haueð iseilet me to him seolf, & mi meiðhad – þet tu ne maht nans-weis, wið weole ne wið wune, wið wa ne wið wontreþe ne wið nan worldlich þing, wenden me ne wrenchen of þe wei þet ich am in bigunne to ganne. & unwurð, þet wite þu, me beoð þine wordes; for him ane ich luuie & habbe to bileue, þe weld & wisseð wið his wit windes & wederes . . .[138]

The second passage, which seems to strive to be a *tour de force* of alliteration on one predominant letter, reminds us of an alliterative past, but also of the distance travelled away from it. Some of the stimuli which operated upon the thirteenth-century author are clearly very different from those which operated upon Aelfric. And it is probably not sufficient to say that Aelfric's 'taste and skill were wanting to his imitators in the twelfth and thirteenth centuries . . .'[139] The later English author was persuaded to intensify an already elaborate method of composition, well-established for homiletic and hagiographical purposes. The nature of these persuasions can partly be judged from the often extremely ornate Latin prose which lies behind the vernacular *Lives*. *St Marherete* is backed by a highly sophisticated Latin life of the Saint, and while it is true that the heavy, obsessive alliteration of the English could not have been prompted directly by the Latin, it is still possible that the English writer was trying for a native equivalent to convey the impressive style of his Latin source:

Cessa, maligne, gemisce horribilis homicida, protector mihi Christus est. Cessa fetor male, fera iniqua, auctor gehenne.

(Cease, O malignant one, groan, horrible homicide. My protector is Christ. Cease, you evil dung, cease, you evil beast, the author of hell.)

Stute nu, earme steorue . . . . for ich habbe to help min healent in heouene . . . . Stute nu, alde monslahe . . . . Stute nu, wleatewile wiht . . .'[140]

The rapid increase during the eleventh and twelfth centuries of the production of treatises of precept and example relating to the fields of poetic and prose-epistolary composition must here be judged extremely important.[141] A greater excitement about the use of the verbal arts of persuasion and beautification resulted in scores of works such as the *De Ornamentis Verborum*[142] of Marbod of Rennes – an author whom we have already encountered when dealing with the possible Latin sources for Laȝamon's long, medially rhymed line (above, p. 59). Marbod composed for a pupil of his this succinct analysis and illustration of the 'schemata verborum' interchangeably applicable to verse or prose:

> Versificaturo quaedam tibi tradere curo
> Scemata verborum studio celebrata piorum
> Quae sunt in prosa quoque non minimum speciosa.　　(col. 1687)

(I take care to hand to you who are about to write verses [rhetorical] schemes celebrated for the zeal of their pious words – which are in prose too not the least dazzling.)

The relevance of this to our English prose treatises is two-fold: not only was one of Marbod's works – a poem called the 'Oratio ad Sanctam Mariam' – translated as 'A Lofsong of ure Lefdi', representing well the style of the so-called 'prose rhapsodies' associated with the 'Katherine Group', but the manual *De Ornamentis* also sets out precisely many of the 'word-schemes' used by the English writers of the whole range of this early thirteenth-century prose, whether narrative or rhapsodic in temper.[143] The English authors seem to have been able to go to Marbod for a good deal of practical material, and for the special means with which to convey it. For in the case of the 'prose rhapsodies' particularly, fervent prayers and meditative exercises for devout nuns, there was little in the English vernacular tradition upon which they could draw even partially. With the *Saints' Lives* we can point to Aelfric, but with these there is nothing except Latin. And these rhapsodies imitate, with great skill and inventiveness, the Latin literature of affective devotion which had been developing since the eleventh century, first on the continent, and then in England too. The models and the theory for pieces such as *The Wooing of our Lord*, for instance, are all in Latin, but the English version is a very competent 'essay' in a particular kind of devotional rhetoric first worked out in Latin. Thus it is interesting to find many of the word-devices discussed and recommended by Marbod in his *De Ornamentis* lavishly used throughout the prose treatises of the *Wooing* group: and we can sometimes find Marbod giving definition and illustration to the most elaborate features of the style in English. Some instruction and imitation has clearly gone on. For example: 1. *Repetitio* (of various forms, often half-rhymed and alliterated)

Tu mihi rex, mihi lex, mihi lux, mihi dux, mihi vindex . . .

Iesu swete, iesu mi leof, mi lif, mi leome, min halwi, min huniter . . .

Iesu swete iesu, mi drud, mi derling, mi drihtin, mi healend, mi huniter, mi haliwei . . .[144]

[Elizabeth Salter's manuscript breaks off here]

3 England and the continent during the thirteenth century: royal and aristocratic patronage

As late as the last decade of the fourteenth century, noble men and women leave, in their wills, copies of books 'en Frauncois'; the Bohun ladies, for instance, Margaret, Countess of Devon, and Eleanor, Duchess of Gloucester, leave, respectively, a book called *Arthur de Bretagne*[1] and 'un Cronike de Fraunce en Frauncois . . . un livre de vices et vertues, et un autre rimeie del "historie de chivaler a cigne" . . . un livre beal et bien enluminee de legenda aurea, en Frauncois . . .'[2] Devotional and leisure reading alike, for the families of magnates such as the Bohuns, seems to have ranged widely in works of continental French; although some of the total list of books in the bequest may have been in Anglo-Norman (the 'livre de vices et vertues', for instance), the romances and chronicle referred to were no doubt written in continental French and produced in France. The specifying of rich bindings ('ove deux claspes d'argent, enamayles ove les armes de duc de Burgoign') and lavish illumination for the *Chronicle* in question and the *Legenda Aurea* leads us in the direction of the French fourteenth-century book-trade in such works, rather than to the English; volumes of Arthurian romance such as Margaret Bohun's *Arthur de Bretagne* are very likely, taking into account the well-known fact that the Bohuns were collectors of fine manuscripts, to have been volumes such as are still extant from the period – neatly-written volumes, made by northern-French workshops, in Paris or Amiens, with a sprinkling of bright, formal little miniatures.[3] The juxtaposition of a French *Lancelot* with the poems of Guillaume de Machaut in the will of Isabella, Duchess of York, who left both books to her son, Edward, in 1392, reinforces this impression of an aristocracy with clearly defined interests in the literature of France, whether of the immediate or more distant past.

It is important to take this fact into account if we wish to gain not only a fully comprehensive picture of English literary taste in the fourteenth century but also some understanding of the creation of a literary context for the greatest international poet of the English Middle Ages – Geoffrey Chaucer. The stubbornly 'foreign' reading habits of the English royal and aristocratic houses during the thirteenth and fourteenth centuries can be interpreted as nothing but manifestations of extreme conservatism – against which English vernacular literature had to battle in order to survive and develop: they can also be seen, however, as challenges which English poets such as Chaucer were to meet, ultimately, by the making of a new English literary medium, fit to receive the subject-matter and the forms of the high vernacular literatures of France and Italy.

For this reason, if no other, we should look at the nature of these royal and aristocratic tastes, taking up the matter again at the end of the twelfth century. We have already (see above, p. 29) suggested that the close of the reign of Henry II (1189) marks the end of a very rich and consistent period of literary patronage, in which the English royal court, under Henry and Eleanor, was a dominant force, not only in this country but in Europe also. It was, moreover, a period in which there were areas of strong similarity between the kinds of work attracted and sponsored by the royal court and by other lesser courts of England – both secular and ecclesiastical. We have noted how frequently authors 'overlap' from one court to another, and how king, bishop and archbishop, earl and nobleman of more provincial location and status seem to share literary tastes. Only, perhaps, the very personal connections of the royal court with French troubadour poets stand out as unique. The interruption of such a unified state of cultural affairs – or, more accurately, its complication – was brought about by political change.

Even before the end of Henry's reign, the rebellion of the 'young king' Henry against him, and the subsequent imprisonment of Eleanor for complicity in this (1173), broke across the continuity of Angevin patronage as it was exercised from an English centre. We do not have to wait until the thirteenth century, with its dramatic record of opposition between royal and baronial parties, to find some divergences in upper-class literary concerns. It has been persuasively argued that the background to the strong and rapid growth of Anglo-Norman romance, during the period 1170–1275, with its double interest in general themes of 'feudal law, administration and justice' and in narratives firmly attached to local family traditions, is baronial, not royal:

Most Anglo-Norman romance dates from the period of resurgent baronial power between the accession of Richard I and the De Montfort rebellion.[4]

This body of romance is of some independence, catering for those who were already feeling themselves at home in England – even, perhaps, developing a sense of national identity as distinct from the international consciousness characteristic of Henry II and Eleanor and their court. It would be too crude an interpretation if we used the Anglo-Norman romances as simple documents of anti-royal sentiment: they are rather, in Rosalind Wadsworth's words, born of 'baronial confidence' (p. 166). But they come out of contexts which produced, by the end of the twelfth century, many increasingly reluctant to commit themselves to military service on behalf of their king in parts of France – Aquitaine, for instance – which were already of remoter interest to them than to their royal master.[5] Only a very late example of the genre takes up a thorough-going attitude of dislike towards the French – the romance of *Guillaume Longespee* (c. 1250), but it is probably significant that one of the earliest expressions of violently nationalistic emotion is to be found there: the French are uniformly 'perfidious and cowardly and go straight to hell'.[6] And it may also be significant that the king who first experienced baronial 'reluctance' to aid him in his battles in France was Richard I, who, being almost totally French in his upbringing, was both poet in the southern-French style of the troubadours, and the focus of interested troubadour comment, whether adulatory or critical.[7] No other king after Richard would be quite so specifically devoted to a continental culture, but there is something of the future here. Taken in combination with the strongly insular nature of the Anglo-Norman romance literature associated with the baronial families of the reigns of Richard, John and even Henry III, Richard's 'foreignness' indicates to us a changing balance of parts in the structure of English upper-class literary patronage. While the royal houses – and especially the queens and duchesses – will have some works addressed to them by native authors, writing in a recognisably native vernacular (Anglo-Norman), they will increasingly look to continental authors, writing in French and Latin, for their literature of entertainment and edification. In many ways, this will only be a continuation of the 'internationalism' – though on a minor scale – of the royal house in the days of Henry II and Eleanor. But by comparison with the growing strength of literature in the native vernaculars, this 'internationalism' will begin to look decisively 'foreign'. And, as never in the time of Henry and Eleanor, it will be possible to debate the respective merits of both kinds of patronal activity.

The evidence for royal literary patronage in the reign of John witnesses rather exactly to a period of transition – as might be expected in a period which saw the final break-up of the Angevin empire of Henry II, and the emergence of England into bitter civil war.[8] John's desperate efforts to retain and then, after failure, to regain the continental possessions of his father were constantly jeopardised by the opposition of his own barons, who ultimately demonstrated their independence by inviting Louis of France to England to claim the throne. Nothing could better illustrate the complexity of English relationships with France, following the loss of Normandy in 1204, than the growing unwillingness of John's barons to support his continental ambitions, yet their willingness to support a continental replacement for him. And complexity is often at the centre of literary, as well as diplomatic and military, situations in this century.

Thus there is something reminiscent of earlier Angevin traditions of learning and patronage in John's reputation as an avid reader and collector of books, no less than in his affiliations with at least two continental poets. Intended for the monastic life, he was removed from the Abbey of Fontevrault by the time he was six years old, and educated at his father's court: the lawyer, Ranulph Glanville, was one of his tutors. A library was built up either for him, or by him, apparently with the co-operation of Reading Abbey: to the Abbot of Reading he acknowledges the receipt of six books, which have been sent to him on loan. They are substantial indeed: an Old and New Testament; Hugh of St Victor on the sacraments; the *Sententiae* of Peter Lombard; Origen on the Old Testament; Candidus Avianus *De Generatione Divina ad Mariam*.[9] On another occasion, the king 'discharged the same abbot from responsibility for the Pliny which had been lent to him'.[10] How much of John's restless adult life could have been spent with such volumes is debatable; we should note, however, that he liked to have books with him, even on campaign. In 1203, 43s. 10d. was paid 'for chests and carts for carrying the king's books beyond the sea'.[11] This looks forward to the travelling habits of French kings in the next century, when John II of France was taken at Poitiers with an expensive manuscript of a *Bible Historiale*.[12] In addition to these works, John is known to have borrowed an unspecified book from St Alban's Abbey;[13] it may not be irrelevant that his chaplain, John of Ford, was a well-known author of theological treatises.[14] Perhaps his reading of history was confined to the French vernacular: he is recorded as requesting Reginald of Cornhill to send him a copy of *Romancium de Historia Anglie*.[15] Giraldus Cambrensis, however, dedicated his Latin *Conquest of Wales* to him, distinguishing John, in his Preface, from 'illiterate princes' who could not understand his writings.[16]

Two important continental poets are connected with John: Savaric de Mauléon and Henry of Avranches – the first a Poitevin seigneur, patron of troubadour poets, and active military man, the second a clerk, perhaps employed on legal business in various European courtly centres, but certainly a prolific writer of verse pieces on the widest variety of topics.[17] The life of Savaric de Mauléon is deeply involved in the history of relations between England and France, 1200–30. He was taken prisoner by John, in 1202, at the raising of the siege of the Castle of Mirabeau, north of Poitiers, where Eleanor of Aquitaine was being attacked by her grandson, Arthur of Brittany. Savaric was brought to England, and kept in Corfe Castle; after his escape and eventual reconciliation with John's cause, he spent most of his life travelling between England and France, collecting honours in both countries, and maintaining a consistent loyalty to John in his efforts to deal with the French and his own rebellious barons. For this he was derided by the troubadour son of Bertrand de Born:

> Savarics, reis cui cors sofranh
> Fara grieu bo envazimen,
> E puois a cor flac, recrezen,
> Ja mais nuls hom en el no ponh.[18]

(Savaric, a king whose heart is weak will hardly conduct a good campaign, and as his heart is soft and recreant, no-one ever puts trust in him.)

This scornful view of John's abilities is expressed even more directly in a *sirventes* meant for the king himself; referring probably to the loss of Poitou and Touraine in 1205, the same poet promises

> Farai un sirventes cozen,
> Que trametrai lai per presen
> A.l rei Johan, que.s n'avergonh.[19]

(I will compose a bitter sirventes, which I will send to King John, that he may feel shame.)

Although the judgement of John by the troubadour is harsh, there would be an occasion in the future when even Savaric de Mauléon, his most faithful adherent, would rebuke John for his faint-heartedness in the face of defeat in France. The episode is recounted by Matthew Paris:

Tu vero, qui regum liberrimus extiteras, sponte te tuumque regnum servituti perpetuae subdidisti, ut tuos protervius homines confunderes naturales.[20]

(You, who were the most free of kings, voluntarily placed yourself and your kingdom in perpetual slavery, that you might the more shamelessly overthrow men who are your natural subjects.)

Savaric was, however, generously rewarded by John: at one time Seneschal of Poitou and Viscount of Southampton, it is not wholly surprising that some contemporary European poets seemed uncertain of his nationality: 'anglais de nation', he is called by Jean de Nostre-Dame; 'inglese, poeta provenzale', by Francesco Redi.[21] But his personal affiliations and those of his own verse-making are with the poetry of Provence and of the Limousin; Bertrand de Born dedicated a *sirventes* to him, and he is particularly remembered for his close ties with four Limousin poets – Gaucelm Faidit, Uc de Bacalaria, Jausbert de Puycibot, and Uc de Saint-Circ.[22]

Most of Savaric's poems have disappeared; what is left tells us of his political allegiances – with the house of Raimon VI, Count of Toulouse, brother-in-law of John of England – and of his literary fellowship – with the Limousins. Thus he addresses Eleanor, wife of Raimon, in one elegant stanza, promising help against his enemies. He takes part in a *jeu-partis* with Gaucelm Faidit and Uc de Bacalaria, which ruefully relates their common love for Guilhelma, Vicomtesse de Benauges, and her heartless behaviour. The decision as to whom the lady favoured most is referred by Savaric to no less an authority than Marie de Ventadorn, 'on bos pretz es', 'with whom is virtue',[23] herself reputed to be a poetess, and a member of that family which had supported a famous court-school of troubadour poets in the twelfth century. In another poem Savaric debates with the Provost of Limoges about his love for Guilhelma, and the circumstances of the debate are preserved for us by Uc de Saint-Circ.[24] The strongly localised and personalised nature of this poetry, with its roots in the aristocratic life of Poitou and Aquitaine, its references to particular lordships (St Macaire, Langon), particular religious houses (St Leonard de Chaumes at La Rochelle), and particular ladies (Marie, Countess of Ventadorn), comments in its own special way upon the political processes that were being worked out so painfully between England and France. Savaric, as Seneschal of Poitou, Viscount of Southampton, Governor of Winchester, Rochester and Bristol Castles, was part of a political world which would end, in all practical terms, by 1213, and the final defeat of

John's continental hopes at the Battle of Bouvines. As French poet, on the other hand, he represented a continental literary world which English royal houses would refuse to relinquish, even after their acceptance of political loss.

No verses presented by Savaric to John remain. But it would be surprising, when we remember his stanza to Eleanor of Toulouse, if he had never addressed his friend and overlord. John's regard for him was more than practical; it was to Savaric that he wrote the day before he died, and an order to the Constable of Norwich is also dated to that day:

Mandamus vobis quod fidem habeatis hiis que Savaricus de Malo Leone, W. comes Aubemarle et Falkes de Breaute vobis dicent ex parte nostra ad commodum et honorem nostrum.[25]

(We command that you shall have faith in the things which Savaricus de Malo Leone, W. Earl of Aubemarle and Falkes de Breaute shall say to you on our behalf to our advantage and honour.)

Moreover, John had other troubadour acquaintances, in Geoffrey and Renaud de Pons, and Robert, Bishop of Clermont;[26] the words of Stubbs, writing of Henry II, 'if the court around him was full of learned men we may safely infer that the central figure was no contemner of learning',[27] may here be adapted to infer that his son, John, was 'no contemner of poetry' composed by his aristocratic Poitevin friends. Nor, perhaps, of that poetry composed by his enemies: the *sirventes* addressed to him by the son of Bertrand de Born[28] assumes his familiarity with the chosen medium if it also calculates upon his displeasure with the sentiments expressed.

A little more is known of the Latin poetry written at the court of John by a quite different sort of artist – the clerk, Henry of Avranches.[29] Henry illustrates the 'internationalism' of the twelfth century as it perpetuates itself in the following century, and on a level of competent rather than fine workmanship. He wrote for a series of illustrious patrons, all over Europe: for Pope Gregory IX he produced the first metrical *Life of St Francis*; for the Emperor, Frederick II, three long eulogies; for Louis of France, a poem on the translation of relics of the Crucifixion to Paris. But he spent a good deal of his wandering life at the English courts of John and his son, Henry III, composing for them and the group of able courtier-administrators and churchmen whose lives spanned both reigns and, frequently, both secular and ecclesiastical office: Eustace de Fauconberg, Treasurer, later Bishop of London; Richard Marsh, Chancellor and Bishop of Durham; Ralph Nevill, Keeper of the Great Seal and Bishop of Chichester; Geoffrey de Bocland, Justiciar; Stephen Langton, Archbishop of Canterbury. He may even have been tutor to the young princes, Henry and Richard: his long metrical treatise on Grammar was perhaps intended for Henry.[30]

Nothing about his poetry is distinguished, but it has an astonishing range, from the highly artful and contrived wit of begging-lines to John –

Nomen habes non inmerito *divina*, Iohannes,
  Gratia, voce sue conveniente rei.
Ergo vel *gratus summo* vel *gratia summi*
  Es: pro parte mea casus uterque facit.
Si *summo gratus*, ergo pietatis alumnus;
  Ergo pauperibus ferre teneris opem:
Ergo michi, cum sim pauper . . .[31]

(You have, John, not undeservedly the title 'divine grace', with a name corresponding to the reality. You are therefore either 'pleasing to the highest' or the 'grace of the highest': either case works to my advantage. If you are 'pleasing to the highest', then you are the pupil of piety; and therefore you are obliged to give help to the poor: and therefore to me, since I am poor...)

to the lively colloquialisms of an abusive dialogue between an Englishman and a German on the subject of national characteristics, such as beer-drinking and the possession of tails.[32] His work for the English court goes well into the reign of Henry III: in 1244 Henry had a certain poem 'quem faciet Magister Henricus uersificator' inscribed upon a ceremonial ring, made in honour of St Thomas a Becket, and carried by the monks of Westminster in a procession 'in uenerationem eiusdem apostoli'.[33] And in 1245 he is recorded to have been given ten marks by the King for the *Lives* of the two royal saints, Edward and George. In fact, Henry III seems to have awarded him for some years a steady annual amount, as if he occupied an official position of 'poet-in-attendance': 'Wine-grants and a definite salary for consoling, amusing and defending the king in verse caused Master Henry's position at the English court to approximate to that of the poets laureate'.[34] Thus, between 1243 and 1260, the English *Rolls* tell us of money, wine and robes granted to Henry by the King and Queen: between October 1243 and 1244, he received 20s. a month; in 1251, he collected 100s. in arrears of his salary; in 1252 he received another 100s. and two gifts of £10.[35] In 1251, a letter close commands that two jars of the best wine should go to 'Magistro Henrico uersificatori'; more is ordered in 1255 and 1256, 'dum vixerit ... ad sustentacionem suam'.[36] In 1257, a letter patent allows him a tun of vintage wine and a tun 'de recko' yearly for life.[37]

Henry's compositions seem to have been occasional and functional: for abbots he provided verses on patron saints; for courtiers, eulogies, often filled with strange punning passages on the name of the dedicatees. His offering to Geoffrey de Bocland raises questions, in some scarce translatable puns and anagrams, about the knowledge and use of English at the royal court of Henry III:

Liberat a viciis liber omnes, liber es ergo,
Cum sis de 'Bocland', de regione libri . . .
O Gaufride, quasi 'fri' gaude, seu quasi liber
Gaude: nam quid 'fri man' nisi liber homo?[38]

(The book frees all men from vices; you are therefore free, since you are from 'Bocland', from the region of the book [i.e. the free] . . . O Geoffrey, rejoice as if 'fri' [Gau-fri-de], or rejoice as if free: for what does 'fri man' mean but free man?)

The pleasures of oral entertainment at both royal and ecclesiastical courts of the thirteenth century are suggested by what we can discover of his 'flyting-match' with another poet, Michael of Cornwall. Unfortunately, Henry's contribution to the contest is lost, but Michael replies by grotesque insults to Henry's apparently contemptuous treatment of his native Cornwall:

> Est tibi gamba capri, crus passeris et latus apri,
> Os leporis, catuli nasus, dens et gena muli,
> Frons vetule, tauri caput et color undique Mauri.[39]

(You have the leg-joint of a goat, the leg of a sparrow, and the flank of a boar, the mouth of a hare, the nose of a puppy, the tooth and cheek of a mule, the brow of an old woman, the head of a bull and the colour all over of a Moor.)

This kind of thing would not be amiss in a courtly society which enjoyed such robust antics as those with which Henry III and his foreign-born jesters are credited: in 1257, Fortunatus de Lucca received new clothes in exchange for those ruined when King Henry threw him into the water; in 1254, John de Blana also received a new suit of clothes in exchange for those torn up by the King.[40]

One of the charges levelled against Henry of Avranches by Michael of Cornwall is his constant habit of versifying older materials – 'vetera metra': we would give a great deal to know what these were. But Michael's accusation fits what can be observed of Henry's abilities: he is a European professional, able to turn his hand to patrons and occasions of any sort. His work for Henry III and his court underlines the essentially European nature of Henry's taste, even if it cannot indicate the quality of that taste as it showed itself in the patronage of painting, embroidery and architecture. When historians call the study of the literary interests of Henry III and his close family circle 'elusive',[41] they refer, of course, to the lack of extant works to match the unusually full record of Henry's payments to his 'official' poet. And it has to be admitted that there is more substantial evidence about Henry's patronage of the arts: here documents and remaining examples of court art match each other fairly precisely.[42] But even if we cannot speak as confidently about the library of Henry III as we can about that of his father, John, for instance, we can build up, from both literary and artistic materials, an impression of an active centre of patronage, receptive to ideas and forms from abroad, at which there is sometimes a very lively interchange between books and royal commissions for painting programmes in particular.

The history of Henry's troublesome dealings with the baronage of England over his plans for the reconquest of continental possessions lost in the reign of his father, and his right to select his own close party of personal advisors and to promote to high office his foreign relatives and those of his Queen, is very complex indeed. Not all of it is closely relevant to a consideration of the cultural milieu of his court at Westminster; as when discussing the reign of John we took care not to identify political movements too narrowly with particular bodies of literature, so here it is necessary to recognise that we cannot equate the recognised status of Henry as a connoisseur of fine objects and workmanship, and the continental direction of his taste, with the existence of a 'foreign' royal party, sharply distinguished from an insular baronial group.[43] But some political allegiances, both at home and abroad, underlie the literary and artistic phenomena associated with his reign. Henry's own marriage, in 1236, to Eleanor, daughter of the Aragonese Count of Provence, Raimon-Bérengar IV (d. 1245), reaffirmed earlier English domestic connections with southern-French culture, although with a differently located part of it – the County of Provence. Raimon-Bérengar himself was a poet – one of the last who might be called a 'seigneur-troubadour' – and he counted poets such as Bertran d'Alamanon, Sordel, Peine Bremon and Blacatz among his friends.[44] And although we cannot be as sure as Jean Audiau that the English court from 1236 onwards became 'un centre littéraire où s'est intensement développée l'influence méridionale',[45] it is impossible to think that the tastes of Eleanor and the Provençal members of her household were not represented. As we shall see, Henry's actions in Europe were closely watched and commented upon by the troubadour-poets of the south. The immediate circle of Henry and Eleanor was a mixture of Provençal, Savoyard and Poitevin relatives and friends, many of whom, in high office, were the objects of considerable political resentment at crucial moments during Henry's reign: the Poitevin Bishop of Winchester, Peter des Roches, and his nephew Peter des Rivaux, Controller of Henry's Household and Treasurer of the Exchequer, in 1233; Peter of Savoy, the Queen's uncle, who was virtually Prime Minister in 1236; Henry's half-brothers, William and Aymer de Valence, from Saintonge, Earl of Pembroke and Bishop of London, respectively. These men could leave their mark upon cultural as well as political matters. Peter of Aigueblanche, for instance, Bishop of Hereford from 1240 to 1268, intimate friend and counsellor of Henry III, who negotiated the marriage of the King's brother, Richard, Duke of Cornwall, to Sanchia of Provence, in 1242, was influential in introducing the newest versions of French Gothic architecture, 'brittle and mannered, with a rather chilly elegance',[46] to the west of England: the north transept of Hereford Cathedral, and his own tomb in that transept, stand as witness to the years of his presence there. It would be helpful to our understanding of some of the English lyric literature produced in the west country at the end of the thirteenth and the beginning of the fourteenth centuries if we could suppose that more than French architectural forms and styles took root during Peter of Aigueblanche's episcopate.[47] In a general sense, the southern familial connections of Henry III are certainly reflected by the increased privileges granted to foreign merchants, bringing through to England the fine wines of Gascony and Provence, and silks from Montpellier and elsewhere.[48]

It was not, of course, Henry's marriage to Eleanor of Provence alone which made him the subject of so much troubadour poetry during the middle years of the thirteenth century. His attempts to strengthen English holdings in France, and to win back what had been surrendered in the time of his father, pre-date his marriage; the troubadours, early on in his reign, saw his continued conflict with the Capetian kings of France as a hope that the independent life of Languedoc, gravely damaged by the armies of Philip Augustus and Louis VIII during the Albigensian Crusades of 1209 and 1226, might be revived.[49] Thus the very moves which were so sceptically regarded by Henry's own baronial advisors and subjects were represented by the troubadours as portents of a glorious future: Guillem Anehir of Toulouse anticipates the victories of his first campaigns of 1224 and 1227:

> ... quar lo reys ditz
> Joves Engles, quez ab colps et ab critz
> Volva cobrar tot quant tenc ses falhida
> Lo pros Richartz, oy er testa partida.[50]

(For the king, the young Englishman, says that with blows and war-cries he will recover without fail all that the brave Richard held, or heads will be split.)

These brave words were not rewarded with victorious results. But the Limousin poets persevered in their praise of Henry's actions; even a well-intentioned but militarily unsuccessful prince deserved poetic support if he was opposed to the common enemy – the King of France. The later events of 1242 – when Henry's bid to take on Louis IX and his formidable mother, Blanche of Castile, was aided by the barons of southern Poitou and the forces of his volatile but undependable relatives, the Lusignans[51] – were celebrated by Peire del Vilar in heroically unrealistic terms:

> Pero si ben vol anparar
> Lo castel, l'ala ni.l bastos,
> Passar pot Escots et Engles,
> Noroecx et Irlans e Gales ...
> E poira cobra Guianes
> E Normandia ...[52]

(But if he wishes to seize the castle, the outworks and the bastions, he can bring Scotch and English, Norwegian, Irish and Welsh . . . he will be able to recover Guienne and Normandy...)

Slightly earlier than this, in 1238, Henry had sent troops to Italy to help his brother-in-law, the Emperor Frederick II of Sicily, who was at war with the city-state of Milan. This practical gesture of friendly alliance was greeted by the troubadours with the same kind of enthusiasm; Uc de Saint-Circ forecast a future for England as splendid and unlikely as that of Languedoc:

Lo falcos, filh de l'aigla, quez es reys dels Frances,
Sapcha que Fredericx a promes als Engles
Que'el lor rendra Bretanha, Anjou et Toarces,
E Peytau e Sayntonge, Lemotges, Engolmes,
Toroinn'e Normandia e Guiana e.l Paes,
E.n venjara Tolzan, Bezers e Carcasses.[53]

(Let the falcon, the son of the eagle, who is King of England, know that Frederick has promised to the English that he will restore to them Brittany, Anjou and the district of Thouars, Poitou and Saintonges, Limoges and Angoulême, the Touraine and Normandy, Guienne and the 'Pays', and that he will avenge the district of Toulouse, Beziers, and the county of Carcassonne.)

Nothing of this was destined to come true: by 1258, in the Treaty of Paris, Henry had surrendered his claims to Normandy, Maine and Poitou, and had done homage to Louis IX for his lordship in Gascony; Raimon, Count of Toulouse, had made his peace with Louis IX, and the Capetian monarchy occupied a solid block of territory in southern France, from Gascony to Provence, with garrisons and officials.[54] But something in the verse of Uc de Saint-Circ is true: Henry's cordial and long-lasting relationship with the Emperor Frederick, who had married Henry's sister, Isabella, in 1235. And it is very possible that in the full account of Henry III as liberal patron of the arts we should not neglect the influence of Frederick as 'precept and example'[55] of more than political significance.

The courts of Frederick II in Sicily and southern Italy not only continued to support the traditions of learning and culture established in the twelfth century by his Norman forebears, but brought those traditions to maturity in a context which now expanded to take in the literature of the vernacular languages of Europe:

Frederick brings the poets of the *Magna Curia* into contact with the troubadours and Minnesinger of his Transalpine dominions, welcomes Theodore the philosopher from Antioch and Michael Scot from Spain, and maintains a learned correspondence with the scientists and philosophers of the various Mohammedan sovereigns of North Africa and the East.[56]

Frederick was also an author in his own right: his Latin treatise on falconry, *De Arte Venandi cum Avibus*, was probably written between 1230–5 and 1240–50.[57] The literary and artistic importance of this text, in both its Latin and later French versions, accompanied by its lavish series of illustrations, cannot be exaggerated.[58] Nothing comparable in the literary field can be even associated with Henry III, but when we are searching for European models to explain the unusually comprehensive and well-organised programmes of art-patronage which can be associated with Henry, his uninterrupted friendship with Frederick may be a factor to take into account.

There are, however, further European models of a distinguished nature. Henry's marriage to Eleanor of Provence reaffirmed another set of connections for the English royal house – with the Capetians of France, the traditional enemy. For Eleanor's sister, Margaret, had married Louis IX of France; another sister, Beatrice, was to marry Charles, Duke of Anjou, brother of Louis IX. In the long and stormy process of negotiations between England and France, from the accession of Louis in 1226 to the peaceful settlement of the Treaty of Paris in 1258, we can trace a changing role for Henry which has some literary and artistic consequences. If, from the point of view of the troubadours of southern France, Henry's reconciliation with Louis IX was disastrous, it was certainly not pure loss, considered as a northern-European event. Powicke describes a meeting in Paris, in 1254, between Louis and Henry, at which the four daughters of Raimon-Bérengar were present, as well as their mother, the Dowager-Countess of Provence; it was a 'family party for Queen Eleanor' of England.[59] It was an occasion of personal and political truce, looking forward to what would be, after the Treaty of Paris, friendship with France for thirty-five years. Henry was able to inspect the Sainte Chapelle, now completed, but begun by Louis in 1243 in order to hold those relics of the Crucifixion for whose translation Henry of Avranches had written his dedicatory verses; he could compare this refined and glittering example of fashionable Gothic architecture from the Ile de France with his own extensive architectural projects in England – in particular, the rebuilding of the church and chapter-house of Westminster Abbey.

Both Louis IX and Henry III have been credited with personal initiative in the creation of a 'court style' in art and architecture, dependent to a great extent upon their royal commissions, and centred upon Paris and London – the Ile de France and Westminster.[60] And although it is debated whether some of the strong similarities between French and English architectural and sculptural forms, and pictorial styles, are not due to parallel evolutionary processes on either side of the Channel, there seems to be very good evidence indeed that in many cases Henry learnt directly from the work done for his Capetian brother-in-law. It is interesting that while the earlier years of his reign were occupied mainly by benefactions to English artisans and institutions, from 1240 onwards he was more deeply preoccupied with commissioning large-scale works on his own account – frequently connected with his special patron-saint, Edward, King and Confessor.[61] This is exactly the time at which he was moving forward to an agreement with Louis IX, and we may speculate that the remarkable energy and breadth of his patronal activities are due in no small measure to his increasing knowledge of, and respect for, what was happening at the Parisian court. Art-historians lay particular emphasis upon that meeting of Henry III and Louis IX, in Paris, in 1254, as a turning-point in the evolution of the English King's taste for the latest styles of French architecture and interior decoration. On this occasion, as Matthew Paris recounts,[62] Henry and his household were lodged first at the Palace of the Old Temple, just outside Paris; the Great Hall there was thickly hung with shields 'according to the continental custom'. And decorative heraldry appears much more frequently in Henry's sculptural schemes after 1254 – those of the nave of Westminster Abbey, done to his order, include shields hung by straps, in the same 'continental' way.[63] The English were escorted, next day, on a tour of the Parisian churches, including the Sainte Chapelle, and that evening dined in the French King's large Palace. The artistic consequences of all this hospitality were probably immediate and long-lasting. Not only did Henry send over, on his return, his master-mason, Henry, to inspect the recent royal building projects around and in Paris, but he seems to have made a fresh start on mural schemes for his audience-chamber and bedroom at the Palace of Westminster – the splendid 'Painted Chamber' (destroyed in the fire of 1834, and now known only from records and illustrations). It has been convincingly suggested that this fresh start was in response to what he saw on the walls of the great Palace of Louis IX.[64] Indeed, the 'decorative martial iconography' of not only Henry's Painted Chamber but also the pages of the *Vie de Seint Aedward le Rei*, dedicated to Henry's Queen, Eleanor, about 1250,[65] has been traced back to the 'finest Parisian work' of the time, whether in murals or illuminated manuscripts.[66] For no doubt Henry was shown, on that same state visit of 1254, examples of the art of the illuminating shops of the French capital as fine as the mid-century *Maciejowski Bible* and Bibliothèque Nationale (Paris) MS fr. 15104, *La Noble Chevalerie du Judas Machabee et de ses Nobles Freres*,[67] both of which have been cited as relevant kinds of source material for English 'court manuscript styles' of a slightly later date. In this very personal way England, in company with the rest of Europe, transplanted the 'seeds of stylistic ideas' from the Paris of Louis IX, 'the symbolic capital of Europe . . . an intellectual, administrative and artistic center'.[68] So many high English modes and rituals of the mid and later part of the century seem to have been deliberately fashioned with Capetian France in mind: Henry's reception of a relic of the Holy Blood, as early as 1247, and his presentation of it to Westminster Abbey recall the arrival of the Crown of Thorns and other relics of the Crucifixion in Paris, in 1239 and 1241, and their eventual enshrinement in the completed Sainte Chapelle. The sermon preached by the Bishop of Norwich makes the nature of the English occasion quite clear:

In possessione tanti thesauri non minus gaudeat et glorietur Anglia quam Francia in adeptione sanctae crucis, quam dominus rex Francorum non immerito diligit.[69]

(Let England take joy and glory in the possession of such a treasure no less than France in obtaining the Holy Cross which my Lord of France rightly esteems.)

We should not, of course, do justice to the achievement of Henry III as patron if we simply stressed the derivative qualities of the art produced to his commissions. There was, especially as the century drew to its last decades, 'fruitful interchange' between English and French artists. The basic importance of Henry's 'obsession with the continent', as it manifests itself in English court art, was no doubt his willingness to learn from continental models such as Frederick

II and Louis IX how to centre patronage upon a court, in a city of capital importance, and to pool talent of all kinds, so that artists could interact powerfully with each other. This was the essential lesson which he absorbed by virtue of that 'foreignness' so distasteful, in a political sense, to his subjects and baronial counsellors. It was a lesson almost impossible to encounter, let alone profit from, except at the very highest social level, and with powerful resources of a financial and administrative kind upon which to draw. It was also a lesson inaccessible to insular ways of thinking.

For, if anything, Henry's taste in the arts was even more eclectic than that of his exemplars; he appreciated the 'weight and grandeur' of English Romanesque as well as the refinements of Parisian Gothic, sometimes turning back to the twelfth-century palaces of his predecessors for inspiration. In one instance we find him ordering wall-paintings modelled upon those at Wolvesey, the magnificent palace of Henry of Blois – that earlier patron-prince whose horizons were also international, and whose 'curial circumstances' were influential upon the whole course of twelfth-century book-illumination.[70] It may be no accident that many of the dramatic qualities of twelfth-century manuscript painting, realised fully in books such as the Winchester Bible, probably made for Henry of Blois, appear in a new 'Gothic' context in the Trinity Apocalypse, probably made for Henry III.[71] This sumptuous treatment of the Vision of St John, commanding in both colour and gesture, could only have been accomplished by a workshop with access to the widest variety of materials and artists: this may most reasonably be identified as Henry's own court-workshop.[72]

We have already remarked that if Henry's patronage is more firmly substantiated for art than for literature, books do play a part in that patronage. It is unlikely that Henry of Avranches received such steady kinds of payment from the King without providing some equally steady literary return – on the lines, probably, of the Latin Saints' Lives for which he is known to have been paid. But Henry, pious as he was, had a more relaxed side to his nature; he evidently enjoyed – and participated in – the entertainments of his jesters, and he was a reader of French romance. In 1237 the Pipe Rolls record a payment for silver hasps and a key to be made for the King's 'magnum librum' of romances.[73] A royal command, in 1250, to Roger de Sandford, Master of the Knights Templar, to hand over a large book kept in his house, containing the 'Gests of Antioch and of the Kings and others', makes clear that this book is 'written in the French language' and is required by those working upon the murals for the 'Queen's low room, in the King's garden at Westminster' – a room which was to be called 'the Antioch Chamber'.[74] We must assume, I think, that the transformation into visual form of manuscript material such as this involved a reading knowledge on the part of Henry and Eleanor as well as a knowledge and approval of whatever illustrative miniatures the book may have contained. The 'Gests of Antioch' dealt with the events of the Third Crusade (1191–2) and the exploits of Henry's uncle, Richard Coeur-de-

Lion; they were favourite subjects with the royal couple – reappearing as painted decoration in a chamber at Clarendon Palace, in 1250, and in the chamber of the King's Chaplain, at the Tower of London, in 1251.[75] We have no reason to suppose that the narrative of a Holy War, intimately concerned with the fame of a colourful member of the family, would not represent fairly well their taste in literature as well as their taste in art – a mixture of piety and romance.[76] The Templars' volume probably contained a version of the Antioch story based upon the *Chanson d'Antioche*, and was doubtless the source for the inscriptions at Westminster of which only fragments survive:

Li reis antiochus entra en egipte a grant ost . . . mut de batailes en gtre [sic] le re tholome de egipte . . . citees garnies & mist tut ala spee e a gref . . .[77]

It is very likely that Henry's 'great book of romances' was also in French, and had Alexander and Tristan stories, with illustrations; murals on the Alexander theme were provided for rooms in Clarendon Palace, and in Nottingham Castle;[78] tiles found in Chertsey Abbey, but originally intended, it is suggested, for one of Henry's palaces, take episodes from a *Tristan*.[79] The floors of these palaces may not have been quite as elaborate as that of the bedchamber of Adela of Blois, described by Baudri of Bourgueil,[80] but they were no doubt in keeping with the lavish quality of the murals. The question of the exact nature of the literary and artistic sources for both the Alexander and the Tristan programmes is an interesting one; Anglo-Norman compositions, as well as 'imported' continental French works, would have been accessible to Henry. Thomas's *Tristan*, made perhaps for Eleanor of Aquitaine, was still being copied in the first half of the thirteenth century;[81] there is also the *Roman de Toute Chevalerie*, by another Thomas, of Kent, which handles the Alexander story very much as an exemplum, and exists in thirteenth- and fourteenth-century manuscripts.[82] One manuscript of *Tristan* was reported to have 'miniatures . . . coarsely executed',[83] but there are two copies of the *Roman de Toute Chevalerie* with extensive and fine illustration, the first probably originally executed in an English workshop of the second quarter of the thirteenth century[84] (Trinity College, Cambridge, MS 0.9.34; later copy in Bibliothèque Nationale MS f. fr. 24364). Its 'martial iconography', though less elaborate than that of the *Vie de Seint Aedward* and Henry's Painted Chamber, is not unworthy of association with it. We cannot, however, be certain that Henry's painters did not work from French poems and their pictures. The comment made by two Franciscan friars, who saw the 'warlike histories of the whole Bible' on the walls of the Painted Chamber in 1322, confirms that the inscriptions were 'beautifully written in French over each battle, to the no small admiration of the beholder, and the increase of royal magnificence.[85] And in this case, given the probable Parisian character of the model for this work, the texts were, most likely, continental French.

We should not neglect, however, to take account of a small but significant number of works in Anglo-Norman known to have been dedicated to the royal family by English authors. John of Howden, clerk of Eleanor of Provence, addressed his graceful and passionate religious poem, *Rossignos*, to her, explaining its title. It was written in a garden:

Rossignos, que il estoit fez et trove en un beau verger flori ou rossignol ades chauntoient.[86]

And, like his Latin poem of the same name, *Philomena*, it set out to captivate the heart into love for Christ: 'Benoit soit qui le lira . . .' Eleanor was an old woman by this time (1272–4) but she is the same queen for whom, twenty years earlier, another 'beau verger' had been created, at Woodstock, by order of the King himself:

Make two good high walls round the queen's garden so that no one can get in, with a suitable and pleasant herb-garden by the king's stew in which she can walk, and with a gate to the garden from the herb-garden.[87]

John of Howden sets out to delight as well as edify the Queen, taking images from many literary gardens for his religious narrative – Christ is conceived by the Virgin 'com en pre violete'.[88] But the poem not only recognises the special nature of its intended reader by adapting the expression of its spirituality; it proclaims itself a work for an international figure – 'la roïne, l'esmeree / Mère au roi Edward, la senée' (lines 5269–70, p. 515) – by its dedications to St Thomas of England, St Denis of France, St Francis, St Patrick, St Brendan. It also provides a series of perspectives for the queen – and for us – upon history and romance: in a closing review of famous men who, however well-armed, were less well-protected than the heart armed by God, it brings to life both Eleanor's most likely reading matter and what must have been her own sense of personal history. The list is extensive, and often accompanied by brief and telling comment, from 'Judas li Makabé', through Hector, Troilus, Caesar, Gawain, Lancelot and Perceval to Richard Coeur-de-Lion and her late husband, Henry, 'qui desrive / En donant com fontayne vive', her son Edward, 'qui a beau viaire / Qui a seul pot Sarrasyn defaire', and names from the past, such as Savaric de Mauléon and Roger of Clifford, men who had assisted English kings in their continental adventures.[89]

It was for Eleanor also that Matthew Paris, chronicler, hagiographer and artist of St Albans, translated into Anglo-Norman the Latin prose life of St Edward the Confessor made for Henry II (see note 65 above). And he seems to have circulated copies of other of his translated *Lives* of English saints – that of *St Thomas of Canterbury*, for instance – among a small number of extremely highborn ladies: the *Life of St Thomas*, in Trinity College, Dublin, MS Ee. 1. 40, has a note on folio 2r:

G., please, send to the Lady Countess of Arundel, Isabel, that she is to send you the book about St Thomas the Martyr and St Edward which I translated and illustrated and which the Lady Countess of Cornwall may keep until Whitsun.[90]

Isabel was of the important Warenne family; the Countess of Cornwall was the Queen's sister, Sanchia of Provence. Apart from this reference, we know nothing of Sanchia's literary interests; nor do we know anything about those of her husband, the King's brother, Richard of Cornwall. Only his well-publicised devotion to the memory of St Edmund of Abingdon and Pontigny, Archbishop of Canterbury from 1233–40, reminds us of the close circle, of which his wife was a member, with its reading of Anglo-Norman *Lives*; the son of Richard and Sanchia was named Edmund, and another of Matthew Paris' works, *La Vie de Saint Edmond, Archeveque de Cantorbery*, is dedicated to Isabel of Warenne, named above as one of the ladies in that favoured group of borrowers.[91] In an indirect way, however, Richard's adventurous life as his brother's 'lieutenant' in Poitou, as Crusader, friend of great continental princes, and, finally, as King of the Romans, furnished important materials for literature and art. His account of four months of spectacular entertainment by the Emperor Frederick II, in the Apennines, in 1241, featuring dancing-girls, baths, feasting and music, inspired Matthew Paris to some of his raciest pages in the *Chronica Majora*.[92] Similarly, his verbal reports of battle-scenes in the eastern world were translated by Matthew Paris into pictures which have been described as 'well-devised, imaginative and first-hand'.[93]

This special area of Anglo-Norman activity which takes in the royal family as well as members of baronial families modifies to some extent the division between royalty and baronage which we have already defined as crucial in the history of English patronage in the thirteenth century. It is interesting to note that, in the case of the Anglo-Norman *Saints' Lives*, the royal patrons and readers are women – Eleanor of Provence and her sister, Sanchia. So, also, in the case of John of Howden's *Rossignos*. Henry III received Latin *Lives* of St Edward and St George from Henry of Avranches. And the essentially continental nature of the habitual secular reading-matter of Eleanor of Provence is well illustrated by John of Howden's long list of heroes in the *Rossignos*: they are all from French romance and *chanson de geste* – Roland, Gawain, Ywain, Perceval, Arthur.[94] When Matthew Paris makes his famous statement of 'English unity' in the *Estoire de Seint Aedward le Rei*,

Now are king, now are barons, and the kingdom, of a common blood of England and of Normandy[95]

he is stating a desirable political hope, which has partly become fact and will be achieved in the following reign, rather than the present. Elsewhere he shows himself more precisely critical of what he regards as Henry III's 'French innovations', and the defects in Henry's character which go with them.[96] What must be said, in retrospect, about the 'court-patronage' of Henry is that, at its richest, it looks to the continent and to continental courts for its patterns, and for a substantial amount of its raw materials. It does, however, provide a centre, an opportunity for some synthesis of native and foreign elements, and no-one would accuse the best of English thirteenth-century court art of being imitative only.

In the sphere of literature, Henry and his family exhibit nothing much more than a standard European taste for hagiography and romance; 'Englishness' here means English saints – Edward, Thomas, Edmund – rather than English heroes, and the acceptability of Anglo-Norman as an occasional alternative to continental French. Literature at this court seems often to serve art, rather than to exist in its own right, and it is not uncommon to find in the royal instructions to painters something of that imaginative excitement which the poetry of Master Henry of Avranches can hardly ever have aroused. A fireplace in the Queen's chamber at Westminster is to be decorated with 'the figure of Winter, which, by its sad look and other miserable portrayals of the body, may be justly likened to winter'.[97] Though they chose that particular winter-image, Henry and Eleanor must have been familiar with another – warming by the fire:[98] thus art and life are brought together in a fitting tableau.

This sensibility does not seem to have been characteristic of Edward I, nor, indeed, did he have to seek the same kind of compensation in art for political turmoil and disappointment as his father had done. The internal strife of Henry III's reign, with King and familial advisors set against baronage, had been worked out through many bitter vicissitudes before he died, in 1272. No doubt, in his memory, the climax of his achievements had been pious and artistic rather than political: the dedication of his new church, at Westminster, on 13 October, 1269 – the special day of his patron-saint, Edward the Confessor, original founder of the Abbey. In this European monument, with its shrine for the bones of Edward, which had occupied him for twenty years, he could afford to see a great positive justification for his much resented 'foreign' bias of interest, his eager involvements across the Channel. And despite the victories of the De Montfort baronial party in the 1260s, standing against French royal intervention in the affairs of England, Henry managed, by the very end of his reign, to leave to his son a situation of stable friendship between the two courts of England and France, which was to last for the most part of Edward's time as king. The Anglo-French royal circle, in which the two kings were first cousins, and the dowager-queen sisters, Eleanor and Margaret of Provence, were still guiding influences, was a powerful force in European politics between 1275 and 1294. Even the recurrence of hostility after that date, when Philip 'Le Bel' moved to challenge English possession in Gascony, was not a long interruption of that friendship. English domestic affairs were also peaceful, by comparison with those of Henry's time. Some of the traditional animosities between baronage and crown were settled –

Edward's daughter, Joan of Acre, was married in 1290 to the Earl of Gloucester, Gilbert de Clare, thereby bringing one of the great mainstays of baronial opposition into the royal family itself.[99]

It is true that we know more of Edward as soldier, statesman and hunter than as patron of the arts and literature; his most enduring monuments are not cathedrals but the castles of Snowdonia, the *bastide* towns of Gascony, and urban foundations such as Kingston-upon-Hull, in England. If he took Louis IX as a model – and he knew him well in his earlier years – it was not for his patronage of new developments in art and architecture but for his noble concept of kingship and its responsibilities. When we discover him issuing personal instructions for the building of something it is, interestingly enough, for the fencing-in of one of his hunting-parks, at King's Langley, and the construction of little lodges in the park, where he could eat and watch both park and game within it.[100] The instructions are given, however, in a letter to his young sons, Thomas and Edmund, and though we may assume, since they were respectively four and five years old at the time, that the essential content was meant to be passed on to appropriate members of the royal household, there is a personal note in the phrasing which runs through many of Edward's extant letters, and allows us an unusual access to his nature. We can tell, from this private correspondence, that he was swift to anger, compassionate, and concerned about his children; writing to 'Margerie de Hausted', on the 12th of September, 1306, he inquires about their development:

Nous vous prions qe vous meismes avisez bien lor estat e coment il cressent e coment il sont juantz, vistes, legiers e menantz . . . et sur tote riens vous prions qe vous avisez bien Alianor, nostre jeofne fille, e nous facez saver pleinement ce qe vous semble de li.[101]

He gives permission for Nicholas Segrave, arrested on return from France, to amuse himself in the meadow of Dover Castle, commenting (as it emerges, with unfounded optimism) –

Nous savons bien qe le chevaler nad mie talent de senfouyr.[102]

Segrave, a headstrong member of an important family, who had challenged Edward's authority by going to France to seek justice in a dispute, did, in fact, escape from Dover.[103] But Powicke's estimate of Edward as a 'conventional man in an age of change'[104] is borne out also by what the letters reveal of his passion for hunting:

Et facez enclore bien et suffisaument le park, si que bestes ny peussent issir. Et facez faire loges en la lande du park, ou nous puissoms manger et eiseement veer nostre deduyt . . .[105]

and, through the easy use of quotation, of his fondness for proverbs: writing to Patrick of Dunbar, Earl of March, he refers sarcastically to the Earl's delay in bringing up his troops:

Quant la guerre fu finee,
Si trest Audegier sespee.[106]

(When the war was over, then Audegier found his sword.)

There is nothing in the letters to discourage us from expecting that, as far as patronal activities are concerned, Edward's role will be that of consolidator rather than innovator; they positively suggest, moreover, that his literary taste will reflect his membership of a European class of royal and aristocratic readers.

Edward was returning from crusade in Syria when, in 1272, he heard the news of his father's death. He and his queen, Eleanor of Castile, had been at Acre; the crusade had been only a partial success, but Edward had demonstrated, by joining it, both his Christian and his family obligations. He had gone in the company of Louis IX and his son, Philip III. But the journey had made room for literary interests. Edward had taken with him a volume of French romances; during the passage out to Acre he had stayed in Sicily, from October 1270 until the spring of 1271. And there Rusticiano da Pisa, working from the volume, produced the earliest compilation of Arthurian romance by an Italian.[107] From Rusticiano's Prologue, as well as from the abridgement itself – which was in French – we can gain some idea of the nature of Edward's book. The circumstances of the work are stated precisely: it was done from

the book of Messire Edward, King of England, at the time that he passed beyond the sea in the service of our Lord God to conquer the Holy Sepulchre.[108]

It is to contain

all the great adventures that befell among the knights-errant of the time of King Uther Pendragon to the time of King Arthur his son, and of the companions of the Round Table . . .[109]

In fact it covers the *Tristan* story, and a part of the *Palamedes*, opening with the romance of *Gyron le Courtoys*, as Rusticiano says 'because he found it at the beginning of "the book of the King of England"'.[110] And it is interesting to find that Edward and Eleanor were reading of the 'testing of King Arthur's court' by a knight of huge stature a century before the author of *Sir Gawain and the Green Knight* made his alliterative version, of this narrative, in the north-west of England, for some kind of aristocratic audience. In this earlier case, the 'tester' is Branor le Brun, an old knight of one hundred years, a member of Uther Pendragon's household, whose bravery is equalled by his piety, and who has come out of Northumberland to Camelot, 'to test the prowess of the knights of the time, to know which were better, young or old . . .' In his Epilogue, Rusticiano tells us that he worked from other sources as well – 'pluseurs hystoires et pluseurs croniques' – at the request of King Edward.[111] It may be that Edward was more of a reader than he has been given credit for;[112] we would give much to know precisely what 'chronicles and narratives' he recommended to the Italian author.

Rusticiano's eagerness to use these materials is understandable in an author whose country had been hospitable to Arthurian themes for nearly two centuries.[113] And that Edward chose to travel to the East with such a book is interesting in the light of what we know about the willingness of the Latin kingdoms of the East to absorb Arthuriana into their courtly rituals. In 1223, Jean d'Ibelin, lord of Beirut, celebrated the knighting of his eldest son with 'auentures de Bretaigne et de la Table ronde . . .'[114] and in Acre, in 1286, only a decade after Edward and Eleanor had been there, the coronation of Henry II of Cyprus as King of Jerusalem included festivities at which 'contrefirent Lanselot & Tristan & Pilamedes & mout d'autres jeus'.[115] It is perhaps only coincidental that Edward's book of romances seems to have concentrated on areas of Arthurian narrative surrounding these three heroes. More than coincidental is the fact that Edward showed himself alive to the part which Arthurian romance could play in the drama of English monarchy; two 'Round Tables', which seem to have mingled jousting and Arthurian tableaux, were held during his reign, one in 1284 to mark the conquest of Wales.[116] In this he was, of course, doing no more than his European peers and their aristocratic vassals: Alfonso of Castile, his brother-in-law, Philip IV of France, his second cousin, the Duke of Brabant, his son-in-law.[117] But he seems to have exploited the Arthurian legend with particular energy, using it as a kind of 'historical (and royalist) propaganda':[118] his much-publicised opening of the tomb of Arthur and Guenevere at Glastonbury, in 1278, and his presentation of Arthur's crown to Westminster Abbey, in 1283, are striking examples of this calculated Arthurian display. The identification of royalist causes and Arthurian themes becomes even more telling when we recall that it is Roger Mortimer, Lord of Wigmore, Edward's most trusted friend, who claimed Arthurian ancestry, and whose own lavish 'Round Table', in 1279, at Kenilworth, may have prompted the King's enthusiasm for such occasions.[119]

Rosalind Wadsworth has suggested that the absence of Arthurian subjects in the Anglo-Norman romances written under the patronage of the barons during the period 1170–1300 reflects this consciousness of a 'royal and Arthurian' cult:[120] the deliberate avoidance of that area of narrative by writers catering for a class of patrons who were frequently in opposition to the crown seems entirely likely. But we may also insist upon the importance of recognising the strong *continental* base for both Edward's and Roger Mortimer's encouragement of Arthurian rituals. As early as the reign of Henry II there are evidences of the Angevin use of Arthurian legend not simply as literature of entertainment but as documentation of dynastic relevance. The first exhumation and reburial of the bodies of Arthur and Guenevere, not actually carried out until 1191, was planned before the death of Henry II (1189), by the monks of Glastonbury, in the context of Henry's quarrel with the Papacy and his disturbed political circumstances; it was intended 'to bolster the ecclesiastical and dynastic claims of their [the Angevin] house . . .'[121] In the intervening period, as we have seen, English kings maintained a lively interest in Arthurian materials.[122] But the institutionalisation of Arthurian legend as political propaganda seems to have belonged to the time of Edward I, and to have been the result, in part, of fresh impetus from the continent. The sense of a community of cultural taste which might still, to some extent, mark out political allegiance is strengthened by the dedication of the French Arthurian romance of *Escanor* to Eleanor of Castile, some time between 1272 and 1290.[123] Girart d'Amiens, its author, worked for a series of royal patrons all over Europe: his *Charlemagne* was 'par le commandement du comte de Valois, le frère du roi de France' – Charles of Valois (1270–1314);[124] *Meliacin* was also probably for one of the royal family of France – two manuscripts have a 'dedicatory' miniature which clearly pictures Philip IV ('le Bel'), his sister Marguerite, the Queen-mother, and the reigning Queen, Jeanne de Navarre. It is appropriate, in these European circumstances, that he should have been at 'la cort au roi de Bretaingne', and there, as he tells us, heard his story from Eleanor herself –

> ... le conte
> que la gentiex dame m'a dit ...
> tres noble dame, bone et sage,
> large ne de gentil corage,
> on le puet bien tele nomer:
> por coi chascuns le doit amer ...[125]

We shall not be surprised, knowing of Edward's manuscript with its romance of Branor le Brun, to find that *Escanor* contains another version of the Gawain narrative, this time actually involving Gawain himself and a mysterious challenger. Nor to find that *Escanor* is full of decorative detail, often reminiscent of what we know to have existed in the palaces of Edward and Eleanor – one room in the castle of Briant les Isles, adversary of Arthur, had all the history of Troy painted on the walls.[126]

There are good grounds for thinking that Eleanor commissioned *Escanor* between 1277 and 1282 – perhaps 'in connection with the Round Table held at Warwick in 1281'.[127] Certain of its historical references, made through heraldry, are precisely traceable to those years. In this, as in so much else, it aligns itself with the usages of contemporary literature; we may be sure, for instance, that its mingling of eminent historical figures with the heroes of Arthur's court did not go unnoticed or unappreciated by Eleanor and her household, who would probably have enjoyed identifying coats of arms of contemporary royalty among those assembled for the tournament in *Escanor* – in this case, the blazons of the houses of Scotland and Wales. The pleasures provided for noble readers by this form of 'heraldic flattery'[128] are frequent enough in continental Arthurian poems such as the *Roman de Ham*, written in 1278 for a literary circle which included the Queen of France, Marie of Brabant, and Count Robert II of Artois, cousin of Edward I.

The same literary circle furnished more than the audience of the poem, for it is a description of an Arthurian gathering and tournament at Hem-Monacu, in which distinguished European royalty played Arthurian 'parts'.[129]

When Edward allowed himself and the great events of his reign such as the conquest of Wales to be associated with the figure of Arthur and the narratives surrounding that 'rex quondam et futurus', he was simply taking to a more calculated conclusion 'a vogue not exclusively English but shared by most of the aristocracies of Christendom in his day'.[130] It is not surprising that in 1316 he is credited, by a Brabançon chronicler, Lodewijk van Velthem, with an elaborate Arthurian tournament and tableau, at which plans for campaigns in 'Cornuaelge, Wales and Irlant' were announced. Nor is it unlikely, allowing for the confusion of fact and fantasy in Lodewijk's account, that this is based upon the real festivities, the Arthurian 'interludes', which took place at his second wedding, in 1299, to Margaret of France, daughter of Marie of Brabant. Certainly, in 1306, at the famous 'Swan Feast' at Westminster, appealing to what must have been a shared sense of the Arthurian past in the European present, Edward vowed, as knights such as Perceval and Gauvain had done in the French literary works which the king must have known, to punish the newly rebellious Scots and to make one final pilgrimage to the Holy Land.[131] Prince Edward vowed 'not to sleep two nights in the same place' and to help his father against the Scots. Fittingly enough, the first repercussions of Edward's 'Swan Feast' of 1306 are European rather than strictly English and involve members of the royal and ducal families of England and France. It was Thiebaut de Bar, Bishop of Liège, brother of Edward's son-in-law, the Count of Bar, a man whom Edward had presented to the rectory of Pagham, in Sussex, who commissioned the *Voeux de Paon* from Jacques de Longuyon, before 1316; the episode in this famous romance in which Alexander and his knights make vows over a roasted peacock must hark back to the 'vowing' of Edward in 1306. Roger Loomis has pointed out that Thiebaut's niece and Edward's grand-daughter, Joan de Bar, married in 1306 to John de Warenne, Earl of Surrey, was present at the 'Swan Feast', and her husband knighted on that same occasion, in company with the future Edward II.[132] The romance of Jacques de Longuyon probably celebrates the real-life romance of the Edwardian 'vowings' at Westminster, long recounted by those who were present to their relatives in France.

Outside romance, only one other literary work is closely connected with the name of Edward – and it is, as we might have anticipated, a treatise on warfare. Translated from the standard text of Vegetius, the *De Re Militari*, it sets out, in Anglo-Norman, a history of Roman chivalry, defines the terms of medieval chivalry, and instructs on methods of making war. It is, in the words of the *incipit*, a prince's hand-book: 'le quel livre chescuns prince de tere devereit aver'.[133] From a short verse passage on one of the end-papers of the only manuscript, it appears that the translation was made by a clerk of Eleanor of Castile for presentation to Edward while they were both in Acre, in 1271–2, on that first crusading venture:

Maistre Richard, vostre clerc, que vostre
livere escrit
En la vile d'Acre sans nul contredit.[134]

Two competent miniatures commemorate the transmission of military wisdom from Vegetius to Edward, and the nature of medieval sea-fighting. All other thirteenth- and fourteenth-century translations of the *De Re Militari* are by Frenchmen such as Jean de Meun, working for French nobility such as Jean de Brienne, Comte d'Eu; it is interesting to find 'Maistre Richard', Eleanor's clerk, writing of his desire, after doing penance in the Holy Land, to return 'a vus, madame, en France' (Thorpe, 'Maistre Richard'). The translation is into Anglo-Norman, and no certain identification of 'Maistre Richard' has been made. The suggestion that he was the 'Master Richard', physician to Prince Edward, who was granted Preston Manor in 1265, cannot be proved or disproved (Thorpe, 'Maistre Richard'). The temptation to connect him with an earlier 'Maistre Richart' who is said, in the manuscripts of the French *Prophécies de Merlin*, to be 'd'Irlande', and attached to the court of the Emperor Frederick II of Sicily, must probably be resisted. The *Prophécies*, it is agreed, were the work of a Venetian Friar Minor, writing between 1272 and 1279.[135] The author, for some reason, hides his identity by the pseudonym. All that can be pressed is the interest of a situation in which two Italian authors, one in Venice, the other in Pisa, were busy making Arthurian compilations in French during those years which saw Edward's crusading journey through Italy to the Holy Land, one author directly indebted to a book owned by Edward, the other using a pseudonym almost identical to the name of a clerk-translator in the employ of Edward and his queen.

As for Eleanor herself, we have record of one other work made specifically at her request: the 'moralizing exposition' in Anglo-Norman of the Pseudo-Dionysian *Celestial Hierarchy*, by John Pecham, Archbishop of Canterbury.[136] Pecham – who maintained a lively correspondence in Anglo-Norman with both Edward and Eleanor – went to Canterbury in 1279; this was his only non-Latin production among a more important corpus of devotional verse writings. His letters to the King and Queen show the close relationship he had with them – fearless, affectionate and personal: he sympathises with them on the death of their son, Alfonso, in 1284; criticises Eleanor for not tempering Edward's harshness; thanks her for gifts of venison; invites her to visit him in Teynham, Kent.[137] The *Jerarchie*, which exists in one manuscript only, in a thirteenth-century hand, and announces quite simply that it is translated by John Pecham 'de latin en frannceis a la requeste la Reine de Englece, Alienore, femme le Rey Edward', is written directly, with 'Madame' always in mind. The 'seigneurial' metaphors are constant: this is devotional instruction for a great secular princess.

Si as baillifs ke gardent les chasteus e les maneres Nostre Seignur, ceo sunt les homes ke sunt fet pur ceo ke Deus en eus se herberge . . .   (*Jerarchie*, p. 83)

Et si vus, Madame, volez sauer diunt ces ordres et ces ierarchies servent, perneit garde que a meynee de Reys apartient treis maneres de genz, aucuns ke sunt ausi cum tuz jurs a curt, e aucuns ke sunt ausi cum tuz jurs hors en lur baillies, e aucuns ke vont e vienent.   (*Jerarchie*, p. 82)

The household accounts of Eleanor give us another kind of insight into her habitual piety: in one year, 1286, she presented brooches or fermails at the shrines of five saints, in England and France; beginning in December, with St Ethelwold, at Cerne, she travelled through March to August, visiting and paying homage to St Richard at Chichester, St Denis at Paris, St Edmund at Pontigny, and St Martin at Tours.[138] Her will makes mention of a bequest to 'Ricardo du Marche, Luminatori . . .'.[139] and on the basis of such a reference alone we might well inquire about the illuminated books made to commission for Eleanor and Edward.

Whether the book of Arthurian romance which accompanied Edward and Eleanor to Acre was a *de luxe* copy, with miniatures, we have no means of knowing. It seems likely that it was one of the numerous manuscripts of secular romance, frequently Arthurian, produced in French workshops from the second half of the thirteenth century onwards, and owned by all the leading noble households of Europe. Edward's manuscript was no doubt impressively comprehensive, but we hear of others: 'un grans roumans a rouges couvertures', belonging to his contemporary, Jean d'Avesnes, Count of Hainault (d. 1304), which contained narratives of 'Mellin et de Lancelot du Lach'; Robert, Count of Artois, confiscated three *Tristan* manuscripts from his wife, Mahaut, in 1316; the Yale copy of *Lancelot*, still extant, belonged to Guillaume de Termonde, second son of Gui de Dampierre, Count of Flanders, who died in 1312.[140] That *Lancelot* is illustrated liberally, and probably belongs to a north-eastern French workshop in the diocese of Therouanne. Other examples of thirteenth-century Arthurian manuscripts – the *Lancelot* cycle, the *Tristan* – with programmes of 200 or more miniatures, unattached to any special patron, but clearly, from their lavish lay-out, intended for distinguished ownership, can be cited.[141] At any rate, given the exceptionally large number of volumes of Arthurian romance, often illustrated, which can be reliably ascribed to French workshop provenance at this date in the thirteenth century, we are not hazarding greatly if we assume that Edward's own Arthurian book was of French origin and style. The only English centre of activity at that time engaged in the illustration, by line-drawing, of French secular texts, was operating on a very small scale compared with centres in France: when we look at its productions – the *Roman de Toute Chevalerie* of Thomas of Kent, the *Chanson d'Aspremont* – their modest size and nature reinforce the opinion that Edward's important volume was made across the Channel.[142]

Liturgical manuscripts associated with Edward and Eleanor, however, seem to have been executed at the 'court school' set up in the reign of Henry III, and clearly still thriving in the later thirteenth century. An exquisite book was executed, probably at Westminster, for an occasion of European importance – the betrothal of Alfonso, their third son, to Margaret, daughter of the Count of Holland. Left unfinished, presumably because of the death of Alfonso in 1284, it was completed for Elizabeth, Alfonso's sister, who married John, Count of Holland, in 1297.[143]

[Elizabeth Salter did not finish this chapter, but she left notes that indicate she would have gone on to deal with early fourteenth-century English literary texts such as those contained in MS Harley 2253]

Part II *Piers Plowman* and alliterative poetry

4 The alliterative revival*

I

IN spite of all that has been written about it, the quickening of alliterative poetry in middle and later fourteenth-century England remains something of a mystery. Neither the theory of a tenuous but uninterrupted 'alliterative tradition' in the west country[1] nor the theory of alliterative verse as an expression of 'baronial discontent'[2] is entirely satisfactory.[3] While it is clear enough that alliterative writing was never abandoned in the western and northern counties of England between 1100 and 1500, 'continuity' alone will not bridge the gap between Layamon's *Brut* and *Winner and Waster* or the *Parliament of the Three Ages*. It is not simply that the evidence for alliterative poetry during those years is thin: there is an immense and still largely unexplored difference in style and tone between the work of 1200 and that of 1350.

J. R. Hulbert's 'Hypothesis concerning the Alliterative Revival' made an attempt to place the alliterative poems of the fourteenth century in a specific political context, seeing them as instruments of powerful baronial families who were in opposition to the king's party. In this view, the old country metres were deliberately utilized as a mark of defiance against the royal court with its more cosmopolitan literary tastes. It is a pity that Hulbert's article finally rested its case upon the special issue of 'baronial opposition', for this is the most easily refutable of its points. In other ways it drew our attention to important matters: the close connection of the alliterative poems with noble families – their literary inclinations, their libraries. Historians confirm that our picture of this fourteenth-century literary 'revival' cannot be completed without more intensive study of the households of the great magnates whose estates lay in the west and north of England.[4] But the same historians cannot be used to support a theory of 'baronial opposition', and this part of Hulbert's argument must now be sceptically received. For the facts seem to be clear: the new flowering of alliterative poetry in the west and north midlands[5] coincides almost exactly with a period of remarkable accord between crown and baronage – the middle years of the fourteenth century. The most distinguished recent history of the times sums up its account of these central years: 'Thus did the winter of baronial discontent give place to glorious summer'.[6]

Revived interest in the writing of alliterative verse is apparent by 1350. We know that Humphrey de Bohun, Earl of Hereford, commissioned the adaptation

* Originally published in *Modern Philology*, 64 (1966), 146–50, 233–7.

of *William of Palerne* about 1351. *Winner and Waster* and the *Parliament of the Three Ages* follow closely. And those very families whose fortunes may turn out to be so intimately connected with the production of alliterative poetry were firmly behind the king in his wars with France: the Mortimers, the Bohuns, the Beauchamps shared in his most splendid victories.[7] The changed times are very well seen in the house of Lancaster. However deeply involved it may have been in 'baronial opposition' to Edward II,[8] by 1337 Henry, Duke of Lancaster and Derby, was destined to become one of Edward III's greatest generals and his constant companion in battle.

Henry of Lancaster was a westerner: he was born at Grosmont – one of the loveliest of the Monmouthshire castles. In later years his main court was at Leicester, but his west country ties were strong. We do not know that he ever concerned himself – as did his contemporary, Humphrey de Bohun of Hereford – with alliterative poetry, but he had a taste for literature as well as for tournaments and the harsher arts of war. His *Livre des Seyntz Medecines*[9] is not only an ingenious allegory of man and his 'physician', Christ, but also a vivid picture of aristocratic life in the middle of the fourteenth century. Although it is written in French (to that extent Henry was old-fashioned, for his native tongue was English[10]), there are many ways in which it is reminiscent of the almost contemporary alliterative poems of the West.[11] Henry's stark sense of mortality does not prevent him from appreciating – even if ruefully – the power and energy of youth: 'et serroit encore, tresdouz Sires, par aventure, si jeo feusse si chaude et si joisnes come jeo soley ...' (*Livre*, p. 78). So the poet of the *Parliament of the Three Ages*[12] is exhilarated by the subject of 'youth'; there is a kind of magnificence about the years of 'orgoil', as Henry of Lancaster knew:

> This hathelle one this heghe horse, with hawke one his fiste,
> He was ȝonge and ȝape, and ȝerninge to armes ...
>
> (*Parliament*, lines 170–1)

And so too, for all his critical view of the times, the poet of *Winner and Waster*[13] draws in the Black Prince with admiration:

> What, he was ȝongeste of ȝeris, and ȝapest of witt,
> þat any wy in this werlde wiste of his age!
>
> (*Winner*, lines 119–20)

Henry of Lancaster's words are almost a gloss on Youth and the Black Prince in those poems:

Ceo estoit quant jeo fui joesnes et me senti fort et legier, et me plesoit ma bealtee et ma taille ou ma gentilesce ...   (*Livre*, pp. 15–16)

But all agree on the ending:

jeo n'atenk forsqe la mort, voir voir la male mort ...   (*Livre*, p. 7)

Makes ȝoure mirrors by me, men bi ȝoure trouthe –
This shadowe in my shewere, shunte ȝe no while.
And now es dethe at my dore that I drede moste.

(*Parliament*, lines 290–2)

Some likeness in material and tone should not surprise us: the works may draw on common kinds of reading, observation, and experience; and the audience of the *Parliament* and *Winner and Waster* may easily have included men similar to the 'friends' who encouraged Henry of Lancaster to begin his *Livre*.[14]

Both Henry of Lancaster and Humphrey de Bohun of Hereford – the one an author, the other a patron – are strong witnesses to the growth of favourable conditions for literary work in provincial courts. They are parts of the same general pattern – but it is a pattern which was not dominated by aggressive political factors. There are no historical grounds for holding that the production of alliterative verse in 1350 was accelerated by 'baronial discontent', for by that time England was already in 'glorious summer'. Whatever the state of affairs in the earlier part of the century,[15] and whatever the later developments, the first signs of renewed activity in this field must surely be seen as one of the results of the optimism, energy, and strongly patriotic spirit of the period which began with victory at Sluys and came to a high peak with the peace of Bretigny in 1360–1. Edward III's barons had every incentive to encourage the composition of poetry in a traditionally English form – as they also had incentive to encourage the illumination of their prayer books and psalters by English artists.[16] But it would be a mistake to interpret either as a gesture of 'provincial defiance' against the king and the metropolis. Allowing for some regional and local characteristics, both poetry and manuscript illumination can be defined in 'national' terms.

Winner and Waster is an excellent example of this. Written, apparently, by some 'westren wy' who did, to some extent, identify himself with western *as distinct from* metropolitan ways of life,[17] it has no critical things to say about Edward III and the Black Prince but is remarkable for its pride in their splendour and prowess, and turns its gaze impartially upon most sections of society, lay and religious.

But the general directions given by Hulbert in his article were sound. Aristocratic patronage is a known feature of the beginning and the end of alliterative verse writing in the Middle English period.[18] It may be that we shall never *identify* the poets, but we already possess some of the materials we need for understanding the forces and conditions which shaped their work.

The thirteenth century provides only the merest of hints that there may have been, by that time, a connection between the longer English alliterative poem and patronage. The 'worthy knight', mentioned in MS Otho C. XIII of Layamon's *Brut*,[19] could have encouraged this immense project. While we can assume that the Fitzwarin family knew and approved the French romance which celebrated their exploits, we know nothing of the social and literary context of the alliterative Fulk Fitzwarin poem.[20]

It is not until the early fourteenth century that we have real proof of a highly literate western nobility and of the part it must have played in collecting the material from which later vernacular poets were to work. Most literary historians mention the books which Guy Beauchamp, Earl of Warwick, gave to Bordesley Abbey (Worcestershire) in 1305; the importance of this gift cannot be overemphasised.[21] For here is a record of a private library which, in range and quality, provides a comprehensive and comprehensible background to some of the most important of alliterative poems written after 1350. If, as seems possible, the authors of these poems were clerks in aristocratic employ,[22] easy access to French and Latin sources was available. Guy of Warwick's books covered a wide area of subject matter: religious meditations and lives of saints, didactic and historical treatises, epic legends, and courtly romances. But most interesting is the way in which certain of the books remind us of extant English alliterative poems:

> un Volum del Romaunce Titus et Vaspasien . . .
> un Volum del Romaunce Iosep ab Arimathie, e deu Seint Grael . . .
> un Volum del Romaunce de Troies . . .
> un Volum de la Mort ly Roy Arthur, et de Mordret . . .
> un Volum del Romaunce d'Alisaundre . . .[23]

The list cannot be used to suggest direct sources. But it does suggest a credible type of background for the alliterative *Titus and Vespasian*, *Joseph of Arimathie*, *Morte Arthure*: the mention of romances of 'Troy' and of 'Alexander' points to important areas of interest in alliterative writing. If the 'Romaunce de Troies' was Benoît de Sainte-Maure's *Roman de Troie*, either this volume or a similar copy was to prove extremely useful to later fourteenth-century poets of the northwest midlands: the *Gest Historiale* seems to have used the Latin translation of Benoît by Guido delle Colonne, but the partially alliterative *Laud Troy Book* and the rhymed *Seege of Troy* (both from the northwest) depend to varying extents upon Benoît. The inclusion of *Ferebras* in the list is significant in view of the *Morte Arthure*, which draws on this as on other French epic legends. In fact, the high proportion of epic legend in Guy Beauchamp's collection (commented upon by M. Blaess, p. 518) leads one to wonder whether the strongly 'heroic' cast of much western alliterative romance was not due to availability of material rather than to 'heroic traditions' of an ancient English past.

In other fields, it is useful to know that among these books was 'un Volum qe est appele l'Apocalips' and 'un Volum de le Enseignement Aristotle, enveiez au Roy Alisaundre', since both of these are probable source books for the finest of all alliterative poems – *Pearl*.[24]

It looks as if some of these books did not remain in seclusion at Bordesley, but found new owners in the west country. A few familiar titles are recorded in the private library of Nicholas of Hereford, Prior of Evesham, who, at his death in 1392, owned over one hundred volumes of religious and secular writings.[25]

No other private libraries have yet been located unmistakably in the west midlands and described for us in such detail. But it is beyond doubt that many noble families with strong interests and commitments in the west were collectors of books: the 'raw materials' for poets. We do not know whether the Bohun family continued to encourage the writing of alliterative verse, but we do know that Humphrey de Bohun's daughter, Eleanor, left a considerable number of books, in French and Latin, to her son. Among these we find 'historie de chivaler a cigne ... en Francois';[26] the alliterative *Chevalere Assigne* comes to mind. Her husband, Thomas of Woodstock, Duke of Gloucester, who died in 1397, had eighty-three books in his possession at Pleshy Castle, Essex. The inventory made after his death lists the *Romance of the Rose*, *Mandeville's Travels*, and Arthurian romance, as well as devotional works, law treatises, and chronicles. Gospels and a bible were in English.[27]

Given the historical data and given, also, the nature of many of the alliterative poems, it is fair to assume that the social and cultural environment in which they were produced was not so very different from that in which John of Trevisa's prose translations were made. His English versions of Higden's *Polychronicon* and Bartholomaeus Anglicus' *De Proprietatibus Rerum* were undertaken while he was Chaplain to the Lords of Berkeley Castle, in Gloucestershire – and, moreover, at their request.[28] Thomas III of Berkeley, like his contemporary, Henry of Lancaster, was a man of varied interests; his physical exuberance must have matched that of the Lord Bercilak in Gawain's adventure:

hee and his brothers have kept out four nights and days togeather with their nets and dogs in hunting of the fox . . . and with this delight of hunting this lord began and dyed . . .[29]

Thomas III was a champion of religion and scholarship as well as of the hunt;[30] the unidentified patrons of the alliterative poets were surely men such as these, whose lives spanned religious and secular worlds. Many authors must have been responding to the sort of influences which could only have been exerted by families similar to the Berkeleys, the Bohuns, and the Beauchamps. It is probably for their sophisticated taste (the complex, glittering Bohun manuscripts are sufficient evidence), for their moral and historical preoccupations (Thomas III of Berkeley was impressed by 'the profit arisynge by histories'[31]), and for their maturing sense of 'Englishness' (Humphrey de Bohun and Thomas of Berkeley felt 'the necessity of translations into the English tongue'[32]) that the west midland and northern clerks in their employ translated and paraphrased into alliterative 'high style' some of the most famous French and Latin works of the age.[33] And those works may already have been lying at hand in their private libraries. The four alliterative poems in MS Cotton Nero A. X – *Patience, Cleanness, Pearl*, and *Sir Gawain and the Green Knight* – with their varied background in the bible and Patristic literature, rhetorical treatises, and French romance, comment eloquently on such a situation.

II

As long ago as 1930, J. P. Oakden suggested that the *Gawain*-poet may have been a retainer of John of Gaunt, living at Gaunt's castle of Clitheroe, in Lancashire.[34] Lancastrian connections were again discussed in 1953 and 1956. J. R. L. Highfield recommended that we should keep under scrutiny 'the south Lancashire and west midland clerks in the household of the Duke of Lancaster'[35] if we wished to solve the 'authorship mystery'. His account of the career of Simon Newton, 'a west-midland man of some importance between 1363 and 1380' was interesting in view of other evidence: *Sir Gawain and the Green Knight* was certainly known to Humfrey Newton, a country squire of Cheshire in the later fifteenth and early sixteenth century.[36]

H. L. Savage, in his study of *Sir Gawain*, was mainly concerned to prove that the poet had connections with Gaunt's brother-in-law, the French Earl of Bedford, Enguerrand de Coucy, but he did not rule out the possibility that 'he served either (or both) of those princes in some administrative or clerical capacity'.[37]

A closer look at the records of the Lancastrian household does not reveal anything conclusive about the identity of the poet, but it does provide rich information about the kind of aristocratic life which might conceivably have shaped both poet and patron – and it does, incidentally, bring the name 'Newton' to our attention once more. Gaunt succeeded by marriage to the lands and title of Henry of Lancaster: his vast properties stretched over England, but, with a few exceptions, his castles lay in the midlands and the north. 'Draw a line across England from the mouth of the Severn to the Wash, and there are scarcely a score of strongholds of importance out of the Duke's hands'.[38] Clearly, Gaunt's influence was strong in those very areas from which the alliterative poems came – the Welsh border, the midlands (west and east), and the north. His practical concern for one English poet needs no underscoring: Chaucer's private and professional links with Gaunt are well known. But it was certainly not only in London, at his palace of the Savoy, that he held court, granted pensions, ordered gifts and entertained. He travelled extensively between his various castles and estates, transacting the business of his immense 'kingdom' as he went. His *Registers* tell us of ceaseless journeying. Men such as Gaunt were as familiar with life in northern and midland settings as with life in London and were as often served by families with roots in Derbyshire, Staffordshire, and Yorkshire as by families of southern origin.[39] The social and cultural situation which these facts suggest must have been responsible in part, at least, for encouraging a form of literature with a strongly regional ground base, but with a live knowledge of affairs in the capital, and a desire to cater to tastes no less subtle than those for which Chaucer provided. Our idea of the alliterative revival as a 'local affair'[40] must allow for the fact that the clerkly poets were probably as well travelled as their noble patrons, on whose business they must often have passed between wild border country and London.

Among Gaunt's castles of the northwest midlands was Tutbury,[41] on the borders of Staffordshire and Derbyshire; it came through his Lancastrian inheritance, in a neglected state, and was enlarged and improved at his wishes for his second wife, Constance of Castile.[42] Gaunt transformed it into a very splendid building – if we are to believe the evidence of a sixteenth-century drawing,[43] which certainly pictures for us a 'castel þe comlokest þat euer knyȝt aȝte' (*Sir Gawain*, line 767). But there is no point in trying to fit any particular poem or poet to Tutbury at this stage in our researches: Tutbury is important because it is a castle within reach of 'Gawain country'[44] and allows us, on the basis of some historical evidence, to recreate for ourselves an image of the life described in the poem. We cannot prove that the author of *Sir Gawain* had connections with Tutbury and was in John of Gaunt's employ, but it is not unlikely that he came from a similar sort of milieu – and had an illustrious patron to encourage his complex and rich art.

The *Registers* of Gaunt mention Tutbury a good deal, and in one case the name 'Newton' is linked with it: an order to the seneschal of Tutbury confirms the grant, in 1382, of 'manoires terres et tenementz' in the counties of Staffordshire and Leicestershire to 'Thomas de Newton' and two other 'chers et bien amez'.[45] The ceremony of life at Tutbury in the later fourteenth century is well documented: in 1380 the *Registers* record a charter granted to 'le roy des ministralx deinz nostre honour de Tuttebury' to enforce the services performed by minstrels at that castle 'dancien temps'.[46] The customs of the castle ranged from the rough sport of 'bull-running' (perhaps introduced by Constance of Castile from her native country, and only abolished in the eighteenth century) to courtly rituals imposed on tenants such as Sir Philip Somerville. He, 'when his lord keepeth Christmas at his castle of Tutbury', was to come to the castle and carve Gaunt's meat for him.[47] The last act of the August hunt of the domestic swine (carried out by Sir Philip and the woodmasters of nearby Needwood Forest) reads almost like an episode in a romance: 'on Holy Rood day the sayd Sir Phelippe shall returne to the castell of Tutbury . . . shall dyne with the Steward . . . and after dynner he shall delyver the horse, saddylle and bercelett to the steward, and shall kysse the Porter and depart'.[48]

Whether Tutbury with its minstrels, its ceremonies, its architecture, and its ducal owners had any claim to be the home of alliterative poetry we do not know. But the *Registers* of Gaunt speak generally (and eloquently) about the 'pure, crude fact' of a life accepted as normal in *Sir Gawain*.[49]

If the New Year's gifts about which the noble knights of the poem 'debated bisyly' (line 68) even remotely resembled those given by Gaunt, on January 2, 1380, they were, indeed, worth some discussion: a crucifix, 'ovesque Marie et Johan,' set with 'diverses pieres et perles', and another 'garnise ovesque un saphire et diverse perles'.[50] The minstrels who announce the beginning of the banquet in *Sir Gawain*

> þen þe first cors come with crakkyng of trumpes . .
> Nwe nakryn noyse with þe noble pipes . . .
>
> *(Sir Gawain, lines 116, 118)*

have their real-life counterparts in Gaunt's account books: Hankyn Fysh, piper, 'bien ame ministralle', and Johan Cliff, drummer, are frequently rewarded for their services. Cliff received 'un peir de nakeres . . . et deux stykkes dargent faitz pur meismes les nakers' in 1381.[51]

The splendid accoutrements of the Green Knight and Gawain ('Gryngolet . . . gurde with a sadel / þat glemed ful gayly with mony golde frenges' [lines 597–8]) are easily rivalled by those of Gaunt's family: his daughter, the Countess of Pembroke, received a 'seel de velvet, enbroudez de lyons', for her appearance at the marriage of Richard II and Anne of Bohemia.[52] The agreement of poem and *Register* is most striking on aristocratic taste in bedroom furnishings: Gawain's 'bryȝt boure, þer beddyng watȝ noble' with its

> . . . cortynes of clene sylk with cler golde hemmeȝ,
> And couertoreȝ ful curious with comlych paneȝ . . .
>
> Tapiteȝ tyȝt to þe woȝe of tuly and tars,
> And under fete, on þe flet, of folȝande sute . . .
>
> *(Sir Gawain, lines 854–5, 858–9)*

is another variation on a real-life theme. Gaunt's gifts and bequests include 'une nostre list palee de blank et de blue, ove les tapites dycel, et la sale de meisme la seute'.[53] His will mentions 'mon grant lit de draps d'or, le champ piers overez des arbres d'or, et juxte chescun arbre un alant blanc',[54] as well as 'draps dor donc la champ rouge satyn raye dor' and 'un covertur d'ermyn'.[55] The adjective 'curious' (*Sir Gawain*, line 855) would clearly have had a precise significance for an aristocratic fourteenth-century audience.

Lastly, the metaphor of *Gawain* (lines 235–6), 'grener hit semed / þen grene aumayl on golde glowande bryȝter', calls to mind not only the dazzling appearance of the Green Knight on horseback but also the dazzling list of precious objects in gold, silver, and enamel ordered by Gaunt from 'Herman goldesmyth' and 'Adam Bamme, orfeour de Londres'; for example, 'une saler dargent par lui fait ove un levrer sur an tarage aymelle de vert'.[56]

If the *Registers* of John of Gaunt do not reveal to us either the poet's or the patron's identity, they do strengthen the conviction that the poem has not emerged from a household of the minor gentry but from a household maintained by a lord of considerable standing.[57]

Whatever errors of judgment there were in J. R. Hulbert's 'hypothesis' about the alliterative revival,[58] it is still true that we are just as likely to be able to 'map' that revival by reference to the estates, the retinues, the account books, and the bequests of the 'higher nobility' of middle and later fourteenth-century England as by references to vague 'western traditions' of alliterative verse. Though it has a ground base of metre with a long and redoubtable ancestry, the distinction of this Middle English verse is its power to invest an old measure with contemporary splendour and relevance. Like the art of the illuminated psalters commissioned by the baronial families, the English poetry written either in or near to their castles has links with the past – but more decisively caters to the tastes of the present. The gold-pinnacled borders of the Bohun manuscripts faithfully repro-duce 'late-decorated' architectural styles: the Green Knight's castle is equally up to date in its features:

> So mony pynakle payntet watʒ poudred ayquere,
> Among þe castel carneleʒ clambred so þik

and so is the 'decorated' art of *Pearl*. We may have to use a word such as 'provincial' to describe the dialect of the Cotton Nero A. X poems: 'archaic' may be appropriate to use about certain parts of the vocabulary – although I suspect that we have overstressed that 'archaic element'. But we have only to look at some of the wall paintings in St Stephen's Chapel, Westminster (1350–63); the fan-vaulted cloisters of Gloucester Cathedral (1351–1407); the Percy Tomb in Beverley Minster (*ca.* 1350); or the Warwick Chantry in Tewkesbury Abbey (1422)[59] to see one thing clearly: even the most elaborate alliterative poem is central to one very important area of fourteenth-century sensibility. And this 'area' has no firm geographical boundaries: there is nothing provincial about it – it spans England even more thoroughly than the Lancastrian or Bohun estates.

Some things are far from clear about alliterative verse. One question, in particular, has not been answered satisfactorily. Exactly how much did its 'pro-vincial dialect' limit its appeal?[60] For though its manuscripts are few and its language 'local', its horizons are often very wide indeed. If the poet of *Winner and Waster*, by his own admission, was a 'westren wy' (line 8), he knew London pretty well,[61] and he envisaged his debate, which involved the king, the Black Prince, and most classes of society, to be of national relevance. *The Parliament of the Three Ages* is no more *narrowly* regional than Henry of Lancaster's *Livre des Seyntz Medecines*. Even the poet of the much later *Mum and the Sothsegger* (*ca.* 1397–1400) writing from the west country–perhaps from Bristol – is as confident about the reception of his 'message' by king and nobleman as Langland, writing from London:

> So rithfully be reson / my rede shuld also
> For to conceill and I couʒthe / my king and the lordis. . . .[62]

There is more work to be done on the dialectal 'spread' of these poems,[63] but it may be that we need to look more closely at the standard critical judgment that the alliterative poems and their techniques were 'completely alien to the poets of the royal court'.[64] The constant movement of lords and officials between Westminster and distant estates in the west and north is something to be taken into serious account: although the revival itself drew on 'local' sources, those concerned with it – as patrons, poets, audiences – were probably frequently on the move.[65] Midland families in Lancastrian employ are met with in London as often as in Staffordshire, Derbyshire, or Leicestershire – the Newtons, for instance.[66] Chaucer's much-quoted words about 'rum, ram, ruf' must be set beside the rare but memorable occasions when he wrote seriously and alliteratively.[67] It would not be sensible to account for all of those occasions in terms of Latin rhetorical usage: neither would it be sensible to conclude that the poet of *Sir Gawain and the Green Knight* and of *Pearl* was committed to alliterative verse for want of knowledge and skill in other ways of handling poetry.

No one would be surprised to find odd echoes of Chaucer in contemporary Latin poetry: Richard Maidstone, Carmelite friar, and confessor to John of Gaunt, has this to say of Richard II in a poem of 1392, which celebrated the king's return to the capital and his reconciliation with the city of London:

> Vernula quam facies fulvis redimita capillis . . .,
> Fulget et ex auro vestis sua rubra colore,
> Quae tenet interius membra venusta nimis,
> Iste velut Troilus, vel ut Absolon ipse decorus,
> Captivat sensum respicientis eum.[68]

The reference to Troilus and Absalom reminds us that Maidstone, as a man about court, probably knew Chaucer and his work. But we might also allow ourselves to be reminded of another literary hero, whose appearance was dazzling, and whose figure was set off to advantage by magnificent robes:

> þe ver by his visage verayly hit semed
> Welneȝ to vche haþel, alle on hwes,
> Lowande and lufly alle his lymmes vnder,
> þat a comloker knyȝt neuer Kryst made hem þoȝt.
>
> (*Sir Gawain*, lines 866–9)

There is no point in suggesting any sort of indebtedness, one to another.[69] But there is point in noticing that Maidstone, Chaucer, and the *Gawain*-poet may have been writing for patrons and audiences of similar tastes and experience. Lancastrian affiliation may override (though never ignore) differences of language, dialect, and geographical setting.[70]

5   *Piers Plowman*: an introduction*

ALLEGORY

The dimensions of the poem

Langland's dominant concern is to expose and clarify the social and religious issues raised by his conscience: whatever allegorical methods he uses are designed to illustrate and elucidate the great themes of the poem. One of the most important functions of his dreamer-figure is to ensure that we should not find our encounters with allegorical journeys, landscapes and debates riddling or enigmatic, but, if anything, over-directed. It is true, for instance, that we need much less initial equipment for 'interpreting' allegorical actions in this poem than in a secular medieval allegory such as the *Roman de la Rose*: there some preliminary knowledge of the concepts and conventions of medieval love-literature is essential if we are to make proper sense of the fictitious narrative of the dreamer, in his progress through the walled garden, with its pool, rose-bush and tableaux of sensuous delight. Again, no allegorical character in *Piers Plowman* is allowed to remain as mysterious and elusive in nature as the guide-maiden in *Pearl*.[1] Holy Church, Reason, Patience, Clergy, and Wit are self-explanatory, in name, form and function. Even the changing significance of Piers Plowman is deducible from the commentary offered by the poem: the last journey towards Piers–

> 'By Crist', quod Consience tho, 'I wol bicome a pilgrime,
> And wenden as wyde as the world regneth
> To seke Peres the Ploghman, that Pruyde myhte destruye'
>
> (C xxiii 380–2)

is not a quest into the unknown, but a long-anticipated movement of the conscience towards spiritual well-being and authority.

It would be a pity, when describing the richness of Langland's allegorical invention, to lose sight of this 'openness' of aim and technique, and to risk creating false barriers between the poem and present-day readers. *Piers Plowman* has sometimes been recommended as a work susceptible of many-levelled interpretation,[2] as if it could command the same kind of attention from us as the text of the Bible from the medieval scholar –

---

* Originally published as pp. 3–58 of the Introduction to the Selections from the C-text of *Piers Plowman*, ed. E. Salter and D. Pearsall, York Medieval Texts (London, 1967); this section was entirely written by Elizabeth Salter.

Blessed are the eyes which see divine spirit through the letter's veil . . .[3]

But its wealth of significance cannot be charted in any very precise and rigorous way. No one would deny that from the moment when the dreamer looks out over his dream province, and recognizes not only the familiar, turbulent scenes of his own day – 'al the welthe of the world and the wo bothe' – but also the symbolic tower of Truth and the deep dale of Death (C I 14ff), *Piers Plowman* engages with some kind of allegorical mode. The rapid and down-to-earth survey of medieval society which follows is broken into by speeches from Conscience and Kind Wit: allegorical characters move easily among the 'bisshopes and bachilers' of fourteenth-century London:

> Conscience and the kyng into the court wenten,
> Where houede an hondred in houes of silke,
> Seriauntes hij semede that seruen atte barre . . . (C I 158–60)

And for all the harsh realism of the closing lines of Passus I, the clamorous invitations of Langland's own world –

> . . . Hote pyes, hote!
> Goode gees and grys, ga we dyne, ga we! (C I 226–7)

Passus II opens with the dreamer offering us *interpretations* of the scene –

> What the montaigne bymeneth and the merke dale
> And the feld ful of folk, I shal you fair shewe. (C II 1–2)

'What it all means' will clearly be one of the major preoccupations of the poem. The first words of Holy Church to the dreamer press home the point that most people who 'passeth on this erthe' see only the confused pattern of their own lives:

> Of othere hevene then here thei halde no tale. (C II 9)

The dreamer's reply is a request for his own – and our – enlightenment: 'what may this be to mene?'

But if, by the mingling of 'real' and 'allegorical' characters, and by frequent references to the 'meaning' of phenomena, Langland very early on in his poem makes us conscious of appearance and its further significance, he is certainly not laying down or taking for granted specific rules for the realization of that significance. No doubt he was familiar with the time-honoured medieval system of Biblical exegesis, which saw, beneath the literal level of the Scriptures, three separable and gradually deepening kinds of spiritual truth – the allegorical, the tropological and the anagogical.[4] If he had not been formally trained in the use of such a method, he would have seen and heard it in operation in the sermon literature of his time.[5] Although it is true that the popularity of the 'fourfold method' of studying the Bible waned somewhat after the 13th century, treatises outlining it were current in Langland's day, and later. But it is by no means certain that any medieval poet, using an allegorical form, did in fact envisage his work as fourfold of meaning, in just that precise way that the fruitfulness of the Biblical text could be demonstrated by a trained scholar.[6] To be told that there are 'four parallel lines of interpretation . . . sometimes simultaneous, sometimes interlinked', but that 'on all four planes the poem is complete',[7] is a challenging introduction for the new reader of *Piers Plowman* and it is some consolation to know that on good historical grounds such a statement is unlikely to be true. A brief acquaintance with the poem makes clear that it is not 'four layered' in any continuous or consistent way: even a comparison of Passus I with Passus II will display the variation of allegorical texture which is an important feature of the whole work.

On the other hand, a completely literal reading of *Piers Plowman* is liable to be an impoverished one; we can be guilty of dogmatism at either extreme:

its literal nature renders it an impossible medium for the fourfold method . . .[8]

For the 'literal nature' of *Piers Plowman* has, first of all, to be defined, and then proved for each part of the poem as we come to it. While it might usefully describe a good deal of Passus I, it would not be helpful, except with changed terms of reference, when applied to Passus II or to Passus XXI.

In the case of Passus XXI, there is a *literal* and agonizing narrative of Christ's passion, just as in Passus I there is a literal narrative of happenings on the Field Full of Folk. But the narrative flow in Passus XXI is constantly disturbed by depth-charges of significance. Often we might say that the full explosion of sense takes place beneath the *literal* surface of the narrative. If it is unlikely that we shall discover a formally layered, quadruple structure of meaning in Langland's poetry, it is certain that we shall discover a range and allusiveness of meaning not easily covered by the term 'literal'.

There are times in *Piers Plowman* when the rich sense of the poetry can be naturally and continually described by means of the 'fourfold method'. Christ's words at the Harrowing of Hell, for instance, coming at the climax not only of the Passion narrative, but also of the dreamer's long, tortuous search for an understanding of God's intent, are simple, and yet charged with powerful meaning. A 'fourfold' expression of that meaning does not overtax or distort the language:

> 'That art doctour of deth, drynke that thow madest!
> For I that am lord of lyf, love is my drynke,
> And for that drynke todaye I deyede, as hit semede.
> Ac I wol drynke of no dische, ne of deep clergyse,
> Bote of comune coppes, alle Cristene soules;
> Ac thy drynke worth deth, and depe helle thy bolle.
> I fauht so, me fursteth yut, for mannes soule sake.
> *Sicio.*

> May no pyement ne pomade ne presiouse drynkes
> Moiste me to the fulle ne my furste slakke
> Til the ventage falle in the vale of Josophat,
> And drynke riht rype must, *resurreccio mortuorum.*'   (C XXI 405–15)

In these words there is the *literal* drama of Christ poised in triumph, with the gates of hell wide open – a vivid and familiar moment for the artists of the Middle Ages, who recorded it on burnished manuscript pages, and on sculpted columns and portals. There is the *allegorical* sense of the Harrowing of Hell and the Resurrection as part of the intimate relationship between Christ and man. The triumph of love and life over sin and death is the special significance of Christ for doomed mankind – this thirsting 'lord of life', who will eventually 'have out of hell all men's souls' (C XXI 417). Further there is a *tropological*, or purely moral sense: the speech prescribes as well as exemplifies a proper way of life. Christ's action holds out hope and establishes a pattern of behaviour:

> 'And al that men mys-dede, I, man, to amenden hit.'   (C XXI 392)

In imitation of the perfect man, mankind can now centre life around selflessness and love, so that

> Adam and alle thorw a tre shal turne to lyve.   (C XXI 401)

Finally, for Langland and some of his readers, there could have been a particular spiritual 'echo' about lines such as

> '. . . love is my drynke,
> And for that drynke todaye I deyede, as hit semede.'   (C XXI 406–7)

The *anagogical* sense would have been appropriate only to the rare and lonely life of the contemplative, who 'dies' to the world ('as hit semede') for the sake of the 'drink' of divine love.[9]

At points like these, a fourfold description of what Langland may have had in mind as he wrote is not extravagant. Other parts of the text do not yield the same kinds of reward, and our assessment of the depth and the nature of symbolic meaning in this poetry must depend on close and sympathetic reading. For it may be that we shall find many sorts of meaning knotted into one crucial passage – as in the Harrowing of Hell speech, above, or in the episode of the Good Samaritan (C XX). At other times, we may find a linear progression – one 'sense' following and developing out of another. Passus II of the poem illustrates this exactly: it shifts rapidly among various sorts of significances. The *literal* action – a conversation between Holy Church and the dreamer about the meaning of the opening panorama – is managed sharply and humorously:

> 'Thow dotede daffe', quod she, 'dulle aren thy wittes;
> To lyte lernedest thow, I leve, Latyn in thy yowthe.'   (C II 139–40)

But the theme of the lady's discourse – the search for, and the means of attaining salvation – is conveyed on different successive levels. Words dealing with salvation in the local and specific context of medieval society –

> 'Kynges and knyghtes sholde kepen hit by resoun,
> Ryden and rappe adoun in reaumes aboute'   (C II 90–1)

follow words setting the search on the highest spiritual plane – the man who walks with Truth

> '. . . is a god by the gospel and graunte may hele . . .'   (C II 86)

In turn, the long perspectives of religious history open out: God's plan for man's salvation is evidenced in the solemn narrative of Lucifer's fall, with its eternal consequences of right set against wrong:

> 'And alle that worchen that wikked is, wenden thei sholle
> After here deth-day and dwelle ther Wrong is,
> And alle that han wel ywrouhte, wende they sholle
> Estward til hevene, ever to abyde
> There Treuthe is, . . .'   (C II 130–4)

Comment on the contemporary scene narrows the field of interpretation:

> 'Aren none hardere ne hungriere then men of holy chirch,
> Averous and evel-willed when thei ben avaunsed'.   (C II 188–9)

Universal statements expand it again to encompass many kinds of truth – religio-historical, moral, mystical:

> 'So love is leche of lyf and lysse of alle payne
> And the graffe of grace and grathest way to hevene'.   (C II 200–1)

The real test is not so much the historical probability of 'multiple meaning' in *Piers Plowman*, but our own experience of the work. If Langland did not see the dreamer's quest as an investigation on four separable planes of significance, he did see it as a search for a Truth which was complex, often contradictory, and cumulative.

It need not then surprise us that his methods of charting that search are most various. We should be sceptical of critics who recommend to us one kind of allegorical writing as 'characteristic' of *Piers Plowman*, or who try to convince us that we have a straight choice between 'allegorical' and 'literal' methods of reading. In fact, a whole spectrum of allegorical modes is characteristic of the poem: it displays almost every type of allegory known to the medieval period. To give a comprehensive account of the sources of Langland's allegory, we should have to range over popular sermon literature, courtly poems in French and English, moral treatises, and, in all probability, illustrations to tracts. Not only can we observe diversity of forms, but also widely differing stages of growth. More-over, even when Langland appears to dispense, temporarily, with allegory, his 'realism' is by no means as simple to define as our first contact with it might suggest.

Allegorical categories and modes

Personification allegory   A vast number of medieval works are usually described as 'allegorical': 'allegory' has to serve as a portmanteau-word for a range of compositions which require some degree of interpretation from the reader, and invite, through their fictions, an inner commentary on the events narrated. Often those are the only common factors: to see *Piers Plowman* and the *Divina Commedia* as allegories, a very flexible frame of reference indeed has to be allowed. Within such a frame, various attempts have been made to sort and regroup allegorical writings. For instance, one of the major methods of procedure in allegory is that of personification, and Langland's poem has been called, in company with other English and French poems, 'personification allegory'.[10] In this, abstract qualities or faculties are given human form, and display their natures or re-enact some experience by means of a typical human activity – a debate, a fight, a feast, a trial, a journey. So, in the *Roman de la Rose*, the experience of falling in love is first abstracted from a particular human situation, and reshaped in terms of personified faculties – Reason, Shame, Jealousy, Idleness, Welcome – who meet, hinder and help the lover in his search for the rose of love. And in the English alliterative poem *Winner and Waster*,[11] man's natural and opposed tendencies to extravagance and miserliness are set before the reader as two figures in debate about their ways of life.

But difficulties arise when we associate them with each other, and *Piers Plowman* with them, as 'personification allegories'. It is true that all three poems 'personify': Langland breaks down the lesson of preserving humility in the face of great provocation into its component parts of patience, reason, anger, and sets them up as characters at a feast (C XVI). But more important is a comparison of how each poet *used* the device of personification: Guillaume de Lorris's poem is a formal tableau of characters in an enclosed garden: *Winner and Waster* is a ceremonious encounter on a tournament field: Langland's Feast episode is a dynamic, wry scene of mounting tensions, insults, and reconciliations, which materializes and disintegrates before our very eyes. Not that this is always the case with *Piers Plowman*: Langland has static debates as well as bustling feasts – between Reason and the dreamer, Holy Church and the dreamer. The point to make is that the category 'personification allegory' is only of limited help in placing *Piers Plowman*, as, indeed, it may be in placing other medieval works. Personification is a weapon for many allegorists, but they can only be properly distinguished by their ability and inclination to handle it.

And, as we shall see, personification is not the whole story: allegory has many faces.

The same difficulty arises when we try to assign *Piers Plowman* to any particular allegorical class or category, and it seems more useful to begin by recognizing its comprehensive allegorical span. This involves not only recognition of the variety of traditional methods Langland draws upon, but also his unique use and combination of those methods.

Dramatic allegory   Usually – and rightly – singled out for attention is the kind of allegory we find in the Lady Meed episodes of *Piers Plowman* (C III–V) or in the Feast of Patience (C XVI). Here a central subject is investigated by means of an actively developing allegorical narrative, with conceptional and fictional elements in perfect, continuous adjustment. The whole sequence of events involving Lady Meed – the arranging of the marriage, the journey to Westminster, the arraignment at the king's court – is dramatically convincing, as well as deeply meaningful. No detail is imprecise in significance, or flat in design. Liar, for instance, evading the King's summons to judgment, is accurately analysed for us, but he leaps into the poetry with the sure energy of an English medieval line-drawing:[12]

> Lyghtliche Lyere lep away thennes,
> Lorkynge thorw lanes, tologged of menye.
> He was nawher welcome for hus meny tales,
> Oueral houted out and yhote trusse,
> Til pardoners hadden pitte and pullede hym to house.
> Thei woshe hym and wypede hym and wonde hym in cloutes,
> And sente hym on Sonnedayes with seeles to churches . . .
>
> (C III 225–31)

It is visually satisfying as well as morally instructive that Lady Meed – the essence of material reward – should be fêted by a 14th-century court, and presented to society by 'a clerk – ich can nouht his name':

> Cortesliche the clerk thenne, as the kynge hyghte,
> Toke Mede by the myddel, and myldeliche here broughte
> Into boure with blysse and by hure gan sitte,
> Ther was myrthe and mynstralcy Mede to plesen . . .   (C IV 9–12)

All gestures are vividly realized, yet full of 'sentence' – Meed, hard pressed, looks to the lawyers to save her from Reason's logic:

> Mede in the mote-halle tho on men of lawe gan wynke,
> In sygne that thei sholde with som sotel speche
> Reherce tho anon ryght that myghte Reson stoppe.   (C V 148–50)

But her faded glamour comes under harsh scrutiny:

And alle ryghtful recordeden that Reson treuthe seyde . . .
Loue let lyght of Mede and Leaute 3ut lasse . . .
Mede mornede tho, and made heuy cheere,
For the comune called hure queynte comune hore.

(C v 151, 156, 160–1)

Similarly, the description of the Feast of Reason, to which the dreamer goes with Conscience, Clergy and Patience, proceeds as a continuous and highly amusing narrative, but skilfully utilizes every property or speech to convey a bitter lesson of endurance. While the learned and pompous friar is fed on delicacies, 'mortrews and poddynges / Braun and blod of the goos, bacon and colhoppes . . .', Patience and the impatient dreamer are more straitly and healthily served by Scripture:

He sette a sour lof, and saide, '*Agite penitentiam*',
And sethe he drow us drynke, *diu-perseverans*:
'As longe', quod he, 'as lyfe and lycame may duyre.'
'This is a semely servyce!' saide Pacience.   (C xvi 56–9)

We should not pass too quickly over the outraged astonishment of the dreamer as Patience accepts his fare *with gratitude*:

Pacience was wel apayed of this propre service,
. . . ac I mournede evere.   (C xvi 63–4)

It is a master stroke of dramatic writing, but it is also a highly appropriate witness to the dreamer's unreformed, and therefore rebellious, state of mind.

In both of these sequences – and in others like them – Langland mingles personifications with 'real' figures: Meed, Falsehood, Liar, Conscience, Peace, and Wrong thread their way through undefined crowds of the medieval world – pardoners, lawyers, soldiers. The words spoken by personifications give glimpses of rough, authentic life; Peace describes Wrong at work, and there behind the personified figure, with his formal Bill of Complaint, is a whole landscape overrun by men on aggressive, everyday business:

'He menteyneth hus men to morthre myn hewes,
And forstalleth myn faires and fyghteth in my chepynges,
And breketh up my bernes dore and bereth away my whete'.   (C v 58–60)

This mixture of personification and vivid local reportage is not new; Langland would have known of it from many earlier poems, in which Truth or Covetousness travel the English countryside:

Coveytise upon his hors he wole be sone there,
And bringe the bishop silver and rounen in his ere.[13]

Winner and Waster do not manage their debate in generalities, but by reference to the stuff of fourteenth-century living:

'... thy wyde howses full of wolle sakkes,
The bemys benden at the rofe, siche bakone there hynges,
Stuffed are sterlynges undere stelen bowndes ...   (250–2)

But such episodes in *Piers Plowman* modulate the 'real' and the personified in an
especially delicate and powerful way; the details of the landscape behind Peace
illustrate but do not dominate the central moral theme of the passage – the
tyranny of violence. In the Feast scene, the particular references to the friar
preaching at St Paul's lead the eye out through an open window to the contemporary scene:

> Hit is nat thre daies don, this doctour that he prechede
> At Poules byfore the peple what penaunce they soffrede ...
>
> (C xvi 69–70)

Nothing outside, however, distracts attention from the essential moral drama
indoors: the discovery of the very basis of patience in willingness to listen to
half-truths delivered by a corrupt man (see C xvi 113).

This is allegory at its most expansive – richly conceived, precisely executed.
But there are growing-points for such writing all the way through the poem –
embryonic allegory. Langland frequently rests on the very brink of 'realizing' an
allegorical sequence. A quotation may suggest to him a theme for development,
and he makes a brief, telling sketch for a larger design. The words 'Multi enim
sunt vocati, pauci vero electi' (Matthew 22:14) are rapidly set as an allegorical
feast-scene:

> *Multi* to a mangerie and to the mete were sompned,
> And whan the peuple was plener come, the porter unpynnede the gate,
> And plyghte in *pauci* pryueliche and leet the remenant go rome.
>
> (C xiii 46–8)

'Iustus vix salvabitur' (I. Peter 4:18) is dramatized, in simple but striking terms, as
a court scene, with 'vix' personified, and interceding for 'justus':

> ... how Ymaginatyf saide
> That *justus* bifore Jesu *in die judicii*
> *Non salvabitur* bote if *vix* helpe ...   (C xvi 21–3)

These little episodes, arrested between concept and allegorical action, and
rich in potential, show how Langland was constantly drawn to allegory (see
C xxiii 134). But the fact that they remain undeveloped is interesting too: if
Langland's movement towards allegory was instinctive, it was also controlled.
For him, allegory vivified and clarified doctrine; its form and scope depended
intimately upon the needs of the sense at any given moment. We can compare his
compact treatment of these quotations with his elaborate drawing-out of a
Biblical quotation in the 'Four Daughters of God' debate which prefaces the

Harrowing of Hell (C xxi 116 ff.). Here Psalm 85, verse 10, 'Misericordia et veritas obviaverunt sibi: iusticia et pax osculate sunt', is expanded into a full-scale encounter and debate on the reasons for man's salvation.[14] The positioning of this debate is all-important: the length and detail of the allegory are closely related to Langland's concern for absolute clarity on the subject of atonement and salvation. Differences between such passages are those of extent rather than of nature: the minuscule sketches are capable of expansion into robust allegorical scenes – they cry out for lively development.

Diagrammatic allegory   But there are forms of allegory in *Piers Plowman* which make no such claims upon us. By comparison, they are flat and unspectacular, and it is all the more important for us to understand their nature and function. Very frequently Langland uses an allegorical mode which is closely connected with a particular kind of medieval art: in fact, 'diagrammatic' is the best descriptive term to use of it. Although no exact sources have been identified, it seems possible that Langland was influenced by schematized drawings when he devised his allegory of the Tree of True-Love, growing in man's heart (C xix 6 ff.). Medieval moral treatises constantly used the image of the tree, formally divided into branches, leaves and fruit, as a way of expressing man's life, and his relationships to God.[15] And Langland could easily have been familiar with some of the more popular handbooks of the Middle Ages, made probably for the clergy, which gave 'clear visual representation, that the reader, in the midst of a complicated world of abstractions, might see and grasp the essentials'.[16] The descriptions of the Court of Truth (C viii 232 ff.) and the Barn of Unity (C xxii 320 ff.) which Piers Plowman builds for his spiritual harvest recall many manuscript drawings of allegorical buildings, quite as stiffly constructed and carefully labelled as Langland's:[17]

> He made a maner morter and Mercy hit hihte.
> And therwith Grace bygan to make a good foundement,
> And watelide hit and wallyde hit with hus peynes and hus passion,
> And of alle holy writt he made a roof after . . .
>
> (C xxii 326–9)

It may be that Langland worked from purely literary materials, and not from the visual arts: allegorical buildings were favourite 'exempla' with medieval preachers,[18] and a well-known 14th-century text such as the *Abbey of the Holy Ghost*,[19] with its meticulous architectural symbolism, might very well have been read and used by Langland. Its stone walls are 'festenande togedir with the lufe of gode', its 'syment or morter' is the 'qwykelyme of lufe and stedfaste by-leve . . .' (p. 323), its foundations are laid by Meekness and Poverty, its walls raised by Buxomness and Misericord (pp. 322–3). Or, again, his debt may be double: he may have gone to illustrated texts which provided him with both 'mental images and actual forms'.[20] His phrasing occasionally suggests direct debts to visual allegory; to a Tree of the Vices, for instance –

> Ac whiche be the braunches that bryngeth men to sleuthe?   (C VIII 70)

and to a Tree of the Vices compounded with a Tree of Life –

> ... Pruyde hit aspide,
> ... greuen he thenketh
> Conscience, and alle Cristene and cardinale uertues,
> To blowen hem doun and breken hem and bite atwo the rotes ...
>
>   (C XXII 337–40)

Here Langland draws upon two two iconographical features – Pride, traditionally at the base of the Tree of Vice, and animals (usually identified as Day and Night) gnawing at the roots of the Tree of Life.[21] The total image, built up from simple parts, is unusually complex.

But if our knowledge of particular sources must remain incomplete, we can still use art to help us define the character of Langland's diagrammatic allegory. For, like the didactic illustrations of the period, it is static, precise, and formalized: what it lacks in evocative power it makes up in faithful accuracy of communication. The description of the way to St Truth, offered by Piers Plowman (C VIII 157 ff.), illustrates this well. It is a route plan, laid before the 'thousand of men' who have been stirred by Repentance to 'go to Treuthe'. The passage has often been dismissed as dull and wooden. But, like the maps and diagrams of medieval religious art, it is not meant to be visualized *in depth*. It is a blue-print for action, not a picture or a full description of the action itself. Similarly, the meticulous setting-out of the tree of 'Trewe-love', planted by the Trinity in man's heart, with its flowers of 'benygne-speche', and its fruits of 'caritas', does not amount to a picture of a tree: it is nearer to an anatomical or botanical abstract of those physical entities, in which our observation is guided to general structural truths, rather than to variations within the species.

The same comment can be made about the final ploughing scene of the poem (C XXII 262 ff.). Piers 'tilling truth', with a team of the four Evangelists, and sowing in man's soul four seeds of the cardinal virtues, only barely achieves any sort of dramatic presence – in contrast to an earlier ploughing scene (C IX 112 ff.) when 'Perkyn with the pilgrimes to the plouh is faren' and we feel his sturdy personality directing the familiar activities of the land:

> Dykers and deluers diggeden up the balkes; ...
> And somme to plese Perkyn pykede aweye the wedes ...
>
>   (C IX 114, 118)

In the later passage, what matters above all is that each component part of the allegory should be accurately labelled and understood. For this vital account of the establishing of spiritual authority on earth, the fictional element is firmly disciplined. The idea that 'Grace gaf to Peers greynes, cardinales vertues/And sewe hit in mannes soule . . .' (C XXII 274–5) has visual and dramatic potential, but the poet is primarily concerned that we should understand what those grains were called, and what were their properties. Such allegory, in which nothing is left to chance, or to the reader's imagination, must be seen as the verbal equivalent of the elaborately inscribed and glossed art of medieval tract illustrations. In fact, it could be said that in its simple, linear quality it bears the same relationship to fully active and rounded allegory (the Meed episodes of C III–V, for instance) as the diagram does to the picture, with its deep perspective and its more complex media of communication.

Non-visual allegory But Langland can, on occasion, deal even more severely with our visual expectations. The way to Truth may have to be 'realized' as a map, and not as a picture, but there are times when his allegorical writing is clearly not meant to be visualized in any form whatsoever. We should be mistaken in trying to make ordinary visual sense out of the descriptions of Book, Wit and Anima:

> Thenne was ther a wihte with two brode yes,
> Boke hihte that beau-pere, a bolde man of speche. (C XXI 240–1)

> He was long and lene, ylyk to noon other. (C XI 114)

> Tyl I seigh, as it sorcerye were, a sotyl thinge withal,
> One withouten tonge and teeth . . . (B XV 12–13)

In these, the eye is refused any help: the details do not build up into a logically and visually acceptable whole, but are isolated symbolic features. Thus the protean shape of Anima – by turns Love, Conscience, Memory, Spirit, Reason – is properly denied a physical identity because this would limit and confine it: it is 'spirit specheles' (B XV 36) and only assumes bodily form to operate God's will in man. The staring eyes of Book refer us directly to the double authority of the opened Gospel pages – an immediate confrontation with the revealed word of authority, rather than with 'a bold man' *representing* authority. Wit is a particularly interesting example; the blocking of a visual response in the second half of the line ensures that the details 'long and lene' are rapidly related to the judicious and sober nature of the faculty of Wit, and not allowed any physical reality.

If, to us, this seems a somewhat cold and intellectualized allegorical mode,[22] we may be taking for granted that visual clarity and forcefulness are always the most effective means of communication for poet or artist. Langland's readers – many of whom were by no means unsophisticated – may have found the very impossibility of visualizing Book a short-cut to grasping its full significance. Clearly Langland could count upon a sensitive response to widely differing allegorical methods, and it is not surprising if, with his comprehensive and complex subject matter, he availed himself of all known devices to capture the understanding.

Allegory through exempla   Somewhere between the full-scale allegorical sequence and the formal allegorical design lie numerous passages of illustrative material, presented very much like parables or 'exempla' in the sermon literature of Langland's time. They do not make use of personification, and they are not diagrammatic: occurring mostly within the speeches of allegorical characters, they are short narratives within narratives. Their function is essentially allegorical; the events they describe are meant to be translated into more significant conceptual terms – and, in fact, are often translated on the spot. But their most distinctive feature is their positioning, for they are experienced by the dreamer at one remove. They are reported allegory. And, like their counterparts in the sermon literature of the Middle Ages, they are vivid and authoritative. Their message is trenchant, but it is also limited: because of their special, circumscribed position in the poem, they can only be developed to a certain extent. Sometimes Langland uses them to make a moral point more tellingly than subtly: the rough effectiveness of the friar's 'forbisene' (C XI 32 ff.) is deliberate. Here sinful man is likened to a man in a boat in peril of the waves and the wind, and 'waggynge of the bote', but saved by the very condition of his humanity, which is set in faith and love. Man falls, but not into the sea; he only stumbles within the boat, and is saved: he sins, but only within the body, which, in its frailty, draws God's compassion to it:

> 'So hit fareth', quod the frere, 'by the ryhtful mannes fallynge;
> Thogh he thorw fondynges falle, he falleth nat out of charite . . .'
> (C XI 41–2)

It is immediately obvious that the 'equivalences' will not stand up to rigorous analysis – the boat as the body is a tricky concept and, indeed, Langland's purpose in the whole episode is to show us a spiritual teacher who is only superficially clever. The friars are a constant butt of his irony and anger for their glib, popular methods and their presumption. But Langland will also use the 'forbisene' in a favourable context, as a swift means of clinching a protracted argument, or as a sudden – but not necessarily final – simplification of a complex debate. So Ymaginatif (in C XV 103 ff.) offers the puzzled dreamer a chance to resolve, temporarily, some of the long-worked-over problems of the debate on salvation by faith, good works, or learning. The man with learning, he says, can be compared to a man in the water who knows how to swim – he is more likely to be able to save himself from sinking, because of his knowledge:

> 'Ryght so,' quath that renke, 'reson hit sheweth,
> That he that knoweth cleregie can sonnere aryse
> Out of synne, and be saf, thow he synegy ofte.'   (C XV 110–12)

The sense of relief, shared by dreamer and reader, when they come upon what seems to be a neat and apt analogy, is short-lived. It soon becomes clear that there is much more to say about 'cleregie', and that Ymaginatif is certainly not envisaging it simply as a useful sort of expertise. Neither is he convinced that it is always as efficacious as his parable would have; his last words dwell upon truth, hope, and love, not upon learning:

> 'And where hit worth other nat worth, the byleyue is gret of treuthe,
> And hope hongeth ay theron to haue that treuthe deserueth;
> *Quia super pauca fidelis fuisti, supra multa te constituam*:
> And that is loue and large huyre yf the lord be trewe,
> And cortesie more than couenant was, what so clerkes carpen.'
>
> (C xv 213–16)

But, as an interim comment, the parable had value: it helped to concentrate the dreamer's diffuse thoughts, and it encouraged him to use his reason as well as his feelings when tackling the thorny problem of salvation for the simple and the learned.

But, if we can distinguish four or five allegorical methods at Langland's easy command, we should not think of them as operating independently of each other. Whatever approach is made – diagrammatic, exemplary, active – it is chosen to display or to investigate subject matter most effectively at that particular point, and may be preceded or superseded by an entirely different kind of approach. The merging of one type of allegory into another is a characteristic of *Piers Plowman*, not shared by many other poems of its time, though frequent enough in some types of devotional prose writing.[23] The most striking example of this comes in C XIX 106 ff. when the static allegory of the Tree of Trewe-love quickens, and in the presence of the dreamer becomes an active allegorical drama of man's subjection to the devil –

> For euere as Elde hadde eny down, the devel was redy,
> And gadered hem alle togyderes, bothe grete and smale,
> Adam and Abraham and Ysaye, the prophete . . .   (C xix 111–13)

and of the decision to save him –

> Thenne moved hym mod *in majestate dei*,
> That *Libera-Voluntas-Dei* lauhte the myddel shoriar
> And hit aftur the fende . . .   (C xix 118–20)

The passage from this to the actual historical moment of the Annunciation –

> And thenne spak *Spiritus Sanctus* in Gabrieles mouthe
> To a mayde that hihte Marie . . .   (C xix 124–5)

is, in one sense, a startling and brilliant move by Langland, but in another sense it is quite natural – a stage in a continuous process of evolution, from design to life, which in its turn is drawn back again to attitude and gesture.

Nor should we think that all in *Piers Plowman* which cannot be categorized as one or other type of allegory is therefore the very reverse of allegory, with only literal or realistic force. In the passages discussed so far, realism has been either subtly adjusted or subordinated to conceptual truth: no problem has arisen. But there are many parts of *Piers Plowman* in which Langland does not appear to be working in any allegorical mode at all. Moreover, it will be obvious that some very important characters in *Piers Plowman* – Piers himself, Abraham, Trajan, the Good Samaritan – are not easily accounted for 'allegorically'. And yet they are hardly to be described as 'real', or 'historical': Trajan is accepted by the poet as 'real', but also as 'symbolic' of salvation by works (C XIII 74 ff.): Abraham is double-named 'Faith' (C XIX 186, 200, 275, etc.).

REALISM AND THE FIGURAL APPROACH TO REALITY

Realism

It is here that we might try to consider more precisely the nature and the context of what often strikes the new reader as the distinctive *realism* of *Piers Plowman*: it is the realism of a good deal of later medieval literature and art. The Tavern scene of C VII springs to mind; Gluttony is diminished to the status of a real-life gluttonous 'cherl', weak-minded, unable to hold his drink, offensive to his fellow revellers. The stale and raucous atmosphere of the ale-house is perfectly captured by the poetry:

> There was leyhing and louryng and 'lat go the coppe!'
> Bargaynes and bevereges bygan tho to awake,
> And seten so til evensong, and songen umbywhile,
> Til Glotoun hade yglobbed a galoun and a gylle.
> His guttes gan to gothly as two grydy sowes ... (C VII 349–53)

And so, too, is the easy corrupt life of worthless beggars:

> In hope to sitte at even by the hote coles,
> Unlouke his legges abrood or ligge at his ese,
> Reste hym and roste and his rug turne,
> Drynke druie and depe and drawe hym thenne to bedde ...
> (C X 142–5)

No other medieval poet writes with such relish of the simple pleasures of a

> loof or half-loof other a lompe of chese ... (C X 150)

There is realism, too, in Langland's opening presentation of his focal character, Piers – a man who, whatever his high destiny, comes bursting into the poem full of ardent certainties, quick to anger and to pity, and humbly reconciled to the hard life of the land he tills:

> 'And a cow with a calf and a cart-mare,
> To drawe afeld my donge the whyle drouth lasteth.
> By this lyflode we mote lyue tyl Lammasse tyme.' (C IX 312–14)

The imaginative realism which makes his account of the Good Samaritan episode in C xx so much more than Biblical paraphrase also enables him to write of the Virgin as

> 'a pure, pore mayde, and to a pore man wedded . . .'

Both historical personage and parable figure come to life as we read; the Samaritan, with his practical charity:

> And to this wey he wente, his woundes to byholde.
> He perseyvede by his pous he was in perel to deye,
> And bote if he hadde recover the rather that ryse sholde he nevere,
> And unbokelede his boteles and bothe he atamede;
> With wyn and with oyle his woundes he can lithe . . .
>
> (C xx 65–9)

and his brisk instructions to the innkeeper:

> 'And that more goth for his medicyne I make the good ageynward,
> For I may nat lette', quod that lede, and lyard he bystrideth.
>
> (C xx 75–6)

Most affecting in its simple brevity is Langland's moment of Christ's crucifixion:

> And nayled hym with thre nayles, naked upon a rode
> And, with a pole, poysen putten up to his lippes . . . (C xxi 51–2)

and of the moment of death:

> '*Consummatum est*', quod Crist, and comsed for to swone,
> Pitousliche and pale, as prisoun that deyeth. (C xxi 58–9)

It would be easy to conclude, from material such as this, drawn from contemporary life, past history, and sacred fiction, that whatever the range and subtlety of his allegorical usages, Langland works most powerfully in literal, realistic modes of expression. In this, he could be associated with many others of his age – artists of all kinds. The increasing regard of the 14th and 15th centuries for familiar and recognizable fact provided the atmosphere in which Chaucer could begin to envisage the Canterbury pilgrims: in which Italian and Flemish painters could visualize Christ, the Virgin and Joseph as a sentient human family. Paintings such as Bellini's *Madonna of the Meadows*, with its pensive woman in an autumn landscape, or Campin's *Merode Altarpiece*, with its town vistas, and the Virgin receiving the angel in a spotless parlour, adjoining Joseph's workshop – these belong to a noonday world, where light falls simply and directly, recording shapes and surfaces without a shadow of implication.

But painting can often signal to us more urgently than poetry that it is dangerous to take an easy view of later medieval realism. The harrowing Crucifixion pictures of the time, the sculpted plague crosses of Germany and Scandinavia, score deep gashes in Christ's body not simply as a reminder of 'man's inhumanity to man' but as a symbol, in all the 'reality' of their depth and width, of the extent of divine compassion for fallen man. The quiet domesticity of Campin's altarpiece is 'real', indeed, but is also richly symbolic. Joseph, in his crowded carpentry shop, refers precisely (and, from the *literal* point of view, quite inappropriately) to the brutal death of the unborn child: he is boring holes in a spike-block, similar to those dragged by Christ in Flemish pictures of the *Road to Calvary*. Many of the tidy 'realistic' objects in Mary's parlour are meant to symbolize the power and innocence of the woman as a receptacle of the divine: the lily in a jug of Delft ware, the shining bronze laver, the candle and candlestick, and the window through which light streams, unimpeded.[24] This double use of realism is something we should entertain for *Piers Plowman* too, even when Langland is not committed to allegory.

Moreover, we should be wise to attend to the larger contexts of realism: here again the painters can achieve at a glance what the poet, with his more complex spatial problems, must take time to establish. But there are strong similarities, for instance, between Langland's use of realism in his tavern scene (C VII 353 ff.) and that of Hieronymus Bosch, in the Hell volet of his *Garden of Delights*.[25]

Bosch, a painter of almost photographic accuracy, but of deeply symbolic import, sets a perfect miniature study of tavern debauchery within a broken egg-shell. The egg-shell is the body of a despairing monster, who is rooted in the murky waters of hell, by two decaying tree stumps of legs. The further implications of *realism* are sharply brought to our attention by the strange, horrifying, and patently *unreal* nature of its setting. Langland's version of the same sort of material, with Glutton superbly rounding out the definition of excess, is not an isolable dramatic episode, but is set into a total vision of sin and redemption, as the words of Repentance, which close the confessions, make absolutely clear:

> 'God, that of thi goodnesse gonne the world make
> And madest of nauhte auhte and man liche thysulve,
> And sethe soffredeste hym to synege, a sykenesse to us alle,
> And for oure beste, as I beleve, what-so the book telle.
> *O felix culpa, O necessarium peccatum Ade!*　　　　　　　(C VIII 123–6)

The same could be said of Langland's picture of the honest poor –

> The wo of this wommen that wonyeth in cotes;　　　　　　　(C X 83)

it is a picture bordered by a larger discussion of divine justice and mercy. Truth's 'perpetual pardon' to Piers and his heirs on earth (C X 3 ff.) is itself a truth which modifies or gives a new perspective upon the terrible social injustices of the medieval peasant's lot.

The figural approach

This easy commerce between a vivid sense of the real, the actual, and an equally vivid sense of spiritual implication is as characteristic of *Piers Plowman* as it is of the whole outlook of the Middle Ages. And when we have finally distinguished and categorized all types of allegory in the poem, we are left with many vigorous creations which, without any loss of their 'reality', may still be intended as 'figures and foreshadowings of great things'.[26] For an understanding of these, we must look not to allegorical processes of thought and composition, but to *figural*.[27] The difference is important: in terms of biblical study, for instance, the allegorical method uses the literal, historical narrative merely as point of departure for various kinds of spiritual interpretation – the figural method maintains the historical truth of Biblical events, while seeing in them, simultaneously, a 'foreshadowing of greater things'. So the Old Testament is 'real', but is also a 'figure' of the New Testament: in its turn, the New Testament, fulfilling the Old, is an incarnation not quite complete. It is itself a promise or augury of the ultimate truth which will be revealed after the Last Judgment. It was an attitude which had far-reaching consequences, in art and literature: 'No student of the Middle Ages can fail to see how it provides the medieval interpretation of history with its general foundation and often enters into the medieval view of everyday reality' (Auerbach, p. 61). It is this which underwrites not only Langland's acceptance of the concrete, historical actuality of the life of Christ ('Jesus Christ on a Jews douhter alight'), of Abraham, or of the life of the patient poor in the 14th century, but also his ability to place them in a 'perspective of eternity' (ibid., p. 42). *Piers Plowman* bases itself firmly on a figural interpretation of reality,[28] upon 'the idea that earthly life is thoroughly real, with the reality of the flesh into which the Logos entered, but that with all its reality it is only *umbra* and *figura* of the authentic, future, ultimate truth, the real reality that will unveil and preserve the *figura*'.[29]

Such a statement makes it easier to understand the whole complex relationship between the real, the literal, the dramatic and the spiritual in *Piers Plowman*. It is easier, in particular, to understand 'characters' such as Abraham, the Good Samaritan, and Piers Plowman himself. For they are not presented as 'allegorical' in the same way as the personified abstractions Clergy, Study, Reason, are presented. On the other hand, they are not dealt with in terms of unequivocal realism. They shift easily between literal and symbolic modes. The simplest example is that of Abraham. He is movingly 'real' as the dreamer meets him –

> And thanne mette ich with a man on Mydlentens Soneday,
> As hor as an hawethorn and Abraam he hihte. (C XIX 183–4)

and hears him describe, almost conversationally, as an old man might, his vision of the Trinity:

128

'Hauest thow seyen this?' ich seide, 'alle three, and o god?'
'In a somer ich seyh hym,' quath he, 'as ich sat in my porche,
Where god cam goynge a-thre, ryght by my gate;
Tres uidit et unum adorauit.
Ich ros up and reuerencede god and ryght fayre hym grette,
Wesh here feet, and wypede hem, and after thei eten . . .'

(C XIX 241 ff.)

The 'reality of the flesh' is here – the accepted historical truth of the wife, the 'faire sone Ysaac', the sacrifice, the blood shed for God:

'Myself and my meyne . . .
Bledden blod for that lordes loue . . .'   (C XIX 254–5)

But equally present is the concept of Abraham as a 'type' of faith. Born in the Old Law, he looks towards, and is fulfilled by the New: he counsels the questioning dreamer in the name of Faith –

'Muse not to muche ther-on', quath Faith, 'tyl thow more knowe,'
(C XIX 200)

and he is explicit about the fact that his worship of God 'wyth wyn and wyth bred bothe/At ones on an auter' is a symbolic reference forwards to the sacrament instituted by Christ:

'And make sacrifice so, somwhat hit bytokneth:
Ich leyue that thilke lorde thenke a newe lawe to make.'   (C XIX 265–6)

The phrase 'somwhat hit bytokneth' ('signifies or symbolizes something') is a pointer to the double aspect of most of Abraham's speech: the father's sacrifice of the son, the blood shed for love, remind us of the event which the dreamer and Abraham are waiting to see completed – the sacrifice of Christ:

'. . . Crist is hus name,
That shal delyuery ous som day out of the deueles powere . . .'
(C XIX 283–4)

Similarly, Langland presents his Good Samaritan in a manner not totally realistic, but certainly not allegorical. Accepting Christ's parable as virtual sacred history, he develops the man warmly and vividly – but we are not allowed to forget that the action of the Good Samaritan is a 'figure' of Christ's rescue of wounded mankind. The Samaritan's words make this quite clear:

'Have hem excused,' quod he, the Samaritan, 'here helpe may nat availe,
Ne no medicyne under molde the man to hele brynge,
Nother Faith ne fyn Hope, so festred aren his woundes.
Withoute the blod of a barn he beth nat ysaved . . .'   (C XX 81–4)

The curiously 'echoic' quality of the language at times springs from the assumption that any 'real' event or action can be deepened and extended in significance by later happenings. Thus the Good Samaritan echoes or anticipates Christ's words when he speaks of the protective power of his doctrine of charity:

> 'For wente nevere man this way that he ne was here yryfled,
> Save mysulve sothly, and suche as I lovede.'   (C xx 90–1)

The 'character' of Piers Plowman might also be regarded as a natural product of figurative thinking. This highly complex creation of Langland's cannot be dealt with in terms of allegory or social realism. Piers comes before us with particular historical and dramatic force: he is rooted in the life of the 14th-century peasant –

> 'Bothe to sowe and to sette, the while I swynke myhte'   (C VIII 186)

He provides all classes of men with the very stuff of their earthly lives – grain *is* life. But from the beginning, we are made conscious that he 'figures' much more than this; he is in touch with mysteries, and it is instantly clear that he has it in his power to provide spiritual sustenance, as well as material. He expounds, to the crowd of waiting pilgrims, not only the Ten Commandments of the Way to God, but also the miraculous heart of the matter – the ultimate recognition of God, dwelling in man:

> 'And yf Grace graunte the to go in this wyse,
> Thow shalt se Treuthe sitte in thy sulve herte,
> And solace thy soule, and save the fram payne . . .'   (C VIII 254–6)

Here he hints at his own 'fulfilment', as incarnate spiritual wisdom and love: at the height of the poem, he comes before the dreamer's astounded gaze as the human 'form' of Christ (C xxi 8, and C xxii 6 ff.). His constant function – for dreamer and mankind – is that of guide to salvation and to the knowledge of God. In fact, when Christ says (in C xxii 260–1)

> 'My prower and my plouhman Peers shall beo on erthe;
> And for to tulye treuthe, a teome shall he haue.'

we accept his words as a confirmation of what has already been understood: Piers is 'incarnate revelation, that part of the divine plan of salvation which . . . is the miracle whereby men are raised above other earthly creatures . . .'[30] But, as is proper and natural to the figurative view, the 'man Piers' is never lost to our sight: indeed, for his complete spiritual fulfilment to take place, he must remain recognizable. What Langland shows us in Piers the Plowman is the operation of God through a man in a state of grace; he is not propounding, by personification, a theological concept of grace in humanity. Consequently, Piers is always famil-iar, always sought-for, acclaimed by the dreamer and other characters – 'the historical reality is not annulled, but confirmed and fulfilled by the deeper meaning' (Auerbach, p. 73).

The most dramatic visual illustration of this comes late in the poem, when the dreamer sees a figure who resembles both Piers and Christ:

> ... and sodeynliche me mette,
> That Peers the Plouhman was peynted al blody,
> And cam yn with a croys byfore the comune peuple,
> And ryght like in alle lymes to oure lord Iesu.   (C XXII 5–8)

Here, coalesced, in one staggering moment of revelation, is the man and the power working through him –

> 'the reality of the flesh into which the Logos entered . . .'

What, then, seems to be true is that some of the most significant parts of *Piers Plowman* cannot be dealt with in terms of allegory: neither can they be satisfactorily dealt with as areas of dramatic or social realism. Allegory provides Langland with a wide variety of literary methods for examining and displaying his wealth of material: it allows him freedom of play in many poetic styles and genres, ranging from fictions of strong visual content to designs of flat diagrammatic clarity. But allegory is no help to us when we come to consider how Langland 'built' his central character, Piers, nor is it helpful to our understanding of Langland's basic attitude to historical and spiritual truth – to his concept of 'reality'.

The essential structure of his thought is figural, with all that this implies about the co-ordination of the real and the spiritual. No-one could have felt more intensely and described more vividly the often claustrophobic 'reality' of later 14th-century England: this did not prevent Langland from 'interpreting' it in a perspective of eternity, both in the first disturbing long shots, and in the last terrifying close-ups of the poem –

the figural structure preserves the historical event while interpreting it as revelation, and must preserve it, in order to interpret it.   (Auerbach, 'Figura', p. 68)

FORM, STRUCTURE AND PROCEDURE

Form

Piers Plowman is related to numerous kinds of medieval literature, but cannot be exactly matched with any one. The most recent long study of the poem proposes 'six forms – three literary and three religious' as the 'genres in which Langland chose to work, and with which he attempted to give structure to his poem'.[31] Those poems range widely: the allegorical dream narrative, the dialogue or debate, the encyclopaedic satire, the complaint, the commentary and the sermon. Elements of all can be recognized – although, according to our own particular reading of the poem, we may differ in judging which genre was most significant. But when we have set out all the possible literary relationships of *Piers Plowman*, we are left with a problem: how can such varied allegiances encourage a poem of structural coherence, much less structural excellence? Critics have written of the 'confusion and even clash of genres'[32] in *Piers Plowman*: they have said that Langland 'hardly makes his poetry into a poem'.[33] It could easily be said that, in encompassing or in sampling from so many medieval genres, Langland abandoned hope of formal success from the very start. It is highly significant that the only writers prepared to describe *Piers Plowman* as no less perfect structurally than the *Divine Comedy* had to base their proof upon improbable theories of the poem's allegorical nature.[34]

Structure

The manuscripts of the poem tell us that *Piers Plowman* is divided into four large sections: in the C-text, they consist of Passus I–X, Passus XI–XVII headed '. . . de Dowel', Passus XVIII–XXI, '. . . de Dobet', and Passus XXII–XXIII, '. . . de Dobest'. It is not, of course, certain that Langland himself was responsible for such rubrics, but they do provide a sensible comment on certain important developments of subject matter and theme. To some extent, therefore, they ask us to consider a fourfold structural pattern in *Piers Plowman*. Passus I–X are mainly introductory – opening up the problems of remedial action, and generally indicating, to the reader as well as to the dreamer, that the road to salvation invites man urgently, but that the journey is painful, dangerous, and difficult. Passus XI–XVII investigate, under the heading of 'Dowel', the immensely complex business of 'doing well', as a guarantee of ultimate salvation: it is a section which probes deeply, often savagely, and it ranges, sometimes confusedly, over a whole area of thought and personal experience, weighing learning against faith, love and patience against knowledge, grace against good works. Passus XVIII–XXI, '. . . de Dobet', is a splendidly clear and positive vision of God's love, centred in the Crucifixion and Harrowing of Hell. 'Dobet' is far removed from the agonized self-searchings and castigation of 'Dowel'. The dreamer has passed beyond doubt and protest to a wondering acceptance of the rightness of God's purpose. Passus XXII–XXIII, '. . . de Dobest', both concludes and restarts the dreamer's search for salvation. The problem he first had stated for him, in the opening Passus, is restated, in grim terms, but 'Dobest' is now clear: the dreamer has his help, in God's Church, and in her ministers, symbolized ideally by Piers the Plowman. Such a summary does rough justice to the poem. The four headings correspond to well-defined stages in the growth of themes: however we may wish to define the central activity of the poem, Passus I–X introduce, Passus XI–XVII explore, Passus XVIII–XXI confirm, and Passus XXII–XXIII both conclude and initiate a fresh beginning.

Problems

But it would not be sensible to try to make a very precise scheme of those headings – 'Dowel, Dobet, and Dobest'. Langland, for instance, discusses all three concepts in the section named 'Dowel': the boundaries are not fixed, and material overlaps from one section into another. As we are told in the A-text, Dobet and Dobest are natural growths out of Dowel:

> Riht as the rose that red is and swote,
> Out of a ragged roote and of rouwe breres
> Springeth and spredeth that spicers desyreth.
> Or as whete out of a weod waxeth uppon eorthe,
> So Dobest out of Dowel and Dobet doth springe   (A x 119–23)

This the poem illustrates perfectly.

Nor are the definitions of those headings or concepts absolute: Langland uses 'Dowel, Dobet and Dobest' to express a number of connected ideas and states. The triple formulation itself would have been attractive and familiar to medieval readers, who would have kept in mind, as Langland developed and reworked his sections, many 'triads': the three 'estates' of labourer, knight and clergy: the three kinds of life – active, contemplative, and the mixed life of the administrative church, part thought, part action: the special categories within the enclosed religious life – the triple division of the contemplative way into active prayer and repentance, illumination, and meditation on the fruits of visionary experience. 'Dowel, Dobet, Dobest' could serve as useful summaries for any or all of these patterns of life and experience: indeed, over the length of the poem, Langland gives us good grounds for believing that this is exactly what he intended we should discover.[35]

It would not be honest, therefore, to base theories of the structure and organization of the poem on 'Dowel, Dobet and Dobest' except in a rather general way.[36] The same could be said of Piers Plowman himself as a structural device: his appearances are most important, his function essential, but he alone is not sufficient to pull together the diverse materials of the poem. It is true that he serves to point the major preoccupations of the four main sections: he is, among other things, successively 'Dowel', the obedient son of the Church, 'Dobet', the man of perfect love, and 'Dobest', the representative of God in his Church on earth. He often acts as a focus of attention, a clearing-house of themes. But he cannot be made to assume heavy responsibility for the ordering and unifying of the poem.[37]

Faced with these problems, some critics have preferred to shift their ground entirely, feeling that the poem's coherence lies in its 'perception of moral values and social principles, and . . . preoccupation with human material'[38] or, simply, in its 'truly imaginative' rather than 'formal . . . unity'.[39]

And yet there is something very compelling about *Piers Plowman*, which makes one dissatisfied with a wholesale contracting out of the matter, or any simple explanation of its structural defects. It is interesting to see how various are the theories put forward to justify what might – on a quick reading – be thought clear faults of construction.

The abruptness of the transitions, for instance, which could be due to Langland's carelessness or ineptitude, has been given much critical attention. There are the sudden switches of scene and subject: in Passus I, when, with a single word of introduction, the 'route of ratones' displace the crowd of lawyers and courtiers surrounding the King and Conscience; in Passus XIX, when Liberum Arbitrium hits out at the devil with the second 'plank' of the Trinity, and the Incarnation begins –

> And thenne spak *Spiritus Sanctus* in Gabrieles mouthe
> To a mayde that hihte Marie . . .,   (C XIX 124–5)

the frequent vanishings and appearances – in Passus XVI, when Piers Plowman speaks, unexpectedly, at the Feast of Patience:

> Quod Peres the Ploghman: '*Pacientes vincunt.*'   (C XVI 138)

These 'phenomena' have been variously explained – as a very deliberate imitation of the irrationality of dream experience,[40] as a literary method akin to photographic or cinematographic technique, with strong dramatic intent,[41] and, most recently, as the result of the influence of the Biblical commentary – 'it is like reading a commentary on an unknown text'.[42] In the case of the rapid comings and goings of Piers Plowman himself, another idea can be put forward. He operates more and more certainly, as the poem progresses, in a revelatory capacity: his 'materializations' will therefore be incalculable, since they are divinely controlled and only *intimations* of truth to the struggling dreamer. The transitory and sudden arrivals of Piers Plowman, in the 'Dowel' section of the poem, are directly related to the muddied state of the dreamer's comprehension: he has not yet won through to a steady vision of the Truth, but is allowed glimpses. Langland's contemporary, Walter Hilton, explains the situation in a different, but parallel, spiritual context – that of the contemplative 'touched' but not stabilized by divine favour:

. . . all such feelings come to them in that state *as it were unwarily*, for they come or they wit it, and go from them or they wit it, and they cannot come thereto again nor wit not where they should seek it . . . for they have not yet no homeliness with them, *but suddenly go and suddenly come* . . .[43]

There is the same sense of loss and fear in the poem when:

> ... wiste no man after
> Where Peres the Ploghman bycam, so priveliche he wente.
> And Resoun ran after and riht with hym yede;
> Save Concience and Clergie I couthe no mo aspye. (C XVI 149–52)

On this one point of structure alone, Langland has been both defended and condemned; the same holds for most of the larger structural features of the poem. Perhaps it is true that 'he could not properly solve his formal problem',[44] but the fact that *Piers Plowman* constantly tempts us to reconsider that 'formal problem' is some testimony to its holding power. It may be that we should regard Langland's loose-woven fabric of procedures not so much as a failure to achieve structural tautness as a way of capturing something of a kaleidoscopic vision of truth. In this sense, indeed, the substance of the poem *is* the form, and the reader of *Piers Plowman* must agree to be 'carried forward not merely or chiefly by the mechanical impulse of curiosity, nor by a restless desire to arrive at the final solution, but by the pleasurable activity of mind excited by the attractions of the journey'.[45]

Thematic versus narrative unity

In the first place, unless we accept that the poem has no proper narrative structure, we are still liable to make unjustifiable demands of Langland's handling of his material. Narrative as a form is utilized in the poem – often for long stretches as in the allegorical narrative of Lady Meed's marriage and trial – but Langland is not committed to a narrative structure in any continuous way. Here the poem differs from many other allegorical works of the period: a knowledge of the *Roman de la Rose* or of religious allegories such as the *Voie de Paradis* could not prepare us for its interrupted and suspended narratives. Langland *is* committed, however, to a continuous development of themes, which may be served, as needed, by various narratives. Thus the narratives of Holy Church and the dreamer (C II), of the Meed trial (C III–V), of the Confessions of the Seven Deadly Sins (C VII–VIII), of the ploughing of the half-acre (C IX), of the Feast of Patience (C XVI 26 ff.), are all, to some extent, isolable. They are illustrative of great moral themes which build up, irresistibly, while characters and *mise-en-scène* change and shift. Holy Church, Meed, Gluttony, Waster, Patience and the doctor of divinity do not reappear outside their own sections as 'characters in a narrative': they do reappear, however, as concepts. The themes of spiritual authority, reward, reformation of sin, patience and love, are constantly developed and enriched, but their narrative exposition frequently alters.

This explains, in part, the long delays and interruptions to which narratives as vital as that of the life of Christ are subjected. Passus XIX–XXI of the C-text cover events from the Annunciation to the Harrowing of Hell, but Langland's eye is as much upon the spiritual hinterlands of that story as it is upon its agonizing and triumphant sequence of events. It is significant that the story is introduced (at XIX 121) almost as an illustration of the allegory of the Tree of Charity and life, whose apples are menaced by the devil: the moral allegory precedes and is confirmed by the historical narrative. As the narrative develops, we are taken through Christ's life to the point when he is led before the Justices –

> Thus Iewes to the Iustices Iesus thei ladden ...   (C XIX 179)

but then the dreamer wakes, 'ner frentik' at the loss of his vision. He engages in a series of meetings and conversations with Abraham, Spes, and the Good Samaritan,[46] and during this time, when he is being taught various important truths about faith, love, the Trinity, temptation, amendment of life, the narrative of the Passion is suspended. There is a sense that something is waiting to be completed, just beyond the dreamer's grasp. All those he meets are on their way to Jerusalem – the Samaritan

> ... rapede hym to ryde the rihte way to Jerusalem.
> Bothe Faythe and his felawe *Spes* folewede faste aftur ...   (C XX 77–8)

but as the dreamer follows after, and interrogates the Samaritan, there is time for lengthy discussion about the nature of the Trinity. Nothing that is said in this discussion is irrelevant to the coming events of the Passion. It is of prime importance that the dreamer should understand the *total* significance of the Crucifixion: what will happen to Christ is an offence (although divinely accepted) against the Father and the Spirit. God is to be crucified for the sins of man:

> 'Ry3t so, faillede the sone, the syre be ne myghte,
> Ne holde, ne helpe, ne hente that he louede.'   (C XX 138–9)

When the dreamer next sleeps (C XXI 4), he still does not resume contact with the Passion narrative. His first vision is of Christ, 'semblable to the Samaritan, and somdeel to Peers the Plouhman', on his triumphal entry into Jerusalem. The sight is a confirmation of the preceding discussion of the Trinity; this knight, 'that cometh to be doubed/To geten his gilte spores ...' and who is to joust with Death in Jerusalem, is backed by the power of God:

> 'For no dynt shal hym dere as *in deitate patris*.'   (C XXI 25)

Before the dreamer rejoins the crowd at the trial of Christ, Faith puts him in possession of all the salient facts about the scenes he is to witness: nothing is left to chance – 'O mors, ero mors tua'. And at last (C XXI 35) the story is taken up again; it continues to the death of Christ, and there (at XXI 115) it again halts. The dreamer is poised on the very brink of the Harrowing of Hell and Resurrection episodes, and then, suddenly,

> ... I saw sothly, *secundum scripturas,*
> Out of the west, as it were, a wenche, as me thouhte.   (C XXI 117–18)

What follows is the well-loved, medieval allegorical debate of the Four Daughters of God. Before Langland will relate the Harrowing of Hell, he insists on making quite sure that his dreamer – and his readers – understand the terms and premises of the redemption of mankind. Before the event, the theory of the event. The debate of Truth, Righteousness, Mercy and Peace ranges over the whole course of sacred history, from the fall of Lucifer to the present moment of Christ's death. Consequently, when the Passion narrative is resumed –

> 'Soffre we', sayde Treuthe, 'I here and se bothe
> A spirit speketh to helle and bit to unspere the gates' –   (C XXI 271–2)

not only does it come with fresh dramatic force, but it can be seen as part of a vast historico-religious plan which will not be completely fulfilled until Judgment Day.

This is a particular instance of a general characteristic of the poem; Langland is always willing to abandon narrative continuity for the sake of greater richness of significance. Narratives for him are illustrative of themes. And if in one important way this reminds us of medieval sermon structure and technique – moral lessons enforced by short narratives, or 'exempla' – in another way it can be seen as the structural consequence of the figural approach to reality, discussed in the last section. For the assumption underlying it is that sequences of events are not laws unto themselves, but are connected, at every point, with other events, past and future, and with an all-embracing divine plan, in which they have always had a timeless existence. So narrative Truth must always be fulfilled by thematic; the narrative of the Passion

is not regarded as a definitive self-sufficient reality, nor as a link in a chain of development in which single events . . . perpetually give rise to new events, but *viewed primarily in immediate vertical connection* with a divine order which encompasses it.[47]

This 'vertical connection' is made explicit in Langland's handling of the Passion episodes: the 'horizontal' or sequential flow is constantly interrupted to point 'vertical' significances. It may even be that here we touch upon another reason for abruptness of movement in the poem: the ordinary causal sequences can, at any time, be violated or at least modified, in the interests of a higher order of truth.

The effects of such an attitude are very clear in medieval art of Langland's own period; the relationship of narrative to theme is particularly well illustrated in the drawings accompanying semi-popular devotional texts of the time. British Museum MS Additional 37049, which is a collection of diagrams, drawings and religious pieces in prose and verse, was probably intended to help less learned clergy in their tasks of instruction; its public may well have overlapped with the lower strata of Langland's clerkly readers. The manuscript has already been mentioned in this Introduction for its allegorical tree diagrams (see pp. 120–1, and plates 5, 6, 7): some of its miniatures range more widely. A double-page miniature, with the Seven Sacraments as its subject,[48] takes various narratives to implement that subject – the Fall of the Angels, the Fall of Man, the Crucifixion, sinners entering Hell and the saved entering Purgatory. But it is not primarily a narrative picture, and the narrative episodes remain isolable, even strangely dislocated, until the eye registers the thematic centre of the whole design: the Seven Sacraments, raying out from the crucified body of Christ. The *theme* of the picture is the salvation of man through Christ's death and the sacraments of the Church: its unity, even its sense, cannot be properly argued on any other formal grounds.

Such parallels can help us to understand Langland's 'shifting organization' of his poem, and the 'paradoxical space'[49] inhabited by the dreamer and his visions. As in the picture, we must not hope for continuous narrative structure: as in the picture, we should envisage space as a concept of timelessness, in which past, present and future coexist, and are equally powerful: 'in transcendence the revealed and true reality is present at all times, or timelessly'.[50] This is as much the 'context' of the sequence of events leading from the discovery of the Tree of True-love to the morning of Resurrection as it is of Holy Church's discourse to the dreamer in Passus II. For that discourse ranges restlessly over the Creation, the Incarnation and Passion: it sees man's present and future in immediate and vital relationship with Lucifer's pride, Adam's disobedience, and Christ's suffering:

> '. . . the fader that formede us alle,
> Lokede on us with love, let his sone deye
> Mekeliche for oure mysdedes, to amende us alle.'   (C II 163–5)

Cohesive elements

The dreamer   But there are certain formal binding elements in *Piers Plowman*. The constant presence of the dreamer should not be undervalued: it has dramatic, didactic and structural significance. In one sense, the dreamer acts as a compass needle held before us as we make our way into the poem: it is not so much that he leads us on a straight course as that he plots and defines for us the inevitable curves and detours of this most elaborate search for truth. Convinced, early on, by his earnest and pressing desire to *arrive* at truth,

> 'Teche me to no tresor, but telle me this ilke,
> How I may save my soule . . .'   (C II 79–80)

we are the more likely to endure the trials of the journey with some measure of good-humour and fortitude. Travelling with the dreamer is a consistent, though not a direct path: incentives and impetus remain constant, while the terrain may change rapidly. It is not simply a dramatic but a structural device to have the dreamer always inquiring for us, pushing ahead for us, taking the weight of our own ignorance and impatience upon himself, and ensuring that our confusion never goes unrecognized, or unattended. Whether we hear him asking our simple questions –

> 'Charite,' quod I tho, 'that is a thyng forsothe
> That maistres comenden moche; where may hit be yfounde?'
>
> (C xvii 284–5)

> 'Wher Sarrasyns,' ich seyde, 'seo nat what is charite?'   (C xviii 150)

protesting our fatigue with lengthy lectures, or brashly revealing our Faustus-like ambition –

> 'Alle the science under sonne and alle sotile craftes
> Ich wolde ich knewe and couthe kyndeliche in myn herte,'
>
> (C xvii 210–11)

he represents our own unbroken relationship with the poem – a predictable (though often fallible) commentator, who never ceases to work for us towards mastering and unifying the diverse materials of the visions.

The dream-vision   Then there is the dream-vision itself. Langland adopts this well-known and well-used medieval literary form, but adapts it for his own more complex purposes. The poem spans a whole series of dreams, and the rhythm of sleeping and waking becomes a familiar part of the process of reading. Both dreamer and reader learn and fall back, despair and understand, in great waves of waking and sleeping experience.

Structurally, the 'dream-device' is both vital and problematic. It serves, in the first place, to give some definition to the poem as a whole: the dreamer falls asleep in the first ten lines of the poem, and wakes in the last. And between those points, the acts and thoughts of one man's life-time are exposed – used as a centre for the widest survey of man and his destiny. This outer demarcation is important: it is not only a formal method of enclosing a vast amount of subject-matter, nor is it only a means of indicating to the reader that his close attention is required. We should give Langland full credit for the words used by the dreamer to describe his first encounter with the dream:

> And merveylousliche me mette, as I may telle.   (C I 9)

The 'miraculous' element in Langland's dreaming is very early stressed: like the contemporary dream poem, *Pearl*, *Piers Plowman* is concerned with revelation, as well as with action and discussion:

> My goste is gon in Godes grace
> In auenture ther meruayles meuen . . .   (*Pearl*, lines 63–4)

Backing Langland's dreams are statements like that of Job 33: 15–17:

In a dream, in a vision of the night, when deep sleep falleth upon men, in slumbering upon the bed; then he openeth the ears of men, and sealeth them in slumber . . .

And, from his own period, the words of Walter Hilton:

Ego dormio, et cor meum vigilat. I sleep and my heart waketh . . . The more I sleep from outward things, the more wakeful I am in knowing of Jhesu and of inward things. I may not wake to Jhesu, but if I sleep to the world . . .[51]

For the dream in *Piers Plowman* can indicate status as well as map out areas in the poem: to sleep may not only be a means of attaining a special vantage-point from which to view great expanses of man's past, present and future, but also a means of attaining a special position of privilege for the interpretation of that view. Though it often takes the dreamer a long time to benefit from what he sees and is told, he is, in sleep, receptive and open to whatever influences may be exerted upon him:

> a reasonable instrument wherein that he (Christ) worketh.[52]

The great dream-boundary of *Piers Plowman* marks out a potential field of revelation: it could be said, at its most significant, to define an area within which grace can freely operate. The last line of the poem:

> And sethe he gradde aftur grace tyl I gan awake   (C xxiii 386)

is therefore particularly meaningful. And this is the general sense in which the dream-device unifies and reconciles all the multifarious events, speeches and transformations in *Piers Plowman*. Langland is not likely to have been concerned with the irrationality of dream experience as a phenomenon, although the poem does appear, at times, to be counterfeiting it. But he did want to establish, within the dream, the possibility (and the acceptability) of a different order of naturalness in a world directly, and miraculously, subject to the workings of the divine will. The mysterious comings and goings of Piers Plowman are as unexpected, and yet as 'natural', as the workings of grace: the final search of the poem is for Piers and for grace in a world which has temporarily lost sight of both. It is 'natural', in this context, that the dreamer only comprehends within the dream, through grace, and often loses all sense of contact with truth and reality when awake:

> . . . 'Slepynge, hadde I grace
> To wyte what Dowel is, ac wakynge nevere!'   (C xiv 218–19)

The mounting urgency of the call towards sleep is a striking dramatic – and thematic – feature of the poem. Leisurely introductions to the dreams, with some concessions to the medieval literary morning of sun, birdsong and running water, give way to brief peremptory references:

... me lust to slepe ... (C XVI 25)

And if sleep, with its invitation to knowledge and understanding, becomes, at certain times, an almost compulsive force, the turning towards sleep is usually a signal of heightened awareness, a directive which *may* be momentous, for dreamer and reader. This, as it occurs over the length of the poem, like a warning-light, switched on and off, has obvious structural importance.

Waking episodes are often simply reflective pauses in the development of the poem: brief, slightly dazed recollections of the crowded and exciting events of the dream. So (C XVI 1–25) the dreamer muses over the long speech of Ymaginatyf, which has revealed to him how learning and humility and grace can be reconciled – 'al worth as god wole'. He picks up a few points made by Ymaginatyf – 'of Kynde and his connynge . . . how lovyng he is to uch a lyf . . . for alle he wisseth and yeveth wit . . .' – but his overriding desire is to sleep and learn more: 'me lust to slepe . . .' What follows, in sleep, is a particularly subtle and valuable lesson on how to put Ymaginatyf's *dicta* into practical use: the Feast of Patience, in which the dreamer is directly confronted with learning devoid of humility and grace, and is asked to make the most of the teaching offered by the doctor of divinity. 'Al worth as god wole' is not a sentiment that comes easily to the dreamer's lips as he sits next to placid Patience, and watches the display of hypocrisy at the high feasting table – 'this goddes gloton, . . . with his gret chekes . . .'

But there are many examples of Langland's use of sleep as an index of change and significance. At one point (C XII 167) the dreamer sleeps again, within his dream:

And in a wynkynge ich worth and wonderliche ich mette.

This second falling asleep is an unmistakable sign of a new direction in argument and procedure. The dreamer is in need of new direction: he has been receiving a substantial amount of teaching on the subject of Dowel, from such 'characters' as Wit, Study, and Clergy. Dame Study's scepticism about his fitness to receive such teaching – expressed with the tartness Langland usually reserves for his allegorical and academic ladies –

... 'Nolite mittere, ye men, margerie-perles
Among hogges that han hawes at wille' (C XII 7–8)

has been counterbalanced by Clergy's willingness to be constructive about Dowel, and to give sensible – if not very original – definitions of the three 'states'. But this in its turn is followed by an unexpectedly savage attack upon the dreamer by Clergy's wife, Scripture, who scorns him, for no apparent reason, only

141

throwing out the phrase 'seipsos nesciunt' as a positive clue (C XII 166). The new dream begins, and it comes in immediate response to the accusation of Scripture that the dreamer is very ill-informed about his inner self. His ability to receive and deal with such information as Wit, Study, Clergy have to offer depends upon a better state of self-knowledge. The dream-within-a-dream marks an attempt by the dreamer to come to closer grips with this problem: it is not a solution of the problem, but it meaningfully shifts the basis of the inquiry on to a deeper, more personal and private plane.

Within this dream, the wilful errors of the dreamer's life are brought under closer scrutiny: he is led by Fortune, seduced by the flesh, comforted by Recklessness:

'Ye, recche the neuere', quath Rechelesnes, stod forth in raggede clothes,
'Folwe forth that Fortune wol, thou hast ful fer to elde.'

(C XII 195–6)

The very serious limitations of his power to understand and reform are displayed, as he repents and corrects his way of life, only to fall into the error of rebuking Reason for apparent lack of attention to human affairs –

'I have wonder in my wit, so wys as thow art holden, . . .
That thow ne reuledest rather renkes then other bestes?'

(C XIV 185, 187)

As a result of his rebuke, he is thrown out of the dream: wilfulness is with him to the end! But all is not on the debit side: if Recklessness speaks, initially, for the dreamer's *selfish* carelessness, he comes to express, in warmest terms, a doctrine of *spiritual* carelessness, or reliance upon God's provision for the dedicated Christian:

'For-sak al and sue me and so is thi beste.'   (C XIII 166)

The long and moving speech of Recklessness 'in a rage' against Clergy argues the sufficiency of grace, and the superior strength of patience, poverty and love: when he comes to an end (at C XIV 128), it is clear that he stands for a double-sided tendency in the dreamer. The same swift extravagance of feeling that leads him to a life of heedless rebellion, to anger and frustration when encountering the 'academic' personnel of his religion – Clergy, Scripture, and Study – leads him also to identify in sympathy with those who will risk everything for God.

Recklessness speaks for the good and the bad in his nature, and the inner-dream episode takes a close-up view of his chances of success in the search for truth. It magnifies – even distorts, by magnifying – a small area of the human organism, and shows us how the instincts may often lead astray, but how some intuitions may be confirmed as sound, and channelled, under guidance, into good.

In such cases, and many others, the dream operates in a clearly defined way. But we should not press its structural importance too far. It is not always true that Langland uses the dream meaningfully. On one occasion at least the dreamer wakes, without ever having slept (C xx 332). There are times when it is difficult to see how Langland distinguished – and expected his readers to distinguish – the different quality of experience received in waking and sleeping states. This would not matter if we could always bring to Langland's defence the idea that he might have deliberately blurred or removed those boundaries in keeping with some concept of psychological or spiritual truth. There is some point, for instance, in thinking that the very easy movement between sleeping and waking in C xxi 471 ff. is significant: the church-bells in the vision of the Resurrection set the dreamer awake, direct him (and his family) to church, and thence back to sleep (C xxii 5). At this stage the dreamer has reached some firm understanding of God's purposes: he is *at one* with his visions, and can sum up their meaning:

> '. . . crepe to the cros on knees and kusse hit for a jewel . . .
> And hit a-fereth the fende, for such is the myhte . . .'

> (C xxi 475, 478)

The flight to sleep as a desperate attempt to draw order out of living chaos is no longer a dramatic necessity, and the dreamer slips again, almost peacefully, into his next vision:

> In myddes of the masse, tho men yeden to offrynge   (C xxii 4)

Examples such as this should not blind us to the fact that Langland's handling of dream-procedures in some parts of the poem is arbitrary. As a structural device it has a variable role, and he seems to have been capable of using it in a purely mechanical as well as a richly significant way. His interest and attention fluctuate.

The search   But this could not be said of another feature of the poem – the search or quest. The basic and recurrent pattern of *Piers Plowman* is that of a journey or a series of journeys – interrupted frequently by static debates, and often halted by allegorical incidents,[53] but always resumed in one form or another. Thus the dreamer – like many of the characters in the poem – is either on the move, or on the brink of movement. He meets others, who sometimes overtake him and pass on, sometimes persuade him to go with them. He sees journeys begun by others, arrested, fulfilled. The last thing he reports from his dream is the resolution of Conscience to 'go on pilgrimage' to find Piers Plowman: the first real advancement of the poem is his own resolution to pursue the goal of Truth.

Between those two moments, the dominant theme and design of the poem is the search: it is no light comment when Ymaginatyf addresses the dreamer as one '. . . that sekest after weyes' (C xv 157). For 'seeking after ways' is the most characteristic and continuous form of action in *Piers Plowman*, and, perhaps, its most positive structural asset. Once the reader has accepted the fact that he, with the dreamer, is not merely a witness to dramas involving others, nor a passive recipient of information, but is expected to engage directly in the gradual discovery of truth for himself, he can be more easily reconciled to the apparent inconclusiveness and deviousness of the poem's movement. That is, once he has accepted and therefore undertaken the journey, he has accepted the conditions of journeying – exhilaration mingled with frustration, a sense of purpose, an apprehension of the unknown shot through with misgiving as the landscape widens and changes unexpectedly.

For Langland, as indeed for the whole medieval world, the metaphor of the journey was both commonplace and extraordinary. It is drawn readily from the everyday business of travelling in the 14th century as an illustration of the different ways of rich and poor towards God (C XIV 33 ff.). Merchant and messenger, we see them dealing with their papers, paying tolls, taking short-cuts through the wheatfields, on their way to Winchester fair. But it is used most seriously in pilgrimage form: the whole of life, from birth to death, was regarded as a pilgrimage, equally beset by perils as by aids to salvation. Christ's life, the pattern for mankind, had been essentially one of wayfaring, and medieval man never forgot that on both the dedicated pilgrimage and on the everyday journey Christ's presence might again, as to the disciples on the road to Emmaus, be revealed:

> 'Witnesse in the Paske-woke when he yeode to Emaus,
> Cleophas ne knew hym nat, that he Crist were,
> For hus poure aparail, and pilgrimes clothes . . .' (C XIII 122–4)

Nor is it surprising that a poem which so much concerns itself with the problem of salvation should take as its dominant structural device that very metaphor of the 'via' used by Christ of himself: 'I am the way, the truth, and the life: no man cometh unto the Father, but by me' (John 14: 6).[54]

The dreamer either sees or takes part in many journeys, as the poem opens out: some can be seen as sections of longer routes, some are tangential: some overlap others. But there is no doubt that they are Langland's happiest solution of the formal problems his vast collection of materials set him. At least six important searches are undertaken in the poem – for St Truth, for Dowel, for Clergy, for Parfitnesse, for Charity, and for Piers Plowman. But it would be wrong to suggest that these are in any way disconnected, or in simple sequence. Although they seem, when baldly defined, to be so disparate in aim, they are closely linked. In fact, the greatest advantage of the search or journey form for Langland is that multifarious paths, involving a variety of travellers, stopping-places and incidents, and setting out, apparently, in different ways, can be gradually or dramatically revealed as similar, even identical in direction and end-point. Thus a vast area of material can be traversed and explored, but a final unified perspective of the whole can be achieved. Many of the searches upon which the dreamer embarks bring him to the same resting place – and in one vital sense all searches in the poem, whether his or not, are variations of the one great search for St Truth, recommended by Holy Church at the very beginning of the poem (C II 203, etc.), again by Reason (C VI 199), and first turned into a practical proposition by Piers himself (C VIII 182 ff.).

Although the pilgrimage to St Truth, as it is envisaged by repentant mankind –

> A thousend of men tho throngen togyderes,
> Criede upward to Crist and to his clene moder
> To have grace to go to Treuthe – god leve that they mote!
>
> (C VIII 155–7)

– is never literally completed, all the searches which succeed it are, essentially, for St Truth or Truth. They unfold out of the first search in a way which is more like a process of organic growth than deliberate literary design. So the search for Dowel is initiated by the words of the Pardon, sent by St Truth to Piers Plowman and the hopeful pilgrims, encouraging them to abandon pilgrimage and stay at home (C X 1–8). The injunction 'Dowel . . . and god shall haue thy saule' (C X 289) formulates, in a different way, the dreamer's first request for help – 'how I may save my soul' – and Holy Church's advice – 'Truth is the best'. Dowel replaces Truth as the dreamer's immediate goal, but as a warning that this is no side-tracking or diminution of great issues, the search for Dowel is almost immediately rephrased in triple terms – Dowel, Dobet and Dobest: Thought replies to the dreamer

> 'Dowel and Dobet,' quod he, 'and Dobest the thridde
> Aren thre fayre vertues and ben nat fer to fynde.' (C XI 76–7)

The dreamer is, in fact, still pursuing Truth, but in its component parts – three 'true' ways of life, states of grace, grades of charity. The problem of 'seeking truth' has been broken down into smaller, more manageable units for investigation. And the various journeys which are recommended and undertaken while the search for 'Dowel, Dobet and Dobest' is still under way – the journeys to Clergy, to Parfitnesse, to Charity – are all exploratory within the terms of that search. Clergy is consulted as the voice of authority on Dowel, and the road to salvation –

> 'To Clergie shult thow neuere come, ne knowe what ys Dowel . . .'
>
> (C XII 113 ff.)

Parfitnesse is sought as an alternative route towards Dowel: the dreamer follows Conscience 'with gret wil', who has already turned against Clergy, and decided

> 'With Pacience wol I passe, parfitnesse to fynde.' (C XVI 184)

But it is Dowel they speak of, as they travel: the search has changed course, but not ultimate direction:

> And as thei wente by the wey, of Dowel gan thei carpe.   (C XVI 190)

And when the dreamer asks for help in his search for Charity –

> 'Leve *Liberum Arbitrium*,' quod I, 'I leve, as I hope,
> Thow couthest telle and teche me to Charite, as I leve?'   (C XIX 1–2)

it comes not only as the climax to numerous affirmations of love as the underlying principle of Dowel, Dobet and Dobest, but is specifically called up by the statement that salvation can only be achieved through belief in Holy Church, which *is* belief in Charity. The dreamer asks

> 'What is holychurche, frend?' quoth ich; 'Charite,' he seyde . . .
> (C XVIII 125)

And the way to heaven is once more opened out:

> 'And that is Charite, my leue childe . . .
> Contrarie hure nauht, as in conscience, yf thou wolt come to heuene.'
> (C XVIII 148–9)

Such words make it clear that the nature of the quest has not really changed since the dreamer first asked Holy Church 'how I may save my soul'. And, indeed, from this point forward, the quest is seen less in triple than in unified concepts, as if the time for diversified exploration is past, and the time for rejoining main routes is near. Although the last two sections of the poem are labelled 'Dobet' and 'Dobest', the activity of the poem from Passus XVIII onwards is increasingly centred upon Charity and upon Piers the Plowman, who exemplifies and encloses within himself the trilogy, Dowel, Dobet and Dobest, and who finally reveals Truth in human form.[55] There is no contradiction in the fact that the poem starts out to seek Truth, and ends by seeking Piers Plowman: Langland is as much concerned to provide means as he is to provide goals. The perplexity of the dreamer, when he is told by Holy Church in Passus II to seek Truth, is gradually replaced by a sense of relief as he realizes he can seek Piers Plowman to reveal that Truth: this is as fine a witness to Langland's penetrating knowledge of the human predicament as it is to his dramatic inventiveness.

Finally, it is important to see that the directions given by Piers for the arrested pilgrimage to Truth (C VIII 204 ff.) are not wasted. They lay down general guiding lines for all later quests. We are meant to find that the dreamer, asking for help as he seeks a variety of goals, receives familiar answers and recognizes old familiar routes. So the journey to Clergy (itself a part of the search for Dowel) proceeds, as Piers had forecast, through humility and patience and avoidance of sin. The dreamer appeals for 'som tokne, for tyme is that I wende', and gets from

Dame Study brief confirmation of what Piers has said – that obedience and active virtue are prime requisites for the pilgrim:

> 'Aske the heye wey,' quath hue, 'hennes to Suffre –
> Bothe-wele-and-moche-wo yf thow wolt lerne . . .
> Bothe wommen and wyn, wratthe, yre, and slewthe,
> Yf thow hem vse other haunte, haue god my treuthe!
> To Clergie shult thow neuere come, ne knowe what ys Dowel.'[56]
>
> (C XII 107–8, 111–13)

And when Clergy is found, his advice about how to reach and recognize Dowel confirms once more Piers' doctrine of obedience to the ten commandments,[57] and belief in the miraculous atoning power of the Incarnation:[58]

> 'By Cryst,' quath Clergie, 'yf thow coueyte Dowel,
> Kep the ten commaundemens and kep the fro synne;
> And by-leyf leelly how godes sone a-lyghte
> On the mayde Marie . . .'
>
> (C XII 142–5)

Perhaps the most significant fact to observe is that whatever the nature of the search, and whoever the guide, whoever the seeker, Langland never allows dreamer or reader to forget the emphatic statements made by Piers, so early on, about love. Love 'roofs over' the court of Truth (C VIII 237–8) and the travellers to that court are urged to discover in their own hearts Truth enshrined in love (C VIII 257–8).

The austere Dame Study recommends love as the 'clue' to Dowel, Dobet and Dobest:

> 'Lerne for to louye, yf the lyke Dowel,
> For of Dobet and of Dobest here doctor is dere Loue.' (C XII 135–6)

Clergy reinforces this in his discussion of Dowel, seeing love as the crown of faith:

> 'Thus Byleyue and Leaute and Loue is the thridde,
> That maketh men to Dowel, Dobet, and Dobest.' (C XII 161–2)

The essence of the search for Parfitnesse is sacrifice of all for love: pilgrims moving on this lonely path must travel by love:

> 'And for goddes loue leueth al and lyueth as a beggere.' (C XVII 105)

It comes as a natural conclusion that when the dreamer asks to be directed to 'charite' (C XIX 1 ff.), he is led to a country called 'cor-hominis', in which the tree 'true-love' grows. Piers' original assurance that the questing for Truth will end in love, in man's own heart – '. . . charge Charite a churche to make/In thyne hole herte, to herborwe alle trewe'[59] – is here confirmed. The dreamer has now, in fact, advanced along that road to Truth sketched out by Piers: he stands in the land of the 'hole herte', 'cor-hominis', and sees Truth and Love face to face –

> 'The tree hatte Trewe-love,' quod he, 'the trinite hit sette'.   (C XIX 9)

But confirmation is also given by the very last search of the poem, announced by Conscience, and set towards Piers Plowman (C XXIII 380 ff.). In a strange and powerful way, the directions first given by Piers are proved not only upon the dreamer's experience, but upon that of Piers also. For in the centre of Piers, as 'Dowel', lie also 'Dobet', love, and 'Dobest', spiritual authority. Piers tells us, and the poem then reveals to us, by his successive appearances and transformations, how Truth and Love live in the heart of man:

> 'For Peres love the palmare, that impugnede ones
> Alle kyne konnynges and alle kyne craftes . . .
> And preveth by puyre skyle inparfyt alle thynges,
> Bote lele love and treuthe. . . .'   (C XVI 131–3, 136–7)

The stirring of Conscience towards Piers Plowman is, in its deepest sense, the stirring of man's desire for regenerative growth: to seek Piers Plowman is not only to seek spiritual authority, the ideal Pope, but to seek the inner sources of good, the materials and energy for reform, the prerequisite for life's journeying.

It has been possible to distinguish for *Piers Plowman* a four-part structure, enclosed and subdivided again by dream-boundaries, threaded through by the constant presence of the dreamer-figure, punctuated by significant appearances of Piers Plowman, and patterned by recurrent forms of search or pilgrimage. Even this complex statement does not give an entirely accurate impression of the experience of reading the poem: an experience we may find both richer and, at times, more confusing than any analysis or abstract can suggest.

Procedures

For Langland's procedures, his manipulative habits, can strike the reader as strange. We may be able to accept the need to look for thematic and not for narrative continuity in the poem, but the building of themes does not go forward in a direct and obvious manner. So many subjects seem to be held under consideration at the same time: Langland's attention is frequently diverted by fresh objects and ideas. We can often detect a leaning to the impromptu in his dealings with chosen material. It is not always clear on what principles he becomes expansive or economical: on the one hand, he shows himself fond of insistent, repetitious treatment of themes; on the other, only too willing to abandon or curtail or interrupt a sequence of thought. Evidence of planning we can discern, but it is clear that Langland had no intention of being constrained by plan. To put this down simply to his unpredictable or idiosyncratic nature would not be just, however. Difficult as he may sometimes be to follow, he had good precedent for the more unfamiliar of his movements – the techniques and procedures of the looser medieval sermon, constructed 'd'après un plan dont la logique nous échappe, nourris d'associations, d'idées qui ne nous semblent ni naturelles ni surtout nécessaires'.[60] Étienne Gilson's analysis of this elusive sermon logic is useful and appropriate to a reading of *Piers Plowman*: Langland often preaches – either openly or through his characters:[61]

> . . . prechours of godes wordes
> Sauen thorgh here sermons mannes soule fro helle. (C VIII 88–9)

It is natural that we should find strong similarities between his poem and the literature of the medieval pulpit, not only in basic material, but also in techniques of exposition.[62]

Sermon techniques

Digressive and diffuse procedures For our present purposes, it is important that the accepted theory of medieval sermon composition, aiming at the fullest possible 'drawing-out' of its themes, allowed and even encouraged sudden departures from plan, and maintained loose-knit unity by a linking system of repetitions, correspondences and cross-references. The frequent twists and abrupt changes of direction in *Piers Plowman* can be quite easily explained in terms of the 'logique interne' of the pulpit, whose theorists were eager to claim freedom from the tyranny of form, when moral fruitfulness was an issue: 'edification of souls is more to be prized than continuity of discourse'.[63] Langland often demonstrates the 'déplacements brusques des prédicateurs', the unannounced flight from a subject in hand 'chaque fois que son zèle pour les âmes propose à son imagination quelque nouvel objet'.[64] What may sometimes look like a wilful disregard for orderly procedure or an inability to control the flow of thought may be based upon a conviction that the impulse to teach must not, on any purely formal or artistic grounds, be resisted. The priorities are spiritual.

On one occasion, at C XXI 360–1, Langland admits that he has digressed from his main theme for the sake of such 'edification'.

> (A litel I over-leep for lesynges sake,
> That I ne sygge as I saw, suynde my teme!)

The example is a decisive one: Langland has apparently been struck by Satan's use of the word 'lesynges' to Lucifer (C XXI 350, 351) and has interrupted the account of the Harrowing of Hell to enlarge on the significance of 'lying' for his own age:

> Beth ywar, ye wyse clerkes and witty men of lawe.　　　　　(C XXI 357)

It is, on a first reading, surprising that Langland should have been willing to delay that magnificent exchange between Lucifer and Christ –

> 'What lord artow?' quod Lucifer. A voys aloud saide . . .

– for such a comparatively minor piece of teaching: on reflection, it seems entirely characteristic, and, within its own terms of reference, quite logical – 'magis . . . aedificatio quam . . . continuatio . . .'

But it is not only dislocation of flow which can be better understood by reference to sermon theory. One of the most characteristic and, to the new reader, most frustrating, features of *Piers Plowman* is Langland's circuitous method of dealing with themes. The long speech by Wit, for instance (beginning at C XI 127), is, to us, a very diffuse answer to the dreamer's desire to know 'wher Dowel and Dobet and Dobest ben in londe . . ./And what lyues they lyuen, and what lawe they usen . . .' (lines 123, 125). An illustrative allegory of the castle of Sir Dowel, man's soul, is interrupted by a description of Kynde, the creator of the castle, and succeeded by a special examination of Inwit, guard of the castle, and rational power of the soul. Those who misused this faculty are reviewed – Lot, Noah, Herod: the attack then widens to take in man's deficiencies in virtuous living and in charity, and the Church's responsibility for failure to enforce the lessons of Christ. By the time Wit returns to this original theme, and gives the dreamer a compact definition of Dowel, Dobet and Dobest, the Fall, the Flood and contemporary marriage-broking have all been dealt with. While nothing in the speech is irrelevant to the three states or lives, it can hardly be called a systematic treatment of the subject.[65]

Langland would probably have offered no defence of this. For a good part of medieval sermon theory and practice would have encouraged him to feel that a theme might be developed quite as usefully and pleasurably in a woven fabric of statement and variation as it might be in simple sequence. If repetition were involved, it served to enforce the message of the theme: if the poet – or the preacher – elected to traverse his material much in the way that the weaver's shuttle traversed the web, he could at least guarantee that his meaning would be covered thoroughly and closely. To accept this is not necessarily to find passages such as those cited above any more attractive to modern taste: they do, however, become more intelligible and seem more responsible in their approach.

Repetitive devices　　But pulpit theory encouraged Langland in other methods of work which actively contributed to the overall unity of the poem. *Piers Plowman* makes full use of those repetitive devices, recommended by sermon manuals as teaching aids – not only within individual passages, as 'word-play', but as 'foretastes and echoes'[66] running the whole length of the poem.

The subject of the Seven Deadly Sins is an obvious example. Lightly touched upon in the first passus,

> ... this wastors with glotony destrueth. (C I 24)

> ... summe putte hem to pruyde ... (C I 25)

> Slep and also slewthe sueth suche ever. (C I 46)

> And leneth it lorelles that lecherye haunten. (C I 75)

it is written in more deliberately in Passus III (lines 79 ff.) where Lady Meed's marriage charter describes a whole world of evil feature and attribute – 'the erldom of enuye and yre', 'the lordshep of lecherye ...' So far, the sins have been viewed objectively, as abstract qualities: in Passus VII, through their confessions, they are personalized, in horrifying detail. This thorough scrutiny of sin, its various faces and its subtle operation, confirms what has gone before, and, for the future, makes it impossible for us to accept even the briefest mention of sin without bringing to it the fearsome associations of Passus VII.

Thus, when Patience sketches the seven deadly sins (in C XVII 44 ff.), proving that they have no strength against poverty, we are able to provide the passage with a deep hinterland of evil and suffering. And, when the poem begins to come full circle, and Antichrist attacks (C XXIII 69 ff.), the fact that many of his officers are deadly sins is grimly familiar. Their re-entry into the poem is dramatically effective –

> And Pryde hit bar baldly aboute (C XXIII 70)

> This Lecherye leyde on with lauhyng chere (C XXIII 114)

> Thenne cam Covetyse ...
> And armed hym in avarice and hungriliche lyvede.
> (C XXIII 121, 123)

But there is, by now, cause for hope as well as for despair: we have already seen them rendered powerless – once by Repentance (Passus VIII) and once by Poverty (Passus XVIII). Their antics can now be more soberly judged than when they first erupted into Langland's vision, on the Field full of Folk.

The presence of these 'foretastes and echoes' – so reminiscent of the verbal correspondences used by preachers to link the various parts of their sermons together – means that Langland's poetry often makes its mark cumulatively. The speech of Christ, after the Harrowing of Hell (C XXI 404 ff.), has been singled out for its great wealth of significance: more precisely, every phrase in it reverberates, drawing verbal and conceptual powers from close surroundings and distant regions of the poem.[67]

A passage such as this, in its relationship to the rest of the work, points to one very characteristic way in which *Piers Plowman* operates upon us. For Langland,

like many medieval preachers, allowed main themes to act as magnets, attracting
to themselves a rich abundance of expressive associations. The central themes of
sin and love are 'expressed' throughout the poem in innumerable variations and
transpositions; though the method may be repetitive, it does ensure that when the
dreamer asks one of his last questions –

> 'Consaileth me, Kynde', quod I, 'what craft be beste to lere?'
>
> (C XXIII 206)

the answer not only rings with immediate authority, but echoes back through the
poem, harmonizing and unifying it:

> 'Lerne to love', quod Kynde, 'and leef alle othere'.   (C XXIII 207)

THE POETRY OF PIERS PLOWMAN

Over the last few years, increased attention has been paid to Langland as a poet:[68]
this means that it is no longer necessary to set out all the old charges against him,
or to proceed entirely on the defensive. It is now possible to claim recognition for
the amount of fine poetry which exists in a work of this size before offering
apologies for the inferior writing. Langland's status is secure enough for us to
bring comments from the *Biographia Literaria* to bear upon our judgment of *Piers
Plowman*:

... a poem of any length neither can be, nor ought to be, all poetry. Yet, if a harmonious
whole is to be produced, the remaining parts must be preserved in keeping with the
poetry.[69]

A case can here be made for Langland, as it can be for Wordsworth in *The
Prelude*, or for Milton in *Paradise Lost*.

It is also possible to recommend Langland's poetry to the modern reader as the
most accessible of medieval verse: lacking the sumptuous vocabulary, the contorted syntax of many other alliterative poems, and the often elaborate metrical
patterning of the Chaucerian 'school', it comes closer than anything else in its
period to modern accentual verse. The approximation of its grammar to that of
ordinary speech, the simple vividness of its language, give us a direct line of
approach to *Piers Plowman*:

> Adam, the whiles he spak nat, hadde paradys at wille,
> Ac when he mamelede aboute mete and musede for to knowe
> The wisdom and the wit of god, he was put out of blisse.
>
> (C XIV 227–9)

It is easy for us to understand and appreciate the flexibility of Langland's line:
it is the most versatile of all medieval forms – able to encompass the free
conversational rhythms of

'What manere mynstralcie, my dere frend,' quath Conscience,
'Hast thou used other haunted al thy lyf-tyme?'   (C XVI 196–7)

as well as the formal, processional movement of Christ's speech at the Harrowing of Hell.

And it is no longer necessary to spend much time proving Langland's poetic ability: when he wished, he could polish and perfect a line – compare his last version of Christ's words to Lucifer

'May no pyement ne pomade, ne presiouse drynkes
Moiste me to the fulle, ne my furste slakke . . .'   (C XXI 412–13)

with his earlier version

'May no drynke me moiste, ne my thruste slake . . .'   (B XVIII 366)

And when he wished, he could avail himself of verbal devices:

'At churche in the charnel, cheorles aren uvel to knowe,
Other a knyght fro a knaue, other a queyne fro a queene.'   (C IX 45–6)

'And riht as the gylour thorw gyle bygiled man formest . . .'   (C XXI 164)

More generally, it is now possible to demand a sympathetic hearing for a poet whose attitude to his art is above all honest, whose principles may not always be conducive to 'fine writing', but will always discourage empty showiness of style. Langland's poetry is at its best when his religion and his imagination are in perfect accord, and direct, jointly, his verbal skills. If his faith had the right to set 'imprimatur' to his poetry, it had also absolute right to inspire and sustain it. In this context, rapid fluctuations of poetic quality from a work which has been justly called 'at once magnificent and impoverished'[70] are to be expected. The great Christian themes of suffering, patience and love, the great Christian mysteries of incarnation and resurrection, constantly fire Langland's verse:

For the hye holygost shall heuene to-cleue,
And loue shal leepe out after into this lowe erthe.   (C XV 84–5)

But his dedication to a primarily religious purpose – 'how I may save my soul' – may, at times, command from him verse in which everything has been reduced to the bare bone of sense. Piers Plowman's directions for the pilgrims to Truth, or Wit's discourse to the dreamer on Dowel, and Kynde and Inwit (C XI 127 ff.), consist of nothing but information to be absorbed by the reader and dreamer. On such occasions – and there are many similar – we are not called upon to be moved or exhilarated, but only edified. We cannot commend the *poet*, but we can, still, respect the man of religion. Whether we like it or not, it is as a man of religion that Langland would have expected his age and succeeding centuries to remember him. It would probably be more rewarding for us to admire the ways in which his devotion so often inspired and nourished his poetry than to regret the ways in which it diminished it.

We should remind ourselves that, in the medieval period, the use of verse did not necessarily commit the writer to 'high art'. For an age in which literature still performed many of its traditional oral functions, verse, rather than prose, was the more usual, the more normal medium of expression. The really complex and difficult works of the period, written for highly specialized groups of readers, were written in prose: The *Cloud of Unknowing*, for instance. Verse covers the whole spectrum of medieval taste. As well as the 'court' poets, such as Chaucer and his equally sophisticated contemporaries, the alliterative poets of English provincial centres, whose work was backed by an expert knowledge of rhetorical techniques, there were many fourteenth-century English writers who used verse only because it was a popular and convenient means of communication. The lesser romance writers, the compilers of verse treatments of sacred history, of saints' lives, the chroniclers, the complaint writers, and many of the so-called 'lyric' writers, do not use verse in preference to prose because of its stronger imaginative and decorative potential: they use it because it is easier to recite and to memorize.

Our expectations of what kind of poetry we are to find in *Piers Plowman* would be more realistic if we associated it less with *The Canterbury Tales*, *Pearl*, or *Winner and Waster*, and more with verse histories of the world, such as the *Cursor Mundi*, treatise poems, such as Robert Mannyng's *Handlyng Synne*, religious allegories, such as Guillaume de Deguileville's *Pèlerinage* poems, or satirical complaints in verse, such as the earlier fourteenth-century *Simonie*. For although *Piers Plowman* was probably designed for a rather more learned public than theirs, and although Langland shows himself capable of, and interested in, a range of poetry quite outside their reach, he shares with them – as he does not share with Chaucer – a basically utilitarian attitude to his art. Verse, for him, is to be used, not specially revered or respected for its own sake.

The famous defence of his position as a poet (B XII 20 ff.) refers to his pleasure in 'makynges', but rests ultimately upon practical considerations: through writing poetry he is searching for spiritual understanding. Of course prayer is of a higher order than writing verse: only the extreme form of his moral dilemma justifies his pursuit of the truth in poetry, or, indeed, in any other way but in total dedication to God:

> 'Ac if there were any wight that wolde me telle
> What were Dowel and Dobet and Dobest atte laste,
> Wolde I neuere do werke, but wende to holicherche.'   (B XII 26–8)

Here the logic of the major changes Langland made in his last version of the poem, the C-text, becomes understandable. The C-text embodies, in the quality of its verse, the spirit of the principles outlined above. When we compare its opening twenty lines with those of the B-text, we may at first only notice Langland's rejection of the drowsy felicities of medieval dream poetry: the hint of enchantment, the hillside, the stream and its chattering waters have disappeared. But in their place we have a poetry of grave and disciplined beauty in which meaning and form are quintessential. It is Langland's peculiar achievement that out of commitments and materials which appear daunting, even prohibitive, and which *proved* to be for many medieval poets, he so often managed to create a poetry finely adjusted to satisfy the moral senses as well as the imagination:

> And seith, 'lo, briddes and bestes that no blisse knoweth,
> And wilde wormes in wodes, thorw wynter thow hem greuest,
> And makest hem wel ney meek and mylde for defaute;
> After than thow sendest hem somere, that is here souereyn Ioye,
> And blisse to alle that been bothe wilde and tame.
> Then may beggers, as bestes, after blysse asken,
> That al here lif hauen lyued in langour and defaute.'   (C XVI 292–8)

But this should not blind us to the fact that there are many stretches of *Piers Plowman* in which Langland is unlikely to be doing more than communicating plain sense as plainly as possible in verse form. This, to him and to his age, would have been permissible and comprehensible. The 'harmonious whole', demanded by Coleridge of the long poem, can be seen in *Piers Plowman* if we are not prejudiced against the groundbass of verse statement and exhortation from which Langland's imaginative poetry takes flight. It is, indeed, 'in keeping' with the finest poetry that it should exist in juxtaposition with the prosaic: it is all in keeping with Langland's honesty about the relationship of his art to his religion.

Significant here is the passage (C X 107 ff.) in which Langland speaks of 'God's minstrels' as distinct from 'alle manere mynstrales' of the secular world. It looks very much as if he may be giving us his own concept of the poet in his highest function – a prophet figure, who speaks to man as inspired by God:

> Ne none muracles maken – ac many tymes hem happeth
> To prophecye of the peple, pleyinge, as hit were, . . .
> For hit aren merye-mouthed men, munstrals of hevene,
> And godes boys, bordyors, as the book telleth.
>
> (C X 113–14, 126–7)

Much that is initially puzzling about the matter and the art of *Piers Plowman* becomes clear if we accept Langland's view of himself as one of 'godes mynstralles and hus messagers'.

With such an outlook, and such allegiances, it should not surprise us that when Langland mentions 'rhetoric', he does not mean poetic rhetoric but that of the pulpit:

> 'Thinge that al the worlde wote wherfore shuldestow spare
> To reden it in retoryke, to arate dedly synne?'   (B XI 97–8)

Many of the devices prescribed by such sermon 'retoryke' are prescribed by the manuals of poetic theory too: Chaucer, like Langland, was interested in various forms of verbal repetition, and both poets use them with skill and assurance. The difference lies in the reason for their use: Langland and the preachers view repetition primarily as a teaching aid, a method of underlining or summing up an important idea.[71] In particular instances, it is true, Langland transforms a teaching device into an illuminative feature: the use of the word 'guile' in the Harrowing of Hell debate (C XXI 315–402) is an obvious example. Musical analogies are not out of place here: the whole episode, from the beginning of the defiant speeches of Satan and Lucifer to the last triumphant words of Christ at their fall, uses language as music uses chords, to transpose from one key into another. 'Guile', first played upon as a single note, is gradually combined with 'life' and 'grace', in different variations, and resolved into the major mode of 'life' and 'love':

> '. . . The olde lawe techeth
> That gylours be bigiled and in here gyle falle' (C XXI 385)

> 'So that with gyle was gete, thorw grace is now ywonne.
> And as Adam and alle thorwe a tre deyede,
> Adam and alle thorw a tre shal turne to lyve' (C XXI 399–401)

> 'For I that am lord of lyf, love is my drynke.' (C XXI 406)

Langland is, by general definition, an 'alliterative poet'; his line is, basically, the four-stress accentual measure of *Sir Gawain*, *Winner and Waster* or the *Parliament of the Three Ages*. Yet many have been impelled to comment upon, and to suggest reasons for, the unique qualities of his verse. So, one of the most recent writers on the poem sums up the situation:

. . . the impression one receives from reading the other alliterative poems enforces the difference between them and *Piers Plowman* . . .[72]

A far less specialized poetic vocabulary and a far freer rhythmical range distinguish *Piers Plowman* immediately from much of the poetry of the 'alliterative revival', which so often gives the impression of having been wrought in stiff brocade, or in glittering cloisonné. It had, of course, a more ordinary style at its command: there are poems and parts of poems from the fourteenth-century alliterative 'school' which are nearer to *Piers Plowman* than *Pearl* or *Sir Gawain*. *Richard the Redeless*,[73] for instance, has something of its toughness and forthrightness:

> A! Hicke Heuyheed! hard is thi nolle
> To cacche ony kunnynge but cautell bigynne!
> Herdist thou not with eeris how that I er tellde. . . .
> (Passus III, lines 66–8)

But no single alliterative poem, in its entirety, reminds us of *Piers Plowman*. It is as if Langland accepted certain basic structural features, and certain stylistic traits of the alliterative poetry he must have known from his youth in the west of England, but totally rejected other features, shaping a verse medium more properly suited to his diverse materials and purposes. Many factors must have operated upon him. Writing in London, for an amorphous clerkly public, and not in a provincial castle, for a particular baronial audience, he would hardly have been tempted to experiment with the encrusted alliterative styles which were so much to the taste of western poets and their patrons. And it is probable, too, that the wide range of his reading – wider, certainly, than that of any other alliterative poet of his time – would have affected his style. In London he must have come into contact with many different kinds of English verse, rhymed, semi-alliterative, popular and instructive, satirical and serious.[74] It is more than likely that the looser, more various rhythmic nature of his verse is in part the result of this contact: it could also have shown him how to utilize alliteration as an index of sense, rather than as an insistent pattern of sound. Few full-scale alliterative poems can offer lines so similar to *Piers Plowman* as this from *The Simonie*, a semi-alliterative poem of London provenance:

And there they clateren cumpelin, whan the candel is oute.   (line 120)[75]

Ultimately, we must restate the singularity of Langland's most impressive verse. Admirable for its dramatic verve, and for its descriptive pungency, it is remarkable – almost inimitable – for the way in which it charges the simplest language with imaginative energy:

Deth cam dryvyng aftur and al to duste paschte
Kynges and knyhtes, caysers and popes.   (C XXIII 100–1)

6 *Piers Plowman* and *The Simonie**

A RECENT article set out to discover 'how much . . . of the considerable quantity of Middle English alliterative verse might have influenced Langland';[1] its conclusions, rightly, were tentative:

Winner and Waster probably, *The Parliament of Three Ages*, *Somer Soneday* . . . and *William of Palerne* possibly – these poems might have inspired Langland to improve upon them . . .[2]

Critics return to the same point about *Piers Plowman* – its singularity:

. . . the impression one receives from reading the other alliterative poems enforces the difference between them and *Piers Plowman* . . .[3]
. . . ostensibly it is written in the alliterative tradition . . . yet the total effect of the poem is strikingly different from that of the ornate, repetitive parallel style most other monuments of the alliterative revival display . . .[4]
. . . His achievement is a new thing . . . neither the built and near-hieratic language of Old English poetry, nor the weaker ornateness and elaboration of the 'Revival' . . .[5]

Explanations of this have been varied: a different public:[6] a different set of aesthetic principles:[7] a different poetic temperament.[8] In fact, all of these may have operated significantly: none are mutually exclusive. But it seems to me that without minimising any part of Langland's immense achievement, we could cast our net more widely for literary antecedents. If the full-scale alliterative poems of the 'Revival' are only partly helpful, we could move outside them to shorter works of varied style, competence and origin.

Langland's reading in earlier and contemporary vernacular poetry may have been free-ranging indeed. He is the only alliterative poet whose knowledge of the capital can fairly certainly be put down to long residence in London,[9] and there is every chance that he was equally familiar with works of eastern and western provenance. It could be that his distinctive style was due, in part, to the width of his reading in the vernacular, for English poetry at 1360 could have suggested an impressive range of alliterative and semi-alliterative usages – especially if we go outside the longer alliterative poem for evidence. There is nothing historical or geographical against the possibility that he knew poems which had found their way into collections such as Harley MS 2253 or into the Auchinleck MS – the one made principally in the West Midlands, the other in London, and both before 1350.[10]

* Originally published in *Archiv*, 203 (1967), 241–54.

Chaucer's knowledge – even possession of – the Auchinleck MS has already been suggested.[11] But Auchinleck contains at least one item relevant to *Piers Plowman* studies – a poem called *The Simonie*.[12] Although it is not, properly speaking, alliterative, employing a stanza form with rhyme, it has as good a claim as any thorough-going alliterative work to be one of those poems which 'might have inspired Langland to improve upon them'.[13] Wells, in *A Manual of the Writings in Middle English*, noted 'its anticipation by perhaps fifty years, of much of the motive and spirit that animated Langland . . .'[14] But we can, I think, be more precise than that, and suggest that Langland had read *The Simonie*, and used it to good effect.

It is important, in the first place, to record the very variable nature of its verse line. Predominantly six-stress, and rhyming,

> Whij werre and wrake in londe . and manslauht is icome
> Whij hungger and derþe on eorþe the pore haþ undernome . . .
> (Auchinleck, fo. 328r, Wright, lines 1–2)

it can at times read just as easily as four-stress: on many of such occasions, its language is strongly alliterative. Thus

> Hit nis noht al for þe calf : þat kow louweþ . . .
> (Auchinleck, fo. 330v, Wright, line 183)
> And þere hij clateren cumpelin : whan þe candel is oute.
> (Auchinleck, fo. 329v, Wright, line 120)

might pass as acceptable lines in a plainer alliterative poem of the fourteenth century; it happens that not only their alliterative, accentual make-up, but also their syntactical structure brings *Piers Plowman* to mind:[15]

> Ac it is nauȝt by the bishop . that the boy precheth . . .   (B Prol. 80)[16]
> And gnawen god with the gorge . whan her gutte is fulle . . .   (B X 57)

But alliteration is not constant: about one third of the lines have some alliterative element, which can vary from light emphasis –

> And if hit be a pore lyf in pouerte and in care . . .
> (Auchinleck, fo. 330v, Wright, line 177)

to stronger weighting –

> þeih dradden more here lond to lese : þan loue of ihesu crist
> (Auchinleck, fo. 334v, Wright, line 450)
> Pride prikede hem so faste : þat nolde þeih neuer haue pes
> (Auchinleck, fo. 334r, Wright, line 433)
> Nu ben þeih so degised and diuerseliche idiht
> (Auchinleck, fo. 331v, Wright, line 255)

Here it is worth recording that the Peterhouse text of the poem (which differs considerably from the Auchinleck version)[17] contains a slightly larger number of alliterative readings: Auchinleck, for instance,

> Among none of þe cardinaus dar he noht be sein
> (fo. 328r, Wright, line 16)

is Peterhouse

> Wt yn þe popes paleys ʒif he myʒt be sayn   (fo. 210r)

which recalls Langland's comment upon Meed:

> In the popis paleys . she is pryue as my-self . . .   (B II 23)

The Peterhouse text is fuller in its criticism of worldly monks, and alliteration points some of the irony:

> swych sorow þei suffre for our lordes loue . . .
> wel þei beth i fed . wt gode flesch and fysch
> and if it ys gode mete . þe lete lytil in her disch
> of þe beste
> þus þei pyneth her bodyes . to hold crystes hest.   (fo. 210v, col. ii)

'Flesch and fysch' is a familiar half-line in *Piers Plowman*, used often in similar contexts – those of over-fastidious and indulgent living: the learned friar rationalises his gluttony, proving that delicate food

> Is noither fisshe ne flesshe . but fode for a penaunte . . .   (B XIII 92)[18]

'To hold crystes hest', a common enough alliterative phrase, reappears in several forms in *Piers Plowman*:

> . . . a-countable to Crist . and to the kyng of heuene,
> That holden mote the heye weye . euene the ten hestes . . .
> (C XIV 67–8)

The greater frequency of alliteration in the Peterhouse version adds force to the idea that *The Simonie*, with its varied line-length and flexible range of alliterative usages, may anticipate some of the special features of Langland's style. We have been reminded that

. . . *Piers* differs (from *Winner and Waster* and *The Parliament of the Three Ages*) not only in greater irregularity in length of line . . . but also in its greater variety . . . in its use of the different types of alliteration . . .[19]

Irregularity of line-length in *The Simonie* will already be apparent: the poem uses anything from four to six stresses in the line, and is not concerned with syllabic regularity:[20]

Anon he wole biginne : to blere þe wiues eiȝe
he wole aske half a pound : to bien spicerie
þe . viij . shillinges sholen up : to þe win and þe ale
and bringe rotes and rindes : bret ful a male
of noht
hit shal be dere on a lek : whan hit is al iwrouht
He wole preisen hit inohw : and swere as he were wod
for þe king of þe lond : þe drink is riche and god
and ȝeue þe gode man drinke : a god quantite
and make him worsse þan he was : euele mote he þe . . .

(Auchinleck, fo. 331r, Wright, lines 223–32)

In heuene y blessyd mut he be . þat herkeneth her a stounde
how plenteþ and al myrþe . for pride is brout to grounde
how stedfastnesse and trewþe . ys torned to trecherye
and all poure mennes song . alas for hunger I dye
up ryȝt
y heried be þe kyng of heuen . such is hys myȝt

(Peterhouse, fo. 210r, col. ii)

The Simonie displays a wide variety of alliterative modes, all of which can be paralleled in *Piers Plowman*. The standard *aa/ax* type is present:

þat þe beste blod of þe lond shamliche was brought to grounde

(Auchinleck, fo. 334r, Wright, line 435)

Alliteration often occurs in final position in the line –

Ac hit is for þe grene gras þat in þe medewe grouweth[21]

(Auchinleck, fo. 330v, Wright, line 184)

as in Langland's

And so ferde ȝe, madame . ȝe couthe namore fynde   (B III 340)

or

Tauerners to hem . told the same tale   (A Prol. 106)

The pattern is frequently *ax/aa*:

And þat euerich biwreied oþer of here wrecchede werkes

(Auchinleck, fo. 328v, Wright, line 36)

Summe bereþ croune of acolite : for þe crumponde crok[22]

(Auchinleck, fo. 329v, Wright, line 115)

For hadde þe clergie : harde holden to-gidere[23]

(Auchinleck, fo. 334v, Wright, line 451)

So Langland on occasion:

Riȝt so, quod Gregorie . religioun roileth   (B X 297)[24]

161

The pattern *aa/bb* is common to both:

> þe clerkes of þe cuntre wolen him faste wowe
> (Auchinleck, fo. 328v, Wright, line 57)

> Hii riden wid hauk and hound . and contrefeten knihtes
> (Auchinleck, fo. 329v, Wright, line 122)[25]

> And if ȝe seche Sapience eft . fynde shal ȝe that folweth . . .
> (*Piers Plowman*, B III 344)

> Ich am to waik to worche . with sykel other with sythe . . .
> (ibid., C VI 23)[26]

And so are patterns *aa/xx, xx/aa*:

> And if the parsoun haue a prest : of a clene lyf . . .
> (Auchinleck, fo. 329r, Wright, line 97)[27]

> That Mede moste be meynpernour . Resoun thei bisouȝte . . .
> (*Piers Plowman*, B IV 112)[28]

> For Coueytise and Symonie han þe worlde to wille . . .
> (Auchinleck, fo. 328r, Wright, line 30)[29]

> I fauȝte so, me threstes ȝet . for mannes soule sake . . .
> (*Piers Plowman*, B XVIII 365)

Both poems allow alliteration on two or four words in the line. *The Simonie* has a good number of the former:

> And þus þeih seruen þe chapele : and laten þe churche stonde . . .
> (Auchinleck, fo. 329r, Wright, line 78)[30]

Piers Plowman can show

> Ouer-lede the comune . ne to the courte sompne . . .   (B III 314)[31]

In *The Simonie*

> So longe lastede þat gamen among lered and lewed . . .
> (Auchinleck, fo. 333r, Wright, line 369)[32]

is comparable to Langland's

> That wikked men, thei welden . the welthe of this worlde,
> And that thei ben lordes of eche a londe . that dute of lawe
> libbeth . . .   (B X 24–5)[33]

The most that can be claimed from this sort of evidence is that if Langland had been conscious of the need to fit his verse for a public far wider than that of a West Midland castle or parish, he could have found in poems such as *The Simonie* something to his purpose. If he had wanted a more flexible and permissive alliterative range, from a line with practically no alliterative content to one with four full stresses, then *The Simonie*, rather than *Winner and Waster*, might have shown him a way.

It is, of course, true that two western alliterative poems, *William of Palerne* and *Joseph of Arimathie*, both written about 1350, could also have demonstrated a freer alliterative system.[34] But we have no conclusive evidence that Langland did read, or was influenced by them:[35] the evidence for his knowledge of *The Simonie* is stronger. Some verbal and syntactical likenesses have already been pointed out:[36] they are by no means isolated cases. The poem is full of familiar phrases and halflines:

> And bringe the bishop silver and rounen in his ere . . .
> (Auchinleck, fo. 328v, Wright, line 62)

> And ritt riȝte to Resoun . and rowneth in his ere . . .   (B IV 13)

> Anon he wole biginne : to blere the wiues eiȝe . . .
> (Auchinleck, fo. 331v, Wright, line 223)

> He bonched hem with his breuet . and blered here eyes . . .   (B Prol. 74)

> And baillifs and bedeles : under the shirreue
> Everich fondeþ hu he may pore men most greue
> þe pore men beþ over al : somouned on assise . . .
> (Auchinleck, fo. 332v, Wright, lines 337–9)

> As sysours and sompnours . shireues and here clerkes;
> Bedelles and bailliues . and brokoures of chaffare . . .   (B II 58–9)

> God sende treuþe into þis lond : for tricherie dureþ
> to longe . . .
> (Auchinleck, fo. 332v, Wright, line 336)

> And that is no treuthe of the trinite . but trecherye of helle . . .   (B I 196)[37]

Even the line

> And nu ben þeih lïons in halle and hares in þe feld . . .
> (Auchinleck, fo. 331v, Wright, line 252)

with its metaphor and its antithetical construction, is reminiscent of Langland writing about the unreformed active man – Haukyn:

> Pore of possessioun . in purse and in coffre,
> And as a lyon on to loke . and lordeliche of speche . . . (B XIII 301–2)[38]

Two of the most significant points to make about *The Simonie* and its possible connection with *Piers Plowman* are its marked use of alliterative language and its acceptability to a London audience in the earlier fourteenth century. Inclusion in a miscellany such as the Auchinleck manuscript proves the latter beyond a doubt. That it was already in circulation in London – in more than one form – argues, for many years before Langland's arrival in the capital, an atmosphere and a public favourable to the sort of poem he was projecting: a poem of satire and complaint, which would mingle criticism with constructive advice, and which would be more preoccupied with lively communication than with elegance or richness of language.

For what Langland may have found 'to his purpose' in *The Simonie* extends far beyond patterns of language and rhythm. It would not be an exaggeration to say that its bitter review of the secular and spiritual ill-health of the earlier fourteenth century comes nearer in subject and in tone to some parts of *Piers Plowman* than any other single extant work. The range of its material is similar to that outlined by Langland in the Prologue and first few Passus of *Piers Plowman*: antipapal denunciation,[39]

> For at þe court of rome . þer treuþe sholde biginne
> Him is forboden þe paleis dar he noht com þerinne . . .
> Among none of þe cardinaus dar he noht be sein . . .
> (Auchinleck, fo. 328r, Wright, lines 9–10, 16)

examination of a corrupt Church at home, the arraignment of worldly priests, cynical bishops, avaricious friars. Lawyers, sheriffs, knights and squires are stringently dealt with, but the Church is held primarily responsible for temporal suffering:

> For hadde þe clergie : harde holden togidere
> And noht flecched aboute : nother hider ne thidere
> But loked where þe treuthe was : and þere have bileued
> þanne were þe barnage hol : þat nu is al todreued
> so wide
> Ac certes engelond is shent þurw falsnesse and þurw pride . . .
> (Auchinleck, fo. 334v, Wright, lines 451–6)

Langland strikes the same sad and stern note:

> Many ferlis han fallen . in a few ʒeris.
> But holychirche and hij . holde better togideres,
> The moste mychief on molde . is mountyng wel faste . . . (B Prol. 65–7)

But it is not simply the wide panorama of criticism, opened up in *The Simonie*, which brings to mind Langland's 'felde ful of folke'; there are times when the handling of the scene is similar. In a general sense, the mingling of abstract concepts and classes of people in a designedly realistic setting is highly suggestive of Langland's method in *Piers Plowman*. And some of the concepts are familiar to readers of the later poem: Truth, Holy Church, Simony, Covetyse, Pride. The operation of Truth in *The Simonie* is particularly interesting; it could have given Langland an idea, in however embryonic a form, for his much more complex 'character' in *Piers Plowman*. Truth functions in *The Simonie* as the ideal, exiled figure who is the remedy for all ills; he has not yet been envisaged as 'Seynt

Treuthe' – 'ther treuthe is in Trinitee, and troneth hem alle . . .' (B1131) but he is extremely important, and presented dynamically:

> . . . at þe court of rome . þer treuþe sholde biginne
> Him is forboden þe paleis dar he noht come þerinne
>   for doute
> and þouh þe pope clepe him in ȝit shall he stonde þeroute[40]
> Alle þe popes clerkes han taken hem to red
> if treuþe come amonges hem þat he shal be ded . . .
>   (Auchinleck, fo. 328r, Wright, lines 9–14)

> God sende treuþe in to þis lond for tricherie dureþ to longe . . .
>   (ibid., fo. 332v, Wright, line 336)

Certain unique stanzas in the Peterhouse version of the poem develop the idea of Truth as a figure 'friendly to poor men':

> . . . he were worþi . to be hanged and drawe
> þat hath dryue trewth out of lond . without proces of lawe
>   alas
> certes whil trewth was in londe . a gode frend he was
> Trewþ was ouer al redy . for pore men to speke
> and now go pore men al adoun . . .   (fo. 211r, col. ii)

Truth in *Piers Plowman* is known first of all by the poor plowman, Piers:

> I know him as kyndely . as clerke doth his bokes . . .   (B v 545)

and later in the poem Divine Truth, in Christ's person, travels 'disguised' as a poor man:

> In a pore mannes apparaille . pursueth us euere,
> And loketh on us in her liknesse . . .   (B xi 180–1)

The urge towards *active* personification in *The Simonie* is strong; Symonye and Coveytyse would not be out of place in the Meed episodes of *Piers Plowman*:[41]

> If symonie may mete wid him he wole shaken his berd . . .
>   (Auchinleck, fo. 328r, Wright, line 18)

> For coueytise and symonie han þe world to wille . . .
>   (ibid., Wright, line 30)

> Coueytise shal stoppen here mouþ and maken hem al stille . . .
>   (Auchinleck, fo. 328v, Wright, line 54)

> And þere shal symonye ben taken bi þe top . . .[42]
>   (ibid., Wright, line 60)

> Coueytise upon his hors he wole be sone þere
> And bringe þe bishop siluer and rounen in his ere . . .
>   (ibid., Wright, lines 61–2)

And þus is coueytise louerd boþe est and west . . .
(Auchinleck, fo. 330r, Wright, line 168)

Holy Church and Meed are not developed as allegorical figures in this way, but the occurrence of their names in that part of the poem which deals with the operation of Truth, Simony and Couetyse stirs memories of *Piers Plowman*:

And þise ersedeknes þat ben set to uisite holichurche
Euerich fondeth hu he may shrewedelichest worche
he wole take mede of þat on and þat oþer . . .
(Auchinleck, fo. 328v, Wright, lines 49–51)

When we read that the sinful priest 'medeþ wid þe clerkes . . .' it is appropriate to remember that it was a clerk of Westminster who

toke Mede bi the middel . and brou3te her into chaumbre . . .   (B III 10)

and his fellows who swore to her

. . . we beth thine owne . . .   (B III 27)

The final scene of *The Simonie*, with Pride riding throughout the land, 'Pride prikeþ aboute wid niþe and wid onde', Peace, Love and Charity fleeing 'out of londe / so faste', the prelates of Holy Church 'ablent wid coueytise', and the threat of total destruction hanging over the world, 'þat god wole fordon þe world we muwe be sore agaste . . .' (Auchinleck, fo. 334v, Wright, lines 448–62) might be a rough sketch for part of Passus xx of *Piers Plowman*:

Antecriste hadde thus sone . hundredes at his banere,
And Pryde it bare . boldely aboute . . .
And pryked forth with Pryde . . .
'He lith and dremeth', seyde Pees . 'and so do many other . . .'
(B xx 68–9, 148, 375)

On many occasions it is difficult not to think that Langland had read and remembered *The Simonie*: both poems, for instance, are deeply compassionate about poverty – the lines

And also muche paieþ anoþer þat pouerte haþ brouht to grounde
And haþ an hep of girles sittende aboute þe flet . . .
(Auchinleck, fo. 332r, Wright, lines 308–9)

may look forward to the moving passage in the C-text about 'poure folke in cotes', who struggle for bare necessities

To a-glotye with here gurles . that greden after fode . . .   (C x 76)

Stanzas in *The Simonie* on famine, which describe how suffering tames men –

> A mannes herte mihte blede for to here þe crie
> Of pore men þat gradden allas for hungger I die . . .

and how the return of plenty means the return of sin –

> Þo god 3er was a3ein icome and god chep of corn
> þo were we also muchele shrewes as we were beforn . . .
> (Auchinleck, fo. 333v, Wright, lines 399–400, 405–6)

could have suggested an outline of the Hunger episode in Passus VI of the B-text:

> Thanne pore folke for fere . fedde Hunger 3erne
> With grene poret and pesen . . .
> By that it neighed nere heruest . newe corne cam to chepynge;
> Thanne was folke fayne . and fedde Hunger with the best,
> With good ale, as Glotoun tau3te . and gerte Hunger go slepe.
> And tho wolde Wastour nou3t werche . . . (B VI 299–304)

So too, *The Simonie* gives the gist of Langland's diatribe against 'lewed prestes' (B XI 289 ff.). The wretched parson

> . . . rat on þe rouwe bible and on oþer bok
> No mo
> But unþank haue þe bishop þat lat hit so go . . .

He is . . .

> a daffe . . .
> þat can noht a ferthing worth of god unneþe singe a masse
> But ille . . .

and the poet sums up indignantly:

> No more wot a lewed prest in boke what he rat
> Bi day
> þanne is a lewed prest no bettre þan a iay . . .
> (Auchinleck, fo. 329r–v, Wright, lines 88–90, 99–101, 106–8)

Langland treats the theme more compactly and effectively, but he makes some of the same points – in some of the same words:

> The bisshop shal be blamed . bifor god, as I leue,
> That crouneth suche goddes kni3tes . that conneth nou3t *sapienter*
> Synge ne psalmes rede . ne segge a messe of the day . . .
> (B XI 303–5)

Comparable also are two passages on legal practices: the famous lines in the Prologue

> Seriaunt3 it semed . that serueden atte barre,
> Plededen for penyes . and poundes the lawe . . .

167

> Thow my3test better mete the myste . on Maluerne hulles,
> Than gete a momme of here mouthe . but money were shewed . . .
>
> (B Prol. 211–12, 214–15)

may have taken some hints from

> And countours in benche þat stondeþ at þe barre . . .
>
> He wole take xl pans for to do doun his hod
> And speke for þe a word or to and don þe litel god . . .
>
> (Auchinleck, fo. 332v–333r, Wright, lines 343, 345–6)

The earlier poem is rough work indeed when set against *Piers Plowman*, but its *potential* is rich. It does not seem to me impossible that out of a reading of

> And þise abbotes and priours don a3ein here rihtes
> Hij riden wid hauk and hound and contrefeten knihtes
> Hij sholde leue swich pride and ben religiouus
> And nu is pride maister in euerich ordred hous
> Iwis
> Religioun is euele i holde and fareþ þe more amis . . .
>
> (Auchinleck, fo. 329v, Wright, lines 121–6)

with their sober, generalised prescriptions, Langland could have fashioned his brilliantly visual

> Ac now is religioun a ryder . a rowmer bi stretes,
> A priker on a palfray . fro manere to manere,
> An heep of houndes at his ers . as he a lorde were . . .
>
> (B x 306, 308–10)

It would not be easy to establish which version of *The Simonie* Langland is most likely to have read. The lines on Truth, quoted above,[43] might weight the balance in favour of the Peterhouse text. One other episode, absent from the Auchinleck MS, would certainly have appealed to him – a derisory picture of well-fed 'monkes, chanouns oþer freres'. It has a few details he might have been able to put to better use for his preaching friar:

> Religion was imaked . penaunce for to drye
> now it is mych torned . to pryde and glotonye
> wer shalt þu fynde . redder men on lerys
> fayrer men oþer fatter . þan monkes chanouns oþer freres
> he will drawe at a draw3t . a gode quart oþer more
> of gode ale and strong . wel ibrowen of þe beste
> and sone þerafter he wol fond for to cach reste . . .
>
> (Peterhouse, fo. 210v, col. ii)[44]

The Simonie is not the only 'popular' semi-alliterative poem Langland might have drawn upon: it is very probable that he was familiar with the *Song of the Husbandman*, from MS Harley 2253, and with *Thomas of Erceldoune's Prophecy*, from the same manuscript collection.[45] Reason's sermon (B ɪᴠ 113 ff.) looks as if it may be based on the 'prophecy' form, and many of the lines in the earlier poem tempt translation into active allegory:

> When wyt and wille werres togedere . . .
> When prude prikes and pees is leyd in prisoun . . .
> When ryþt and Wrong ascenteþ to-gedere . . .[46]

The *Song of the Husbandman* has the evocative line 'þus wil walkeþ in lond . . .'[47] a simple starting point, indeed, for the labyrinthine dream-journeys of *Piers Plowman*.[48]

Many lost or only half-remembered English poems must lie behind Langland's comprehensive work: a single line sometimes asks us to reflect upon the crudity of the materials offered to Langland by his age – a *Harrowing of Hell*, in jingling couplets

> ȝef þou revest me of myne
> y shal reve þe of þyne . . .[49]

is both near to and remote from the fine long alliterative lines of Passus xᴠɪɪɪ of the B-text:

> If he reue me my riȝte . he robbeth me by maistrye   (B xᴠɪɪɪ 274)

The Simonie had more to show such a poet, but even there it is the quality of Langland's transforming imagination rather than his indebtedness which must be given final credit.

7 Alliterative modes and affiliations in the fourteenth century*

T HERE is every reason to suppose that the subject of the 'alliterative revival of the fourteenth century' will continue to attract scholars and students, as much for what appear to be its silences and enigmas as for its articulate triumphs. But there is, equally, every reason to suppose that the most promising lines of present-day and future research lie, not through areas sign-posted, as in the past, by a kind of scholarly patriotism, but through those which direct our attention to features of extreme detail in the literary landscape. Nothing is now to be gained by the reiteration of heroic commonplaces about the reassertion of heroic – and Anglo-Saxon – spirit in the alliterative poetic line of the mid- and later fourteenth century.¹ But much is still to be gained by further investigation of the contexts and the affiliations of alliterative writing over the whole span of the late Old English and Middle English periods: more of a precise nature can certainly be said about processes of transmission, about patrons and audiences, and about literary relationships in all their variousness and complexity.

It is no longer possible to write usefully upon the 'origins of the alliterative revival' with the assumption that we are confronting a common inherited poetic tradition: it is not even possible to write accurately of an 'alliterative revival' in any but a very limited sense, for, as an objective survey of the evidence will show, innovation – even renovation – has no significant part to play in accounting for the existence of a large body of unrhymed and loosely alliterative composition from the fourteenth century. English alliterative verse had a wide range of particular, and probably differing, literary and social backgrounds; it defines its separateness from other forms of composition with a flexibility of practice which we should do well to observe and respect. The set of circumstances and connections which we may find helpful in coming to an understanding of the shaping and the shape of any one alliterative poem may not necessarily aid us in our approach to another. It is clear, for instance, that alliterative poets must have been as much influenced by a number of diverse 'models' – Latin, French, Anglo-French and English, verse and prose – as they were by some general agreement as to what constituted alliterative verse form: the obvious stylistic differences between, say, the *Destruction of Troy*, *William of Palerne* and *Piers Plowman* suggest the fragile grounds upon which we have to rest arguments for a cohesive and identifiable 'school' of alliterative poetry in the fourteenth century.² But equally fragile are the grounds

* Originally published in *Neuphilologische Mitteilungen*, 79 (1978), 25–35.

upon which we have to rest arguments for the occurrence of a deliberate and widespread 'revival' of alliterative composition in the 1350s. There may be departments of alliterative verse-writing which lay some genuine claim to self-conscious literary 'antiquarianism', or to other forms of self-conscious literary refinement upon older patterns newly rediscovered. But there are others whose part in a 'revival' is less well-defined, and whose affiliations – not by any means exclusively poetic – speak rather of transformatory processes, no less rich and interesting for the fact that they are hardly mysterious.

By far the most valuable recent contributions to the study of medieval alliterative poetry have been those which have stressed the diversity of its origins and nature, and the easy commerce it traditionally maintained – at least since the days of Aelfric and Wulfstan – with other forms of composition: Angus McIntosh, who laid the foundations in 1949 for this approach by his British Academy Sir Israel Gollancz Memorial Lecture,[3] has recently emphasized, for work on the 'alliterative tradition', 'the need to look not only at verse in the strict sense, but also at other examples of the use of rhythmic patterns in compositions wherein we can scarcely be said to be involved with verse at all, and where we certainly cannot always say that they are being used to *poetical* ends'.[4] Norman Blake's important essay on 'Rhythmical Alliteration' proposes that Middle English alliterative poetry was created out of the situation which resulted when 'the boundary between prose and poetry became blurred in the eleventh and twelfth centuries'.[5] This blurring of the boundaries of prose and poetry is no doubt one of the most continuously significant of all medieval literary phenomena; reluctance to take its full consequences into account has certainly distorted our view of the development of alliterative composition during the twelfth, thirteenth and fourteenth centuries, and may easily be responsible for the invention of the whole concept of an 'alliterative revival'. It seems increasingly useful, therefore, to pay close attention to those works which, either in part or in whole, lie on the very boundaries of prose and alliterative, accentual verse. In particular, it would be helpful to see whether they can dispose of, or at least reduce, some of the 'silences and enigmas' which have usually been rendered acceptable parts of the patchily-written history of medieval alliterative verse, by reference to a primarily oral tradition, and poems unrecorded.

The problem has never been that of finding evidence of the widespread use of alliteration in rhymed verse of various kinds throughout the supposedly lean years of the thirteenth and early fourteenth centuries. Alliterative materials are common in thirteenth-century prayers and hymns, are elaborately represented in many of the secular poems of a famous early fourteenth-century collection such as MS Harley 2253, and are lavishly worked into the stanzaic verse of the so-called 'Rolle School', before 1350. All of this is proof of a well established alliterative verse usage which increased its strength as the period progressed: it exists as both a norm and as high art – in both the work-a-day devotional pieces of the Vernon manuscript, of 1400, and in the contemporary and sophisticated *Pearl*. When Richard Maidstone, Carmelite Confessor to John of Gaunt, and writer of elegant Latin ceremonial verses, paraphrases the *Penitential Psalms*, he does so in a version of the same sturdy alliterative style used by many other anonymous Psalm translators of the period:

> Mercy lord of my misdeede
> after þy mercy that mechel is
> lette þy pite sprynge and sprede
> Of þy mercy þat I nouȝt mys
> After gostly grace I grede
> Gode god now graunte me thys . . .'[6]

The relationship of Maidstone's alliterative language to that of William Langland – both were London poets of the later fourteenth century – is worthy of further study. What we have to consider more urgently is whether vernacular alliterative usages, in an unrhymed format, were readily available as working models for later thirteenth- and fourteenth-century poets.

Some evidence exists for the continued reading and use of the major alliterative – and predominantly unrhymed – poem of the thirteenth century, Laȝamon's chronicle, the *Brut*, by vernacular poets, working from monasteries in the west of England, not long after the turn of the century.[7] But although this tells us something quite exact about possible centres of literary activity in south-western England and, moreover, about likely channels of transmission of material from one century to another, it tells us nothing to our purposes about a continued interest in the *form* of the long, unrhymed alliterative line: Robert of Gloucester's *Chronicle* turns whatever it takes from Laȝamon's *Brut* into the familiar rhymed septenary couplet. And, in fact, all the considerable body of vernacular texts coming from the south-west at this time – translations of the Old Testament, parts of the New, homiletic and legendary material, the *Chronicle* itself – are in couplet form of one kind or another.[8] If we search in this rhymed couplet verse for traces of the older – or contemporary – alliterative verse which may lie at one remove from it, we are rewarded thinly; odd fragments occur, but there is no sense of their continuing life – they seem to be encapsulated in alien materials. Thus two lines of alliterative verse, in a metrical form recognizable as that of the later Old English period, are 'quoted' in the thirteenth-century *Life of St. Kenelm*, part of the important *Southern Legendary* collection. The poet interrupts his septenary couplets to give us what he clearly regards as a special, and unusual piece of verse – 'without rhyme':

> And for to tellen it without ryme þeos wordes it were:
> In Klent Cowbache Kenelm kyngues sone
> Lith under haweþorne, is heued him bireued.[9]

These commemorative lines on the death of St Kenelm which can be found independently, in Latin Chronicles dealing with the Kenelm material, deliver the Old English line to the thirteenth century, but release none of its life to the practising poet.

On the other hand, when short passages of what appears to be alliterative verse occur 'embedded' in prose texts, the impression is quite different. Richard Rolle's prose Epistle, *Ego Dormio*, written and dedicated in Yorkshire, about 1340, contains ten lines of such composition – introduced without comment, in the natural sequence of his argument. The 'verse' is not of the strictest alliterative kind, showing a tendency to fall into the patterns *aa/xx*, and, in one case, when it uses a whole-line alliterative component, to an *aa/aa* pattern. The punctuation of the manuscripts emphasizes these features, which are interesting in the context of alliterative verse usages after 1350:

> It wanes into wrechednes. Þe welth of þis worlde.
> Robes and ritches . rotes in dike.
> Prowde payntyng . slakes into sorow.
> Delites and drewryse . stynk sal ful sone.
> Þair golde and þaire tresoure . drawes þam til dede.
> Al þe wikked of þis worlde . drawes til a dale.[10]

In fact, it may be that this very association of unrhymed alliterative writing (punctuated often in the manuscripts into units which compose, however rough-ly, the medially-divided, long alliterative verse line) with prose texts and contexts, is of vital importance to our knowledge of the preservation of an 'alliterative tradition'. English prose, from the days of Aelfric onwards, had always shown itself hospitable to the stylistic and rhythmical features of English poetry,[11] and that poetry, being basically accentual as well as alliterative, could, by its very nature, sustain such flexible relationships with other, freer forms of composition. Prose could, therefore, provide a continuum, in which the existence of the unrhymed alliterative line, either conceived of as a separate, essentially poetic form, or as a much more loosely articulated rhythmical unit, was guaranteed. The processes involved in the apparent 're-emergence' of the long alliterative line, in the hands of fourteenth-century poets, would often be better described as closer, therefore, to 'restoration' and 'formalization', although we have been at pains to stress that what may hold good for one kind of alliterative poet may not necessari-ly fit the case of another, whose immediate models and persuasions may be very different.

There is, of course, no one simple formula to describe the way in which the long alliterative and accentual line preserves its life within the 'body' of another kind of text. The texts themselves, loosely defined as 'prose', are extremely varied – sometimes allowing little more than the potential of the alliterative line to be discerned, but, at other times, its full shape. This is interestingly demonstrated by the mid-fourteenth-century translation made by a monk of St Mary's Abbey, York, John Gaytryge, of the Archbishop of York's Latin treatise addressed to his clergy, instructing them in the fundamentals of Christian belief and practice.[12] Gaytryge's version, expanded out of Thoresby's Latin, is written in a form which, even when it is recorded in the manuscripts as continuous composition, is frequently punctuated into its basic rhythmical and metrical units: in some manuscripts it is recorded in a long verse-line format.[13] As the following extract shows, the characteristic pattern is of lines with a predominantly four-beat structure, very variably emphasized by alliteration: occasionally a line will emerge in full accentual and alliterative strength:

> He made skilwise creatures angels and man.
> Of witt and of wisdome to knaw god al-myghten.
> And thurg þair knawyng loue him and serue him.
> And so come to that blisse that thai were made to.
> This maner of knawyng had oure forme fadyrs.
> In þe state of innocentz that thai were made in . . .
> For þe knawyng that thai had of god almighten.
> Thai had it of goddes gift at thaire begynnyng.
> Withouten travaile or trey or passyng of tyme.
> And all þe knawyng þat we haue in þis world of him.
> Is of heryng and leryng and techyng of othir
> Of þe lawe and þe lare þat langes till hali kirke.
> The whilke al creatures that loues god almighten.
> Awe to knawe and to kun and lede þaire lyue aftir.
> And so com to þat blisse þat neuer more blynnes.[14]

Particular lines are no less recognizable as alliterative verse than many from accepted fourteenth-century 'alliterative poems':

> aghe to gyfe þaim gudely to godes seruyse
>   (*Treatise*, Tr. Coll. Cbg. MS B. 10. 12, fo. 59r)
>
> ne lyfe in lykynge ne luste þat þe flesche ȝernes   (loc. cit.)
>
> thurgh prelates and prestes þat has þe powere   (ibid., fo. 61r)
>
> withouten whilke no synful man saule may be sauede   (loc. cit.)
>
> þe grace and þe gyftes of þe haly gaste   (ibid., fo. 61v)
>
> withouten any lesynge whils þair lyfes lastes   (ibid., fo. 62v)
>
> þat wisses us to be ware with wathes of þis werlde   (ibid., fo. 64r)
>
> ffor methe is mesure and mett of al þat we do   (loc. cit.)
>
> to fulfil þe lykynges and þe lustes of þe flesche   (ibid., fo. 65v)

Gaytryge's *Treatise* was widely known in the North, in East Anglia and the Midlands generally; whatever problems it may present to the modern reader, it had none for the medieval, who was evidently able to recognize and accept its hybrid stylistic nature, and to adapt its materials to changing needs over the fourteenth and fifteenth centuries.[15] These two verifiable facts – its acceptability and its extensive circulation – are important, if we are interested in improving our knowledge of the more unspectacular literary forms in which an unrhymed, alliterative line could manifest itself quite unselfconsciously, in the years of the mid-century.[16]

In this connection, it is worth recording that particular verbal groupings in the *Treatise* are loosely reminiscent of lines in *Piers Plowman*, not only reminding us of the fundamental subject matter common to both works – the Commandments, Sacraments, Virtues, Graces, Vices – but also prompting speculation about Langland's familiarity with some version of the *Treatise*. The likenesses may occur, fleetingly, in a half-line, or may be spread more generally over a passage:

> Awe to knawe and to kun and lede þaire lyue after
>> (*Register* text, ed. Simmons & Nolloth, line 31)
>
> And hadden leue to lyen al hire lif after
>> (*Piers Plowman*, B Prol. 49)[17]
>
> ffor it kens us to knaw þe gude fra þe ille
>> (Tr. Coll. Cbg. MS B. 10. 12, fo. 64r)
>
> kenne me by som craft to knowe þe false　　(B II 4)
>
> Of þe whilke synne many spyces sprynges and spredes
>> (MS B. 10. 12, fo. 65r)
>
> Springeth and spredeth that spicers desyreth　　(A IX 121)

Comparison of the sections which deal with the Deadly Sins reveals minute but important verbal resemblances, sometimes displaced, sometimes 'anchored' identically: thus in the *Treatise* it is Wrath to whom the 'gret othes' of Langland's Gluttony ('Thanne goþ Gloton In and grete oþes after', B V 306: 'glotoun wiþ grete oþes', B XIII 400) are attached:

> With many fals and many foule and many gret othes
>> (Tr. Coll. Cbg. MS B. 10. 12, fo. 65r)

But Gluttony in both works attracts a scattering of similar concepts and expressive language; varieties of Gluttony in the *Treatise* are enumerated:

> Ane is ouere arely or ouere late and oure oftsythes
> ffor to ete or for to drynke bot if nede gart it.
> another is for to lyfe dilicately . . .
>> (Tr. Coll. Cbg. MS B. 10. 12, fo. 65v)

In *Piers Plowman*, the confession of Glotoun is clearly based on something of this sort, at, perhaps, several removes; there is a sense of general equivalence, rising sometimes to the exact word:

'I, Gloton . . . gilty me yelde
That I haue trespased with my tonge . . .
There no nede was . . .
And ouer seyen me at my soper and som tyme at Nones . . .
Ouer *delicatly* on [feeste] dayes *dronken and eten bope*,
And sat som tyme so longe þere . . .'
(B v 367–8, 370, 371, 374–5. See also B v 184:
'*drynke nat ouer delicatly* . . .')

In the same way, we are bound to wonder whether, when Langland was allegoriz-
ing the ten commandments into a journey, the phrasing of his line 'And hold wel
þyn haliday heighe til euen' (B v 579) did not owe something to the memory of
this earlier, even drier prescriptive statement: 'The third is that we sal *hald* and
halowe our *haliday*' (*Register* text, line 187).

There would be little point, on such evidence, in suggesting that Langland
learnt any of his considerable craft from such a rough piece of English composition as Gaytryge's *Treatise*. Rather, we can suggest that the *Treatise* illustrates the
probable nature of some of the old raw materials from which Langland would
have been able to refine his good verse line. If we are allowed to entertain the idea
that the curious passage in the C-text of *Piers Plowman* (I 95–124), part of which
is almost devoid of alliteration, is not necessarily the result of scribal corruption
or interpolation, but is Langland's own work, then we may here, perhaps, come a
little closer to such 'raw materials' at that moment before Langland had been able
to subject them to his characteristic poeticizing processes. There is nothing
unusual or remarkable about the passage if we compare it with Gaytryge's
Treatise: both demonstrate exactly the same arbitrary movement between a free
verse line, with no alliterative content, and a line with effective, though never
elaborate, alliteration:

'For the synne of Ophni . and of Finées hus brother
Thei were disconfit in bataille . and losten *Archa Dei*;
And, for hure syre sauh hem syngen . and soffrede hem don ille,
And no3t chased hem ther-of . and wolde no3t rebuke hem,
A-non, as it was ytold hym . that the children of Israel
Weren disconfit in bataile . and *Archa Dei* ylore . . .'   (C I 107–12)

And if the passage is not Langland's, but an interpolated piece, it has still a good
deal of interest to tell us about the continued life of such a mode of composition,
in the later years of the fourteenth century, and about medieval standards of
stylistic propriety which differ greatly from ours.[18]

The usefulness of Gaytryge's *Treatise* to the study of Langland's verse is that it
provides another example of the kind of English writing which may have been
part of his normal reading matter. We have proposed elsewhere that he was
thoroughly familiar with, and made use of, homiletic and satirical poems in

rhymed alliterative format:[19] additional evidence which helps us to understand his choice of a long *unrhymed* line for his extensive project is welcome.[20]

It may not be entirely without significance that there are other hybrid prose and verse texts from the later decades of the fourteenth century, which associate themselves, either by subject matter or style, with *Piers Plowman*. Thus, a volume of sermons, found in British Library Additional MS 41321, and dated by its editor to about 1380,[21] from the Cheshire area, contains passages which are directly, and strikingly, reminiscent of the poem:

Also in this blyndenesse beth þoo that bileuen that for a bulle purchasid of a fals pardoner, þoru a fals suggestion and symonye of selver (and thei paie him thanne a peny, and leie hit on hire hevedes) thei beth asoiled of alle hire synnes, as thei witterli wene.
(Additional MS 41321, fo. 85r, ed. Cigman, pp. 95–6: compare *Piers Plowman* B Prol. 68 ff.)

Prelates þat ben now a daies han many dyuerse castellis and maners, as rial as þe kynge himselfe . . . ʒea, þouh it be to visite his pore scheep, he mut ride wiþ foure or fyve score hors, proudeli apareiled at alle poyntes, his owne palfrai, for his bodi, worþ a 20 or 30 pound, al bihangid wiþ gliterynge gold as þouʒ it were an hooli hors; himself aboue, in fyn scarlet or oþer cloþ as good as þat, and wiþynne as good pelure as þe quene haþ any in hire gowne; hire persones and hire clerkis rydynge aboute hem al in gult harneise, wiþ bastard swerdis overgild bi hire sides hangynge . . .
(Additional MS 41321, fo. 100v, Cigman, p. 267: compare *Piers Plowman* B X 306–16)

It is sometimes, however, in short, telling correspondences that the complex relationships between Langland's poem and other religious materials of the age are suggested: Langland's celebrated allegory of Life, turning to triviality in the face of disaster – 'And rood [so to] revel, a ryche place and a murye' (B XX 181) – is glossed more simply by the Sermon picture of vain ecclesiastics, 'proude men of this world but principalli prelatus and prestis' who travel like 'a kynge rydinge toward a revel . . .'

Considerable passages fall naturally into alliterative verse lines – a fact which is commented upon, in a marginal (and contemporary) hand, on folio 72v of the manuscript: 'ista prosa est edita instar cadencie'. The first quotation which follows has been arranged in lines, but with editorial punctuation: the second has manuscript punctuation:

Þis is no poynt of pride, if it be wel ipreued.
And þenke also on þin eende: how peinful it schal be,
Grunnynge and gronynge and grisbatynge of teþ,
And sauerynge vnsoteli to hem þat sitteþ aboute.
Whan þou art deed, þus delfeli deluen þou schalt be,
And iwastid wiþ wormes, be þou neuer so worþi.
Wiþ þe mynde of þis matere þou mai make good dunge
To make þe rote of riʒtwis werkis the rathlier to growe . . .
(Additional MS 41321, fo. 66r, Cigman, pp. 41–2)

> It is good to be busi and bidde fast to god.
> For al hangeth in his hond . oure hap and oure hele.
> Bothe at mateyns and at messe . for that myche auayleþ
> And wiþ þe perfite pater noster . for þat preier pleseþ god /
> But thanne comeþ his muk in his mynde and marreþ him amydde
> And seiþ leef þi labour for a litill tyme.

> (ibid., fo. 74v, Cigman, p. 64)

It is, of course, not only of poems such as *Piers Plowman* that the echoes are strong:

> Thus auarice ouergoþ abstinence and unableth it to frute

> (fo. 74v, Cigman, p. 65)

More elaborate alliterative compositions come to mind in 'lines' such as 'to fiȝte wiþ hire foule flesch þat is so fayn to falle . . .' (loc. cit.) as well as Chaucerian descriptive detail in accounts of worldly 'prelatus and prestis', with their 'gingelinge brideles' and their 'grete fatte hors fed for the nones' (ff. 1ʳ–1ᵛ, Cigman, p. 2).

This richness of reference leads us to question, once more, the nature of the relation between English homiletic prose and English poetry during the thirteenth and fourteenth centuries, looking particularly, however, to the way in which this prose may not simply 'echo' or 'reflect' the great named works of the age, but may provide both their staple materials *and* some of their basic metrical forms. For a poet of ability to refine and regularize the 'line' of Gaytryge, or the 'line' of the anonymous sermon-writer of MS Additional 41321 would have been no difficult task; we have certainly no guarantee that the processes we are trying to recover always operated as a diffusion of verse into looser prose formats.

The field is ripe for investigation, and many of the texts hardly touched.[22] Michigan State College, MS I, for instance, an early fifteenth-century manuscript,[23] contains an independent and hitherto unnoticed partial translation of the widely influential *Meditationes Vitae Christi*. The translation, which was probably made, as were other partial English translations, during the fourteenth century,[24] is sporadically alliterative throughout. But with the lament of the Virgin over the dead Christ, it moves into a more substantially alliterative style. While, as the following extract will show, this lament cannot often be arranged into regular alliterative lines of a standard *aa/ax* pattern, the manuscript punctuation helps to define a structure which works predominantly to a long-line, alliterative format, even if composed of varied basic parts:

> My swete sone my dere derlyng full of dole.
> I behold þe dede lying in my lapp.
> þi doleful dede hase dygth a deuorse
> Betwene us two . a meruelous mygth.
> A lufly lykyng . and lyf withowten lackyng

178

Alliterative modes and affiliations

Wase betwen us two . . .
In þi dolefull dede . þi frendes were few.
And in þi feruent fygth . þi foyes wer full fell.　　　　(fo. 72r)

Here dyede dulefully my dere worthy derlyng.
Here sufferde my sone woundes full wyde.
Here blede he hys blode of hys blyssede body.
Here was his fayre flech rent on þe rode.　　　　(fo. 73r)

179

8   The timeliness of *Wynnere and Wastoure**

THE opinion of Sir Israel Gollancz that *Wynnere and Wastoure* 'is, in fact, a topical pamphlet in alliterative verse on the social and economic problems of the hour'[1] has never been seriously challenged. Nor has the dating finally settled upon by Gollancz – 'England in the year 1352':[2] a date arrived at by an attempt to correlate the poem's descriptive and satiric detail with historical fact. But it is no less true now than in 1921, when J. M. Steadman confirmed the findings of Gollancz (after sifting and reordering his evidence), that 'the question of the date of *Wynnere and Wastoure* has . . . important bearings on the study of the whole group of alliterative poems . . .'[3] and it is worth re-examining, therefore, some of the grounds upon which decisions as to the nature of the poem and its 'local habitation' have been traditionally based.[4]

In 1920, just before Gollancz produced his second edition,[5] J. R. Hulbert, writing on 'The Problems of Authorship and Date of *Wynnere and Wastoure*', proposed that even when the apparent authenticity of some of the poem's historical materials had been taken into account, there was no proper reason for restricting its composition to anything but a span of years, ranging from 1351– 66.[6] Much of Hulbert's supporting argument for this judgement was extremely sound, and it is curious that it has never gained wider currency.[7] An article published as late as 1972 accepts at the outset that 'internal evidence conclusively fixes its date at 1352–3',[8] not only working to confirm that date, but finding a precise historical event – the Parliament convened at Westminster in January 1352 – to be the motive for the writing of the poem. Professor Bestul's study, of 1974, footnotes Hulbert's view with some approval, but is only interested in a more liberal attitude to dating in so far as it aids his central thesis – that 'the poem is best seen as a topical poem, but one which records an experience shaped and formed by the welcome pressures of tradition . . .'[9]

It would not be profitable to review all the evidence brought forward in these earlier articles, and to attempt a critique of their respective methods of dealing with it. But it is important to question the premises upon which the collection and the presentation of such evidence were made, and to suggest that if editors and critics had not been so prematurely convinced of 'the timeliness of the poem and its significance as a pamphlet of the hour',[10] they might have been more judicious in both recognising and interpreting its 'historical materials'. Certainly they

* Originally published in *Medium Aevum*, 47 (1978), 40–65.

might have been less confident about assigning it to a particular year in the fourteenth century, and less confident, too, about identifying its 'characters' in a way which would support a particular set of 'historical' referents. We may set about this questioning by considering in detail some of the difficulties we encounter in the poem when we try to regard it as a 'most timely poem of the hour'[11] and expect its content to match contemporary history with exactitude. For it is upon the proof of such exactitude that the possibility of an exact date of composition must depend.

Lines 126–133, interpreted by Gollancz as a 'distinct allusion to the Statute of Treasons (1352) evidently recently promulgated',[12] have, on the whole, been accepted as this by later commentators. They occur in the speech of the knight who challenges the armies of Wynnere and Wastoure, drawn up aggressively against each other; the command is:

> That no beryn be so bolde one bothe his two eghne,
> Ones to strike one stroke ne stirre none nerre
> To lede rowte in his rewme, so ryall to thynke,
> Pertly with ʒoure powers his pese to disturbe.
> For this es the vsage here and euer schall worthe:
> If any beryn be so bolde with banere for to ryde
> Withinn þe kyngdome riche, bot the kynge one,
> That he schall losse the londe and his lyfe aftir.

The first important fact to be recognised about the situation as the poet of *Wynnere and Wastoure* presents it to us is that the opposing armies are concerned only with each other, and are not 'leading rout' against the King of the realm. The King himself is made to acknowledge this, when in line 106 he commands 'that they neuer neghe *nerre togedirs*'. We are, therefore, dealing with a situation in which the peace of the realm is threatened by the aggressive behaviour of rival armed bands, whose quarrel is with each other, and not with the King. If we wish, with Gollancz – and, by association, with most successive commentators – to relate this exactly to the Statute of Treasons of 1352, we are immediately faced by the problem of line 133, which states as the penalty for such behaviour, 'that he schall losse the londe and his lyfe aftir' – that is, forfeiture of lands and capital punishment. One of the most important objects of the Statute of Treasons was 'to establish a clear distinction between high and petty treason, and to settle the rules about forfeiture'.[13] High treason, for which the appropriate penalty would be that ultimate severity described in line 133, was defined under six heads: the situation in *Wynnere and Wastoure* comes into none of the stated categories. Whereas 'levying war against the King' could be regarded as high treason, the offence of fighting between rival armed bands was specifically defined as non-treasonable by that very Statute which has been used to gloss and to date the poem:

And if percase any Man of this Realm ride armed covertly or secretly with men of Arms against any other, to slay him or rob him, or take him or retain him till he have made Fine or Ransom for to have his Deliverance, it is not the Mind of the King nor his Council that in such case it shall be judged Treason, but shall be judged Felony or Trespass, according to the ancient law of the land.[14]

In the light of such a statement, there seems to be no doubt that, in 1352–3, from a legal point of view (and the Statute of Treasons had, as one of its primary objects, legal clarification) the offence of Wynnere and Wastoure and their followers would have been considered strictly felony, and not either high or petty treason. The punishment proposed so unequivocally, in language which is lightly reminiscent of the phrasing of the Statute,[15] as 'the vsage here and euer schall worthe . . .' (line 130) would, in the years immediately following the passing of the Statute, have appeared excessively severe, not to say impossibly so, since that Statute had been designed against a background of controversy and animosity concerning the attempts of the Crown, during the first half of the fourteenth century, to extend the definition of treasonable activities.[16] If, therefore, we are to see the poem as a comment upon the Statute of Treasons, 'recently prom- ulgated', and to place it in that precise historical context, the words of the knight to the armies poised for battle misrepresent one of the major intentions of the Statute.

We could, of course, go further, and ask whether they misrepresent the intentions of the 'comliche kynge' (line 86) of the poem. This is another question. For, if we feel obliged to concern ourselves with proper historical implications, Bellamy has reminded us of the reasons for believing that 'the crown could ignore any contradictory section of the Statute if it wanted to . . .'[17] and that in spite of the distinctions established in 1352, 'the crown . . . throughout the fourteenth and fifteenth centuries continued to hold that it only needed an act of arms and a banner displayed to make riot an act of treason . . .'[18] One of the crucial consid- erations in the matter was the nature of the forfeiture of land involved; if the offence were defined as felony, it was legally forfeited to the culprit's lord: if defined as treason, to the king. We have no clue in the phrasing of *Wynnere and Wastoure* which could help us determine whether its culprits would 'losse the londe' to crown or to mesne lord: we are probably unreasonable if we demand one. But we should notice that we are dealing with uncertainties, both historical and literary: not with clear situations and clear references which direct us to the legislation of a particular year in the fourteenth century.

The issue could be complicated further by historical developments during the reign of Richard II. In 1381, a Parliamentary Statute extended the law of treason: 'And the King straitly defendeth to al manner of People, upon Pain of *as much as they may forfeit against him in Body and Goods*, that noone from henceforth make nor begin any manner Riot and Rumour, nor other like. And if any the same do, and that duly proved, it shall be done of him as of a Traitor to the King and to his said Realm.'[19] It would seem, then, that from a strictly legalistic point of view, the only reign during which the activities of Wynnere and Wastoure could unequivocally have been interpreted as treason, and punishable to the harshest degree of the law, 'ils purront forfaire devans lui en corps e en biens',[20] was that of Richard II, and, even then, after 1381. Bellamy considers that while 'most English Kings of the period (1352–1485) were happy to abide by the definitions of treason embodied in the act of 1352 . . . the only king who may have had ideas of extending the law of treason was Richard II. He sought to preserve, define and even increase the royal prerogative...'[21] We may fairly observe, from these conflicting materials, that if lines 131–3 refer to the Statute of Treasons of 1352, line 133 shows how loosely, even inaccurately, the poet, in the person of the knight, construed the provisions of the Statute. There are, however, other possibilities. The poet may not have intended any precise reference to the Statute, either because he was composing freely, with literary licence, and attending only to dramatic effect, or because the Statute had not yet been passed. He may, alternatively, have been remembering the terms of the Statute at some distance of time, later in the century, when conditions and, perhaps, kings, had changed. Whatever the truth (and it is probably irrecoverable) we must be reluctant to assign the poem to any particular date on such grounds.

We should look equally carefully at what has traditionally been claimed as the most impressive piece of 'historical' evidence for the favoured 1352 dating of the poem: lines 317–18, spoken by Wastoure in his capacity as representative of 'sadde men of armes / Bolde sqwyeres of blode...'[22] which refer angrily to lawyers in general and to Sir William Shareshull in particular, Chief Justice of the King's Bench from 1350–61:

> That alle schent were those schalkes, and Scharshull itwiste,
> Þat saide I prikkede with powere his pese to distourbe . . .

The verbal echo here, of Shareshull's own complaint in his opening speech to the Parliament of January 1352, about 'les destourbours de la Pees et meintenours des quereles et des riotes',[23] was striking evidence for earlier scholars, in search of a decisive date for the poem's composition. It would indeed be more than striking if we could prove that this is the first record of the phrase 'disturbance of the peace' in the English vernacular: the possibility of a direct translation of Shareshull's original Anglo-French would be considerably strengthened. In fact, although the phrase, in various grammatical forms, is far more commonly in use in the later fourteenth century (in the works of Gower, Trevisa, Wyclif), it is recorded at c. 1300–25, from the south-west, – in Robert of Gloucester's *Chronicle*,[24] for instance. But even if we concede that here we have a precise, though small, verbal equivalence, we must admit that it exists in a larger context of imprecision, and it is not clear what ultimate importance to attach to it. We discover, for example, that it was Sir William Shareshull who was largely responsible for 'the most vital measure' in the legislation of the Statute of Treasons – 'the clear-cut distinction between treason and other felonies...'[25] This is, of course, the particular distinction about which, as we have seen, the poet of *Wynnere and Wastoure* shows himself to be quite vague. If we are asked to believe that the poet's acquaintance with Shareshull's words and actions was so thorough as to suggest that he wrote as an on-the-spot reporter of contemporary events in which the Chief Justice was involved, recalling in detail his 1352 speech to Parliament, it is curious that he should display any degree of vagueness about one of Shareshull's most remarkable legal achievements, in that very year which is canvassed as the year of the poem's composition.[26] Further, the dating of *Wynnere and Wastoure* on the basis of its author's accurate knowledge of the allegiances and sympathies of Sir William[27] is complicated by a closer look at the poem in relation to Shareshull's life and career.

We may assume, from the text before us, that Wastoure presents a large view of the military classes, from magnates down to 'bowemen many', and is not simply an embodiment of the wasteful and destructive elements in that comprehensive section of mediaeval society. The questions put by Wastoure to Wynnere –

'Woldeste þou hafe lordis to lyfe as laddes on fote?'
'Schold not a ladde be in londe a lorde for to serue?'[28]

should not be read simply as deliberate attempts to give us unfavourable insights into Wastoure's 'ethic'. They are orthodox elements in mediaeval social philosophy – harsh, hierarchical, but, for the period, just. Wastoure's hostility to Shareshull – 'that alle schent were those schalkes, and Scharshull itwiste' – does, admittedly, refer us to the historical fact that he was unpopular, in his capacity as Chief Justice, with 'those violent elements in the population that were of some social importance':[29] we have records not only of his instigation of criminal proceedings against 'unruly knights' such as the notorious Sir Hugh de Wrottesley, of Shropshire and Staffordshire (in 1353), but also of personal assaults on his property and servants by similar gentlemen of Staffordshire and Oxfordshire during the years 1333–58.[30] But Shareshull had friends enough among the magnates and the 'substantial landowners' of England to qualify him, on other counts, as Wastoure's ally: his connections with William Montacute, Earl of Salisbury, were particularly strong.[31] His contribution to the framing of the Statute of Treasons, and especially his work on the redefinition of treason and felony, with its important consequences for forfeiture of land, were grounds enough for his popularity with the higher echelons of the knightly classes:

those who benefited from the termination of the vague and elastic periphery of Treason were the magnates. If the Statute was adhered to by the King, they would receive as mesne lords, after a year and a day, lands which would previously have gone to the Crown for good...[32]

It is also relevant to note that in real life, Shareshull's name seems to have been abused by a variety of people, and in a variety of places, on account of his part in restrictive legislation of all kinds. His involvement with the devising of the Ordinance and the Statute of Labourers (1349, 1351) was commemorated in 1358, in Hertfordshire, when a clerk and a group of men, some of whom may have been labourers, were indicted 'for various offences, including the clerk's words that he and the others would gladly strike Shareshull...'[33]

If, therefore, we invoke history to explain the invocation of Shareshull's name, in lines 317–18 of *Wynnere and Wastoure*, it leads us to a period of years, during which the naming might have been powerful and appropriate, rather than to a particular year. Shareshull's active legal life extended from the 1330s well into the 1360s: made Chief Baron of the Exchequer in 1344, Chief Justice of the King's Bench in 1350, he was still presiding over sessions in Warwickshire and Worcestershire in 1367.[34] Moreover, it looks as if the attitude expressed in *Wynnere and Wastoure* was part of a more generally prevalent view – which may even have hardened retrospectively into something of a tradition: 'it was inevitable that in his life-long fight against humble and powerful law-breakers alike he should have become an object of hatred to the turbulent elements in all classes of society...'[35]

If the close scrutiny of some of the most notable 'historical references' in *Wynnere and Wastoure* diminishes our confidence in their power to date the poem exactly, there may be grounds for a fresh look at other supposedly firm evidence. The corroborative strength of a literal reading of lines 205–6, with their significant claim of 'twenty-five years' service to the king',

> Wele knowe we the kyng: he clothes vs bothe,
> And has vs fosterde and fedde this fyue and twenty wyntere ...

can be both confirmed and questioned by reference to other poems, alliterative and non-alliterative, of the fourteenth century. An interpretation of these lines as an accurate pointer to 'the twenty-fifth year of the reign of Edward III' (i.e., 1352) could be supported by the traditional reading of lines 78–9, Passus III, of *Mum and the Sothsegger*,[36]

> Þey bablid with her billis / how þei bete were,
> And tenyd with twiggis / two and twenty ȝeris ...

as a description of the events of 1399, when the 'nedy nestlingis' of England turned to the 'egle', Bolingbroke, and complained of the wrongs inflicted upon them by Richard II. But even if we are convinced that we have, in both poems, a looser verbal equivalent of the authoritative, 'regnal date' formula of official documents, we must still be cautious about the propriety of identifying the usages of *Wynnere and Wastoure* with those of *Mum and the Sothsegger*, a poem of very different mode and intention, which is full of undisputed historical reference.

The fact that the numerical formula in *Wynnere and Wastoure* is familiar in mediaeval contexts of great diversity, some less serious than others, might also caution us.[37] The difficulty of assessing the precise status of any such formulas, in mediaeval English vernacular works, is demonstrated, rather than clarified, by the variant forms of the trenchant lines on summary punishment in the reign of Richard II, both of which use an unequivocal 'regnal date' formula, but with entirely different numerical units:

> Þe stool was hard, þe ax was scharp,
> þe iiij ȝere of kyng Richard

> The ax was sharpe, the stokke was harde,
> In the xiiij ȝere of kyng Richarde[38]

In *Piers Plowman*, some distinction seems to be made between dating formulas of some precision, such as that used by Hawkin, 'the actyf man', in his reference to the year 1370, 'whan Chichestre was maire', as 'noȝt longe ypassed',[39] and looser temporal statements, such as that used by the poet-dreamer, in his confession that 'coueitise of eiȝes' 'folwed me fourty wynter and a fifte moore' (B xi 46–7). In these circumstances, it would be hasty to place absolute reliance upon the factual value of the *Wynnere and Wastoure* lines as a proof of its date of composition, although they cannot, of course, be discounted.

Nor is it difficult to question the part played in dating procedures by the historical identification of 'characters' in the poem. The proposal that we must understand Pope Clement VI (1342–52) as the 'Pope of Rome' to whom Wynnere is directed, in lines 460–1,[40]

> Wende, Wynnere, þi waye ouer þe wale stremys,
> Passe forthe by Paris to the Pope of Rome . . .

is strikingly at odds with historical fact. The reputation of this particular Pope, 'aristocrate de l'esprit, grand seigneur de l'Eglise, confidant du roi de France', would more naturally set him among the ranks of Wastoure than among those of Wynnere. He employed the finest Italian and French artists to decorate his oratory and private apartments with brilliant scenes of religious legend and courtly diversion: he spent more than his two predecessors combined on works of art and sumptuous robes: he bought the château of Visan as well as the town of Avignon. 'Les gouts fastueux du pontife ont transformé l'atmosphère de sa cour, lui ont donné une mondanité qui a probablement engendré des excès...'[41] If, however, the poet may be thought to intend a general allusion to the ways in which the Papacy extracted money from the English Church, and lived luxuriously upon the proceeds of 'winning', his grievance takes its place in a century full of similar complaints: they occur in any decade, provoked rather by a continuing situation than by an identifiable Head of the Church. That this is a more likely reading of the lines is suggested by the poet's use of the phrase 'þe

Pope of Rome': it sounds traditional, certainly unspecific – contrasting with the deceptively specific opening of the line:

> Passe forthe by Paris to þe Pope of Rome . . .

We are reminded of that earlier poem of the fourteenth century, *The Simonie*, which would be just as resistant to dating by means of associating its references to a 'court of Rome' with the misrule of any particular Pope:

> For at the court of Rome, ther treuthe sholde biginne,
> Him is forboden the paleis, dar he noht com therinne . . .[42]

Even more important is a re-assessment of the evidence upon which historical portraits of Edward III and the Black Prince have been discovered in the poem and made to work in favour of a 1352 dating. In fact, we should probably scrutinise the procedures by which three of the poem's noble characters have been identified, either wholly or partially: the two knights, introduced at lines 70 and 101, and the king, introduced at line 86. In the case of the first knightly figure to appear, at line 70, we are given some clues in the form of a blazon of arms on the mantling attached to the wearer's helm; it seems to constitute an expansive version of the technical heraldic description of the arms of Edward III, assumed by the king in 1340 – 'Quarterly France Ancient and England':[43]

> . . . casten ful clenly in quarters foure,
> Two with flowres of Fraunce before and behynde,
> And two out of Ynglonde with sex grym bestes,
> Thre lebardes one lofte and thre on lowe undir . . .   (77–80)

The desire of the poet to be as accurate as possible may even account for the defective alliterative scheme in line 79. But there is no compelling reason for us to accept Gollancz's suggestion that the man may be the Garter Herald.[44] Nor, indeed, should we be persuaded towards any alternative theories on the basis of Gollancz's emended reading of line 83, 'And by the cabane I knewe the k[nyght]e that I see', which invents a certainty of identification where the MS reading, 'And by the cabane I knewe the kynge that I see', only intends an expectation of the eventual appearance of the king.[45] Whoever this first figure is meant to represent, the only facts we have at our disposal are the royal arms on the decorative accessory to his crest, and the lion of England on the cap of maintenance above his helm:

> With ane helme one his hede, ane hatte appon lofte,
> And one heghe one þe hatte ane hateful beste,
> A lighte lebarde and a longe, lokande full kene,
> 3arked alle of 3alowe golde in full 3ape wyse . . .   (72–5)

It may be observed that the description could be precisely illustrated by the helm, cap and crest of the Black Prince, still to be seen among his funeral achievements in Canterbury Cathedral.[46] And we could suppose that the lack of a specific naming rested upon the poet's confidence in his readers' ability to supply a name for themselves; the royal arms were borne by someone whose special claim to them needed, perhaps, no explanation. But we must insist that the account of the arms as they appear upon the mantling could not, of itself, prove that we should limit our own search for candidates to the reign of Edward III. The lines would also be appropriate as a description of the arms of Richard II, even as late as 1394. Only at this date do we have the first evidence, from a seal, of Richard's additions of the arms of his 'patron', Edward the Confessor, to those of Edward III: 'the Confessor impaling Quarterly France Ancient and England'.[47] They would also, in fact, be appropriate as a description of the arms of Henry IV, who adopted those of Edward III, changing the number of fleur-de-lis in the French quarters to three, but retaining the 'sex grym bestes' of England: 'Quarterly France Modern and England'.[48]

The persuasion that we are, in spite of this, reading a description of the arms of Edward III must draw support from other kinds of corroborative 'evidence'; some more precise than others. The 'portrait' of the King himself, in lines 86–98, is certainly not inappropriate for Edward III, with its attention to decorative costume-motifs, drawn from falconry, 'Fawkons of fyne golde flakerande with wynges' (line 92) and followed as it is by what seems to be the poet's own admiring speculation about the king's enthusiasm for hawking along river-banks: '... full selly me thynke, / But if this renke to the reuere ryde vmbestounde' (lines 99–100). In sequence with the clear identification of the Garter motto on the king's pavilion (line 68), it probably makes best sense as a reference to Edward III, whose hunting pleasures are historically vouched for, and whose dress, on at least one occasion, in 1351, is recorded to have had bird and garter embroidery.[49] If, however, the poem makes such supposition possible, it does not allow us to deduce anything about the intended age of Edward which would be of help in dating the poem. Gollancz's recourse to MS Cotton Nero D.vi, for 'portraits' of Edward III, representing him in the 1350s, which supposedly corroborate detail such as that of line 91, 'bery brown was his berde', is of little value. For in two of the historiated initials which depict Edward, his beard is painted white or predominantly grey-white;[50] it is clear from Gollancz's note that he consulted inaccurate reproductions of the historiated initials, rather than the manuscript itself.[51] Neither the poem nor the manuscript can therefore demonstrate conclusively that the king of *Wynnere and Wastoure* was intended to appear 'of early middle-age'; much less can their information be used as part of an argument for a date of composition.

In the case of the identification of the second knight, who appears at line 101, as 'a beryn by hym þat stondeth' we should proceed with even greater caution. It is not that Gollancz's identification – Edward, the Black Prince – is totally out of the question: rather, it is that we have been misled into believing that the supporting evidence is historically secure, and, as a consequence, that it provides further evidence for a specific dating of the poem. The crux of the matter is the escutcheon on the knight's jupon, which, if we take what it tells us literally, consisted of a heraldic charge of three wings:

> Thre wynges inwith wroghte in the kynde,
> Vmbygon with a golde wyre . . .   (117–18)

Gollancz's desire to read this as 'the Prince of Wales's feathers'[52] raises many problems. The distinction between the Black Prince's use of the royal arms and that of the ostrich-feather badge is made substantially clear by the passage in his will which orders that both devices should figure in his funeral procession – 'l'un pur la guerre de nos armes entiers quartellez et l'autre pur la paix de nos bages des plumes d'ostruce . . .'[53] We have, however, no record of his wearing 'bages des plumes d'ostruce' on a jupon; existing evidence points rather to his use of the royal arms in such a position – the historiated initial on fo. 31 of BL MS Cotton Nero D.vi, the gilt-bronze effigy and the jupon itself, both in Canterbury Cathedral. Even if we could suppose that he did, on occasions such as tournaments, for instance, substitute his 'badge for peace' for his royal blazon, we have still to suppose that the poet of *Wynnere and Wastoure* would have chosen to introduce him in this way: the illuminator of the Cottonian MS clearly 'identifies' him by the royal arms of England. And, indeed, the acceptance of Gollancz's interpretation means that we must also accept a curious discrepancy in the poet's methods: clear, unambiguous heraldic description for the mantling of the first knight (lines 76–80) but obscure heraldic description for the second knight's surcoat.

The use of 'wynges' is in itself significantly puzzling, if we are to accept the word as a clear indication that we are dealing with the Black Prince's ostrich feather badge. The earliest fourteenth-century documents which refer to that badge use, in the vernacular, 'plume' or 'fether'. Thus the will of the Black Prince (1376) specifies twice, among the directions for his funeral ceremonies, and for the decoration of his Chapel in Canterbury Cathedral, 'nos bages des plumes d'ostruce', 'our badges of ostrich feathers'.[54] And again in 1376, the English surgeon, John Arderne, whose earlier family connections associate him with the Black Prince, but whose subsequent career associates him even more reliably with Henry of Lancaster and John of Gaunt, writes in his Latin treatise, *Practica de Fistula in Ano*, of the way in which the Black Prince came upon the ostrich feather device – 'et sic assumpsit sibi illam pennam quae dicitur "Ostrich fether"'.[55] The story told by Arderne, suspect though it may seem to modern scholarship for its romantic picture of the Black Prince taking the feather from the dead King of Bohemia, on the battlefield of Crécy, – 'et illam pennam conquisivit de rege Boëmio, quem interfecit apud Cresse in Francia'[56] – does at least draw our attention to the fact that the customary fourteenth-century translation of Latin 'penna', in heraldic contexts, was 'plume/fether' and not 'wyng'.[57]

The phrase 'in the kynde' also poses problems: we might suspect that it is a translation of a technical French or Anglo-French heraldic term, but no satisfactory original has been offered. The occurrence of a similar phrase, in a mid-fifteenth-century heraldic context – 'Sable two spotted lebardys of sylwyr in her kynde' – is initially suggestive of meanings connected, perhaps, with the concepts of 'in natural colours or form',[58] and, indeed, as we shall see, one of those meanings can ultimately be supported.

Even more difficult, in the context of the Black Prince's ostrich-feather badge, is it to read 'Vmbegon with a golde wyre' as 'bound together with a gold wire or band', and to understand it as a reference to the scroll which traditionally encircles the Prince of Wales's feathers. Escutcheons on the Black Prince's tomb at Canterbury display three feathers *in separate arrangement*: 'sable, three ostrich feathers, their quills passing through escrolls argent, bearing the words Ich Dien'.[59] Not until the sixteenth century do we find clear examples of the three feathers gathered within a single scroll or other enclosing device: the move seems to have been made by Edward VI, while still Prince.[60] It is of interest, however, that a roof boss in the cloisters at Canterbury Cathedral commemorates the arms of John of Gaunt, Duke of Lancaster, with a complex device 'surrounded by two Ostrich feathers, each having a chain along the quill...'[61] – a detail which reminds us that it is not immediately obvious what the poet intends us to visualise for 'Vmbegon *with a golde wyre*'. It must even be admitted that there seems to be some doubt as to how early the ostrich feathers were formalised into a triple design for the Black Prince: some of his seals, engraved in the 1360s, including that for the Duchy of Aquitaine, use two feathers, placed either side of a central motif.[62] Arderne's account of the episode on the battlefield of Crécy has some interest here for its marginal sketch of a *single* feather – 'penna Principis Walliae' – with a blank scroll placed upon the quill.[63]

In any case, a clear vote for the identification of this figure as the Black Prince has to take into account the extensive use of the ostrich feather device by members of the royal family and the nobility throughout the fourteenth century. The origin of the ostrich feather as a device for royal and aristocratic badges seems to lie with the European houses of Bohemia, Luxembourg and Hainault, and it has been suggested that the early record (not long after 1369) of 'a black escutcheon with ostrich feathers', enamelled at the base of a silver gilt dish belonging to Queen Philippa, wife of Edward III,[64] explains why not only Edward III himself, but almost all of his sons made use of the ostrich feather in seals and varieties of badges. Thomas of Gloucester displayed it, with garter and buckle, and the Lancastrian adoption of the feather device, in both double and triple format, is extremely well-documented. John of Gaunt's memorial window, in Old St Paul's, placed there in 1398, contained 'a sable shield charged with three

ostrich feathers ermine, the quills and escrolls or'.[65] His son, Henry Boling-
broke, both before and after his accession to the throne, used ostrich feathers
entwined with garters, carrying the motto 'Souerayne', for his seals: his second
seal, as Henry IV, bears a shield with three ostrich feathers on the obverse side.[66]
In fact, all descendants of the sons of Edward III showed a liking for ostrich
feather devices in some form or another: Richard II 'made frequent use of the
feathers, and granted them as marks of special favour to Thomas Mowbray,
Duke of Norfolk'.[67] The Beauforts, legitimised family of John of Gaunt, laid
claim to them, as did also Sir Roger Clarendon, natural son of the Black Prince.[68]
There is then, no evidence for the exclusive appropriation of the triple feather
device by Edward, the Black Prince, and even supposing that we assume 'thre
wynges' in line 117 to mean 'three ostrich feathers', there is at least one other
contender among the sons of Edward III for the right to be recognised as the
knight in question.

It is possible, however, that in our anxiety to discover one kind of historical
truth in the 'portrait', we fail to recognise another. We have already taken note of
the poet's apparent desire for accuracy when describing the royal arms borne by
the first knight to be introduced: we should probably credit him with a similar
desire for accuracy in the passage now under discussion.[69] And this must mean
that we seriously envisage the jupon of the second knight to have been blazoned
with a charge of three wings, and not three feathers. The simplicity of such a
proposal has much to recommend it. Nothing in the presentation of this figure
forces us to conclude that we are dealing with a king's son, and, by inference, the
Black Prince. We may observe that his function in the poem seems very reminiscent of that of the mediaeval herald: he acts as king's messenger (the term
'sandisman' is used for him in line 204) and also as what might be termed
'impresario' for the would-be combatants, recognising them by their banners,
and providing a brief history for each section of the host.[70] Moreover, once we
have abandoned the search for the Prince, we are free to search afresh for
fourteenth-century families whose heraldry may be more precisely represented
in the poet's words. Wings are not so unusual as heraldic charges in the
fourteenth century as to make the interpretation of 'thre wynges' in our present
context, as 'feathers', a natural procedure.[71] In fact many of the problems which
we meet when we attempt to read 'thre wynges inwith wroghte in the kynde /
Vmbygon with a golde wyre' as a description of the feather badge of the Black
Prince disappear when we consider the lines more directly, as a possible description of the armorial bearings of one of the most famous families in royal and ducal
employ throughout the fourteenth and fifteenth centuries.

Camden's reference to the Wingfields of Wingfield and Letheringham, Co.
Suffolk, as 'famous for their knighthood and ancient nobility'[72] leads us back to
the households of Edward III and the Black Prince, as well as to Rolls of Arms for
the reign of Richard II. Several of the Wingfields were prominent in the martial

and political life of the mid and later fourteenth century.[73] Sir John Wingfield, who died in 1361, was closely connected with both Edward III and the Black Prince: T. F. Tout traces his career in some detail, from early service with William Montacute, second Earl of Salisbury, to his exploits at Crécy and Poitiers, 'among the king's own followers', and to his rising importance in the Black Prince's household, 'governor of the prince's business', 'attorney', 'virtually the Prince's lieutenant'.[74] He acted for the Prince, and sometimes for the king, moving between London, Gascony, and his Suffolk estates.[75] His brother, Sir Thomas Wingfield, who died in 1378, made his career in the service of members of higher nobility such as the Arundels: he served with Richard Fitzalan, Earl of Arundel, in the Crécy campaign. Their cousin, Sir William, who lived on until 1398, having taken a distinguished part in the parliamentary affairs of two reigns, gave evidence in the London hearing of the Scrope-Grosvenor controversy (1389), in the company of Sir John Clanvowe and Geoffrey Chaucer.[76]

There is no lack of fourteenth-century evidence for the Wingfield arms: 'argent on a bend gules cotised sable three pairs of wings conjoined in lure of the field'.[77] The seal of the College of Priests, at Wingfield, Suffolk, founded in 1362 in memory of Sir John Wingfield, by his wife, the Lady Alienor, and his brother, Sir Thomas, had, at its base, three pairs of wings on a bend.[78] The memorial brass for Sir John Wingfield (son of Sir Thomas) who died in 1389, shows quite clearly, in Cotman's engraving, the same charge; interestingly enough, for *Wynnere and Wastoure*, it occurs on a sleeveless jupon worn over armour.[79]

There is, then, a distinct possibility that the poet of *Wynnere and Wastoure* expected his readers to recognise the 'thre wynges' on the 'jupown full juste' of the second knight as a distinguishing feature of some precision, and not as a curiously oblique reference to the feather-badge of the Black Prince. It should follow, if this is so, that other obscurities in the two crucial lines (117–18) are capable of clarification. And this, indeed, proves to be the case. The phrase 'wroghte in the kynde', which, as we have seen, is difficult to translate in the context of the Black Prince's ostrich-feathers, makes better sense in the context of the Wingfield arms. For whereas there seems to have been only one standard way of depicting the feather or plume in heraldic blazonry, wings, either alone, or as component parts of a charge featuring a bird (such as an eagle, for instance), appear in many diverse forms, some highly stylised, and others which are, indeed, as the *Wynnere and Wastoure* poet tells us, portrayed 'according to nature', 'wroghte in the kynde'.[80] The Wingfield arms show three pairs of wings 'conjoined in lure', that is, 'joined together with their tips downward', and it is possible that the poet is contrasting this heraldic format with others more elaborate and 'unnatural', in which the wings are formalised into an almost abstract patterning.[81] Some such sense may be reinforced by the only other recorded use of the phrase in a mid-fifteenth-century heraldic setting: 'sable two spotted lebardys of sylwyr in her kynde...'.[82] Here, too, the meaning 'according to (their) nature, in natural form' could be intended: the distinction remarked upon is probably that which exists between the 'lion-leopardé', or the stylised heraldic lion of the royal arms of England, for instance (*Wynnere and Wastoure* line 80, 'thre lebardes on lofte'), and the life-like, or spotted leopard – 'two spotted lebardys of sylwyr...'[83]

Some retrospective light may be shed upon these fourteenth- and fifteenth-century usages by a treatise on arms, published in 1586 – the *Blazon of Gentrie*.[84] In the course of a discussion of heraldic charges, the question of 'natural' and 'unnatural' representation is raised. Here the objection that an 'eagle displaid checquie' (an eagle with wings and legs spread out on either side, the wing-tips upward, chequered in two colours) was 'unnaturally borne', is countered by a firm statement that 'although things borne according to their nature or colour beene very commendable, yet is there as good misteries and honourable intendements in coats wherein be borne beasts, foules, fishes etc. different from their nature...' The imperial eagle of Rome, for example, was borne 'not to the nature of the bird'.[85] It is interesting that the same treatise, when commenting upon the Wingfield coat of arms, 'that beareth Argent, on a bend G(ules), three paire of wings', makes clear the 'verie honourable and ancient' status of the blazon, and seems to imply a certain simplicity in its wing-format: 'it is ynough to call them wings and say no more'.[86]

In a similar way, the phrase 'vmbygon with a golde wyre' (line 118) which, for good historical reasons, proved resistant to interpretation as a reference to the encircling scroll of the Prince of Wales's badge, has far greater persuasive force as a reference to the way in which the charge of three wings would have been, in normal mediaeval practice, embroidered and then appliquéd upon the knight's jupon. 'Vmbygon' may, of course, be used here in the familiar sense of 'encircling or surrounding', although there is some support for a more general use in the sense of 'ornamenting, or decorative'.[87] 'Golde wyre' is an accepted M E alternative to 'fildore' as a translation of the Latin 'filum aureum', the gold-thread used so lavishly in mediaeval embroidery.[88] It is possible to envisage the phrase, therefore, as a description either of the decorative outlining of the charge of three wings by 'a golde wyre' or 'a gold thread', or, perhaps, of the overall 'tinselling' of the embroidered devices upon the jupon.[89]

We are now in a stronger position to deal with the fact that one of the major internal 'signals' for the identification of the Black Prince in this portrait was provided for us not by the poet of *Wynnere and Wastoure* but by Sir Israel Gollancz, in one of his boldest emendations: the replacement of the M S reading, in line 108, 'Yis lorde saide þe lede while my life dures' by '[Y serue,] lorde saide þe lede, while my life dures'. The emendation, which substitutes an 'englished' version of the Black Prince's own motto, 'Ich Dien' for the simple 'Yis', has nothing to recommend it except its convenience to Gollancz's particular historical argument about the dating and the siting of the poem. The use of 'yes' as a response to a command or summons is perfectly regular in fourteenth-century practice, especially when emphasis is required; it is instanced in texts as diverse as the *Cursor Mundi, Sir Tristram,* Chaucer's *Book of the Duchess,* and the *Canterbury Tales.*[90] Gollancz's assertion that the original reading may have been 'y ser', employing a northern variant of 'serue' in a contracted form, and that this could have suggested 'Yis' to the scribe of the unique copy of the poem in the Thornton manuscript,[91] is not borne out by linguistic evidence from within the poem or from elsewhere. Other occurrences of the verb 'serue' are recorded in the poem (lines 177, 388, 492), two of which use the familiar *er* contractions. If northern 'ser' variants lie behind these, the Thornton scribe seems to have had no difficulty in adapting them.[92]

Similarly, Gollancz's inference of a grammatical model for his emended line in *Piers Plowman* A XI 101–2,

> ȝour man shall I worþe,
> For to werche ȝour wil while my lif duriþ

is challengeable. The original MS reading, 'Yis lorde said þe lede while my life dures' need not be grammatically defective, but may depend upon our recognition of another model – that, perhaps, of the heraldic motto, or of the 'devise', with its elliptical structure: 'dum varior', 'whyll lyff lastyth'.[93]

It must be said, in conclusion, that no 'historical' reference in *Wynnere and Wastoure* is in the same category as the celebrated passage from *Piers Plowman,* quoted above (p. 186), which clearly specifies the year 1370 as 'noȝt longe ypassed'.[94] Even in the present sampling, any line-by-line correlation of the poem with the verifiable data of historical record tends to give a picture of some complexity. We may with reason begin to suspect that the purpose of the poet was less exact than the literal and contemporary reporting of the political, economic and social conditions of any given year, and that a close examination of other areas of the poem, outside the scope of this present study, would prove such suspicions well-grounded. Materials relating to the treatment of the merchant classes in the debate might be particularly responsive to examination. What follows inevitably, however, is that we should be unwise to accept, any longer, a categorical dating for the composition of *Wynnere and Wastoure,* and that we should, therefore, define its formative role in the development of fourteenth-century alliterative poetry very tentatively indeed. The traditional assumption that it pre-dates the A-text of *Piers Plowman,* for instance, with all that this implies for Langland's deliberate 'purifying' of an established and elaborate alliterative style, should be questioned afresh.[95]

On the other hand, we should be alive to the fact that among the materials of the poem there may be some which are of particular and special 'historical' relevance. The function of heraldry in the illuminated manuscripts of the fourteenth and fifteenth centuries is often precise and significant; so is it also in many

German, French and Anglo-French poems of the same years.[96] It is difficult to believe that heraldry in *Wynnere and Wastoure*, as it attaches to non-allegorical characters, does not reveal something of the history of the poem, even if it is a more dangerous guide to the history of the period. The exact relationship of certain kinds of English alliterative verse to aristocratic patronage is a complex matter, still under debate. No less problematic is the acceptability of this verse to patrons and audiences in widely-dispersed areas of the country – in London, East Anglia, and Yorkshire, as well as in the West and North-west Midlands. It may be premature to claim that just as the late alliterative poem, *Scotish Feilde*, with its explicit Stanley heraldry, was written for that family, so too, more than a century earlier, *Wynnere and Wastoure*, with its Wingfield heraldry, was written for a Wingfield.[97] We can, however, speculate about the contexts in which such 'patronage' might have been exercised.

We should not overestimate the difficulty of associating an alliterative poem with a family whose main estates, during the fourteenth century, lay in Suffolk, but whose professional commitments would so often bring them to London. It is worth noting that, in 1352, Sir John Wingfield was granted lands in Cheshire by William Montacute, Earl of Salisbury, and that several branches of the Wingfield family were settled in Derbyshire and Shropshire by the mid-fifteenth century.[98] After the death of her husband in 1389 (Sir John Wingfield, nephew of the above), Margaret Wingfield married Sir John Russel, of Strensham, Worcester-shire, and these Worcestershire family connections were maintained by her son, Sir Robert Wingfield, who married a Russel heiress.[99] That the London house-hold of a Wingfield, in the fourteenth century, should contain a 'westren wy', capable of writing a poem such as *Wynnere and Wastoure*, and of using it to pay a graceful compliment to his master, does not seem impossible. There is good historical evidence for the employ of clerks from western families in royal and aristocratic service during these years; such service would of necessity involve them in travel between the west-country and the capital, and substantial resi-dence in both areas.[100] The double allegiances of *Wynnere and Wastoure*, with its references to the life and, less certainly perhaps, to the literary traditions of the west of England (lines 8–10, 24–8) and its references to the life and topography of mediaeval London (lines 476ff.) would suggest some such background – a secular counterpart to the background we have come to accept for William Langland, that other 'westren wy' who appears to have written his alliterative poetry in the heart of the capital. The vocabulary of *Wynnere and Wastoure* is not, in its present form, remarkable for its western character and, in any case, London readers, if we are to judge by the earlier fourteenth-century Auchinleck miscel-lany, were already used to being presented with texts of a strongly 'provincial' nature.[101]

We have, of course, no means of telling which fourteenth-century member of the 'verie honourable and ancient' family of Wingfield may have been the object of the *Wynnere and Wastoure* poet's complimentary attention. Nor is it possible to be absolutely sure whether that attention was directed from a contemporary or from a retrospective viewpoint. The career of Sir John Wingfield, Lord of Wingfield in Suffolk, was illustrious on the battle-field and in the council-chamber. At first in the service of John Warenne, Earl of Surrey, and later in that of William Montacute, Earl of Salisbury, he fought at Crécy and at Poitiers. By the time of the battle of Poitiers, however, he had already passed several years in the service of the Black Prince: the decade 1351–61 sees him active on royal business. He appears in Gascony, accompanying the Black Prince on his campaigns of 1355–7, and writing letters home with detailed accounts of military operations in southern France;[102] he reappears in England, authorising letters 'from his bed', or 'from the chimney-corner' of his London house.[103] As the governor or the lieutenant of the Black Prince's household, 'his name was of itself authoritative' (Tout, *Chapters*, V, 388) – a truth borne out by the amount and the variety of important transactions he is recorded as managing on behalf of the Prince (Tout, V, 386–8, 394, *Register*, IV *passim*). Dying suddenly of the plague, in 1361 – 'invadens mors pestifera'[104] – he left money for the foundation and endowment of a College of Priests at Wingfield: at his death, his lands lay in Suffolk, Norfolk and Cheshire. His daughter, Katherine, married Michael de la Pole, favourite of Richard II, who made him Earl of Suffolk in 1385. The Wingfield and de la Pole alliance, thus formed, was strong and lasting: it was the 'dominating influence governing the Parliamentary representation of the country for the greater part of Richard II's reign'.[105] The de la Poles quartered the Wingfield arms with their own;[106] it was Michael de la Pole who, in 1384, obtained a licence to make a castle of his manor-house at Wingfield. Did the de la Pole sense of participating, by marriage, in a distinguished family past extend to the literary commemoration of that distinguished ancestor, Sir John?[107]

There are, however, other eligible Wingfield family contexts in which to imagine the composition of *Wynnere and Wastoure*. Sir Thomas Wingfield, Sir John's younger brother, acquired, by marriage to an heiress of the Suffolk family of Bovile, not only the main Bovile seat of Letheringham, with its Church and Priory of Austin Canons[108] but much other valuable property. His career was associated to some extent with that of his brother, Sir John, but he had independent connections with magnates such as the FitzAlans, Earls of Arundel.[109] Though less is recorded of his life than of that of his brother, he was clearly, as his will of 1378 reveals,[110] a man of wealth and standing. His bequests of money to religious houses include the Priory Church at Letheringham and the aristocratic Austin Nunnery of Campsey in Suffolk.[111] To the Priory Church he also gave a silver cross, and 'vestimenta de armis comitis Warenne' – a reminder of the early Wingfield-Warenne links. The main part of his estate, with a 'golden cross', went to his son John, but his Confessor, Brother John Kynyngham, was remembered, and so also were Sir William Hoo, and his wife Elizabeth.[112] The mention of the

Hoo family, tenants of St Albans, with estates in Bedfordshire, evokes not only the dangerous events of the next decade, when Sir William helped to arrange Michael de la Pole's escape to Calais,[113] but also the quieter realities of fourteenth-century book-collections: an A-text of *Piers Plowman* was in Hoo ownership before 1399.[114]

Indents only remain in the Church at Letheringham for the lost brasses of Sir Thomas Wingfield, and Margaret, his wife. But that of his son, Sir John Wingfield, who died in 1389, is still to be seen there, clearly displaying the 'three wings' of the Wingfield arms on a sleeveless jupon (see above, p. 192 and n. 79). It is suggestive, if no more, to find the fifteenth- and sixteenth-century descendants of Sir Thomas Wingfield appearing in connection with families such as the Stanleys, powerful land-owners in Cheshire and Lancashire, whose role, over those centuries, as owners of manuscripts and patrons of literature, operates for both alliterative and non-alliterative verse. The famous 'Chaucerian' Miscellany, MS Fairfax 16, has been reliably associated with Thomas, Lord Stanley (1405–59) whose sister-in-law, Elizabeth Goushill, was married to Sir Robert Wingfield, great-grandson of the fourteenth-century Sir Thomas. By the early seventeenth century, the MS was owned and signed by another 'Robert Wingfield': it has been suggested that it may have passed into Wingfield hands before the close of the fifteenth century.[115] Remembering evidence that the Stanleys and some of their tenants took a strong interest in the copying and even in the composition of alliterative poetry,[116] it is tempting to speculate that some members of the Wingfield family may have assisted the preservation of the text of *Wynnere and Wastoure* into the fifteenth century.[117]

But one last fourteenth-century Wingfield deserves our consideration: Sir William Wingfield, cousin of Sir John and Sir Thomas, who by 1349 is recorded as lord of the manor of Dennington, in Suffolk.[118] His early years were spent in the service of Sir Baldwin de Botetourt, 'knight bachelor' of the Black Prince; by 1360, when Sir Baldwin died, he was already 'yeoman' of the Black Prince, and keeper of the manor of Newport for him. After 1361, he seems to have transferred to the service of Thomas de Vere, Earl of Oxford, who granted him manors in Berkshire and Northamptonshire. He was a man of distinguished career: giving evidence in the Scrope-Grosvenor controversy of 1389, he refers to his presence at the sea-fight against the Spaniards, off Winchilsea (1350) and at the winter campaign of 1359–60, 'devant Parys', with the best of Edward III's captains.[119] He was nine times Knight of the Shire for Suffolk, in collaboration with Sir Richard Waldegrave, and was especially prominent during the Good Parliament of 1376, attacking ministerial corruption. His particular involvement with the case against John Neville, Lord of Raby, who was accused of corrupt practices in wool-transactions, is interesting in view of his links with London property and London merchant life. His wife, Joan, was widow of Ellis Fraunceys, a member of that powerful London family of mercers, who were heavily involved in the syndicates of Edward III, emerging with property in four counties and a substantial city estate.[120] His son, William Wingfield, married Kathcrinc Hadley, daughter of John Hadley, the 'great merchant capitalist of London' (John, p. 687). It is Sir William Wingfield whom we can sometimes place very precisely in London settings: in 1382, for instance, when he testified on behalf of his friend, Sir William Waldegrave, that two coffers had been stolen from him at the 'Swerd on the Hoope' inn, in Fleet Street.[121] Sir William's circle of close acquaintances must have been drawn from influential men; it is a pity that his will, proved in 1398, is only fragmentary, for it might have contained further evidence of those who were part of his busy and interesting life.[122]

Much remains to be discovered about the historical and literary affiliations of *Wynnere and Wastoure*. The fact that its Prologue, among general reminiscences of Latin and vernacular poetry, contains lines which are more closely reminiscent of a passage in the Prologue to the Chandos Herald's *Vie et Gestes du Prince Noir*,[123] a work which its editors date to 1385 – must surely continue to give us thought. The sentiments, and the expression of those sentiments turn similarly upon regret for the passing of a situation in which responsible patrons were served by worthy poets, and contempt for the present situation, in which

> on teigne plus grant acompte
> D'un janglour ou d'un faux menteur,
> D'un joglour ou d'un bourdeour (*Vie*, lines 16–18)

> Bot now a childe appon chere, withowtten chynwedys . . .
> Fro he can jangle als a jaye and japes telle
> He schall be leuede and louede. (*Wynnere*, lines 24, 26–7)

Here we may only be referred to a commonplace of mediaeval literary tradition;[124] poems such as the *Dis des Estas dou Monde*, by the earlier fourteenth-century Hainault poet, Jean de Condé, whose work was certainly being read in cultivated English circles during the fourteenth century,[125] give stern advice to 'menestrés' on the standards they should try to maintain:

> Ne te faices teil appieller
> C'on die tu soies gengleres.
> Soies conteres u jougleres
> U menestrés d'autre maniere.[126]

But it has been suggested that there may be, in the Chandos Herald's lines, a direct indebtedness to Jean Froissart's complaint, that 'plusieur gongleour et enchanteour . . . corromput par les chancons et rimes controuvées le just et vraie histoire . . .':[127] whatever the precise source for the *Wynnere and Wastoure* version of this comment, we seem to be led, in our search, to French and Anglo-French materials, some of which were produced at the English court, in association with aristocratic, even royal, patrons. To such circles of authors and patrons, the poet of *Wynnere and Wastoure* and the Wingfields of Suffolk need not have been strangers.[128]

9 A Complaint against Blacksmiths*

A⊤ some time before 1450 a blank folio of a thirteenth-century Norwich Cathedral Priory manuscript (now British Library MS Arundel 292)[1] was half-filled with a lively alliterative composition on the theme of blacksmiths and their exasperating practice of working at night; written out in continuous format, it is punctuated into long-line units:[2]

> Swarte smekyd smeþes smateryd wyth smoke .) dryue me to
> deth wyth den of here dyntes .) Swech noys on nyghtes ne
> herd men neuer .) what knauene cry & clateryng of knockes .)
> þe cammede kongons cryen after col col .) & blowen here
> bellewys þat al here brayn brestes .) huf puf seyth þat on haf
> paf þat oþer .) þei spyttyn & spraulyn & spellyn many
> spelles .)[3] þei gnauen & gnacchen þei gronys to gyder .)
> and holdyn hem hote wyth here hard hamers .) of a bole hyde
> ben here barm fellys .) her schankes ben schakeled for þe
> fere flunderys .) heuy hamerys þei han þat hard ben handled .)
> stark strokes þei stryken on a stelyd stokke .) lus. bus. las.
> das. rowtyn be rowe .) sweche dolful a dreme þe deuyl it to
> dryue .) þe mayster longith a lityl & lascheth a lesse .)
> twyneth hem tweyn and towchith a treble .) tik . tak . hic .
> hac . tiket . taket . tyk . tak .) lus . bus . lus . das . swych lyf
> þei ledyn .) Alle cloye[4] merys cryst hem gyue sorwe .) may
> no man for brenwaterys on nyght han hys rest.

General agreement as to the interest of this piece guarantees its regular appearance in anthologies,[5] but commentary upon it has always ranged uneasily. Much admired for its 'magnificent realism',[6] it has been used as material evidence by both literary and social historians, who have seen in it a proof of the vigour of alliterative verse 'on the eve of the alliterative revival' no less than an account of the actual conditions of English urban life in the later Middle Ages.[7] But its random association with a variety of writings, from short popular verse satires and civic documents to texts as distinguished as Chaucer's *Miller's Tale*, and its equally random association with the fourteenth and fifteenth centuries for probable dates of origin,[8] point to continuing difficulties in the establishment of its historical and literary affiliations. Such affiliations may only be partially recoverable – but the business of attempting recovery in this case illustrates particularly well the nature of the problems often set for us by medieval vernacular texts, in which an impression of strong but unlocalised life urges us to work towards reducing some of the uncertainties of authorship, intention and status.

* Originally published in *Literature and History*, 5 (1979), 194–215.

Nothing so far written about this *Complaint against Blacksmiths* makes quite clear the curiosity of its appearance as a late entry in a thirteenth-century Norwich Priory manuscript, or the curiosity of its reminiscences of widely-differing historical and literary texts. The importance of the fact that we have no knowledge either of the type of circumstance in which it was first composed, or of that in which it was transcribed, has hardly been recognised: we have not even fully established the literary *genre* to which it belongs. Only, however, by accepting the meaningfulness of our perplexities and by exposing the issues raised by them can we hope to replace something of that 'common body of knowledge and expectation'[9] which the original author, scribe and reader of the alliterative lines would have shared, and which we so signally miss when we try to describe or to appraise them in a substantial medieval context.

The point may be made, in a comparative way, by emphasising how simply another later addition to Arundel MS 292, the so-called *Chorister's Lament*,[10] can be 'contexted'. This wry and technically expert satirisation of the rigorous training imposed in monastic or cathedral song-schools presents no problems as an item in a miscellany of monastic provenance: moreover, the clerkly and essentially orthodox tradition of impudent criticism to which it subscribes provides it with a network of relationships in an established literary mode.[11] But the relationships already proposed for the alliterative *Complaint* lead immediately into more controversial areas and prompt serious questions: about the materials and motives of its author, about the significance of its East Anglian religious – and probably urban – provenance, and about the propriety of accepting it without hesitation as a realistic account of how one particular 'profit-making concern on overtime . . . kept a fifteenth-century poet . . . in furious wakefulness...'[12]

Most recent citations of the *Complaint* accept its historical authenticity and utilise it as corroborative evidence for a variety of practical purposes. This is not without hazard. It is, indeed, tempting to draw upon it for annotation of a work such as Chaucer's *Miller's Tale* which builds a crucial part of its narrative about the fact that medieval blacksmiths kept nocturnal business hours. 'Derk was the nyght as pich or as the cole' when Absolon, in fourteenth-century Oxford, found the smith Gerveys sharpening 'shaar and kultour' for the next day.[13] And it is tempting, also, to associate it with a London document of 1394, to provide additional proof that in the *Miller's Tale* Chaucer was not in any way 'sacrificing truth to the exigencies of fiction'.[14] But it is in this very process of assembling literary and documentary texts for a common purpose that interpretative problems begin to appear, and 'what is truth?' becomes, once more, a relevant question. The dilemma can easily be illustrated.

Since the London document of 1394 (see below, p. 203) requests approval for Guild legislation against night-forging, it is possible to extract from it different kinds of evidence according to whether we lay emphasis upon a common practice which required legislation or upon a reformed practice which resulted from legislation. And, in fact, this is exactly what has happened: the same document has been pressed into service by literary historians to illustrate the 'contemporaneousness' of Chaucer's reference to night-forging in the fourteenth century, and by social historians to illustrate the successful resistance to night-forging in the fourteenth century.[15] Clearly, neither poem nor document can be considered in isolation if the corroborative value of one to the other is to be settled beyond reasonable doubt. Our view of the authority of Chaucer's account must be influenced by our knowledge of the existence of numerous European analogues for his drama of mistaken identity and painful retribution – in all of which a night-setting and a forge in full action were essential to the conduct of the narrative.[16] Our assessment of the authority of the London document must be based upon a knowledge of its place in a sequence of similar legislative materials. And it follows that our understanding of the literal or imaginative fidelities of the alliterative *Complaint* cannot be achieved except through a series of explorations, designed to test out its relationship to historical fact and historical convention, to literary and, perhaps, to devotional tradition. Nothing can be taken for granted if we wish to be in a position not only to appraise it but also to make use of it in critical argument.

One convenient access to historical fact lies, we might think, in documents which deal in various ways with the same basic theme as the *Complaint*: the night-working habits of the metal-crafts during the Middle Ages. But, as we have already briefly anticipated, these documents – the Craft *Ordinances* of London and other medieval cities – do not automatically serve to verify the historical status of the *Complaint*; instead, they face us with their own range of enigmas and uncertainties. Some light, indeed, they shed upon the choice of subject matter and the attitudes of the unknown author; there is no doubt that an anxiety to curb night-activity is common to all. But in many important ways they serve to underline, rather than to score-out, our difficulties. While they can persuade us, even to the extent of providing occasional verbal reminiscences, that *Complaint* and civic document stand in some kind of relationship to the facts of medieval urban life, they cannot clarify that relationship entirely. Indeed this should, on reflection, hardly surprise us, since the questions they themselves raise for us – their own reliability as a guide to contemporary practice, their authentic, as opposed to their apparent, motivation, even their class of authorship – are the same questions raised by the *Complaint* itself. As Sylvia Thrupp insists, when dealing with these Craft *Ordinances*:

it was a convention to frame public policies in the name of general principles . . . to advance a special interest, it was almost a necessity to declare that it coincided with the public interest, a claim that might or might not be taken at its face value . . .[17]

A recognition of the distance, often considerable, between 'face value' and 'inner intent' is salutary, but uncomfortable, for the literary historian who seeks endorsement from documentary sources for his task of dating and defining literary texts.

If, for instance, we relied uncritically upon this official kind of testimony, it would be possible to hold that at any time between 1261 and 1394 night-forging was being vigorously prohibited, and by responsible authorities, for the general good of the community.[18] As early as 1261, the *Ordinances* of the Lorimers of London (makers of bridles, bits and other articles of horse-equipment), presented 'par commun consail' of the Craftsmen and approved by the Mayor, William FitzRichard, and the Aldermen of the City, laid down decisively 'qe nul du mester ne forge ne oevre de nuyt nule manere de overaigne de lormerie; ne qe nul oevere jettee ne fundue mette en oevreyne; pur ceo qe est freinante chose et maveise...'[19] It would be hard to say whether we have in these words any early hint of the existence of that kind of public resentment of night-smithying which appears to inspire the alliterative piece. The most common – and obviously acceptable – justification of the drive against night-work was that it helped to maintain the production of goods of highest quality. Identical resolutions – but without the comment 'freinante chose et maveise' ('disruptive and harmful') – were being passed by other crafts at the time: the *Articles* of the Saddlers and Joiners lay down that 'nul fuster oevre de son mester de nuyt mes tantsoulement de jour...'[20]

Later documents are more expansive but not necessarily unambiguous; in a case brought before the Mayor's Court of the City of London, in March 1298–9, we seem to come a little closer to some acknowledgement, however differently angled, of the social attributes displayed by the *Complaint*. In the context of what has been described as an 'effervescence of craft-formation'[21] during the early years of the reign of Edward I, seventeen London smiths were called to answer the City and the Commonalty of London for their making of a parliament and a confederacy 'in contempt of the King and to the harm of the City'.[22] The smiths admitted that they had indeed instituted a central fund for charity-relief of their trade-members, and that they had made an *Ordinance* 'that none should work at night on account of the unhealthiness of the sea-coal and damage to their neighbours; that their doors should be closed all the year at the first stroke of Curfew at St Martins-le-Strand'.[23] Their acquittal on all charges is certainly a witness to the strength and 'ferocious spirit of solidarity'[24] in the Craft-movement of this decade, which saw the Crafts moving at last into political action with their general assemblies, confederacies and strikes. And the concern expressed in this document for the well-being of the urban community may have been genuine. When Queen Eleanor was in Nottingham, in 1257, she was forced to depart suddenly, 'owing to the smoke of the sea-coals';[25] we may be able to see, here, a responsible reaction to the unpopularity of forge-activities in increasingly crowded town conditions. But it is the various nature of the reasons given, over the later thirteenth and fourteenth centuries, for repeated legislation against night-working which must cause us some uneasiness, and which brings to mind Sylvia Thrupp's warning about the scepticism with which the contemporary 'pulpit and parliament' sometimes received the assurances of the Craft Guilds that they legislated only 'for the profit of the people'.

Constant among such reasons is always the necessity to control working hours in order to preserve the standard of craftsmanship; the *Articles* of the Spurriers, in 1345, speak for many other Crafts when they set down that 'no man can work so neatly by night as by day', substantiating their claim by particularising how 'many persons of the said trade who compass how to practise deception in their work, desire to work by night . . . and then they introduce false iron, and iron that has been cracked, for tin . . .'[26] But they move on to give a startling account of other reasons for action: the socially unacceptable practices of the metal-workers. The picture they present, of riotous and extravagant behaviour, is strongly reminiscent of the alliterative *Complaint* in some of its detail:

many . . . are wandering about all day, without working at their trade; and then, when they have become drunk and frantic, they take to their work to the annoyance of the sick and of all their neighbourhood . . . And then they blow up their fires so vigorously, that their forges begin at once to blaze, to the great peril of themselves and of all the neighbourhood around. And then too all the neighbours are much in dread of the sparks, which so vigorously issue forth in all directions from the mouths of the chimneys in their forges . . .[27]

And it is this same 'social unacceptability' which is advanced as a primary persuasion to reform in 1394, when 'the reputable men of the trade of Blacksmiths of London . . . delivered unto John Hadley, the Mayor, and the Aldermen of the City' certain articles 'entreating that the same might be granted, for the common profit and advantage of the said city . . .'[28]

In the first place, for as much as the folks of the said trade of Blacksmiths are oftentimes indicted at divers wardmotes from ward to ward, and warned to quit their houses, by reason of the great nuisance, noise and alarm experienced in divers ways by the neighbours around their dwellings; – it is ordained that noone of the said trade shall work by night, but only from the beginning of daylight to 9 of the clock at night throughout all of the year, except between the Feast of All Hallows and the Feast of Candlemas, between which Feasts they shall work from 6 of the clock in the morning until 8 of the clock at night . . .[29]

The fact that these documents so frequently support their case for legislation on grounds ranging from a coolly-expressed regard for quality to a highly-charged indictment of anti-social, almost vicious, behaviour, is bound to invite inquiry as to their motives and their candour. Indeed, all that emerges with absolute clarity from them is the apparent difficulty of enforcing any restriction upon the working day of the metal Crafts of London, over the later thirteenth and fourteenth centuries.[30] Unwin comments upon the significant difference between the earlier *Articles* which the Craft Guilds presented to the Civic Authorities, with proposals for the 'regularisation of their calling', and the later *Charters of Incorporation* under Edward IV and Henry VII: the former are 'almost entirely silent as to the social machinery by means of which the regulations were to be enforced'.[31] When, therefore, we try to use such documents in order to do two things – to verify the historical standing of the alliterative *Complaint* and to suggest a possible date for its composition – we quickly discover the limits of their usefulness. In a century and a half of attempts to legislate against patterns of night-working, documents and *Complaint* can doubtless be seen as proof of the continued strength of the resistance to that legislation. As guides to the actual historical conditions which, in any given year, made legislation necessary, they are best handled with caution.

The slender evidence upon which we have to proceed, for instance, when we try to relate Guild *Ordinances* to the specific problems of the year in which they were issued makes it unlikely that we shall find any indisputable way of associating the *Complaint* with a document of one particular date rather than of another. There is no objective method of determining whether urban affairs in London in 1345 would have been more likely than affairs in 1394 to stimulate both legislation and *Complaint*. We can only say that the clustering of documents of legislation in the fourteenth century, and the comparative silence of the fifteenth century on this subject, may indicate a date before 1400 for a set of conditions sufficiently provocative to encourage both political and literary activity. With regard to the latter, and in a choice between 1345 and 1394, it is other evidence, of an internal nature, which tips the balance in favour of 1394.[32]

And as for the establishment of a date of composition, so also for the verification of historical standing: recourse to Guild documents does not solve the problem of how to judge the *Complaint* as a record of factual event, but it does help in the accurate definition of the problem. It suggests, for instance, that 'historical authenticity' should best be sought as 'authenticity of witness' to a complex historical situation, in which cross-currents of conflicting interests were powerfully locked. Any restoration of 'historical life' to the *Complaint* must take into account this complexity, recognising what the study of civic documents teaches us – the need to see beyond official formulations to the bitter inter-class struggles which they attempt, with only partial success, to simplify and even to misrepresent. In these struggles, merchant oligarchies, Guild-masters and journeymen-workers played effective, but by no means simple, parts. Thus, if as a general rule the merchant oligarchy exercised major control over institutions of urban authority, and were often in conflict with the Craft-Guilds,[33] there were other occasions on which merchants and master-craftsmen in the Guilds were at one in their desire to see the markets protected from over-production, and from the consequence of falling prices, by agreement on the strict limitation of working-hours. 'Medieval evidence being what it is, examples are all a historian can produce';[34] beyond the 'evidence' of the documents of the English Craft-Guilds we can point to incidents in Italy and France when reprisals were taken against metal craftsmen, from within their own fraternity, for working too early and too late.[35] It is easy to see how Guild documents, made-up by clerks for the purposes of Guild masters, might seek to conceal, in orthodox and socially palatable statements, actual situations of high tension which were often caused, as we know from precise instances, by the persistence of ordinary craftsmen in working overtime. And this was especially so in occupations where to supplement meagre earnings was an absolute necessity.[36]

We are right, therefore, in suspecting that there is frequently more than meets the eye in these documents of legislation, with their apparent care for the maintenance of high standards, their apparent sense of social responsibility, and their marshalling of vivid and pejorative detail to justify both. There may also be more than meets the eye in the *Complaint*, although we do not have to propose that its centre of concern is identical to that of the documents, or that it uses similar detail for precisely the same ends. The association of documents and *Complaint* indicates, rather, how wide is the area of speculation as to the materials and the motives which went to their composition. Thus, while the Craft *Ordinances* may initially persuade us that the *Complaint*, like them, is a direct product of later medieval social and economic change, accelerated by the strained conditions of urban employment, the *Complaint* has something to contribute, in return, about factors of a different kind which were almost certainly influential upon it, and which cannot be ruled out of operation, even if in a very minor capacity, for the shaping and expression of the *Ordinances* themselves.

We are alerted to these factors by one very special circumstance – the manuscript provenance of the *Complaint*. No attempt to reconstruct the cultural milieu of a medieval literary text can afford to ignore what clues this may provide both as to its genesis and to its continuing life within the period. In this respect, the *Complaint*, as distinct from the civic documents, offers us two opportunities for speculation. Its unique appearance in a monastic miscellany from Norwich Cathedral Priory must raise with us the possibility, in the first place, that its vehement denunciation of blacksmiths and their working practices may have been fed, in part, by older religious attitudes and, in the second place, that such attitudes may account, at the very least, for its preservation in a strongly traditional and moral setting. The force of these considerations is strengthened by the discovery of the inserted phrase 'ech of hem at othyrs', above those words of the *Complaint* which deal with the noisy tale-swapping of the blacksmiths: 'spellyn many spelles'. If we have here a reference to the opening of Chaucer's *Pardoner's Tale*, with its equally vehement denunciation of the riotous youth of Flanders – 'And ech of hem at otheres synne lough' – then we have some evidence that either author or scribe associated the devilish nature of the activities in Flemish taverns with that of activities in the forge-workshop. No doubt he would not have missed the point of Chaucer's metaphor, as he goes on to describe the 'verray develes officeres' who 'kyndle and blow the fyr of lecherye' in the 'develes temple.'[37]

The long history of the treatment of the smith in medieval literature takes us back to sources of some antiquity. The account, in Book VIII of the *Aeneid*, of the forging of a shield for Aeneas by Vulcan and his Cyclopes in the 'vaults of Aetna', is an impressive testimony to the mixture of admiration and awe with which the dark arts of the armourer were traditionally regarded:

> . . . validique incudibus ictus
> auditi referunt gemitus, striduntque cavernis
> stricturae Chalybum et fornacibus ignis anhelat, . . .
> . . . alii ventosis follibus auras
> accipiunt redduntque, alii stridentia tingunt
> aera lacu. gemit impositis incudibus antrum.
> illi inter sese multa vi bracchia tollunt
> in numerum versantque tenaci forcipe massam.
>
> (lines 419–21, 449–53)

References in the Old Testament to those arts are predominantly unfavourable; the smith, as befits, perhaps, the descendant of Tubalcain, son of Cain and 'faber in cuncta opera aeris et ferri' (Genesis, Ch. 4, v. 22), is most frequently an image of idolatrous and corrupt creation:

Faber ferrarius lima operatus est; in prunis, et in malleis formavit illud, et operatus est in brachio fortitudinis suae: esuriet at deficiet, non bibet aquam, et lassescet.

(Isaiah, Ch. 44, v. 12)

Ecce ego creavi fabrum sufflantem in igne prunas, et proferentem vas in opus suum, et ego creavi interfectorem ad disperdendum. (Isaiah, Ch. 54, v. 16)

Defecit sufflatorium, in igne consumptum est plumbum, frustra conflavit conflator: malitiae enim eorum non sunt consumptae. (Jeremiah, Ch. 6, v. 29)

It is not difficult to imagine how direct or indirect knowledge of Classical and Biblical writings such as these, reinforced by a well-developed concept of the Devil as black in colour,[38] could have provided the basis for certain kinds of medieval Christian literature: from the diabolical island landscapes of the widely circulated and much-translated *Navigatio Brendani Sancti*, with their savage smiths and blazing forges,[39] to those legends of the smith and his formidable wife whose cruel part in the preparation of nails for the Crucifixion is so vividly portrayed by vernacular passion poem, drama and art.[40] Indeed, the image of Christ as an anvil, worked-upon by sinful smiths, becomes a typological commonplace in the fourteenth and fifteenth centuries through the influence of the *Speculum Humanae Salvationis*, which illustrates, by juxtaposition, the prefiguring of the Crucifixion in Tubalcain's forge.[41] Of course the favourable side of Tubalcain's skills was never entirely neglected; medieval hagiography represents the work of the smith in both culpable and innocent aspects. Two famous Saints, Dunstan and Eligius, are associated with skill in different kinds of metal-craft, as well as minor religious figures such as the ninth-century monk Cwicwine, of Crayke in Yorkshire, who took his relaxation at the smithy:

Mireficis fratrem licat memorare loquelis ferrea qui domitans potuit formare metalla diversisque modis sapiens incude subactum malleus in ferreum peditat, stridente cambo . . .[42]

But in contrast to this are the stories which stress the aggressive, profane behaviour of smiths; when Egwin of Evesham attempted to preach at Alcester, in the eighth century, it was the smiths who deliberately drowned his words with their hammering:

gens incredula . . . incudes ferreis malleis quibus maxime abundabat per plateas et vicos castri circumquaque tanto strepitu continue percutiebat, ut beati viri sermo non audiretur et ut a castro recedere cogeretur.[43]

It is also possible that we should pay some attention to the particular religious significance of the issue of night-labour which, as Jacques Le Goff has shown, powerfully outraged orthodox opinion during the fourteenth century not only because of its economic and social repercussions, but also because of its radical denial of 'le temps religieux, celui des *horae canonicae*.[44] When we try to analyse the struggle recorded in the civic documents, we must not forget that there were many painful religious consequences of the changeover, during the fourteenth century, from a predominantly rural to an urban economy. Although the old God-given truths about the separation of day and night were reaffirmed throughout the fourteenth and fifteenth centuries –

> And now in my blyssying I twyne tham in two,
> The nighte euen fro þe day, so þat thai mete neuer,
> But ather in a kynde courese þaire gates to go
> Bothe þe nighte and þe day . . .[45]

– they could be most convincingly demonstrated for a world that was rapidly passing away, for 'une économie encore dominée par les rythmes agraires, exempte de hâte, sans souci d'exactitude, sans inquiétude de productivité . . . et une société à son image, *sobre et pudique*. . .'[46] There must have been many who saw in the new working-habits encouraged by patterns of town life a disturbing reversal of religious values: 'dans ce contexte naturel, et rural, le travail de nuit est une sorte d'hérésie urbaine'.[47] We cannot be sure that the strongly emotional phrasing of a document such as that of the London Spurriers, in the year 1345 (above, p. 203), was not partly influenced by some sense of 'urban heresy' and by a sense of the sinister as well as the inconvenient nature of the metal-workers' activities. But we are on even better ground for supposing that they may have been among the various credible reasons for either the composition of the *Complaint* or its copying into a Norwich Priory manuscript. There may be more than casual significance in 'cryst hem gyue sorwe'.

We have not yet considered, however, what more can be determined about the origins and character of the *Complaint* from a study of its contemporary literary affiliations. The first observation must be that the versified derivatives of documentary materials have nothing relevant to offer for comparison. When the Craft Guilds abandon prose for something more literary, they produce – or have produced for them – the kind of modest clerkly work we might expect: the later fourteenth-century *Constituciones Artis Gemetrie Secundum Euclyde*. Among the rhymed *Articles* of the Guild of Masons, the question of night-labour comes up but it is treated in a plain expository fashion:

> The eleventhe artycul . y telle þe .
> þat he ys boþe . fayre and fre .
> For he techyt . by hys mygth .
> That no mason . schulde worche be ny3th .
> But 3ef hyt be . yn practesynge of wytte . . .[48]

If, however, we take our search-directions from the most striking stylistic feature of the *Complaint* – its exuberant alliteration – we are poorly rewarded. There is, for instance, little evidence to suggest that its most intimate connections are with the language and literary forms of those western or north-western areas usually regarded as the home of medieval English alliterative verse. Since 1930, when J. P. Oakden characterised the language of the unique copy as 'south-east midland', more rigorous and comprehensive analysis has established that its present dialect is that of west Norfolk and, in all likelihood, north-west Norfolk, in the neighbourhood of King's Lynn[49] – a circumstance which recalls the East Anglian provenance of MS Arundel 292. Indeed, certain features of vocabulary might argue composition, as well as copying, in East Anglia. The author's use of 'brenwaterys' as a derisive term for blacksmiths finds recorded confirmation only from the Cambridge area, in the thirteenth century, where it appears as a surname.[50] Another compound 'barmfellys' (leather aprons) is only elsewhere recorded in John Lydgate's translated work, *The Pilgrimage of the Life of Man*.[51] 'Cammede' (pug- or snub-nosed) has a predominantly East Anglian provenance[52] and so has 'gnacchen'.[53] None of this constitutes irrefutable proof of an East Anglian origin, but what can certainly be said is that the author's 'excessive alliteration'[54] – designed, we may note, for a literate public of the east of England – owes little or nothing to the set formulae of 'classical' alliterative verse of the fourteenth- and fifteenth-century west. Standard collocations are rare, and the most inventive alliterative usages – 'cammede kongons', 'gnauen and gnacchen', 'spyttyn and spraulyn' – are not constructed out of vocabulary with a special alliterative range.[55] Compound word-formations are made according to traditional patterns, but two examples – 'fere flunderys' (fire-sparks) and 'cloye merys' (mare-lamers) – are not otherwise recorded.

We can widen our area of comparison to include a variety of looser alliterative and non-alliterative works which, at first sight, resemble the *Complaint* in their satiric or burlesque purposes. We can associate it – for its confident transposition of outrage into a mode of the literary absurd, and for its brilliant improvisation upon commonplaces of alliterative style – with the burlesque poems and prose pieces of the fifteenth century which exploit alliterative language in the service of high comedy.[56] But it does not take long to discover that the fundamentally unserious nature of such compositions, which more often than not set their limited powers to the production of alliterative nonsense – whether blasphemous, abusive or fantastic – distinguishes them significantly from the *Complaint*. If, on the other hand, we are tempted to associate it, for the greater degree of serious-ness which informs its outlook, with complaint literature in general, its moral vantage point still seems elusive of definition; poems such as the early *Satire on the Retinues of the Great*,[57] which pursue an ingenious line of abuse in vigorously alliterative language, are stabilised quite differently, and far more explicitly, by their homiletic function. Alone among these texts the *Complaint* is remarkable for allowing its readers access to serious preoccupations and observations, at the same time as it invites them to share its ironic perspectives and to relish the quality of its stylistic performance.

For we should not fail to notice its zest for a degree of precise technical reference; although it is a predominantly unsympathetic, even enraged, account of smithying, there is nothing imprecise about its characterisation of major workshop activities[58] – the immense effort needed for the operation of the bellows and for the wielding of the heavy hammers,[59] the dexterity of the master-smith, probably engaged in welding-processes.[60] Its picture of the smiths themselves, with their thick leather aprons and blackened skin, is both traditional and verifiably exact.[61] This interested attention to detail may prompt our memory of passages in the metrical romances and popular *Saints' Lives* – the description of 'smethymen' and their foundry in *Sir Isumbras*, for example,[62] or that of the carpenters and 'smyghtes . . . both robyn and Iohn' who 'hewe and blewe ful soore' to prepare the wheel for St Katharine's Martyrdom in John Capgrave's fifteenth-century *Life* of that Saint, written, we may note, from the Austin Friary of Lynn, in west-Norfolk.[63] No romance or *Saint's Life*, however, accumulates detail in quite so systematic and deliberate a way, calling up not simply the circumstances surrounding a particular incident, but persuading us that here, for a moment, we are admitted to the very substance and texture of the working life of the medieval Crafts. Nor, of course, does romance or hagi-ography set that detail into the kind of dramatic and personalised context we have here. It will be obvious that, on both counts, there are reasons for associating the *Complaint* with certain kinds of later fourteenth- and earlier fifteenth-century English poetry in which the 'world of work' is both chronicled and subjected to criticism.[64] Half-way between Langland's grudging admission of the thriving energies of that world –

> Baksteres and Brewesteres and Bochiers manye,
> Wollen webbesters and weueres of lynnen,
> Taillours, Tynkers and Tollers in Marketts,
> Masons, Mynours and many oþere craftes;
> Of alle kynne lybbynge laborers lopen forþ somme,
> As dykeres and delueres þat doon hire ded[e] ille
> And dryueþ forþ þe longe day with 'Dieu saue dame Emme'.[65]

– and Chaucer's 'neutral and detailed enumeration of the daily duties'[66] of those who emerge from it to be Canterbury Pilgrims, lies the *Complaint*, with its appreciation of professional expertise, its susceptibility to professional resentment, and its desire to express all of this as a vignette of urban life, personally experienced. Something similar can be found in Hoccleve's *Preface* to the *Regement of Princes*;[67] his sleepless nights were passed, he tells us, in the heart of London, at 'Chestre ynne, right fast be the stronde, / As I lay in my bed . . .' (lines 5–6), and by day he contrasts the boisterous working noises of London outside his window with the cramping silence of the office of the Privy Seal in which he was a reluctant clerk:

> This artificers, se I day be day,
> In the hotteste of al hir besynesse
> Talken and syng, & make game and play,
> And forth hir labour passith with gladnesse;
> But we labour in travaillous stilnesse:
> We stowpe and stare vpon þe shepes skyn
> And keepe must our song and wordes in. (st. 145, p. 37)

So far we have managed to isolate certain elements in the historical and literary make-up of the *Complaint*. But part of our difficulty in dealing with it as an entry in a manuscript collection belonging to a Cathedral Priory stems from an inability to determine the precise *genre* in which it was composed. And it is no less true for the medieval than for the classical period that 'until the *genre* of the particular piece is known, many assessments of the motives, methods or merits of its author are bound to be subjective.'[68] Our search for indications of *genre* has concentrated, in the main, upon medieval literary forms in the vernacular. But as part of a monastic miscellany the *Complaint* may lay partial claim to some kinds of literary precedent in Latin. And here we are bound to recall that the theme of disturbance in the City, and especially night-disturbance on account of trade activity and traffic, is richly developed in Classical poetry. Horace, Juvenal and Martial complain bitterly about the life of a poet in Rome – 'nocte pistores / aerariorum marculi die toto . . .' ('by night the bakers: the hammers of the coppersmiths all day . . .').[69] Only the rich can sleep soundly through the night-noises of the city: 'magnis opibus dormitur in urbe . . .' Moreover, urban crime keeps the black-smiths at their clangorous work – forging fetters: '. . . qua fornace graves, qua non incude catenae? / Maximus in vinclis ferri modus . . .'[70]

The unlikelihood of the direct influence of such satire upon medieval poetry is not essentially a question of the availability of Classical texts: the Roman satirists were well-known and well-used by Latin poets of France and England during the late eleventh and twelfth centuries.[71] It is a question of changed historical circumstances and, in particular, of the fragmentation of that antique urban culture which had supported urban satire. The old dichotomies of the Classical world, town and country, were replaced by a shifting series of medieval alternatives which, from a base of reality, operated diversely within literary forms: monastery and desert, castle and feudal domain, court and wilderness. Only gradually did the city re-establish itself among such alternatives and, even then, the pivotal and determining factor in its role was quite as often its relationship with the court or with the University as with the countryside.[72] In natural response to this, and for most of the medieval period, urban satire was replaced by curial. Up to the fourteenth century, when the full and uncomfortable effects of urban growth could once more be expected to register in literature as in life, complaint from literary men about the adverse conditions under which they worked focussed upon the court, and upon distracting noise as a small but inevitable part of court-experience.[73]

From Peter of Blois, writing in retrospect about the English court of Henry II,[74] to the lyric poet Walther von der Vogelweide, still uncomfortably situated at the thirteenth-century court of the Margrave of Thuringia, we hear the same story: what peace can be achieved amidst the crowds of tradesmen, entertainers and parasites who throng the courts of the great? 'grôz wunder ist daz iemen dâ gehoeret . . .' ('it is amazing that anybody hears anything at all . . .'); '. . . ein schar vert ûz, diu ander in naht unde tac . . .' ('one lot pours out, another in, night and day').[75] While, therefore, any resemblances, superficial or otherwise, between the urban complaint of Classical Rome and that of fourteenth-century England are much more likely to be the product of similar stimuli to composition than the product of literary imitation, there is no reason why the English author of the *Complaint against Blacksmiths* should not have been familiar with a medieval tradition of anti-curial satire which had an essential point or two in common with Classical complaint and may, indeed, have been indebted to it. Strongly represented by the Latin literature of twelfth- and thirteenth-century England, this anti-curial satire would have been easily accessible to fourteenth-century readers in monastic and cathedral libraries.

There is also no reason why the author should not have been familiar, through the same libraries, with another medieval tradition quite as well represented by the Latin literature of England in the twelfth and thirteenth centuries – that of instruction in the arts of composition. These manuals frequently provide illustrative exercises in special features of poetic and epistolary style, and it is interesting to find in the *Poetria Nova* of Geoffrey of Vinsauf, for instance, a fifteen-line 'exercise' on the activities of blacksmiths engaged in the making of armour.[76]

The passage has a particular function in the treatise – it is designed to illustrate one of the 'difficult ornaments' of style: the metaphorical use of verbs by transposition from their original human context to that of inanimate objects. Consequently, Vinsauf's Latin verse pictures the violence of the forge exclusively in terms of the instruments and equipment of the smithy; the blacksmiths themselves are absent – the 'magister' is not the 'mayster' or 'master-craftsman' of the English piece but the 'magister malleus', or 'master hammer'. The highly-wrought description of Vinsauf's 'exercise' confirms the dignified status of armament in the encyclopaedic traditions of the Middle Ages, and its re-spected position as one of the 'mechanical arts'.[77] To that extent it is remote from the English *Complaint*, which refers, in one contemptuous phrase, to smithying on the most everyday level of horse-shoeing – the work of the medieval 'marshall' smith.[78] But when we also say that the *Complaint* is partly concerned to celebrate, in richly echoic language, the rapid skills and the massive energies of craftsmen and craft-processes, we come a little nearer to the nature and intent of the Latin exercise. In the light of the East Anglian manuscript provenance of the *Complaint*, it is worth stressing that a knowledge of Vinsauf's treatise and a general attentive-ness to prose and poetic rhetoric can be illustrated from Norfolk collections and Norfolk authors of the later medieval period. A copy of 'Galfridus, de artificio loquendi' – Vinsauf's *Poetria Nova* – was noted by Bale, in his *Index Scriptorum*, as having belonged to one of the Norwich libraries – perhaps that of a Friary, rather than a monastic house.[79] The Prior of Ingham in Norfolk – either John of Norwich or John of Blakeney – wrote a *Tractatus de Modo Inveniendi Ornata Verba* before 1450.[80] The *Complaint* preserves its independence of the traditional alliterative poetic of the west and north-west of England. But proficiency in other kinds of alliterative writing must have been a common accomplishment in the East Anglian area – the drama of the '*N-Town*' *Cycle* is a slightly later but obvious example.[81] A situation can be envisaged in which varieties of alliterative style could have been freshly devised, drawing upon familiarity with those rougher vernacular forms which served the writers of the East Anglian plays in their attempts to convey the vaunting malice of Satan or Herod, but responding also to the stimulus of elaborate Latin exercises such as those of Vinsauf. In such a situation, an author, as well as a collector, from some East Anglian religious house is more than likely.

This speculation as to a probable literary context for the *Complaint* does not, of course, rule out speculation as to particular and topical reasons for its original composition. And we are still left with the fact that only the civic documents of London appear to offer us any decisive leads in this area of our inquiry. It would probably be unrealistic to expect any East Anglian urban centre to produce legislative records of an exactly similar kind. The metal-trades never played a very prominent part in the civic economy of Norwich, for instance, which was above all a textile town. Although King's Lynn had a greater variety of such trades than Norwich, its metal-workers and their affairs do not seem to have attracted much civic attention.[82] The point should be made, however, that in municipal administration, provincial cities freely admitted to being guided by the practice of London, and knowledge of the formulations of the London Craft *Ordinances* can certainly be assumed for centres such as York, Bristol and Norwich. This is made clear by the *Composition* of Norwich in 1415, which covered all Crafts, and looked specifically to London for its precedents.[83]

When dealing with the East Anglian provenance of the *Complaint*, both Norwich and King's Lynn have been mentioned. And although the text is preserved in a monastic miscellany, there is no guarantee that it was not first composed in another kind of religious setting. The importance of the Friars in the history of the writing of medieval English religious literature is too familiar to need more than brief mention. But we may reflect that the same combination of learning, social consciousness and interest in forms of vernacular literature which characterises them as a class, could also be said to characterise the unnamed author of the *Complaint*. The immense libraries of the Augustinian Friars, for example, within their essentially urban foundations, and their intimate involvement with urban politics – in some recorded cases the politics of the Craft Guilds, who often rented Friary premises for conducting their business[84] – might encourage us, if we are anxious to localise both author and *Complaint*, to follow up the clue provided by the analysis of its language (see above, p. 208 and n. 49). We could, it seems to me, hazard a guess that its place of origin was not dissimilar to the Augustinian Friary at King's Lynn. The distinguished record of that Friary, during the fourteenth and fifteenth centuries, for the training of scholars and the production of religious literature is only rivalled by its record for close relationships with the working life of the people of Lynn.[85]

But whether, in fact, the *Complaint* confronts us with the work of Friar or monk and directs us to King's Lynn or Norwich, we are now in a better position to imagine how motives of some urgency could have found convenient sanctions in a well-known rhetorical 'set-piece'. The wit of the *Complaint* may reside most exactly in an appreciation of the distance between its ostensible theme – a common nuisance, of some social and moral resonance – and the dignified framework of Latin rhetorical exercise into which it is so neatly and divertingly set. If this is the measure of the skill of the author, we need not be surprised to find in his work fleeting reminiscences of some of the advanced literary forms of the later fourteenth and early fifteenth centuries, as well as acknowledgements of more traditional literary modes.

Nor need we devalue the authority of the *Complaint* as one of those important 'témoignages littéraires . . . touchant le rôle du forgeron, son autorité sociale, sa popularité . . .'[86] in order to emphasise a different and special kind of authority it may draw from its manuscript provenance. The folio of Arundel MS 292 on which it is written down is followed by a text of the *Purgatorium Patricii*.[87] We shall never know whether scribe or author, utilising a blank space in a thirteenth-century manuscript, was moved to associate his composition, deliberately, with this immensely popular vision of hell as a vast smelting-furnace under the direction of yelling demon-smiths, in which the damned endure torture by molten metals and hammered nails. But we can be fairly sure that readers of the manuscript in medieval Norwich would have done so.

Part III   Chaucer

10   *Troilus and Criseyde: a reconsideration**

ALTHOUGH many academic critics have expressed 'second thoughts' about
C. S. Lewis's overall view of *Troilus and Criseyde* – 'a great poem in praise of love'[1]
– I suspect that most readers will continue to find him a precise and sensitive
guide to Chaucer's meaning:

> It semed hire he wiste what she thoughte
> Withouten word, so that it was no nede
> To bidde hym ought to doon, or ought forbeede;
> For which she thought that love, al come it late,
> Of alle joie hadde opned hire the yate.[2]

It would be difficult, under the influence of *The Allegory of Love*, to miss the
significance of those lines: original to Chaucer, they are offered as a tribute to the
seriousness rather than to the fretting urgency of human love, which is poised at
that moment in the poem between recognition and fulfilment. Criseyde surely
refers back to 'such sober certainty' when she later tells Troilus

> Ne hadde I er now, my swete herte deere,
> Ben yold, ywis, I were now nought heere!   (III, 1210–11)

and it is an eccentric gloss which requires us to hear her words as an admission of
connivance.[3]

In spite of the challenges thrown down by more recent criticism, the centrality,
the 'passionate sanity'[4] of C. S. Lewis's writing on *Troilus* has not been obscured
or outdated: there are few important works which are not indebted in some way to
the comparative methods of study he advocated in 'What Chaucer really did to *Il
Filostrato*'[5] or to the wider interpretative modes of the *Allegory of Love*. If there is
still a need to 'reconsider' *Troilus and Criseyde*, it is not because his directions
were substantially wrong, but because many of these directions have not been
fully explored. Intensive studies of *Troilus*[6] and its sources have not mined ore of
the same quality as his short and exemplary article in *Essays and Studies*, and
learning quite as impressive as his has been misapplied to the understanding of
the poem, since it could not draw on the same kind of literary responsiveness
which distinguished and stabilized *The Allegory of Love*.[7]

It is still possible to see the main area of *Troilus* criticism divided between

---

* Originally published in *Patterns of Love and Courtesy. Essays in Memory of C. S. Lewis*, ed. John
Lawlor (London, 1966), pp. 86–106.

writers whose effort is simply to demonstrate more precisely the 'grete worthynesse' of Chaucer's work, and those who are set to disturb traditional attitudes by exercising ingenuity at the expense of common sense and sensibility. But close attention to the form and texture of Chaucer's verse – an attention which marked all of C. S. Lewis's commentary – makes either extreme reverence or extreme inventiveness unnecessary. Much remains to be said about *Troilus and Criseyde*, but I doubt whether we shall improve on his way of encountering the poem.

No real confidence, for instance, could now be placed in judgements of the poem which are not prepared to take into account Chaucer's dealings with his sources. Minute or major changes, redispositions of material, are crucial to our understanding of 'the poet at work', and, ultimately, to our understanding of the work itself. A simple and yet immensely important example of this occurs at the end of Book III. Chaucer's refusal to conclude this Book with Boccaccio's ominous lines –

> Ma poco tempo durò cotal bene,
> Mercé della fortuna invidiosa,
> ... Crisëida gli tolse e'dolci frutti,
> e' lieti amor rivolse in tristi lutti[8]

is the climax of a series of actions designed to seal off that section of the narrative from its bleak hinterlands of violence and betrayal. So, too, the whole of Book II, with its perplexing heroine and its uncertain narrator, must first be seen as a struggle with materials only partially tractable to the poet's emerging purposes. The logical conclusion of an unbiased study of 'Chaucer at work' in *Troilus* may not yet have been fairly represented. The acceptability of such statements as 'he achieves a symmetry, a balance, in episode and detail', or 'he communicates to us a view of the whole in which tolerance and critical perception are harmoniously blended',[9] has still to be proved. For *Troilus and Criseyde* shows unmistakable signs of conflicting purposes, unresolved difficulties. And it is, above all, a striking example of a medieval poem which forbids the easy use of terms such as 'unity', 'consistency'. It would be possible to say that the very magnitude of what Chaucer attempted to do in *Troilus* was the guarantee of some measure of failure, and that, unless we allow for this, we minimize his imaginative strength, demonstrated with such special triumph in Book III of the poem.

The situation in *Troilus* is similar to that in other major poems of Chaucer's: given a narrative which cannot be *radically* altered, Chaucer proceeds to treat that narrative in ways which demand, for the sake of unity and consistency, just that radical action denied to him. And if the text is given close scrutiny, it is hard to resist the conclusion that Chaucer's dealings with his material were often arbitrary, and certainly not always the result of premeditated design. The greatest problem of *Troilus and Criseyde* is not the character of Criseyde, nor the adjustment of Boethian philosophy with courtly love, but the poet Chaucer – for his workings are, at times, most problematic.[10]

In brief outline, *Troilus* displays to us a poet whose gradually changing purposes involve him in greater and greater difficulty with his sources. Warnings, in Book I, of possible clashes of substance and interpretation are confirmed by Book II: this is perhaps the most confused and at the same time the most interesting of all five Books from the point of view of 'poet at work'. Out of its near-chaos comes the great resolution of Book III, which justifies, retrospectively, the uneven conflicts of Book II. And here I think Chaucer intended his readers to accept a break, a pause in the movement of the poem. Books IV and V can also be seen in terms of conflict: the poet's gradual – and at times extremely painful – accommodation to the dictates of his narrative. So the ending of *Troilus* has, indeed, been prepared for throughout the poem, but mainly in the sense that it is an urgent declaration of a predicament in which Chaucer began to find himself as early, perhaps, as Book I: a predicament born of the decision to free his imagination, and to write about the love of Troilus and Criseyde not simply as a gay, sensual episode, nor as an ennobling example of 'amour courtois', nor indeed as a proof of 'worldes brotelnesse', but as an embodiment of 'the holiness of the heart's affections'.[11] For the unique excellence of *Troilus and Criseyde* is not, surely, to be counted the creation of 'characters' such as Pandarus and Criseyde, nor the weaving of a rich and many-stranded poetic fabric, but, more basically, the growth and release of a poet's imagination.

In *Troilus*, triumphing momentarily over both his story and his age, Chaucer is in his element –

> . . . for his bounty,
> There was no winter in it: an autumn 'twas
> That grew the more by reaping . . .

But the operative word is 'momentarily'. It should not, nowadays, be anything but a commonplace to say that a medieval poet's conception of 'unity' in a work of art could differ sharply from that of later writers. The 'unity' of Malory's *Morte D'Arthur*, of *The Canterbury Tales*, of a cycle of Miracle Plays is loose-knit, and not easily categorized in terms acceptable to post-Renaissance criticism. In *Troilus* certain kinds of unity can be recognized immediately: the narrative completes the curve described by Chaucer in Book I –

> In which ye may the double sorwes here
> Of Troilus in lovynge of Criseyde,
> And how that she forsook hym er she deyde;   (lines 54–6)

there is a general unity of verisimilitude in the movement of the main characters in the context of the poem; and there is undoubted unity in the perfectly sustained quality of the verse over all five Books. But recognition of this need not make us anxious to press for a more comprehensive and thorough unity. Chaucer shows here and elsewhere that he is only too willing to work for local effectiveness at the expense of total consistency and continuity.[12] In a poem which still accepted oral recitation as a possible mode of delivery – 'And red wherso thow be, or elles songe' – discrepancies of tone, of attitude, of reference would not appear to be of paramount importance. We should not, however, fail to notice that they exist.

To take one isolated example: Chaucer's references at the close of the poem to 'payens corsed olde rites', 'what alle hire goddes may availle', 'Jove, Appollo . . . Mars . . . swich rascaille' (v, 1849, 1850, 1853) depend for their effectiveness on the reader's consent not to range back meticulously over the length of the poem, inquiring whether the poet's strictures are supported by the evidence of his work. They depend on an inaccurate recollection of the whole substance of Book III, and on the poet's right to establish a local forcefulness without regard to total congruity. However ingenious our arguments, the relationship between the ending of *Troilus* and Book III remains uncertain: the elevation of Boccaccio's terrestrial passion to 'love, that his hestes hath in hevenes hye . . .', a process which occupies a good part of Books II and III, is not so much comprehended as misrepresented by the final judgements of Book V. The stanza in question is not only suspiciously vehement but careless,[13] and I doubt if we should spend much energy trying to justify what Chaucer himself preferred to ignore – or at most to notice cursorily.

Then also, we should allow for a considerable element of wilfulness in Chaucer's methods of procedure. The progress of his poem does not seem to have been controlled by steady consciousness of an overall plan. Book II, in particular, is a piece of writing in which sudden, happy improvisation jostles with hesitation, and recklessness is followed by uncertainty. Here sometimes the poet's imagination is allowed to leap forward at a heedless pace, and the verse records the very uneasy commerce of creative invention with narrative discretion. But the vital point to make is that Chaucer assumes his right to take sudden decisions about the development of his work in mid-career. Book I gives only slight indication of what was soon to begin stirring his creative processes and setting his poem so decisively apart from Boccaccio.

Two factors must weigh in a fresh consideration of *Troilus and Criseyde*. There is a strong possibility that Chaucer's view of his poem allowed for discontinuity of attitude and mode of presentation as well as for the preservation of other kinds of continuity. There is the equally strong possibility that Chaucer's purposes were not entirely clear to him even when the poem was well under way: the graph of *Troilus* records sudden advances and recessions, as the poet realizes – and pauses to consider – where his independence is leading him. This is not to brush aside the significance of Chaucer's revisions of the poem, but simply to ask whether they do, in fact, argue his grasp of 'the parallels and the symmetry of the poem's structure'.[14] Such an approach need not seek to isolate *Troilus* from the rest of

Chaucer's work. It is proper to recall *The House of Fame*, in which the tendency to sudden and arbitrary action is most freely – and perhaps disastrously – indulged: to recall also *The Canterbury Tales*, in which impromptu and disruptive episodes (the Canon's Yeoman episode is a brilliant example) are part of a complex pattern of continuities and discontinuities operated on narrative, dramatic and thematic levels.

Although Book I of the poem does not pose any very serious problems, it is clear, even as early as this, that Chaucer does not intend to allow his preordained narrative to keep him from ways of writing which may, ultimately, come into conflict with it. The narrator's advice to lovers is a case in point. The tone of the passage is not ironic: advice is plainly given, and it bases its argument on the power and the virtue of love:

> Now sith it may nat goodly ben withstonde,
> And is a thing so vertuous in kynde,
> Refuseth nat to Love for to ben bonde ...   (I, 253–5)

Boethian insights are already present:

> ... Love is he that alle thing may bynde,
> For may no man fordon the lawe of kynde ...   (I, 237–8)

Already Chaucer shows his inclination to write for the moment: the disastrous outcome of love – 'Swich fyn hath, lo, this Troilus for love!' – is not remotely in mind, as Chaucer invites his audience to honour the 'fall' of Troilus –

> Blissed be Love, that kan thus folk converte!   (I, 308)

and his dedication to a life of love, service and 'vertu':

> Dede were his japes and his cruelte,
> His heighe port, and his manere estraunge,
> And ecch of tho gan for a vertu chaunge.   (I, 1083–5)

This high valuation of human love, which the more prudent Boccaccio did not suggest, is confirmed by words given – incongruously, perhaps – to Pandarus. The Italian heroine's 'aptness' for love is turned by Chaucer from a cynical and slightly vulgar appraisal of woman's nature into a dignified statement about the proper sequential relationship of love 'Celestial, or elles love of kynde' (I, 979). This is the first time in the poem that earthly love is clearly set into some kind of cosmic pattern, and the significance of Chaucer's action cannot be over-emphasized. For not only is he anxious (we may think) to protect Criseyde from the casual lash of Boccaccio's remark: he seems also to be eager to establish high status for the quality and import of love between creatures. The dramatic unlikeliness of the words, coming from Pandarus, is a sure sign of their *thematic* relevance:

It sit hire naught to ben celestial
As yet, *though that hire liste bothe and kowthe* . . .   (I, 983–4)

The potentialities of Criseyde, and, through her, the potentialities of human kind, moving from terrestrial to heavenly love – these are the points at stake. If they have little to do either with the character of Pandarus or with the 'double sorwe' of Troilus, Chaucer is not greatly perturbed. It could be claimed that already there are signs of his reluctance to feel himself wholly committed by accepting the story in its main essentials. As Book I closes, we cannot forecast exactly what he intends: Troilus 'dryeth forth his aventure', but the line gives no distinct foreboding of ill fortune, and could be hinting at happiness which 'vertu' will come to deserve. We can forecast, however, that the dignifying and deepening of the concept of human love will make for a more complex poem, and that the handling of betrayal and disillusion may be correspondingly difficult. It would be impossible to say how far Chaucer anticipates, or, indeed, cares to consider this.

The Proem to Book II, which he apparently added to his first draft of the poem, raises questions for the reader. If the value of its opening stanzas as high-styled apostrophe is undebatable, its main function is not so easily described. It seems to spring from a need to say something about artistic responsibility; it may be read, in part, as Chaucer's (retrospective) admission of the problems inherent in his treatment of the story. The desire to shed some responsibility for the nature and conduct of the poem is clearly pressing him, and when we remember how Book II develops, it is hardly surprising that he felt bound to make some kind of comment. Direct discussion of artistic motive and predicament is rare in Chaucer's period: there is no real precedent for him. But in these words which preface Book II a strong sense of Chaucer's uneasiness about the progress of his poem makes itself felt:

Wherfore I nyl have neither thank ne blame
Of al this werk, but prey yow mekely,
Disblameth me, if any word be lame,
For as myn auctour seyde, so sey I . . .   (II, 15–18)

We need not deny that the stanzas are cast in the familiar rhetorical form of *dubitatio*, nor that their overt conclusion is 'In sondry londes, sondry ben usages'. What is crucial here is that Chaucer should return to enforce the point about 'myn auctour' (line 49): his anxiety to invoke his sources can be interpreted as a recognition, not a solution, of the 'cas' he finds himself in as Book II moves erratically to its precipice of suspense –

– O myghty God, what shal he seye?

For it is, surely, in Book II that Chaucer begins to put his powers of independent action to the test: the angle of divergence from Boccaccio widens, and the passages which convey the poet's increasing – and not always happy – awareness of the situation are more prominent. Although there have been intimations of change in Book I, Book II marks a quickening of the tempo of change: fresh energy is released to the business of adaptation, and the poetry swings dramatically between 'drede and sikernesse', showing doubt and confidence in the propriety of what is being done. This is particularly clear in the case of Criseyde: Chaucer's dealings with her in this Book are sometimes bold and imaginative, sometimes timorous in the extreme. She struggles to emerge from the poetry, but if she remains largely an enigma, this is less the result of subtle characterization than of an imperfect fusion of old and new material.

The nature of her reply to the first unmistakable suggestion that she should *love* Troilus is important here. The violence of her outburst is surprising in the immediate context; Pandarus has been calculating with her in terms of 'tendre wittes' (II, 271): she has appeared demure, complaisant, a little playful and a little curious – 'I shal felen what he meneth, ywis . . .' – and Chaucer has shown no great interest in developing the serious note he introduced in Book I. But the words she uses to Pandarus, in rebuke, are serious indeed – much too serious for the narrative as it has been forecast, and for the events which follow almost immediately. Her severe, intelligent complaint belongs to a narrative which might take a different course, to a woman who might either be steadfast in chastity, or prove worthy of a man's virtuous love, and faithful to him. At this point Chaucer does not resist the prompting of his imagination; the speech is magnificently inappropriate:

> What! is this al the joye and al the feste?
> Is this youre reed? Is this my blisful cas?
> Is this the verray mede of youre byheeste?
> Is al this paynted proces seyd, alas!
> Right for this fyn? . . . (II, 421–5)

It is hardly relevant to debate whether Criseyde is genuinely outraged or not: the interesting fact is that Chaucer considered such language fitted to the occasion. The incisive quality of the verse is not so much a measure of his concern to save the reputation of Criseyde as a measure of his growing dissatisfaction with the nature of Boccaccio's narrative.

This dissatisfaction seems to centre more and more on the *status* of the love he is to celebrate in Book III. For it must be increasingly clear to him that if he is to write solemnly, even responsibly, about this love, the Italian heroine, who makes most of her decisions on the basis of expediency and desire, will not do. He has already revealed something of the context in which he wishes to set this 'love of kynde'; it is a commitment which is both exciting and perturbing him by Book II. His efforts to manipulate Criseyde, so that she may be a serious participant in his changing concept of the poem's theme, occupy a good part of Book II, but they are efforts often balked by the sheer weight of substance of the original. Chaucer may have felt free to deepen the reactions of this woman, to give her sharp protests of disillusioned wisdom: he did not feel free – nor, in all probability, did he feel obliged – to attempt a total recasting of her. The importance of the stanzas in question is thematic, rather than psychological: they belong as much to the poet and his readers as to Criseyde, and function as a warning that the gradient to love will be steep. By stating and then rejecting what his Italian source so patently deals in (a 'paynted proces'), Chaucer establishes his right to ask for a different valuation of the affair, even if he cannot re-order events.

So he proceeds, with a mixture of confidence and nervousness: his confident invention of the scene in which Criseyde sees Troilus riding back from battle 'so lik a man of armes and a knyght', and finds her fears about love assuaged by his sobriety as well as by his valour, is followed by a display of artistic misgivings. Suddenly he loses conviction about what is now superbly evident – that Criseyde is not approaching love easily, but with difficult self-adjustment. The comment by the narrator –

> Now myghte som envious jangle thus:
> This was a sodeyn love; how myght it be
> That she so lightly loved Troilus . . .   (II, 666–8)

is quite gratuitous from the dramatic point of view: it is highly significant, nevertheless, as a comment on Chaucer's creative battles, already partly over and won. That he feels it necessary is a gauge of the pressures constantly at work on him throughout this critical stage of the poem's development. For it is vital to his writing in the coming Book that some kind of transformation should be effected now: a transformation of values, since it cannot, in the medieval contract, be a total transformation of material.

And in all these dealings, it is surely on Book III, no further, that his vision rests. The conquests being won so hardly are for near objectives, and will require fresh campaigning as the poem turns to its conclusion. There is no evidence that in the restless manoeuvring of Book II Chaucer had anything more than Book III in sight:

> For for o fyn is al that evere I telle . . .   (II, 1596)

The 'fyn' he refers to here is certainly not that of Book V: it is closer, more immediate. This emerges again in the elaborate Deiphebus episode. No one could deny that here, in the busy intriguing of Pandarus, Chaucer allowed himself splendid opportunities for dramatic verse – 'O verray God, so have I ronne!' He also, for very practical purposes, allowed the innocence of Criseyde to be enmeshed by Pandarus in his less endearing, slightly more sinister capacity – 'But Pandarus thought, "It shal nought be so . . ."' (II, 1296).

But the episode has another special claim on our attention as a preparation for Book III. It marks a decisive severing of allegiance to the standards and expectations of the original Italian. It comes as a sudden burst of free composition after a period of uneven progress, and demonstrates the imaginative strength of the poet, who is now so confidently at variance with his original that he can allow himself a major addition to the narrative – and, in some respects, a redirection of the narrative. For the Deiphebus episode begins to intimate to the reader how love will grow uncorrupted out of the centre of intrigue:

> Lo, hold the at thi triste cloos, and I
> Shal wel the deer unto thi bowe dryve . . .   (II, 1534–5)

The transformation of values has been achieved, and Criseyde goes to Troilus freed of responsibility for events, and untouched, except by compassion for a man she has begun to trust:

> Al innocent of Pandarus entente,
> Quod tho Criseyde, 'Go we uncle deere'.   (II, 1723–4)

It is significant that Pandarus conjures Criseyde to behave with pity towards Troilus

> On his half which that soule us alle sende,
> And in the vertu of corones tweyne . . .   (II, 1734–5)

Such language, with its particular Christian references and its nuptial imagery, is not only, of course, anachronistic, but uncharacteristic of the speaker: it is only appropriate to the developing theme of the poem. The general tone is right, if the dramatic context is not, and confirmation of this will not be long delayed. It says as clearly as it can that whatever *events* the narrative is destined to recount, the *theme* of the central part of the poem will be honourable and legitimate love. And if the breathless concluding line of the Book is not patently Christian in phrasing, it carries sufficient religious associations to act as a bridge to the Proem of Book III:

> . . . O myghty God, what shal he seye?

In this Proem, for the first time, religious language has an unambiguous part to play. Books I and II mingle pagan and Christian references in a way which is sometimes of obvious importance, and sometimes quite fortuitous. But now Chaucer takes the opportunity not only to reposition material from his Italian source, but to recast some of it in strongly Christian terms. The impulse towards change and the nature of the change are both notable. The first stanza of the Proem,

> O blisful light, of which the bemes clere
> Adorneth al the thridde heven faire . . .

could be dealing with the highest form of *amour courtois*: the second stanza could

Chaucer

not. After translating Boccaccio's Boethian lines, 'Il ciel, la terra ed il mare e lo'nferno/ciascuno in sé la tua potenza sente ...' (op. cit., p. 90), Chaucer gives us plain words:

> God loveth, and to love wol nought werne,
> And in this world no lyves creature
> Withouten love is worth, or may endure.   (III, 12–14)

The passage in Boccaccio is quite differently set:

> e gli uomini e gl'iddii; né creatura
> sanza di te nel mondo vale o dura.   (loc. cit)

The substitution of 'God' for 'gods', and the assertion of heavenly benevolence in the matter of human love are both remarkable, and should not be passed over. In width of concept and precision of language the whole stanza bears comparison with many statements in orthodox religious treatises of Chaucer's own day:

... from out the great ring which represents the Eternal Godhead, there flow forth little rings, which may be taken to signify the high nobility of natural creatures ...[15]

For this was showed: that our life is all grounded and rooted in love, and without love we may not live: and therefore ... the soul ... of this special grace seeth so far into the high marvellous goodness of God, and seeth that we are endlessly joined to him in love ...[16]

The effect of this stanza is felt throughout the Proem and beyond. It lends warmth and seriousness to the poet's invocation –

> How I mot telle anonright the gladnesse
> Of Troilus, to Venus heryinge?
> To which gladnesse, who nede hath, God hym bringe!   (III, 47–9)

But it is particularly interesting as a deliberate – and, in all likelihood, later – declaration of progress and intent. There can be no doubt now about Chaucer's desire to clarify and confirm his position. The tentative, exploratory move in Book I towards a definition of love which could touch simultaneously human and celestial boundaries[17] is here followed through with assurance – 'God loveth, and to love wol nought werne ...' With these words Chaucer crowns his efforts to achieve a 'reformation of feeling' in his poem. For they define the outer limits of the love that is to be the subject of the coming Book, and they announce a new mood of reconciliation – not simply the reconciliation of pagan and Christian elements in that cosmic dance described in this and surrounding stanzas, but the reconciliation of Chaucer with his poetic materials and his inclinations. The words are a manifesto of intention about the conduct of the next stage of the story and, further, a manifesto of Chaucer's status as a creative artist. They establish his right to present his narrative according to his imaginative convictions, and not according to the dictates of his original or the narrower doctrines of his age. He

224

will not be subject to Boccaccio, nor to the homilists, and, indeed, throughout this Book he demands from his readers an unqualified sympathy with 'the high nobility of natural creatures'. He has won for himself freedom of action in a situation where freedom was scarcely to be expected, and he has won it by widening the perspectives of his poetry[18] to a degree uncalled for, and even unjustified, by his given material, with its evanescent delight and its sombre outcome. Book III is dedicated, in defiance of the known ending of the story, to what Spenser described in his *Epithalamium* as 'the safety of our joy', and the strength of the poetry is directly related to Chaucer's new-found security: 'God loveth, and to love wol nought werne.'

For Book III has, in a special sense, an independent existence, and Chaucer must have expected his readers to accept this. Not that, even now, there is total consistency of attitude and subject-matter: it is typical – and, in the long run, unimportant – that Chaucer should allow the odd jarring note to be heard. The careful and delicate phrasing of Criseyde's promises to Troilus –

> Bysechyng hym, for Goddes love, that he
> Wolde, in honour of trouthe and gentilesse,
> As I wele mene, eke menen wel to me . . .   (III, 162–4)

and the equally fastidious account of her capitulation by Pandarus –

> For the have I my nece, of vices cleene,
> So fully maad thy gentilesse triste,
> That al shal ben right as thiselven liste . . .   (III, 257–9)

are followed by that jaunty passage in which Troilus offers

> . . . my faire suster Polixene,
> Cassandre, Eleyne, or any of the frape . . .   (III, 409–10)

to Pandarus in return for his services. It is a careless adjustment of old and new.[19]

But much more noticeable is the confidence of the writing. It is confidence – based on persuasions of the goodness and legitimacy of this relationship – which allows Chaucer to take Book III at such a leisurely pace. The period between Criseyde's long-awaited words

> . . . I wol wel trewely
> . . .
> Receyven hym fully to my servyse . . .   (III, 159, 161)

and their fulfilment is slowly and compassionately charted: their love is proved first in service and companionship. It is no accident that some of the most moving poetry about human love in this Book comes well before that 'blisful nyght, of hem so longe isought', and that an atmosphere of 'concorde and quiete' announces the central act of the story –

That to ben in his goode governaunce,
So wis he was, she was namore afered ...   (III, 481–2)

It is also no accident that the bitter outcry of Criseyde against the 'brotel wele of mannes joie unstable ...'[20] cannot really disturb the sense of safety which pervades the Book. The movement between momentary 'drede' and 'sikernesse' is simple, and Criseyde's sadness is easily transformed into a positive desire to solace Troilus:

'Hadde I hym nevere lief? by God, I weene
Ye hadde nevere thyng so lief!' quod she.   (III, 869–70)

From that point to the end of the Book the poem's development is one of expanding certainty: the setbacks experienced by the lovers are minimal, their humorous setting acceptable, because so many serious assumptions have already been made. And seriousness grows in exact proportion to the sensuousness of the poetry: every new move is endorsed by religious language.[21] When Troilus takes the final step towards happiness, it is with a benediction:

This Troilus, with blisse of that supprised,
Putte al in Goddes hand,[22] as he that mente
Nothyng but wel; and sodeynly avysed,
He hire in armes faste to hym hente ...   (III, 1184–7)

After this, it cannot seem inappropriate that Criseyde's generosity in love should be praised in devout words:

For love of God, take every womman heede
To werken thus, if it comth to the neede,[23]   (III, 1224–5)

nor that the excited description of her beauty should be followed by a fresh affirmation of the cosmic power of love:

Benigne love, thow holy bond of thynges ...

The poet writes, and the characters act, out of a deep assurance of propriety; for all its delighted 'concreteness'[24] the dominant mood of the poetry is 'pees' and 'suffisaunce', and the dominant movement is *andante cantabile*:

... myn owen hertes list,
My ground of ese, and al myn herte deere,
Gramercy, for on that is al my trist!   (III, 1303–5)

Even at the very centre of misery, the moment of 'disseveraunce', reconciliation is suggested: the immediate pressure of pain is reduced by wide-ranging allusions to Creation, Order, Purpose:

O blake nyght, as folk in bokes rede,
That shapen art by God this world to hide
At certeyn tymes wyth thi derke wede . . .

Thow rakle nyght, ther God, maker of kynde . . .

Ther God thi light so quenche, for his grace . . .

(III, 1429–31, 1437, 1456)

Criseyde comforts Troilus in an ascending series of passionate and religious statements, and it would be a perverse reading of the poetry at this stage which could find intended irony in her juxtaposition of

by God and by my trouthe . . .   (III, 1512)

It is not surprising that the warnings of Pandarus, next day, about 'discretion', 'moderation' are, in the circumstances, not so much portentous as inadequate. In the lighter Italian text they had a significant part to play, but in this changed context their concern with

Be naught to rakel . . .

Bridle alwey wel thi speche and thi desir . . .   (III, 1630, 1635)

seems peripheral. Even the additions to the Italian – 'For worldly joie halt nought but by a wir . . .' (III, 1636) are not strong enough to shake the belief that 'hire hertes wel assured were'. They witness more to Chaucer's sense that the original words fall short of touching the new situation than to an anxious sense of approaching doom. For they come between the lovers' dedication to each other, and Troilus's total dedication not simply to love but to love as the divine principle of the universe. Only one line gives a hint that all may not ultimately be well, and this is so firmly embedded in the celebration of 'suffisaunce . . . blisse . . . singynges . . .' (III, 1716) that Chaucer cannot have intended that it should halt his readers for long:

And thus Fortune a tyme ledde in joie
Criseyde, and ek this kynges sone of Troie.   (III, 1714–15)

The last stanzas of the Book, by their additions and omissions, ratify all that has gone before. Writing his own *finis* to this part of the story, Chaucer invokes religious philosophy of the highest and most solemn kind. By setting Troilus to associate (not, it must be noted, to identify) his love with

Love, that of erthe and se hath governaunce,
Love, that his hestes hath in hevenes hye,
Love, that with an holsom alliaunce
Halt peples joyned . . .   (III, 1744–7)

he makes his most moving case for 'the high nobility of natural creatures' and their 'holsom alliaunce'. No irony plays about his comprehensive statement of the interlocking of human and divine loves:

> So wolde God, that auctour is of kynde,
> That with his bond Love of his vertu liste
> To cerclen hertes alle, and faste bynde . . .   (III, 1765–7)

The spirit of the words is hardly different from that of Julian's 'we are endlessly joined to him in love'. After this, Boccaccio's summary announcement of impending disaster would have been completely out of tune: its omission, and transference to the Proem of Book IV, is of greatest importance to our understanding of Chaucer's intentions. His admission that he has deliberately altered Boccaccio's ending is candid but unrepentant:

> My thridde bok now ende I in this wyse . . .   (III, 1818)

And so it is in 'lust and in quiete' that the Book fulfils its promise. Giving religious sanction to a love which originally asked and needed none, Chaucer gave sanction to a freedom of imaginative movement hard to equal in any work of his age which dealt with 'love of kynde'. It is both a sad and a triumphant fact that the only medieval writings on love which rival the grace and intensity of Chaucer's language in Book III of *Troilus* are religious treatises, and Chaucer had to win the release of his full imaginative powers for this difficult subject by religious means. The word to stress is 'full': medieval literature abounds in descriptions of human love – sensual, casual, refined, ritualized, practical and brutal – but few artists found ways to take full imaginative grasp of this complex human condition, to admit its dignity as well as its vulnerability, and to give serious status to bodily as well as spiritual compassion.

But the cost of this to Chaucer in *Troilus and Criseyde* should not be underestimated. If Book II records, by a series of surface disturbances, a deep turmoil of decisions, and if Book III records the confident outcome of decisions taken, the two remaining Books record a gradual, difficult readjustment to authority in the shape of the original narrative. By the end of Book III, Chaucer has worked certain transmutations: the rest of the poem must be a process of disenchantment. Expectations encouraged by Book III must be refused to the reader, and the divergence of narrative and presentation, by now wide and serious, must be reduced. With the beginning of Book IV, Chaucer tackles fresh problems: problems which he has, to a large extent, created for himself by energetic development of unsuspected potential in his sources. The admirable recklessness of his actions has to be paid for.

The unpalatable nature of what lies before him is the real subject of his Proem to Book IV, and we should see in it not only regret for the tarnishing of his bright image of Criseyde,

> Allas! that they sholde evere cause fynde
> To speke hire harm ...   (IV, 19–20)

but also his reluctance to begin the closing-down of the great imaginative vistas of Book III. From now on the story will lay strongest claims to his allegiance, and he will have only a small area for freedom of operation. The deepest 'drede' which fills him at this point is fear of imaginative restriction by the events henceforth to be 'matere of my book'.

The poem is, indeed, entering a new phase, and Chaucer warns his readers to look for decisive changes – not only in the way his characters must behave, but also in the attitudes he and they must begin to adopt towards such behaviour. Nothing he has so brilliantly evoked in Book III can be any help towards *understanding* what will happen: he has ensured that the rift between love and betrayal will now be unbridgeable except in terms of strictest narrative necessity. Consequently the poem must now be concerned with providing answers and consolations which may prove expedient in a situation otherwise unbearable and unacceptable. In Books IV and V, Chaucer ranges widely in search of philosophic and religious vantage-points from which to view his 'matere' with some compo- sure: his imaginative range, however, is strictly narrowed by what he has to do. The great passages on Fate, Necessity, and Free Will function seriously as the poem moves to its bitter conclusion, but they give, in many respects, 'a comfort serves in a whirlwind'; we should not mistake philosophic and religious recon- ciliation for imaginative committal. The sad bewilderment with which Chaucer watches his poem shrink to a tale of treachery cannot be wholly remedied: like Troilus, seeing Criseyde's love fade from him, he can only state, in all truth, what *was*:

> ... I ne kan nor may,
> For al this world, withinne myn herte fynde
> To unloven yow a quarter of a day!   (V, 1696–8)

But answers to the extreme dilemma of the narrative have to be attempted.

The crux of the matter lies in the last answer Chaucer chose to give – his closing stanzas. E. T. Donaldson has shown conclusively that the poetry from line 1750 onwards reveals 'the narrator's quandary'.[25] Anxiety and evasiveness are strongly apparent: the only conclusion left is one which is not congenial. And when at length Chaucer comes to draw that conclusion, it is with a surprising and terrible forcefulness:

> Swych fyn hath, lo, this Troilus for love ...   (V, 1828)

Now he makes obeisance to the medieval theme of *vanitas vanitatum*, and the severity of his expression can be seen as a measure of the reluctance he has shown, in the central part of his poem, to give any weight to that theme. It is, in fact, in this severity, rather than in conciliatory references to 'floures faire',[26] that we can discern Chaucer's recollection of what he achieved in Book III. Having enriched and deepened the implications of the Italian narrative, he is now forced to erase the memory of his actions. The pounding of his rhetoric is meant to still questioning, but we may inquire more thoughtfully than Chaucer's readers could about the relevance of that stanza

> Lo here, of payens corsed olde rites,
> Lo here, what alle hire goddes may availle . . .   (V, 1849–50)

It is a revealing and, at the same time, a problematic stanza: revealing, because it shows quite clearly that Chaucer hopes we will not question this palpably unsatisfactory account of what we have just read or heard; problematic, because it is difficult to believe that any artist of integrity could turn his back on his work quite so decisively. 'Payens corsed olde rites', 'what alle hire goddes may availle', 'the fyn and guerdoun for travaille/Of Jove, Appollo, of Mars, of swiche rascaille', give poor coverage for the deliberate evocation of Christian belief and feeling in Books II and III. As an explanation of 'double sorwe' it is woefully inadequate, and we must not miss the fact that Chaucer offers it as an explanation:

> *Lo here*, what alle hire goddes may availle . . .
> *Lo here*, the fyn and guerdoun for travaille
> Of Jove, Appollo, of Mars . . .

The automatic listing of the gods (not all of them, as several critics have pointed out, properly operative in the poem) is in itself indicative of Chaucer's haste to be done with a troublesome matter. Automatic also is his dismissal of 'the high nobility of natural creatures' –

> Lo here, thise wrecched worldes appetites . . .

It was not this view which drew from him some of his finest poetry.

In short, Chaucer could never have intended his poem to be seen as a unified whole, except in the crudest narrative sense. It is a work of variable and fluctuating allegiances, of co-ordinate rather than complex construction, which relies on significant breaks and pauses between its separate parts. Beginning simply, it develops into a subtle and devout study of human 'worthynesse': ending simply, it fails to relate its findings meaningfully, and is even forced to revoke some of them – though not without some distress.

Like many of Chaucer's answers to complicated problems, the final answers given in *Troilus* do not match the intelligence and energy of the questions asked, the issues raised. For Chaucer, in the struggle between narrative authority and imaginative penetration, authority must win – 'all/ Life death does end, and each day dies with sleep'. But we should not be afraid to recognize the struggle, nor to admit that while authority could literally conclude his poems for him, it could never conclude the business his imagination loved to engage in.

11 *Troilus and Criseyde*: poet and narrator*

It was E. Talbot Donaldson who first accurately diagnosed the literary symptoms of 'a kind of nervous breakdown' toward the end of *Troilus and Criseyde*.[1] Where others had ignored or explained away the uncomfortable signs of distress – distracted skirmishes, rapid changes of mood and direction – he treated the situation as one of crisis. His analysis of the last eighteen stanzas of the poem was precise and subtle. And more than this: his affirmation of serious disturbance in a key area of Chaucer's poetry not only was startling but raised questions of far-reaching importance about the process which went to the making of this most distinguished and, in many ways, most enigmatic of Chaucer's works.

The authoritative account offered by Donaldson of the 'shifts and turns' in the business of ending *Troilus and Criseyde* defined, as no earlier study had done, the reader's difficulties with this section of the poem. It left us sensitized to the inconsistencies, the oddities even, in Chaucer's handling of the denouement of his 'tragedye'. The defence which was also offered, based upon the argument that we have here a brilliantly dramatic demonstration of the poet-narrator relationship – 'Chaucer has manipulated a narrator capable of only a simple view of reality in such a way as to achieve poetic expression of an extraordinarily complex one' (p. 43) – was itself a brilliant demonstration of problem solving. It effectively located tension in the narrator, not in the poet, and sought to prove that the 'emotional storm-centre' of the narrator's trouble with his story is made to generate energy for the 'great complexity of the poem's ultimate meaning' (p. 34). But for some of us it was the convincing nature of the analysis of the narrator's 'trouble' which encouraged an uneasiness about the attractive neatness of the solution.

The theory of the 'fallible first-person singular', with its corollary of an interesting ambiguity of relationship between the author and his narrator, has been richly applied to medieval narrative fiction. Developed out of 'the conventions of the dream-vision, and extending to other fourteenth century poetry narrated in the first person',[2] it seems to have given both Chaucer and Langland a controlled range of approach to their subject matter; 'the poet behind the narrator'[3] manipulates a series of situations which encourage, resist, and challenge the hopeful reader. And the same theory has had an even more fruitful

---

* Originally published in *Acts of Interpretation: The Text in its Contexts 700–1600. Essays on Medieval and Renaissance Literature in Honor of E. Talbot Donaldson*, ed. M. J. Carruthers and E. D. Kirk (Norman, Oklahoma, 1982), 281–91.

application to postmedieval narrative fiction, in which the presence of 'seriously flawed narrators'[4] has the authority of the authors themselves: if we are forced to deduce the working of the theory from the poetry of Chaucer and Langland, we can find it discussed in the notebooks of Henry James. There can be no question that author–narrator dualism is skilfully exploited by Chaucer in his early dream poems and again in *The General Prologue* to *The Canterbury Tales*. But the operation of this 'dualism' in *Troilus and Criseyde* seems to me more difficult to accept – at least, without doing some damage to the poet's deep involvement with his poem. Indeed, the discovery of unreliable narrators in medieval fictional narratives could already have become more convenient than true; just such a state of affairs was reached in twentieth-century criticism of the novel, where over-reaction to 'extreme unreliability' in a whole series of famous witnesses provoked statements from authors: 'If he means the narrator, then it is me'.[5]

We do not have to imagine Chaucer putting his case in quite those words if we say that there may still be room for debate about the modes of narration in *Troilus and Criseyde*. The debate must focus largely upon the extent to which the 'quandaries', so persuasively described for us by Donaldson, can be said to be engineered by the poet for his narrator, in the service of a higher and all-embracing interpretation of the story. One of the alternatives is to persist in attributing most of the quandaries to the poet himself, as he makes his difficult way through a major recasting of his Italian source and 'annotates', both for his contemporaries and for posterity, his progress. There are many different modes of address in *Troilus and Criseyde*, suggesting that Chaucer anticipated many different readings of his poem – attentive and inattentive, courtly and learned. But one mode of address is, surely, that of the poet to his art; one important reading concerns his dealings with older European narratives of the *Troilus* story and the gradual evolution of his 'myght to shewe in som manere' what he could offer, uniquely, to that European tradition.

To observe that even the most privileged members of Chaucer's public could not have assessed the exact nature and quality of his contribution does not, of course, deny that his anticipated public was influential at certain levels of his artistic calculations. And clearly it was responsible for some of his most careful commentary upon the developing narrative. Those of his listeners or readers who were unacquainted with any particular literary version of the Troy story would have had the firmest of views about the unalterable sequence of events constituting the 'double sorwe of Troilus'; any substantial variation, however temporary in effect, would have required some explanatory glossing, some authorial reassurance. Later readers, with their more comprehensive knowledge of Chaucer's materials and their different historical perspective upon his methods of procedure, may find a number of those glosses and reassurances curious rather than crucial. But what remains of permanent interest is the way in which all readers are given some access, from the very beginning of the poem, to the inner drama of its growth. We should, indeed, be cautious about concluding that we can identify the voice which speaks to us throughout the work as that of a simple narrator, used dramatically by an inventive poet, or that we can easily recognize a division of the narrational voice between poet and narrator.[6]

The careful arrangement of *Troilus and Criseyde* into five books, reminiscent of classical precedent and a departure from the more varied canto structure of the *Filostrato*, inadequately disguises a work which evolves gradually, according to decisions taken during the act of composition. Chaucer's changing purposes, or, to put it more positively, his capacity for change, give the poem some of its most remarkable characteristics.[7] But this is a matter of authorial responsibility, and we miss the creative excitement at the heart of the matter if we continue to think in terms of a poet–narrator arbitration as the over-all controlling and justifying device. For here may be the first time in English literature when the poet goes some way toward an acknowledgment, both to himself and to his public, of the controversial and troublesome part he finds himself bound to play in the handling of his received 'matere'. We are allowed, even encouraged, to speculate upon 'workshop activity'. And, if, indeed, the poem makes any use of narrator as distinct from author, it does so at the same time as it engages in a process of transformation: the medieval fiction of 'naive narrator', already given a particular Chaucerian likeness in his earlier poems, is made to cope with the pressing problems of the poet himself, as he presents a freshly thoughtful version of a narrative familiar to all in general outline if not in literary detail. In *Troilus and Criseyde* (to imitate a famous aphorism of C. S. Lewis) the narrator died into reality, enabling the poet to speak out with a kind of freedom hitherto denied to him.

This 'death' was not immediate, however, and we hear, from time to time, that voice from *The Book of the Duchess* or *The Parliament of Fowls*, protesting mock-humble attitudes; what is there in the Proem to book I (lines 15–16):

> For I . . . / Ne dar to love, for my unliklynesse[8]

comes again in the Proem to book II (lines 19–21):

> Ek though I speeke of love unfelyngly,
> No wonder is, . . .
> A blynd man kan nat juggen wel in hewis.

And in book III (lines 1408–10), even after the assured treatment of the 'blisful nyght, of hem so longe isouht':

> For myne wordes, . . .
> I speke hem alle under correccioun
> Of yow that felyng han in loves art. . . .

The lingering usefulness of such protestations may be more closely related to contemporary social circumstance than we have recently been asked to believe.

But it is significant that by book III they do not appear in the cruder forms of books I and II;[9] even the lines quoted above from book III are prefaced by a confident statement about the way in which the source material may, 'at loves reverence', have been 'eched for the beste' (lines 1405–7) – that is, 'expanded and improved'. It is an author's piece of self-advertisement, and not in the same world as that of the polite disclaimer which follows. The poet, not the narrator, is in the ascendant; if he is a learner, he is clerk to no sublunary court of love but to the goddess herself, as the strong Proem to book III makes very clear (lines 39–42):

> Now lady bryght, for thi benignite,
> . . .
> Whos clerk I am, so techeth me devyse
> Som joye of that is felt in thy servyse.

The problems to which this clerk addresses himself are those of art, not of experience, and at such points his humility is proper in a high creative context, rather than in that of medieval rhetorical convention or medieval courtly society. This is confirmed by the end of the poem, when Chaucer places his work in an antique literary tradition and defines his 'modesty' as a dignified act of obeisance to 'the storied past' (V, 1786, 1790–2):

> Go litel book, go, litel my tragedye,
> . . .
> But subgit be to alle poesie,
> And kiss the steppes, where as thow seest pace
> Virgile, Ovide, Omer, Lucan and Stace.

It is important, therefore, that in our search to identify the 'fallible narrator', concerned and confused about the way in which events are turning out, we do not fail to recognize what may be the poet, making his own statements, tentative as they may sometimes be, about the problematic background to his artistic decisions and procedures. We cannot miss the significance of the signal at the end of book III, when we are given direct information about the poet's changes in the original Boccaccian sequence division (III, 1818):

> My thridde book now ende ich in this wyse . . .

But we could miss, by attributing the stanzas to a reluctant and inconsistent narrator, the significance of the Proem to book IV, when we are certainly introduced to a poet's sense of dilemma – a prescribed 'matere' now seriously at variance with the situation and characters as he has chosen to develop them (IV, 15–21):

> For how Criseyde Troilus forsook,
> Or at the leeste how that she was unkynde,
> Moot hennes forth ben matere of my book,

> As writen folk thorugh which it is in mynde.
> Allas! that they sholde evere cause fynde
> To speke hire harm! and if they on hire lye,
> I wis, hem self sholde han the vilanye.

This could be read as the narrator's wilful, inexplicable refusal to face what the omniscient poet must arrange to happen. But it could just as easily be understood as the poet's own lament for the inevitable tarnishing of a lady whose special brightness had been his deliberate creation. It could also be the poet's bid to his readers, or listeners, for a more reflective attitude to coming events than was traditionally accorded – 'as writen folk thorugh which it is in mynde' – to the narrative of Criseyde's betrayal of Troilus. The poet, in fact, may be sharing with them, and with us, his mixed feelings about the largely unequivocal materials with which he must henceforth work and preparing us, by unexpectedly raising the question of their veracity – 'and if they on hire lye' – for the possibility, at the very least, of an opinion about, rather than a simple judgment upon, Criseyde's perfidy. And this is what book IV goes about to demonstrate. Much of Chaucer's energy is here devoted to the crossing and recrossing of the plain story line with invitations to reflect upon the complex relationship between Criseyde's motives and her actions (IV, 1415–21):

> And treweliche, as writen wel I fynde,
> That al this thyng was seyd of good entente;
> And that hire herte trewe was and kynde
> Towardes hym, and spak right as she mente
> . . .
> And was in purpos evere to be trewe,
> Thus writen they that of hir werkes knewe.

Here he refers to authorities other than Boccaccio, and, indeed, some of his boldest departures from the Italian text in this book serve to delay as long as possible the moment of our final disillusionment with Criseyde. The transference to her of the speech 'For trusteth wel, that youre estat roial / Ne veyn delit . . . / This made, aboven every creature / That I was youre, and shal, whil I may dure' (IV, 1667–82), which was originally given to Troilus in the Italian,[10] is a move in keeping with his assurance of her 'good entente' – it contains some of his best and warmest writing (lines 1672–3):

> 'But moral vertu, grounded upon trouthe,
> That was the cause I first hadde on yow routhe.'

And here, although it may be objected that there is some inaccuracy in Criseyde's memory of the first occasion when she 'had pity' upon Troilus, there is no inaccuracy in the poet's recollection of his labour – and some would say his almost perverse labour – over the preceding books, to make her into the kind of woman who might meditate so tenderly upon the long days of falling in love.

There are other places in the poem where we may be in danger of mistaking poet for over-anxious narrator: the comment, for instance, in book II about the 'suddenness' of Criseyde's attraction to Troilus (II, 666–8):

> Now myghte som envious jangle thus:
> 'This was a sodeyn love; how myghte it be
> That she so lightly loved Troilus . . .?'

The comment is not only redundant but reductive, for nothing could be further from a proper description of the slow process by which Pandarus and circumstance bring her to love than the word 'lightly'. What anxiety is displayed here, however, belongs to the poet, not the narrator, who has worked to transform the 'light loving' of his Italian heroine into something more hardly won. It is, no doubt, the poet who remembers Boccaccio's Criseida, 'already . . . stricken by love' ('trafitta gia', *Fil.* II, stanza 66), even as Pandarus puts the suit of Troilus to her: Boccaccio's Criseida, standing invitingly at one of her windows, 'suddenly taken' with the sight of the young man, 'so that she desired him beyond any other good' ('E si subitamente presa fue, / che sopra ogni altro bene lui disia', *Fil.* II, stanza 83).

The stanzas in question (lines 666–79) offer a surface record of the deeper troubles encountered by the poet as he wrought decisive changes in his source.[11] No apology was needed, in reality, for the newly delicate account of Criseyde's first step toward capitulation – we accept the naturalness of 'Who yaf me drynke?' because we have been prepared so well. But Chaucer's own loss of confidence is both real and understandable; he labours a point already made, partly because he still has in mind the Italian source, and partly because he is only too conscious of the difficult task he has set himself – that of asking his readers to take a more generous view of Criseyde. The lines permit us to assess just how much effort he is expending, in this crucial book, upon the conversion, not just the translation, of the *Filostrato*.

It is in this light that we must view that later loss of confidence – the 'nervous breakdown' of the approach to the ending of the poem. Nothing in book V, as it goes about its stern and often patently distasteful business of charting the ruin of all that Troilus believed in, could lead us to doubt that we are meant to understand ourselves in the hands of the poet from start to finish. The only 'fallible voice' within this book, as, indeed, within all the preceding books, is that of Pandarus, whose narrow involvement with the build-up and breakdown of the affair does truly give us a commentary from a 'seriously flawed' viewpoint. But in book V the authorial voice is strong and purposeful throughout; in no other part of the work are we so constantly kept in touch with the assembly of materials and the craft of the poet as he deploys them.[12] And it is interesting that these references correlate with Chaucer's increasing use of other versions of the Troy story to augment the Italian. It is to Benoît de Sainte-Maure that he often turns to 'flesh out' the otherwise psychologically bare account of Criseyde's treachery; his borrowings, which begin in book IV but become more frequent and significant in book V, serve to stress both the intolerable pressures upon her in the Greek camp and the shocking realities of her behaviour, once she has taken 'a purpos for tabyde' (V, 770).

We are again encouraged, in book V, to consider the internal workings of the poem and the problems faced by the poet as he attempts to make sense – and, more accurately, all kinds of sense – out of his authorities. The magnitude of those problems can be gauged by the variousness of the commentary, which not only reminds us of the presence of 'olde bokes' behind the English text but also reveals to us a good deal of the mind of Chaucer, questioning, assessing, synthesizing, and interpreting what those books contained. Thus Benoît's lines describing Criseyde's 'compassionate' surrender to Diomede are put into a freshly ambiguous context by the addition of 'I not' (V, 1049–50):[13]

> And for to hele hym of his sorwes smerte,
> Men seyn, I not, that she yaf hym hire herte.

The indication, in the *Roman de Troie*, that two years elapsed before that surrender was complete, is used to suggest some slight mitigation of her guilt (V, 1091–2):

> For though that he bigan to wowe hire soone,
> Or he hire wan, yit was there more to doone.

Most striking, however, is an unusually direct passage which introduces the possibility of modifying what 'the storye wol devyse' by a sense of pity for Criseyde (V, 1093–4, 1097–9):

> Ne me ne list this sely womman chyde,
> Forther than the storye wol devyse.
> . . .
> And if I might excuse hire any wise,
> For she so sory was for hire untrouthe,
> I wis, I wolde excuse hire yit for routhe.

Even at this late stage of harsh certainty, a desire to refer fact to opinion persists; speculation is invited in the most hopeless contexts: the second, empty letter of Criseyde to Troilus, for example – was it prompted by some stirring of her easy compassion? The parenthetical phrase seems to suspend the decision (V, 187–8):

> For which Criseyde upon a day, for routhe –
> I take it so . . .

But none of this can, I think, be relegated to a sentimental narrator. The commentary in *Troilus and Criseyde* carries the burden of authorial doubt and

237

assurance, thought and afterthought. It records the poet's busy – and sometimes not entirely happy – engagement with his medieval materials, with his medieval public. It records also the poet's struggle to express something of what he dimly understood about the new kind of life he had given to his characters. This is particularly relevant to Criseyde, whose gradual transformation from the shallow girl of Boccaccio's poem to the intriguing and baffling woman of the English work was such an expensive though triumphant experiment for Chaucer. For, ironically enough, in the process of rewriting an old story, he made the near discovery of a way of viewing and presenting human beings which led, logically, to the abandonment of commentary altogether, whether by poet or by narrator. There are long stretches of *Troilus and Criseyde* in which the narrating voice is virtually eliminated and the characters act out their parts uninterrupted by anyone whose function is to 'stand in the gaps to teach you / The stages of the story'.[14] This direct exposure of scene and dialogue is essentially dramatic in method; it is often highly successful, especially when the relationships in question admit some degree of enigma. Thus passages of dialogue between Criseyde and Pandarus in book II and between Criseyde and Troilus in book IV stand independent, evoking rather than dictating our responses and, as in drama, allowing obscurities to exist without comment: '. . . the unfocussed aspects of character work within the minds of those who encounter them, like yeast in bread'.[15]

The potential of such a discovery could not, of course, be fully realized within the bounds of a medieval narrative form – especially one which was to present itself as a 'tragedye'. The necessity of meeting obligations to a clearly prescribed story sequence and of providing some interim as well as final statements which could lighten obscurities, resolve all problems, was absolute. It was this necessity, to make all clear, in a description and a reading of life inevitably at odds with his subtler perceptions of the 'breeding of causes'[16] in human nature, which precipitated Chaucer's 'nervous breakdown' as he came to the ending of his poem. After some desperate manoeuvres he turned to the conclusion of another of Boccaccio's works, the *Teseida*, to achieve that clarity of judgment alien to his poetic (and dramatic) imagination. It is his own 'Ode to Duty', his dismissal of the 'uncharted freedom' which had withheld nothing from him in this poem except repose.

12 Chaucer and Internationalism*

Boccaccio, in his *Trattatello in Laude Dante*, describes the special part which Dante had played in elevating the Italian vernacular to a high literary status:

Which vernacular . . . he first exalted and brought into repute amongst us Italians, no otherwise than did Homer his amongst the Greeks, or Virgil his amongst the Latins. Before him, though it is supposed that it had already been practised some short space of years, yet was there none who . . . had the feeling or the courage to make it the instrument of any matter dealt with by the rules of art . . . But he showed by the effect that every lofty matter may be treated in it; and made our vernacular glorious above every other.[1]

Whether Chaucer knew this statement or, indeed, any of Dante's more complex pronouncements upon the nature and the potential of the vernacular for literary purposes, it can stand as an exemplary definition of the kind of context in which he must have viewed the development of his own poetry: a context essentially European, not narrowly insular, which offered both theory and precedent for the creation of high-prestige vernacular literature, often involving curial patronage of some distinction. He certainly knew of the achievements of the French within that context; even at the beginning of his career in an aristocratic household he would have had good reason to attend to the internationally famous poetry of Machaut and his contemporaries and to understand, also, how important was the process of translation as a proof of confidence in the capacity of a language to express matters of learned as well as courtly significance. Before the great series of translations commissioned by Charles V of France – the French versions of Aristotle's *Ethics*, *Politics*, and *Economics*; Augustine's *City of God*; John of Salisbury's *Policraticus* – his father, Jean II, had ordered a translation of Livy and of the Bible with its Commentaries.[2] The learned interests of the French royal house throughout the middle and later years of the fourteenth century – witnessed by the magnificent collection of royal books which became the library of the Louvre – were served by the conviction of kings and their translators that the French language was adequate to encounter the difficult content and the 'merveilleus stille'[3] of Latin originals.

To the old question of 'why did Chaucer write in English?' we can nowadays return better answers than those traditionally based upon a fighting notion of the 'triumph' of English. Not, of course, that the fourteenth century lacked such notions: a surprisingly varied assortment of people, from the eminent friar,

* Originally published in *Studies in the Age of Chaucer*, 2 (1980), 71–9.

Robert Holcot, to anonymous romance and sacred-history writers and members of Parliament, identified the English language with an aggressive sense of English nationality, which often found expression in strong and understandably anti-French terms. The resentment clearly heard in the *Cursor Mundi*, 'Selden was for ani chance / Praised Inglis tong in France . . .'[4] comes out curiously in Holcot's equation of 'learning French' and 'learning to tell lies';[5] it fosters suspicion in Parliament in the 1340s, when the Chancellor of England, Sir Robert Sadington, announced what he knew of the invasion plans of the French:

'Et si est il en ferme purpos a ce que nostre Seigneur le Roi et son Conseil ont entendu en certeyn, a destruire la lange Engleys et de occuper la terre d'Engleterre . . .'[6]

Such sentiments, stimulated no doubt by propagandist needs of a moral as well as a political nature, have little to do with Chaucer's decision to deal in English. The undistinguished verse of the *Cursor Mundi* reminds us that most of the advances made during the first half of the fourteenth century in the use of English as a literary medium are of negligible meaning as far as quality is concerned. The Auchinleck manuscript,[7] the first large collection of vernacular verse to show a solid preference for English over Anglo-French, produced in London about 1330 for an urban middle-class consumer market, records the utility and the wide intelligibility of English. But if it establishes a convention for the future, it lays down nothing in the way of standards for that convention. While the scope of English as a literary language is being enlarged, no claims are as yet being made upon it for excellence. Exactly as in the case of the growing demand by the literate laity for historical reading matter – a demand which activated Franciscan scholars during the early fourteenth century – the quality of the market set a ceiling to the quality of the output.[8] The emergence of new and influential 'bourgeois' readers had important consequences for the stabilization of English as a dominant vernacular; it operated also to limit its potential as an art-form. This piece of literary history tells us nothing of value about Chaucer, whose motives were affected by movements in quite different levels of a society both English and European.

Two recent discussions of 'Chaucer at court' have raised again the interesting problems of 'what the aristocracy contributed directly to the court culture which produced (him) . . .' and how, in a 'French-speaking court' he could have come to write *The Book of the Duchess* in English.[9] The problems are crucially interconnected, and there may be some reason for further thought about the composition of that 'court culture' and the precise way in which it may have led him towards the use of English for his major poetry. There is nothing controversial about the nature of the international and courtly world in which Chaucer received his training and spent his mature life: the household of Elizabeth of Ulster, wife of the Duke of Clarence; war-service in France and ransom as a distinguished prisoner; various positions as 'professional royal servant',[10] interleaved with less easily specified forms of royal business, throughout two reigns. It is not difficult to suppose that his earliest verse may have been written in French[11] – a likely enough hypothesis for the aspirant work of a young man at the English court during the fifties and sixties of the fourteenth century.

For these were the cosmopolitan years which saw the translation of leading members of the French court to England: the capture of Jean le Bon at Poitiers in 1356 meant that not only French books but French artists and poets came in his train.[12] The king, whose household had included Guillaume de Machaut, who had received Petrarch, and who had commissioned the splendidly illuminated *Bible de Jean de Sy* from the Parisian Bondol workshop,[13] still functioned as a patron of literature and the arts during his English captivity. One of his painters, Girard d'Orléans, 'valet de chambre', accompanied him to London, and for two years at least pursued his varied work for Jean.[14] It is thought that the polyptych, depicting Jean, Edward III, the Emperor Charles IV, and the Dauphin Charles, of which now only the portrait of Jean remains, was ordered and carried out at this time.[15] On the literary side, Jean's chaplain, Gace de la Buigne, began, at the king's request, a long poem which combines a debate between the rival merits of hunting with dogs or birds and a moral treatise on the battle of the vices and virtues. This *Roman des Deduis*, intended by Jean for the instruction of his fourth son, Philip of Burgundy, contains one striking indication of the amicable relations which must have been established between the royal prisoner and his court-in-exile and the court of Edward III; Edward is handsomely complimented as huntsman and soldier:

> 'Aussi pour servir Eddouart,
> Le roy Anglais, qui bien scet l'art
> Des Deduis, et si n'est sur terre
> Nulz plus vaillant roy pour la guerre . . .'[16]

Jean found it easy to buy French texts in England: a *Roman de Renart* was purchased from book-sellers in Lincoln; a *Garin le Loherain* and a *Tournoiement de l'Antechrist* from dealers in London.[17] Book-binders were busy on his behalf in London, as well as illuminators;[18] he took an interest in the famous religious places of the capital – endowing the shrine of St Erkenwald, at St Paul's, in 1360.[19] A glimpse of more relaxed court occasions is afforded by his gift of 'iii escuz', in 1359, to 'Philippe, roy des menestereulx'.[20] When he returned to France, in 1360, it was on condition that his place was taken by three of his sons – among whom was the prince who was to become the greatest collector and patron of the whole medieval period – Jean, Duc de Berry. For Jean's departure to England, where he remained, except for periods of parole, until 1367, Machaut wrote his elegant *Dit de la Fonteinne Amoureuse*, in which de Berry appears as a 'lordly lover . . . bewailing his separation from his lady' and 'comforted by a poet-stranger'.[21] The literary côteries of England during these years would have contained, as a matter of course, French and English patrons, with French and English poets attached, in a variety of ways, to their households. It is no accident, but a consequence of definable historical circumstances, that Chaucer's first large-scale English poem, *The Book of the Duchess*, delicately adapts the basic situation of the *Dit de la Fonteinne* for a prince who must have been well known to Jean de Berry – John of Gaunt. With such distinguished French visitors in England – men whose upbringing encouraged them in the composition as well as the reading of courtly verse[22] – the transmission of high-class French materials to this country must have been easy and continuous.

Not only was French poetry being written in England for patrons-in-exile; it was being written for members of the English royal family, by continental poets in their regular employ. Jean Froissart, who first came to England in 1359, and presented to Edward's Queen, Philippa of Hainault, a verse account of the years following the battle of Poitiers,[23] returned in 1361, and stayed as 'clerc de la chambre' to the Queen until her death in 1367. While in her household and patronage, he proceeded with his French prose continuation of the *Vrayes Chroniques* of Jehan le Bel, composed a number of occasional poems of some local interest[24] and began on his long verse-romance of *Meliador*, in which so much of the English history of Edward III's reign is thinly disguised.[25] Even if Chaucer had left the service of Elizabeth of Ulster by the time Froissart was in residence in the household of her mother-in-law, Philippa, he could hardly have avoided knowledge of, and contact with, Froissart. Chaucer's own Hainaulter wife, Philippa, was also a member of the Queen's household, and he himself continued to be connected with royal and ducal affairs in one capacity or another. James Wimsatt's proposal that Froissart's *Dit dou Bleu Chevalier* was influenced by Chaucer's *The Book of the Duchess*[26] seems, in such interlocking social and administrative contexts, entirely plausible, and as natural as the fact that, like Chaucer, Froissart also lamented the death of Blanche of Lancaster, in his *Joli Buisson de Jonece* of 1373. The same kind of context, at a slightly later date, must have ensured Chaucer's familiarity with the person and the poetry of the Savoyard knight, Oton de Granson, who was in Lancastrian employ from 1374.[27]

It is obvious that the structure of this courtly society allowed for the support of a great range of household officers, who often appear to have had a variety of duties and occupations; poets and chroniclers whose professional designation may be that of chaplain or 'clerc de chambre': 'knights and esquires of the chamber' who may also be poets.[28] In fact, the first answer to the query about the 'direct contribution' of the aristocracy to the court culture which 'nourished' Chaucer must be a simple one: it provided a framework within which that culture could develop. Even if we leave aside the exercise of patronage and the shaping of taste, it offered a reason for, and a means of, bringing people together in situations which might conceivably be as productive artistically as they certainly were in a social and political sense. This must have been particularly true of the royal courts, whose clientèle at any given moment of the year depended very much upon the decision of the King himself, and in which rigid distinctions between political and cultural activities cannot ever have really existed. The disassociation of the upper echelons of the nobility and the royal family from the court as an administrative body is quite artificial if we are trying to assess what pressures there may have been upon Chaucer in his emergent, as well as his mature, years as King's esquire, royal servant, and man of letters.

The fact, for instance, that the libraries of English royalty and nobility are almost exclusively, at this time and even much later in the century, made up of French literature is not irrelevant as evidence of those pressures. A recognition of the international status of French as a literary vernacular, witnessed in the reading materials and reading habits of his employers and their continental peers, could have urged Chaucer towards both early conformity (and perhaps some composition in that medium) and later experiment with English in emulation of French. The step taken by Chaucer when he wrote *The Book of the Duchess* in English marks his clear understanding of himself as 'nourished' by European traditions which had long been concerned to demonstrate the power of the vernacular languages for high and refined literary purposes: in these traditions, aristocratic patronage had played no mean part. Many have commented upon the way in which *The Book of the Duchess* sets itself decisively apart, in style and narrative strategy, from any earlier English work of the century. It is a poem such as would have been acceptable to all who were accustomed to reading in the sophisticated *demandes*, *saluts*, and *complaintes d'amour* of contemporary France. When we feel the need to specify a particular class of audience for *The Book of the Duchess* – or indeed for Chaucer's subsequent English verse – we should still allow for the fact that his efforts seem to have been so patently directed towards the provision of alternatives for the same wide range of public which had hitherto been satisfied by courtly literature in French only.

We have, for instance, no certainty that 'the court in its wider sense'[29] was much more interested than the aristocracy (and therefore a stronger determining influence upon Chaucer) in an English rather than a French courtly mode. The tastes of the aristocracy are frequently mirrored in those of their national administration: kings, magnates, royal tutors, clergy, and civil servants read the *Roman de la Rose*. Two of the texts bought by Jean le Bon in England – a *Roman de Renart* and a *Garin le Loherain* – are listed as part of a bequest, left in 1365 by a member of the Chapter at Langres.[30] It is not quite true that there is a radical class-distinction between the 'old-fashioned French romances' prized by the English aristocracy and the 'dits amoureux' prized by Chaucer and his closer friends. Isabella, Duchess of York in Chaucer's lifetime, read the poems of Machaut as well as a prose *Lancelot*. On the last folio of a fourteenth-century manuscript of the works of Baudouin and Jean de Condé, the names 'Herford, Holand, Cliffort, Stury' are inscribed.[31] The Condés, Hainaulter poets, were read and patronized, like that other Hainaulter, Jean Froissart, by the Avesnes family, Counts of Hainault, Holland, and Zeeland – a family to which Queen Philippa of England belonged. Such facts suggest that aristocratic reading tastes are too often assumed to be limited to pious works and romances. Even the collection of books confiscated from Thomas, Duke of Gloucester, in 1397, usually characterized by literary historians as highly orthodox in its predilection for romances, may contain, under deceptively general titles, verse of the Condé-Machaut-Froissart kind: 'j large livre de Tretes amoireux et moralite3 et de carolles frannceis bien eslumine3'.[32] This is not unlike the description given by Froissart of the handsome volume of poems which he presented to Richard II in July 1394: 'tous les traités amoureux et de moralité que . . . je avoie par la grasce de Dieu et d'Amour fais et compilés . . .'[33]

In our desire to correct the insubstantial documentation of older accounts of Chaucer as court-poet, with patrons among the innermost circles of the English royal family, we should not be tempted to spring so far in the opposite direction as to exclude the possibility that those innermost circles were, in fact, influential upon the development of his literary as well as his professional activities.[34] There is much plain historical evidence about the overlapping of circles of society at the English courts of the fourteenth century; the implications of such evidence are very various. Chaucer's friends Clanvowe and Clifford, for instance, were Chamber Knights of Richard II and in daily attendance upon the King; it is difficult to believe that Richard knew little of Chaucer's poetry, and cared less. It may be objected that all the 'innermost circles' of the English royal court can indicate of literary taste and talent is the (lost) French poetry of John Montagu, third Earl of Salisbury and personal friend of Richard II. The truth is, surely, that the French works of Montagu and the English works of Chaucer are natural products of the same situation, in which the stubbornly 'foreign' reading expectations and practices of royalty and aristocracy, no less than those of their respected servants, are a force to be reckoned with. Chaucer, however, learnt a more truly international lesson from the admiration which a great vernacular literature of Europe could continue to command among the upper classes of his own country and their households. His use of English is the triumph of internationalism.

Part IV Literature and the visual arts

13 Medieval poetry and the visual arts*

A STRIKING feature of critical writing about medieval English poetry in the last decade has been its increasing use of medieval art not simply to elucidate or to confirm its references, but also to clarify its principles of composition and, even further, to interpret its meaning.

Three large areas of Chaucer's poetry have been examined in terms of art: character-creation, setting and structure. The form of the *Canterbury Tales* was 'substantially defined' in 1957 by reference to art-historians, who were describing the aesthetics of Gothic art.[1] A precedent had been established: recent studies of 'Gothic unity and disunity' in Chaucer have used the characteristics of Gothic art, and in particular, of Gothic architecture, as the basis for analysis of a highly professional and rigorous nature.[2] The whole of Chaucer's work has been placed for us in a cultural context which owes as much to the researches of Panofsky as to the theology of St Augustine: D. W. Robertson's *A Preface to Chaucer*[3] sets medieval art and literature in closest connection. So, Chaucer's exuberance and seeming illogicality of procedure are explained as features of a special English variety of 'Gothic', and related to fan-vaulting and manuscript painting of the fourteenth century. Convention and realism in the make-up of many of Chaucer's characters are defined, significantly, as 'iconography' and 'delineation from life', and illustration is again drawn from sculpture and manuscript painting. The problematic settings of the *Canterbury Tales* are said to be the result of a 'typically Gothic disregard for spatial unity' and specific analogues are suggested – gold leaf for the empty settings, iconographic pictorial schemes for those of a more detailed kind.[4]

These analogies and, in some cases, identifications with the visual arts are as stimulating as they are wide-ranging, but they raise many questions. It would be unwise to assume that they can do much more than act suggestively, or evocatively, upon the reader; they cannot be used to provide exact proofs. While they should never be regarded as precision instruments, they may, in fact, turn out to be double-edged weapons of some peril, both for the critic and for the poetry he examines. This is not to say that even when they are wrongly applied they are useless; they may reveal unexpected truths which, although complex and inconvenient, will press for admittance.

We may take, for instance, the relating of character-creation and verisimilitude

---

* Originally published in *Essays and Studies*, 22 (1969), 16–32.

of setting in Chaucer's poetry to certain characteristics of Gothic art. It is a good corrective to the persistent view of Chaucer's characters as psychologically convincing and life-like to be reminded that their sudden lapses from dramatic realism and their retreat into stereotype not only occur, but are familiar and meaningful in terms of the isolating tendencies of Gothic art.[5] And it would have spared us a good many essays on 'character-contradictions' if direct communication with the listener or the viewer had been recognized as a natural medieval alternative to indirect communication via overhead or overseen words and actions – an alternative used frequently, with little or no explanation. Nothing could be a better warning of the danger of expecting consistent dramatic illusion in Chaucer's poetry, and of the flight to disappointment or to ingenuity which must follow, than the page of a fourteenth-century manuscript, or the sculpted front of a Gothic cathedral, the canopy of a Gothic tomb, with their figures of the Holy Family, Saints or Kings, juxtaposed but isolated from each other, gazing out of the spatial setting they share to some remote realm of truth, beyond us. So in an early fourteenth-century Psalter illustration,[6] the Virgin and St Christopher, each with their divine burden, stand side by side in the same arcaded setting, but have no contact with each other; the mounded water in which St Christopher stands almost laps the Virgin's robe, but she is insensible of it. They confront us directly with their separate roles in God's narrative. So, sometimes, Chaucer's characters, Walter and Griselda, Palamoun and Arcite, Criseyde, Troilus and Dorigen do not converse so much as speak out beyond their narrative setting with a consistency which is local and isolable, not part of a 'nexus of dramatic or psychological interactions'.[7] Dorigen's unlikely rehearsal of just a few of the 'thousand stories' she could tell about wronged women,[8] Criseyde's protestations of fidelity, when all hope of fidelity has gone,[9] are presented not so much for their naturalness in a particular human dilemma as for their appropriateness in an ideal moral situation.

And yet, for all that, Gothic art of the fourteenth century should help us to question the idea that what we instinctively and persistently register as 'realism' in Chaucer can be adequately described as skill in conversational English, and verisimilitude in detail of setting.[10] More than a 'sense of immediacy' is involved. For it is not simply an increasing degree of verisimilitude which we notice in some areas of fourteenth-century painting and sculpture. This in itself is impressive enough to make us uneasy about agreeing that 'realism was alien to the artistic expression of the period generally'.[11] Realism and formalism coexist, in art as in literature; a fourteenth-century pattern-book, such as the Pepysian Sketch Book,[12] records among mythical, zodiacal and symbolic creatures a whole world of English game and domestic animals, more closely observed and naturally set than any in Chaucer's major or minor poems. Chanticleer, striking though he is when first introduced to us, is most accurately associated with courtly painting of elaborate French style – an art of hard, brilliant substance and formal stance:

His coomb was redder than the fyn coral,
And batailled as it were a castel wal;
His byle was blak, and as the jeet it shoon;
...
And lyk the burned gold was his colour.[13]

The miniatures in an early fifteenth-century French manuscript, containing a translation of Bartholomew the Englishman's *De Proprietatibus Rerum*,[14] provide perfect equivalents; the cockerel on folio 177 is closer to Chaucer's description of Chanticleer than the cockerel of the Pepysian Sketch Book, which is a recognizable farmyard bird. Here Chaucer's detail is meant to dazzle rather than to convince by its familiarity. Only when he begins to involve his bird-characters in action does he change to a mode of naturalism: the edgy, amorous relationship of Chanticleer and Pertelote is portrayed in rounded, human terms.

And here fourteenth-century art is still relevant: side by side with patterns of isolation and juxtaposition, it shows us more complex patterns of relationship – persons and objects in dramatic inter-connection. A scene from a Bohun Psalter[15] of the later fourteenth century pictures Christ's journey to Calvary as an embryonic but moving drama of weariness and derision; an earlier fourteenth-century Peterborough Psalter displays the whole Passion sequence as a series of stylized events, held still in a luminous spiritual atmosphere.[16] The Lytlington Missal,[17] made for an abbot of Westminster between 1383–4, contains a crucifixion scene packed with incident and movement of actors; the Job paintings in St Stephen's Chapel, of the same date, must, from what we can still see, have been impressively dramatic in conception. So, Chaucer's Griselda is not entirely Petrarch's emblem of patient fortitude; occasional comments show her reacting sharply and directly to the cruelty of Walter's testing.[18] Criseyde and Pandarus engage in convincing manœuvres of inquiry and dissimulation.[19] Arcite and Palamoun are given formal, complementary speeches, but they also seize and capitalize on each other's words.[20]

There is, in fact, room in later fourteenth-century art and literature to accommodate the widest variety of expressive modes: the Italianate-English, dramatic styles of the Bohun manuscripts, of the Lytlington Missal and the paintings in St Stephen's Chapel correspond to the even more highly developed dramatic styles to be found in Chaucer's *Troilus* and in parts of the *Canterbury Tales*. Having said this, we must admit that recession to other less dramatic methods is frequent in both painting and poetry; there is less dramatic interconnection between Criseyde and Troilus than between Criseyde and Pandarus. Chaucer's treatment of his hero is more formal by far. Consistency of procedure would not have recommended itself to the medieval artist or poet as much as variety. A fair reading of the *Clerk's Tale* or of *Troilus and Criseyde* depends upon our willingness to admit that the value of his symbolic material is frequently – though temporarily – obscured for Chaucer by his sense of dramatic immediacy,[21] and that the poems, like many fourteenth-century manuscripts, screen-paintings or tomb-canopies, are chequer-boards of styles and approaches. The art of his time cannot be used to support any particular theory about Chaucer as 'realist' or 'symbolic moralist', although it can suggest to us the complexity, and even the uncertainty, of the relationship between the two. While it will certainly not rule out the possibility that Chaucer's poetry is 'concerned primarily with ideas',[22] it will also indicate the possibility that some of his finest, and most original work might be in the field of 'dramatic or psychological interactions'.

On the vexed question of the backgrounds and settings of poetry, art is again an unpredictable ally. Attempts have been made to explain the contrast between background emptiness or vagueness and foreground detail in both Chaucer and Langland by means of book-illumination and altar-painting – the 'floating' of religious subjects against gold, as in the Avignon Pietà, the Wilton Diptych, or in innumerable miniatures of the period.[23] But the comparisons will not stand scrutiny, and we are left feeling that gold leaf is a fashionable remedy for critical doubt about spatial concepts in the work of medieval poets. In the first place a background of gold leaf, or indeed, of gold paint, hardly ever gives an impression of emptiness; it is a very assertive feature of manuscript painting, whether used, with tooled decoration, as a back-drop of substantial splendour, recommending the pictured events of the foreground to the viewer, or in the case of religious subjects, as a symbolic comment upon their divine meaning and context:

the glittering surface, which changes in brightness with the smallest movement on the spectator's part . . . effectively destroys all visual association with this world; it creates a celestial envelope of light, in which bodies have no corporeality . . .[24]

Neither function is relevant to the *Canterbury Tales*. If we are anxious to find a more exact parallel between painted backgrounds and the setting of Chaucer's poetry, we can point to the *Book of the Duchess* with its dream-description of a May-morning:

> And eke the welken was so fair, –
> Blew, bryght, clere was the ayr, . . .
> Ne in al the welken was no clowde . . .[25]

This is a precise verbal equivalent of another convention of medieval art – the intense, plain, blue background which is often an alternative to plain gold. The exquisite, formal landscapes illustrating Jean Corbechon's *Proprietez des choses*[26] are frequently backed by 'blew, bryght, clere' and cloudless skies. In both cases, art and poetry, we are dealing with a visual and thematic convention, rather than with a version of naturalism. The purely decorative value of blue as a foil for landscape details in green, white and red is fully realized; there are also signs that it is used, like gold, to represent the changeless spiritual ether which backs and surrounds all created things. So, again, it cannot be said to give an effect of 'emptiness', if that is what we are seeking: it vibrates with deep colour and meaning. The clearest examples of this significant use of blue backing come from eleventh- and twelfth-century religious painting, from books such as the Sacramentary of Limoges[27] and the Bury Bible.[28] But in its extensive use by later medieval painters, in more naturalistic contexts, it is still possible to see symbolic and decorative purpose. Both are present, unmistakably, in the backing to Giotto's frescoes in the Scrovegni Chapel, Padua. Both can, perhaps, be discovered in the backing to the Calendar pictures of the *Très Riches Heures*, made for Jean, Duc de Berry, in the early fifteenth century: the deep blue of heaven, through which the chariot of the sun drives, and the constellations shine, passes imperceptibly to become the unchanging back-drop of man's seasonal pageant.[29] And in Chaucer's poem, a blue, bright, cloudless setting may symbolize something of the theme: consolation is offered not by disguising the fact of the death of the Duchess, but by presenting human fidelity in love in an ideal and changeless form.[30]

The background to the *Canterbury Tales* is at once a more and less complicated matter. Each of the *Tales* has, of course, its own setting and orientation; we are led to look at the world of each one as through the open windows of many later medieval pictures – from the frame, the window-sill, we see a various landscape. But for the Canterbury Pilgrimage itself, with its stress – uneven, admittedly – upon points along a route rather than upon landscape, we should expect to find visual equivalents in medieval maps, rather than in paintings. We are dealing with something nearer to geography than landscape-description, although medieval maps sometimes seem to be a curious combination of the two, with cartographic and pictorial elements. The map of Great Britain, made about 1360, and known as the Gough Map,[31] was a fourteenth-century traveller's guide, and could have been familiar to Chaucer. It provides fairly accurate information on the road-network of medieval England, based, it is thought, on well-tried itineraries between main cities; it also includes stylized 'vignettes' for towns and important castles, with spires, towers, crenellated walls and a few houses. Chaucer's references to particular places on the way to Canterbury are brief, but deliberate; the background is only empty in the same way as the background to a mapped-itinerary might be called 'empty'. It is to common knowledge of a map that he appeals.

Finally, we may turn from space to structure, and consider how the application of the structural principles of Gothic art to the *Canterbury Tales* can help to demonstrate the nature and the unity of the whole work. Comparisons with Gothic form in other branches of the arts are always instructive, but not always amenable to particular critical theories. Certainly the break-up of a total design into separate, juxtaposed units of composition, and the arrangement of such a structure as a 'sequential procession',[32] can be recognized as a familiar procedure and pattern in Gothic art and architecture. We meet it in the frontal designs of Gothic cathedrals, in the 'window-pages' of manuscripts of the thirteenth and fourteenth century, which dispose a continuous narrative into separate pictures, each framed – and therefore isolable – but set within a larger enclosing frame. An intricate piece of carving such as the Neville Screen[33] in Durham Cathedral is based upon the same principles; with its series of elaborately-worked niches, surmounted by delicate spires and pinnacles, it is an essay in repetitious, co-ordinate design. It spans the nave, however, as an entirely convincing and confident whole work of art. But comparison of any of these with the *Canterbury Tales* produces as many problems as solutions. It is easy to see that the 'collection of stories', envisaged as a medieval art-form, must, basically, be a Gothic co-ordinate construction: Boccaccio's *Decameron*, the moral collections such as the *Book of the Knight of la Tour Landry*, and Chaucer's own *Legend of Good Women* use, in a very simple way, sequential techniques. The works build cumulatively, through their separate and equal parts, to full size. Essentially, then, it is possible to see a familiar pattern in Chaucer's collection of *Canterbury Tales*, each representing a well-received genre of medieval literature, and each part of a sequentially-ordered whole: the larger structure of the pilgrimage. If there were no more to the *Canterbury Tales* than a variety of tales told at various points along a journey, and illustrative of the entire range of medieval taste and experience, we could legitimately compare them with other examples of Gothic art, to discover a unity which accommodates discrete parts: 'the basic structural procedure . . . is the inorganic one of additive collocation'.[34]

But in fact the *Canterbury Tales* is much more difficult to describe and account for than this would suggest. Much hinges upon the need of the present-day critic to find 'unity' in the whole work. But it is worth remembering that the concept of unity is far more flexible for the medieval period than for our own: even its desirability is not always apparent. In some ways, the skeleton structure of the *Canterbury Tales* is very similar to that of the manuscript collection of diverse materials – the 'miscellany', which had no other reason for existing than its diversity of content. While some collections work to a particular theme, others are built up simply on the principle of variousness. The fourteenth-century Vernon manuscript is an example of the first type, all of its contents gathered under one general heading, 'Salus anime, and in englysh tonge Sowlehele'. Of the second type, there are innumerable examples from the fourteenth and fifteenth centuries: British Museum MS Additional 16165, written by the fifteenth-century 'publisher', John Shirley, has everything from treatises on hunting and on the Passion to Chaucer's translation of Boethius and love-complaints. It would be perverse to discuss the 'unity' of the Vernon manuscript except in the most general thematic terms and even more perverse to discuss that of the miscellany proper, although all could be said to illustrate, in a very free way, the medieval tolerance of a compendious structure (which may be no more than the material entity of the manuscript itself) of extremely various parts. There is less pressure upon the medieval writer than upon later writers to demonstrate over-all unity by any sort of cohesive methods; there is also no very sharp distinction between the compiler of materials written by others, and the creative artist.

The relevance of this to the *Canterbury Tales* is cautionary; we must beware of assuming it necessary to prove the unity of the whole composition by sophisticated aesthetic theory, since it is possible that Chaucer felt himself to be more in the position of the compiler of a miscellany than, for instance, in that of the architect of a Gothic cathedral. He may, in any case, have been more casually concerned with what, to later ages, has become a compelling problem – unification. His *Legend of Good Women* is a work which stands low in modern critical estimation for the mechanical way in which it brings together a collection of stories about unfortunate women, and for the rather listless execution of the scheme. It is doubtful whether medieval readers had any of our reservations about the crudity of the formal structure, any more than they had reservations about the structure of a collection of Saints' Legends, each accompanied by its commemorative picture of Saint and symbol.

But, of course, the *Canterbury Tales* is a very different proposition from the *Legend of Good Women*. Chaucer deliberately encourages us to think of it as more than just a miscellany of stories, or as a panoramic survey of the variety of medieval life. The *General Prologue*, with its announcement of dramatic verisimilitude in the telling of the *Tales* (lines 725–36), the reinforcement of this in the *Miller's Prologue* (lines 3170–5), and the provision of the Links to the *Tales* raise different expectations, and set up different standards of judgment. While no one could deny that these innovations of Chaucer's inspired his finest dramatic writing, they also involved him in serious problems of organization. Left as a 'miscellany' with a purely formal introduction, the *Canterbury Tales* would, indeed, have invited straightforward comparisons with other fourteenth-century art forms, or with the manuscript compilation, for its principles of construction and its concepts of unity. As it comes down to us, it is a far more complex work, and, if it invites comparison with medieval art, takes us to fields in which the proof of unity is a far more hazardous activity.

For it is not only the marked fluctuation of literary quality in the *Canterbury Tales* – the *Second Nun's Tale* against the *Clerk's Tale*, the *Parson's Tale* against the *Pardoner's* – which should make us uneasy about comparisons with examples of Gothic art in which technical excellence is sustained throughout all parts of the design: the west-front of Wells Cathedral, the Neville Screen, the Psalter of Robert de Lisle.[35] We might, however, expect the 'unity' of a painted manuscript page or of a cathedral front to be questioned if the standard of workmanship varied as much as that of the *Tales*. We can go further than this, and ask whether there is not a more serious kind of fluctuation in the *Canterbury Tales* – a fluctuation of purpose, described conveniently, though crudely, as an uncertain movement between narrative and dramatic principles of organization. If this is true, it does not rule out the propriety of comparison with some forms of Gothic art, but not, on the whole, with those which manifest unity of composition most strikingly.

The characteristics of Gothic art after 1400 have been described as 'unbalance . . . conflict . . . disintegration of elements . . . lack of coherence'.[36] But even before 1400 it had shown signs of such tendencies. One department alone of English fourteenth-century art – that of manuscript illumination – often poses us the problem of deciding whether the written and decorated page is still a total artistic unit, or has already begun to disintegrate. 'Conflict and unbalance' are as often properly descriptive of the relationship between parts of the whole decorative scheme as 'diversity within unity'. We are not yet at the point when the border designs threaten to dominate the page entirely, taking precedence over the main picture and invading even the area originally reserved for the script: that will come, in the next century. But a number of elements are clearly in conflict in some manuscript painting of the fourteenth century – the Luttrell Psalter,[37] the Grey-FitzPayn Hours[38] show, beside pages where text, main picture and border design are relevantly balanced and linked, pages where border designs admit interest, in artist and patrons, difficult to interpret as anything but secular, dramatic, even comic by nature, and therefore intrusive.

Much effort has been expended upon proving that such secular 'irrelevances' are, in medieval terms, symbolically relevant. But we tread dangerous ground here if we are not prepared to consider the whole field of manuscript painting. It is dangerous to resort to ingenious symbolic explanations, in order to make disparate kinds of subject matter on a page of manuscript illumination exact echoes of each other.[39] For the manuscripts in which an 'implicit relationship' between main initial picture and border decoration can be shown to exist, an equal number, of the same date, deny such a relationship. The lavishly decorated Metz Pontifical,[40] of the earlier fourteenth century, uses the widest variety of marginal subjects, some overtly religious, some problematic, and some certainly secular. The relationship of border to initial picture is not particularly meaningful – initials taking standard types of subject which offer no scope for comparison, implicit or explicit, with the often wildly imaginative marginal subjects.[41]

But it is not only in subject-relationship that the illustrative schemes of fourteenth-century book painting exhibit conflicting elements; space-concepts are also a problem. As such schemes become more ambitious in scope, the problem of unifying the 'space-illusion' for the whole page of text, central-picture and margin becomes more acute. The 'inner conflict between the conception of the book-page as a primarily planimetric organism and its treatment as an opening into a recession of depth'[42] was only ever partially resolved by French and English artists of the fourteenth century. It is not uncommon to find sharp differences of viewpoint, scale and perspective, with margin and main subject unrelated, in spatial terms, to each other, and to the flat surface of the page of text.[43] The room for manœuvre was wide; in one powerful fifteenth-century attempt at a solution, the framing border is deliberately given an intensity of focus denied to the central scene – even when that scene is of the Crucifixion: 'we get the illusion that the marginal zone is alive, and the scene in the centre only a picture'.[44]

An increasingly dispersive relationship between the components of the manuscript page might indeed be expected from what we know of the changing conditions under which book painting was carried out during the fourteenth century. By the middle years, the secular and professional *atelier* had come to stay and there are many clear cases of division of labour – the text written in a monastic centre, but its illustration and decoration carried out by secular artists, to the demands of a lay patron.[45] Such circumstances do not strongly favour unity of design and theme – not even unity of opposed but meaningful parts. They can, at worst, encourage a self-willed, somewhat indulgent diversity. The Pepysian Sketch Book[46] gives evidence of the profusion of decorative material which the fourteenth-century book-painter was expected to be able to provide for his patron's tastes – dogs hunting, cats washing, pheasants and mallards, rabbits, dragons, mermaids, saints, zodiacal beasts and a Pelican in its Piety. And a manuscript such as the Grey-FitzPayn Hours, which we know to have been decorated by lay artists, confirms that such tastes were successfully met.

If we take a wider view of Gothic art, looking not only at architecture of the high Gothic period, but at painting over the span of the Gothic centuries, it is impossible to deny that the basic structural principle of 'additive collocation' with its inevitable 'detachability of parts',[47] could only too easily result in disparity and unbalance of parts. The fifteenth century did, in fact, see 'the breakdown of the aesthetic equilibrium of Gothic book decoration'[48] but the warning signs of the breakdown were already apparent in Chaucer's day and earlier.

The importance of this to the *Canterbury Tales* is considerable. Chaucer's problem in that work of multiple parts is, like that of the book-painters, one of accommodation – of new materials, forms and impulses with older. 'Additive collocation' describes the various *Canterbury Tales* – juxtaposed, opposed, illustrative in content and genre of the variety of the medieval world. It cannot properly describe their frame, and their relationship with it – a relationship of pilgrim and tale which is, by turns, brilliantly maintained as dramatic illusion, halting and uncertain, and even non-existent. The *General Prologue* and, even more, the Links to the *Tales* draw upon sources of material and energy quite untapped by other medieval poets, and, perhaps, by any poet before Shakespeare. And as fourteenth-century illuminators often found licence, in their borderwork, to experiment fruitfully with new dramatic themes and forms,[49] so Chaucer innovated, unchecked, in his 'borders' to the *Tales*. Our anxiety to praise Chaucer should not prevent us from recognizing the unique nature of what he – imperfectly – attempted: the creation of 'free-standing characters' who could as actors function before an audience. The creation of the Wife of Bath involved Chaucer in something akin to the dramatist's 'imaginative feat of detachment';[50] this urge to give independent life to characters, although it was frequently withdrawn, or hesitatingly offered, is the final distinguishing mark of Chaucer's art. It distinguishes the *Canterbury Tales* from the *Legend of Good Women* and from the *Confessio Amantis*, as it distinguishes *Troilus and Criseyde* from *Il Filostrato*.

But we cannot pretend that it makes for balance and unity. Its vehemence is liable to erupt through older surfaces, to disturb older patterns with sudden improvisation, as the Canon and his Yeoman gallop to join the pilgrimage, the Cook and Maunciple brawl, and the Wife of Bath so takes control of her *Prologue* that it ceases to be a medieval 'confession' and persuades us to speculate about hidden motive, and partially-revealed nature: 'the unfocussed aspects of character work within the minds of those who encounter them, like yeast in bread'.[51] The powerful effort to evoke the pilgrims and their world in the Links, and sometimes in individual *Prologues*, is more often abandoned than sustained in the *Tales*: we may compare the depth of focus in the portrait of the monk, in the 'merry words of the Host to the monk', with the flat mode of the *Tale*. It is a testimony to the vigour of these creations that critics have always been active to disguise difficulties by elaborate theories of dramatic irony, and, more recently, by theories of 'Gothic juxtaposition'. But these are false resolutions of the central problem, which is one of proportion and equilibrium. Like many illuminated pages of later medieval books, the *Canterbury Tales* does not properly adjust border material to main subjects. The frame, like the wide, packed, and errant borders of many manuscripts, contains or fails to contain, an explosive life of its own, secular and dramatic; such a life advances upon the more static and conventional material of many of the *Tales*, encroaching, without ever bidding for complete take-over.

That Chaucer might allow this to happen, we might predict from the statements of dramatic intent in the *General Prologue* and in the *Prologue* to the *Miller's Tale*. These should not be taken as humorous disclaimers of art[52] but, on the contrary, as serious passages, laying claim to art of a particular nature – that art of the dramatist which 'involves a kind of abdication'.[53] That Chaucer would not wish, or be able, to take a fully dramatic view of all of his material, we might also predict, from what we know of his immediate environment, and of the limitations imposed upon him by his age and training. But as in many later medieval book paintings, the uneasy tensions in the *Canterbury Tales* between different sorts of material and different approaches, the conflicts between narrative statement and dramatic exploration are defining elements in the make-up of the whole work.

The freedom for dramatic experiment allowed to the illuminators in the marginal area of their pages can often be proved to bear fruit, finally, in the increased liveliness of central page compositions.[54] It is doubtful whether, without the possibility of experiment in the frame-space, Chaucer's superbly complex presentation of the Wife of Bath, in her own *Prologue*, would have been achieved. This *Prologue* very decidedly represents the invasion of a narrative area by dramatic forms; the subsequent *Tale* is a mere appendage to what can only be described as a mature character-study. Similarly, in the whole relationship of border to main subject, frame to *Tale*, Chaucer and the illuminators often give us the impression 'that the marginal zone is alive, and the scene in the centre only a picture'. The many qualitative contrasts of pilgrim portraits, Links and *Tales* are not always to be dismissed as 'Gothic paradox', or 'juxtaposition of contrasting parts': they tell us of a problem of adjustment, rather than of a mastery of the problem. In a miniature from the early fifteenth-century Hours of Marguerite of Orléans (plate 1), the opening words of the prayer, 'Obsecro te domina', are accompanied by a picture of the countess, kneeling in front of the Virgin and Child. The scene is gorgeously but flatly presented, the group backed by ornate, glittering fabrics, their attitudes still and formal. But almost encircling prayer and picture, in a deep and profuse border, is a pilgrimage: knights, ladies on horse-back, palmers on foot travel a winding road, through little woods, past flowers and butterflies, to a chapel, and beyond that, to the spires of a distant town. The pilgrimage is, indeed, 'alive . . . the scene in the centre only a picture': the world of the border is fully-dimensioned, and vigorously presses against the enclosed area of prayer and picture, as if it can hardly be contained. Drama restlessly stalks narrative over the manuscript page.

14 *Piers Plowman* and the visual arts*

COMPARED with the poetry of Chaucer, which is lavishly provided with references to the visual arts, Langland's *Piers Plowman* is economical enough; if we relied upon encouragement from the poet to persuade us that his work is deeply indebted to painting and sculpture for its imagery or for its larger descriptive conventions, we should be badly off. It is typical of Langland, scrupulously concerned to make beauty present its credentials in a world of moral values, that he should have his dreamer condemned for long dealings with 'couetyse-of-eyghes', that 'foule lust of the ey3en' which traditionally featured in medieval attacks on the arts as stimulants of 'veyne ioye and glorie'.[1] The dreamer is beguiled from true vision by *concupiscentia oculorum*, a handmaid of Fortune:

> Coueytise-of-eyes . conforted me ofte,
> And seyde, 'haue no conscience . how thow come to gode . . .[2]

To this austere view, patronage of the arts must, indeed, be a proving-ground for conscience; wall-paintings and stained-glass windows become, understandably, part of a shady 'spiritual' transaction between a friar-confessor and the devious, expensive Lady Meed, whose offer to

> . . . 3owre cloystre do maken,
> Wowes do whiten . and wyndowes glasen,
> Do peynten and purtraye . and paye for the makynge . . .   (B III 60–2)

is repudiated as 'superbia vitae'[3] (pride of life)

> On auenture pruyde be peynted there . and pompe of the worlde . . .
> (B III 66)

Even the exquisite calligraphic skills of the Middle Ages Langland only dares to mention, admiringly, in connection with the Ten Commandments and their commentary:

> This was the tixte trewly . I toke ful gode 3eme:
> The glose was gloriously writen . with a gilte penne . . .   (B XVII 12–13)

It is not, therefore, surprising that when he does seem to acknowledge a direct link with a contemporary art-form, it is with the illustrations to manuals of

---

* Originally published in *Encounters. Essays on Literature and the Visual Arts*, ed. John Dixon Hunt (London, 1971), pp. 11–27.

religious instruction; his allegorical trees, buildings, garments and documents are naturally related to this art of 'clear visual representation', which intended 'that the reader in the midst of a complicated world of abstractions might see and grasp the essentials'.[4]

But the rather modest claims made by the poet himself have not deterred the critics from going to far more elaborate areas of mediaeval painting in order to elucidate and define some of the characteristics of his poetry. The sequential dream-structure of *Piers Plowman* – not one, but many dreams – has been generally described as 'Gothic': he 'breaks up the poem, in Gothic fashion, into a series of dreams . . .'[5] The spatial concepts which support, or *fail* to support the movement of the poem, have been likened to the 'empty' backgrounds of gold in sophisticated works such as the Wilton Diptych or the Avignon Pietà.[6] The 'paradoxical space',[7] in which the poem exists, has been compared with that of contemporary Italian fresco and panel painting: 'a strained, disharmonious unity of plane and space, line and mass, colour and shape'.[8]

Clearly, there is some kind of dilemma here. The poem itself sanctions attention to a very limited field of the visual arts: the readers of the poem are drawn to wider and more exciting terrain, as they try to express, for themselves and for others, their actual experience of Langland's dream-allegory. On the one hand, we are bound to act responsibly towards the text of *Piers Plowman*, pursuing our investigations with the same vigour that the poet himself uses in his own pursuit of truth: on the other hand, we are bound to take note of the fact that the poem sometimes appears to keep more distinguished company in the visual arts than its author is prepared, or able, to admit. Both courses of action are open to criticism: both promise discoveries and disappointments: both are necessary and, indeed, interdependent exercises.

The problem with analogy-making as opposed to source-hunting is only partly that of securing general agreement, for there is also the danger that agreement may be won by the striking nature of analogies rather than by their fitness. So, the suggestion that the un-localized settings of episodes in *Piers Plowman* can be likened to gold backgrounds in mediaeval manuscript and panel paintings is attractive. But this cannot be approved entirely, for the suggestion is based on the idea that both in the paintings and in the poetry, backgrounds are 'empty'.[9] While this may easily be true of Langland's presentation of his central narratives, it is far from true of the relationship of the gold 'backdrop' in the Wilton Diptych to its varied foreground subjects. The effect of gold-leaf, or gold paint, whether plain, diapered or tooled in ornate designs, is hardly ever that of 'emptiness'; when it is not present simply to provide a substantial, glittering screen, against which foreground events may be seen to greater advantage, it functions as a spiritual comment, enveloping the particular moment – Deposition, or Resurrection – in a haze of significant light. It is almost the reverse of 'emptiness'. Only one episode in *Piers Plowman* could legitimately call to mind the use of gold-leaf in manuscript illumination – the Harrowing of Hell.[10] Here Langland deliberately introduces the theme of blinding light: Christ approaches Hell as a spirit clothed in splendour –

> And now I se where a soule . cometh hiderward seyllynge
> With glorie and with grete li3te . god it is, I wote wel . . .
>
> (B XVIII 304–5)

The whole of the drama is envisaged as the confrontation of light and the 'dukes of this dym place'; whatever the precise source of Langland's imaging, the impression given by this whole section of his poem is not falsely conveyed in terms of those miniatures of the Harrowing of Hell and the Resurrection which float the triumphant Christ in a concentrate of gold light to the walls of Hell, or out of the confines of the tomb (plate 2).[11] But for most of the time, the 'emptiness' of Langland's backgrounds is better represented in visual terms by the plain, empty space of the manuscript page, as it appears behind and through the line-drawings of humbler mediaeval book-illustrators, who are similarly concerned with the essential shape of an act, or an episode, rather than with all of its supporting and corroborative detail. In this respect, we would come nearer to some of Langland's attitudes and procedures by studying a work such as the fourteenth-century Holkham Bible Picture Book:[12] here the contrast between the vigorous, dramatic rendering of Biblical scenes from Creation to Last Judgement, in strokes equivalent for their energy and decisiveness to Langland's strong language –

> 'Consummatum est,' quod Cryst . and comsed forto swowe
> Pitousliche and pale . as a prisoun that deyeth;
> The lorde of lyf and of li3te . tho leyed his eyen togideres.
> The daye for drede with-drowe . and derke bicam the sonne . . .
>
> (B XVIII 57–60)

and the bare unsubstantiated background to those scenes (plate 3) is reminiscent of the way in which *Piers Plowman* holds parts of the Biblical narrative in solution, as it were, taken out of their particular historical context, and exhibited to the eye of faith alone.

The Holkham Bible Picture Book is too simple a production to be of more than momentary interest to the reader of *Piers Plowman*. Its limited material means that it can have limited usefulness as a comment on the organizational problems presented to Langland by his all-embracing visions of life, death and salvation as they are revealed in religious history and moral allegory. And it is the complex and shifting nature of the 'spatial environments'[13] in *Piers Plowman* which has prompted comparison with some major Italian painting of the mid- and later fourteenth century. Frescoes which depict the violent and contrarious sensations of a country afflicted by bubonic plague, guilt, fear and anguished spirituality, are said to share with the English poem 'paradoxical space, a rejection of perspective, and a tension between the natural and the unnatural, the physical and the abstract'.[14] But no Italian fresco adequately represents the variety of Langland's dealings with space and location. Traini's *Triumph of Death*, in the Campo Santo, Pisa,[15] with a theme similar to that of Passus XX of *Piers Plowman* –

> Deth cam dryuende after . and al to doust passhed
> Kynges and kny3tes . kayseres and popes;
> . . .
> Many a louely lady . and lemmanes of knyghtes
> Swouned and swelted . for sorwe of Dethes dyntes . . .
> (B XX 99–100, 103–4)

has something of that 'inconsequence of spatial relations' observed in the poem: groups of people, each oblivious of the other, are disposed over the picture-area, engaged in separate activities – ladies seated in a grove, knights riding in cavalcade, hermits praying and meditating in rustic seclusion. Their existence in a common picture-space is rather summarily indicated; the relationship between grove, rocky countryside and open meadow is not explored realistically. A sense of tragic isolation pervades, which only death will, ironically, dissolve. The fresco is, however, far simpler to grasp than the equivalent section of *Piers Plowman*: there is some structural logic to its 'broken terrain' landscape, as there is also some logic to its time-scheme. Its events are embedded in space and time at the same depth. In *Piers Plowman* there are no such certainties. The attack of Death takes place within a dream, and, further, within the context of the coming of Anti-Christ. The boundaries of present and future are continuously blurred, as we move from contemporary reference – the accommodating Friars, the terrors of the Black Death – to apocalyptic forecast; we are left, designedly, uncertain whether Anti-Christ already reigns, in the fourteenth century, or whether the dreamer is being admitted to a vision of the Last Days. The battles that rage, between Anti-Christ and Conscience, between Death and Humanity, between Sin and Virtue, have not one, but many grounds of action; they take place about the 'barn of Unity', the historical Church of post-apostolic and mediaeval times, in the Westminster of Langland's day, in the labyrinths of man's interior world.[16] The transitions are unremarked; they are hardly difficult to make, for no substantial, visualizable, setting is provided, either in terms of allegory or literal realism. The 'broken terrain' of Langland's composition, we might say, is that of the mind; the locus of action is as changeable, as unlimited as the growing capacity of the dreamer's vision to 'wander through eternity', or to interpret the images in the troubled 'mirror of middle-earth'.[17] The only control exercised over the choice, disposition and relating of materials is spiritual; it is not so much an 'insecurity of . . . structure'[18] that we find in *Piers Plowman* as a deliberate attempt to work on a principle familiarly expressed by Langland's contemporary, the author of *The Cloud of Unknowing*:

'Wher then', seist thou, 'schal I be? Nowhere bi thi tale!' Now trewly thou seist wel: for there wolde I have thee . For whi nowhere bodely is everywhere goostly . . .'[19]

Langland's reluctance to show his reader, or his dreamer, any sympathy for that irritable question – 'Where, then . . . am I to be? Nowhere, according to you!' – is crudely understood as an admission that stability and security are lost. Rather, it is a direction towards a new stability – a coherence to be discovered only fragmentarily in history or fiction, regarded as sequential narratives, but most fully in the great spiritual themes that inform them.

The search for similar statements, similar procedures is rewarded more positively by the art of the earlier mediaeval period than by that of Langland's own day. The Carolingian Utrecht Psalter,[20] made near Rheims in the ninth century, is not only remarkable for the literal nature of some of its pictorial commentary on the psalms, verse by verse. Its most significant features relate to concepts of space and time. For here, in a single picture-space, disparate subjects are irrationally, but unquestioningly juxtaposed: the light, impressionistic backgrounds of late-antique landscape painting are used to suggest, but never to define, some common ground inhabited by all created beings. They are, however, metaphors rather than representations of space – as English artists, copying the Psalter in the twelfth century, recognized.[21] Their later versions of the manuscript go one stage further in the translation of landscape into pure calligraphy: their figures, dancing, fighting, praying, lamenting in isolable groups, are presented in a context which is, simultaneously, as shallow as the manuscript page, and as deep as the total, realizable meaning of the Psalmist's text – 'nowhere bodely is everywhere goostly . . .' For here, seeming irrationality can only ever be resolved by the words of the psalms in their literal and figural senses; a picture which contains, within a single frame, and in a single space, episodes from Old and New Testament history, from contemporary life, and from religious legend clearly asks to be 'read' not as a continuous and self-sufficient narrative, but as an exploration of deeper harmonizing truths.

So, the logic of a scene which could otherwise appear meaningless, or at best enigmatic, is found in the text inspiring it, and in the range of meanings offered by that text. Space and time are flexible concepts, accommodating the phenomena of the material world to the larger realities of a spiritual universe. The abrupt proximity of unrelated actions and events in an illustration of Psalm LXXXV[22] – ploughing and reaping, the Visitation, the Virgin and Child, men protected by angels – is 'explained' by the text of the psalm:

terra nostra dabit fructum suum.   (v. 12)

(Our land shall give her increase).

misericordia et veritas obviaverunt sibi: justitia et pax osculatae sunt.   (v. 10)

(Mercy and Truth are met together: Righteousness and Peace have kissed each other.)

veritas de terra orta est: et justitia de caelo prospexit.   (v. 11)

(Truth has sprung out of the earth; and Righteousness has looked down from heaven.)

ostende nobis, Domine, misericordiam tuam: et salutare tuum da nobis   (v. 7)

(Show us thy mercy, O Lord, and grant us thy salvation.)

But the picture achieves its proper unity at a deep level of significance: the Psalm and its illustration, allegory, history, and genre realism, are synthesized in a timeless and untramelled process of prophecy and fulfilment. It is the benignity of God – 'Etenim Dominus dabit benignitatem' (v. 12) (Yea, the Lord shall give that which is good) – witnessed in the life and words of the Psalmist himself, in the fact of the Incarnation and in the yearly rewards of man's labour on earth, which provides true sustaining continuity.

Similarly, the choice and arrangement of subjects for Psalm XVI (plate 4)[23] – Christ raising Adam and Eve out of Hell, the three Maries at the tomb, a company of Saints, Christ praised by angels and human beings asleep – result, superficially, in an inconsequence not only spatial. The very process, however, of interpreting

... non derelinques animam meam in inferno: nec dabis sanctum tuum videre corruptionem ...

(v. 10)

(... Thou wilt not leave my soul in hell; neither wilt thou suffer thine Holy One to see corruption ...)

as the Harrowing of Hell and the Resurrection, argues for an underlying view of space and time in which text and illustration are of vital, linked consequence; the Psalmist's premonition of truth was confirmed by providential Christian history. To such a view the range of reference, from ordinary human life to the life of Christ, from the Saints on earth to the angels rejoicing in Heaven, is not unacceptably wide, nor are the forms taken by such reference particularly surprising. Man's intuition is instructed of divine purpose, in sleep – 'usque ad noctem increpuerunt renes mei' (v. 7) – (and in the night my inmost self instructs me ...) as his waking understanding is instructed by Scripture and legend and holy example.

In Langland's *Piers Plowman* the dreamer arbitrates between the poet, the reader and the materials of vision; he is involved, commenting upon the variety, pace, and often unexpected quality of the action – the sudden disappearances:

And whanne he hadde worded thus . wiste no man after,
Where Peers Plouhman by-cam . so priueliche he wente ...

(C XVI 149–50)

– the sudden transformations:

> And thanne called I Conscience . to kenne me the sothe.
> 'Is this Iesus the Iuster?' quod I . 'that Iuwes did to deth?
> Or it is Pieres the Plowman! . who paynted hym so rede?'　　(B XIX 9–11)

And so, too, in the Psalter illustrations, the Psalmist is constantly present as an onlooker, a participant, an eye upon events or an actor in one episode of the drama; this agile figure, trampling upon the unjust, supplicating God, threatening and praising, is hardly a unifying agent, in a strict sense. But he does, like the dreamer of *Piers Plowman*, provide a focus of attention in a world of diverse and, if only initially, perplexing forms.

The art of the Utrecht Psalter and its copies can have nothing but associative value for studies of Langland's art: a more specific indebtedness could never be in question. It does, however, usefully remind us, when we are tempted to compare his structures adversely with the 'strong geometry [or geography]'[24] of the *Divine Comedy* and the *Canterbury Tales* that surface irrationality may not indicate confusion of outlook, but rather a different mediaeval attitude to the ways in which the poet and artist can express the relationship of phenomenal and spiritual truth. In this case, a method of Biblical illustration throws light, from afar, upon Langland's methods: in other cases, using simpler art-forms within his probable reach, we might expect to be rewarded more exactly and, indeed, more richly. The confidence which recent writers have shown in going to treatise-illustration for the sources of Langland's imagery is well-founded; his own phrasing is clearly directive – to a Tree of the Vices:[25]

> Ac whiche be the braunches . that bryngeth men to sleuthe? . . .　　(C VIII 70)

– to a Wheel of the Virtues:[26]

> . . . take Pacience,
> And bere hit in thy bosom . abowte wher thou wendest,
> In the corner of a cart-whel . . .　　　　　　　　　(C XVI 160–2)

Manuscripts best described as 'spiritual encyclopaedias', which provided, for all levels of the later mediaeval devout reading public, poems and prose-pieces accompanied by drawings, could have given him exemplars.[27] Turning their pages, we are confronted by many of the raw materials of Langland's allegory: king, knight and bishop, their hearts touched with death's spear:[28] Christ leading 'the cart of the fayth', packed with believers, and threatened by devils, to his heavenly harvest (plate 5):[29]

> And whan this dede was done . Grace deuised
> A carte, hyȝte Cristendome . to carye Pieres sheues;
> And gaf hym caples to his carte . Contricioun and Confessioun . . .
>
> 　　　　　　　　　　　　　　　　　　　　　　　(B XIX 326–8)

trees of life, attacked at the roots by time and death, trees of the vices, rooted in pride –[30]

> ... Pruyde hit aspide,
> And gadered hym a gret ost . greuen he thenketh
> Conscience, and alle Cristene . and cardinale uertues,
> To blowen hem doun and breken hem . and bite a-two the rotes ...
>
> (C XXII 337–40)

lamps of good-works, fed with the oil of charity –[31]

> For-thi chastite with-oute charite . worth cheyned in helle;
> It is as lewed as a laumpe . that no liȝte is inne ...   (B I 186–7)

Concerned only with clarity of exposition, this is a world in which the grotesque or the bizarre has no place;[32] when Langland comes to his central allegory of the Tree of Charity, he has his guide-figure, Piers, shake humanity from the branches, like apples, and the devil gather them up, like an orchard-thief:

> For euere as thei dropped adown . the deuel was redy,
> And gadred hem alle togideres . bothe grete and smale ...
>
> (B XVI 79–80)

And when the manuscript artists present us with the Tree of Life, man is the ripening fruit for whom time, death, and damnation greedily watch (plate 6).[33]

But we should be mistaken if we imagined that by such detailed comparisons we could do more than indicate how knowledge of certain pictorial formats may have worked in the poet's imagination. This is most clearly proved by the section of the poem in which the dreamer's desire to understand 'what charite is to mene' (B XVI 3) is answered by exposition and visionary experience of a Tree of Charity. Here, in a very important sense, Langland tells us that source-hunting is not enough – although his warnings have not been properly heeded by the critics, who persist in trying to elucidate the passage in terms of particular kinds of mediaeval tree-models.[34] For while any of the manuscripts already mentioned, and a wide variety of others similar, could have given Langland his exemplar for the tree as it is first described to the dreamer (B XVI 4–16), brief and plain, like a simple line-drawing, no manuscript illustration and no religious treatise could account for his translation of picture into active drama. It is as if the poet impatiently turned from the manuscript page, with its three-fold trees of love (plate 7),[35] its loaded trees of life, its burgeoning hearts of contemplation,[36] and substituted experience of love and life in a visionary re-creation of the story of the Fall, and the Redemption. What, in the cold words of the first expositor, Anima, is nothing but a formula, becomes a living substance in the words and movements of the second guide, Piers Plowman, for he takes the dreamer down to a deeper level of spiritual consciousness (B XVI 19–20) and makes the tree-allegory *work*.

The intervention of the dreamer, by his continued questioning of the tree's structure –

> 'Pieres', quod I, 'I preye the . whi stonde thise piles here?'. . .   (B XVI 24)

and of Piers, by his decisive action against the apple-robber –

> And Pieres for pure tene . that o pile he lauȝte,
> And hitte after hym . happe how it myȝte . . .   (B XVI 86–7)

leaves pictorial allegory far behind, as the tree is metamorphosed into Christian history, and love becomes incarnate:

> And thanne spakke *Spiritus Sanctus* . in Gabrieles mouthe,
> To a mayde that hiȝte Marye . a meke thinge with-alle . . .   (B XVI 90–1)

In fact, whether we look to the rich art of the Middle Ages, or to its poorer relations, for help with understanding *Piers Plowman*, the usefulness of our studies must nearly always stop short of Langland's poetry. So, a single manu-script painting may elucidate some of the processes which went to the making of his famous metaphor of love as the 'plant of peace':

> Loue is the plonte of pees . and most preciouse of vertues;
> For heuene holde hit ne myȝte . so heuy hit semede,
> Til hit hadde on erthe . ȝoten hym-selue[37] . . .   (C II 149–51)

In a fifteenth-century prayer-book, decorated sumptuously for the Talbot-Beauchamp family (plate 8),[38] the Virgin and Child, ringed with bright gold, are supported in the bell of a slender lily which rises from a green mound. Langland's words are brought to mind by the strange growth of body out of plant, woman and child out of symbolic purity: by the paradox of heavenly symbol rooted in earth, and humanity lifted to heaven. But nothing in the painting can suggest that further imaginative act of the poetry which transmutes plant, flesh and blood into shivering leaf and into needle-point, so that we may be left with a sense of the mystery of the Incarnation and not simply with a picture of its beauty:

> Was neuere lef vp-on lynde . lyghter ther-after,
> As whanne hit hadde of the folde . flesch and blod ytake;
> Tho was it portatyf and pershaunt . as the poynt of a nelde,
> May non armure hit lette . nother hye walles . . .   (C II 152–5)

For like the greatest religious painter of Northern Europe in the next century, Hieronymus Bosch, Langland was always more preoccupied with power than with beauty of concept. Far-fetched as the comparison may at first seem, it is Bosch alone, among later mediaeval artists, who matches the range and some of the special quality of Langland's invention. The relevance of Bosch's *Haywain*[39] triptych to the opening of *Piers Plowman* is very clear: in both picture and poem man's life, in its sensual confusion, is poised between Heaven and Hell. Langland's description of his 'field full of folk',[40] with its tumbling crowds of beggars, merchants, churchmen and labourers is rapid and impressionistic: in this it differs from Bosch's presentation of his fallen world, which is observed with acute, almost photographic precision. But the informing vision is common to both: 'all the wealth of this world, and also the misery',[41] the headlong rush of man, once destined for greatness, into the 'deep dale' of hell, where nothing but death awaits him –

> . . . deth, as ich lyuede,
> Wonede in tho wones . and wyckede spiritus . . .   (C I 17–18)

And only the hideous procession of the central panel of *The Haywain*, where demon trudges shoulder to shoulder with doomed man, can properly remind us of Langland's Deadly Sins, mingling as friends with all classes of society:

> I, Wrath, rest neuere . that I ne moste folwe
> This wikked folke . for suche is my grace . . .   (B V 151–2)

The paintings of Bosch can offer us explicit, arresting statements of themes which in *Piers Plowman* are developed in a more leisurely, discursive manner. The egg-monster in the Hell volet of *The Garden of Delights* triptych[42] reveals an ale-house, within its cracked body; Langland's Glutton is beguiled into a tavern on his way to confession.[43] In Bosch's picture no hope is held out to the revellers, who can only climb in and out of the dark waters of Hell: Langland's sinners are eventually allowed the knowledge that

> . . . goddes mercye is more . than alle hise other werkes . . .   (B V 289)

But behind both scenes lies the controlling idea of conviviality blind to damnation; both artists work energetically and ironically to demonstrate the truth that sin is already hell, and that hours in the ale-house are snatched from salvation.

Most important is the way in which both Bosch and Langland move boldly to question and disturb accepted boundaries of the ordinary and the extraordinary. Bosch's studies of saints in prayer or meditation surround the dreaming or semi-conscious man with landscapes fashioned strangely from inner and outer reality: the phantasmagoria of the spiritual world, shapes of good and evil, invade that 'mighty world of eye and ear' with life and substance.[44] So, in Langland's poem, the dreamer is admitted, in a solitary dream, to a land which accommodates, without apology, the sights and sounds of contemporary England, the events of Biblical history and the allegories of man's moral existence. Neither poet nor painter allows sharp distinction to be made between waking and dreaming. What the waking senses might receive as customary, becomes, in the dream, material for wonder:

265

I seigh the sonne and the see . and the sonde after,
And where that bryddes and bestes . by here makes thei ȝeden,
Wylde wormes in wodes . and wonderful foules,
With flekked fetheres . and of fele coloures . . .   (B XI 318–21)

Conversely, the material of vision is often adjusted to everyday reality, as when Langland's dreamer questions Abraham about his meeting with the Trinity:

'Havest thow seyen this?' ich seide . 'alle thre, and o god?'
'In a somer ich seyh hym', quath he . 'as ich sat in my porche,
Where god cam goynge a-thre . ryght by my gate . . .'   (C XIX 241–3)

The variousness of the phenomena presented to the reader or the viewer is never less than challenging, and is often bewildering. Access to understanding lies only through the dreamer or the saint, in whose experience the poem or painting lives. The eye constantly retreats from Bosch's paradoxical landscapes, crowded with diabolic and heavenly symbolism, to the holy figures who, in their hours of trial and trance, call up, suffer, and finally resolve the confusion. So, too, it is only by resting upon the efforts of Langland's dreamer, who by turns invites, resists and accepts the evidence of his vision, that wilderness and paradise can be seen, even temporarily, in meaningful harmony.

Bsecro te domina
sancta maria ma
ter dei pietate ple
nissima summi regis filia ma

1 Virgin and Child, Pilgrimage. Hours of Marguerite of Orléans, Paris, BN, MS Lat. 1156 B, fo. 25r; French, after 1426.

3   Crucifixion. Holkham Bible Picture Book, London, BL, MS Add. 47682, fo. 32v; English, first half of 14th cent.

2   Harrowing of Hell. 'Paduan Psalter', Cambr., Fitz. Mus., MS 36/1950, fo. 103v; German, Italianate style, c. 1260.

4 Events surrounding Resurrection. Cambr., Trinity Coll., MS R.17.1, fo. 24r; Canterbury, c. 1150.

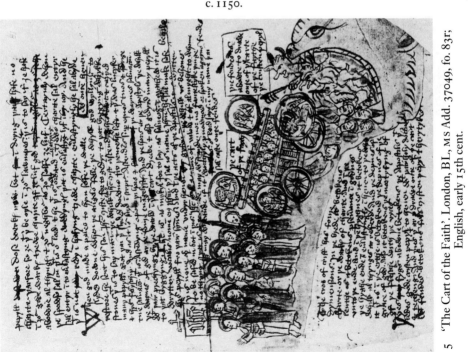

5 'The Cart of the Faith'. London, BL, MS Add. 37049, fo. 83r; English, early 15th cent.

6 'The Tree of Life'. London, BL, MS
Add. 37049, fo. 19v.

7 'The Tree of Love'. London, BL, MS
Add. 37049, fo. 25r.

8 Virgin and Child. Talbot Hours, Cambr., Fitz. Mus.,
MS 40/1950, fo. 73r; French, c. 1450.

9 *Troilus* Frontispiece. Cambridge, Corpus Christi College, MS 61, fo. 1v; English, first quarter of 15th cent.

10 Copy of the Limbourgs' *Itinerary*
(French, c. 1410), now lost. Lithograph of
Auguste, Comte de Bastard d'Estang.

11 Ascension. Breviary of Jean sans Peur,
London, BL, MS Harley 2897, fo. 188v;
French, c. 1413–17.

12 Adam de la Halle, *Oeuvres*, Paris, BN,
MS f. fr. 25566, fo. 10r; French, c. 1300.

13 Machaut, *Poésies*, Paris, BN, MS f. fr.
22545, fo. 75v; French, c. 1380.

14 Deguileville, *Pèlerinage de vie humaine*, London, BL, MS Add. 38120, fo. 1r; French, c. 1415.

15 Deguileville, *Pèlerinage*, Paris, BN, MS f. fr. 376, fo. 1r; French, c. 1420.

16a Detail from the *Troilus* Frontispiece (in reverse).

16b Paris, BN, MS f. fr. 12420, fo. 54r; French, 1402.

16c Paris, BN, MS f. fr. 598, fo. 54v; French, 1402–3.

17a　Detail from the *Troilus* Frontispiece.

17b　Paris, BN, MS f. fr. 12420, fo. 73r.

18a　Detail from the *Troilus* Frontispiece.

18b–d　Paris, BN, MS f. fr. 12420, fos. 31r, 60v, 165r.

15   The *Troilus* Frontispiece*

I T has become traditional to believe that the full-page miniature on folio I V of M S 61 in Corpus Christi College, Cambridge (see plate 9), which portrays two incidents in the life of medieval aristocratic society – a formal meeting outside a castle gateway and an open-air recital in a wooded parkland – describes, with retrospective authority, not only the historical role of Chaucer as court-entertainer, delivering his poetry to a sophisticated and appreciative audience, but also a particular moment in the 1380s, when *Troilus and Criseyde* received its first public reading from the poet himself, in front of Richard II and his immediate family circle.[1] And although the insecurity of such a belief must be exposed, it is beyond doubt that, on grounds of costume alone, the picture cannot refer to a period later than the second decade of the fifteenth century.[2] It is also beyond doubt that it stands as a Frontispiece to the text of Chaucer's *Troilus*, which begins on the facing folio; it appears to be an integral part of the design of the whole manuscript – a design allowing for the presentation of the poem in a spacious format already established by continental traditions of secular book illumination, but unprecedented in the history of the publication of any major English work before this time. Apart from the completed Frontispiece, spaces are left in the sequence of the poem for ninety further pictures, and we may suppose that a lavish programme of illustration was planned – of a similar scope, perhaps, to those which had been developed over the thirteenth and fourteenth centuries in Italian and French manuscripts of Benoît de Ste Maure's *Roman de Troie* and its derivatives.[3]

In the absence of certain information, however, it is the Frontispiece itself and its significance as an element in the *ordinatio* of the Corpus Christi manuscript which must continue to occupy our attention. No other Chaucer manuscript contains such an elaborate prefatory miniature; even the copy of *Troilus and Criseyde*, made for Henry V while still Prince of Wales, has nothing comparable. And the quality of the only extensive illustrative materials provided for the *Canterbury Tales* (in the Ellesmere and Cambridge University Library Gg. 4.27 M S S, for instance) serves to throw into high relief the unique circumstance recorded by Corpus Christi M S 61: the introduction of a medieval English poem by an exceptional piece of international Gothic painting.[4]

In 1928, Eric Millar wrote of the Frontispiece: 'the miniature is somewhat of a

* Originally published in *Troilus and Criseyde. A Facsimile of Corpus Christi College Cambridge M S 61*, introductions M. B. Parkes and Elizabeth Salter (Cambridge, 1978), pp. 15–23.

puzzle . . . it may be said to stand by itself in English art'.[5] And although this judgement was made in an art-historical context, a similar acceptance of the complexity of the issues raised by the miniature is still the best basis for any study of its wider affiliations and of its particular function within the Corpus Christi manuscript. Indeed, the confidence of literary historians to pronounce upon these matters has sometimes been won at the expense of that very stylistic and iconographic analysis which might have prevented them from asking and answering over-simple questions about the content and the meaning of the picture. The impulse, for instance, to make it yield up inappropriately exact messages about Chaucer and the social contexts in which his poetry was delivered, and the reactive impulse to deny it access to any substantial degree of historical life[6] must both be checked against what we know of the nature of medieval Frontispiece composition. The following discussion will propose that international rather than narrowly English perspectives require us to take a liberal view of the involvement of history, art-history and literary-history in the relationship between poem and picture.

We should not be surprised that our first impression of the Frontispiece as an ambitious and comprehensive attempt to convey some sense of high occasion should be succeeded, on closer scrutiny, by a recognition of its intricate, composite iconography. The medieval workshop convention by which the prefatory miniature of a de-luxe manuscript was carried out as a special commission, often by the major artist of that workshop, reflects quite accurately its important status as an introduction to the volume and often, in the case of religious manuscripts, as a dedication to the collaborative purposes of author, artist and patron. The further convention that such a miniature might be, in part or in whole, a compilation of motifs drawn from earlier or contemporary exemplars not only expresses a respect for authority but also a taste for ingenuity and variousness which did not need to seek exclusive delight in fresh invention.[7] In the case of the *Troilus* miniature, there is particular reason for remarking upon such things, for here we are dealing with the special requirements of a secular text – a situation which customarily prompted a more intensive process of borrowing and adaptation from iconographic patterns of religious origin.[8]

For purposes of analysis, the Frontispiece may be divided into two main component parts, probably derivative from quite different iconographic materials: a diagonal line of soft-modelled rock separates off a scene of encounter between two elegant retinues from a scene of public recital, staged quite as elegantly. The relationship of one section to the other is more that of companion-pieces than that of background and foreground subjects; the retinue scene, with its winding procession, ornate castle gateway and twin tower-crowned peaks, occupies nearly half the picture space and is identifiably based upon some version of a famous set of exemplars – the *Itinerary* miniatures devised in the early fifteenth century by the Limbourg brothers for three of the most splendid manuscripts of Jean, Duc de Berry, to accompany prayers for his safe journeying (see plate 10).[9] The exact model for the open-air recital scene is less easy to define but it is based, ultimately, although with interesting variation of individual features, upon a preaching-group: this is decisively signalled by the lack of text in front of the speaker, and by his familiar hand-gestures as he looks down from his portable, draped 'pulpit'.[10]

We should, however, give a false impression of the novelty of the adjustment of religious format to secular purposes in this lower section of the miniature if we failed to note that the artist may easily have been influenced by the established iconography for prefatory pictures to a celebrated fourteenth-century vernacular poem – the first recension of Guillaume de Deguileville's *Pèlerinage de Vie Humaine*.[11] Here, over the later fourteenth and early fifteenth centuries, in direct response to the wording of the opening lines of the poem in which Deguileville, a Cistercian monk of the Royal Abbey of Chaalis, near Senlis, addressed himself to 'riche, povre, sage et fol / soient roys, soient roynes / pelerins et pelerines . . .',[12] we can trace the development of a lively 'recital' scene, with poet–monk addressing an appropriately mixed audience from his pulpit. Of special importance to the *Troilus* Frontispiece is the earlier fifteenth-century elaboration of this scene as a courtly, outdoor idyll, complete with landscape detail of a stylised type, and intricate castle architecture (see plates 14 and 15).[13] There had been, of course, no lack of pictorial conventions in the fourteenth century for representing the poet in communication with his public – manuscripts containing the poetry of Adam de la Halle, Guillaume Machaut, and Jean Froissart bear this out (see plates 12 and 13).[14] But the responsibility for adapting and then standardising the preaching formula favoured by the *Troilus* artist most probably lies with the Deguileville illuminators, whose manuscripts were widely disseminated in France and in England.[15]

If in certain important ways the iconography of the Frontispiece directs us to models from late fourteenth- and early fifteenth-century France, its style confirms that direction. Here first, however, we must distinguish between borders and main miniature. Both the inner border, with its fleshy, curled stems and shaded insets of flowers and leaves, and the outer border, with its freer, more delicate foliate sprays, can be paralleled by similar examples from workshops centred upon early fifteenth-century London and East Anglia.[16] But it is difficult to be convinced that either the immediate or the ultimate influences upon the stylistic modes of the miniature itself are to be sought anywhere but in that Parisian work of the late fourteenth and early fifteenth centuries to which so many brilliant Italian and Flemish artists contributed.[17] Not only in its overall composition – a strongly diagonal design, accommodating two significant areas of subject interest – can it remind us of Gethsemane and Nativity miniatures by artists such as Jean de Limbourg and the Brussels Initial Master.[18] And not only in its choice of a widely various range of figure and facial types – by turn stocky, fleshily-nosed, sinuous and sharp-etched – can it remind us of the anonymous Bedford Master and productions of the 'Bedford Trend'.[19] It can 'quote' in greater detail than this; from architectural forms and landscape features distinctively Limbourgian, and almost certainly to be located in the *Belles Heures*, completed for Jean de Berry before 1409 (see plates 10 and 11);[20] from lavishly or gracefully costumed figures and facial characteristics already part of the repertoire of artists such as the Coronation and Brussels Initial Masters, working for French kings and princely patrons during the first years of the fifteenth century, when the Limbourg brothers arrived in Paris, to learn from them a new refinement of their art (see plates 16 to 18).[21]

Such observations about the international relationships and possible lineage of the Frontispiece cannot encourage us to support a very straightforward view of the picture's overtly English historical references. If it is, in fact, a 'gate-way to untravelled paths of truth',[22] it issues something of the same contradictory invitation to the optimistic traveller as that other gateway, in Chaucer's *Parliament of Fowls*. With its rich reminiscences of continental landscape and figure painting, its mosaic of stylish iconographical motifs, and its typically English border-work, it must be accounted both less and more than a confirmatory report upon Chaucer and his authentic audience for *Troilus and Criseyde*. Less, because neither art-historical nor palaeographical evidence[23] suggests the possibility of finding in it recognisable 'portraits of fourteenth century celebrities'[24] and a specifically English comment about Chaucer's position as poet at the court of Richard II.[25] More, because it speaks to us, though we may as yet understand imperfectly, of historical sequences and situations which compose its larger and wealthier cultural context. The royal and aristocratic *dramatis personae* whose literal presence in that crowded parkland may be so unlikely are still part of the total history of the painting; like their counterparts on the continent, it is they and their fifteenth-century heirs who brought artists travelling across frontiers to work for them and for their courtly circles, and whose own travels, on errands of war and peace, must often have charted the passage of books and forms of art between one country and another.[26]

The precise circumstances in which the Corpus Christi manuscript was first commissioned and furnished with its Frontispiece are not known; we can, however, be reasonably confident, from the purity of its text[27] and the unusually high standard of its prefatory picture, that the circumstances were informed by a proper understanding of what may have been due not only to the patron but also to the poem and, retrospectively, to its author. We cannot give ourselves the pleasure of believing in the local and contemporary realism of the Frontispiece, but we can believe in its hold upon certain kinds of historical and imaginative truth. Far from allowing our identification of the sources of its pictorial vocabulary to discredit that 'truth', we should rather admire the way in which it asks such vocabulary to express matters newly and traditionally relevant to the poem. For in addition to building-back, out of the *Proheme* to *Troilus and Criseyde*, a dazzling image of that very moment of formal yet intimate discourse which Chaucer's words seem deliberately to invoke –

> But ye loveres, that bathen in gladnesse,
> If any drop of pyte in yow be,
> Remembreth yow . . .   (lines 22–4)

– it uses the celebrated *Itinerary* motif to suggest not only a continuum of courtly existence, but also, perhaps, to recall another moment from the sad narrative of the poem, when the heroine, Criseyde, now no more than a pawn in the game of war, is escorted from the gates of Troy to be exchanged for Antenor and meets, for the first time, the 'sodeyn Diomede'.[28]

To these questions, some undisputed facts about the fifteenth-century provenance of the Corpus Christi manuscript may write a postscript.[29] It was, at one time or another, in the hands of John Shirley, who, over the course of his long life (1366–1456), saw service as a member of the retinue of Richard Beauchamp, Earl of Warwick, was book dealer, publisher, prolific scribe and, not least, purveyor of much engaging information about the literary and aristocratic figures of his day. It may also have been owned, among other de-luxe volumes, by Anne Neville, Duchess of Buckingham (c. 1410–80), granddaughter of John of Gaunt and distant relative, by marriage only, of Chaucer's wife, Philippa de Roet.[30] Such facts will not automatically convince us of the possibility that we can 'trace the history of the *Troilus* copy back to the reign of Richard II'.[31] But they do suggest that patterns for the original commissioning of the manuscript and its distinguished Frontispiece should be sought among families at least as eminent as the Beauchamps, the Beauforts, the Nevilles, and the Staffords. Without heraldic clues, the field of choice is impossibly wide; only the unique nature of the miniature in the context of early fifteenth-century English art suggests, further, that our search should concentrate upon families whose connections with France, during those years, were particularly close, and whose taste for French book-painting was particularly strong.[32] In this sense, the 'enigmatic' quality of the Frontispiece may, eventually, guarantee the identification of both workshop and patron: meanwhile, if we cannot accept it as a historical document, there is nothing to prevent us from accepting it as a moving expression of historical respect.

16 The Annunciation to the Shepherds in later medieval art and drama*

INTRODUCTION

WHAT I have to say concerns two active and controversial areas of research in medieval studies: first of all, the degree to which secularisation of devotional forms can be detected in later medieval art and literature, and the adequacy of our processes of 'detection' – in some cases this comes down to no more than a crude contrast between 'realism' and 'symbolism'; and second, the interconnections between medieval art and literature, and the propriety of using one to corroborate and demonstrate characteristics or developments in the other. I am taking, as a means of exploring these issues, the subject of the Annunciation to the Shepherds in the vernacular drama and the visual arts of later medieval England and France. My purpose is to ask questions and suggest, but not prescribe, answers. I propose to look at a large variety of literary and artistic evidence in order to examine the problematic nature and function of the shepherd materials, especially those materials which substantiate the rustic life of the shepherds before they depart for Bethlehem to adore the child Christ.

This essay will be moving towards a statement – though we may never arrive at that statement – that we may be mistaken to try and read an elaborate symbolism into the rustic conversations and 'goings-on' among the Annunciation shepherd groups of the later Middle Ages; and that playwrights, whether they are English or French, are like their contemporaries the painters in taking the opportunity to move into new fields of secular comedy, complaint and social observation which will allow them eventually to celebrate and concentrate on rustic life without any need for clerical or devotional imprimatur. This would be a process similar to that by which, as Gombrich put it, 'Venus conquered her commentators' and arrived in Botticelli's paintings free from medieval lascivious associations.[1]

There are, of course, problems likely to be encountered in the analogical study of literature and art. We should, in the first place, try to be clear as to whether relationships are inherent in the nature of the materials we encounter, or whether they are, partially or wholly, of our own making. We are, for instance, often quietly trying to find relationships where none exist. We should be honest about the amount of trouble we are prepared to take in order to understand the nature of the materials we are relating: how much of an art-historian, for instance, are we

---

* This essay is published here for the first time: its provenance is described in the Preface above, see p. xiii.

prepared to become if we wish to examine medieval poems on the assumption that they obey laws and proceed according to principles similar to those operating in medieval architecture or medieval manuscript illumination? It is all too easy to misunderstand and misrepresent the qualities and the historical contexts of one or another of the arts in order to make an effective, clarifying statement about literature.

We should, in the second place, be clear about our motives. When we explore these 'problematic' relationships, are we really interested in discovering, testing out a provable relationship between literature and the other arts: that is, do we want to engage in an activity which may turn out to be expert, scholarly and circumscribed? Or are we really interested in processes far more closely identifiable with our work as teachers, interpreters and propagandists? As literary specialists we may, if we are honest, be ultimately concerned to communicate the power and beauty of literary texts by recourse to the widest variety of artistic forms. If we imagined, for example, that we were saying anything about a *real* relationship between art and literature when we speak of 'Gothic Chaucer', we would be deluded:[2] what we are saying is something striking and provocative which may make two kinds of complexity seem temporarily connected and give us the impression that to some extent a mystery is being reduced.

the hazards . . . are only too obvious. No man can master more than one fairly limited field; every man has to rely on incomplete and often secondary information whenever he ventures *ultra crepidam*. Few men can resist the temptation of either ignoring or slightly deflecting such lines as refuse to run parallel, and even a genuine parallelism does not make us really happy if we cannot imagine how it came about.[3]

But it is not simply that the establishment and exploration of analogical relationships between literature and the other arts are difficult to manage in a way which is entirely fair to all disciplines involved, and which protects us from René Wellek's charge of 'drearily speculative analogizing between the arts';[4] it is also that the very business of trying to define these analogical processes sets up vibrations in every single area of cultural support.

In my experience we cannot properly deal with the relationship between literature and the other arts unless we also take into account many other cultural relationships. Within the literary context, we have to distinguish and compare a variety of distinct literary traditions, not least those of the English, Anglo-Norman and French languages; we may also have to extend the range of our investigations beyond the arts altogether to the religious, social and economic history in which our literary and artistic phenomena are securely embedded. Our *real* problem, therefore, is perhaps to determine at what point our responsibility to truth, as total as that can be, inhibits the possibility of making even interim pronouncements about the nature and significance of the strands in this web of literature, art and history. My illustration of this problem is drawn from the particular area of literature and art that centres upon the theme of the Annunciation to the Shepherds.

My proposition – however inadequate to the complexities of the situation – is that in looking at the vernacular drama and art of England and France during the fourteenth and fifteenth centuries, we can see what appear to be interestingly parallel – and perhaps ultimately related – ways in which the *mise-en-scène* of the Annunciation to the Shepherds was built up. I propose that all of this was dependent upon a devotional realignment which took place in the twelfth and thirteenth centuries, a realignment for which Cistercian and Franciscan spirituality was mainly responsible; and I propose that the processes involved can be expressed similarly, whether we are dealing with art or literature: the processes provided for the creation of a 'picture-space' within which artists, dramatists and poets could work with new freedom.

SHEPHERDS AND EXEGETES IN THE MIDDLE ENGLISH DRAMA

The pastoral life has always been richly drawn upon by religious writers to express spiritual concepts and processes; from an early period the Middle Ages found, in Biblical texts which dealt with the shepherds literally, such as Luke 2, or metaphorically, such as John 10, 'veiled words, full of topics of inquiry, pregnant with sacramental signs'.[5] Later, however, devotional literature, both Latin and vernacular, witnesses to the growth of an interest in the literal, as opposed to the metaphorical, significance of the Biblical Shepherds of the Gospel of St Luke. I will be tracing first of all some of the particular socio-literary as well as devotional consequences of this for the Annunciation to the Shepherds plays in the vernacular drama of later medieval England; for I believe that in this drama we begin to see a kind of confrontation, perhaps even a conflict, between traditional roles and newly-emergent shaping forces – forces born first of all of changes in affective piety, but after that of the enthusiasms of the dramatists moving into independent and experimental areas of creative work. This development may easily result in an assortment, even an ill-assortment, of materials and themes.

Examples of both a metaphorical and a literal treatment of shepherds and their flocks are clearly provided by the Old Testament, with its images of Israel as the 'flock of the Lord' and 'Yahweh' as the 'shepherd',[6] but also its narration of the lives of the great proprietors of flocks such as Job and Nabal, or the lives of the servants of the great, where the real hardships of pastoral care are described: 'Day and night was I parched with heat, and with frost'.[7] In the early commentaries on the Bible, moreover, both metaphor and literal reality are kept in mind. St Augustine, dealing with Christ's metaphorical use of the figure of the shepherd in John 10 and extending the shepherding metaphors of Christ as the good shepherd to Christ as sheep also – 'he was led as a sheep to the slaughter', 'Behold the Lamb of God' – refers briefly and tellingly, I think, to the actual life of the shepherd 'in the way we are accustomed to know and to see shepherds'.[8] He offers just a glimpse into a real pastoral of the fifth century.

But 'real pastorals' are very far from the minds of the authors of the Latin liturgical drama of the Middle Ages when, in their twelfth- to fourteenth-century *pastores* plays, they use the shepherds of the New Testament to accomplish a number of important things: first, to witness to the angelic song; second, to discuss its meaning; third, to proceed to the manger in order to adore the Christ-child, in some cases singing an antiphon based on the angels' song;[9] in this adoration they confirm the fulfilment of prophecy in his birth. The exegetical texts which supply them with their attitudes are conveniently collected in the *Catena aurea* of Thomas Aquinas, and include Origen, St Gregory, Bede and Ambrose. Most of them 'interpret' the simple shepherd narrative of the Gospel of St Luke as an allegory of Christ's revelation to the church, that is, to the 'masters' of the spiritual flocks who wake in meditation 'while others sleep' and by their teaching fulfil the duties of their pastoral office. St Gregory writes:

It was *in a mystery* that the angel appeared to the shepherds while they were watching, and the glory of the lord shone around them, implying that they who take a watchful care of their faithful flock are thought worthy above the rest to see divine things . . .

and Bede:

in a mystery those shepherds and their flocks signify certain teachers and guides of faithful souls. The night in which they were keeping watch . . . indicates the dangerous temptations from which they never cease to keep themselves . . .

Origen goes further in dissolving all literal historical sense of the episode:

but if we would rise to a more hidden meaning, I would say that there were certain shepherd angels, who direct the affairs of men, and while each one of them was keeping his watch, an angel came at the birth of his lord, and announced to the shepherds that the true Shepherd had arisen.[10]

In deference to such readings of the Biblical texts, the liturgical drama instructs its clerical actors to reveal the 'inner truth' of the Annunciation to the Shepherds by playing 'shepherds-as-exegetes': they wear ecclesiastical robes and carry other occasional iconographical objects which hint at 'a realism of common life' but do not arrest the attention of the audience – the robed shepherds of the Rouen Christmas Play, for instance, also have staffs;[11] appropriately, the Latin Shepherd Play from the *Codex Burana* involves theological debate, and the 'shepherd' figures stress their special clerkly status by the *frater* (brother) form of address.[12] The vernacular drama of the fourteenth and fifteenth centuries in northern Europe preserves something of this approach, although in a thinner and less learned form; and scholars such as D. W. Robertson and Bernard Huppé, with A. C. Cawley in agreement, see the shepherds of the Wakefield *Prima* and *Secunda pastorum* as '*types* of the clergy who seek and find Christ through the study of Scripture'.[13] In what Catherine Dunn calls a 'curiously learned dialogue' which ranges over Biblical and classical prophecy and even takes on typological exegesis, the shepherds of the Wakefield *Prima pastorum* discuss and expound the Fourth Eclogue of Virgil;[14] the Middle Ages regarded this as messianic prophecy – and the Augustinian Friary at York, for instance, contained two copies of Virgil's *Eclogues, Georgics* and *Aeneid*.[15] The shepherds also announce the typological significance of the burning bush, a prefiguration of Mary's virginity (lines 359–63), and explain the appearance of the fourth man with the three whom Nebuchadnezzar threw into the fiery furnace:

> That fygure
> Was gyffen by revalacyon
> That God wold have a son;
> This is a good lesson
> Us to consydure. (lines 354–8)

More than one critic has found that in this particular play the Wakefield Master 'chose to make his shepherds the vehicle of the exegesis'.[16] Other English Shepherd Plays remind us of an earlier learned strain in 'shepherd functions', as when the Chester *Adoration of the Shepherds* allows its shepherds to prophecy as they present their gifts, 'prophets did tell, thou shold be our soccour . . .';[17] the Coventry *Shearmen and Tailors' Pageant* also gives its shepherds the ability to discern prophecy's fulfilment in the Angel's Salutation and at the Birth itself.[18] And, finally, the *N-Town Plays* present a very serious and instructed shepherd company, able to call up Biblical material at will and acquainted with the traditional symbolic imagery for Christ and Mary – the pearl, the rose, the star:

> Heyle floure of flourys fayrest i-fownde
> Heyle perle peerles prime rose of prise
> heyl blome on bedde we xul be un-bownde
> with þi blody woundys and werkys full wyse[19]

The injunction laid upon the shepherds to broadcast the news of the birth is almost reminiscent of the later injunction laid upon the apostles to preach the Gospel of Christ.

But of course there is much more to say about the Annunciation shepherds in the English vernacular drama than this, and it is interesting to find the Wakefield Master seemingly acknowledging as much when, in the *Prima pastorum*, he allows one of the shepherds, John Horne, to jeer at his companion's learned interpretation of Virgil's fourth Eclogue:

> Virgil in his poetré sayde in his verse,
> Even thus by grameré, as I shall reherse: (lines 386–7)

What we may have here is the playwright's own admission that there is some element of incongruity in the spectacle of rough Yorkshire countrymen expounding Latin as if they were clerks or priests; the moment is electric as John Horne shouts out at the grave words:

> Weme! tord! what speke ye here in myn eeres?
> Tell us no clergé! I hold you of the freres;
> Ye preche. (lines 388–90)

The very fact that we can describe these shepherds as 'Yorkshiremen' signals that this play, like at least two of its companions, the Wakefield *Secunda pastorum* and the Chester *Adoration of the Shepherds*, has already established a picture of the Annunciation shepherds which hardly prepares us for their role of 'shepherd-exegetes', exegetes in thin disguise, drawn from an earlier tradition of Latin liturgical drama and exegetical literature. For, even if these same plays develop into pious and learned testimonies to salvific history, they open, challengingly, with pictures of English rural life in the fourteenth and fifteenth centuries, raw with specific references to the ills of the agrarian lower classes and authentic enough to provide some modern historians with material evidence about the state of the English peasantry at the end of the Middle Ages.

Of course the implications of paying such 'realistic' attention to the harsh detail of peasant life are complex. There are symbolic justifications for such literal presentation of the shepherds' suffering on earth before the birth of Christ the redeemer, and such justifications to some extent offer a means of circumscribing and controlling the more problematic issues raised by such 'realism'. Do these shepherd portraits therefore depict 'the realistic consequences of Adam's Fall as suffered by the contemporary audience'?[20] Are the learned authors here drawing upon texts such as Isaiah 56:11?

the shepherds themselves knew no understanding. All have turned aside into their own way, every one after his own gain, from the first even to the last.

Or are they, on the other hand, providing for its own sake evidence of 'the conditions and the grievances of the agrarian lower classes' in 1425 round Wakefield?[21]

The complaints of the Annunciation shepherds through which such pictures of English rural life come into focus are, of course, very mixed in content and origin. They cover a wide range, from topics of traditional complaint and satire such as anti-feminism and ugly or aggressive wives, to topics of particular relevance to shepherd life such as bad weather and footrot – topics which may nevertheless be part of another literary tradition exemplified in the *Georgics*.[22] But the shepherds' complaints also range from the social and economic oppressions of the fourteenth and fifteenth centuries – taxation, harsh landlords, insolent treatment from the retinues of the great, the special evil of 'purveyance'[23] – to hints of possible religious dissent. We find, then, in the opening sections of these plays on the 'shepherds' watch' elements which cannot be totally accounted for as the long-hallowed material of complaint and satire, but which find clearer echoes in certain topical themes of protest and dissent.

There is a great deal of social discontent expressed in the Wakefield *Prima pastorum*, for instance:

> Fermes thyk ar comyng, my purs is bot wake,
> I haue nerehand nothyng to pay nor to take.
> I may syng
> With purs penneles
> . . .
> Is none in this ryke, a shepard, farys wars.
> Poore men ar in the dyke and oft-tyme mars.   (lines 30–3, 92–3)

And in the *Secunda pastorum* complaint is sustained over several stanzas about the exploitation of the small farmer and the injustices of the lord's hired men, 'thyse gentlery-men' (line 18). But this play also appears to draw on contemporary religious dissent when one shepherd adds 'That men say is for the best, we fynde it contrary'.[24] Hinted here may be a rejection of the Church's orthodox justifications for social inequality, poverty and suffering, largely through promises of reward and equality to follow in heaven; such a rejection may have been made possible by the long-term unsettling effect of Wycliffe's attack upon the Church's unchallenged and priestly authority to 'interpret' God's meaning for the benefit of men in general. Certainly, if the line in question means anything, it means something quite radical.

At this point, however, an essential question presents itself: how is the author of the play identifying, if at all, with the nature of such sentiments? We may first of all, perhaps, compare with these materials in the drama similar literary episodes, for example, the address of Pees to the king against Wronge in *Piers Plowman*:

> How Wronge ageines his wille had his wyf taken,
> And how he ravisshed Rose Reginoldes love,
> And Margarete of hir maydenhode maugre here chekis.[25]

We may compare too the 'sermon' of John Ball before the Peasants' Revolt of 1381, as reported by Froissart:

We be all come from one father and one mother, Adam and Eve: whereby can they say or shew that they be greater lords than we be, saving by that they cause us to win and labour for that they dispend? They are clothed in velvet and camlet furred with grise, and we be vestured with poor cloth: they have their wines, spices and good bread, and we have the drawing out of the chaff and drink water: they dwell in fair houses, and we have the pain and travail, rain and wind in the fields; and by that that cometh of our labours they keep and maintain their estates: we be called their bondmen . . .[26]

It seems likely that there is also a core of authentic protest material behind this passage from Walsingham's *Historia Anglicana*:

[John Ball] began a sermon in this fashion: 'Whan Adam dalf, and Eve span, Wo was thanne a gentilman?' And continuing his sermon, he tried to prove by the words of the proverb that he had taken for his text, that from the beginning all men were created equal by nature, and that servitude had been introduced by the unjust and evil oppression of men, against the will of God ... Let them consider, therefore, that He had now appointed the time wherein, laying aside the yoke of long servitude, they might, if they wished, enjoy their liberty so long desired ... And when he had preached these and many other ravings, he was in such high favour with the common people that they cried out that he should be archbishop and Chancellor of the kingdom.[27]

But what assumptions did such authors make about how their readers would understand these expressions of social discontent? If Langland's sympathies were to an important degree with the poor, Froissart, as in his *Chronicles* generally, almost certainly expected his aristocratic readers to take a very unfavourable view of sentiments such as those he attributes to John Ball; and Walsingham leaves no doubt at all on the question.

Rodney Hilton records an interesting witness to the contemporary phenomenon of the small tenant farmer dissatisfied with the traditional rates of payment due to the overlord, and the overlord in turn frustrated by the difficulty of obtaining payment: on the estates of the Earl of Warwick in the 1390s the traditional labour services of the tenants were relaxed without payment of any dues, and it was with reference to this that notes were recorded on documents in the later fourteenth and again in the early fifteenth century that rents would not be paid 'until the world is set to rights'.[28] The landed classes recognised the power of the people to refuse payment. But what does the fact that the note is phrased in such semi-apocalyptic or political language give witness to? On the one hand, to the strength of the resistance to the established order; but on the other hand, perhaps also to a religious vision which presented and thus circumscribed that resistance as part of a larger decay, a falling-off in standards and virtues. It may be, then, that the Wakefield playwright, like Froissart, Walsingham or the steward of the Warwick estates, also sees the complaint of the shepherds as a symbolic 'sign of the times'.

There were of course many apparently orthodox writers of the fourteenth century who felt themselves in dilemmas: Langland, for instance, was at times satisfied with the idea that poor shepherds go straight to heaven –

> Souteres and shepherdes, suche lewed Jottes
> Percen with a *pater-noster* the paleys of hevene. (B X 460–1)

– at another time tortured with the idea that there may be some uncertainty –

> Ac pore peple, thi prisoneres, lorde, in the put of myschief ...
>
> Now, lorde, sende hem somer and some manere joye,
> Hevene after her hennes goynge, that here han suche defaute! (B XIV 174, 164–5)

Both Langland and the authors of the religious plays, to some degree and in some areas, are uneasy about the preservation of the status quo; both raise awkward questions, whether or not they calculated clearly over the total implications of their questioning. In *Piers Plowman* certainly orthodoxy and the querying of orthodoxy are left juxtaposed. One could dispose of the difficulty by pointing out that Langland's possible unorthodoxy is offered as part of the incomplete vision of a fallible dreamer, and again that dissent in the plays is always offered from within the bounds of dramatic character; it remains unclear how far we should trust the shepherds as witnesses – are they fallible witnesses? In all of these cases we are inevitably prompted to ask questions about the angling and presentation of this material of protest and dissent, and about the extent to which the author identifies with it.

These new materials in the shepherd drama indicate that there may be several ways of portraying the shepherds of the Annunciation in the English religious drama of the later Middle Ages: one is dependent upon older, orthodox traditions of exegesis on the Scriptures, and probably upon those traditions as they are contained in the Latin liturgical drama; another is dependent upon – what? If we say that it is dependent upon a tradition of complaint and satire, familiar enough in Latin and vernacular texts throughout the period we are considering, we have not really gone far enough. Rodney Hilton's book on the medieval English peasantry seems to me to be an essential guide to the ways in which the main-line creative literature of the Middle Ages is or is not 'a mirror of contemporary society',[29] giving us clues as to how we may distinguish the proportions of traditional, received material from the fresh, particularised material in the work of, say, Gower, Chaucer, Langland and the English Mystery dramatists. For the shepherd episodes in the plays it seems clear that we need Hilton's general thesis about the nature of social change in the fourteenth and fifteenth century – 'a period of considerable self-confidence, even assertiveness . . . not checked by the defeat of the 1381 rising', in which we can find 'if not . . . a peasant class-consciousness, at any rate (a) political awareness . . . quite apparent in 1381, and . . . in the 1440s' (p. 18). Perhaps we also need Hilton's careful 'reading' of the various shepherd and rustic characters in the plays, and his provision of a precise economic context for them. He distinguishes, for example, between shepherds in the Wakefield *Secunda pastorum*, describing the first shepherd as a land-owning husbandman, but the third shepherd as a labourer, a 'manoeuvrier' (pp. 21–3, 35–6). Such readings allow us to gauge not only who the shepherds are, but also how the poet might possibly regard them individually.

We still need to determine, however, how it was possible for shepherd–exegetes to become shepherd–complainers and satirists, shepherd–protesters and even dissenters in the drama of the later Middle Ages. It is ironic, I think, that the answer is to be found in a perfectly orthodox devotional 'realignment' associated with Cistercian and Franciscan spirituality of the twelfth and thirteenth centuries, a realignment which created for artists and dramatists, just as it did for writers of the lyric and meditative prose, a 'picture-space' within which they could work with increasing freedom and inventiveness. This realignment resulted from the much greater emphasis laid in devotional Latin texts of the twelfth and thirteenth centuries upon the sacred humanity of Christ,[30] and from the increasing prominence given to the fact that the first manifestation of Christ incarnate was to the shepherds and not to the Magi. We are not so much concerned with the symbolism which identifies the shepherds and the Magi with either the clergy or even the Jews and the Gentiles: rather the shepherds are being identified with the poor and the ordinary, those who bring with them into the constantly rewritten Biblical story all their moving imperfections and who will involve the Nativity scene, indeed invade the Nativity scene, with the attitudes, the feel, the very smell of the secular world they inhabit – whatever kind of secular world that turns out to be.

A text which very well expresses the quality of this realignment is the thirteenth-century Latin *Meditationes vitae Christi*, at one time attributed to St Bonaventure. Originally written in Italy, this very important Latin text was soon widely disseminated and translated into all the major European vernaculars.[31] A passage from the English translation reads:

Wolt thou knowe his peple? That is of whom speketh Dauid in the psawter and seith: Lorde / to the is bylaste the pore puple . . . Wherfore cristes innocens and childhode conforteth not jangeleres and grete spekeres . . . his symple clothinge conforteth not hem that gone in proude clothynge; and his stable and cracche conforteth noght hem that louen first seetes and worldes worschippes. And also the aungels in cristes Natiuite apperynge to the wakynge scheephirdes conforten none othere but the pouere travailloures; and to hem tellen they the ioye of newe light / and noght to the riche men that haven her conforte here.[32]

Nothing here, of course, would directly justify the 'complaining' or 'protesting' shepherd, but it would open the door for later artists to portray not just the innocence of the 'pouere travailloures', but also their culpable and moving attempts to understand the harsh contexts in which they are inescapably and really trapped. It opens the door to realism, with all its well-known artistic advantages and its politico-religious dangers. This new devotional realignment created a new 'picture space' within which writers, and of course artists, could work. It gave sanction to a concentration upon the realities of shepherd existence. The simple pastoral watch on the night of Christ's birth could be seen to reflect the simplicity and suffering of Christ's own 'watch' upon earth, but it gave sanction also to a freedom of creative invention which could scarcely be resisted.

The waiting shepherd-space would eventually be inhabited by creatures marvellously authentic, but sometimes surprisingly independent of the orthodox ways of thinking that had first given them life; indeed, the shepherd-space would finally become hospitable to opinions and doctrines inimical to that orthodoxy.

The creation and amplification of this 'picture-space' might be compared with contemporary rhetorical technique, especially the diversification, expansion and illustration of themes found in pulpit rhetoric.[33] But the eventual result in the English Shepherd Plays, with their strong contrasts of different shepherd materials, seems to have been an intersection of older exegetical and newer devotional approaches to Biblical narrative in the thirteenth century; we might even go so far as to say that they register a collision rather than an intersection. How, therefore, can we deal with the two distinct types of role assumed by the shepherd inhabitants of the Annunciation Plays? Should we regard the shepherds as exegetes even in their complaints, witnessing to the divine fulfilment of promise and teaching us of the fallen state of man which can always be restored by divine grace, as they move from the rainy hillsides of Cheshire and Yorkshire to the unlocalised country of the crib and the 'unspeakable mystery on the bestial floor'? Or should we regard the shepherds as evidence of two divergent interests, perhaps irreconcilable in theological terms, but uneasily partnered in the vernacular literature of the dangerous decades of the fifteenth century?

But before answering these questions, I would like to look at the Annunciation to the Shepherds in the drama and visual arts of fourteenth- and fifteenth-century France. I want to demonstrate here a parallel process in the gradual augmentation of a 'picture-space' devoted to shepherd life, first under a religious imprimatur, and then, perhaps, under sanctions less overtly religious than freely imaginative. In both the plays and the pictures, this 'picture-space' seems to become almost an independent zone, attracting into it materials and themes, originally quite alien to its nature and purposes, which will eventually take it over.

SHEPHERDS AND COURTLY PASTORAL IN FRANCE

Later medieval France offers a particularly coherent body of information about the situation in which French drama and manuscript illumination were produced, a body of information such as we cannot really find for England. The shepherd drama and art were being created in social contexts which are at least basically definable in relation to French medieval society as a whole; we know a good deal about the identity of dramatists, painters, patrons and audiences. And we know a good deal about the processes by which the dramatists and painters went about 'augmenting' their shepherd scenes.

In France there was already in existence a literary tradition of shepherd material in pastoral and *bergerie* poetry: this material was varied and found in both lyric verse and drama.[34] The twelfth-century *pastorela* of the Provençal poet Marcabru, for instance, takes place 'jost' una sebissa' ('beside a hedge'), and narrates how its robust and sensible heroine, 'Cap'e gonel' e pelissa Vest e camiza treslissa, Sotlars e caussas de lana' ('wearing a hooded cape, a skirt and fur lined coat and an open-weave blouse, shoes and woollen stockings'), rebuffs the

19 Annunciation to Shepherds. Psalter, Cambr., Trinity Coll., MS B. 11.4, fo. 100v; English, early 13th cent.

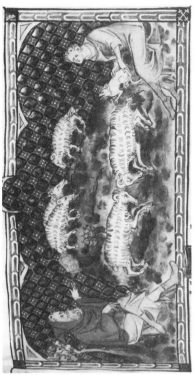

20b Aries. London, BL, MS Roy. 2.B.VII, fo. 74r.

20a Annunciation to Shepherds. Queen Mary's Psalter, London, BL, MS Roy. 2.B.VII, fo. 112r; English, early 14th cent.

21 Nativity, Annunciation to Shepherds. Breviary of Blanche of France, Rome, Vat. Lib., MS Urb. Lat. 603, fo. 127; French, c. 1320–5.

22 Annunciation to Shepherds. Hours of Jeanne d'Evreux, New York, Cloisters, fo. 62r; French, c. 1325–8.

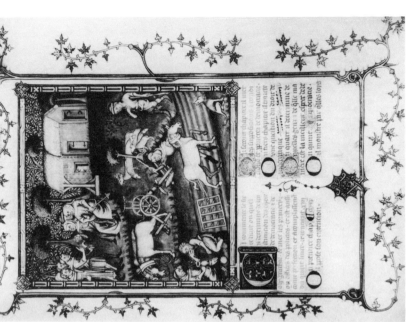

23 Annunciation to Shepherds. Hours of Yolande of Flanders, London, BL, MS Yates Thompson 27, fo. 70v; French, c. 1350–60.

24 Work in the Fields. Brussels, Bibl. Roy., MS 11201–2, fo. 241r; Paris, c. 1376.

25a, b Bridges of Paris. Details of *Vie de Saint Denis*, Paris, BN, MS
f. fr. 2092, fos. 18v and 2v; French, 1317.

26 Annunciation to Shepherds. Brussels Bibl. Roy., MS
11060–1, fo. 82; French, before 1407.

28 Annunciation to Shepherds. Cambr., Fitz. Mus., MS 63, fo. 60v; French, c. 1460–70.

27 Annunciation to Shepherds, Pastoral scene. Oxford, Bodl., MS Douce 144, fo. 68v; French, 1407.

29   Annunciation to Shepherds, Nativity. De Lévis Hours, Vienna, Nat.-bibl., MS 1855, fo. 65v; French, c. 1420–2.

30   Annunciation to Shepherds. De Buz Hours, Cambr., Mass., Houghton Lib., MS
Richardson 42, fo. 52r; French, c. 1415.

32 Annunciation to Shepherds. Mercadé, *Passion d'Arras*, Bibl. d'Arras, MS 697, fo. 28v; French, mid-15th cent.

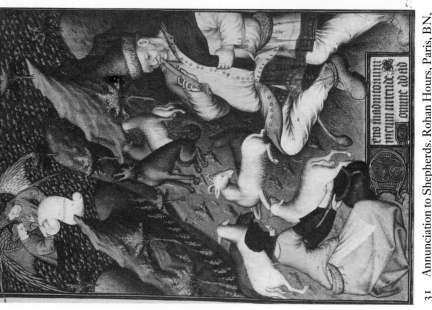

31 Annunciation to Shepherds. Rohan Hours, Paris, BN, MS Lat. 9471, fo. 85v; French, c. 1420–30.

knight's offer of presents and 'amistat de coratge' ('sincere friendship'); this *pastorela* is much more overtly didactic than many, and its shepherdess provides a sturdy lesson on keeping to one's own place in society – 'Don, tot mon ling e mon aire Vei revertir e retraire Al vezoig et a l'araire' ('Sir, all my lineage and my kin do I see going back and returning to the sickle and the plough'); she recommends the quality of 'mezura' ('what is fitting') and refers the knight to the words of 'la gens anciana' ('the Ancients').[35] Here an essentially fabricated pastoral situation is used to teach a lesson on human behaviour, in which the shepherdess is idealised as a receptacle of human wisdom, but of a secular sort. The late thirteenth-century drama *Le Jeu de Robin et de Marion* written by the Arras poet Adam de la Halle probably for Robert II, Count of Artois, portrays rustic life in an idyllic way no doubt entirely acceptable to courtly patrons.[36] Richard Axton speaks of this as a world of 'straw hats, apples and cheeses . . . bagpipes and dances, comic brawling, dainty exchanges of love-tokens and vows . . . a refined, aristocratic image of idealised country sports'.[37]

A distinctive aspect of the French situation is the amount of interest taken in versions of the rustic life focussed upon shepherds by authors and painters working for aristocratic patrons, and by the aristocratic patrons themselves.[38] This interest is manifest in idealising remarks reportedly made by Charles V to his brother, Louis of Anjou, that 'le pauvre et sage est plus digne d'estime que le riche déréglé' ('the one who is poor and wise is more worthy of esteem than the wealthy dissolute').[39] This interest of the aristocracy is equally manifest in the half-affectionate mockery of Guillaume de Machaut's *Dit dou lyon*, where the 'gens de vilages, Norris de lais et de frommages, De chos, de feves, de naviaus' ('people from the villages, fed on milk and cheeses, cabbages, beans and turnips') with names like Robin and Marote come to the orchard of love to perform country dances – rustics with faces so strange, Machaut observes, that no artist could properly portray them.[40] Some of the contrasting and even contradictory perspectives of an aristocracy that both revered and condescended to the idea of the shepherd are found in *Le Bon Berger*, a work dedicated by Jehan de Brie to Charles V, but whose significance remains extremely hard to place.[41] A treatise on the art of *bergerie*, it claims that 'Le mestier de la garde des oeilles est moult honnorable et de grant auctorité' ('the profession of shepherding is honorable and of high status'), though Henri Martin also described it as a guide 'for the use of the people' (pp. 38, xv and xxi–xxii). Its points of reference are often symbolic – the shepherd's 'houlette' or crook, for instance, is described as equivalent to a bishop's crozier or a soldier's sword (pp. 75–8); but they are also practical – these shepherds also have tar boxes, needles, scissors and lunchpacks (pp. 71–3). Above all, however, in *Le Bon Berger* the shepherd's pure life, uncorrupted by pubs or brothels, is seen to be 'sobre, chaste et débonnaire', as St Paul says (p. 69). The virtuous life of the symbolic and real shepherd alike offers a moral ideal to the French aristocracy. It is perhaps not so surprising that Philip of Burgundy, the brother of Charles V and Jean de Berry, had the famous sculptor, Claus Sluter, carve himself and his duchess, Margaret, 'in domestic costume, seated under an elm tree, surrounded by sheep'.[42]

What we find, when we come to the shepherd episodes with which the French dramatists of the fourteenth and fifteenth centuries prefaced their Passion Plays, is that the whole literary tradition of *bergerie* is exploited to provide materials for this rustic interlude while we wait for the first manifestation of Christ to his people.[43] We have already observed that in the Latin liturgical plays the shepherds tend to function as guides to the meaning of the Angel's Salutation – they are clerks, scholars and exegetes, not ordinary men. But from the later thirteenth century onwards, after the appearance of the Latin *Meditationes vitae Christi*, in fact, the effect of the new freedom allowed to medieval writers in picturing the shepherd scene begins to make itself felt in French vernacular drama.

In the shepherd scenes of the Passion Plays there are not only shepherds, but also shepherdesses, and the sweetheart, the 'doulce amie' is often present; the weather is always good, for this is the 'joyeux temps' and the 'doulce saison'; there are games, song contests, dancing, flute and bagpipe playing, crowning with garlands, the picking of flowers and eating – impromptu picnics of apples, nuts, milk and eggs. The whole episode is usually a light-hearted one, as they go off to Bethlehem with their dogs and simple presents – a spoon, a flute, a basket, a knife or a shepherd's 'houlette'; in the *Passion de Semur* they go off running, 'En Bethleam alons courant'.[44] The shepherd scenes in the Passion Plays are a gay affair. What we see here may to some extent be typical of a larger tendency certainly found in the literature of the period to amplify not only the religious drama but also other dramatic and literary works from *bergerie* traditions; the play entitled the *Estoire de Griseldis*, for instance, contains inserted shepherd episodes.[45] Nevertheless, to amplify the religious drama with such *bergerie* materials must surely also indicate a gradual movement towards the secularisation of these religious forms.

It is worth remarking the interest taken by the French kings in the production of these plays. In 1402 Charles VI signed letters patent for the Confrérie de la Passion to play in Paris, with the result that a permanent theatre was established there;[46] some time previously, in 1373, Charles V had had a 'Passion notre seigneur' 'rimée par personnages' in his library.[47] It is also worth remarking the status and learning of those who wrote and copied these plays: Eustache Mercadé, author of the fifteenth-century *Passion d'Arras*, for instance, was a bachelor of theology, doctor of law, and an official of the Abbey of Corbie;[48] Arnoul Gréban, author of a later *Mystère de la Passion*, was choirmaster at Notre-Dame in Paris, and after 1456 a bachelor of theology;[49] Jehan Floichot, who wrote out the *Passion de Semur*, was the 'notaire royale' of Semur.[50] When we turn to the visual arts, moreover, we should note right away that the artists are working for people similar to, if not the same as, those we have already seen taking an interest in shepherd poetry, treatise and drama – that is, the royal house of France in the fourteenth and fifteenth centuries, Jean de Berry, his brother Charles V, Charles VI, Philip of Burgundy, Louis of Anjou and his descendants.[51]

For at the same period in the visual arts, artists are, seemingly like the dramatists, filling in the 'picture-space' of comparable shepherd episodes. In the art of the twelfth and thirteenth centuries, the shepherds are grave, attentive figures, subordinated in size and position to the angels, usually pointing or directing the observer in some way to the angelic message (see plate 19).[52] In the fourteenth century all this changes. The sources of shepherd iconography in the visual arts must of course be in many respects different from those of the drama. After all, much of the shepherd material found in the Annunciation to the Shepherds scenes arrives by a process special to the visual arts, for the painters frequently assemble new materials first of all in the borders of their pictures, and only later on do they allow them to make their way into the main pictures. The shepherd images enter by stages, as if to mark their initially problematic nature, alien to the Biblical episode; nevertheless, their eventually-permitted entry is part of the gradual elaboration of illuminated shepherd scenes in the manuscripts of the fourteenth and fifteenth centuries, as artists augmented and substantiated them from the seething margins and bas-de-page areas characteristic of the Pucelle manuscripts (see plates 21, 22 and 23).[53]

Nevertheless, it seems possible that here too we are seeing the secularisation of certain religious forms; it is possible to see the scene of the Annunciation to the Shepherds well on its way to becoming a rustic festival, a shepherd's calendar, or a pastoral landscape with shepherds (see plates 26, 27, 28).[54] There exist a number of shepherd pictures where the Annunciation simply seems to have been left out (plates 20a, 20b[55] and 30, for instance); a fourteenth-century miniature of Work in the Fields illustrating Oresme's translation of Aristotle's *Politics* includes among the agrarian labourers a shepherd with a pipe, seven sheep under a tree, and a dog looking up and round – just as dogs do in many pictures of the Annunciation to the Shepherds (plate 24;[56] also plates 22 and 23); Marcel Thomas has suggested that, among other possibilities, one model for the shepherdess of the Rohan Hours Annunciation to the Shepherds (plate 31) can be found in the calendar picture for July from the *Très Riches Heures*.[57]

A wealth of evidence, however, also exists to illustrate the augmentation of shepherd scenes in the French manuscripts of the fourteenth and fifteenth centuries with other materials possibly from 'life', though we cannot always prove it, but some of them certainly from literary traditions of *bergerie*. Indeed, there is an increasing tendency in the fifteenth-century pictures to take these *bergerie* materials from a drama which may have already assimilated aspects of that *bergerie* from a secular literary world.[58] One very valuable, if late, proof of this relationship was pointed out by Gustave Cohen: in a printed edition of the Hours of Simon le Vostre, dated around 1501, the illustration of the Adoration of the Shepherds has written in the names Mahault and Alison for the two shepherdesses who are giving a lamb and an apple to the baby, and the names Aloris and Isambert for two of the shepherds; in the Shepherd Play of MS Chantilly 617 two shepherdesses called Mahauls and Alison also give respectively a lamb and an apple; and in *Le Mystère de la passion* of Arnoul Gréban there are two shepherds called Aloris and Isambert.[59] We might set against this, however, a manuscript of Eustache Mercadé's *Passion d'Arras* where the text of the drama is illustrated imprecisely, by a set of visual stereotypes; here, despite its juxtaposition with the drama, the art has preserved its own independently developed shepherd formats (see plate 32).[60]

Comparisons of French and English shepherd materials in the drama have led in the past to fairly simple, succinct conclusions that are nevertheless suggestive about the relative cultural situations in the two countries, and relevant not only to the drama but also to the visual arts:

French and English Shepherd Plays developed quite independently, the English plays according to current popular and religious ideas, and the French plays according to pastoral traditions which have no place in the English plays.[61]

We could generalise about the immediately observable differences between the French shepherds who, humble as they are, are presented in terms acceptable to the literate gentry, and the grotesque, touching, quarrelsome, clumsy peasants of English fourteenth- and fifteenth-century plays, whose normal preoccupations are assumed by their probably clerkly creators to be socio-economic and domestic. The French drama peasants are on the whole as agreeably rustic as those the Limbourg brothers put into their equally 'acceptable' landscape versions of the real, harsh medieval world of northern Europe for Jean de Berry. The dominant image is that 'of the happy shepherd spending his carefree days singing, dancing, and playing',[62] only interrupted by the normal perils of country life, such as the episode of the sheep almost stolen by Ysangrin the wolf in Gréban's *Passion*.[63] Such elements offer just so much sharp realism as will not disturb the mood of that pastoral world with its expensive contemporary furnishings and distinct echoes of the classical past.

We could illustrate the different status and style of the shepherd drama in France and England by a comparison of the kinds of music which accompany and embellish the plays. The five-part *Requiescant* and the three-part *chanson* in the 1474 Rouen *Mystère de l'incarnation* or the 'dialogued rondeaux' in Gréban's *Passion* indicate the complexity and subtlety of the French tradition;[64] the music extant for the York and Chester cycles is not naive, but it lacks this kind of sophistication.[65] Above all, we could contrast the well-documented, immensely long tradition of French literary pastoral and *bergerie* forms with the much more fragmentary and confused vernacular tradition in England. Clearly the shaping influence of a strong secular *bergerie* tradition upon fifteenth-century French religious drama is beyond doubt: the existence, in the late thirteenth century, of an accomplished pastoral play with music such as Adam de la Halle's *Robin et Marion* must have mattered – there is nothing comparable for the English dramatists of the later fourteenth- and early fifteenth-century cycles.

We do have tantalising references to pastoral or *bergerie* elements in the medieval English drama, but how 'low class' this is compared with the evidence from France! In 1447 the city chamberlains at York made a payment to 'j ludenti cum Ioly Wat and Malkyn', for instance.[66] These same names Joly Wat and Mal, of course, also appear in the fifteenth-century carol and dialogue in MS Oxford, Balliol College 354, Richard Hill's commonplace book;[67] and what are we to make of all the patchwork materials in the late fifteenth-century *Assembly of Gods*, whose 'classical' scenarios are more like a pantomime transformation scene?

> The rewde god Pan, of shepherdys the gyde,
> Clad in russet frese, & breched lyke a bere,
> With a gret tar box hangyng by hys syde.
> A shepecrook in hys hand he sparyd for no pryde.
> And at hys feete lay a prykeryd curre.
> He ratelyd in the throte as he had the murre.[68]

Although the shepherd scenes in the Holkham Bible Picture Book have Anglo-Norman 'captions', they also contain an English snatch describing the songs apparently sung by the shepherds in imitation of the angels' song:

> Songen alle wid one stevene
> Also the angel song that cam fro hevene:
> *Te Deum et Gloria.*[69]

But were these verses ever part of an English Shepherd Play? There is, after all, little way of knowing how much Anglo-French and English secular drama from the thirteenth and fourteenth centuries we have lost, even if we know for certain that there indeed were other English Shepherd Plays.[70]

SHEPHERDS IN MEDIEVAL DRAMA, ART AND SOCIETY

Even if the broad distinctions which have been drawn between English and continental shepherd materials will stand, however, it remains essential to deal with all of these materials in their own terms. I have been drawing a connection between the importation of subjects and motifs into the shepherds scene, whether in drama or painting, from the world of secular literature and from the world of real, historical existence. But how can we be certain of identifying even these? In discussing the English Shepherd Plays, for instance, I assume that the filling of the 'shepherd space' often implies a fairly straightforward passage of 'the real' and realistic techniques of presentation into a more formal world of religious truths which was traditional, orthodox and symbolically resonant; but while it is possible that the subplot material of a play such as the Wakefield *Secunda pastorum* is drawn from the brawling, vigorous world of quarrelling men and wives and babies, shivering northern nights, peasant protest and complaint, it could also be part of a world of grotesque fantasy and parody. When we consider the problem more closely, it is immensely difficult to generalise about the nature and origin of the various materials imported, and again about the psychology that underlies their importation.

This discussion has now also raised crucial questions about the 'analogising' of art and literature, and the imposition of interrelations between the 'shepherd spaces' of the pictures and the drama. In discussing the visual arts, for example, I suggest that the movement of materials from the border area to the main miniatures represents a variety of processes comparable to those we have witnessed in the drama. The margins certainly contrast with the restrained and formal composition of the main pictures; the free composition, improvisation and even commentary on the main pictures found in the margins mean that they do offer opportunity for more spontaneous, individualistic expression, though whether of social observation, comment and satire, fantastic invention and parody, or even simply of sacred imagery, it is sometimes difficult to say.[71] Since often the marginalia and the main pictures were done by the same artist, or else the subject matter of the marginalia was dictated by the artist of the main picture to a team of artists working under him, it seems likely that some form of control was exercised over the materials found in both the borders and the main miniature; the manuscript page must frequently have been designed as a whole with a coherent significance.[72] Any images which get integrated into the main pictures from manuscript borders, therefore, may be derived from 'life', from fantasy, or from a more controlled allegorical iconography. Goats, for example, are often found in marginalia and in shepherd scenes, but they are also a commonplace of the medieval bestiary and so possess their own potential symbolism.[73]

Both drama and art, then, illustrate the augmentation of orthodox religious themes and narratives with material which looks different, even alien, in origin and spirit. How are we to know whether the new shepherd materials are part of a total plan, possessing a sacred, symbolic significance, or whether they reveal artistic inventiveness running riot? Many of the playwrights and manuscript illuminators, for instance, develop the motif of the shepherds singing and playing musical instruments. Are the songs and bagpipes simply a secular importation of 'genre' material, low-life reportage lifted from the margins into the main pictures? Or is this music a reference to the traditional dichotomy of the 'old song' of fallen Mankind and the 'new song' of man redeemed, referred to by the psalmist when he says 'sing to the Lord a new song'?[74] At the birth of Christ the shepherds move from the unredeemed world to the redeemed world; and in an analogous way, the bagpipe, a common symbol for human sensuality, becomes 'bagpipes for the lord';[75] in the Chester *Adoration of the Shepherds* and the Wakefield *Secunda pastorum* the shepherds' cracked voices imitate and approximate to the heavenly song of the angels.[76] Inviting the once marginal rustics into the plays and into the main pictures, in other words, becomes an invitation to redemption. And, like the Mak episode in the Wakefield *Secunda pastorum*, the peasant with the bagpipe or flute can be regarded as either super-realistic or highly symbolic.

Perhaps, however, this discussion of French and English shepherd materials cannot simply be left as a matter of literary and artistic form and iconography; perhaps in order to understand the 'psychology' of the inhabited rustic 'space' which I have located in the drama and the visual arts, one has to take account of many differing factors – political, social, religious, some, no doubt, conflicting. It is necessary not only to identify the differences between the French and English materials, but also to speculate on how they came about. The evidence is too rich and diverse and often too contradictory for us to be satisfied with observation and description alone.

Some kind of overall picture of twelfth- to thirteenth-century attitudes to-wards the peasantry, for example, seems essential. The shepherd materials that we possess result mostly from the interaction of urban patronage, authorship and workshop with a rustic subject matter; indeed, many medieval attitudes towards the peasantry could be loosely characterised as urban attitudes, and therefore part of the complex relationship between the cities and the peasantry in the later Middle Ages.[77]

A range of distinct attitudes towards the peasantry can be documented from sources other than the drama and the visual arts. Learned and clerkly tradition, for instance, formulates various views of the peasant class between the twelfth and fifteenth century. William of Conches and John of Salisbury certainly theorised in the twelfth century about the role of man as an artisan, *homo faber*, in a divinely-fabricated universe and society;[78] Jacques Le Goff says that John of Salisbury's *Policraticus* offers a 'perspective dynamique' which restores to rural workers a role and a place in society alongside the urban artisans as part of a total, unified plan: 'the image of human society . . . must integrate all working human beings'.[79] But there is also from the twelfth century onwards a goliardic and clerkly tradition of mockery and contempt for the peasant, which sees him, according to Le Goff, as some rustic devil – 'oraisons dérisoires' in which all the worst things imaginable are wished upon him;[80] such is this thirteenth-century comic German 'Declinatio rustici':

Nom.	hic vilanus	hi maledicti
Gen.	huius rustici	horum tristium
Dat.	huic tferfero	his mendacibus
Acc.	hunc furem	hos nequissimos
Voc.	o latro	o pessimi
Abl.	ab hoc depredatore	ab his infidelibus[81]

Related to this tradition of clerkly mockery and contempt must be the anger of the professional learned classes, such as the minstrels, at the upstart peasants who hire themselves out with their simple musical instruments, the bagpipe and the tabour, and do the minstrels out of work:

> Merveille est de cest monde comme torne bouele:
> A tort et sans reson use chose et rebele,
> Quar s'uns bergiers de chans tabore et chalemele,
> Plus tost est apelé que cil qui bien viele.[82]

(It's astonishing how the world is upside-down: things are contradictory and reason and order are overturned, for if a shepherd from the fields plays the tabour and the bagpipes, he is more in demand than the one who fiddles properly.)

And in fact fifteenth-century records from Norwich confirm in a non-literary context the existence of just such economic rivalry between professional musicians and peasants when they record an almost identical complaint:

Many unskilled rustics and artificers ... pretending that they are our own minstrels, by the use of their livery and by colour of the said art or occupation, deceitfully collect and receive great exactions of moneys ... although they are by no means skilled or expert in that art or occupation . . .[83]

But perhaps we should also be studying economic and social interrelations and tensions between urban and rustic elements in the medieval cities. Le Goff surely describes the peaceful interaction of these elements when he points out that 'the medieval town was impregnated with the countryside':[84] inevitably the town was victualled from the surrounding land, and for its food, Paris depended on the peasants.[85] Nevertheless there were tensions too in the more irritable relationship between the city and vagrant life from the countryside, a floating population which had come to the towns for a variety of economic reasons; Bronislaw Geremek documents how the legislation against vagabondage in Paris became increasingly severe over the fourteenth century.[86] Contemporary manuscript illumination illustrates something of this: in the early fourteenth-century manuscript of the *Vie de notre Seigneur S. Denis* made for Philippe le Long of France there are pictures of sheep being driven into Paris over the bridges of the Seine, in which we can see shepherd and labourer life penetrating deep into the heart of the capital; and yet in the same streets there are also beggars and cripples (plates 25a and 25b[87]). How, after all, was the vagrant to be distinguished from the rustic?

The French shepherd materials which we are considering also demand that we take into account the complex and mixed attitudes behind the interest in rustic life shown by the French aristocracy and royal house. If works such as Adam de la Halle's *Robin et Marion* or Machaut's *Dit dou lyon* express what is essentially an affectionate contempt for the peasantry, a text such as *Le Bon Berger* or remarks allegedly made by Charles V provide, as we have seen, a far more idealised version of rustic life. In the thirteenth century Blanche of Castile actually patronised a peasant insurrection in a very curious historical episode of at least initial aristocratic support for the 'pastoureaux'.[88] Nevertheless, even if French pastoral literature and art were shaped within courtly contexts, these contexts are still part of larger social and economic groupings. The responsibility of the great lords for their estates meant that all the people for whom the poet Deschamps worked and for whom the Pucelle workshop catered also had practical pre-occupations with their peasant tenants. The development of towns such as Paris meant that the interest taken in the countryside by these distinguished literary and artistic patrons could on the one hand be quite distanced, both patronising and idealising, but could on the other hand be absolutely down-to-earth and engaged.

In England, however, a different geography and economic history were bound to influence representations of shepherd life. The fact that there was much more sheep farming in England than in France makes it likely that English writers know more about the actual conditions of the shepherd world;[89] it would have been difficult for a dramatist, for example, to impress a local Yorkshire or East Anglian audience with a picture of 'nuts in May' when all they would have known would have been the realities of rain, footrot, and pig's trotters to eat. The harsh season in which the shepherds of the English drama are portrayed is quite unlike the 'doulce saison' of southern Europe; and we have already noticed how the very specific grievances expressed in the English drama relate to known conditions among the agrarian classes in the fourteenth and fifteenth centuries – their exploitation by landlords and subjection to 'purveyance', for instance.

Due to the nature of English social and urban development, moreover, patterns of patronage were different from those documented for France. In contrast to the diversified Parisian patronage of university, mercantile classes and court, English literary patronage in the thirteenth and fourteenth centuries was, especially outside London, to a greater degree dominated by the ecclesiastical establishment;[90] and the entirely different socio-economic context in which the English drama was produced even in the fifteenth century must have militated against the entry of much courtly *bergerie* material into the Annunciation to the Shepherds scenes. Similarly, the very limited production of luxury and illuminated manuscripts in England from the mid-fourteenth century onwards contrasts with the very large output at the same period in France, and offers little scope for the ornate and decorative visual illustration of the pastoral life which we find in France.[91] And yet, although this cultural and social situation resulted in relatively limited work on shepherds in the visual arts, it did produce the dynamic English shepherd drama, with its intimate and first-hand understanding of the sheep-farming peasantry.

In contrast, the French shepherd materials perhaps confirm that a really rich and varied pastoral art and literature cannot be produced except from sophisticated and prosperous urban centres, organised to cater for the needs of wealthy patrons. The social and economic situation of artists and their relationship with their patrons is immensely complex, and a whole series of workshops produced for aristocratic and royal patrons the shepherd pictures we have been looking at: the Pucelle workshop was active in the early and mid-fourteenth century in Paris; in the later fourteenth century there were *ateliers* in Paris, Bourges and Troyes working for Jean de Berry, Philip of Burgundy, Charles V and VI of France and Louis of Anjou. The gradual elaboration of the shepherd scenes in the French manuscripts produced under the patronage of succeeding generations of the French royal house, whether fed by contemporary fact and event, by literary *bergerie*, or simply by conventions of visual iconography, are bound to reflect enormously varied interests and persuasions. Many illuminators, for example, undoubtedly used 'workshop pattern books, a repertoire of decorative figures in lively poses from which the master and his assistants diversified the pages of these manuscripts made for noble ladies and their lords;[92] nevertheless it seems unlikely that we can deal with the development of the shepherd scenes and their infiltration by the material of the margins simply in terms of such pattern books. What number of assumptions are tacitly made between these Parisian patrons and the Parisian workshop masters who control the work? If we compare the physiognomy of the two foremost shepherds in the Annunciation of the Hours of Jeanne d'Evreux (plate 22) to those of the Passion attendants in the same manuscript, what attitudes can we deduce from the similarity between these figures?[93] Clerkly and aristocratic contempt, fear and condescension in response to the rough rustic? We might also note the similarities between these shepherds and the beggar and vagabond images in the same manuscript;[94] what social attitudes underlie such likenesses? While this may simply be a case of the switching-about of workshop pattern books, it may also surely reflect urban resentment of the miscellaneous, dispossessed population which invaded the towns from the countryside.

What, however, seems to me to be undeniable about all these shepherd scenes is that they provide receptive ground for the changing preoccupations of artists, clerks, poets and ecclesiastics over the medieval centuries, whether these are focussed on politics and social discontent in fifteenth-century England or the fashion for *bergerie* and even for landscape painting in the French courts of the later Middle Ages. Both the immense, absorbed peasant of the Rohan Hours (plate 31),[95] and the equally dominating figures of the shepherd-rustics in the Wakefield Shepherds' Plays, offer a moving witness to processes of cultural change which took place over the thirteenth to fifteenth centuries. And yet they do not witness identically, nor can they be made to do so by later desires for neat and cogent documentation: both 'fill the space' – but with what different lineages and messages?

Notes

Introduction

1. E. R. Panofsky, *Meaning in the Visual Arts* (Garden City, NY, 1955), p. 19.
2. Thomas Hoccleve, *Regement of Princes*, ed. F. J. Furnivall, EETS, ES 72 (1897), 1, 2077.
3. Dryden, *Preface to the Fables*, in *Poetical Works*, ed. G. R. Noyes (Boston, 1909), p. 744.
4. Matthew Arnold, 'The Study of Poetry', in *Essays in Criticism*, second series (London, 1888), pp. 1–55 (p. 32: 'We are to adopt a real, not a historic, estimate of poetry').

1 Cultural patterns in twelfth-century England

1. G. O. Sayles, *The Medieval Foundations of England* (London, 1948), p. 270.
2. Ibid., p. 276.
3. See, in particular, M. D. Legge, 'La Précocité de la littérature anglo-normande', *Cahiers de Civilisation Médiévale*, 8 (1965), 327–49 (p. 349).
4. The classic statement of such continuity is R. W. Chambers, *On the Continuity of English Prose*, EETS 191A (1932), but Chambers has had many followers, including e.g. B. Cottle, *The Triumph of English* (London, 1969).
5. For this 'international scene', see C. H. Haskins, *The Renaissance of the Twelfth Century* (Cambridge, Mass., 1927).
6. G. Zarnecki, '1066 and Architectural Sculpture', *PBA*, 52 (1966), 87–104 (p. 102).
7. F. Wormald, 'Style and Design', in F. W. Stenton, *The Bayeux Tapestry* (London, 1957), pp. 25–36.
8. See R. R. Darlington, 'Anglo-Norman Historians', Inaugural Lecture delivered 20 May 1947 (London, 1947): 'England was *patria nostra* to them all . . .' (p. 18).
9. See Legge, 'Précocité', p. 344.
10. See R. M. Wadsworth, 'Historical Romance in England' (unpublished PhD thesis, York, 1972), p. 360.
11. *De Gestis Regum Anglorum*, ed. W. Stubbs, 2 vols., Rolls series 90 (1889), II, 283. ('I, however, since the blood of both nations runs in my veins . . .')
12. See Darlington, 'Anglo-Norman Historians', p. 18.
13. R. R. Bezzola, *Les Origines et la formation de la littérature courtoise en Occident (500–1200)*, 3 parts, Bibliothèque de l'Ecole des Hautes Etudes, part 1, fasc. 286 (1944), part 2, fasc. 313 (1960), part 3, fasc. 319–20 (1963), II, 417.
14. E. Jamison, 'The Sicilian Norman Kingdom in the Mind of Anglo-Norman Contemporaries', *Proc. British Academy*, 24 (1938), 237–85 (p. 243).
15. R. L. Poole, 'The Appointment and Deprivation of St William, Archbishop of York', *EHR*, 45 (1930), 273–81.
16. See G. R. Barnes, 'The Riddarasögur: a Literary and Social Analysis' (unpublished PhD thesis, London, Univ. College, 1975).

17. See R. W. Southern, *The Making of the Middle Ages* (London, 1953), pp. 226 ff., 232 ff.
18. See O. Pächt, 'The Illustrations of St Anselm's Prayers and Meditations', *JWCI*, 19 (1950), 68–83.
19. Ibid., p. 81, n. 3.
20. W. Dugdale, *Monasticon Anglicanum*, 3 vols. (London, 1655, 1661, 1673), II, 213–14 (Dugdale's printing of the Anglo-Norman account of the foundation of Wigmore priory).
21. T. S. R. Boase, *English Art 1100–1216* (Oxford, 1953), p. 78.
22. Ibid., pp. 81–3, and G. Zarnecki, *Later English Romanesque Sculpture 1140–1210* (London, 1953), pp. 10–13. For illustrations of the carvings in these Herefordshire churches, including Fownhope and Brinsop, mentioned below, see Boase, *English Art*, pls. 22a and 26a (Kilpeck), pl. 26b (Shobdon), pl. 24a (Fownhope), pl. 24b (Brinsop); and Zarnecki, *Sculpture*, pls. 19–24 (Kilpeck) and pl. 31 (Brinsop).
23. For Andrew of St Victor, see B. Smalley, 'Andrew of St Victor, Abbot of Wigmore: a Twelfth-Century Hebraist', *Récherches de théologie ancienne et médiévale*, 10 (1938), 358–73; also Smalley, *The Study of the Bible in the Middle Ages* (Oxford, 1952), pp. 112–95.
24. See *The Complete Peerage*, ed. G. E. C[okayne], vol. IX, ed. H. A. Doubleday and H. de Walden (London, 1936), pp. 273–83.
25. C. H. Haskins, 'Henry II as a Patron of Literature', *Essays in Medieval History presented to T. F. Tout*, ed. A. G. Little and F. M. Powicke (Manchester, 1925), pp. 71–7 (p. 77).
26. C. Bullock-Davies, 'Professional Interpreters and the Matter of Britain', lecture delivered at a Colloquium of the Departments of Welsh in the University of Wales, June 1965 (Cardiff, 1966), p. 8.
27. Bezzola, *Origines*, II, 449.
28. *De Gestis Regum Anglorum*, ed. Stubbs, II, 519. See also *Arthurian Literature in the Middle Ages*, ed. R. S. Loomis (Oxford, 1959), p. 80.
29. Boase, *English Art 1100–1216*, p. 93.
30. See Bezzola, *Origines*, II, 451, and *Arthurian Literature*, ed. Loomis, pp. 80, 88–9.
31. Legge, 'Précocité', p. 327.
32. Bodleian Library, Oxford, MS Digby 23.
33. M. D. Legge, 'Archaism and the Conquest', *MLR*, 51 (1956), 227–9 (p. 229).
34. *Chanson de Roland*, lines 2331–2.
35. See Legge, 'Archaism', p. 228, and 'Précocité', p. 332.
36. For the hands at work in the Albani Psalter, see M. Rickert, *Painting in Britain: The Middle Ages* (London, 1954), pp. 78–80.
37. Ibid.
38. M. D. Legge, *Anglo-Norman Literature and its Background* (Oxford, 1963), p. 4.
39. Bezzola, *Origines*, II, 448, n. 1, citing E. Faral, *La Légende Arthurienne*, 3 vols., Bibliothèque de l'Ecole des Hautes Etudes, fasc. 255–7 (1929), III, 72.
40. Bezzola, *Origines*, II, 447–8, citing Faral, *Legende*, III, 72.
41. William of Malmesbury, *De Gestis Regum Anglorum*, ed. Stubbs, II, 494.
42. *PL* 171, col. 1660.
43. *PL* 171, col. 290.
44. Hugh of Fleury-sur-Loire, *Historia Ecclesiastica*, Preface: 'quoniam estis litteris erudita, quod est gentilitium sine civilitas magna' (quoted Bezzola, *Origines*, II, 378, n. 1).
45. Bezzola, *Origines*, III, 458, n. 3.

46. For Baudri de Bourgueil, see Bezzola, *Origines*, II, 371–6, and *Les Oeuvres Poétiques de Baudri de Bourgueil*, ed. P. Abrahams (Paris, 1926).
47. 'Adelae Comitissae', no. 196 in *Oeuvres*, ed. Abrahams, lines 37–42 (p. 198).
48. 'Ad Eadem pro Cappa quam sibi Promiserat', no. 197, in *Oeuvres*, ed. Abrahams, lines 9–12 (p. 254).
49. 'Adelae Comitissae', no. 196 in *Oeuvres*, ed. Abrahams, lines 85–6.
50. See C. Dodwell, *Painting in Europe 800–1200* (London, 1971), pp. 7–9; Abrahams, *Oeuvres*, notes to 'Adelae Comitissae', pp. 248–9. Their evidence is more useful than Bezzola's celebration of the poem as a precise description of a real chamber (*Origines*, II, 376).
51. Bezzola, *Origines*, II, 373. But see the warning remarks by P. Dronke, in *Medieval Latin and the Rise of European Love-Lyric*, 2 vols. (Oxford, 1965), I, 210–12.
52. Bezzola, *Origines*, II, 369, n. 1.
53. See C. Luttrell, *The Creation of the First Arthurian Romance: A Quest* (London, 1974), pp. 20–5.
54. See Abrahams, *Oeuvres*, pp. xx–xxi.
55. See L. Voss, *Heinrich von Blois* (Berlin, 1932); D. Knowles, *The Monastic Order in England, 940–1216* (Cambridge, 1940), pp. 286 ff.; and for Henry as a patron and collector, Boase, *English Art 1100–1216*, pp. 169–74.
56. See Dodwell, *Painting in Europe*, pp. 173–6.
57. Giraldus Cambrensis, *Opera*, ed. J. S. Brewer *et al.*, Rolls series 21 (1861–91), VII, 45.
58. Bezzola, *Origines*, II, 376.
59. Boase, *English Art 1100–1216*, pp. 170–1 and notes.
60. Giraldus Cambrensis, *Opera*, VII, 47.
61. F. Wormald, *The Winchester Psalter* (London, 1973), pp. 107–8.
62. Ibid., p. 83.
63. Ibid., p. 90.
64. John of Salisbury, *Historiae Pontificalis*, ed. R. L. Poole (Oxford, 1927), p. 81. See also G. B. Parks, *The English Traveler to Italy*, vol. I: The Middle Ages (Rome, 1954), pp. 105–6.
65. For 'Benedeiz' and his *Voyage*, see Legge, *Anglo-Norman Literature*, pp. 8 ff., and 'Précocité', pp. 330–1.
66. Legge, 'Précocité', p. 331.
67. Amatus of Monte Cassino, quoted and translated by E. Jamison, 'The Sicilian Norman Kingdom' (see n. 14 above), p. 251.
68. See C. H. Haskins, *The Renaissance of the Twelfth Century* (Cambridge, Mass., 1927), p. 61.
69. See Jamison, 'Sicilian Norman Kingdom', p. 275; Parks, *English Traveler*, p. 145; the quotation is from *Otia Imperialia*, in *Scriptores Rerum Brunsvicensium*, ed. G. W. Leibniz, 3 vols. (Hanover, 1707–11), I, 881–1006 (p. 964).
70. Quoted and translated by Parks, *The English Traveler*, p. 145.
71. John of Salisbury, *Metalogicon*, III, quoted (in translation) by Parks, *English Traveler*, p. 114.
72. Jamison, 'Sicilian Norman Kingdom', p. 272.
73. John of Salisbury, *Entheticus de dogmate Philosophorum*, line 1640, in *Opera Omnia*, ed. J. A. Giles, 5 vols. (Oxford, 1848), V, 291.
74. Peter of Blois, *Epistolae*, quoted in Haskins, *Renaissance*, p. 50.
75. See W. Stubbs, 'Learning and Literature at the Court of Henry II', in *Seventeen Lectures on Medieval and Modern History* (Oxford, 1886; 3rd edn 1900), pp. 142–6.

76. F. J. E. Raby, *A History of Christian–Latin Poetry* (Oxford, 1953), p. 336.
77. Honorius of Autun, translated by J. Le Goff, *Les Intellectuels au Moyen Age* (Paris, 1957), p. 64.
78. Ibid., p. 65.
79. For detailed examination of this theme, see R. Lejeune, 'Rôle littéraire d'Aliénor d'Aquitaine et de sa famille', *Cultura Neolatina*, 14 (1954), 5–57.
80. R. Lejeune, 'The Troubadours', in *Arthurian Literature*, ed. Loomis, pp. 393–9 (p. 397).
81. Legge, *Anglo-Norman Literature*, pp. 49 ff.
82. E. Hoepffner, 'The Breton Lais', in *Arthurian Literature*, ed. Loomis, pp. 112–21 (p. 116). And see C. Bullock-Davies, 'Marie, Abbess of Shaftesbury, and her Brothers', *EHR*, 80 (1965), 314–22.
83. Lejeune, 'The Troubadours', p. 394.
84. Gottfried von Strassburg, *Tristan*, trans. A. T. Hatto (London, 1967), p. 44.
85. R. S. Loomis, 'The Oral Diffusion of the Arthurian Legend', in *Arthurian Literature*, ed. Loomis, pp. 52–63 (p. 61).
86. R. Lejeune, 'Rôle littéraire de la famille d'Aliénor d'Aquitaine', *Cahiers de Civilisation Médiévale*, 1 (1958), 319–37 (p. 329).
87. Stubbs, *Seventeen Lectures*, p. 136.
88. C. H. Haskins, 'Henry II as a Patron of Literature' (note 25 above).
89. See the list printed by Haskins, ibid., pp. 74–6.
90. R. R. Bezzola, 'Guillaume IX et les origines de l'amour courtois', *Romania*, 66 (1940), 145–237 (see p. 161).
91. J. F. Benton, 'The Court of Champagne as a Literary Center', *Speculum*, 36 (1961), 551–91 (see pp. 555–8).
92. Ibid., p. 590.
93. See R. W. Eyton, *Court, Household and Itinerary of King Henry II* (London, 1878), and Lejeune, 'Rôle littéraire d'Aliénor', pp. 20–1, 50–7.
94. Lejeune, 'Rôle littéraire d'Aliénor', p. 20.
95. Quoted by Haskins, 'Henry II as a Patron of Literature', p. 76.
96. C. Appel (ed.), *Bernart von Ventadorn: Seine Lieder mit Einleitung und Glossar* (Halle, 1915), pp. xxxiv ff., lvi ff.
97. H. J. Chaytor, *The Troubadours and England* (Cambridge, 1923), p. 37.
98. Ibid., p. 40.
99. Quoted by Chaytor, ibid., p. 36.
100. According to the English poet, Laʒamon, in his version of Wace, the *Brut*, ed. G. L. Brook and R. F. Leslie, 2 vols., EETS 250, 277 (1963, 1978), lines 21–3 (MS Cotton Caligula A.ix only). For Wace, see U. T. Holmes, 'Norman Literature and Wace', in *Medieval Secular Literature*, ed. W. Matthews (Berkeley and Los Angeles, 1965), pp. 46–67.
101. Holmes, ibid., p. 65.
102. Benoît de Sainte-Maure, *Roman de Troie*, ed. L. Constans, 6 vols., SATF (1904–12), lines 13468, 13465.
103. Lejeune, 'Rôle littéraire d'Aliénor', p. 24.
104. Baudri de Bourgueil, 'Adelae Comitissae' (note 49 above).
105. *Chronique*, ed. F. Michel, Surtees Society, 11 (1840). See I. Macdonald, 'The Chronicle of Jordan Fantosme', *Studies in Medieval French presented to A. Ewert* (Oxford, 1961), pp. 242–58.
106. See H. L. D. Ward, *Catalogue of Romances in the Department of Manuscripts in the British Museum*, vol. 1 (London, 1883), p. 365, and C. E. Pickford, 'Miscellaneous

French Prose Romances', *Arthurian Literature*, ed. Loomis, pp. 348–57 (see p. 348).
107. See Bezzola, *Origines*, II, 456–61.
108. For Henry of Huntingdon, see Bezzola, *Origines*, II, 458–9; and for Geoffrey of Monmouth, see J. J. Parry and R. A. Caldwell, 'Geoffrey of Monmouth', in *Arthurian Literature*, ed. Loomis, pp. 72–93 (see pp. 75–9).
109. See below, p. 33.
110. See Legge, *Anglo-Norman Literature*, pp. 36–42, and Bezzola, *Origines*, II, 455–6.
111. See D. M. Williamson, 'Ralf son of Gilbert and Ralf son of Ralf', *Lincolnshire Architectural and Archaeological Society, Reports and Papers*, n.s. 5 (1953), 19–27.
112. For Gaimar's translation, and the circumstances surrounding it, see Legge, *Anglo-Norman Literature*, pp. 27–36. The circulation of Geoffrey of Monmouth's *Historia* seems to have been predominantly within the class of literate laymen, and W. G. East, in an unpublished dissertation, 'De Contemptu Britonum: A History of Prejudice' (PhD thesis, Yale, 1974), goes so far as to propose that many manuscripts of the *Historia* were copied, not in monastic scriptoria, but in courts and centres of lay activity, by scribes 'used to writing documents but not to producing books' (Chap. I, p. 8).
113. See C. H. Haskins, 'Adelard of Bath and Henry Plantagenet', *EHR*, 28 (1913), 515–16 (p. 515), and K. Norgate, *England under the Angevin Kings*, 2 vols. (London, 1887), I, 334, 375.
114. *Epistle* no. 66, to the Archbishop of Palermo: see *PL* 207, col. 198.
115. For Peter of Blois, see C. L. Kingsford, in *DNB*; C. H. Haskins, 'Henry II as a Patron of Literature', pp. 72, 75; M. M. Davy (ed.), Pierre de Blois, *Un Traité de l'Amour du XIIe Siècle* (Paris, 1932), Part I, Chap. I (pp. 13–28). For the poems, prose works and letters, see *PL* 207, *passim*.
116. For these and other details, see M. Schlauch, 'Literary Exchange between Angevin England and Sicily', *Romanic Review*, 14 (1923), 168–88.
117. For consideration of knowledge of the classical drama in England, in the twelfth and thirteenth centuries, see e.g. R. S. Loomis, 'Were there Theatres in the Twelfth and Thirteenth Centuries?' *Speculum*, 20 (1945), 92–5; Dino Bigongiari, (same title), *Romanic Review*, 37 (1946), 201–24; M. H. Marshall, 'Boethius's Definition of "Persona" and Mediaeval Understanding of the Roman Theatre', *Speculum*, 25 (1950), 471–82.
118. For illustration of this, see F. Wormald, 'English Art and the Mediterranean' (Guide to the Photographic Exhibition), The Warburg Institute (London, 1941), pp. 37, 39, and O. Demus, *The Mosaics of Norman Sicily* (London, 1949), p. 450.
119. See E. Jamison, 'The Sicilian Norman Kingdom', pp. 254–6, and M. Schlauch, 'Literary Exchange between Angevin England and Sicily', pp. 176–8.
120. This romance is dated to the later twelfth century by R. Lejeune, 'Rôle littéraire de la famille', p. 331, and to the mid-thirteenth century (1250–75) by A. Micha, 'Miscellaneous French Romances in Verse', in *Arthurian Literature*, ed. Loomis, pp. 358–92 (p. 383).
121. For *Ipomedon*, see Legge, *Anglo-Norman Literature*, pp. 85–96, and the edition by E. Kölbing and E. Koschwitz (Breslau, 1889).
122. Hue de Rotelande, *Ipomedon*, ed. Kölbing, line 10569.
123. See above, p. 24.
124. Legge, *Anglo-Norman Literature*, p. 95.
125. Hue de Rotelande, *Protheselaus* (ed. F. Kluckow, Göttingen, 1924), lines 12707–11.
126. See below, p. 69 (the Bohun family).

127. See Boase, *English Art 1100–1216*, p. 205. For illustrations of the Rochester tympanum and the Barfreston doorway, see Boase, pls. 68a and 68b.
128. Ibid., p. 183.
129. Ibid., p. 187.
130. See C. M. Kauffmann, *Romanesque Manuscripts 1066–1190* (London, 1975), p. 28. For illustrations of the initials of the Winchester Bible, see Kauffmann, figs. 34, 38, and pls. 229–32, 235–9.
131. Ibid., p. 27. For illustrations of the Becket and Bosham books and their imitators, see Kauffman, fig. 15 and pl. 287, and Boase, pl. 67.

2 Culture and literature in earlier thirteenth-century England

1. D. Pearsall, *Old English and Middle English Poetry* (London, 1977), p. 90.
2. Ibid., Chap. 3.
3. G. O. Sayles, *The Medieval Foundations of England* (London, 1948), p. 387.
4. See R. M. Wadsworth, 'Historical Romance in England: Studies in Anglo-Norman and Middle English Romance' (unpublished PhD thesis, Univ. of York, 1972).
5. See H. J. Chaytor, *The Troubadours and England* (Cambridge, 1923), p. 40.
6. Count Raimon-Bérengar IV, of Provence (1200–45), is an outstanding example of 'poet-prince': he was father of Henry III's wife, Eleanor of Provence.
7. See J. Audiau, *Les Troubadours et l'Angleterre* (Paris, 1927), p. 31, n. 1. For text of the poem, see *Chrestomathie du Moyen Age*, ed. G. Paris and E. Langlois (Paris, 1897), pp. 283–6.
8. For texts and a summary of the debate, see F. de Labareyre, *La Cour Littéraire de Dauphin d'Auvergne des XIIe et XIIIe siècles* (Clermont-Ferrand, 1976), pp. 40–52.
9. Sayles, *Medieval Foundations*, p. 276. See above, p. 5.
10. See F. M. Powicke, *The Thirteenth Century 1216–1307* (Oxford, 1953; 2nd edn 1962), pp. 1–15.
11. Ibid., pp. 14–15.
12. Ibid., p. 97.
13. See A. Jeanroy, 'Un Sirventes Politique de 1230', in *Mélanges d'Histoire du Moyen Age offerts à F. Lot* (Paris, 1925), pp. 275–83.
14. Sayles, *Medieval Foundations*, p. 146.
15. Ibid., p. 397.
16. Powicke, *The Thirteenth Century*, p. 149.
17. See H. E. Allen, 'The Mystical Lyrics of the *Manuel des Pechiez*', *Romanic Review*, 9 (1918), 154–93 (p. 174).
18. M. D. Legge, *Anglo-Norman Literature and its Background* (Oxford, 1963), pp. 233–5.
19. See ibid., pp. 225–6, and her edition of the poem, 'John Pecham's *Jerarchie*', *Medium Aevum*, 11 (1942), 77–84.
20. See Legge, *Anglo-Norman Literature*, Chap. VII, and Wadsworth, 'Historical Romance'.
21. See I. S. T. Aspin (ed.), *Anglo-Norman Political Songs*, ANTS, 11 (Oxford, 1953), nos. 2, 3, 7, 8, 10.
22. See Legge, *Anglo-Norman Literature*, p. 213, n. 1; H. E. Allen, 'Two Middle-English Translations from the Anglo-Norman', *MP*, 13 (1916), 741–5.
23. Prologue, lines 1–6, cited in M. Y. H. Aitken, *Etude sur le Miroir ou Les Evengiles des Domnées de Robert de Gretham* (Paris, 1922), p. 105.
24. Allen, 'Two Middle-English Translations', p. 742.

25. See S. H. Thomson, *The Writings of Robert Grosseteste, Bishop of Lincoln 1235–53* (Cambridge, 1940), p. 149; Legge, *Anglo-Norman Literature*, pp. 222–3. For a general account of Grosseteste, see D. A. Callus (ed.), *Robert Grosseteste, Scholar and Bishop: Essays in Commemoration of the Seventh Centenary of his Death* (Oxford, 1955).

26. *Le Chasteau d'Amour de Robert Grosseteste*, ed. J. Murray (Paris, 1918), lines 26–8.

27. 'The Castle of Love', in K. Sajavaara (ed.), *The Middle English Translations of Robert Grosseteste's Chasteau d'Amour*, Mémoires de la Société Néophilologique de Helsinki, vol. 32 (Helsinki, 1967), p. 260.

28. Aspin, *Anglo-Norman Political Songs*, no. 8, pp. 86, 92.

29. D. L. Douie, *Archbishop Pecham* (Oxford, 1952), p. 109.

30. See R. M. Wilson, *Early Middle English Literature* (London, 1939), p. 11.

31. Allen, 'Mystical Lyrics', p. 171.

32. Walter Map, *De Nugis Curialium*, ed. M. R. James, Anecdota Oxoniensia, Mediaeval and Modern Series, Part XIV (Oxford, 1914), p. 18.

33. *Compendium*, cap. VI, in *Opera*, ed. J. S. Brewer, Rolls series 15 (1859), I, 433.

34. Allen 'Mystical Lyrics', p. 178.

35. Ibid., p. 164.

36. Ibid., p. 165.

37. V. H. Galbraith, 'Nationality and Language in Medieval England', *TRHS*, 23 (1941), 113–28 (p. 124).

38. See E. Faral, *Mimes Françaises du XIIIe siècle* (Paris, 1910), pp. 41–2, and Faral's Introduction to the poem, pp. 31–9.

39. Ed. M. R. James, Roxburghe Club (London, 1920), from CUL MS Ee.3.59.

40. From the dedication (*Estoire*, lines 3846 ff.), as translated by M. R. James, p. 13.

41. See M. Rickert, *Painting in Britain: The Middle Ages* (London, 1954), p. 120, and pl. 107B.

42. Ed. E. G. Stanley, Nelson's Medieval and Renaissance Library (London and Edinburgh, 1960).

43. Latin text from *Poetae Latini Aevi Carolini*, ed. E. Duemmler, 2 vols., MGH (Munich, 1978), I, 272. Translation by H. Waddell, *Mediaeval Latin Lyrics* (London, 1929), p. 87.

44. E.g. Pearsall, *Old English and Middle English Poetry*, pp. 91, 94.

45. See, for instance, Walter Map's 'Dialogus inter Aquam et Vinum', in T. Wright (ed.), *Latin Poems of Walter Mapes*, Camden Society (1841), pp. 87–92. See also H. Walther, *Das Streitgedicht in der lateinischen Literatur des Mittelalters* (Munich, 1920); F. J. E. Raby, *A History of Secular Latin Poetry in the Middle Ages*, 2 vols. (Oxford, 1934; 2nd edn, 1957), II, 282–308.

46. P. Dronke, 'Peter of Blois and Poetry at the Court of Henry II', *MS*, 38 (1976), 185–235 (p. 213).

47. Text and translation from Dronke, 'Peter of Blois', p. 208.

48. Ibid., p. 209.

49. Ibid., p. 209.

50. Ibid., p. 234.

51. See, for instance, Peter's own letters to the clergy of Henry II's court, demonstrating what Dronke (p. 193) calls the 'sic et non' and the 'odi et amo' of his thought upon courtly life.

52. The Oxford MS was very likely copied from an exemplar which resembled the British Library MS. See B. Hill, 'The History of Jesus College, Oxford, MS 29', *Medium Aevum*, 32 (1963), 203–13, and 'Jesus College, Oxford, MS 29, Addenda', *NQ*, 22

(1975), 98–105. Note also that R. M. Wilson, in 'More Lost Literature, II', *LSE*, 6 (1937), 30–49 (p. 31), points to a (lost) Tichfield MS of Geoffrey of Monmouth's *Historia Britonum* which contained a copy of *De conflictu inter philomenam et bubonem in anglicis*.

53. Ed. B. S. Merrilees, *Le Petit Plet*, ANTS, XX (Oxford, 1970). For discussion of this and other poems by Chardri, see Legge, *Anglo-Norman Literature*, pp. 192–201.

54. *Les Set Dormanz*, lines 57–9, cited in Legge, *Anglo-Norman Literature*, p. 196.

55. *Owl and the Nightingale*, lines 1746, 1752–3; see the section on 'The Author' in Stanley's Introduction, ed. cit., pp. 19–22. Dronke, 'Peter of Blois', p. 214, n. 70, makes a strong case from Latin literature of the twelfth century to support the reference to 'Maister Nichole' as an authorial naming. One other poem in the Jesus College MS has a dedication to a cleric – the Anglo-Norman *Vie de Tobie*, by Guillaume le Clerc, written for William, sub-prior of St Mary's, Kenilworth, between 1214 and 1227. See Hill, 'History of Jesus College MS 29', pp. 203 ff., and Legge, *Anglo-Norman Literature*, p. 224.

56. John of Howden's *Philomena*, for instance (see Legge, *Anglo-Norman Literature*, p. 233), or the debate poem, *The Thrush and the Nightingale* (in *English Lyrics of the XIIIth Century*, ed. C. Brown, Oxford, 1932, no. 52) and the 'notes suete of nyghtegales' in 'Lenten is come with love to toune' (in Brown, no. 81).

57. See, for instance, the February picture from the *Très Riches Heures de Jean de Berri*, painted before 1417 for the great French prince by the Limbourg brothers.

58. The Owl's association with Athene is not entirely lost in the Middle Ages: see E. A. Armstrong, *The Folklore of Birds* (London, 1958), pp. 117–24. Much stronger, however, is its symbolic identification with darkness and heresy: see, for instance, the use made of it in the paintings and drawings of the fifteenth-century painter, Hieronymus Bosch, e.g. in association with Pilate in the *Ecce Homo*, and on the head of one of the tormenting demons in the centre panel of *The Temptation of St Anthony* (see W. S. Gibson, *Hieronymus Bosch*, New York, 1973, p. 22 and pls. 9, 128). For the double aspect of the Nightingale, see note 56 above.

59. See P. Tristram, *Figures of Life and Death in Medieval English Literature* (London, 1976), pp. 162–7.

60. The texts upon which this section of the poem is based are the *De Remediis* of Seneca and Ecclesiasticus 3:22. It is impossible not to be reminded of Passus XIV and XV of Langland's *Piers Plowman* (B-text), in which Patience instructs the dreamer in God's providence – 'For lente neuere was lyf . bote lyflode were shapen / Wherof or wherfore . or whereby to lybbe' (B XIV 39–40) – and Reason rebukes him for his 'curiositas': 'Thanne artow inparfit . . . and one of Prydes knyʒtes' (XV 50). See *The Vision of William concerning Piers the Plowman, in Three Parallel Texts*, ed. W. W. Skeat, 2 vols. (Oxford, 1886).

61. Pearsall, *Old English and Middle English Poetry*, p. 94.

62. See, for instance, R. W. Chambers, *On the Continuity of English Prose*, EETS 191A (1932), where the *Brut* is cited (pp. lxvi–lxvii) as a link – albeit a weak one – in the continuous chain of alliterative verse stretching from the eleventh to the fourteenth century.

63. E. G. Stanley, 'Laʒamon's Antiquarian Sentiments', *Medium Aevum*, 38 (1969), 23–37 (p. 33).

64. Line 21 (Caligula MS only) in Laʒamon, *Brut*, ed. G. L. Brook and R. F. Leslie, EETS 250, 277 (1963, 1978). Brook and Leslie print the texts of the Caligula MS and of MS Cotton Otho C. xiii parallel. Citation below is always of Caligula unless otherwise specified. For Wace, see above, p. 22.

65. Stanley, 'Laȝamon's Antiquarian Sentiments', p. 30.
66. On Laȝamon's sources, see below, pp. 58–70.
67. Pearsall, *Old English and Middle English Poetry*, p. 112.
68. Old English alliterative verse is almost invariably written out by scribes in a 'continuous' format: so is the later rhythmical homiletic prose of Aelfric and others which may also be part of Laȝamon's heritage.
69. Stanley, 'Laȝamon's Antiquarian Sentiments'; Friedlander, 'Early Middle English Accentual Verse', *MP*, 76 (1979), 219–30.
70. See A. C. Gibbs, 'The Literary Relationships of Laȝamon's *Brut*' (unpublished PhD thesis, Cambridge, 1962), p. 101.
71. *Le Roman de Brut*, ed. I. Arnold, SATF (Paris, 1938–40), lines 11207–24.
72. Repetition, for a variety of stylistic effects, is as characteristic of Old English poetry (see the *Seafarer* or the *Charms*) as it is of the Old French *Chanson de Roland*. But an increased emphasis upon elaborate forms of verbal rhetoric, and in particular upon those which use the device of *repetitio*, is discernible first in Latin precept and example of the twelfth century, and then in vernacular imitations. See E. Salter, 'The English Tradition of Prose Translation', Chap. VI in *Nicholas Love's 'Myrrour of the Blessed Lyf of Jesu Christ'*, Analecta Cartusiana, 10 (Salzburg, 1974), pp. 179–263.
73. *Proverbs of Alfred*, in *Specimens of Early English*, ed. R. Morris, 2 vols. (Oxford, 1882), I, 146–52 (lines 17–32).
74. See Pearsall, *Old English and Middle English Poetry*, pp. 79–80.
75. Ed. J. Normand and G. Raynaud, SATF (Paris, 1877).
76. See below, pp. 59–60.
77. Pearsall, *Old English and Middle English Poetry*, p. 72.
78. Entry for 1086, on the death of William the Conqueror: see *Two of the Saxon Chronicles Parallel*, ed. J. Earle, rev. C. Plummer, 2 vols. (Oxford, 1892–9), I, 221.
79. Entry for 1036, on the presentation of Aelfred the Aetheling: see ibid., I, 158.
80. Entry for 975: see ibid., I, 119.
81. Ibid., I, 220.
82. Twelfth-century MSS such as Bodley 343, Corpus Christi College, Cambridge, 303, B. L. Cotton Vespasian D.xiv and Cotton Tib. C.i(2), thirteenth-century MSS such as Lambeth Palace Library 487, and eleventh-century MSS such as Bodleian Hatton 113–15 and Junius 121, were all glossed by the 'tremulous hand' of a thirteenth-century Worcester scribe and scholar. See N. R. Ker, 'The Date of the "Tremulous" Worcester Hand', *LSE*, 6 (1937), 28–9.
83. *The Homilies of Aelfric: A Supplementary Collection*, ed. J. C. Pope, 2 vols., EETS, 259–60 (1967–8), I, 105.
84. N. F. Blake, 'Rhythmical Alliteration', *MP*, 67 (1969), 118–24.
85. Aelfric has occasional examples of this: Pope cites from the *Cuthbert* homily, 'se ðe ðone heofenlican fodan him brohte and ðaes eorðlican ne rohte . . .' (I, 115).
86. Legge, *Anglo-Norman Literature*, p. 22.
87. Cited in ibid., p. 20.
88. See R. H. Fletcher, *Arthurian Material in the Chronicles*, Harvard Studies and Notes in Philology, X (Boston, 1906), pp. 143–4.
89. Legge, *Anglo-Norman Literature*, p. 77.
90. Among the poets of the fourteenth century so-called 'alliterative revival', in very different ways, the poet of *Winner and Waster* and William Langland himself work with 'compromise'.
91. Legge, *Anglo-Norman Literature*, p. 137.

92. See P. Clemoes, 'Aelfric', in *Continuations and Beginnings*, ed. E. G. Stanley (London and Edinburgh, 1966), pp. 176–209 (p. 203).
93. See, for instance, H. S. Davies, 'Laȝamon's Similes', *RES*, n.s.11 (1960), 129–42.
94. Wace, *Roman de Brut*, ed. I. Arnold, 2 vols., SATF (Paris, 1938–40), line 912.
95. Geoffrey, *Historia Regum Britanniae*, ed. A. Griscom (London, 1929), Book VI, Chap. XVI (p. 379). In the *Historia*'s range of short similes, warriors are likened to lions and wolves preying upon sheep, to wild boar chasing hounds, to lightning striking, to the west wind driving back the tide. Laȝamon clearly benefited from a knowledge of some of these.
96. *Roman de Brut*, lines 8517–20: the Britons, under king Uther Pendragon, savage the Saxons 'like proud lions, famished for prey, killing lambs and ewes, whether fully-grown or not'.
97. E.g. *Historia*, X, 11 (ed. Griscom, p. 493).
98. *Historia*, VII, 3 (ed. Griscom, p. 387); translation by S. Evans (1903), rev. C. W. Dunn (New York, 1958), p. 141.
99. Trinity College, Cambridge, MS 0.9.34, fo. 15v. Compare the miniature in B.L. MS Royal 20.A.v, fo. 71v, reproduced in D. J. A. Ross, *Alexander and the Faithless Lady: A Submarine Adventure*, inaugural lecture delivered at Birkbeck College, 1967 (London, 1968), fig. 2.
100. The solution proposed by H. S. Davies (see note 93 above) – a lost English source for Laȝamon – is quite without supporting evidence.
101. *Chanson de Roland* (ed. G. J. Brault, University Park, Pa. and London, 1978), lines 1111, 1529. The alternative solution proposed by Pearsall (*Old English and Middle English Poetry*, p. 112) – Laȝamon's indebtedness to Old French poetry – also lacks supporting evidence.
102. See R. R. Bezzola, *Les Origines et la formation de la littérature courtoise* (see note 13 in Chapter 1 above), III, 145–6, 404–6, and G. Cary and D. J. A. Ross, *The Medieval Alexander* (Cambridge, 1956), pp. 63–4.
103. For Joseph of Exeter, see Bezzola, *Origines*, III, 146–7, 149, and W. B. Sedgwick, 'The *Bellum Troianum* of Joseph of Exeter', *Speculum*, 5 (1930), 49–75. See also the translation by G. Roberts (Cape Town, 1970).
104. Latin text in *Joseph Iscanus: Werke und Briefe*, ed. L. Gompf, Mittellateinische Studien und Texte, Bd. IV (Leiden and Köln, 1970), I, 299–305; translation (by Roberts), p. 9.
105. Latin text, VI, 443–50; translation, p. 75.
106. *Alexandreidos*, in *PL*, 209, cols. 459–574, Book I, col. 465; Book III, col. 487; Book II, col. 476.
107. See A. Cameron, *Claudian* (Oxford, 1970), p. 427.
108. *Thebaid*, ed. J. H. Mozley, Loeb Classical Library (1928), I, 340–506, II, 2–446.
109. See Claudian, *De Raptu*, ed. M. Platnauer, Loeb Classical Library (1922), I, 24–97, II, 292–372.
110. See E. R. Curtius, *European Literature and the Latin Middle Ages* (first publ. in German, Bern, 1948), trans. W. R. Trask, Bollingen Series XXXVI, 1953 (Princeton, 1967), pp. 36, 49–52, 160.
111. Virgil, ed. H. R. Fairclough, Loeb Classical Library (1918), *Aeneid*, X, 264–6.
112. *Oeuvres de Rigord et de Guillaume le Breton*, ed. H.-F. Delaborde, 2 vols. (Paris, 1882–5), *Philippidos* (vol. II), VIII, 842–9.
113. See, for instance, *Georgics*, IV, 67–87, in which the martial behaviour of bees is described, and *Aeneid*, I, 430–4, 'apes . . . augmine facto'.

114. Quotation and translation from T. Wright, *The Political Songs of England*, Camden Society (1839), p. 26.
115. See J. S. P. Tatlock, *The Legendary History of Britain* (Berkeley and Los Angeles, 1950), p. 487.
116. For accounts of Areley, see T. R. Nash, *Collections for the History of Worcestershire*, 2 vols. (London, 1781–2), II, 166–70, and the *Victoria County History of Worcester*, 4 vols. (London, 1901–24), IV, 227–30.
117. Nash, *Worcestershire*, II, 166.
118. See *Register of Bishop Godfrey Giffard*, ed. J. W. Willis Bund, 2 vols., Worcestershire Historical Society (1902), II, 174 (entry for year 1283).
119. By that time, the records show, a new priest had taken over: in that year, 'William, rector of the church of Arleg [Areley Kings]' was granted dispensation 'not to be compelled to make personal residence there, while undertaking the duties of Master Thomas de Cantilupe'. See ibid., I, 3 (entry for year 1268).
120. See above, pp. 9–10.
121. See M. Blaess, 'L'Abbaye de Bordesley et les livres de Guy de Beauchamp', *Romania*, 78 (1957), 511–18.
122. See M. Blaess, 'Les manuscrits français dans les monastères anglais au Moyen Age', *Romania*, 94 (1973), 321–58 (p. 330).
123. See A. F. Cameron, 'Middle English in Old English Manuscripts', in *Chaucer and Middle English Studies in Honour of R. H. Robbins*, ed. B. Rowland (London, 1974), pp. 219–29.
124. *Homilies of Aelfric*, ed. Pope, I, 186.
125. See T. W. Williams, 'Gloucestershire Medieval Libraries', *Transactions of the Bristol and Gloucestershire Archaeological Society*, 31 (1908), 78–195 (pp. 139–78).
126. See Carleton Brown, 'A Thirteenth Century Manuscript from Lanthony Priory', *Speculum*, 3 (1928), 587–95.
127. Williams, 'Gloucestershire Libraries', pp. 134, 156.
128. R. H. Hilton, *A Medieval Society: the West Midlands at the end of the Thirteenth Century* (London, 1967), pp. 24–5.
129. See R. M. Clay, *The Hermits and Anchorites of England* (London, 1914), pp. 37, 57.
130. *Victoria County History of Worcester*, IV, 231.
131. J. C. Dickinson, *The Origins of the Austin Canons and their Introduction into England* (London, 1950), pp. 111–12, 143.
132. See the relevant section, reproduced by Hilton, *A Medieval Society*, plate 4.
133. E. J. Dobson, *The Origins of the Ancrene Wisse* (Oxford, 1976), p. 135.
134. Ibid., p. 170.
135. E.g. Chambers, *Continuity* (see note 62 above).
136. See above, pp. 7–8.
137. Dobson, *Origins*, p. 132.
138. Aelfric, 'Passio Sancti Vincenti', in *Aelfric's Lives of the Saints*, ed. W. W. Skeat, 2 vols., EETS, OS 76, 114 (1881, 1900), II, 436; *St Marherete*, ed. F. M. Mack, EETS, OS 193 (1934), p. 10.
139. D. Bethurum, 'The Connection of the Katherine Group with Old English Prose', *JEGP*, 34 (1935), 553–64 (p. 563).
140. Latin version of the Life of St Margaret, in *St Marherete*, ed. Mack, pp. 127–42 (p. 135); *St Marherete*, ed. Mack, p. 28.
141. See E. Faral, *Les Arts poétiques du XIIe et du XIIIe siècle*, Bibliothèque de l'Ecole des Hautes Etudes, fasc. 238 (Paris, 1924), p. xiii.
142. *PL*, 171, cols. 1687–92.

143. See Salter, *Nicholas Love's 'Myrrour'* (see note 72 above), pp. 206 ff.
144. *De Ornamentis Verborum*, col. 1687; 'On Ureisun of ure Louerde', in *The Wohunge of ure Lauerd*, ed. W. Meredith Thompson, EETS, 241 (1958), p. 1; 'The Wohunge of ure Lauerd', ed. cit., p. 20.

3 England and the continent during the thirteenth century: royal and aristocratic patronage

1. See *Testamenta Vetusta*, ed. N. Harris Nicolas, 2 vols. (London, 1826), I, 127.
2. Will printed in *A Collection of all the Wills . . . of the Kings and Queens of England*, ed. J. Nichols (London, 1780), pp. 181–2.
3. Compare Bodleian Library, Oxford, MSS Douce 215 (France, c. 1300: *Lancelot*), Digby 223 (France, late thirteenth century: *Lancelot, Graal, Mort Artu*), and Pierpont Morgan Library, New York, MS 805 (France, c. 1300: *Lancelot*). See also Bodl. Lib. MS Douce 178 (N. Italy, early fourteenth century: *Merlin*).
4. R. M. Wadsworth, 'Historical Romance in England: Studies in Anglo-Norman and Middle English Romance' (unpublished PhD thesis, York, 1972), pp. 168–9.
5. See A. L. Poole, *From Domesday Book to Magna Carta 1087–1216* (Oxford, 1951), pp. 370–1.
6. See Wadsworth, 'Historical Romance', pp. 160–1.
7. See H. J. Chaytor, *The Troubadours and England* (Cambridge, 1923), pp. 43–68.
8. See Poole, *From Domesday Book*, Chaps. XI–XIII.
9. See M. Bateson, *Mediaeval England* (London, 1904), p. 156; Poole, *From Domesday Book*, p. 243; J. C. Russell and J. P. Heironimus, *The Shorter Latin Poems of Master Henry of Avranches relating to England* (Cambridge, Mass., 1935), p. 32; and *Rotuli Litterarum Clausarum*, ed. T. Duffus Hardy, 2 vols. (London, for the Public Records, 1833–44), I, 108. (The first two works cited here also give general accounts of John's upbringing and education.)
10. Russell and Heironimus, *Poems of Henry of Avranches*, p. 32.
11. See Pipe Roll for 5 John, ed. D. M. Stenton, Pipe Roll Society, LIV (London, 1938), p. 139.
12. Now B.L. MS Royal 19.D.ii.
13. See W. Stubbs, 'Learning and Literature at the Court of Henry II', in *Seventeen Lectures on the Study of Mediaeval and Modern History* (Oxford 1886; 3rd edn, 1900), p. 141.
14. See Russell and Heironimus, *Poems of Henry of Avranches*, p. 32.
15. Bateson, *Mediaeval England*, p. 156; Poole, *From Domesday Book*, p. 243.
16. See *The Historical Works of Giraldus Cambrensis*, ed. T. Wright (London, 1863), p. 177.
17. See H. J. Chaytor, *Savaric de Mauléon: Baron and Troubadour* (Cambridge, 1939); Russell and Heironimus, *Poems of Henry of Avranches*.
18. Quoted and translated in Chaytor, *Savaric de Mauléon*, p. 16.
19. Text and translation from Chaytor, *Troubadours and England*, pp. 69–70.
20. *Historia Anglorum (Historia Minor)*, ed. F. Madden, Rolls series 44, 3 vols. (London, 1866–9), II, 152, cited in translation by Chaytor, *Savaric de Mauléon*, p. 28.
21. Chaytor, *Savaric de Mauléon*, p. 76. See J. Audiau, *Les Troubadours et l'Angleterre* (Paris, 1927), p. 25, n. 3.
22. Chaytor, *Savaric de Mauléon*, pp. 70–1.
23. See Chaytor, *Savaric de Mauléon*, p. 70, and the text in Appendix 7, pp. 87–90.
24. See Chaytor, *Savaric de Mauléon*, pp. 72–4, and the text in Appendix 8, pp. 90–3;

also *Poésies de Uc de Saint-Circ*, eds. A. Jeanroy and J.-J. Salverda de Grave, Bibliothèque Méridionale, series 1, vol. XV (Toulouse, 1913), nos. I, VI, VII.

25. Quoted by Chaytor, *Savaric de Mauléon*, p. 36, n. 2.
26. Audiau, *Les Troubadours et l'Angleterre*, pp. 25–6, n. 4.
27. Stubbs, *Seventeen Lectures*, p. 141.
28. See above, text at note 18.
29. See J. C. Russell, 'Master Henry of Avranches as an International Poet', *Speculum*, 3 (1928), 34–63, and Russell and Heironimus, *Poems of Henry of Avranches*.
30. See Russell and Heironimus, *Poems of Henry of Avranches*, pp. 56–9.
31. Russell, 'Master Henry of Avranches', p. 39.
32. Ibid., p. 39.
33. Quoted from the Close Rolls for 1244 by Russell, ibid., p. 46.
34. Ibid., p. 52.
35. Ibid., p. 50.
36. Ibid., p. 51.
37. Ibid., p. 51.
38. Poem no. 42, 'Ad Galfridum de Boclandia', lines 1–2, 7–8, in Russell and Heironimus, *Poems of Henry of Avranches*, p. 54.
39. Quoted ibid., p. 153.
40. See A. E. Stamp, 'Some Notes on the Court and Chancery of Henry III', *Historical Essays in Honour of J. Tait*, ed. J. G. Edwards, V. H. Galbraith and E. F. Jacob (Manchester, 1933), pp. 305–11 (p. 310).
41. Russell and Heironimus, *Poems of Henry of Avranches*, p. 142.
42. See R. Kent Lancaster, 'Artists, Suppliers and Clerks: the Human Factors in the Art Patronage of Henry III', *JWCI*, 35 (1972), 81–107, and T. Borenius, 'The Cycle of Images in the Palaces and Castles of Henry III', *JWCI*, 6 (1943), 40–50.
43. See F. M. Powicke, *The Thirteenth Century 1216–1307* (Oxford, 1953; 2nd edn, 1962), p. 41: 'There was no formal party of barons, as barons, opposed to the Crown, but a movement of fluctuating groups within a large family'.
44. See Audiau, *Les Troubadours et l'Angleterre*, pp. 31–2.
45. Ibid., p. 33.
46. G. Henderson, 'Studies in English Manuscript Illumination', Part I: 'Stylistic Sequence and Stylistic Overlap in Thirteenth-Century English Manuscripts', Part II: 'The English Apocalypse, I', *JWCI*, 30 (1967), 71–104, 104–37 (p. 98). For illustrations of the tomb of Peter of Aigueblanche and of the north transept of Hereford Cathedral (see text following), see P. Brieger, *English Art 1216–1307* (Oxford, 1957), pls. 31 and 73b.
47. The 'foreignness' of Peter of Aigueblanche is directly commented upon in the *Chronicle of England* of Robert of Gloucester: the English poet gives a hostile account of how Peter was turned out of his church during the uprising of 1262–3 against Henry's French relatives and ministers: 'A Freinss bissop þer was at Herefordе þo, / Sir Peris de Egeblaunche, þat hii dude also wo'. He knew no English. See *Early Middle English Verse and Prose*, eds. J. A. W. Bennett and G. V. Smithers (Oxford, 1966), no. XI, lines 51–2, 60–1 (pp. 160–1).
48. Chaytor, *Troubadours and England*, pp. 24–7.
49. See Powicke, *The Thirteenth Century*, pp. 96–103; also J. R. Strayer, *The Albigensian Crusade* (New York, 1971), pp. 139–40, 163–70.
50. Chaytor, *Troubadours and England*, p. 79.
51. Henry's mother, Isabella of Angoulême, had married, as second husband, Hugh le Brun of Lusignan, Count of La Manche.

52. Chaytor, *Troubadours and England*, p. 81.
53. Ibid., pp. 78–9.
54. See Strayer, *Albigensian Crusades*, Chapters VIII–IX.
55. Powicke, *The Thirteenth Century*, p. 97.
56. C. H. Haskins, *The Renaissance of the Twelfth Century* (Cambridge, Mass., 1927), p. 61.
57. Edited by C. A. Wood as *The Art of Falconry*, by Frederic II (Stanford, 1943).
58. See O. Pächt, 'Early Italian Nature Studies and the Early Calendar Landscape', *JWCI*, 13 (1950), 13–47 (pp. 22–4).
59. Powicke, *The Thirteenth Century*, p. 119.
60. See R. J. Branner, *St Louis and the Court Style in Gothic Architecture* (London, 1965).
61. Kent Lancaster, 'Artists, Suppliers and Clerks', p. 81.
62. Matthew Paris, *Historia Anglorum (Historia Minor)*, ed. F. Madden, Rolls series 44, 3 vols. (1866–9), III, 342, quoted in translation in P. Tudor-Craig, 'The Painted Chamber at Westminster', *Archaeological Journal*, 114 (1957), 92–105 (p. 104).
63. Ibid., p. 104.
64. Ibid., pp. 104–5.
65. Cambridge University Library MS Ee.3.59; facsimile reproduction, ed. M. R. James, Roxburghe Club (London, 1920). There are illustrations from the *Vie*, as well as reproductions of early watercolours and drawings of the Painted Chamber, in Tudor-Craig, 'The Painted Chamber', pls. XVI–XXIII.
66. See Henderson, 'Studies in English Manuscript Illumination' (see note 46 above), p. 85.
67. See Tudor-Craig, 'The Painted Chamber', p. 105; Henderson, 'Studies', p. 85; and, for the *Noble Chevalerie* (Bibliothèque Nationale MS fr. 15104), M. A. Stones, 'Secular Manuscript Illumination in France', in *Medieval Manuscripts and Textual Criticism*, North Carolina Studies in the Romance Languages and Literatures, 173 (Symposia, No. 4), ed. C. Kleinhenz (Chapel Hill, 1976), pp. 83–102 (p. 87). Stones has an illustration from MS 15104 as her pl. 4.
68. See *Transformations of the Court Style: Gothic Art in Europe 1270–1330* (Catalogue of an exhibition by the Dept. of Art, Brown University, Providence, R.I., 1977), p. 10.
69. Matthew Paris, *Chronica Majora*, ed. H. R. Luard, Rolls series 57, 7 vols. (1872–83), IV, 642.
70. See p. 15 above.
71. Trinity College, Cambridge, MS R.16.2. See the facsimile reproduction, ed. M. R. James, *The Trinity College Apocalypse*, Roxburghe Club (London, 1909).
72. Henderson, 'Studies', p. 126.
73. See W. R. Lethaby, 'English Primitives, IV: The Westminster and Chertsey Tiles and Romance Paintings', *Burlington Magazine*, 30 (1917), 133–40 (p. 138).
74. Ibid., pp. 138–9, and T. Borenius, 'The Cycle of Images' (see note 42 above), p. 45.
75. See Lethaby, 'English Primitives, IV', pp. 138–9; Borenius, 'Cycle of Images', p. 45; Kent Lancaster, 'Artists, Suppliers and Clerks', p. 105.
76. M. D. Legge's assertion (*Anglo-Norman Literature and its Background*, Oxford, 1963, p. 108) that we know 'absolutely nothing' of Henry's literary interests seems exaggerated.
77. Quoted by W. R. Lethaby, 'English Primitives: The Painted Chamber and the Early Masters of the Westminster School', *Burlington Magazine*, 7 (1905), 257–69 (p. 263).
78. Lethaby, 'English Primitives, IV', p. 139: Borenius, 'Cycle of Images', pp. 44–5.
79. See R. S. Loomis, 'Illustrations of Medieval Romance on Tiles from Chertsey

Abbey', *Univ. of Illinois Studies in Language and Literature*, 2 (1916), 243–338 (p. 263).
80. See p. 14 above.
81. See Legge, *Anglo-Norman Literature*, pp. 57–8.
82. Ibid., pp. 105–7.
83. Ibid., p. 57.
84. See D. J. A. Ross, 'A Thirteenth-Century Anglo-Norman Workshop Illustrating Secular Literary Manuscripts?' *Mélanges offerts à Rita Lejeune*, 2 vols. (Gembloux, 1969), I, 689–94 (see p. 690).
85. See Loomis, 'Illustrations of Medieval Romance', pp. 264–5.
86. See Legge, *Anglo-Norman Literature*, pp. 233–4, and L. W. Stone, 'Jean de Howden, poète anglo-normande du xiiie siècle', *Romania*, 69 (1946–7), 496–519 (p. 501).
87. 34 Henry III, 20 June 1250, in *Calendar of the Liberate Rolls*, vol. III: Henry III, 1245–51 (London, 1937), p. 292.
88. Stone, 'Jean de Howden', p. 502 (line 28).
89. Ibid., pp. 509–12 (lines 3969–4048).
90. Quoted in Henderson, 'Studies', p. 79; see also A. T. Baker (ed.), 'La Vie de Saint Edmond, Archevêque de Cantorbéry', *Romania*, 55 (1929), 332–81 (pp. 338–40).
91. See Baker, 'Vie de Saint Edmond', p. 338.
92. Matthew Paris, *Chronica Majora* (ed. cit. note 69 above), IV, 146–7.
93. Henderson, 'Studies', p. 72.
94. *Rossignos*, lines 3979–4010, cited in Stone, 'Jean de Howden', pp. 509–10.
95. *Estoire*, ed. James (see note 65 above), p. 13 (from the dedication, as translated by James).
96. E.g. *Chronica Majora* (see note 69 above), IV, 226–33, V, 231, 329, 514–15, 674, VI, 403.
97. 20 January 1240, in *Calendar of the Liberate Rolls*, Vol. I: Henry III, 1226–40 (London, 1916), p. 444.
98. February-by-the-fire motifs were no doubt among the stone reliefs of the Months on the hood of the fireplace in the Queen's Chamber at Clarendon Palace, ordered in 1251. See Lethaby, 'English Primitives, IV', p. 139.
99. See Powicke, *The Thirteenth Century*, p. 268.
100. See P. Chaplais, 'Some Private Letters of Edward I', *EHR*, 77 (1962), 79–86 (pp. 84–5).
101. Ibid., p. 86.
102. Ibid., p. 80.
103. Powicke, *The Thirteenth Century*, p. 268.
104. Ibid., p. 230.
105. Chaplais, 'Some Private Letters', p. 85. See also his letters to Robert de Bavent, King's Yeoman, 'sur des questions de vénerie', ed. F. J. Tanquerey, *BJRL*, 23 (1939), 487–503.
106. Chaplais, 'Some Private Letters', p. 80. See further J. Stevenson, *Documents illustrative of the History of Scotland 1286–1306*, 2 vols. (Edinburgh, 1870), II, 468, and J. Bain, *Calendar of Documents relating to Scotland*, 4 vols. (Edinburgh, 1881–8), vol. II (1272–1307), p. 382 (item 1461).
107. See E. G. Gardner, *The Arthurian Legend in Italian Literature* (London, 1930), pp. 46–7, and C. E. Pickford, 'Miscellaneous French Prose Romances', in R. S. Loomis (ed.), *Arthurian Literature of the Middle Ages* (Oxford, 1959), pp. 348–57 (pp. 350–2).
108. Pickford, (see n. 107), p. 351.

109. Gardner, *Arthurian Legend*, p. 47. See the printing of the *preambule* to Rusticiano's compilation (Bibl. Nat. MS fr. 6961) in P. Paris, *Les manuscrits françois de la Bibliothèque du Roi*, 7 vols. (Paris, 1836–48), II, 356–7, and in the Appendix to E. Löseth, *Le Roman en Prose de Tristan, le Roman de Palamède, et la compilation de Rusticien de Pise: analyse critique* (Paris, 1891), p. 423.
110. Gardner, *Arthurian Legend*, p. 49.
111. From the printing of the epilogue to the compilation of Rusticiano in Löseth, *Le Roman*, p. 472.
112. See T. F. Tout, *Edward I* (London, 1893), p. 71.
113. See Gardner, *Arthurian Legend*; R. S. Loomis, 'Chivalric and Dramatic Imitations of Arthurian Romance', in *Mediaeval Studies in Memory of A. K. Porter*, ed. W. R. W. Koehler, 2 vols. (Cambridge, Mass., 1939), I, 79–97 (p. 80).
114. Loomis, 'Chivalric and Dramatic Imitations', p. 79.
115. Ibid., p. 80. H. Buchthal, *Miniature Painting in the Latin Kingdom of Jerusalem* (Oxford, 1957), provides evidence of a manuscript-illuminating shop in Acre, several manuscripts from which are still in existence (pp. 48–93), and which may also have done Arthurian manuscripts (p. 86).
116. Loomis, 'Chivalric and Dramatic Imitations', p. 81.
117. Ibid., p. 81.
118. Wadsworth, 'Historical Romance in England' (see note 4 above), p. 323.
119. See R. S. Loomis, 'Edward I, Arthurian Enthusiast', *Speculum*, 28 (1953), 114–27 (pp. 116–17).
120. Wadsworth, 'Historical Romance in England', p. 325. *Fergus* is the only exception.
121. See W. A. Nitze, 'The Exhumation of King Arthur at Glastonbury', *Speculum*, 9 (1934), 355–61 (p. 355).
122. See Loomis, 'Edward I, Arthurian Enthusiast', p. 115; also id., 'Tristram and the House of Hujon', *MLR*, 17 (1922), 24–30.
123. See A. Micha, 'Miscellaneous French Romances in Verse', in *Arthurian Literature of the Middle Ages*, ed. Loomis, pp. 358–92 (p. 389); Loomis, 'Edward I, Arthurian Enthusiast', p. 116. The romance is edited by H. Michelant, *Der Roman von Escanor von Gerard von Amiens* (Tübingen, 1886).
124. See *HLF*, 31 (1893), pp. 152, 189–90. See also M. A. Stones, 'Secular Manuscript Illumination in France' (see note 67 above), p. 88, where a dedicatory copy (Bibl. Nat. MS fr. 1633) is described as having been made for Marguerite of France, some time between 1285 and 1291.
125. *Escanor*, lines 25904, 48–9, 25915–18; see also *HLF*, 31 (1893), p. 167.
126. See Micha, in *Arthurian Literature*, ed. Loomis, p. 390. This last detail may, however, be based upon similar features in Chrétien de Troyes. See *HLF*, 31 (1893), p. 168.
127. G. J. Brault, 'Arthurian Heraldry and the Date of *Escanor*', *Bulletin Bibliographique de la Société Internationale Arthurienne*, 11 (1959), 81–8 (p. 88).
128. Ibid., p. 86.
129. See Loomis, 'Chivalric and Dramatic Imitations', pp. 92–5, and id. 'Edward I, Arthurian Enthusiast', pp. 114, 121.
130. Loomis, 'Edward I, Arthurian Enthusiast', p. 114.
131. Ibid., pp. 118–22, where the chronicle of Lodewijk and the events of the 'Swan Feast' are treated in detail.
132. Ibid., p. 125.
133. See L. Thorpe, 'Maistre Richard: A Thirteenth Century Translator of the "De Re Militari" of Vegetius', *Scriptorium*, 6 (1952), 39–50 (p. 41).

134. Ibid., p. 40.
135. See C. E. Pickford, 'Miscellaneous French Prose Romances' (note 107 above), p. 352; R. Taylor, *The Political Prophecy in England* (New York, 1911), p. 150.
136. See M. D. Legge, 'John Pecham's *Jerarchie*', *Medium Aevum*, 11 (1942), 77–84.
137. See D. L. Douie, *Archbishop John Pecham* (Oxford, 1952), p. 52.
138. See [T. H. Turner], *Manners and Household Expenses of England in the Thirteenth and Fifteenth Centuries*, Roxburghe Club (London, 1841), p. lxix.
139. Ibid., p. 103.
140. M. A. Stones, 'Secular Manuscript Illumination in France', pp. 85–7.
141. Ibid., pp. 84–5.
142. See Ross, 'A Thirteenth Century Anglo-Norman Workshop' (note 84 above).
143. B.L., London, MS Add. 24686. See M. Rickert, *Painting in Britain: The Middle Ages* (London, 1954), pp. 139, 161.

4 The alliterative revival

1. Based on the definitive work of R. W. Chambers, *On the Continuity of English Prose*, EETS, OS 191A (1932).
2. J. R. Hulbert, 'A Hypothesis Concerning the Alliterative Revival', *MP*, 28 (1931), 405–22.
3. See the remarks by W. Matthews, *The Tragedy of Arthur* (Los Angeles, 1960), pp. 151–2; and by M. W. Bloomfield, 'Sir Gawain and the Green Knight: An Appraisal', *PMLA*, 76 (1961), pp. 9 ff.
4. See M. McKisack, *The Fourteenth Century* (Oxford, 1959), pp. 525–6: 'much remains to be discovered of the knightly and aristocratic households of the north and midlands, where such poets must have found their audiences'.
5. It seems likely that the north-east midlands as well as the west midlands are concerned here; A. McIntosh, 'The Textual Transmission of the Alliterative *Morte Arthure*', in *English and Medieval Studies presented to J. R. R. Tolkien*, ed. N. Davis and C. L. Wrenn (London, 1962), pp. 231–40, finds some evidence for associating the poem with Lincolnshire.
6. McKisack, *The Fourteenth Century*, p. 254.
7. Ibid., p. 254: 'Emblazoned on his roll of honour were names which in the past had spelt turbulence and treason . . .'
8. Thomas, Earl of Lancaster and Derby, was beheaded outside Warwick in 1322.
9. Written in 1354; ed. E. J. Arnould (Oxford, 1940).
10. '. . . pur ceo qe jeo sui engleis et n'ai pas moelt hauntee le franceis . . .' (*Livre*, p. 239).
11. It is worth remarking that his prose is frequently alliterative; see M. D. Legge, *Anglo-Norman Literature and its Background* (Oxford, 1963), pp. 219–20.
12. Ed. M. Y. Offord, EETS, OS 246 (1959).
13. Ed. I. Gollancz, *Select Early English Poems* 3 (Oxford, 1930).
14. Henry of Lancaster was godfather to Thomas, Earl of Warwick, whose father, Guy, gave his considerable library to Bordesley Abbey in 1305.
15. The very real period of 'baronial discontent' under Edward II did, indeed, produce some poems in the vernacular, but they are only partially alliterative, popular in tone, and clearly not inspired by aristocratic patrons: see T. W. Ross (ed.), 'On the Evil Times of Edward II', *Anglia*, 75 (1957), 173–93.
16. The Bohun family, in particular, were active patrons of artists as well as of poets: see

309

M. R. James, *The Bohun Manuscripts*, Roxburghe Club 200 (London, 1936); and the will of Eleanor Bohun, Duchess of Gloucester, with its reference to 'un psauter bien et richement enlumines' (J. Nichols, *A Collection of all the Wills . . . of the Kings and Queens of England*, London, 1780, p. 181). Guy Beauchamp of Warwick had a Romance of Alexander 'ove peintures'; and Thomas of Woodstock, Duke of Gloucester, owned an *Alexander* 'tresbien esluminez' and a *Speculum Humanae Salvationis* 'plein de ymagerie'.

17. 'Dare neuer no westren wy, while this werlde lasteth, / Sende his sone southewarde to see ne to here . . .' (*Winner and Waster*, lines 8–9).

18. See C. A. Luttrell, 'Three North West-Midland Manuscripts', *Neophilologus*, 42 (1958), 38–50.

19. 'He wonede at Ernleie wid þan gode cnihte / Uppen Seuarne . . .' (MS Otho C.XIII, lines 3–4).

20. The original (and lost) Fulk Fitzwarin poem probably dated from the later thirteenth century; the only extant version is in Anglo-Norman prose, and is thought to have been written before 1314, for Fulk V, by a monk of New Abbey, Alberbury, Shropshire. Leland's account of 'an old Englisch boke yn Ryme of the Gestes of Guarine and his Sunnes' allows us to recognise a lost alliterative work, which may have been a free adaptation of the Anglo-Norman prose *Fulk*. For this complex situation, see Legge, *Anglo-Norman Literature*, pp. 171–5, and J. Leland, *De Rebus Britannicis Collectanea* (1770), I, 230 ff.

21. The document recording the gift, 'escrites au Bordesleye le premer Iour de May, le An du Regne le Roy Edward trentime quart . . .' is one of the items in Lambeth MS 577, fo. 18v. It was first printed by H. J. Todd, *Illustrations of the Lives of Gower and Chaucer* (London, 1810), pp. 160–2. Since that time, some confusion seems to have arisen as to the date (and, therefore, as to the donor) of the gift. Todd himself put it at 1360, assuming that the King Edward in question was Edward III; R. M. Wilson, *The Lost Literature of Mediaeval England* (London, 1952), p. 117, took the date 1315, assuming that the gift was a *bequest* and that the reign was that of Edward I; McKisack, *The Fourteenth Century*, p. 258, seems to accept a date of approximately 1361. My colleague, D. A. Pearsall, has pointed out to me that the description of the donor as 'Counte de Warwick' in the MS makes it much more likely that the Guy Beauchamp concerned is the Earl who died in 1315, and who was a great benefactor of Bordesley Abbey. His testament directs that his body should be buried there, and also refers to 'books pertaining to his Chapell' (see W. Dugdale, *The Antiquities of Warwickshire*, 1656, repr. 1765, p. 315). The later Guy Beauchamp, who died at Vendôme in 1361, was only *heir* to the Earl of Warwick; moreover, his testament makes no mention of Bordesley nor of books. This date and identification is confirmed by M. Blaess, 'L'Abbaye de Bordesley et les livres de Guy de Beauchamp', *Romania*, 78 (1957), 511–18.

22. A well-documented example of this in the field of prose is John of Trevisa, who made several of his translations at the request of his 'employers', the Lords of Berkeley, in Gloucestershire.

23. Blaess, *Romania*, 78, pp. 513–14.

24. See *Pearl*, ed. E. V. Gordon (Oxford, 1953), p. xxv: 'The poet of *Pearl*, like most English poets of the fourteenth century, seems to have drawn on his foreign reading for his material. There is little trace of debt to any known English writing.' For his description of the jewelled dream landscape, it has been suggested that the poet drew on some account of the Wonders of the East: one would have been available to him in *Alexander's Letter to Aristotle*. The Apocalypse is an obvious source (see line

944); and the metaphor in line 1026, 'glent as glayre' ('glittered like white of an egg') makes one think that the poet may have been remembering some richly illuminated Apocalypse MS, in which the Holy City was decorated with gold leaf ('glayre' was the normal fixative for gold leaf). The Trinity College, Cambridge, Apocalypse (thirteenth century) has a splendid example (fo. 16r).

25. See W. A. Hulton, *Documents relating to the Priory of Penwortham*, Chetham Society 30 (1853), p. 94. Nicholas had a copy of the *Secreta Secretorum* – that source book for some of the elaborate 'seasonal rhetoric' of medieval poetry.

26. See Nichols, *Collection of Wills*, p. 181.

27. See W. H. St John Hope, *Archaeological Journal*, 54 (1897), 300–3, for a transcript of the inventory; and, for some discussion of it, M. V. Clarke's article 'Forfeitures and Treason in 1388' in her *Fourteenth Century Studies*, ed. L. S. Sutherland and M. McKisack (Oxford, 1937), pp. 115–45.

28. See J. Smyth, *The Lives of the Berkeleys, 1066–1618*, ed. Sir J. Maclean, 3 vols. (Gloucester, 1883). Trevisa began his work in the days of Thomas III of Berkeley (d. 1361) and finished it in 1398 during his grandson's lifetime, 'the year of my lord's age Sir Thomas Lord of Berkeley that made mee to make this translacion, the 47th' (Smyth, II, 22).

29. Ibid., I, 324.

30. He gave an annual grant to William of Stinchcomb, 'an hopefull scholler', and founded numerous chapels and chantries (ibid., I, 333). His grandson, Thomas IV, left 'to the sisters of Mary Magdalens hospital by Bristoll . . . one psalter with a glosse, and the legends of Saints in English' (ibid., II, 19).

31. Ibid., I, 343.

32. Ibid., I, 343.

33. These seem to have been the conditions under which the *Gest Historiale of the Destruction of Troy* was translated, at the request of an unknown knight, 'out of latyn into englysshe', as the Index to the MS tells us.

34. J. P. Oakden, *Alliterative Poetry in Middle English*, 2 vols. (Manchester, 1930–5), I, 257–61.

35. J. R. L. Highfield, 'The Green Squire', *Medium Aevum*, 22 (1953), 18–23.

36. See R. H. Robbins, 'A Gawain Epigone', *MLN*, 58 (1943), 361–6.

37. H. L. Savage, *The Gawain Poet* (Chapel Hill, N.C., 1956), p. 11.

38. S. Armitage-Smith, *John of Gaunt* (London, 1904), p. 207.

39. See Highfield's article, 'The Green Squire'. He mentions the Burtons and the Newtons. We might add the fact that Thomas of Tutbury was Gaunt's treasurer and then passed into the service of Henry IV. See T. F. Tout, *Chapters in the Administrative History of Mediaeval England*, 6 vols. (Manchester, 1920), IV, 202, n. 1.

40. J. A. Burrow, 'The Audience of *Piers Plowman*', *Anglia*, 75 (1957), p. 374.

41. I first heard Tutbury Castle associated with the *Gawain* poet by the late Laura Hibbard Loomis. As I understood her argument, however, she hoped to prove that the description of Sir Bercilak's castle (*Sir Gawain*, lines 767 ff.) was in fact a description of Tutbury. I have not seen any of her findings in published form.

42. For the history of Tutbury and accounts of its customs, see R. Plot, *The Natural History of Staffordshire* (Oxford, 1686), pp. 434–6; S. E. Bridges and S. Shaw, *The Topographer for the Years 1789–91* (London, 1789–91), I, 24–6 and II, 169; and Sir O. Mosley, *A History of the Castle, Priory and Town of Tutbury* (London, 1832).

43. Public Record Office, London, MS MR.17; reproduced in R. Somerville, *The History of the Duchy of Lancaster* (London, 1953), facing p. 86.

44. Professor A. McIntosh, of the University of Edinburgh, has localised the language of

the poem as it stands in MS Cotton Nero A.X in a very small area either in south-east
Cheshire or just over the border in north-east Staffordshire (lecture delivered to the
staff of the Department of English Language, University of Edinburgh, 18 November 1959). This would point to Gaunt's castle of Newcastle-under-Lyme rather
than to Tutbury.

45. *John of Gaunt's Register, 1379–1383* (hereafter cited as *Gaunt's Register*), ed. E. C.
Lodge and R. Somerville, 2 vols., Camden Society, 3rd series 56–7 (1937), I, 698,
pp. 225–6. Thomas de Newton appears in the *Calendar of Close Rolls*, Richard II, vol.
IV, 1389–92 (London, 1922), as 'escheator in Notynghamshire and Derbyshire'
(February 23, 1390). In 1392 (July 1) Thomas de Newton was confirmed sheriff of
London, after the previous mayor and sheriffs had been dismissed and fined by
Richard II. See *Calendar of Close Rolls*, Richard II, vol. V, 1392–6 (London, 1925), p.
88, and n. 70 of this article, below.

46. *Gaunt's Register*, I, 1077, p. 341.

47. Plot, *Natural History of Staffordshire*, p. 443.

48. W. Dugdale, *The Baronage of England* (1676), II, 108.

49. Much can also be gleaned from the *Register of Edward the Black Prince*, 4 vols.
(London, 1932), which substantiates aristocratic life at a slightly earlier period, that
of the first 'revival' poems, *Winner and Waster* and the *Parliament of the Three Ages*.

50. *Gaunt's Register*, I, 327, pp. 109–13. Crucifixes such as these must have been in the
mind of the earlier alliterative poet of *Winner and Waster* when he likened the feast
tables of the great to 'a rayled rode with rynges and stones' (line 343).

51. *Gaunt's Register*, I, 643, p. 209. The Black Prince's minstrels were also well rewarded
with silver-gilt pipes and sometimes with horses. See the *Register of Edward the Black
Prince*, IV, 67, 73.

52. *Gaunt's Register*, I, 714, p. 230.

53. Ibid., I, 528, p. 170. The parallel phrasing is worth noticing: 'of folȝande sute' / 'de
meisme la seute'.

54. Armitage-Smith, *John of Gaunt*, p. 427. M. V. Clarke points out in 'Forfeitures and
Treason in 1388', in her *Fourteenth Century Studies*, ed. L. S. Sutherland and M.
McKisack (Oxford, 1937), p. 117, that beds and their hangings were 'the most
valuable secular articles' in a nobleman's house. Robert de Vere, Duke of Ireland,
according to the Inventory of 1388, owned a bed of 'blue camoca, embroidered in
gold with owls and fleur-de-lys', valued at £68 13s. 4d. See also the list of 'litz dor et
de soye' in the Inventory of Thomas of Woodstock (*Archaeological Journal*, 54, 1897,
289 ff.), which tells of hangings decorated with 'wodewoses joustantȝ a chival',
'papegayes de vert tartryn', etc.

55. Armitage-Smith, *John of Gaunt*, p. 426.

56. See *Gaunt's Register*, I, 556, 557, 715, etc., pp. 179–83, 231–3.

57. A similar distinction could be made in terms of art: the quality of the finest of the
Bohun manuscripts is superior to that of the Grey-Fitzpayn Hours (Fitzwilliam
Museum, Cambridge, MS 242), made before 1308 for Sir Robert Grey of Codnor,
Derbyshire: see D. D. Egbert, 'The Grey-Fitzpayn Hours', *Art Bulletin*, 18 (1936).
Recent suggestions for the 'home' of *Sir Gawain* are various as ever: the household
of the Earl of Arundel, at the castle of Holt, Cheshire (G. Mathew, 'Ideals of
Knighthood in Late Fourteenth Century England', *Studies in Mediaeval History
presented to F. M. Powicke*, Oxford, 1948, p. 356); any of several Lancastrian house-
holds in the west and north-west midlands (Highfield, 'The Green Squire');
Dieulacres Abbey, near Leek, on the Cheshire–Staffordshire border (R. W. V.
Elliott, 'Sir Gawain in Staffordshire', *Times*, 21 May 1958).

58. J. R. Hulbert, 'A Hypothesis concerning the Alliterative Revival', *MP*, 28 (1931), 405–22. See above, 'The Alliterative Revival, I'.
59. See pls. 27, 41, 79 and 84 in J. Evans, *English Art 1307–1461* (Oxford, 1949).
60. It would be tempting to rely on John of Trevisa's comments on the state of the English language in the later fourteenth century (in his translation of Ranulph Higden's *Polychronicon*, ed. J. R. Lumby, 9 vols., Rolls series 41, 1865–86, II, 159–63). But, while we can accept as genuine evidence his endorsement of Higden's point about the greater ease with which midlanders understand both northern *and* southern speech, we must use with great caution his categorical statement that 'we souþerne men may þat longage unneþe understonde' (i.e. the language of 'þe northumbres'), since the observation was first made by William of Malmesbury in the twelfth century and repeated by Higden.
61. This is also true of the poet of *St Erkenwald*, which is set in London.
62. *Mum and the Sothsegger*, ed. M. Day and R. Steele, EETS, OS 199 (1936), lines 48–9.
63. The recent association of the *Morte Arthure* with the Lincoln area points to the kind of redistribution that may, in some cases, prove to be necessary. See the essay by McIntosh cited in n. 5 above.
64. A. C. Cawley (ed.), *Sir Gawain and the Green Knight* (London, 1962), p. x. See also Burrow, 'The Audience of *Piers Plowman*', p. 374 and elsewhere.
65. *Piers Plowman* raises problems too complex and numerous for treatment within this general and exploratory article. But it is worth some reflection that a west-country poet, writing in London, should never have questioned the acceptability of an alliterative mode outside the west and north-west midlands. Although it is true that he tends to avoid the specialised vocabulary of other western poets (see Burrow's article), his work remains sufficiently alliterative to give signs of his knowledge of poems such as *Winner and Waster*, the *Parliament of the Three Ages*, *William of Palerne*, and possibly others too. See S. S. Hussey, 'Langland's Reading of Alliterative Poetry', *MLR*, 60 (1965), 163–70. The circulation of *Piers Plowman* manuscripts argues a vast network of communications and the accessibility of one 'literary and dialectal area' to another. For interesting comment on this, see M. L. Samuels, 'Some Applications of Middle English Dialectology', *English Studies*, 44 (1963), 81–94.
66. The careers of Sir John Stanley (controller of the royal household from 1397 to 1399) and of his kinsman, Thomas Stanley (keeper of the rolls from 1397 to 1399), sketch a similar, though not Lancastrian, pattern, in which Staffordshire, Cheshire, Lancashire, and London are significant points. The house of Stanley was celebrated in the last of the alliterative poems, *Scotish Feilde*, written after 1515. See Tout, *Chapters in Administrative History*, IV, 199, and *Scotish Feilde*, ed. J. P. Oakden, Chetham Society, n.s. 94 (Manchester, 1935).
67. See *The Knight's Tale*, lines 2605–16; *The Legend of Good Women*, lines 635–48; and some striking single instances: *The Man of Law's Tale*, line 460; and *The Nun's Priest's Tale*, line 3398. Lines such as 'With knotty, knarry, bareyne trees olde' (*The Knight's Tale*, line 1977) and 'And heterly they hurtelen al atones' (*The Legend of Good Women*, line 638) show some knowledge of special alliterative vocabulary and a willingness to use it for particular poetic effects. See D. Everett, 'Chaucer's "Good Ear"', *Essays on Middle English Literature* (Oxford, 1955), pp. 139–42.
68. *Super Concordia Regis Ricardi et Civium Londoniensium*, ed. T. Wright, in *Political Poems and Songs*, 2 vols., Rolls series 14 (1859), I, 285. Maidstone was a prominent anti-Lollard writer, whose work is almost completely in Latin. *Seven Penitential*

Psalms in English exist in three Bodleian manuscripts. He is probably the 'Fratri Ricardo' to whom payment is recorded on 31 March 1372, in *Gaunt's Register, 1371–1375*, ed. S. Armitage-Smith, 2 vols., Camden Society, third series 20–1 (1911), II, 969, p. 48. See *DNB*, XII, 783–4.

69. It is tempting to see in *vernula quam facies* and 'þe ver by his visage' a striking parallelism: *vernulus* (adj.) should strictly mean *vernacular* (A. Blaise, *Dictionnaire Latin–Français des Auteurs Chrétiens*, Turnhout, 1954, s.v. *vernulus*) or *du pays*. By 1200, *vernula* (subst.) had come to mean 'faithful follower' (J. H. Baxter and C. Johnson, *Mediaeval Latin Word List*, Oxford, 1934, p. 452). But, considering how frequently the phrase *vernalis facies* occurs in classical and medieval Latin (Augustine, Boethius, Fortunatus), and considering also that interchange of the forms *vernalis* and *vernulus* seems to be common by the thirteenth century (Du Cange, *Glossarium Mediae et Infimae Latinitatis*, London, 1887, VIII, 283), it is possible that Maidstone meant to convey the sense of 'springlike' by *vernula* rather than 'faithful'. Such a sense would fit the context of the passage, which is a eulogy of Richard's physical beauty and splendour.

70. Thomas de Newton, Gaunt's 'most dear friend' (see above, n. 45), was sheriff of London in 1392 and would certainly have witnessed Richard's entry. Perhaps he also knew Maidstone's poem?

5 *Piers Plowman*: an introduction

1. The dream-poem probably to be ascribed to the author of *Sir Gawain and the Green Knight*, and contemporary with *Piers Plowman*: ed. E. V. Gordon (Oxford, 1953). [The quotation practice of the original Introduction is followed here. Passages are quoted in the form in which they appeared in the ensuing Selections; if they did not appear there, the source is *The Vision of William concerning Piers the Plowman, in Three Parallel Texts*, ed. W. W. Skeat, 2 vols. (Oxford, 1886), which is also the source for quotations from the A- and B-texts. Line citations are all to Skeat's edition.]

2. In particular, by D. W. Robertson and B. F. Huppé, in *Piers Plowman and Scriptural Tradition* (Princeton, 1951).

3. Quoted from Claudius of Turin by B. Smalley, *The Study of the Bible in the Middle Ages* (Oxford, 1952), p. 1.

4. Langland's contemporary, Walter Hilton, gives a clear definition of these 'kinds' in his *Scale of Perfection*, ed. E. Underhill (London, 1923), Bk II, Chap. 43, p. 445: 'By the letter, that is lightest and most plain, is the bodily kind comforted; by morality of Holy Writ, the soul is informed of vices and virtues . . . by mystihood it is illumined for to . . . apply words of Holy Writ to Christ our head, and to Holy Kirk that is his mystical body. And the fourth, that is heavenly, longeth only to the working of love, and that is when all soothfastness in Holy Writ is applied to love; and for that is most like to heavenly feeling, therefore I call it heavenly.'

5. See G. R. Owst, *Literature and Pulpit in Mediaeval England* (Cambridge, 1933), Chap. 2, 'Scripture and Allegory', pp. 57 ff.

6. See M. W. Bloomfield, 'Symbolism in Mediaeval Literature', *MP*, 56 (1958), 73–81.

7. N. Coghill, Introduction to *The Visions of Piers Plowman*, a verse rendering of the B-text of the poem by H. W. Wells (London, 1935), p. xvii.

8. R. W. Frank, 'The Art of Reading Mediaeval Personification Allegory', *ELH*, 20 (1953), p. 249.

9. Compare *The Cloud of Unknowing*, ed. P. Hodgson, EETS, OS 218 (1944), pp. 107–8.
10. Frank, 'The Art of Reading', pp. 238 ff.
11. Ed. Sir I. Gollancz (London, 1930).
12. Some of the crude but vigorous scenes from the Holkham Bible Picture Book come to mind: produced in the earlier fourteenth century, it represents a kind of illustrative art with which Langland might easily have been familiar. See the facsimile edition by W. O. Hassall (London, 1954) and plate 134 in M. Rickert, *Painting in Britain: the Middle Ages*, Pelican History of Art (London, 1954).
13. *The Simonie*, Auchinleck MS, fo. 328v, ed. T. Wright, *The Political Songs of England*, Camden Society, 6 (London, 1839).
14. He had many precedents for this in art and literature: the verse had been dramatised and illustrated from the ninth century onwards. See A. Katzenellenbogen, *Allegories of the Vices and Virtues in Mediaeval Art* (New York, 1964), pp. 40–1 and plate xxv, fig. 44.
15. The origins of the tree image are various, but Matthew 7:17 must have been a central text: 'Every sound tree bears good fruit, but the bad tree bears evil fruit... Thus you will know them by their fruits.' See Katzenellenbogen, *Allegories*, pp. 63–8. M. W. Bloomfield, in *'Piers Plowman* and the Three Grades of Chastity', *Anglia*, 76 (1958), 245–53, makes suggestions about the particular sources of Langland's tree.
16. Katzenellenbogen, *Allegories*, p. 63. British Museum MS Additional 37049 is a fine example of such a book: its allegorical trees range over the vices and virtues, religion, love, etc. It may be significant for Langland's tree of 'cor-hominis' that many of them are rooted in man's heart. (See pls. 5, 6, 7.)
17. The 'turris sapientiae', for instance, on fo. 20v of British Museum MS Arundel 507, a fourteenth-century collection of texts and drawings, owned by a monk of Durham.
18. Owst, *Literature and Pulpit*, pp. 77 ff.
19. Ed. C. Horstmann, *Yorkshire Writers: Richard Rolle of Hampole* (London, 1895), I, 321–37.
20. Katzenellenbogen, *Allegories*, p. 73.
21. British Museum MS Additional 37049 has examples of both kinds of trees, on fo. 48r and fo. 19v respectively. (See pl. 6.)
22. Such non-visual allegorical 'picturing' is to be found in some of the Latin literature of the earlier fourteenth century; see B. Smalley, commenting upon the work of the Franciscan John Ridevall: '... all this fancy is verbal, not visual; the "pictures" will serve as aural aids to preaching' (*English Friars and Antiquity*, Oxford, 1960, p. 118).
23. See, for instance, the section on Love in the thirteenth-century spiritual guide, the *Ancrene Wisse*, ed. G. Shepherd, Nelson's Medieval and Renaissance Library (London and Edinburgh, 1959), pp. 21–3. This work was highly influential in the fourteenth and fifteenth centuries.
24. See the article in the *Metropolitan Bulletin of Art*, 16, No. 4 (December, 1957), by M. B. Freeman, 'The Iconography of the Merode Altarpiece'.
25. In the Prado, Madrid: painted before 1516. See *Hieronymous Bosch, The Garden of Delights*, ed. W. Hirsch (Amsterdam, 1954), which reproduces the tavern scene in Hell with excellent detail.
26. Quoted and translated from Lactantius, *Divinae Institutiones*, by E. Auerbach, in his essay 'Figura', *Scenes from the Drama of European Literature* (New York, 1959), p. 35.
27. The best short exposition of the figural outlook is by Auerbach, in the essay noted above. But see also C. Donahue, 'Patristic Exegesis: Summation', in *Critical*

Approaches to Mediaeval Literature, ed. D. Bethurum (New York, 1960), p. 81, who comments perceptively that the figural or typological approach 'might turn imaginative writers towards realism rather than towards allegory'.
28. See the clear 'figural' statement about Christ at C xv 38–9:

> Lawe of loue oure lorde wrot, longe er Crist were.
> And Crist cam *and confermede*, and holy kirke made . . .

29. Auerbach, 'Figura', p. 72. The figural or typological view of history is especially clear in the double row of personages and events from the Old and the New Testaments in medieval choir stall carvings, for instance, and in the series of Old Testament episodes chosen for the Miracle Play Cycles.
30. Auerbach, 'Figura', p. 75, writing of Beatrice, in the *Divine Comedy*.
31. M. W. Bloomfield, *Piers Plowman as a Fourteenth Century Apocalypse* (New Brunswick, NJ, 1963), p. 34.
32. Ibid., p. 8.
33. C. S. Lewis, *The Allegory of Love* (Oxford, 1936), p. 161.
34. Robertson and Huppé, *Piers Plowman and Scriptural Tradition*, p. 247.
35. See S. S. Hussey, 'Langland, Hilton and the Three Lives', *RES*, n.s. 7 (1956), 132–50, for an enlightened discussion of Langland's intentions: '. . . the various definitions (of Dowel, Dobet and Dobest) are not mutually exclusive, but complementary . . .' (p. 148).
36. H. W. Wells, in 'The Construction of *Piers Plowman*', *PMLA*, 44 (1929), 123–40, proposed Dowel, Dobet and Dobest as dominant organising factors in the poem.
37. N. Coghill's article, 'The Character of Piers Plowman considered from the B-Text', *Medium Ævum*, 2 (1933), 108–35, encouraged this idea.
38. A. H. Smith, *Piers Plowman and the Pursuit of Poetry* (London, 1950), p. 19.
39. J. Lawlor, 'The Imaginative Unity of *Piers Plowman*', *RES*, n.s. 8 (1957), p. 126.
40. R. Woolf, 'Some Non-Mediaeval Qualities of *Piers Plowman*', *Essays in Criticism*, 12 (1962), p. 118.
41. J. Lawlor, *Piers Plowman: An Essay in Criticism* (London, 1962), p. 263.
42. Bloomfield, *Fourteenth Century Apocalypse*, p. 32.
43. *Scale of Perfection*, Bk II, Chap. 29, p. 355.
44. Bloomfield, *Fourteenth Century Apocalypse*, p. 34.
45. Coleridge, *Biographia Literaria*, Chap. 14.
46. Although these apparently begin in a waking interval, Langland infers, at C xx 332 ('and therwith ich awakede'), that they are part of the dreamer's sleeping experience.
47. Auerbach, 'Figura', p. 72.
48. Fos. 72v–73r. Reproduced by F. Wormald, 'Some Popular Miniatures and their Rich Relations', *Miscellanea Pro Arte, Festschrift für H. Schnitzler* (Düsseldorf, 1965), pls. CLVI and CLVII.
49. C. Muscatine, 'Locus of Action in Mediaeval Narrative', *Romance Philology*, 17 (1963), p. 122.
50. Auerbach, 'Figura', p. 72.
51. *Scale of Perfection*, Bk II, Chap. 40, p. 424. See also *The Book of Privy Counselling*, ed. P. Hodgson, EETS, OS 218 (1944), pp. 151–2.
52. *Scale of Perfection*, Bk II, Chap. 24, p. 318.
53. So the ploughing of the half-acre 'delays' the first search for Truth (C ix 2 ff.).
54. Quoted by Langland at C xi 255: 'For ich am *uia et ueritas*, and may auaunce hem alle.'

55. In Passus XXII, when Christ assumes a form acclaimed by the dreamer as that of Piers (lines 6–8) and when he delegates his power on earth to Piers (lines 182 ff.).
56. Compare, specifically, C VIII 261 ff.: 'Be war thenne of Wrath, that wikkede shrewe . . .'
57. Compare C VIII 213 ff.
58. Compare C VIII 251–2:

> A ful leel lady unlek hit of grace,
> And she hath the keye and a clycat, thogh the kynge slepe.

59. C VIII 257–8.
60. E. Gilson, *Les Idées et les lettres* (Paris, 1932), p. 95.
61. See, for instance, C VI 114 ff., C XIII 40 ff.
62. See Owst, *Literature and Pulpit*, Chap. IX; E. Salter, *Piers Plowman: An Introduction* (Oxford, 1962), Chap. II; and A. C. Spearing, *Criticism and Mediaeval Poetry* (London, 1964), Chap. IV.
63. 'Magis enim amanda est animarum aedificatio quam sermonis continuatio', quoted by Gilson, *Les Idées*, p. 143.
64. Ibid., p. 144.
65. See the long speech by Ymaginatyf, C XV 1 ff.., which attempts to expose the folly of the dreamer's presumptuous behaviour to Reason, and, appropriately, though discursively, winds through magisterial statements about salvation to a thoughtful and inconclusive end – 'al worth as god wole'. And see also the whole of C XI.
66. The phrase is that of Professor Nevill Coghill, who used it in 'The Pardon of Piers Plowman', *Proceedings of the British Academy*, 30 (1944), p. 312, without relating it to sermon practice.
67. See the detailed exposition of this, using the B-text, in Salter, *Piers Plowman*, pp. 49–52.
68. See E. T. Donaldson, *Piers Plowman: the C Text and its Poet* (New Haven, 1949), Chap. 3, 'The Art of the C Reviser'; Salter, *Piers Plowman*, Chap. 2, 'The Art of *Piers Plowman*'; Lawlor, *Piers Plowman: An Essay in Criticism*, Part II, 'The Poetic Techniques'; and Spearing, *Criticism and Mediaeval Poetry*, Chap. 3, 'The Art of Preaching and *Piers Plowman*'.
69. *Biographia Literaria*, Ch. XIV.
70. Spearing, *Criticism and Mediaeval Poetry*, p. 87.
71. For further comment on sermon and poetic rhetoric, see Salter, *Piers Plowman*, pp. 26–40, and Spearing, *Criticism and Mediaeval Poetry*, pp. 88–92.
72. S. S. Hussey, 'Langland's Reading of Alliterative Poetry', *MLR*, 60 (1965), p. 170.
73. Ed. W. W. Skeat, *Piers the Plowman in Three Parallel Texts and Richard the Redeless*, 2 vols. (Oxford, 1886), pp. 603–28.
74. See E. Salter, '*Piers Plowman* and *The Simonie*', *Archiv*, 203 (1967), 241–54.
75. 'And there they gabble compline, when they've put out the light' – a reference to the idle priest and his mistress. Compare Langland's 'And gnawen god with the gorge, whan her gutte is fulle' (B X 57).

6 Piers Plowman and The Simonie

1. S. S. Hussey, 'Langland's Reading of Alliterative Poetry', *MLR*, 60 (1965), 163–70.
2. Ibid., p. 170.

3. E. T. Donaldson, *Piers Plowman: The C Text and its Poet* (New Haven, 1949), p. 44.
4. M. W. Bloomfield, *Piers Plowman as a Fourteenth Century Apocalypse* (New Brunswick, NJ, 1963), pp. 34–5.
5. J. Lawlor, *Piers Plowman: An Essay in Criticism* (London, 1962), p. 201.
6. J. A. Burrow, 'The Audience of *Piers Plowman*', *Anglia*, 75 (1957), 373–84.
7. E. Salter, *Piers Plowman: An Introduction* (Oxford, 1963), pp. 24 ff.
8. Lawlor, *Essay in Criticism*, pp. 201–2.
9. See G. Kane, *Piers Plowman: The Evidence for Authorship* (London, 1965), pp. 63–4 and elsewhere.
10. For Harley MS 2253, see K. Böddeker, *Altenglische Dichtungen des MS. Harley 2253* (Berlin, 1878). For the Auchinleck MS (Advocates MS 19. 2. 1, National Library of Scotland) see L. H. Loomis, 'The Auchinleck MS and a Possible London Bookshop of 1330–1400', *PMLA*, 57 (1942), 595–627, and A. J. Bliss, 'Notes on the Auchinleck Manuscript', *Speculum*, 26 (1951), 652–8.
11. See L. H. Loomis, 'Chaucer and the Auchinleck MS: *Thopas* and *Guy of Warwick*', *Essays and Studies in Honor of Carleton Brown* (New York, 1940), pp. 111–28.
12. The Auchinleck text was printed by T. Wright, *The Political Songs of England*, Camden Society, 6 (1839), pp. 323–45. The poem exists in two other manuscripts – Peterhouse, Cambridge, MS 104, and Bodley MS 48. The Bodley version is incomplete, and differs considerably from the other two texts: it is possible, although not certain, that it is a later redaction, with a new opening and conclusion. Bodley MS 48 is a fifteenth-century miscellany of prose and verse. T. W. Ross has printed *The Simonie* from this MS in *Anglia*, 75 (1957), 173–93.

    Quotation in this article is made from the two earlier MSS. Peterhouse MS 104 contains, in a later fourteenth-century hand, the Latin Sermons of Ralph Acton, preacher and theologian of the reign of Edward II. (See *DNB*, I, 68–9, and A. B. Emden, *A Biographical Register of the University of Oxford to A.D. 1500* (Oxford, 1951), p. 12.) *The Simonie* follows Acton's Sermons at fo. 210r.

    The MS was given to Peterhouse before 1418 by the executors of Thomas of Exeter, youngest son of John of Gaunt by Catherine Swynford (see M. R. James, *A Descriptive Catalogue of the Manuscripts in the Library of Peterhouse, Cambridge* (Cambridge, 1899), pp. 9 and 120–3). Legitimised by Richard II in 1397, he was granted Castle Acre, Norfolk, in the same year; he held important positions in the employ of his half-brother, Henry IV, and was buried at Bury St Edmunds (see *DNB*, XI, 49–50). The manuscript is therefore connected with the East Midlands: T. W. Ross, *The Simonie*, p. 176, suggests that the language of the Bodley text is east midland, with some western influence. It seems likely, taking into account the certain London provenance of the Auchinleck MS, that *The Simonie* came to Langland's notice in London and not in the west country.
13. Hussey, 'Langland's Reading', p. 170.
14. J. Wells, *A Manual of the Writings in Middle English, 1050–1400* (New Haven, 1916, repr. 1930), p. 232. It is interesting that G. R. Owst in *Literature and Pulpit in Mediaeval England* (Cambridge, 1933; 2nd edn, Oxford, 1961) frequently juxtaposes sermon material of Ralph Acton and *Piers Plowman* (see pp. 344, 561, 569 in particular). Peterhouse 104 may indicate an even wider area of indebtedness for *Piers Plowman* than at first appears.
15. Line 120 has also something of Langland's bold, ironic way with metaphor; see *Piers Plowman*, B III 309–10:

    Prestes and persones . with *placebo* to hunte,
    And dyngen vpon Dauid . eche a day til eue.

[In this essay, *Piers Plowman* is quoted from the parallel-text edition of W. W. Skeat, 2 vols. (Oxford, 1886)]

16. See also *Piers Plowman*, B I 36–7, for lines of similar structure.
17. See Wells, *Manual of the Writings*, p. 231.
18. Cf. also B VI 312, B XV 424 etc.
19. Hussey, 'Langland's Reading', p. 163, paraphrasing J. P. Oakden, *Alliterative Poetry in Middle English*, 2 vols. (Manchester, 1930–5), II, 166f.
20. The punctuation in both of the MSS from which quotation is made should be noted. The medial point in Peterhouse MS 104, and the frequent *punctus elevatus* in Auchinleck comment clearly on the fact that the line demands a medial pause: Wright, by modernising the punctuation of Auchinleck, obscured the rhythmical make-up of the poem.
21. See also line 433, quoted above, p. 159. Line 184 might be compared with *Piers Plowman* B XI 357: 'And how amonge the grene grasse . grewe so many hewes'.
22. See also Wright, *Political Songs*, lines 117, 180, 255, 313.
23. A line verbally reminiscent of *Piers Plowman*, B Prol. 66 'But holychirche and hij . holde better togideres'.
24. See also A Prol. 106, quoted above.
25. See also Wright, *Political Songs*, lines 151, 369, 389, 397, 402.
26. See also B X 422, B XI 81, 83.
27. See also Wright, *Political Songs*, lines 88, 150, 226.
28. See also C IV 122, A III 98.
29. Compare C XIII 228 for verbal likeness: 'And hauen the worlde at here wil . other-wyse to lyue . . .'
30. See also Wright, *Political Songs*, lines 216, 252, 270, 308.
31. See also B Prol. 11.
32. See also Wright, *Political Songs*, line 272.
33. See also B X 207, 255.
34. See Oakden, *Alliterative Poetry*, I, 168–70.
35. See Hussey, 'Langland's Reading', p. 165, on *Piers Plowman* and *Joseph of Arimathie*; p. 166, on *William of Palerne* and *Piers Plowman*.
36. See above, pp. 159–62.
37. See also C I 12: 'Of truythe and of tricherye . of tresoun and of gyle . . .'
38. Possibly also reminiscent of B XV 197–8:

> 'And to pore peple . han peper in the nose,
> And as a lyoun he loketh . there men lakketh his werkes . . .'

39. *The Simonie* may have been first circulated in a period of strong anti-papal protest: William of Ockham's *Octo Quaestiones super Potestate ac Dignitate Papali* (written between 1339 and 1342), Edward III's note to the Pope about foreigners in high office in the English Church (sent in 1343: see M. McKisack, *The Fourteenth Century* (Oxford, 1959), p. 273) and the record of a Joust at Smithfield in 1343, with challengers dressed (satirically?) as the Pope and Cardinals (see Glynne Wickham, *Early English Stages, 1300–1660* (London, 1959), p. 20) witness to national feeling on various levels. *The Simonie* also testifies to the atmosphere of the times, in a very wide frame of reference.
40. It is important, in view of these lines, that in *Piers Plowman* B II 23–4, Meed is 'pryue' in the 'popis paleys' against the will of 'sothenesse':

> 'In the popis paleys . she is as pryue as my-self,
> But sothenesse wolde nou3t so . . .'

41. Nor in B XX 125ff., where Coueityse is sent by Symonye on important missions, among which 'he Iugged til a Iustice . and Iusted in his ere . . .' (133)
42. Wright reads 'taken bi þe cop . . .', which is clearly mistaken, and obscures an alliterative phrase.
43. See above, p. 165.
44. Cf. B XIII 77: '"Ac this goddes gloton", quod I. "with his gret chekes" . . .'
    B XIII 98–9: '. . . this doctour, / As rody as a rose . rubbed his chekes . . .'
    B XIII 103: '"Dowel?" quod this doctour –. and toke the cuppe and dranke . . .'
45. Printed by R. H. Robbins (ed.), *Historical Poems of the XIVth and XVth Centuries* (New York, 1959), pp. 7–9 and 29.
46. Ibid., p. 29. The events in Passus IV of the B-text which lead up to Reason's sermon involve such 'characters' as Pees, Wronge, and Witt (cf. lines 47, 48, 76 etc.).
47. Robbins, *Historical Poems*, p. 8, line 31.
48. Compare B XV 148: 'I haue lyued in londe,' quod I . 'my name is Longe Wille . . .' and B XIII 2: 'And as a freke that fre were . forth gan I walke . . .'
49. W. H. Hulme (ed.), *The Middle English Harrowing of Hell and Gospel of Nicodemus*, EETS, ES 100 (1907), p. 11. See also pp. 9–10, where the debate between Satan and Christ involves the concept of 'reason', and is distantly reminiscent of *Piers Plowman* B XVIII 328, 337, and 347. The poem exists in three MSS, two of which are Harley 2253 and the Auchinleck MS. Knowledge of such a poem could have been gained in the west or in London: like *Piers Plowman* later, it defies regional compartmentation.

7 Alliterative modes and affiliations in the fourteenth century

1. See, for instance, C. Moorman, 'The Origins of the Alliterative Revival', *Southern Quarterly*, 7 (1969), 345–71.
2. The relationship between alliterative prose and verse in Latin and the vernacular languages is still not sufficiently explored: Richard Rolle's *Canticum Amoris*, which uses heavy alliteration and a medial caesura, has an as yet undefined importance to his vernacular alliterative usages; the poet of *Patience* used the alliterative Latin of Marbod of Rennes' *Naufragium Jonae Prophetae* (*PL*, 171, cols. 1675–8) as part of his source material; Arthurian prose romances, in alliterative Latin, with a taste for richness of synonyms, were being written on the English–Welsh border during the later thirteenth century (*Historia Meriadoci, De Ortu Walwani*, ed. J. D. Bruce, Göttingen, 1913). This does not exhaust the variousness of the background evidence.
3. 'Wulfstan's Prose', *PBA*, 35 (1949), 109–42.
4. 'Early Middle English Alliterative Verse', a lecture delivered in the Faculty of English, University of Cambridge, 1 February 1974.
5. 'Rhythmical Alliteration', *MP*, 67 (1969–70), 118–24 (p. 121).
6. Richard Maidstone, *Penitential Psalms*, Bodley MS Digby 102, fo. 131r. Compare the denser alliterative style of the anonymous paraphrase of Psalm 51 in BL MS Additional 31042 (Thornton MS), fo. 102r:

    > God þou haue mercy on mee
    > After thi mercy mekill of mayne
    > God þou haue mercy on me
    > And pourge my plyght with penaunce playne . . .

7. For the monasteries as the main agents of preservation and transmission of allitera-

tive texts, and as the main centres of fresh alliterative composition, see the important forthcoming article by D. A. Pearsall, 'The Origins of the Alliterative Revival' (lecture to the Conference on Alliterative Poetry held at Binghamton, NY, October 1975) [now published in *The Alliterative Tradition in the Fourteenth Century*, ed. B. S. Levy and P. E. Szarmach (Kent, Ohio, 1981), pp. 1–24].

8. See M. Görlach, *The Textual Tradition of the South English Legendary*, Leeds Texts and Monographs, n.s. 6 (1974), p. 45.

9. Quoted in extract VII in *Early Middle English Verse and Prose*, ed. J. A. W. Bennett and G. V. Smithers (Oxford, 1968), p. 104, lines 186–8.

10. *Ego Dormio*, ed. H. E. Allen, *English Writings of Richard Rolle* (Oxford, 1932), p. 64; punctuation from CUL MS Dd.v.64, fo. 246r.

11. Cf. McIntosh, on Aelfric's prose style in his *Lives of the Saints*: 'it reflects the basic alliterative structure of classical verse in a remarkable if idiosyncratic way...' ('Early Middle English Alliterative Verse', p. 4).

12. For Gaytryge's translation, see the edition of the two MSS by T. F. Simmons and H. E. Nolloth, EETS, OS 118 (1901), curiously entitled *The Lay Folks' Catechism*. See also *Religious Pieces in Prose and Verse*, ed. G. G. Perry, EETS, OS 26 (1889), which prints a text of the *Treatise* from the Lincoln Cathedral Library Thornton MS.

13. The recording of medieval English verse in a continuous format raises questions of manuscript convention only, and not those of literary genre. Trinity College, Cambridge, MS B.10.12 records Gaytryge's work by a mixed convention – beginning 'continuously' on fo. 56r, but switching to the long line at fo. 57v. Corpus Christi College, Oxford, MS 155 and BL MS Harley 1022 favour the long line. The text in Archbishop Thoresby's *Register* (Borthwick Institute of Historical Research, York, fos. 295r–297v) is written continuously, but the punctuation, which is the most significant guide, defines a line-by-line structure.

14. Gaytryge's *Treatise*, text with original manuscript punctuation, from Thoresby's *Register*, fo. 295, printed by Simmons and Nolloth, *Lay Folks' Catechism*, lines 12–17, 24–32.

15. For the later fifteenth-century developments of the Gaytryge *Treatise* see *Quattuor Sermones*, ed. N. F. Blake (Heidelberg, 1975), Introduction, pp. 12–15.

16. If we are convinced that the monasteries were the most important agents of preservation and transmission of an 'alliterative tradition', the status of Gaytryge, as Benedictine monk, is significant.

17. Quotations from *Piers Plowman* are, for the A- and B-texts, from the editions by G. Kane, *Piers Plowman: The A Version* (London, 1960), and by G. Kane and E. T. Donaldson, *Piers Plowman: The B Version* (London, 1975). For the C-text, the three-text edition by W. W. Skeat (Oxford, 1886) is used.

18. The opinion expressed by G. H. Russell, in 'Some Aspects of the Process of Revision in *Piers Plowman*' (*Piers Plowman: Critical Approaches*, ed. S. S. Hussey, London, 1969, 27–49), that the passage is 'demonstrably corrupt' (p. 29) seems to me to over-simplify the matter. His unfavourable comparison of the lines in question with the regularised version of the Ilchester manuscript rests upon the assumption that we are to accept a metrical norm for Langland's work similar, or identical to that proposed by Kane and Donaldson for their edition of *Piers Plowman: The B Version* (Introduction, pp. 130 ff.). Such an acceptance, with its corollary of extensive emendation on metrical grounds, will not be universally approved.

19. See E. Salter, '*Piers Plowman* and *The Simonie*', *Archiv*, 203 (1967), 241–54. (See above, pp. 158–69.)

20. It is not, for instance, totally clear why poems conventionally dated to the early

1350s, such as *William of Palerne* and *Winner and Waster*, should have given Langland the precedent he needed. In any case, the published evidence for the date of
Winner and Waster is by no means reliable; it would be perfectly possible to suggest
that the poem belongs to the next decade and is more nearly contemporary with, or
later than, the A-text of *Piers Plowman*. See my forthcoming study in *Medium Aevum*.
[See the essay following, here.]

21. See G. R. Cigman, 'An Edition of Sermons 1, 8, 9, 10 from British Library
Additional MS 41321' (unpublished B.Litt. diss., University of Oxford, 1968). The
sermons were briefly noticed in the *British Museum Quarterly*, 1 (1926), 49–51.

22. G. R. Owst's *Literature and Pulpit in Medieval England* (Cambridge, 1933) is full of
quotations from alliterative sermon-materials which differ only slightly from accre-
dited 'alliterative verse'. Worcester Cathedral MS F.10 would clearly repay further
study (Owst, p. 38). The *Jack Upland* texts, from the late fourteenth and early
fifteenth century, also deserve fresh scrutiny in this context: see *Jack Upland: Friar
Daw's Reply: Upland's Rejoinder*, ed. P. L. Heyworth (Oxford, 1968), which usefully
prints the materials, but is, in my opinion, mistakenly persuaded that they illustrate
the decay and debasement of a once regular and vigorous alliterative technique
(Introduction, p. 29).

23. Formerly Phillipps MS 1054, sold in the Harmsworth sale of October, 1945, lot
2135, as 'Meditations on the Passion of Christ'. In 1949 it was acquired by Michigan
State College.

24. For some account of the range of English translations, partial and complete, of the
Meditationes, see E. Salter, *Nicholas Love's 'Myrrour of the Blessed Lyf of Jesu Christ'*,
Analecta Cartusiana 10 (Salzburg, 1974).

8   The timeliness of *Wynnere and Wastoure*

1. *A Good Short Debate between Winner and Waster*, ed. I. Gollancz, Select Early English
Poems III (Oxford, 1930), Preface.

2. So J. M. Steadman, 'The Date of *Wynnere and Wastoure*', *MP*, 19 (1921), 211–19.
J. M. Anderson, 'A Note on the Date of *Winnere and Wastoure*', *MLN*, 43 (1928),
47–9; G. Stillwell, '*Wynnere and Wastoure* and the Hundred Years War', *ELH*, 8
(1941), 241–7; and D. Moran, '*Wynnere and Wastoure* – an Extended Footnote',
Neuphilologische Mitteilungen, 73 (1972), 683–5 confirm this area of dating, within a
year or so. T. H. Bestul, *Satire and Allegory in 'Wynnere and Wastoure'* (Nebraska,
1974), p. 1, n. 1, shows some uneasiness about Gollancz's dating, but does not
pursue the matter at length.

3. Steadman, 'The Date of *Wynnere*', p. 211.

4. In preparing this article, I have been helpfully advised by my colleagues R. B.
Dobson, D. A. Pearsall and M. G. A. Vale. And I acknowledge special debts of
gratitude to two past students of mine – Helen Houghton and Charles Kightley.

5. The first edition appeared in the appendix to his edition of *The Parlement of the Thre
Ages* (Roxburghe Club, 1897).

6. Hulbert, *MP*, 18 (1920), pp. 36, 37.

7. The probable reason was Hulbert's own recantation of his dating, expressed briefly
in a footnote to Steadman's article, 'The Date of *Wynnere*', p. 211, n. 4.

8. Moran, 'Extended Footnote', p. 683.

9. Bestul, *Satire and Allegory*, p. 23.

10. Steadman, 'The Date of *Wynnere*', p. 219.

11. Gollancz (ed.), *Winner and Waster*, Preface.
12. Ibid., Preface.
13. M. McKisack, *The Fourteenth Century* (Oxford, 1959), p. 257.
14. *Statutes of the Realm* (1810, repr. 1963), I, 320. It is worth recording that Gollancz, when quoting this passage as a footnote to line 130, omitted the central section, thereby destroying the point it was attempting to make.
15. 'Selonc la lei de la terre ancienement usee . . .' (ibid., I, 320).
16. See J. G. Bellamy, *The Law of Treason in England in the later Middle Ages* (Cambridge, 1970), pp. 74–5, 79 ff, and M. H. Keen, 'Treason Trials under the Law of Arms', *Transactions of the Royal Historical Society*, 12 (1961), 87 ff.
17. Ibid., p. 94.
18. Ibid., p. 48.
19. *Statutes of the Realm*, II, 20.
20. Ibid., II, 20.
21. *The Law of Treason*, pp. 136, 137.
22. *Wynnere and Wastoure*, lines 193–4.
23. Quoted from *Rotuli Parliamentorum*, II, 236–7, by B. Putnam, *The Place in Legal History of Sir William Shareshull* (Cambridge, 1950), p. 147.
24. See *MED* under 'distourbaunce', 2a, 5c; 'distourben', 3b; 'distourbinge', 1c; 'distourbler'.
25. *The Law of Treason*, p. 86.
26. See, for instance, in *The Law of Treason*, p. 93, examples of Shareshull's rulings which firmly distinguished cases before him as felony, not treason.
27. A possibility which recommended itself strongly to Gollancz, and which has found support from most subsequent commentators, including B. H. Putnam in her study of Sir William Shareshull, *Place in Legal History*, pp. 146–7.
28. *Wynnere and Wastoure*, lines 375, 388.
29. Putnam, *Place in Legal History*, p. 147.
30. Ibid., pp. 147–8.
31. Ibid., p. 146.
32. *The Law of Treason*, p. 87.
33. Putnam, *Place in Legal History*, p. 148.
34. It has never been noted in this context that Sir William Shareshull's grandson, of the same name, was Sheriff of Staffordshire, was knighted in 1399, and died in 1400, without issue. See W. A. Shaw, *The Knights of England* (London, 1906), II, 11.
35. Putnam, *Place in Legal History*, p. 156.
36. Ed. M. Day and R. Steele, EETS, OS 199 (1936). I am indebted in this section of the argument to John Scattergood, whose critical comment first compelled me to recognise the complexity of the situation and then assisted me in its presentation.
37. The use of a numeral below ten in combination with 'twenty' to express numerical concepts of both exact and inexact nature is well-illustrated by the *OED* entry 'twenty', A.1.b. In some cases it is only equivalent to 'many': see, for instance, as a contrast to the quotation from *Mum and the Sothsegger*, lines 78–9, 'Robyn dwelled in grene wode Twenty yere and two' from stanza 450 of *A Gest of Robin Hood* (c. 1400), ed. R. B. Dobson and J. Taylor (London, 1976), p. 111. See also *The Book of the Duchess*, lines 454–5, where (if the MS reading is correct) 'of the age of foure and twenty yer' is used to give the general sense of 'ryght yong therto': at the time of his wife's death, John of Gaunt was, in fact, twenty-nine.
38. See R. H. Robbins, *Historical Poems of the XIVth and XVth Centuries* (New York, 1959), pp. 54 and 273.

39. *Piers Plowman: the B Version*, ed. G. Kane and E. T. Donaldson (London, 1975), XIII 270, 264.
40. Gollancz (ed.), *Winner and Waster*, Preface, and note to lines 461–5: this identification was accepted by Steadman, 'The Date of *Wynnere*', p. 213.
41. See B. Guillemain, *La Cour Pontificale D'Avignon, 1309–76* (Paris, 1962), pp. 137–40.
42. *The Simonie*, printed by T. Wright, *The Political Songs of England*, Camden Society, 6 (1839). It is perhaps worth recording that Wright did, in fact, attempt a dating of this poem by its 'historical' evidence: see p. 399 of his *Political Songs*.
43. *Boutell's Heraldry*, revised by C. W. Scott-Giles and T. P. Brooke-Little (London, 1950), p. 206, plate V.
44. Gollancz, note to lines 70–1. The office of Garter King of Arms is not recorded until 1417: no doubt, however, some kind of herald officiated at Garter feasts and ceremonies before that date. See Sir Nicholas Harris Nicolas 'Observations on the Institution of the Most Noble Order of the Garter', *Archaeologia*, 31 (1846), p. 138, where payment to 'William Valaunt, King of the Heralds... of the King's gift, for his good services at the Feast of St. George' (1358) is recorded.
45. This entirely convincing restoration of the MS reading was proposed by Basil Cottle, who supported the original line by reference to *Piers Plowman* B XI 235, 'Cleophas ne knew hym noȝt þat he crist were', and to the *Parlement of the Thre Ages*, ed. M. Y. Offord, EETS, OS 246 (1959), line 501, 'And what selcouth he se þe soth he shuld telle'.
46. See Plate VII in W. H. St John Hope, *The Atchievements of Edward, Prince of Wales... in the Cathedral Church of Canterbury, Vetusta Monumenta* (1895), VII, pt 2.
47. Ibid., pp. 207–8, plate XXVII. For a detailed account of the evidence which shows that Richard's public assumption of the new armorial device in 1397–8 was preceded by its use for special purposes between 1394 and 1396, see M. V. Clarke, 'The Wilton Diptych', in *Fourteenth Century Studies*, ed. L. S. Sutherland and M. McKisack (Oxford, 1937), pp. 274–6.
48. *Boutell's Heraldry*, p. 207.
49. See Gollancz's notes to lines 90 and 100. It is worth noting that the Chaplain to King John of France, Gace de le Buigne, who began his *Roman des Deduis* 'a Heldefort en Engleterre l'an mil CCCLIX', during the King's captivity in England, makes special mention, at the conclusion of this poem which debates the rival merits of hunting with 'chiens et oiseaux', of 'Eddouart / Le Roy angloiz qui bien scet l'art / Des Deduis...'. The poem also makes clear, however, that lines 99–100 of *Wynnere and Wastoure*, which appear to refer personally to the English King's known pleasure in riverside falconry, are entirely conventional. See *Le Roman des Deduis*, ed. A. Blomqvist (Karlshamn, 1951), lines 12163–5, 6058–63, 6311–14.
50. MS Cotton Nero D.vi, fos. 4 and 31: the date of the MS, which is a Statute Book, is after 1386.
51. He refers to Joseph Strutt, *Regal and Ecclesiastical Antiquities of England*, ed. J. R. Planché (London, 1842), which may well have misled him.
52. (ed.), *Winner and Waster*, notes to lines 117–18.
53. See J. Nichols, *A Collection of all of the Wills of the Kings and Queens of England* (London, 1780), p. 68.
54. Ibid., pp. 68, 71. The article by Sir Nicholas Harris Nicolas, 'Observations on the Origin and History of the Badge and Mottoes of Edward Prince of Wales', *Archaeologia*, 31 (1846), pp. 350 ff., gives a useful résumé of evidence which can, however, be supplemented by later research.

55. *Treatises of Fistula in Ano* by John Arderne, ed. D'Arcy Power, EETS, OS 139 (1910), p. xxvii, n. 1. For Arderne, see *DNB*, I, 548–9, and *Forewords* to D'Arcy Power's edition, pp. xff.
56. Ibid., p. xxvii, n. 1.
57. If we are content to abandon the effort to place the description accurately, by heraldic reference, it may be relevant that there is some evidence for an alternation between 'fetheres / pennys / wynges' as a late fourteenth-century translation of the Vulgate *pennae*, meaning 'wings'. See *OED* 'pen', sb.², I.l.b. The traditional dating of *Wynnere and Wastoure* in the 1350s would not readily associate it with such usages, of course, which are found in the Wicliffite Biblical Versions.
58. See *MED* 'kinde' 4(c). The later heraldic term for 'in natural colour' is 'proper', which dates only from the sixteenth century: see *OED* 'proper', 3. Comparable terms recorded from the thirteenth and fourteenth centuries seem to have been 'tout plain', 'tout pur', meaning 'of single colour or tincture': see G. J. Brault, *Early Blazon* (Oxford, 1972), p. 283.
59. See *Boutell's Heraldry*, p. 77, fig. 196, and Harris Nicolas (see n. 54), p. 357.
60. *Boutell's Heraldry*, p. 165 and Harris Nicolas, p. 371.
61. See Harris Nicolas, p. 363.
62. Ibid., pp. 361–2.
63. See D'Arcy Power, *Treatises*, p. xxvii, n. 1, and *DNB*, VI, 510. The MS in question is BL Sloane 56, fos. 70 and 74: the ostrich-feather occurs as a marginal device, closely associated with the description of the origin of the Black Prince's 'badge for peace'. It also occurs in similar position in another fourteenth-century MS copy of Arderne's treatise – Sloane 335, fo. 68. The marginal drawings in MS Sloane 56 are extremely interesting: on fo. 71 occurs a helmet, surmounted by a lion rampant, and on fo. 73v, a shield with charge of three birds.
64. See Harris Nicolas, p. 354.
65. Ibid., p. 363.
66. Ibid., pp. 365–6: see also *Boutell's Heraldry*, p. 165 and A. C. Fox-Davies, *Heraldic Badges* (London, 1907), p. 47.
67. *Boutell's Heraldry*, p. 165, Fox-Davies, *Heraldic Badges*, p. 47.
68. *Boutell's Heraldry*, pp. 121, 165.
69. We should, in any case, attend to the literary tradition within which the poet of *Wynnere and Wastoure* may have been writing – a tradition probably as much French and Anglo-French as English. For the importance of 'heraldic identification' in French poetry of the thirteenth and fourteenth centuries, see A. R. Wagner, *Heralds and Heraldry* (London, 1956), Chap. VI, and Appendix B: 'the blazon of a knight's arms comes to be an integral and almost necessary part of the description, with which he is brought on the scene' (p. 46).
70. See Wagner, *Heralds and Heraldry*, Chap. IV, 'The Rise of the Heralds'.
71. Apart from the Wingfield family discussed in this article, the Fitzpaynes also bore a charge of 'silver a pair of wings gules'. See *The Ancestor*, 7 (1903), p. 215.
72. Cited in E. Burke, *The General Armory of England, Scotland, Ireland and Wales* (London, 1884), p. 1123.
73. Documentation for this is usefully provided by E. L. T. John, *The Parliamentary Representation of Norfolk and Suffolk* (unpublished thesis, University of Nottingham, November 1959). See also below pp. 195–8.
74. T. F. Tout, *Chapters in the Administrative History of Mediaeval England*, 6 vols. (Manchester, 1920), V, 386–91.

75. See T. Rymer, *Foedera*, 4 vols. (London, 1816–69), III, i, 504; II, ii, 1048; III, i, 326, 443, 482, 504. And see also the *Register of Edward the Black Prince*, 5 vols. (1930–3), vol. IV (1351–65) passim.

76. See N. Harris Nicolas, *The Controversy between Sir Richard Scrope and Sir Robert Grosvenor* (1832), I, 173–4, II, 396–7.

77. See Burke, *General Armory*, p. 1123.

78. See Viscount Powerscourt, *The Ancient Saxon Family of Wingfield* (1894), pp. 13–14, and plate facing p. 24: W. Page, *The Victoria County History of Suffolk* (1907), II, 152.

79. The brass is still to be seen in Letheringham Church, 'fastened to a board on the north wall'. See J. Blatchly, 'The Lost and Mutilated Memorials of the Bovile and Wingfield Families of Letheringham', *Suffolk Institute of Archaeology*, 33 (1975), 181. For an engraving, see J. S. Cotman, *Engravings of Sepulchral Brasses in Suffolk* (London, 1838), p. 6, and plate. Richard Gough, in *Sepulchral Monuments in Great Britain*, 2 vols. (London, 1786–96), II,i,218, gives an account of two Wingfield tombs of the fourteenth and fifteenth centuries, at Letheringham Church, Suffolk, abundantly ornamented with the Wingfield arms.

80. See *Boutell's Heraldry*, pp. 74 ff.

81. The appearance of wings in some of the varieties of the eagle blazons, for instance, 'wings elevated and displayed', 'wings elevated and addorsed', may be in the poet's mind. See *Boutell's Heraldry*, p. 75. The Wingfield wings, conjoined, were considered suitable for the sculptured ornamentation of the canopied Wingfield tombs at Letheringham. See Gough, *Sepulchral Monuments*, II, i, 218, and Blatchly, 'Lost and Mutilated Memorials', pp. 183–4.

82. See *MED* 'kynde', 4(c), *Book of Arms*, 1456.

83. For this heraldic distinction, see *Boutell's Heraldry*, p. 65.

84. By John Ferne (1586). I am very grateful to Helen Houghton for drawing my attention to this treatise.

85. *The Blazon of Gentrie*, p. 192.

86. Ibid., p. 233.

87. *OED* 'umbego', Vb. obs., *Laud Troy Book* 9468, 'courbel, beme and euery a ston / With riche gold was vmbegon' and MS Bodley 423, fo. 186b, 'A weddynge cote … vmbigoon with diuersitees of uertus'.

88. Thus, where *Sir Gawain and the Green Knight* line 189 has 'folden in with fildore', *Ywaine and Gawaine* line 2967 has 'wirkand silk and gold wir'. And the *OED* for 'wyre', sb., I.i.(a) records *Cath. Angl.* 161/2, 'gold wyre, filum Aureum'. I would only tentatively, at this stage, and without extensive study of the Thornton MS suggest that the original reading of the line may have been 'vmbegon with golde wyre'. But compare *Sir Gawain* line 189 above, and *Laud Troy Book* line 9468, 'with riche gold was vmbegon'.

89. Both interpretations gain support from the analysis of medieval methods of fabricating the individual charges and the subsequent fixing of them upon the jupon. Such a convenient analysis can be found in W. H. St John Hope (n. 46 above), p. 5, where first the embroidery of leopards and fleurs-de-lys 'upon velvet *with gold thread*' is described, and then their application to the quarters already in place upon the jupon. It is also interesting to note that the same writer stresses that the seams of the jupon were '*covered with gold cord*' (my italics). Plates VIII and IX of the study illustrate clearly the way in which gold thread or cord was used both to outline designs and to conceal joins in the material.

90. See *OED*, 'Yes' 3(a) and *A Concordance to the Complete Works of Geoffrey Chaucer* by

J. S. P. Tatlock and A. G. Kennedy (1927; repr. Gloucester, Mass., 1963), 'Yes', p. 1106.

91. Gollancz (ed.), *Winner and Waster*, note to line 108. The MS in question is BL Add. 31042, one of the famous 'Thornton Miscellanies', probably written between 1422 and 1460, for the private use of the Thornton family of East Newton, in Yorkshire.

92. It is significant, also, that the only instance of the 'ser' form noted by the *OED* for the period before 1500 is the past tense 'serd', from Henry's *Wallace*: *OED* 'serue', vb. 20(c). The same text records 'serff' for the present plural form: *OED* 'serue', vb. 8.

93. See *Elvin's Handbook of Mottoes*, rev. R. Pinches (London, 1971), pp. 49, 229.

94. *Piers Plowman* B XIII 265–71.

95. The death of Sir William Shareshull, in 1370, might still be regarded as an ultimate date for the poem's composition: as we have seen, however, the conditions under which the reference to his name might have been perpetuated, in the west-country especially, are by no means clear to us.

96. This is effectively demonstrated in the unpublished doctoral dissertation by S. Cain Van D'Elden, 'Peter Suchenwirt and Heraldic Poetry' (University of Minnesota, 1974). G. J. Brault's article 'Arthurian Heraldry and the Date of *Escanor*' (*Bulletin Bibliographique*, 11, 1959, 81–8) underlines the importance of faithful description to the 'heraldic flattery' of poems intended for noble patrons – in the case of *Escanor*, such a patron was the wife of Edward I, Eleanor of Castile.

97. The Stanley arms are represented, in *Scotish Feilde*, as embroidered upon jupons; see lines 230–2: 'euery bearne had on his brest brodered full fayre / a foote of the fayrest fowle that euer flew on winge / with three crownes full cleare all of pure gold...' (ed. J. P. Oakden, *Remains Historical and Literary connected with the Palatine Counties of Lancaster and Chester*, Chetham Society, n.s. 94 (Manchester, 1935).

98. See Tout, *Chapters*, V, 387, n. 6, and the Wingfield genealogy printed by Powerscourt, *The Ancient Saxon Family of Wingfield*. The Wingfields also began to acquire land in the Midland counties of Rutland, Berkshire and Northamptonshire as early as the fourteenth century. See below, p. 197.

99. See Blatchly, 'Lost and Mutilated Memorials', pp. 181–2.

100. See for instance, Tout, *Chapters*, IV, 202, V, 389. For suggestions as to the possible literary implications of the make-up of the households see J. R. L. Highfield, 'The Green Squire', *Medium Aevum*, 22 (1953), 18–23 and E. Salter, 'The Alliterative Revival', *MP* 64 (1966–7), 146–50, 223–7. (See above, pp. 101–10.)

101. Poems of strongly northern character, such as the *Four Foes of Mankind*, from the Auchinleck manuscript (National Library of Scotland MS 19.2.1. fo. 303), come to mind. See Carleton Brown, *Religious Lyrics of the Fourteenth Century* (Oxford, 1924, repr. 1970), pp. 32–5. In the absence of a published study of the language of *Wynnere and Wastoure*, it is worth recording that it shares some of its more unusual vocabulary with texts as widely-spaced from a regional point of view as *Sir Gawain and the Green Knight*, the *Ormulum* and the Chaucerian translation of the *Roman de la Rose*.

102. See G. F. Beltz, *Memorials of the Most Noble Order of the Garter* (London, 1841), pp. 77–8, 390, and H. J. Hewitt, *The Black Prince's Expedition of 1355–57* (Manchester, 1958), pp. 78–81.

103. See PRO documents, MBE, TR E 36/278 fo. 124, 'en sa chambre en son hostel en loundres ... le dit S' J' estoit en son lit', and E 36/279 fo. 164, 'en sa chambre denz son hostel a londs' devant la chamyne'.

104. See Powerscourt, *The Ancient Saxon Family*, pp. 13–14.

105. See E. L. T. John, *Parliamentary Representation*, p. 683.

106. See Sir W. H. St John Hope, *Stall Plates of the Knights of the Order of the Garter* (London, 1901), plate 50: the arms of Sir William de la Pole, Duke of Suffolk, KG, grandson of Michael de la Pole and Katherine Wingfield.

107. The literary interests of a later de la Pole, William, Duke of Suffolk, friend and 'jailer' of the poet Charles d'Orléans (at Wingfield, among other places), are well-known. Grandson of Michael de la Pole, his wife granddaughter of Geoffrey Chaucer, he was himself heir to the estates of William Wingfield, Lord of the Manor of Dennington (d. 1418).

108. Founded by the Boviles in the twelfth century; see the *Victoria County History of Suffolk*, ed. W. Page (1907), II, 108, and Blatchly, 'Lost and Mutilated Memorials', p. 168.

109. He was, for instance, involved with the Warennes as early as 1347, when he was made Keeper of the lands of John Warenne, late Earl of Surrey, See John (n. 73 above), p. 675.

110. The will is now housed in the Norfolk Record Office at Norwich (Heydon 154).

111. For Campsey and its history, see *VCH Suffolk*, II, 112–15.

112. I am greatly indebted to Lena Andrew for providing me with a precise transcript of Sir Thomas's will.

113. Sir William Hoo was Captain of Oye Castle in the Calais March: deprived of his post by the Appellants, in 1388, for his support of Richard II's party, he went on pilgrimage to Jerusalem. See J. J. H. Palmer, *England, France and Christendom, 1377–99* (London, 1972), p. 111.

114. See G. Kane, *Piers Plowman: the A-Version* (London, 1960), pp. 6–7. The MS in question is BL Harley 6041.

115. See E. Seaton, *Sir Richard Roos* (London, 1961), pp. 84–5. In addition to drawing my attention to this Wingfield connection with MS Fairfax 16, John Scattergood has pointed out Wingfield ownership of several other important later medieval MSS: Egerton 2733 (*Charters* relating to Peterborough Abbey), owned by Sir Robert Wingfield in 1636; Pierpont Morgan Library, M. 815 (*Hours*, illuminated in Paris for Henry VII), owned by Sir Robert Wingfield during the sixteenth century; New York Public Library, Spencer Collection 3 (*Hours* and *Psalter* – a composite MS of which part II, the *Psalter*, was originally written and illuminated for Lady Anne Neville, Duchess of Buckingham), owned by Sir Richard Wingfield, KG, soldier and diplomat, and descendant of Sir Thomas Wingfield, of Letheringham, about 1520. For this last manuscript, see H. M. Nixon, 'French Bookbindings for Sir Richard Wingfield and Jean Grolier', *Gatherings in Honor of Dorothy E. Miner* (Baltimore, 1974), pp. 301–5. A. I. Doyle notes that the arms of Sir John Wingfield (great-great-grandson of Sir Thomas Wingfield) and of Elizabeth his wife occur in Trinity College, Dublin, MS 93 (*Psalter* and *Hymns*) and that the *ex libris* of Dame Anne Wingfield, their daughter-in-law, is to be found in MS Harley 4012, an English Miscellany written about 1460. This is probably the same 'Dame . . . Wyngefelde' who borrowed John Paston's 'Boke of Troylus', after 1474: see *The Paston Letters*, ed. J. Gairdner (1872–5), no. 869, and 'A Middle English Manuscript at Coughton Court, Warwickshire and British Library MS. Harley 4012' by E. Wilson, *Notes and Queries*, 222 (1977), 299–303.

116. Hunterian MS V.2.8. contains the only copy of the alliterative *Destruction of Troy*, copied by Thomas Chetham, bailiff of Thomas Stanley, Earl of Derby, in the early sixteenth century: *Scotish Feilde* (c. 1516) extols the exploits of the Stanleys at the battle of Flodden. See C. A. Luttrell, 'Three North-West Midland Manuscripts', *Neophilologus*, 42 (1958), 38–50.

117. Robert Thornton, the probable scribe and collector of the 'Thornton manuscript' in which *Wynnere and Wastoure* is uniquely recorded, was a minor Yorkshire landowner, who was dead by 1465. He seems to have gathered many of his materials from the north midlands, and it would be interesting to pursue the relationship between what Angus McIntosh tentatively regards as the 'dialect' area of the surviving text of *Wynnere and Wastoure* (central Nottinghamshire) and the fifteenth-century spread of the Wingfield estates.

118. See John, *Parliamentary Representation*, pp. 682–700.

119. See N. Harris Nicolas, *Controversy*, I, 174, II, 397.

120. See Gwyn A. Williams, *Medieval London* (London, 1963), p. 140.

121. See A. H. Thomas, *Calendar of Select Pleas and Memoranda of the City of London* (Cambridge, 1932), p. 11.

122. The will is housed in the Norfolk Record Office, at Norwich (Harsyk 249, 255): Lena Andrew assures me that, when complete, it must have been of great length.

123. Ed. M. K. Pope, E. C. Lodge (Oxford, 1910, repr. 1974) and D. B. Tyson (Tübingen, 1975). Compare *Vie*, lines 1–24 with *W.W.*, lines 20–30.

124. See Francisque-Michel, *Le Prince Noir* (1883), Introduction, pp. x–xi and pp. 296–8.

125. See J. I. Wimsatt, *Chaucer and the French Love Poets* (Chapel Hill, 1968; repr. 1972), pp. 65–9: see also the interesting evidence of MS 9411–26, of the Bibliothèque Royale, Brussels, which has the names 'Herford, Holand, Cliffort, Stury' on fo. 1v. See A. Scheler, *Dits et Contes de Baudouin de Condé et de son Fils, Jean de Condé* (Brussels, 1866), II, xiii–xiv.

126. Scheler, *Dits et Contes*, II, 377, lines 190–4.

127. See Francisque-Michel (see n. 124) and Tyson, *Vie du Prince Noir*, p. 33: for the relevant passage in the *Chroniques* of Froissart, see the edition by S. Luce, G. Raynaud (Paris 1869–99), II, 265.

128. Froissart's position as poet and 'official historian' in Queen Philippa's household, as early as 1361, is well-attested: he travelled with the Black Prince to Bordeaux in 1366 and 1367. Sir John Wingfield and Sir John Chandos were closely associated with each other and with their lord, the Black Prince (Hewitt, *Black Prince's Expedition*, pp. 80–1): it is interesting to find in the *Register*, IV, 167, a record of a payment made in 1355, 'on the information of Sir John de Wengefeld', of 55s. 10d. 'as a gift from the Prince to Hanneray, herald-of-arms who came from beyond the seas in the company of Sir John Chaundos'. This may be the first mention of the poet of the *Vie . . . du Prince Noir*.

9   *A Complaint against Blacksmiths*

1. See N. R. Ker, 'Medieval Manuscripts from Norwich Cathedral Priory', *Transactions of the Cambridge Bibliographical Society* (1949–53), part I, pp. 11, 18, and A. McIntosh, 'The Language of the Extant Versions of *Havelok the Dane*', *Medium Aevum*, 45 (1976), pp. 40–1, notes 10 and 11.

2. The text is here reproduced for the first time in its original manuscript format, since in important ways its mode of presentation may prove to be part of its total history. The adoption of a 'continuous' format for the *Complaint* is unusual in the context of the recording of Middle English alliterative verse; it is more often the rule for freer kinds of alliterative composition, embedded within prose literature (see E. Salter, 'Alliterative Modes and Affiliations', *Neuphilologische Mitteilungen*, 79, 1978, 25–35, and above, pp. 170–9). The manuscript punctuation, which will form the subject of

a separate study, makes use of the point in medial positions: three other signs are employed, without discrimination, to mark-out a long alliterative line-unit.

3. Above '& spellyn many spelles', in a paler ink but in the same hand, occur the words 'ech of hem at othyrs'. If, as Basil Cottle has pointed out to me, this is a reminiscence of line 14 of Chaucer's *Pardoner's Tale*, 'And ech of hem at otheres sinne lough', we have added reason for dating the composition of the *Complaint* in the later, not the earlier, fourteenth century. See p. 204, and note 8 below.

4. All previous printed versions of the *Complaint* have accepted 'cloþe merys' (mare-clothiers), as the proper reading here. The manuscript distinctly reads 'cloye merys' (mare-lamers); see B. Colgrave, *MLR*, 48 (1953), p. 51.

5. First printed in *Reliquiae Antiquae* (ed. T. Wright and J. O. Halliwell, 2 vols., London, 1841–3), I, 240, it has been chiefly edited by K. Sisam, in *Fourteenth Century Verse and Prose* (Oxford, 1921; repr. 1948 etc.), pp. 169–70, and by R. H. Robbins, *Secular Lyrics of the XIV and XV Centuries* (Oxford, 1952; repr. 1961), pp. 106–7; it appears in a modernised form in A. R. Myers, *English Historical Documents, 1327–1485* (London, 1969), p. 1055, no. 612.

6. See, for instance, J. P. Oakden, *Alliterative Poetry in Middle English: A Survey of the Traditions* (Manchester, 1935; repr. 1968), p. 12: Robbins, *Secular Lyrics*, p. 265.

7. Oakden, *Alliterative Poetry*, pp. 10, 14. And see also G. G. Coulton, *Chaucer and his England* (London, 1950), p. 101; J. A. W. Bennett, *Chaucer at Oxford and Cambridge* (Oxford, 1974), p. 41.

8. The view of J. P. Oakden, in *Alliterative Poetry in Middle English: The Dialectal and Metrical Survey* (Manchester, 1930, repr. 1968), p. 45, that 1300–25 is a possible date of composition, has never been conclusively rejected: on the other hand F. R. H. Du Boulay, in *An Age of Ambition* (London, 1970), p. 49, assumes that we have here a 'fifteenth century poet'.

9. F. Cairns, *Generic Composition in Greek and Latin Poetry* (Edinburgh, 1972), p. 7.

10. See F. L. Utley, *Speculum*, 21 (1946), pp. 194 ff.

11. Vernacular poems such as 'The Schoolboy's Wish', found in Lincoln Cathedral MS 132, between two grammatical treatises by John of Garland, point emphatically towards the orthodox and self-critical impetus of these compositions. See Robbins, *Secular Lyrics*, p. 105.

12. Du Boulay, *Age of Ambition*, p. 49.

13. *The Miller's Tale*, ed. F. N. Robinson, *The Poetical Works of Chaucer* (Cambridge, Mass., 1957), lines 3731, 3760 ff.

14. See E. P. Kuhl, 'Daun Gerveys', *MLN* 29 (1914), p. 156.

15. See, for instance, John Harvey, *Medieval Craftsmen* (London, 1975), p. 58, confirming L. F. Saltzman, *English Industries of the Middle Ages* (Oxford, 1923), p. 318, as against Kuhl, 'Daun Gerveys', p. 156.

16. See Stith Thompson, 'The Miller's Tale', in *Sources and Analogues of Chaucer's Canterbury Tales*, ed. W. F. Bryan and Germaine Dempster (London, 1941), pp. 106 ff.

17. S. L. Thrupp, *The Merchant Class of Medieval London* (Ann Arbor, 1962), p. 98.

18. This conclusion might be drawn from a number of references to special dispensations for night-work in the metal trades; in 1387, the Spurriers and Lorimers of York were forbidden 'night-work and Sunday work except for travellers and when the King is in the North' (*York Memorandum Book*, Part I (1376–1419), ed. M. Sellers, Surtees Society, 1912). In the preceding century (1243), similar allowances were made to Carpenters at Windsor for wainscoting 'by day and night' so that a special chamber should be ready 'by Friday, when the King shall come there'. (See D.

Knoop, G. P. Jones, *The Medieval Mason*, Manchester, 1933; rev. 1967, p. 15. And for fifteenth-century instances, ibid., p. 108.) Harvey, *Medieval Craftsmen*, pp. 59–60, cites the Chamberlain's Accounts of Norwich Cathedral Priory, which record the purchase of candles for late work by Carpenters, in 1304–5, and 1321–2. A more recent attempt to curb night and Sunday work in a Yorkshire blacksmith's forge is recorded in the *Whitby Gazette* for 28 August 1978; exception was allowed for 'the business of a farrier' only.

19. *Munimenta Guildhallae Londoniensis*, ed. H. T. Riley, 3 vols., Rolls Series, 12 (1860), II, pt I, p. 78.
20. Ibid., p. 81.
21. Gwyn A. Williams, *Medieval London* (London, 1963), p. 265.
22. *Calendar of Early Mayor's Court Rolls, AD 1208–1307*, ed. A. H. Thomas (Cambridge, 1924), p. 33.
23. Ibid., p. 34.
24. Williams, *Medieval London*, p. 265.
25. *Annales Monastici*, ed. H. R. Luard, Rolls Series 36 (1866), III, 203–4: 'apud Notingham . . . propter fumum carbonum maris nullo modo potuit demorari.'
26. See H. Riley, *Memorials of London and London Life* (London, 1868), p. 226. See also pp. 218–19, 241–4, 239, for similar statements from the Cutlers, the Pewterers and the Hatters.
27. Riley, *Memorials*, pp. 226–7.
28. Ibid., p. 537.
29. Ibid., pp. 537–8.
30. A restriction which was sought by many other Crafts, as appears in their *Ordinances*: see L. F. Saltzman, *English Industries*, pp. 321 ff., G. Unwin, *The Gilds and Companies of London* (London, 1908), p. 89, and Harvey, *Medieval Craftsmen*, p. 60.
31. Unwin, *Gilds*, p. 169.
32. See note 3 above, and pp. 200–3.
33. Knoop and Jones, *The Medieval Mason*, p. 157.
34. M. M. Postan, *The Medieval Economy and Society* (London, 1975), p. 25.
35. See *The Cambridge Economic History of Europe*, ed. M. M. Postan (Cambridge, 1963), III, 275.
36. See Jacques Le Goff, 'Le temps du travail dans la "crise" du xiv siècle: du temps médiéval au temps moderne', *Le Moyen Age*, 69 (1963), 600–1, in which he deals with the same situation in Paris in the earlier fourteenth century: 'un premier expédient cherché par les ouvriers pour pallier la crise des salaires . . .' See also S. L. Thrupp, 'Medieval Industry', *The Fontana Economic History of Europe*, ed. C. M. Cipolla (London, 1972), pp. 252–3.
37. *The Pardoner's Tale*, lines 470, 480, 481.
38. This is established by the sixth century: see, for instance, the Apocryphal *Acts of Thomas*, ed. M. R. James, *The Apocryphal New Testament* (Oxford, 1924, 1972), pp. 390, 394.
39. Ed. C. Selmer (Notre Dame, Ind., 1959), Chapter 23. This episode of the 'island of blacksmiths' is clearly based upon a conflation of passages in the *Aeneid*, Books III and VIII, which represent different aspects of the legend of the Cyclopes. The meeting of Aeneas with Polyphemus and the Cyclopes, on the island of Sicily (III, 588 ff.), emphasises the Homeric tradition of the Cyclopes as a race of savage one-eyed giants: the description of Vulcan supervising the making of a shield for Aeneas by the Cyclopes (VIII, 416 ff.) emphasises their later role as servants of the God, forgers of the thunderbolt. The conflation was probably crucial to the develop-

ment of literature and folk-lore concerning the smith in the Middle Ages; the *Navigatio* acted here as an important channel of transmission, as well as an agent of transformation for classical materials. It is not impossible, for instance, that the author of the *Complaint* knew the partially alliterative English version of the *Navigatio*, with its 'swart and brenninde' blacksmiths, in the *South English Legendary* (ed. C. Horstmann, EETS, OS 87, 1881, lines 470–97). The West-Norfolk MS, Laud Misc. 108, contains a text of the *Legendary*.

40. For examples of and references to literary treatments of this in French and English, see F. A. Foster, *The Northern Passion*, EETS, OS 145 (1913), pp. 168–73, and *The Northern Passion*, EETS, OS 147 (1916), pp. 64–5, 119–20, and note, p. 190. To this should be added E. Norris, *The Ancient Cornish Drama* (Oxford, 1959), I, 433 ff. Representations in fourteenth-century art range from the delicate productions of the French Pucelle school of manuscript painting to cruder but vigorous English work: see fo. 70v of the *Hours* of Yolande of Flanders, c. 1353, reproduced K. Morand, *Jean Pucelle* (Oxford, 1962), pl. xxa and *The Holkham Bible Picture Book*, c. 1330, ed. W. O. Hassall (London, 1954), fo. 31.

41. See, for instance, lines 3897–8 in *Le Pèlerinage de la Vie Humaine*, ed. J. J. Stürzinger, Roxburghe Club (1893). And the commentary on the typology in F. P. Pickering, *Literature and Art in the Middle Ages* (London, 1970), pp. 271–3, and pl. 27a.

42. See Aethelwulf, *De Abbatibus*, ed. A. Campbell (Oxford, 1967), Chap. X, 'De Fratre Cuicuino ferrario', lines 278–81.

43. *Chronicon Abbatiae de Evesham*, ed. W. D. Macray, Rolls series 29 (1868), p. 26.

44. Le Goff, 'Le temps du travail', p. 599.

45. *York Plays*, ed. L. T. Smith (1885; repr. New York, 1963), 'The Creation and the Fall of Lucifer', lines 153–6.

46. Le Goff, 'Le temps du travail', p. 599.

47. Ibid., p. 599.

48. British Library MS Roy. 17. A.1, edited by D. Knoop, G. P. Jones, D. Hamer, *The Two Earliest Masonic Manuscripts* (Manchester, 1938), pp. 116–18. The work, which has Gloucestershire connections, was probably composed in the last quarter of the fourteenth century. To this should be added the interesting rhymed *Debate of the Carpenter's Tools* – a later fourteenth-century dialogue, in which the shortcomings of the artisan and his implements are dramatised. Here, it is the reluctant tool which urges against long hours: 'Mayster, wyrke not oute off sesone, / The day is vary long of reson'. Ed. J. O. Halliwell, *Nugae Poeticae* (London, 1844), pp. 13–20.

49. McIntosh, 'The Language of the Extant Versions of *Havelok the Dane*', p. 48, n. 11. Professor McIntosh writes to me that 'there is nothing that would rule out a provenance from a little south-west of King's Lynn.'

50. 'Roberti Brennewater', *Calendar of Close Rolls of the Reign of Henry III, 1251–3* (London, 1927), p. 217. The document concerns property in Caxton, a parish eleven miles west of Cambridge. East Anglia seems to have been particularly rich in surnames (deriving from nick-names) which refer to occupations in a humorous or derisive manner: see Bo Seltén, *Early East-Anglian Nicknames*, 3, Scripta Minora Regiae Societatis Humaniorum Litterarum Lundensis, 1974–5 (Lund, 1975), pp. 57–8, who cites 'Rotenhering' and 'Surale' as examples.

51. See *Pilgrimage*, ed. F. J. Furnivall, EETS, ES 77, 83 (1899, 1901), lines 15820 ff., where the subject is smith's equipment possessed by the allegorical figure, Tribulation – 'forgeresse' of Paradisal crowns: 'A barmfell off a smyth / At hyr brest she hadde vp-bounde...' (line 15828). It is also interesting that the term 'swarte', which sets the tone of the alliterative piece, and which has a limited range of usage in

Middle English, is used twice by Lydgate for his description of the smith Vulcan: in his translation of *Les Echecs Amoureux*, line 3791, 'his smotry, swarte face' (see *Reason and Sensuality*, ed. E. Sieper, EETS, ES 84, 1901); and his *Troy Book*, II, 5803 (ed. H. Bergen, EETS, ES 97, 1906).

52. See *MED*, II, 27, which cites East-Anglian texts such as the fifteenth-century *Promptorium Parvulorum*, John Metham's treatise on *Physiognomy*, and *Palladius on Husbandry*. In the form 'kamus', the term is used by Chaucer for his description of the Miller's daughter of Trumpington, near Cambridge. We might find some special East-Anglian significance in this (the Reeve himself comes from Norfolk) were it not that it also occurs in Gower's *Confessio Amantis*, V, 2479.

53. See *MED*, IV, 180, which cites fifteenth-century usage in Capgrave's *Life of St Gilbert* and in the *Promptorium Parvulorum*.

54. Oakden, *Alliterative Poetry: the Dialectal and Metrical Survey* (see note 8), p. 150.

55. 'Kongon' ('conjon', *MED*, II, 515) is widely used in Middle English verse and prose, but is not markedly characteristic of central alliterative texts apart from *Piers Plowman* and *Mum and the Sothsegger*. 'Gnauen' (*MED*, IV, 182) appears only twice in fully alliterative works – *Piers Plowman* and *The Parliament of the Three Ages*. 'Gnacchen' (*MED*, IV, 180) and 'cammede' (*MED*, II, 27) find no alliterative placement. In its more boisterous alliterative modes the *Complaint* is reminiscent of the vernacular religious drama of the north-east of England: 'þou bes lassched, lusschyd and lapped; 3a, rowted, russhed and rapped...' (*York Plays*, 'Second Trial Before Pilate', lines 154–5). And it has some verbal reminiscences of *Piers Plowman* (cited from *Piers Plowman: The B Version*, ed. G. Kane and E. T. Donaldson, London, 1975): compare B Prol. 226 with 'knauene cry', and B XVII 331 with 'cryst hem gyue sorwe'. It is interesting that line 331, 'that crist gyue hym sorwe', occurs in a passage dealing with 'smoke and smolder', and the 'blowing-up' of a fire.

56. This is well-illustrated by the texts printed in *Reliquiae Antiquae*, I, 81–5.

57. From British Library MS Harleian 2253: edited by R. H. Robbins, *Historical Poems of the XIV and XV Centuries* (Oxford, 1959), pp. 27–9.

58. A fact which sets it apart from some figurative, and suitably generalised, treatments of blacksmithying in medieval Latin texts such as the Prologue to the *Rota Nova*, by the Bolognese notary, Guido Faba (c. 1226), which describes a period of study in the Law Schools of Bologna in terms of an apprenticeship to the craft of the smithy. See E. H. Kantorowicz, 'An Autobiography of Guido Faba', *Medieval and Renaissance Studies*, I (1943), pp. 267–8, 278–9.

59. So vehement is the emphasis upon the physical force involved in the operation of both bellows and hammers that we might be excused at times for imagining the *mise-en-scène* to be a smelting-smithy rather than a forge-workshop. H. R. Schubert's account of the processing of the crude iron in order to make it 'fit for use by the blacksmith' lays stress upon the 'repeated hammering' and 'intermittent reheating' to a temperature of 1400°c at the *stringhearth*; operations here were considered more laborious than at any other kind of hearth. The bellows required for generating such heat were very large, and the blast was often provided by the efforts of four 'blowers', 'three of whom worked at a time, while the fourth stood ready to replace...' (*A History of the British Iron and Steel Industry*, London, 1957, pp. 131, 146). Both smelting-foundries and forge-workshops would be familiar parts of the urban setting we may wish to propose for the *Complaint*, and, in fact, were sometimes situated together. See Du Boulay, *The Age of Ambition*, pp. 48–9.

60. The lines 'þe mayster longith a lityl ... towchith a treble', which have always given editors interpretative problems, may be intended to convey quite precisely medieval

welding processes – in constant use for the fabrication of a variety of household and decorative objects. See J. Starkie Gardner, *Ironwork, Part I. From the Earliest Times to the End of the Mediaeval Period*, Victoria and Albert Museum Handbooks, 98M (3rd edn., London, 1914), part I, p. 100. We might translate: 'The master-smith beats out a small piece of metal, and flattens an (even) smaller piece, (hammers) the two together, turning them edgewise . . .' The words 'and towchith a treble' may refer to nothing more elaborate than the high-pitched ringing noise of hammer upon metal during forge-activities; they may conceivably, with their musical metaphor, be a reminiscence of the widely-known passage in Macrobius, *In Somnium Scipionis Libri II*, Bk II, Chap. I, which describes how Pythagoras worked out the theory of musical intervals by listening to the sounds made by hammers of different weight in a blacksmith's shop. See *Macrobius: Commentary on the Dream of Scipio*, trans. W. H. Stahl (New York, 1952), pp. 186–7. I am indebted to Brian Donaghey for this suggestion.

61. The stout leather apron is a standard feature of all medieval representations of the blacksmith, grotesque or serious. See the references in note 40 above. The nailsmith in the Passion sequence of the *Hours* of Jeanne de Navarre (Bibliothèque Nationale MS lat. nouv. acqu. 3145, fo. 111, c. 1350) has blackened face and legs. Extracts in Lucien Febvre's 'Une Enquête: La Forge de Village' (*Annales D'Histoire Economique et Sociale*, 7, 1935, pp. 603–4) describe the rural blacksmith in terms unchanged from those of the medieval author: 'le Cyclope enfumé et redoutable dans sa forge noire . . . les reins ceints de la traditionnelle barette de cuir . . . constamment noir . . .' (p. 604).

62. ed. G. Schleich, *Palaestra*, 15 (Berlin, 1901), lines 397–417.

63. ed. C. Horstmann, EETS, OS 100 (1893), lines 1299–302. See D. A. Pearsall, 'John Capgrave's *Life of St Katharine* and Popular Romance Style', *Medievalia et Humanistica*, n.s. 6 (1975), 121–37.

64. J. Mann, *Chaucer and Medieval Estates Satire* (Cambridge, 1973), p. 13.

65. *Piers Plowman*, B Prol. 219–25.

66. Mann, *Chaucer and Medieval Estates Satire*, p. 15.

67. ed. F. J. Furnivall, EETS, ES 72 (1897). I am indebted to John Scattergood for this reference.

68. Cairns, *Generic Composition*, p. 31.

69. Martial, *Epigrams*, ed. & trans. C. A. Ker, Loeb (1920), XII, LVII, 5–6. See also Juvenal, *Satires*, ed. & trans. G. G. Ramsay, Loeb (1940), III, 234 ff. and Horace, *Epistles*, ed. A. S. Wilkins, Loeb (1892), II, 2, 65–86.

70. Juvenal, *Satires*, III, 309–10.

71. See F. J. E. Raby, *A History of Secular Latin Poetry in the Middle Ages* (Oxford, 1934), I, 317 ff., II, 90 ff.

72. See Jacques Le Goff, 'The Town as an Agent of Civilization', *Fontana Economic History of Europe* (n. 36 above), pp. 71–95, and the references to further reading in the Bibliography, pp. 96–106.

73. See Claus Uhlig, *Hofkritik im England des Mittelalters und der Renaissance* (Berlin, 1973).

74. See *Epistola* xiv, *PL*, 207, cols. 48B, 49A, B.

75. *Die Gedichte Walthers von der Vogelweide*, ed. H. Kuhn (Berlin, 1965), 20, lines 9, 8.

76. ed. E. Faral, *Les Arts Poétiques du XII⁴ et du XIII⁴ Siècle* (Paris, 1923), pp. 222–3, lines 813–29. The whole passage runs as follows:

Aut si fabriles ritus hoc ore loquamur:
Ad folles 'vigilant' flammae, 'sepelitur' in igne
Massa rudis, coctam 'transmittit' ab igne recenti
Forceps incudi, 'dat verbera' crebra magister
Malleus et duris 'praecorripit' ictibus illam
Sicque quod optat agit: vel cassidis 'elicit' orbem,
Utile consilium capiti, vel 'procreat' ensem,
Legitimum socium lateri, vel corporis hospes
Loricae procedit opus; 'connascitur' illis
Ocrea subterior, clypeo quam tibia 'sumat',
Et stimulus scitator equi, quem talus 'adoptet',
Et species aliae ferri quas armat acumen.
'Exhaurit' ferrum facies tam dissona rerum,
Tam variae species armorum. Malleus ictum
'Supprimit'; incudes 'respirant' calle peracto
Ad metam 'subsistit' opus 'finitque' diaetam.

Translated by Jane Baltzell Kopp, in *Three Medieval Rhetorical Arts*, ed. J. J. Murphy (Los Angeles, 1971), pp. 62–3:

The flames 'wake' to the bellows; the unformed mass is 'buried' in the fire; a pair of tongs 'transmits' the fired mass from the freshened fire to the anvil. The hammer, as teacher, administers frequent 'blows', and vigorously 'corrects' it with hard strokes, so that it performs as he wishes. Either he 'entices' from it the circle of a helmet, useful 'counsel' for the head, or he 'fathers' a sword, lawful 'companion' for a man's side, or work proceeds on a coat of mail, 'host' for the body. The more lowly greaves are 'born' together with these, a 'shield' which the shins 'elect', and the spur, the horse's 'instigator', which the ankle 'adopts'; and likewise the other kinds of armor which cunning prepares. Such a 'dissonant' array of things, such varied kinds of arms, 'exhaust' the iron. The hammer then 'restrains' its blow; the bellows, their journey ended, 'pant'; the work 'crosses the finish line', and 'completes its meal'.

77. As, for instance, in Book II of Hugh of St Victor's *Eruditionis Didascalicae Libri Septem* (*PL*, 176, Ch. xxi, col. 760), trans. J. Taylor (New York, 1961), pp. 74–5.
78. See note 4, above.
79. See the Appendix by M. R. James to H. C. Beeching's article, 'The Library of the Cathedral Church of Norwich', *Norfolk Archaeology*, 19 (1917), p. 108.
80. The treatise is to be found in British Library MS Royal 12. B. XVIII, fos. 53v–57v, which also contains Vinsauf's *Poetria Nova*, and a variety of texts on Latin rhetoric and dictamen. It can be localised in Cromer, Norfolk.
81. The '*N-Town*' Cycle of plays in British Library MS Cotton Vespasian D. VIII was compiled in central East-Anglia, probably in the 1460s and 1470s. See H. R. L. Beadle, 'The Medieval Drama of East Anglia: Studies in Dialect, Documentary Records and Stagecraft' (unpublished PhD thesis University of York, 1977), I, Chap. IV.
82. I am here specifically indebted to Helen Sutermeister, of the Centre for East Anglian Studies, Norwich, for permission to consult her unpublished work on medieval Norwich.
83. See *Records of the City of Norwich*, ed. W. Hudson and J. C. Tingey (Norwich and London, 1910), I, 93 ff.
84. See F. Roth, *The English Austin Friars, 1249–1538* (New York, 1966), I, 211–12.

85. Ibid., I, 298 ff., II, 214.
86. Lucien Febvre, 'Une Enquête', p. 614.
87. See C. M. van der Zanden, *Etude sur le Purgatoire de St. Patrice* (Amsterdam, 1928). The Latin text of Arundel MS 292 is printed on pp. 159–78.

I gratefully acknowledge helpful discussion and correspondence with David Aers, Richard Beadle, Sid Bradley, Jane Geddes and Rodney Hilton during the writing of this article.

10   *Troilus and Criseyde*: a reconsideration

1. *The Allegory of Love* (Oxford, 1936), p. 197.
2. *Troilus and Criseyde*, III, 465–9, ed. F. N. Robinson, *The Poetical Works of Chaucer* (Cambridge, Mass., 1957).
3. See D. W. Robertson, *A Preface to Chaucer* (Princeton, 1963), p. 491.
4. J. A. W. Bennett, 'The Humane Medievalist', An Inaugural Lecture (Cambridge, 1965), p. 27.
5. *Essays and Studies*, 17 (1932), 56–75.
6. For example, the study by Sanford B. Meech, *Design in Chaucer's Troilus* (Syracuse, 1959).
7. D. W. Robertson's treatment of the poem in his article 'Chaucerian Tragedy', *ELH*, 19 (1952), 1–37, and in *A Preface to Chaucer*, pp. 472–502, is often invalid for this reason.
8. *Il Filostrato*, ed. V. Pernicone (Bari, 1937), p. 94.
9. Meech, *Design*, pp. 424, 427.
10. Two essential articles on Chaucer's methods of work are: D. S. Brewer, 'Love and Marriage in Chaucer's Poetry', *MLR*, 49 (1954), 461–4, and E. T. Donaldson, 'The Ending of Chaucer's *Troilus*', *Early English and Norse Studies Presented to Hugh Smith*, ed. A. Brown and P. Foote (London, 1963), pp. 26–45 [repr. in his *Speaking of Chaucer* (London, 1970), pp. 84–101].
11. This will not mean that the ending of the poem is 'not a part of the whole . . . is detachable at will . . . one need not of necessity consider it at all in an interpretation of the drama' (W. C. Curry, *Chaucer and the Mediaeval Sciences*, 2nd edn, New York, 1960, p. 298). It remains an integral part of the poem, not least because it focuses our attention on the pressing and largely unresolved artistic problems which Chaucer faced throughout his work.
12. *The Canterbury Tales* seem to me to illustrate this point most aptly.
13. Curry, *Chaucer and Mediaeval Sciences*, p. 295, noted some of its improprieties.
14. C. A. Owen, 'The Significance of Chaucer's Revisions of *Troilus and Criseyde*', *MP*, 55 (1957–8), p. 5.
15. Henry Suso, *Life*, trans. T. F. Knox (London, 1915), Chap. lvi.
16. Julian of Norwich, *Revelations of Divine Love*, ed. G. Warrack (London, 1923), p. 103.
17. I, 977 ff.
18. T. P. Dunning, in 'God and Man in *Troilus and Criseyde*', *English and Mediaeval Studies Presented to J. R. R. Tolkien*, ed. N. Davis and C. L. Wrenn (London, 1962), pp. 164–82, holds that in Book III 'the narrator narrows the perspective . . .' (p. 179).
19. Chaucer deliberately refined Boccaccio's cruder language for lines 257–9:

i' ho dal cuor di Criseida rimosso
ogni vergogna e ciaschedun pensiero

che contra t'era, ed hol tanto percosso
col ragionar del tuo amor sincero . . .   (op. cit., p. 71)

But he did not bother to refine Troilus's offer.

20. It is, of course, an outcry provoked by false representation, and the poet knows that his audience will take it less seriously than they otherwise might.
21. See lines 1052–3, 1165–6.
22. The phrasing recalls that of Walter Hilton, in his *Scale of Perfection*, ed. E. Underhill (London, 1923), pp. 395–6: 'Other men that stand in the common way of charity, and are not yet so far forth in grace, but work under the bidding of reason . . . have not put themselves all fully in God's hand.'
23. The point is even clearer in some MSS of the poem which read 'whan it comth to the neede': see *The Book of Troilus and Criseyde*, ed. R. K. Root (Princeton, 1926), p. 201.
24. Lewis, *The Allegory of Love*, p. 196.
25. 'The Ending of Chaucer's *Troilus*', p. 37.
26. Ibid., p. 42.

11   *Troilus and Criseyde*: poet and narrator

1. E. Talbot Donaldson, 'The Ending of Chaucer's *Troilus*', in *Early English and Norse Studies Presented to Hugh Smith*, ed. A. Brown and P. Foote (London, 1963), p. 34.
2. George Kane, 'The Autobiographical Fallacy in Chaucer and Langland Studies', *Chambers Memorial Lecture* (London, 1965), p. 16.
3. Donaldson, 'The Ending of Chaucer's *Troilus*', p. 36.
4. Wayne Booth, *The Rhetoric of Fiction* (Chicago, 1961), p. 346.
5. Henry Miller, quoted by Booth, *Rhetoric of Fiction*, p. 367.
6. As, for example, the division proposed by G. T. Shepherd between the voice of the *narratio* and that of the *argumentum*. See 'Troilus and Criseyde', in D. S. Brewer (ed.), *Chaucer and Chaucerians* (London, 1966), pp. 65–87.
7. Elizabeth Salter, '*Troilus and Criseyde*: A Reconsideration', in *Patterns of Love and Courtesy*, ed. J. Lawlor (London, 1966), pp. 86–106 (see above, pp. 215–30).
8. *The Book of Troilus and Criseyde*, ed. R. K. Root (Princeton, 1926), lines 15–16.
9. See, for instance, the examples at III, 1319–20 and IV, 801–5.
10. Canto 4, stanzas 164–6: 'Non mi sospinse ad amarti bellezza', *Filostrato*, ed. M. Marti, *Giovanni Boccaccio: Opere minori in volgare* (Milan, 1970).
11. The transposition of Criseyde's somewhat calculating thoughts, so that they follow her sight of Troilus from the window rather than, as in the Italian, precede it, is just such a 'decisive change', which helps win her a moment of grace, however temporary.
12. See, for instance, lines 19, 272, 799, 834, 1037, 1044, 1050, 1051, 1088, 1089, 1094, 1562, 1758, 1765, 1777, 1786–99.
13. *Roman de Troie*, ed. L. Constans, SATF (1907; repr. 1968), lines 20208–9.
14. *Pericles*, IV, iv, 8–9.
15. M. C. Bradbrook, *English Dramatic Form* (London, 1965), p. 13.
16. See V, 1027–8.

12   Chaucer and Internationalism

1. *The Early Lives of Dante*, trans. P. H. Wicksteed (London, 1904), p. 39. For the Italian text, see *Giovanni Boccaccio, Opere*, ed. P. G. Ricci (Milan and Naples, 1965), pp. 595–6.

2. See L. Deslisle, *Recherches sur la librairie de Charles V*, 2 vols. (Paris, 1907; repr. Amsterdam, 1967), I, 326–36.
3. Deslisle, I, 114–15.
4. Ed. R. Morris, EETS, OS 57 (1874), lines 245–6.
5. Quoted in B. Smalley, *The English Friars and Antiquity in the Fourteenth Century* (Oxford, 1960), pp. 162–3.
6. *Rotuli Parliamentorum*, Vol. II, p. 147, col. ii.
7. National Library of Scotland MS 19.2.1. See the Introduction to the facsimile edition by I. C. Cunningham and D. A. Pearsall (London, 1978).
8. See Smalley, *English Friars*, p. 26.
9. D. A. Pearsall, *Old and Middle English Poetry* (London, 1977), p. 193, and R. H. Robbins, 'Geoffroi Chaucier, Poète Français, Father of English Poetry', *ChauR*, 13 (1978), p. 100.
10. Olive Coleman, 'The Collectors of Customs under Richard II', *Studies in London History Presented to P. E. Jones* (London, 1969), p. 194.
11. See Robbins, 'Geoffroi Chaucier', pp. 100 ff.
12. Taken with him at Poitiers were a *Bible Historiale*, now BL MS Roy. 19.D.II, and, most probably, a *Miracles de Notre Dame*, now in the Bibliothèque Séminaire at Soissons.
13. Now BN MS fr. 15397.
14. He was both mural and panel painter. See M. Meiss, *French Painting in the Time of Jean de Berry: The Fourteenth Century and the Patronage of the Duke* (London, 1967), p. 380, n. 5.
15. See Meiss, *French Painting*, p. 62 and fig. 507.
16. *Le Roman des Deduis*, ed. A. Blomqvist (Karlshamn, 1951), lines 12163–6.
17. Deslisle, *Recherches sur la librairie*, p. 331.
18. See J. V. LeClerc, *Histoire Littéraire de la France au quatorzième siècle* (Paris, 1865), pp. 191–2.
19. W. Dugdale, *History of St. Paul's Cathedral* (London, 1658; repr. 1818), pp. 15, 16, 20.
20. LeClerc, *Histoire Littéraire*, pp. 191–2.
21. J. Wimsatt, *Chaucer and the French Love Poets* (Chapel Hill, 1968), p. 116.
22. Jean de Berry contributed, as did many of his aristocratic friends, to the *Cent Ballades* of 1389. See the edition by G. Raynaud (Paris, 1905).
23. *Chroniques*, ed. S. Luce, G. Raynaud, 15 vols. (Paris, 1869–99), I, 210.
24. The charming *Débat du Cheval et du Levrier*, for instance, which is 'set' on Froissart's return journey from Scotland, in 1365: 'Froissars d'Escoce revenoit / Sur un cheval qui gris estoit. . . .'
25. See A. H. Diverres, 'Froissart's *Meliador* and Edward III's Policy towards Scotland', *Mélanges Offerts à Rita Lejeune*, 2 vols. (Gembloux, 1969), II, 1399 ff.
26. Wimsatt, *French Love Poets*, pp. 129 ff.
27. See A. Piaget, *Oton de Grandson, sa vie et ses poésies* (Lausanne, 1941).
28. See G. Doutrepont, *La Littérature française à la Cour des Ducs de Bourgogne* (Paris, 1909), p. 470, for comment upon the 'écrivains bourgignons' who were professionally 'écuyers, hérauts d'armes, prévots . . . chevaliers'. Into this continental situation, Chaucer, Clanvowe, Froissart, Gace de la Buigne, Oton de Granson fit perfectly.
29. Pearsall, *Old and Middle English Poetry*, p. 194.
30. LeClerc, *Histoire Littéraire*, pp. 334–5.
31. See K. B. McFarlane, *The Nobility of Later Medieval England* (Oxford, 1973), p. 236, n. 5. And see *Dits et Contes de Baudouin de Condé et de son Fils, Jean de Condé*, ed. A.

Scheler, 3 vols. (Brussels, 1866), II, xiv. We have here the names of Henry Boling-broke, Duke of Hereford; John or Thomas Holand, half-brothers of Richard II and Earls of Huntingdon and Kent, respectively; Sir Lewis Clifford and Sir Richard Sturry, Chamber Knights of Richard II, friends of Chaucer, Froissart, and Eustache Deschamps.

32. See Viscount Dillon and W. A. St John Hope, 'Inventory of the Goods and Chattels Belonging to Thomas, Duke of Gloucester, and Seized in his Castle at Pleshey . . .', *Archaeological Journal*, 54 (1897), p. 303.

33. *Chroniques*, ed. J. Buchon, 3 vols. (Paris, 1835), III, 198.

34. In a forthcoming study of English court life in the later Middle Ages, R. F. Green considers the significance of the loss of those very Household Ordinances, between 1318 and 1471–2, which would have told us about royal interest in literary and cultural matters generally. [Published as *Poets and Princepleasers* (Toronto, 1980)]

13 Medieval poetry and the visual arts

1. Charles Muscatine, *Chaucer and the French Tradition* (Berkeley and Los Angeles, 1957), pp. 167–9.
2. See R. M. Jordan, *Chaucer and the Shape of Creation: the Aesthetic Possibilities of Inorganic Structure* (Cambridge, Mass., 1967).
3. D. W. Robertson, *A Preface to Chaucer* (Princeton, 1963). See, in particular, Chap. 3, 'Late Medieval Style'.
4. Ibid., pp. 257–9.
5. Robertson, *A Preface to Chaucer*, p. 269.
6. Corpus Christi College, Cambridge, MS 53, the Peterborough Psalter, fo. 16r.
7. Robertson, *A Preface to Chaucer*, p. 272.
8. *Franklin's Tale*, lines 1355–1455.
9. *Troilus and Criseyde*, V, 1590–1631.
10. Robertson, *A Preface to Chaucer*, pp. 278–80.
11. Ibid., p. 277.
12. Magdalene College, Cambridge, MS 1916.
13. *Nun's Priest's Tale*, lines 2859–61, 2864.
14. Fitzwilliam Museum, Cambridge, MS 251.
15. National Library of Scotland, MS Adv. 18.6.5, fo. 25v.
16. Corpus Christi College, Cambridge, MS 53, fos. 12r–15v.
17. Westminster Abbey Library.
18. *Clerk's Tale*, lines 852 ff.
19. See the whole episode in Book II, lines 85–595.
20. *Knight's Tale*, lines 1123 ff.
21. See Robertson, *A Preface to Chaucer*, p. 280.
22. Ibid., p. 279.
23. Ibid., p. 258: 'the pilgrims might just as well be seen moving against a background of gold leaf'.
24. R. Hinks, *Carolingian Art* (London, 1935), pp. 38–9.
25. Lines 339–40, 343: the whole passage is highly reminiscent of pictorial conventions – the 'glade gilde stremes' (line 338) of the sun must surely refer to its gold-rayed appearance in manuscript painting.
26. See n. 14 above.
27. Bibliothèque Nationale, MS Lat. 9438, made about 1100.
28. Corpus Christi College, Cambridge, MS 2, made between 1121 and 1148.

29. Only in the picture for the month of February is there any serious attempt to render the wintry subtleties of the northern-European sky.
30. See J. Lawlor, 'The Pattern of Consolation in *The Book of the Duchess*', *Speculum*, 31 (1956), 626–48.
31. Facsimile printed with Introduction by E. J. S. Parsons (Oxford, 1958).
32. Muscatine, *Chaucer and the French Tradition*, p. 168.
33. Given to the Cathedral in 1380, by Lord John Neville.
34. Jordan, *Chaucer and the Shape of Creation*, p. 238.
35. British Museum MS Arundel 83, a composite Psalter, finely illuminated between c. 1300 and 1339.
36. Muscatine, *Chaucer and the French Tradition*, p. 245.
37. British Museum MS Additional 42130, made before 1340.
38. Fitzwilliam Museum, Cambridge, MS 242, made about 1308.
39. Robertson, *A Preface to Chaucer*, pp. 251–2.
40. Fitzwilliam Museum, Cambridge, MS 298.
41. See the Roxburghe Club edition of the Pontifical, ed. F. S. Dewick (London, 1902), for detailed descriptions of the decorative schemes.
42. O. Pächt, *The Master of Mary of Burgundy* (London, 1948), p. 25.
43. See O. Pächt, 'A Giottesque Episode in English Medieval Art', *JWCI*, 6 (1943), p. 52.
44. Pächt, *The Master of Mary of Burgundy*, p. 28.
45. See D. D. Egbert, 'The Grey FitzPayn Hours', *Art Bulletin*, 18 (1936), pp. 531 ff.
46. Magdalene College, Cambridge, MS 1916: see n. 12 above.
47. Jordan, *Chaucer and the Shape of Creation*, p. 239.
48. Pächt, *The Master of Mary of Burgundy*, p. 19.
49. See examples of this in the border designs of Jean Pucelle: K. Morand, *Jean Pucelle* (Oxford, 1962), p. 16.
50. M. C. Bradbrook, *The Rise of the Common Player* (London, 1962), p. 128.
51. M. C. Bradbrook, *English Dramatic Form* (London, 1965), p. 13.
52. See Jordan, *Chaucer and the Shape of Creation*, p. 122.
53. Bradbrook, *The Rise of the Common Player*, p. 128.
54. See above, pp. 252–3.

14 *Piers Plowman* and the visual arts

1. *The Mirrour of the Blessed Lyf of Jesu Christ*, ed. L. F. Powell (Oxford, 1908), p. 70.
2. *The Vision of William concerning Piers the Plowman*, ed. W. W. Skeat, 2 vols. (Oxford, 1886; repr. 1954), B XI 51–2.
3. 1 John 2:16.
4. A. Katzenellenbogen, *Allegories of the Virtues and Vices in Mediaeval Art*, 2nd edn, trans. A. J. P. Crick (New York, 1964), p. 63.
5. M. W. Bloomfield, *Piers Plowman as a Fourteenth Century Apocalypse* (New Brunswick, NJ, 1963), p. 19.
6. Ibid., pp. 41–2.
7. C. Muscatine, 'Locus of Action in Mediaeval Narrative', *Romance Philology*, 17 (1963), p. 122.
8. M. Meiss, *Painting in Florence and Siena after the Black Death* (Princeton, 1951), p. 165.
9. Bloomfield, *Piers Plowman*, p. 19.

10. *Piers Plowman*, B XVIII 137.
11. See, in particular, fo. 103v of the 'Paduan Psalter', Fitzwilliam Museum, Cambridge, MS 36/1950, and fo. 96r of the Peterborough Psalter, Corpus Christi College, Cambridge, MS 53.
12. BL MS Additional 47682. Facsimile ed. W. O. Hassall (London, 1954).
13. Muscatine, 'Locus of Action', p. 120.
14. Muscatine, 'Locus of Action', p. 122.
15. Reproduced by Meiss, *Painting in Florence and Siena*, pl. 85.
16. B XX 72 ff, 132 ff.
17. B XI 8.
18 Muscatine, 'Locus of Action', p. 122.
19. *The Cloud of Unknowing*, ed. P. Hodgson, EETS, OS 218 (1944; repr. 1958), chap. 68, p. 121.
20. Utrecht University Library, Cod. 32. Facsimile ed. E. T. De Wald, *The Illustrations of the Utrecht Psalter* (Princeton, 1932).
21. See C. R. Dodwell, *The Canterbury School of Illumination* (Cambridge, 1954), chap. IV.
22. The Canterbury Psalter, Trinity College, Cambridge, MS R.17.1, fo. 150v. Facsimile ed. M. R. James (London, 1935).
23. Ibid., fo. 24r.
24. Muscatine, 'Locus of Action', p. 120.
25. See E. Salter and D. Pearsall (eds.), *Piers Plowman: the C Text*, York Medieval Texts (London, 1967), Introduction, p. 15 [and above, p. 121].
26. See R. E. Kaske, '*Ex vi transicionis* and its Passage in *Piers Plowman*', in *Style and Symbolism in Piers Plowman*, ed. R. J. Blanch (Knoxville, 1969), pp. 258 ff.
27. Such compilations are found in BL MSS Arundel 507 and Additional 37049, for instance, and, in a more learned context, in an Apocalypse picture-book in the Wellcome Museum, London.
28. MS Additional 37049, fo. 36r: cf. *Piers Plowman*, B XX 99–100, quoted above.
29. Ibid., fo. 83r.
30. Ibid., fos. 19v and 48r.
31. Ibid., fo. 82v: 'the oyle in the lawmpes betokens charyte . . .'
32. A point completely misunderstood by some readers: see D. Mills, 'The Role of the Dreamer in *Piers Plowman*', in *Piers Plowman: Critical Approaches*, ed. S. S. Hussey (London, 1969), pp. 200–4.
33. BL MS Additional 37049, fo. 19v. See also the Tree of Vices, with 'human fruit', threatened by death, in an English psalter of the fourteenth century in the Walters Library, Baltimore.
34. See, for instance, the account of earlier work and the new suggestions in B. H. Smith, *Traditional Imagery of Charity in Piers Plowman* (The Hague, 1966), chap. III.
35. BL MS Additional 37049, fo. 25r. Compare *Piers Plowman*, B XVI 23, 63.
36. BL MS Cotton Faustina B. vi, part ii, fo. 22v.
37. 'Till it had begotten itself upon an earthly body'.
38. The Talbot Hours, Fitzwilliam Museum, Cambridge, MS 40/1950, fo. 73r.
39. *L'Opera Completa di Bosch*, ed. D. Buzzati and M. Cinotti (Milan, 1966), Tav. XVI–XVII.
40. B Prol. 17, C I 19.
41. C I 10.
42. *Hieronymus Bosch: The Garden of Delights*, ed. W. Hirsch (London, 1954), plate facing p. 42.

43. B V 304 ff.
44. See, in particular, *St John the Baptist in Meditation: Opera Completa*, Tav. XLI.

15 The *Troilus* Frontispiece

1. Definitive statements of this interpretative tradition are to be found in A. Brusendorff, *The Chaucer Tradition* (London and Copenhagen, 1925; repr. Gloucester, Mass., 1965), pp. 19–23 and in M. Galway, 'The Troilus Frontispiece', *MLR*, 44 (1949), 161–77. For a sceptical treatment of the tradition as it relates to Chaucer criticism, see D. A. Pearsall, 'The *Troilus* Frontispiece and Chaucer's Audience', *Yearbook of English Studies*, 7 (1977), 68–74.
2. The small, neat female head-dresses point significantly to a date of not much later than c. 1415; compare, for instance, the portrait of Jeanne de Boulogne, on fo. 91v of the *Belles Heures* (New York, Cloisters: c. 1405–8) with that of Anne de Bourgogne, on fo. 257v of the *Bedford Hours* (British Library MS Additional 18850: c. 1422). Datable English examples of costume and head-dress styles similar to those of the Frontispiece are: donor portraits on fo. 23v of the *Beaufort Hours* (British Library MS Roy. 2.A.xviii: c. 1401–10); St Helena figure in Henry V's Charter to the Borough of Colchester (1413).
3. See H. Buchthal, *Historia Troiana: Studies in the History of Medieval Secular Illustration* (London, 1971). Both the twelfth-century verse *Roman de Troie* and its thirteenth-century Latin prose derivative, the *Historia Destructionis Troiae*, were often generously supplied with cycles of narrative miniatures, ranging in number from 50 to 200, and illustrating martial and amatory episodes. It must have been to programmes of this scale rather than to those of a more modest nature, worked out for some copies of Boccaccio's *Filostrato* and its French prose translation, the *Roman de Troyle*, that the organisers of the Corpus Christi manuscript looked for models of pictorial aggrandisement. Copies of the *Historia* were widely circulated in fourteenth- and fifteenth-century England.
4. The Campsall manuscript of *Troilus* (Pierpont Morgan Library MS M.817), which bears the arms of the Prince of Wales on fo. 2r, has only decorative border-work and one historiated initial. See *Supplement to the Census of Medieval and Renaissance MSS in the United States and Canada*, ed. C. U. Faye and W. J. Wilson (New York, 1962), p. 360. For a detailed discussion of illumination in MSS of the *Canterbury Tales* by M. Rickert, see J. M. Manly and E. Rickert, *The Text of the Canterbury Tales* (Chicago, 1940; repr. 1967), I, 561–605.
5. E. G. Millar, *English Illuminated Manuscripts of the XIVth and XVth centuries* (Paris and Brussels, 1928), p. 37.
6. See, for instance, the articles by Galway and Pearsall, cited above, n. 1.
7. For detailed corroboration of these workshop conventions as they relate to Frontispiece composition during the very early fifteenth century by the French Virgil and Coronation Masters, see M. Meiss, *French Painting in the Time of Jean de Berry: The Boucicaut Master* (London, 1968), pp. 63–5, and plate 458; *French Painting in the Time of Jean de Berry: The Limbourgs and their Contemporaries* (London, 1974), pp. 408–9 and pls. 388, 389. An early fifteenth-century document giving elaborate directions to the illuminator for a Frontispiece (with out-door setting) to Sallust's *Catilina* is printed by J. Porcher in *Mélanges offerts à Frantz Calot* (Paris, 1960), p. 38.
8. See, for recent comment upon this process, M. A. Stones, 'Sacred and Profane Art:

Secular and Liturgical Book-illumination in the Thirteenth Century', *The Epic in Medieval Society*, ed. H. Scholler (Tübingen, 1977), pp. 100–12.

9. See Meiss, *French Painting in the Time of Jean de Berry: The Limbourgs*, pp. 108–10, and pls. 403–5.

10. For a convenient selective list of 'preaching miniatures', see D. A. Pearsall, 'The *Troilus* Frontispiece', p. 71, note 3.

11. Written in 1330, and, twenty-five years later, cast into a second version. M. Lofthouse's useful but unsympathetic study, *'Le Pèlerinage de Vie Humaine* by Guillaume de Deguileville', *Bulletin of the John Rylands Library*, 19 (1935), 170–215, should be supplemented by R. Tuve, *Allegorical Imagery* (Princeton, 1966), Chap. 3.

12. Ed. J. J. Stürzinger (London, 1893), lines 4–6.

13. If, as seems possible, Deguileville's narrative – which relates how the author, after a vision of the Holy City, determined to journey to it – suggested to the illuminators this extension of the scope of the Frontispiece, we may have an interesting parallel to, or model for, the *Troilus* situation, where landscape and architectural detail may have been dictated similarly, by events within the narrative.

14. See, for instance, poet and audience miniatures in Bibliothèque Nationale MS f. fr. 25566 (*Oeuvres de Adam de la Halle*; c. 1300) fos. 10, 37, 49; Bibliothèque Nationale MS f. fr. 831 (*Poésies de Froissart: 1362–91*), fo. IV.

15. The Prefatory 'preaching/reciting' picture belongs, in the main, to manuscript copies of the first recension of the poem; in the second recension, changes made in the wording of the Prologue reduce the appropriateness of such a picture, and its omission argues for a traditionally close relationship between text and illustration in this position. For extensive lists of manuscripts and early printed editions of the *Pèlerinage*, see Stürzinger and Lofthouse (notes 11, 12, above) and Tuve, *Allegorical Imagery*, p. 147, n. 2. Chaucer's *A.B.C.* poem witnesses to his knowledge of the *Pèlerinage*; Lydgate translated it entire. Fifteenth-century English interest in the *Pèlerinage* produced a prose-redaction, one manuscript of which, Bodleian Library MS Laud Misc. 740, probably made for Sir Thomas Cumberworth, of Somerby, Lincs., has the familiar Prefatory miniature of a recital scene on folio 2r. See Tuve, *Allegorical Imagery*, pp. 146–50. Other texts besides Chaucer's *Troilus* were provided, during the years 1410–30, with the 'preaching/recital' picture as a statement of an 'author/public' relationship: see folio 112v of Bibliothèque Royale, Brussels, MS 9093, a copy of Corbéchon's French version of the *De Proprietatibus Rerum*.

16. The distinctive inner border is a tightly-organised version of elements characteristic of manuscripts from the English-based Scheere-Johannes workshop: nearest to the Corpus format are certain varieties of border in British Library MSS Additional 42131 (Hours and Psalter made for John, Duke of Bedford, c. 1420) and Additional 50001 (Hours, probably first owned by Cecily Neville, Duchess of Warwick, d. 1450).

17. The fullest account of this period of French workshop activity is to be found in the three studies by M. Meiss: *French Painting in the Time of Jean de Berry: the Late Fourteenth Century and the Patronage of the Duke* (London, 1967) and the two companion volumes referred to in note 7 above.

18. See, for instance, the *Agony in the Garden* from folio 123r of the *Belles Heures* of Jean de Berry, plate 496 in Meiss, *Limbourgs*, and the *Adoration of the Magi* from folio 67r of Hours, British Library MS Additional 29433, plate 760 in Meiss, *Late Fourteenth Century*.

19. See the comments in Meiss, *Limbourgs*, pp. 363–4 [see pl. 29].

20. Strong similarities to the architectural detail of the Frontispiece can be found in the

work of Jean and Paul de Limbourg for folios 186r and 74r of the *Belles Heures*; see plates 417 and 452 in Meiss, *Limbourgs*. The triple format for the upper part of the *Troilus* Frontispiece – two rocky peaks with turreted buildings and a prominent castle-gateway – seems to have been definitively established by the Limbourgs, although the *Adoration of the Magi* miniature by the Brussels Initial Master (note 18, above) has a rudimentary version of it; see pl. 10 and Meiss, *Limbourgs*, pl. 405. It is, however, a copy of the Limbourg design by the Master of the Breviary of Jean sans Peur of Burgundy (executed 1413–17) which comes closest to the Frontispiece in its general and particular disposition (pl. 11).

21. The standing figure in the elegantly decorated houpelande, a member of the 'recital group' of the Frontispiece, is clearly copied from earlier French exemplars to be found, for instance, in the *Adoration* miniature of the Brussels Initial Master (note 18, above) and in the Coronation Master's miniature on folio 73r of Premierfait's *Des Cleres et Nobles Femmes*, presented to Philippe Le Hardi, in 1403. The same manuscript provides suggestive 'models' for facial and figure detail.

22. Galway, 'The Troilus Frontispiece', p. 177.

23. See M. B. Parkes, 'Palaeographical Description and Commentary' in *Troilus and Criseyde. A facsimile of Corpus Christi College Cambridge MS 61*, introductions M. B. Parkes and E. Salter (Cambridge, 1978), pp. 2, 11.

24. Galway, 'The Troilus Frontispiece', p. 161.

25. Ibid., passim, but particularly pp. 176–7.

26. The outstanding example of this during the fourteenth century is the visit in 1390 of William, Duke of Guelders, cousin of Richard II, to England on diplomatic business, accompanied by two heralds: it is convincingly proposed that it was on this occasion that the painter, Herman Scheere, first came to England and determined to set up a workshop. See, for the latest statement of this, G. M. Spriggs, 'The Nevill Hours and the School of Herman Scheere', *JWCI*, 37 (1974), 113–15. The movement of people and books between England and France during the earlier fifteenth century can be briefly illustrated by Bibliothèque Nationale MS lat. 1158 – a book of Hours, illuminated in the style of the French Bedford Master, and acquired in France by a member of the Neville family, who had English 'portrait' folios of Joan Beaufort, Ralph Neville and their family added (fos. 27v, 34v). A finely written copy of the *Poésies* of Froissart (Bibliothèque Nationale MS f. fr. 831) was in the hands of Richard Beauchamp, Earl of Warwick (d. 1439) in the earlier fifteenth century; its prefatory miniature of poet and audience is noted above (n. 14). John, Duke of Bedford, Regent of France (1422–35), commissioned de-luxe manuscripts from workshops in Paris and London; Charles, Duc d'Orléans, royal prisoner in England from 1417 to 1440, took a *Liber Precum*, Bibliothèque Nationale MS lat. 1196, written in England, and provided with one striking initial from the Scheere-workshop, back to France with him after his release (Spriggs, 'The Nevill Hours', pp. 119–20). And it is the brother of Charles, Jean d'Angoulême, who purchased and annotated a copy of the *Canterbury Tales* while in similar captivity (Bibliothèque Nationale MS f. anglais 39).

27. See R. K. Root, *The Book of Troilus and Criseyde* (Princeton, 1926), p. liii.

28. This would be a slight departure only from the familiar fourteenth- and fifteenth-century pictorial convention of the author composing, accompanied by the events and personages of his literary work; see Bibliothèque Nationale MS f. fr. 1586, folio 30v (Machaut composing the *Remède de Fortune*); Kettaneh MS 1. i (Boccaccio composing, with scenes from *De Casibus*) reproduced as plate 379 in Meiss, *The Boucicaut Master*; Bodleian MS Douce 213, folio 1r (Boccaccio composing the

Decameron) reproduced as plate 55, no. 717, in *Illuminated Manuscripts in the Bodleian Library, Oxford*, ed. O. Pächt and J. J. G. Alexander, 3 vols. (Oxford, 1966–73); Bibliothèque Royale, Brussels MS 9466, folio 4r (Martin Le Franc, composing *Le Champion des Dames*; Dijon, Bibliothèque Municipale MS 493, folio 45r (Virgil composing the *Georgics*).

29. See Parkes, 'Palaeographical Description', p. 11.
30. Ibid., p. 12. The identification of Anne Neville, Duchess of Buckingham, daughter of Joan Beaufort and Ralph Neville, Earl of Westmorland, as the owner in question, must rest upon the occurrence of another name on folio 108r, 'Knyvett'; Joanna, daughter of Anne Neville, married, as her second husband, Sir William Knyvett of Norfolk. But it is tempting to find her ownership of the *Troilus* particularly convincing in the courtly contexts of the mid-fifteenth century in England; she was, in company with ladies such as Jaquetta, Lady Rivers, and Alice de la Pole, Duchess of Suffolk (granddaughter of Chaucer) 'in frequent attendance' at the court of Henry VI and Margaret of Anjou. She was certainly owner of part II of the splendidly illuminated Wingfield Hours (New York Public Library MS Spencer 3), and she has been tentatively associated with Glasgow University Library MS Hunterian V. 3.7, the unique manuscript of the *Romaunt of the Rose*, as well as with the original Psalter, later divided to form British Library MS Royal 2.A.XVIII and Bibliothèque Municipale, Rennes, MS 22. She may also be the kneeling figure represented on folio 3v of Bibliothèque Nationale MS lat. nouv. acqu. 3145, a fifteenth-century English painting bound into the *Heures de Jeanne de Navarre*, since the accompanying scroll, 'mercy and grace', repeats identical scrolls on folio 68v of the Wingfield Hours. See E. Seaton, *Sir Richard Roos* (London, 1961), pp. 303, 312; M. Rickert 'The So-Called Beaufort Hours and York Psalter', *Burlington Magazine*, 104, no. 711 (1962), 238–46: A. I. Doyle, Appendix B in *The Epistle of Othea*, ed. C. F. Bühler, EETS 264 (1970).
31. Brusendorff, *The Chaucer Tradition*, p. 21.
32. Apart from suggesting, as in note 26, above, that we should take into account the movement of books and patrons between England and the Continent, we should also, no doubt, reflect upon the significance, for the hybrid nature of the *Troilus* miniature, of fifteenth-century English workshops employing 'foreign' artists or artists trained abroad. See, for manuscripts of a slightly later date than Corpus Christi 61, K. L. Scott, 'A Mid-Fifteenth Century English Illuminating Shop and its Customers', *JWCI*, 31 (1968), 170–96, and the remarks of M. Rickert, in *Painting in Britain: The Middle Ages* (London, 1954), pp. 197–8, and n. 5, on British Library MS Harley 4605, written, as the colophon says, by a Frenchman, Pierre Delafite, in London, the year 1434.

16 The Annunciation to the Shepherds in later medieval art and drama

1. E. H. Gombrich, *Symbolic Images* (London and New York, 1972), p. 64.
2. D. S. Brewer, 'Gothic Chaucer' in *Writers and their Background: Geoffrey Chaucer*, ed. D. S. Brewer (London, 1974), pp. 1–32.
3. E. Panofsky, *Gothic Architecture and Scholasticism* (Latrobe, Pa., 1951; repr. Cleveland, Ohio, 1957), pp. 1–2.
4. 'The Parallelism between Literature and the Arts', *English Institute Annual*, 1941 (New York, 1942), 29–63 (p. 63).
5. St Augustine, *Tractate 45 on the Gospel of St John* in *A Select Library of the Nicene and*

Post-Nicene Fathers of the Christian Church, ed. and trans. P. Schaff, D.D., LL.D., 14 vols. (New York, 1887–92; repr. Ann Arbor, 1969–74), VII, 251.

6. Zachariah 10.3; Isaiah 40.10–11; Jeremiah 13.17 and 31.10.

7. See Job 1.3 and I Samuel 25; for the citation, Genesis 31.40.

8. St Augustine, *Tractate 46 on the Gospel of St John* in *A Select Library*, VII, 256.

9. See R. Axton, *European Drama of the Early Middle Ages* (London, 1974), p. 187; and M. H. Marshall, 'The Dramatic Tradition Established by the Liturgical Plays', *PMLA*, 56 (1941), 962–91 (pp. 965–9).

10. *S. Thomae Aquinatis Catena aurea in quatuor evangelia*, ed. P. Angelicus Guarientus, O.P., 2 vols. (Turin and Rome, 1953), II, 31–2.

11. See K. Young, *The Drama of the Medieval Church*, 2 vols. (Oxford, 1933), II, 12–13; and M. H. Marshall, 'Aesthetic Values of the Liturgical Drama', *English Institute Essays, 1950* (New York, 1951), pp. 89–115; repr. in *Medieval English Drama: Essays Critical and Contextual*, ed. J. Taylor and A. H. Nelson (Chicago and London, 1972), pp. 28–43 (p. 37).

12. See Young, *The Drama of the Medieval Church*, II, 187; and Axton, *European Drama*, p. 187.

13. E. C. Dunn, 'The Prophetic Principle in the Towneley *Prima pastorum*' in *Linguistic and Literary Studies in honor of Helmut A. Hatzfeld*, ed. A. S. Crisafulli (Washington, DC, 1964), pp. 117–27 (p. 118); D. W. Robertson and B. F. Huppé, *Piers Plowman and Scriptural Tradition* (Princeton, NJ, 1951), pp. 152–3; *The Wakefield Pageants in the Towneley Cycle*, ed. A. C. Cawley (Manchester, 1958), p. 102; H. Cooper, *Pastoral: Mediaeval into Renaissance* (Ipswich, 1977), pp. 87–90.

14. Dunn, 'The Prophetic Principle', pp. 122–3. All references to the *Wakefield Plays* will be to the edition cited in note 13.

15. 'The Catalogue of the Library of the Augustinian Friars at York', ed. M. R. James in *Fasciculus Ioanni Willis Clark dicatus* (Cambridge, 1909), pp. 2–96, 500 Ab and 507 Aj.

16. Dunn, 'The Prophetic Principle', p. 127.

17. *The Chester Plays*, ed. H. Deimling and Matthews, 2 vols., EETS, ES 62 and 115 (1892 and 1916), I, 132–60 (line 568); see M. M. Morgan, ' "High Fraud": Paradox and Double-Plot in the English Shepherds' Plays', *Speculum*, 39 (1964), 676–89 (pp. 682–5).

18. *Two Coventry Corpus Christi Plays*, ed. H. Craig, EETS, ES 87 (1902), pp. 1–32, lines 242–77, 307–31.

19. *Ludus Coventriae or The Plaie called Corpus Christi*, ed. K. S. Block, EETS, ES 120 (1922), pp. 146–51 (lines 90–3). It has also been argued that many of the apparently homely gifts of the shepherds to Christ are symbolic, see L. Réau, *Iconographie de l'art chrétien*, 3 vols. (Paris, 1955–9), vol. II, part 3, p. 234; L. J. Ross, 'Symbol and Structure in the *Secunda Pastorum*', *Comparative Drama*, 1 (1967–8), 122–43; repr. in *Medieval English Drama: Essays Critical and Contextual*, pp. 177–211 (pp. 181–99).

20. Ross, 'Symbol and Structure', p. 208.

21. V. J. Scattergood, *Politics and Poetry in the Fifteenth Century* (London, 1971), pp. 360–2 (p. 360).

22. On sheep diseases in particular, *P. Vergilii Maronis Bucolica et Georgica*, ed. T. E. Page (London, 1898), *Georgicon* III, 440–77; on the Hellenistic and Roman works on agriculture behind the *Georgics*, see L. P. Wilkinson, *The Georgics of Virgil* (Cambridge, 1969), pp. 223–5, and on sheep disease, pp. 259–60; on the later influence of the *Georgics*, pp. 270–90. Subsequent Latin works on agriculture include that of Columella in the first century, that of Palladius in the fourth

(translated into English in the fifteenth century) and that of Petrus Crescentius in the thirteenth (widely translated in medieval Europe). See also Walter of Henley's thirteenth-century Anglo-Norman *Husbandry* (transcribed and translated E. Lamond, London, 1890, pp. 1–38; for the Middle English translation, pp. 39–58; on this and the Latin translation, pp. xxi–xl); in one family of manuscripts 'there is a lengthy insertion on some of the diseases of sheep, which is still further amplified in the translations' (p. xxvi; for the insertion, see pp. 36–8); and Jehan de Brie's fourteenth-century French *Le Bon Berger*, cited below, n. 39, devotes Chaps. xxi–xlv to sheep diseases. On these texts, see Lord Ernle, *English Farming Past and Present*, introductions G. E. Fussell and O. R. McGregor (6th edn, London, Melbourne and Toronto, 1961), p. 33, and on sheep disease, pp. 15–16.

23. See M. Carey, *The Wakefield Group in the Towneley Cycle* (Göttingen and Baltimore, 1930), pp. 155–7.
24. Line 21; Carey makes a similar observation (*The Wakefield Group*, p. 147).
25. *The Vision of William concerning Piers the Plowman*, ed. W. W. Skeat, 2 vols. (Oxford, 1886), B IV 48–50. All citations from *Piers Plowman* will be from this edition.
26. R. B. Dobson, *The Peasants' Revolt of 1381* (London, 1970), p. 371.
27. Dobson, *The Peasants' Revolt*, pp. 374–5.
28. R. H. Hilton, *The English Peasantry in the Later Middle Ages* (Oxford, 1975), p. 66.
29. Hilton, *The English Peasantry*, p. 20.
30. See F. Vernet, *Mediaeval Spirituality*, trans. The Benedictines of Talacre (London, 1930), part II, chaps. 1 and 2; E. Salter, *Nicholas Love's 'Myrrour of the Blessed Lyf of Jesu Christ'* (Salzburg, 1974), Chap. 5.
31. *Meditations on the Life of Christ*, trans. and ed. I. Ragusa and R. B. Green (Princeton, NJ, 1961). On the text and its influence, see Salter, *Nicholas Love's 'Myrrour'*, pp. 39–46. For its influence on French religious drama, see E. Roy, *Le Mystère de la passion en France du XIVe au XVIe siècle*, 2 parts (Dijon and Paris, 1903–4), pp. 92*–99*, 243–62; for its influence on French drama and visual art, E. Mâle, *L'Art religieux de la fin du moyen âge en France* (Paris, 1908; repr. Paris, 1969), pp. 27–51; for its influence on English religious drama, R. Woolf, *The English Mystery Plays* (London, 1972), Chaps. 8–10.
32. Nicholas Love, *The Mirrour of the Blessed Lyf of Jesus Christ. A Translation of the Latin Work entitled Meditationes vitae Christi*, ed. L. F. Powell (Oxford, 1908), p. 48. Love's plain and undetailed version of the shepherd episode (ed. Powell, pp. 48–50) contrasts with that of a French version, dated by its editors around 1390: 'et du chant et de la melodie que faisoient les angels si grant, ilz se s'emerveillerent si grandement que ce povoit estre, et mectoient la main sur le front davant les yeulx en regardant vers le ciel, tous esbahiz … Et de joye qu'ilz eurent l'un print a mener sa musete, l'autre sa fleute, et l'autre faisoit ung sault sur la houlette, c'est le baston des pastours' (*La Vie de Nostre Benoit Sauveur Ihesuscrist & La Saincte Vie de Nostre Dame*, ed. M. Meiss and E. H. Beatson, New York, 1977, p. 17). Does the French translation reveal the influence of contemporary miniature painting, or vice versa?
33. See G. R. Owst, *Literature and Pulpit in Medieval England* (Cambridge, 1933); J. J. Murphy, *Rhetoric in the Middle Ages* (Berkeley, Los Angeles and London, 1974), pp. 310–55; compare A. C. Spearing, 'The Art of Preaching and *Piers Plowman*' in his *Criticism and Medieval Poetry* (London, 1964; 2nd edn, 1972), pp. 107–34.
34. See I. Siciliano, *François Villon et les thèmes poétiques du moyen âge* (Paris, 1934), Chap. 6; A. Hulubei, *L'Eclogue en France au XVIe siècle* (Paris, 1938), Chap. 5; Cooper, *Pastoral*, Chap. 2. For the visual and plastic arts, see J. Evans, *Art in Mediaeval France 987–1498* (Oxford, 1948), pp. 183–4; and M. Meiss, with the assistance of S. off

347

Dunlap Smith and E. H. Beatson, *French Painting in the Time of Jean de Berry: The Limbourgs and their Contemporaries*, 2 vols. (London, 1974), I, 55–61.

35. *Poésies complètes du troubadour Marcabru*, ed. and trans. J.-M.-L. Dejeanne (Toulouse, 1909), pp. 137–43; trans. L. T. Topsfield in *Troubadours and Love* (Cambridge, 1975), pp. 88–91.

36. Adam de la Halle, *Le Jeu de Robin et de Marion*, ed. K. Varty (London, 1960); translated in *Medieval French Plays*, trans. R. Axton and J. Stevens (Oxford, 1971), pp. 257–302.

37. *European Drama*, p. 141.

38. See Siciliano, *François Villon*, pp. 415–17; J. Huizinga, *The Waning of the Middle Ages*, trans. F. Hopman (London, 1924), pp. 117–23.

39. Jehan de Brie, *Le Bon Berger . . . réimprimé sur l'édition de Paris (1541)*, notice by P. Lacroix (Paris, 1879), p. xvii.

40. *Oeuvres de Guillaume de Machaut*, ed. E. Hoepffner, 3 vols., SATF (Paris, 1908–21), II, 159–237 (lines 1523–86).

41. *Le Bon Berger* only exists in the sixteenth-century version reproduced in the edition cited above.

42. M. J. Hughes, 'The library of Philip the Bold and Margaret of Flanders, first Valois duke and duchess of Burgundy', *Journal of Medieval History*, 4 (1978), 145–88 (p. 173); see also H. David, *Claus Sluter* (Paris, 1951), pp. 138–40.

43. See Carey, *The Wakefield Group*, pp. 132–42; O. Jodogne, 'La Pastorale dramatique française du XVe siècle', *Studi Francesi*, 8 (1964), 201–13. On this drama in general see G. Frank, *The Medieval French Drama* (Oxford, 1954), Chaps. 14 and 17.

44. See *Mystères inédits du quinzième siècle . . . d'après le MS unique de la Bibliothèque Ste.-Geneviève*, ed. A. Jubinal, 2 vols. (Paris, 1837), II, 71–77; *Mystère de la nativité* in *Mystères et moralités du manuscrit 617 de Chantilly*, ed. G. Cohen (Paris, 1920), pp. 3–23, lines 64–145; *La Passion bourguignonne de Semur* in Roy, *Le Mystère de la passion*, I, 3–203, lines 2565–839 (line 2685); Eustache Mercadé, *Le Mystère de la passion*, ed. J.-M. Richard (Arras, 1891), lines 1624–1702, 2113–2363; Arnoul Gréban, *Le Mystère de la passion*, ed. O. Jodogne, Mémoires, Académie royale de Belgique, classe des lettres, 2e série 12, fasc. 3 (Brussels, 1965), lines 4620–835, 4932–55, 5147–212, 5453–699; *Mystère de l'incarnation et nativité de notre sauveur et rédempteur Jésus-Christ représenté à Rouen en 1474*, ed. P. Le Verdier, 2 vols. (Rouen, 1884–86), interspersed throughout the *Deuxième journee*. For a brief summary of the motifs mentioned here see Carey, *The Wakefield Group*, p. 140.

45. Ed. B. M. Craig (Lawrence, Kansas, 1954), lines 1091–235, 2041–66, 2548–608; see also p. 8; the play was dramatised from Philippe de Mézières' prose version of the story, possibly by Mézières himself, and may have been presented to Charles VI of France (see Frank, *The Medieval French Drama*, Chap. 15). Compare also *La Pacience de Job: Mystère anonyme du XVe siècle ([Paris, Bibliothèque Nationale] ms. fr. 1774)*, ed. A. Meiller (Paris, 1971), lines 1188–1430. For further references see Siciliano, *François Villon*, pp. 415–16.

46. Roy, *Le Mystère de la passion*, p. 12*; see also Frank, *The Medieval French Drama*, pp. 146–7, 165.

47. Roy, *Le Mystère de la passion*, p. 65*; Roy also notes that a Passion was performed before Charles VI in 1381.

48. Eustache Mercadé, *Le Mystère de la passion*, pp. vii–viii; Frank, *The Medieval French Drama*, p. 179.

49. Arnould Greban, *Le Mystère de la passion*, ed. G. Paris and G. Raynaud (Paris, 1878; repr. Geneva, 1970), pp. i–xi; Frank, *The Medieval French Drama*, pp. 182–3.

50. Roy, *Le Mystère de la passion*, pp. 74*–76*.
51. Roy comments on an image commissioned by Charles V and his wife which portrays Christ crucified between the Synagogue and the Church, just as he appears in the Crucifixion Play of the Bibliothèque Ste-Geneviève manuscript (*Le Mystère de la passion*, p. 66*).
52. See also H. Swarzenski, *Early Medieval Illumination* (London, New York, Toronto and Sydney, 1951), pl. 12 and fig. 4; but compare the livelier shepherd figures in the late thirteenth-century Peterborough Psalter, see L. F. Sandler, *The Peterborough Psalter in Brussels and other Fenland Manuscripts* (London, 1974), pl. 18.
53. 'A little shepherd in the top left-hand corner [of pl. 21] actually seems to have trespassed into the holy scene ... His presence does, however, suggest a potentiality for enlivenment of the traditional scenes through the integration of marginal experiments, and his rugged earthy quality anticipates genre details of a much later period' (K. Morand, *Jean Pucelle*, Oxford, 1962, p. 6). Morand also comments on the movement of material from the *bas-de-page* through the initial and into the main picture in pls. 22 and 23 (p. 23). Compare also M. Meiss, *French Painting in the Time of Jean de Berry: The Late Fourteenth Century and the Patronage of the Duke*, 2 vols. (2nd edn, London and New York, 1969), pp. 17, 162, 167.
54. On the *bas-de-page* of plate 27 here, Meiss comments 'the episode looks like the traditional "occupation" in April' (in his *French Painting in the Time of Jean de Berry: The Boucicaut Master*, with the assistance of K. Morand and E. W. Kirsch, London and New York, 1968, p. 36). An actual rustic festival can be found in Bodleian Library, Oxford, MS Douce 93, fo. 28r, reproduced as the frontispiece to this volume; see also the Annunciation to the Shepherds in the Hours of Charles d'Angoulême, Paris Bibliothèque Nationale, MS Lat. 1173, fo. 20v (frontispiece of Cooper, *Pastoral*).
55. The signs of the zodiac here 'have been modeled into a sort of second cycle of months' (O. Koseleff, 'Representations of the Months and Zodiacal Signs in *Queen Mary's Psalter*', *Gazette des Beaux-Arts*, series 6, 22, 1942, 77–88; citation p. 86).
56. See C. Gaspar and F. Lyna, *Les Principaux manuscrits à peintures de la Bibliothèque Royale de Belgique*, 2 parts (Paris, 1937–47), I, 362–65; on this and other similar manucripts, see C. R. Sherman, 'Some Visual Definitions in the Illustrations of Aristotle's *Nichomachean Ethics* and *Politics* in the French translations of Nicole Oresme', *Art Bulletin*, 59 (1977), 320–30.
57. *The Rohan Book of Hours*, introduction M. Meiss, introduction and commentaries M. Thomas (London, 1973), p. 25, pl. 46; *Les Très Riches Heures du Duc de Berry*, introduction and legends J. Longnon, preface M. Meiss (London, 1969), pl. 8.
58. For the influence of the drama on the visual arts and even the involvement of artists in the production of medieval mystery plays, see G. Cohen, *Histoire de la mise en scène dans le théâtre religieux français du moyen âge* (Paris, 1906), Book III, Chap. 3; Mâle, *L'Art religieux de la fin du moyen âge*, Chap. 2, especially pp. 42–54.
59. *Histoire de la mise en scène*, pp. 116–18, pl. 6; Mâle, *L'Art religieux de la fin du Moyen Âge*, pp. 53–4.
60. See Mercadé, *Le Mystère de la passion*, p. vi.
61. Carey, *The Wakefield Group*, p. 142.
62. See H. M. Brown, 'Musicians in the *Mystères* and *Miracles*' in his *Music in the French Secular Theater 1400–1550* (Cambridge, Mass., 1963), pp. 42–57; repr. in *Medieval English Drama: Essays Critical and Contextual*, pp. 81–97 (p. 84).
63. Arnoul Gréban, *Le Mystère de la passion*, ed. Jodogne, lines 4750–65.
64. See Brown, 'Musicians in the *Mystères*', p. 86.

65. See J. Stevens, 'Music in Mediaeval Drama', *Proceedings of the Royal Musical Association*, 84 (1957–8), 81–95; and E. Winternitz, *Musical Instruments and their Symbolism in Western Art* (London, 1967), Chap. 11. On music in the Wakefield Second Shepherds' Play, see N. C. Carpenter, 'Music in the *Secunda Pastorum*', *Speculum*, 26 (1951), 696–700; repr. in *Medieval English Drama: Essays Critical and Contextual*, pp. 212–17.
66. *Records of Early English Drama. York*, ed. A. F. Johnston and M. Rogerson, 2 vols. (Manchester, 1979), pp. 70, 748.
67. 'The Jolly Shepherd Wat' in *Songs, Carols, and other Miscellaneous Poems, from . . . Richard Hill's Commonplace-Book*, ed. R. Dyboski, EETS, ES 101 (1907), pp. 16–18.
68. John Lydgate (attrib.), *The Assembly of Gods*, ed. O. L. Triggs, EETS, ES 69 (1896), lines 324–9.
69. W. O. Hassall, *The Holkham Bible Picture Book* (London, 1954), fo. 13r and pp. 89–91; also reproduced in Cooper, *Pastoral*, pl. I; see Axton, *European Drama*, p. 188.
70. See, for instance, the Shepherd Play of 'The Shrewsbury Fragments' in *Non-Cycle Plays and Fragments*, ed. N. Davis, EETS, SS 1 (1970), pp. 1–7 (pp. 1–2).
71. See L. M. C. Randall, *Images in the Margins of Gothic Manuscripts* (Berkeley and Los Angeles, 1966).
72. See Morand, *Jean Pucelle*, pp. 6, 23, 47–8; Meiss, *French Painting in the Time of Jean de Berry: The Late Fourteenth Century*, pp. 117–18, 136, 162–3.
73. *The Book of Beasts: Being a Translation from a Latin Bestiary of the Twelfth Century*, trans. and ed. T. H. White (London, 1954), pp. 40–3, 74–6; F. McCulloch, *Mediaeval Latin and French Bestiaries* (Chapel Hill, 1960), pp. 120–1; H. Cooper, 'The Goat and the Eclogue', *Philological Quarterly*, 53 (1974), 363–79 (p. 369).
74. Ps.32.3. See D. W. Robertson, *A Preface to Chaucer* (Princeton, NJ, 1962), pp. 126–37, figs. 29–42; see also Stevens, 'Music in Mediaeval Drama'; E. A. Bowles, 'The Role of Musical Instruments in Medieval Sacred Drama', *Musical Quarterly*, 45 (1959), 67–84.
75. On bagpipes as symbol of the fallen nature of man, G. F. Jones, 'Wittenwiler's *Becki* and the Medieval Bagpipe', *JEGP*, 48 (1949), 209–28; E. A. Block, 'Chaucer's Millers and their Bagpipes', *Speculum*, 29 (1954), 239–43; compare also Eustache Deschamps, *Balade 923* in his *Oeuvres complètes*, ed. De Queux de Saint-Hilaire and G. Raynaud, SATF, 11 vols. (Paris, 1878–1903), V, 127. On bagpipes as a symbol of divine harmony, Winternitz, *Musical Instruments and their Symbolism*, Chaps. 4 and 10, 'Bagpipes for the lord'.
76. *Adoration of the Shepherds*, *The Chester Plays*, line 458, but also lines 369–458; *Secunda Pastorum*, *The Wakefield Pageants*, lines 656–64; W. O. Hassall observes of *The Holkham Bible Picture Book* that, although the shepherds imitate the angels' song at the Annunciation with 'Glum glo ceo ne est rien', by the time they reach the Nativity 'Gloria in excelsis deo et in terra' issues 'rather miraculously' from their mouths (p. 90). See also V. A. Kolve, *The Play called Corpus Christi* (London, 1966), pp. 169–72.
77. On the connection between the towns and the intellectuals in the later Middle Ages, J. Le Goff, *Les Intellectuels au moyen âge* (Paris, 1969), pp. 9–10, 68.
78. Le Goff, *Les Intellectuels*, pp. 63–5.
79. *Les Intellectuels*, p. 64; *The Statesman's Book of John of Salisbury: Being the Fourth, Fifth, and Sixth Books, and Selections from the Seventh and Eighth Books, of the Policraticus*, trans. J. Dickinson (New York, 1927), p. 243.

80. *The Town as an Agent of Civilisation, c. 1200–c. 1500*, trans. E. King (London and Glasgow, 1971), p. 5.
81. *Les Poésies des goliards*, ed. O. Dobiache-Rojdestvensky (Paris, 1931), p. 166. A more complexly sympathetic attitude is adopted by the fifteenth-century Italian 'Alfabeto dei villani' (*Poesia del Quattrocento e del Cinquecento*, ed. C. Muscetta and D. Ponchiroli, Turin, 1959, pp. 365–8); these and others are discussed in F. Novati, *Carmina medii aevi* (Florence, 1883), p. 25–38.
82. 'Des Taboureurs' in *Jongleurs et trouvères*, ed. A. Jubinal (Paris, 1835), pp. 164–9, lines 1–4.
83. *The Records of the City of Norwich*, ed. W. Hudson and J. C. Tingey, 2 vols. (Norwich and London, 1906 and 1910), II, 328.
84. *The Town as an Agent of Civilisation*, p. 14.
85. *Histoire de la France rurale*, ed. G. Duby and A. Wallon, 4 vols. (Paris, 1975–6), I, 530–3; see also Hilton, *The English Peasantry*, p. 15.
86. 'La Lutte contre le vagabondage à Paris aux XIVe et XVe siècles', in *Ricerche storiche ed economiche in memoria di Corrado Barbagallo*, ed. L. de Rosa, 3 vols. (Naples, 1970), II, 213–36.
87. For reproductions of all of the bridge scenes in the manuscript, see V. W. Egbert, *On the Bridges of Mediaeval Paris* (Princeton and London, 1974).
88. R. Hilton, *Bond Men Made Free* (London, 1973), pp. 100–2; E. Berger, *Histoire de Blanche de Castille, Reine de France* (Paris, 1895), p. 396.
89. E. Power, *The Wool Trade in English Medieval History* (Oxford, 1941), pp. 12–19, 31–5.
90. See D. Pearsall, *Old English and Middle English Poetry* (London, 1977), Chaps. 4 and 5.
91. See E. G. Millar, *English Illuminated Manuscripts of the XIVth and XVth Centuries* (Paris and Brussels, 1928), p. 41.
92. See Morand, *Jean Pucelle*, pp. 19, 24, 26–30; Meiss, *French Painting in the Time of Jean de Berry: The Boucicaut Master*, p. 35.
93. Compare the soldier who seizes Christ in the Betrayal or the attendants of the Crucifixion (Morand, *Jean Pucelle*, pl. IXc and p. 16; pl. Xc).
94. Compare, for instance, the seated shepherd of pl. 23 here with a *bas-de-page* beggar (Morand, *Jean Pucelle*, pl. VIIIb).
95. 'The dancing figure comes from some marginal decoration' (J. Porcher, *The Rohan Book of Hours*, London, 1959, p. 22).

Bibliography of the published writings of Elizabeth Salter

Under the name Elizabeth Zeeman

'Nicholas Love – a Fifteenth-century Translator', *Review of English Studies* n.s. 6 (1955), 113–27.

'Continuity in Middle English Devotional Prose', *Journal of English and Germanic Philology* 55 (1956), 417–22.

'Punctuation in an Early Manuscript of Love's *Mirror*', *Review of English Studies* n.s. 7 (1956), 11–18.

'Two Middle English Versions of a Prayer to the Sacrament', *Archiv* 194 (1957), 113–21.

'Continuity and Change in Middle English Versions of the *Meditationes Vitae Christi*', *Medium Aevum* 26 (1957), 25–31.

'*Piers Plowman* and the Pilgrimage to Truth', *Essays and Studies* 11 (1958), 1–16.

Under the name Elizabeth Salter

Chaucer: the Knight's Tale and the Clerk's Tale, Studies in English Literature 5 (London, 1962).

Piers Plowman: an Introduction (Oxford, 1963).

'The English Vernacular', *The Listener* 70 (1963), 652–4, 695–7.

'Ludolphus of Saxony and his English Translators', *Medium Aevum* 33 (1964), 26–35.

'The Alliterative Revival', *Modern Philology* 64 (1966), 146–50, 233–7.

'*Troilus and Criseyde*: a Reconsideration', in *Patterns of Love and Courtesy: Essays in Memory of C.S. Lewis*, ed. John Lawlor (London, 1966), pp. 86–106.

'Piers Plowman and "The Simonie"', *Archiv* 203 (1967), 241–54.

(with Derek Pearsall) *Piers Plowman*, selections from the C-text, ed., York Medieval Texts (London, 1967).

'Medieval Poetry and the Figural View of Reality' (Sir Israel Gollancz Memorial Lecture, British Academy, 1968), *Proceedings of the British Academy* 54 (1968), 73–92.

'Medieval Poetry and the Visual Arts', *Essays and Studies* 22 (1969), 16–32.

'*Piers Plowman* and the Visual Arts', in *Encounters: Essays on Literature and the Visual Arts*, ed. John Dixon Hunt (London, 1971), pp. 11–27.

(with Derek Pearsall) *Landscapes and Seasons of the Medieval World* (London, 1973).

'Courts and Courtly Love' and 'The Mediaeval Lyric', Chaps. 12 and 13 in *The Mediaeval*

World, ed. David Daiches and Anthony Thorleby, Literature and Western Civilisation (London, 1973), pp. 407–44, 445–84.

Nicholas Love's 'Myrrour of the Blessed Lyf of Jesu Christ', Analecta Cartusiana 10 (Salzburg, 1974).

'Henry Adams and W. H. Auden: "The Age of Anxiety" ', *Notes and Queries* 24 (1977), 454–5.

'The "Troilus Frontispiece" ', pp. 15–23 of Introduction to *Troilus and Criseyde: a Facsimile of Corpus Christi College, Cambridge, MS 61* (Cambridge, 1978).

'The Timeliness of *Wynnere and Wastoure*', *Medium Aevum* 47 (1978), 40–65.

'Alliterative Modes and Affiliations in the Fourteenth Century', *Neuphilologische Mitteilungen* 79 (1978), 25–35.

'Langland and the Contexts of *Piers Plowman*', *Essays and Studies* 32 (1979), 19–25.

'*A Complaint against Blacksmiths*', *Literature and History* 5 (1979), 194–215.

'Chaucer and Internationalism', *Studies in the Age of Chaucer* 2 (1980), 71–9.

(with Derek Pearsall) 'Pictorial Illustration of Late Medieval Poetic Texts: the Role of the Frontispiece or Prefatory Picture', in *Medieval Iconography and Narrative: A Symposium*, edited by Flemming G. Andersen, Esther Nyholm, Marianne Powell and Flemming Talbo Stubkjaer (Odense, 1980), pp. 100–23.

'The Manuscripts of Nicholas Love's *Myrrour of the Blessed Lyf of Jesu Christ* and Related Texts', in *Middle English Prose: Essays on Bibliographical Problems*, ed. A. S. G. Edwards and Derek Pearsall (New York, 1981), pp. 115–27.

'*Troilus and Criseyde*: Poet and Narrator' in *Acts of Interpretation: The Text in its Contexts 700–1600: Essays . . . in Honor of E. Talbot Donaldson*, ed. Mary J. Carruthers and Elizabeth D. Kirk (Norman, Okla., 1982), pp. 281–91.

Fourteenth-Century English Poetry: Contexts and Readings, ed. Derek Pearsall and Nicolette Zeeman (Oxford, 1983).

Index

Index

71; Boethian elements 217, 219, 224; Christian references 223–4, 226–9; consideration of views of E. T. Donaldson 231–8; of C. S. Lewis 215–30; the ending of the poem 231, 236–8; the frontispiece in Corpus Christi College, Cambridge, MS 61 267–71, 341–5 *passim*; relationship of poet and 'narrator' 231–8; Troy story in European tradition 232–3, 236–7; use of Benoît de Sainte-Maure 236–7; use of Boccaccio, *Il Filostrato* 216, 218–25, 227–8, 230, 232–6, 238, 336 n. 19, 337 n. 11

Chaundos family, of Brockworth 69

Chaytor, H. J. 296 nn. 97–9, 298 n. 5, 304 nn. 17–24, 305 nn. 25, 48, 50, 306 nn. 52–3

Chertsey Abbey, tiles 89

Chester cycle of mystery plays 286, 346 n. 17; Adoration of the Shepherds 276–7, 289, 350 n. 76

Chetham, Thomas 328 n. 116

Chevalere Assigne 105

Chorister's Lament, The 200

Chrétien de Troyes 9, 15, 17, 20, 308 n. 126; *Erec* 15; *Lancelot* 20

Chronicon Abbatiae de Evesham 332 n. 43

Cicero 69

Cigman, G. R. 177–8, 322 n. 21

Cinotti, M. 341 n. 39

Cipolla, C. M. 331 n. 36

Cistercian spirituality 274, 280

Clanvowe, Sir John 192, 244, 338 n. 28

Clare family 24, 26; *see also* FitzGilbert

Clare, Gilbert de, Earl of Gloucester 93

Clarendon Palace 89; Queen's Chamber 307 n. 98

Clarendon, Sir Roger 191

Clarke, M. V. 311, n. 27, 312 n. 54, 324 n. 47

Claudian 14; *Contra Rufinum* 63–5; *De Raptu Proserpinae* 63–5, 302 n. 109

Claudius of Turin 314 n. 3

Clay, R. M. 303 n. 129

Cleanness 105

Clement VI, Pope 186

Clemoes, P. 302 n. 92

Clifford, Sir Lewis 244, 339 n. 31

Clitheroe Castle, Lancashire 106

Cloud of Unknowing 2, 154, 260, 315 n. 9, 341 n. 19

Cluny Abbey 15–16

Codex Burana, shepherd play 275

Coghill, N. 314 n. 7, 316 n. 37, 317 n. 66

Cohen, G. 285–6, 348 n. 44, 349 n. 58

Cokayne, G. E. 294 n. 24

Colchester, borough charter given by Henry V 342 n. 2

Coleman, O. 338 n. 10

Coleridge, Samuel Taylor, *Biographia Literaria* 152, 155, 316 n. 45, 317 n. 69

Colgrave, B. 330 n. 4

Columella 346 n. 22

Complaint against Blacksmiths, A, provenance, date and social background 199–214, 329–35 *passim*

Conflictus Veris et Hiemis, attrib. Alcuin 37–8

Constance of Castile, second wife of John of Gaunt 107

Constans, L. 296 n. 102, 337 n. 13

Cooper, H. 346 n. 13, 347 n. 34, 349 n. 54, 350 n. 73

Corbechon, Jean, *Proprietez des choses* 248, 343 n. 15

Corfe Castle 78

'Coronation Master', The 270, 342 n. 7, 344 n. 21

Cotman, J. S. 326 n. 79

Cottle, B. 293 n. 4, 324 n. 45, 330 n. 3

Coulton, G. G. 330 n. 7

Coventry Mystery Plays, Shearmen and Tailors' Pageant 276

Craig, B. M. 348 n. 45

Craig, H. 346 n. 18

Crécy, Battle of 189, 190, 192, 196

Crescentius, Petrus 347 n. 22

Crick, A. J. P. 340 n. 4

Crisafulli, A. S. 346 n. 13

Cumberworth, Sir Thomas, of Somerby, Lincs. 343 n. 15

Cunningham, I. C. 338 n. 7

Curry, W. C. 336 n. 11

Cursor Mundi 154, 194, 240

Curtius, E. R. 302 n. 110

Cwicwine, monk of Crayke 206–7

Dante, *Divine Comedy* 116, 132, 239, 262, 316 n. 30

Dares Phrygius 69

Darlington, R. R. 293 n. 8

Dauphin d'Auvergne, son of Guillaume VII 30

David, H. 348 n. 42

Davies, H. S. 302 nn. 93, 100

Davis, N. 309 n. 5, 336 n. 18, 350 n. 70

Davy, M. M. 297 n. 115

Day, M. 313 n. 62, 323 n. 36

Debate of the Carpenter's Tools 332 n. 48

Deguileville, Guillaume de 343 nn. 13–15;

359

Hours of Simon le Vostre 286
Hours of Yolande of Flanders, *see* Manuscripts,
 London, BL Yates Thompson 27
Hudson, W. 335 n. 83, 351 n. 83
Hue de Rotelande, *Ipomedon* 26, 297 n. 122;
 Protheselaus 26, 297 n. 125
Hughes, M. J. 348 n. 42
Hugh of Fleury-sur-Loire, *Historia
 ecclesiastica* 294 n. 44
Hugh of St Victor 71, 77, 335 n. 77
Huizinga, J. 348 n. 38
Hulbert, J. R. 101, 103, 108, 180, 309 n. 2,
 313 n. 58, 322 nn. 6–7
Hulme, W. H. 320 n. 49
Hulton, W. A. 311 n. 25
Hulubei, A. 347 n. 34
Humphrey de Bohun, Earl of Hereford, *see*
 Bohun, Humphrey de
Huppé, B. F. 275–6, 314 n. 2, 316 n. 34, 346
 n. 13
Hussey, S. S. 313 n. 65, 316 n. 35, 317 n. 72,
 318 n. 13, 319 nn. 19, 35, 321 n. 18, 341
 n. 32

Ilchester manuscript, *see* Manuscripts, London,
 Univ. Lib. V. 88
Ingham Priory, Norfolk 212
Ipomedon, see Hue de Rotelande
Isabel of Warenne, Countess of Arundel 91
Isabella, Duchess of York 75, 243
Isabella of Angoulême, mother of Henry
 III 305 n. 51
Isabella, wife of Frederick II of Sicily 85
Isidore of Seville 14, 15
Italy, literature of 1, 31–2, 75; painting in,
 14th and 15th centuries 126–7

*Jack Upland: Friar Daw's Reply: Upland's
 Rejoinder* 322 n. 22
Jacob, E. F. 305 n. 40
Jacques de Longuyon, *Voeux du Paon* 97
James, Henry 232
James, M. R. 299 n. 39, 306 nn. 65, 71, 307
 n. 95, 310 n. 16, 318 n. 12, 331 n. 38, 335
 n. 79, 341 n. 22, 346 n. 15
Jamison, E. 293 n. 14, 295 nn. 69, 72, 297
 n. 119
Jaquetta, Lady Rivers 345 n. 30
Jausbert de Puycibot 79
Jean d'Angoulême 344 n. 26
Jean d'Avesnes, Count of Hainault 99
Jean de Brienne, Comte d'Eu 98
Jean de Condé 243–4; *Dis des Estas dou
 Monde* 198
Jean de Meun 98; *see also Roman de la Rose*
Jean de Nostre Dame 79

Jean de Sy, Bible de, see Manuscripts, Paris, Bibl.
 Nat. fr. 15397
Jean d'Ibelin, Lord of Beirut 95
Jean, Duc de Berry, *see* Berry, Jean, Duc de
Jean le Bon, *see* John II, King of France
Jeanne de Navarre, Queen of France 96
Jeanne de Navarre, Hours of, *see* Manuscripts,
 Paris, Bibl. Nat. lat. nouv. acqu. 3145
Jeanne d'Evreux, Hours of, *see* Manuscripts,
 New York, Metropolitan Museum of Art,
 Cloisters Collection
Jeanroy, A. 298 n. 13, 305 n. 24
Jean sans Peur, Duke of Burgundy 344 n. 20
Jehan de Brie, *Le Bon Berger* 283, 290, 347
 n. 22, 348 nn. 39, 41
Jerarchie, see Pecham, John
Joan, daughter of Henry II 18, 20, 25–6
Joan de Bar, grand-daughter of Edward I 97
Joan 'of Acre', daughter of Edward I 93
Jodogne, O. 348 n. 43
'Johannes', English painter 343 n. 16
John, Count of Holland 100
John de Blana 82
John de Warenne, Earl of Surrey 97, 196, 328
 n. 109
John, E. L. T. 325 n. 73, 327 n. 105, 329
 n. 118
John, King of Bohemia 189
John, King of England 30–1, 77–82, 304
 n. 9; literary patronage of 77–81
John II, King of France (Jean le Bon) 239; his
 interest in books 78; exercise of
 patronage while in captivity in
 England 241–3
John of Ford, chaplain to John II of France 78
John of Garland 330 n. 11
John of Gaunt, Duke of Lancaster 106–10,
 189–91, 242, 271, 311 n. 39, 312 n. 44,
 314 n. 70, 318 n. 12, 323 n. 37; his
 Registers 106–8, 312 nn. 45–6, 50–3, 56,
 314 n. 68
John of Howden 32; *Philomena* 90, 300
 n. 56; *Rossignos* 32, 90–1
John of Lancaster, Duke of Bedford 343
 n. 16, 344 n. 26
John of Salisbury 16, 18–19, 64, 295 nn. 64,
 73; *Metalogicon* 295 n. 71; *Policraticus*
 239, 289
John of Trevisa 105, 183, 310 n. 22, 311
 n. 28; translation of *De Proprietatibus
 Rerum* 105; translation of Higden's
 Polychronicon 105, 313 n. 60
John, Prior of Ingham, Norfolk 212
Johnson, C. 314 n. 69
Johnston, A. F. 350 n. 66
Jones, G. F. 350 n. 75

Index

Jones, G. P. 330 n. 18, 331 n. 33, 332 n. 48
Jordan, R. M. 339 n. 2, 340 nn. 34, 47, 52
Jordan Fantosme, *Chronique de la Guerre entre les Anglois et les Ecossois* 23, 54, 59–60
Joseph of Arimathie 104, 163, 319 n. 35
Joseph of Exeter, *De Bello Troiano* 21, 63–5, 70, 302 nn. 103–5
Jubinal, A. 348 n. 44, 351 n. 82
Julian of Norwich, *Revelations of Divine Love* 224, 228, 336 n. 16
Juvenal, *Satires* 210, 334 nn. 69–70

Kane, G. 318 n. 9, 321 nn. 17–18, 324 n. 39, 328 n. 114, 333 n. 55, 337 n. 2
Kantorowicz, E. H. 333 n. 58
Kaske, R. E. 341 n. 26
'Katherine Group', The 70–4
Katzenellenbogen, A. 315 nn. 14–16, 20, 340 n. 4
Kauffman, C. M. 298 nn. 130–1
Keen, M. H. 323 n. 16
Kenelm, Life of St (in the *South English Legendary*) 172–3
Kenilworth, 'Round Table' 95
Kennedy, A. G. 326 n. 90
Ker, C. A. 334 n. 69
Ker, N. R. 301 n. 82, 329 n. 1
Kettaneh manuscript, of Boccaccio, *see* Manuscripts, New York, Kettaneh Collection
Kightley, C. 322 n. 4
Kilpeck Church, Herefordshire 8, 294 n. 22
King, E. 351 n. 80
Kingsford, C. L. 297 n. 115
King's Langley, royal park at 93
King's Lynn 212–13; Austin Friary 213
Kingston, Treaty of (1217) 31
Kingston-upon-Hull, royal foundation of 93
Kirsch, E. W. 349 n. 54
Kleinhenz, C. 306 n. 67
Kluckow, F. 297 n. 125
Knoop, D. 330–1 n. 18, 331 n. 33, 332 n. 48
Knowles, D. 295 n. 55
Knox, T. F. 336 n. 15
Knyvett, Joanna, daughter of Anne Neville 345 n. 30
Knyvett, Sir William 345 n. 30
Koehler, W. R. W. 308 n. 113
Kölbing, E. 297 nn. 121–2
Kolve, V. A. 350 n. 76
Kopp, J. Baltzell 335 n. 76
Koschwitz, E. 297 n. 121
Koseleff, O. 349 n. 55
Kuhl, E. P. 330 nn. 14–15
Kuhn, H. 334 n. 75

Kynyngham, John, confessor to Wingfield family 196

Labareyre, F. de 298 n. 8
Lacroix, P. 348 n. 39
Lactantius, *Divinae Institutiones* 315 n. 26
Lamond, E. 347 n. 22
Lancaster, Blanche, Duchess of, *see* Blanche, Duchess of Lancaster
Lancaster, Henry, Duke of, *see* Henry, Duke of Lancaster
Lancaster, John, Duke of, *see* John of Gaunt
Lancaster, John, of, *see* John of Lancaster, Duke of Bedford
Lancaster, R. Kent 305 n. 42, 306 nn. 61–75
Lancaster, Thomas, Earl of, *see* Thomas, Earl of Lancaster
Lancelot, French prose 75, 99, 243
Langland, William, *Piers Plowman* 109, 111–78, 194–5, 197, 209–10, 231–2, 248, 278–80, 300 n. 60, 301 n. 90, 313 n. 65, 314 nn. 1, 4, 315 nn. 12, 15–16, 323 n. 39, 324 n. 45, 327 n. 94, 333 n. 55, 334 n. 65, 347 n. 25; allegory in 111–25; analogies with visual arts 137–8, 256–66, 340–1; dreamer and dream-vision in 138–43, 261–2; figural approach to 125–31, 137; form, structure and procedures 131–52; importance of search or quest 143–8; manuscripts of 313 n. 65; poetry of 152–7; realism and the figural approach 125–31, 137, 316 nn. 27–9; relationship to Maidstone 172; to other alliterative poetry 170; to sermons and sermon-techniques 123, 149–52, 155–6, 177–8; to *The Simonie* 154, 157, 158–69, 176–7, 318 nn. 12, 14–15, 319 nn. 21–40, 320 nn. 41, 44, 46, 48; to *Winner and Waster* 194; reminiscences of Gaytryge's *Treatise* 175–7; role of dreamer in 138–43, 261–2; role of Piers Plowman in 133–5, 146–8; 'spatial environments' 258–9; use of narrative 135–8; use of exempla 123–4, 137
Langlois, E. 298 n. 7
Langton, Stephen, Archbishop of Canterbury 71–80
Lanthony Priory 69
Laon Cathedral 15
Latimers 9
Latin, writing in England in the 12th and 13th centuries in 6–7, 9–15, 17–21, 23–5, 28, 34–9, 49, 54, 58–9, 61, 63–7, 70, 73, 77, 80–2, 85, 88, 98; in the 14th century 104–5, 110, 211; on

365

Rennes
  Bibl. Municipale 22   345 n. 30
Rome
  Vat. Lib. Urb. Lat. 603 (Breviary of
    Blanche of France)   pl. 21
San Marino, California
  Huntington Library Ellesmere
    26.C.12   267
Soissons
  Bibl. Séminaire, *Miracles de Notre
    Dame*   338 n. 12
Utrecht
  University Library, Codex 32   260–2,
    341 n. 20
Vienna
  Nat.-bibl. 1855   pl. 29
Winchester
  Cathedral Library, Winchester Bible   27,
    88, 298 n. 130
Worcester
  Cathedral Library F.10   322 n. 22
Map, Walter   21, 23, 34; *De Nugis
  Curialium*   299 n. 32; 'Dialogus inter
  Aquam et Vinum'   299 n. 45
Marbod, Bishop of Rennes   12–13, 17, 59; *De
  Ornamentis Verborum*   73–4; *Naufragium
  Jonae Prophetae*   320 n. 2; 'Oratio ad
  Sanctam Mariam'   73
Marcabru   19–20, 282–3
March, Patrick of Dunbar, Earl of, *see* Patrick of
  Dunbar
Marcilhac, France   8
Margaret, daughter of Count of Holland   100
Margaret, Duchess of Burgundy   284
Margaret of Anjou, wife of Henry VI   345
  n. 30
Margaret (Marguerite) of France, second wife
  of Edward I   97, 308 n. 124
Margaret of Provence, wife of Louis IX of
  France   86, 92
Margaret, St, Queen of Scotland   12
'Margerie de Hausted'   93
Marguerite of France, *see* Margaret of France
Marguerite of Orléans, Hours of, *see*
  Manuscripts, Paris, Bibl. Nat. lat. 1156B
Marie, Abbess of Shaftesbury   20
Marie de Brabant, Queen of France   96
Marie, Countess of Champagne   15, 20–1
Marie, Countess of Ventadorn   79
Marie de France   9, 20; *Lais*   23
Marsh, Richard, Bishop of Durham   80
Marshall, M. H.   297 n. 117, 346 nn. 9, 11
Marti, M.   337 n. 10
Martial, *Epigrams*   210, 334 n. 69
Martianus Capella   15
Martin, Henri   283

Martley, Worcs.   67
Mathew, G.   312 n. 57
Mathilda, Countess of Tuscany   7
Matilda, daughter of Henry II   20
Matilda (*also* Maud), empress   10, 67
Matthew Paris, *see* Paris, Matthew
Matthews, W.   309 n. 3
Maud, *see* Matilda
Maud, wife of Henry I   12–13, 15, 17
Meditationes vitae Christi (formerly attrib. St
  Bonaventure)   281–2, 284; translations
  and influence of   347 nn. 31–2; French
  translation, *La Vie de Nostre Benoit Sauveur*,
  etc.   347 n. 32; Middle English
  translation in Michigan State College MS
  I   178–9
Meech, S. B.   336 nn. 6, 9
Meiller, A.   348 n. 45
Meiss, M.   2, 338 nn. 14–15, 340 n. 8, 341
  n. 15, 342 n. 7, 343 nn. 9, 17–20, 344
  n. 28, 347 nn. 32, 34, 349 nn. 53–4, 57,
  350 n. 72, 351 n. 92
Mercadé, Eustache, *Passion d'Arras*   284, 286,
  348 nn. 44, 48, 349 n. 60, pl. 32
Merode altarpiece, *see* Campin, Roger
Merrilees, B. S.   300 n. 53
Metham, John, *Physiognomy*   333 n. 52
Metz Pontifical, *see* Manuscripts, Cambridge,
  Fitzwilliam Museum   298
Micha, A.   297 n. 120, 308 nn. 123, 126
Michael of Cornwall   82
Michel, F.   296 n. 105, 329 n. 124
Michelant, H.   308 n. 123
Millar, E. G.   267–8, 342 n. 5, 351 n. 91
Miller, Henry   337 n. 5
Mills, D.   341 n. 32
Milton, John   40, 152
Moissac, France   8
Montacute (Montagu), William, 2nd Earl of
  Salisbury   184, 192, 195–6
Montagu, John, 3rd Earl of Salisbury   244
Montgomery, Robert, Count of Shrewsbury   6
Moorman, C.   320 n. 1
Moran, D.   322 n. 2
Morand, K.   332 n. 40, 340 n. 49, 349 nn. 53–
  4, 350 n. 72, 351 nn. 93–4
Morgan, M. M.   346 n. 17
Morris, R.   301 n. 73, 338 n. 4
Morte Arthure, alliterative poem   23, 104, 313
  n. 63
Mortimer family   8, 102
Mortimer, Hugh de, Lord of Wigmore   7–8,
  71
Mortimer, Roger de (*fl.* 1175–1200)   67, 71
Mortimer, Roger de, Lord of Wigmore (*fl.*
  1279)   95